D0213401

MICROSOFT® VISUAL C#® 2015

AN INTRODUCTION TO OBJECT-ORIENTED PROGRAMMING, SIXTH EDITION

SIXTH EDITION

MICROSOFT® VISUAL C#® 2015

AN INTRODUCTION TO OBJECT-ORIENTED PROGRAMMING

JOYCE FARRELL

CENGAGE
Learning·

Australia · Brazil · Mexico · Singapore · United Kingdom · United States

CENGAGE Learning

Microsoft® Visual C#® 2015: An Introduction to Object-Oriented Programming, Sixth Edition
Joyce Farrell

Product Director: Kathleen McMahon

Product Team Manager: Kristin McNary

Senior Product Manager: Jim Gish

Senior Content Developer: Alyssa Pratt

Product Assistant: Abigail Pufpaff

Marketing Manager: Eric LaScola

Senior Production Director: Wendy Troeger

Production Director: Patty Stephan

Senior Content Project Manager:
Jennifer K. Feltri-George

Managing Art Director: Jack Pendleton

Cover image(s):
© Bennyartist/Shutterstock.com

Unless otherwise noted all screenshots are
courtesy of Microsoft Corporation

Unless otherwise noted all tables/figures
exhibits are © 2016 Cengage Learning®

© 2016 Cengage Learning
WCN: 01-100-101

ALL RIGHTS RESERVED. No part of this work covered by the copyright herein may be reproduced, transmitted, stored or used in any form or by any means graphic, electronic, or mechanical, including but not limited to photocopying, recording, scanning, digitizing, taping, Web distribution, information networks, or information storage and retrieval systems, except as permitted under Section 107 or 108 of the 1976 United States Copyright Act, without the prior written permission of the publisher.

For product information and technology assistance, contact us at
Cengage Learning Customer & Sales Support, 1-800-354-9706

For permission to use material from this text or product, submit all requests online at **www.cengage.com/permissions**
Further permissions questions can be emailed to
permissionrequest@cengage.com

Library of Congress Control Number: 2015937974
ISBN: 978-1-285-86023-7

Cengage Learning
20 Channel Center Street
Boston, MA 02210
USA

Cengage Learning is a leading provider of customized learning solutions with employees residing in nearly 40 different countries and sales in more than 125 countries around the world. Find your local representative at **www.cengage.com/global**

Cengage Learning products are represented in Canada by Nelson Education, Ltd.

For your course and learning solutions, visit **www.cengage.com**

Purchase any of our products at your local college store or at our preferred online store **www.cengagebrain.com**

Notice to the Reader

Publisher does not warrant or guarantee any of the products described herein or perform any independent analysis in connection with any of the product information contained herein. Publisher does not assume, and expressly disclaims, any obligation to obtain and include information other than that provided to it by the manufacturer. The reader is expressly warned to consider and adopt all safety precautions that might be indicated by the activities described herein and to avoid all potential hazards. By following the instructions contained herein, the reader willingly assumes all risks in connection with such instructions. The publisher makes no representations or warranties of any kind, including but not limited to, the warranties of fitness for particular purpose or merchantability, nor are any such representations implied with respect to the material set forth herein, and the publisher takes no responsibility with respect to such material. The publisher shall not be liable for any special, consequential, or exemplary damages resulting, in whole or part, from the readers' use of, or reliance upon, this material.

Printed in the United States of America
4 5 6 7 8   21 20 19 18 17

Brief Contents

Contents

CHAPTER 3 Using GUI Objects and the Visual Studio IDE . **101**

CHAPTER 4 Making Decisions **137**

viii

x

xiv

Preface

Microsoft Visual C# 2015, Sixth Edition provides the beginning programmer with a guide to developing programs in C#. C# is a language developed by the Microsoft Corporation as part of the .NET Framework and Visual Studio platform. The .NET Framework contains a wealth of libraries for developing applications for the Windows family of operating systems.

With C#, you can build small, reusable components that are well-suited to Web-based programming applications. Although similar to Java and C++, many features of C# make it easier to learn and ideal for the beginning programmer. You can program in C# using a simple text editor and the command prompt, or you can manipulate program components using Visual Studio's sophisticated Integrated Development Environment. This book provides you with the tools to use both techniques.

This textbook assumes that you have little or no programming experience. The writing is nontechnical and emphasizes good programming practices. The examples are business examples; they do not assume mathematical background beyond high school business math. Additionally, the examples illustrate one or two major points; they do not contain so many features that you become lost following irrelevant and extraneous details. This book provides you with a solid background in good object-oriented programming techniques and introduces you to object-oriented terminology using clear, familiar language.

Organization and Coverage

Microsoft Visual C# 2015 presents C# programming concepts, enforcing good style, logical thinking, and the object-oriented paradigm. Chapter 1 introduces you to the language by letting you create working C# programs using both the simple command line and the Visual Studio environment. In Chapter 2 you learn about data and how to input, store, and output data in C#. Chapter 3 provides a quick start to creating GUI applications. You can take two approaches:

- You can cover Chapter 3 and learn about GUI objects so that you can create more visually interesting applications in the subsequent chapters on decision making, looping, and array manipulation. These subsequent chapters confine GUI examples to the end of the chapters, so you can postpone GUI manipulation if you want.

- You can skip Chapter 3 until learning the fundamentals of decision making, looping, and array manipulation, and until studying object-oriented concepts such as classes, objects, polymorphism, inheritance, and exception handling. Then, after Chapter 11, you can return to Chapter 3 and use the built-in GUI component classes with a deeper understanding of how they work.

In Chapters 4, 5, and 6, you learn about the classic programming structures—making decisions, looping, and manipulating arrays—and how to implement them in C#. Chapters 7 and 8 provide a thorough study of methods, including passing parameters into and out of methods and overloading them.

Chapter 9 introduces the object-oriented concepts of classes, objects, data hiding, constructors, and destructors. After completing Chapters 10 and 11, you will be thoroughly grounded in the object-oriented concepts of inheritance and exception handling, and will be able to take advantage of both features in your C# programs. Chapter 12 continues the discussion of GUI objects from Chapter 3. You will learn about controls, how to set their properties, and how to make attractive, useful, graphical, and interactive programs. Chapter 13 takes you further into the intricacies of handling events in your interactive GUI programs. In Chapter 14, you learn to save data to and retrieve data from files.

Features

This text focuses on helping students become better programmers and understand C # program development through a variety of key features. In addition to chapter Objectives, Summaries, and Key Terms, these useful features will help students regardless of their learning styles.

Using Shortcut Arithmetic Operators

You Do It

YOU DO IT follows each major concept. Each "You Do It" section walks students through program development step by step.

67

Performing Arithmetic

In the following steps, you add some arithmetic s

1. Open a new C# program file named **Der** following statements to start a program operations:

   ```
   using static System.Console;
   class DemoVariables2
   {
       static void Main()
       {
   ```

2. Write a statement that declares seven int two of the variables; the values for the ot Because all of these variables are the sai statement to declare all seven integers. F commas between variable names and pla You can place line breaks wherever you v could use as many as seven separate de

   ```
   int value1 = 43, value2 = 10,
       sum, diff, product, quotient,
   ```

3. Write the arithmetic statements that calc between, product of, quotient of, and re variables.

   ```
   sum = value1 + value2;
   diff = value1 - value2;
   product = value1 * value2;
   quotient = value1 / value2;
                        ue2;
   ```

   diff, prod

   alue1 and

   ents to

   and {1}

   betweer
   2, dif
   {0} {1}"

NOTES provide additional information—for example, another location in the book that expands on a topic, or a common error for which to watch out.

CHAPTER 2 Using Data

The prefix and postfix increment operators are **unary operators** because you use them with one operand. Most arithmetic operators, like those used for addition and multiplication, are binary operators that operate on two operands.

66

When all you want to accomplish is to increase a variable's value by 1, there is no apparent difference between using the prefix and postfix increment operators. However, these operators function differently. When you use the prefix ++, the result is calculated and stored and then the variable is used. For example, in the following code, both b and c end up holding 5. The WriteLine() statement displays "5 5". In this example, 4 is assigned to b, then b becomes 5, and then 5 is assigned to c.

```
b = 4;
c = ++b;
WriteLine("{0} {1}", b, c);
```

In contrast, when you use the postfix ++, the variable is used, and then the result is calculated and stored. For example, in the second line of the following code, 4 is assigned to c; then, *after* the assignment, b is increased and takes the value 5.

```
b = 4;
c = b++;
WriteLine("{0} {1}", b, c);
```

This last WriteLine() statement displays "5 4". In other words, if b = 4, then the value of b++ is also 4, and that value is assigned to c. However, after the 4 is assigned to c, b is increased to 5.

> When you need to add 1 to a variable in a stand-alone statement, the results are the same whether you use a prefix or postfix increment operator. However, many programmers routinely use the postfix operator when they could use either operator. This is probably a mistake because the prefix operator is more efficient. You will see an example that proves the superior efficiency of the prefix operator in the chapter "Looping."

A prefix or postfix **decrement operator** (--) reduces a variable's value by 1. For example, if s and t are both assigned the value 34, then the expression --s has the value 33 and the expression t-- has the value 34, but t then becomes 33.

Watch the video *Using Shortcut Arithmetic Operators*.

VIDEO LESSONS help explain important chapter concepts. Videos are available for student and instructor download at CengageBrain.com.

TWO TRUTHS & A LIE

Using Arithmetic Operators

1. The value of 26 % 4 * 3 is 18.

2. The value of 4 / 3 + 2 is 3.

3. rice is 4 and tax is 5, then the value of price - tax++ is −1.

The false statement is #1. The value of 26 % 4 * 3 is 6. The r part of the expression, 26 % 4, is 2, because 2 is the remainder when 4 is divided into 26. Then 2 * 3 is 6.

xviii

TWO TRUTHS & A LIE quizzes appear after each chapter section, with answers provided. The quiz contains three statements based on the preceding section of text—two statements are true and one is false. Answers give immediate feedback without "giving away" answers to the multiple-choice questions and programming problems later in the chapter.

CHAPTER 1 A First Program Using C#

4

TWO TRUTHS & A LIE

Two of the following stat
and explain why it is false

1. A high-level programm
   such as *read, write, c
   these tasks.

2. Each high-level progra

3. Programmers use a c
   into a high-level langu

to translate their

Procedural and Ob

Two popular approaches to wr
object-oriented programming.

When you write a **procedural**
to create and name computer i
steps or operations to manipul
contain instructions similar to

```
get hoursWorked
pay = hoursWorked * 10.0
output pay
```

Named computer memory loc
because they hold values that i
by using a one-word name (an
location referenced by the nam
for different employees. During
the name **hoursWorked** might

THE DON'T DO IT ICON illustrates how NOT to do something—for example, having a dead code path in a program. This icon provides a visual jolt to the student, emphasizing that particular figures are NOT to be emulated and making students more careful to recognize problems in existing code.

Using Compound Expressions in **if** Statements

x	y	x && y
True	True	True
True	False	False
False	True	False
False	False	False

Table 4-1 Truth table for the conditional && operator

155

For example, the two code samples shown in Figure 4-14 work exactly the same way. The **age** variable is tested, and if it is greater than or equal to 0 and less than 120, a message is displayed to explain that the value is valid.

```
// using the && operator
if(age >= 0 && age < 120)
   WriteLine("Age is valid");

// using nested ifs
if(age >= 0)
   if(age < 120)
      WriteLine("Age is valid");
```

Figure 4-14 Comparison of the && operator and nested **if** statements

Using the **&&** operator is never required, because nested **if** statements achieve the same result, but using the **&&** operator often makes your code more concise, less error-prone, and easier to understand.

It is important to note that when you use the **&&** operator, you must include a complete Boolean expression on each side of the operator. If you want to set a bonus to $400 when **saleAmount** is ...00 and under $5000, the correct statement is as follows:

```
... > 1000 && saleAmount < 5000)
0;
```

...tatement is incorrect and will not compile:

```
... > 1000 && < 5000)
0;
```

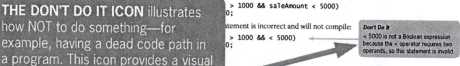

Don't Do It
< 5000 is not a Boolean expression because the < operator requires two operands, so this statement is invalid.

...grammers prefer to surround each Boolean expression that is part of a ...ean expression with its own set of parentheses. For example:

```
...t > 1000) && (saleAmount < 5000))
0;
```

Assessment

PROGRAMMING EXERCISES provide opportunities to practice concepts. These exercises increase in difficulty and allow students to explore each major programming concept presented in the chapter. Additional programming exercises are available to instructors on the Companion Site.

Review Questions

414

1. An object is a(n) _____ of a class.
   a. child
   b. institution

2. A class header or class
   a. an optional access
   b. the keyword clas
   c. an identifier
   d. initial field values

3. Most fields in a class a
   a. public
   b. protected

4. Most methods in a cla:
   a. public
   b. protected

5. Instance methods that static methods.
   a. always
   b. usually

6. To allocate memory fo
   _____
   a. mem
   b. alloc

7. Assume that you have constructor can be ___
   a. public void M'
   b. public MyClas:
   c. Either of these can
   d. Neither of these ca

REVIEW QUESTIONS test student comprehension of the major ideas and techniques presented. Twenty questions follow each chapter.

Exercises

Programming Exercises

265

For each of the following exercises, you may choose to write a console-based or GUI application, or both.

1. Write a program named **ArrayDemo** that stores an array of eight integers. Until the user enters a sentinel value, allow the user three options: (1) to view the list in order from the first to last position, (2) to view the list in order from the last to first position, or (3) to choose a specific position to view.

2. Write a program named **TemperatureList** that accepts seven int values representing high temperatures for seven consecutive days. Display each of the values along with a message that indicates how far it is from the average.

3. Write a program named **ScoresComparison** that allows a user to input four integer quiz scores ranging from 0 through 100. If no score is lower than any previous score, display a message that congratulates the user on making improvement, and then display the scores in the order they were entered. If every score is lower than the previous one, display the scores in the order they were entered, display an appropriate message about the scores' descent, and then display the scores in the more desirable reverse order. If the scores neither increase nor decrease consistently, display an appropriate message along with the scores.

4. Write a program named **CheckZips** that is used by a package delivery service to check delivery areas. The program contains an array that holds the 10 zip codes of areas to which the company makes deliveries. Prompt a user to enter a zip code, and display a message indicating whether the zip code is in the company's delivery area.

5. Write a program called **DeliveryCharges** for the package delivery service in Exercise 4. The program should again use an array that holds the 10 zip codes of areas to which the company makes deliveries. Create a parallel array containing 10 delivery charges that differ for each zip code. Prompt a user to enter a zip code, and then display either a message indicating the price of delivery to that zip code or a message indicating that the company does not deliver to the requested zip code.

6. The Chat-A-While phone company provides service to six area codes and charges the per-minute rates for phone calls shown in Figure 6-25. Write a program named **ChatAWhile** that stores the area codes and rates in parallel arrays and allows a user to enter an area code and the length of time for a call in minutes, and then display the total cost of the call.

DEBUGGING EXERCISES are included with each chapter because examining programs critically and closely is a crucial programming skill. Students can download these exercises at CengageBrain.com. These files are also available to instructors through *sso.cengage.com*

Exercises

Debugging Exercises

1. Each of the following files in the Chapter.02 folder of your downloadable student files has syntax and/or logical errors. In each case, determine the problem program. After you correct the errors, save each file using the with *Fixed*. For example, DebugTwo1.cs will become Fix

   a. DebugTwo1.cs
   b. DebugTwo2.cs
   c. DebugTwo3.cs
   d. DebugTwo4.cs

CASE PROBLEMS provide opportunities to build more detailed programs that continue to incorporate increasing functionality throughout the book.

Case Problems

1. In Chapter 1, you created two programs to display the motto for the Greenville Idol competition that is held each summer during the Greenville County Fair. Now write a program named **GreenvilleRevenue** that prompts a user for the number of contestants entered in last year's competition and in this year's competition. Display all the input data. Compute and display the revenue expected for this year's competition if each contestant pays a $25 entrance fee. Also display a statement that indicates whether this year's competition has more contestants than last year's.

2. In Chapter 1, you created two programs to display the motto for Marshall's Murals. Now write a program named **MarshallsRevenue** that prompts a user for the number of interior and exterior murals scheduled to be painted during the next month. Compute the expected revenue for each type of mural. Interior murals cost $500 each, and **exterior murals cost $750 each. Also display the total expected revenue and a statement** that indicates whether more interior murals are scheduled than exterior ones.

Features

Microsoft Visual C# 2015 is a superior textbook because it also includes the following new features:

- *C# 6.0 in Visual Studio 2015*—This edition is written and tested using the latest edition of C#.

- *The Developer Command Prompt* —Using the Developer Command prompt for console-based programs eliminates the need to understand `class` and `classpath` commands that previous versions of Visual Studio required.

- *Simplified `Console` statements*—The new version of C# allows `Read()`, `ReadLine()`, `Write()`, and `Writeline()` statements to be used without referencing the `Console` class in each statement.

- *String interpolation*—This version of C# provides a new, more intuitive format for displaying strings.

- *Exercises*—Each chapter concludes with meaningful programming exercises that provide additional practice of the skills and concepts you learned in the chapter. Several new exercises appear in each chapter of this edition, and all the replaced exercises and solutions are available to instructors to provide as additional student assignments or to use as the basis for lectures.

Microsoft Visual C# 2015 also includes the following features:

- *Early GUI applications*—Students can begin to create GUI applications in Chapter 3. The earlier introduction helps engage students who have used GUI applications their entire lives. In subsequent chapters on selections, loops, arrays, and methods, students apply concepts to applications in both console and GUI environments. This approach keeps some examples simple while increasing the understanding that input, processing, and output are programming universals, no matter what interface is used. The book is structured so that students who want to skip Chapter 3 until they understand object-oriented programming can do so with no loss of continuity.

- *Objectives*—Each chapter begins with a list of objectives so you know the topics that will be presented in the chapter.

- *Notes*—These tips provide additional information—for example, an alternative method of performing a procedure, another term for a concept, background information on a technique, or a common error to avoid.

- *Figures*—Each chapter contains many figures. Code figures are most frequently 25 lines or shorter, illustrating one concept at a time. Frequently placed screen shots show exactly how program output appears. In this edition, all C# keywords that appear in figures are bold to help them stand out from programmer-created identifiers.

- *Summaries*—Following each chapter is a summary that recaps the programming concepts and techniques covered in the chapter. This feature helps you to check your understanding of the main points in each chapter.

- *Key Terms*—Each chapter includes a list of newly introduced vocabulary, shown in the order of appearance in the text. The list of key terms provides a review of the major concepts in the chapter.

- *Two Truths and a Lie*—This short quiz appears after each main chapter section, with answers provided. This quiz contains three statements—two true and one false—and the student must identify the false one. These quizzes provide students with immediate feedback as they read, without "giving away" answers to the existing multiple-choice and programming problem questions.

- *Review Questions*—Each chapter contains 20 multiple-choice review questions that provide a review of the key concepts in the chapter.

- *Debugging Exercises*—Each chapter contains four programs that have syntax and/or logical errors for you to fix. Completing these exercises provides valuable experience in locating errors, interpreting code written by others, and observing how another programmer has approached a problem.

- *Cases*—Each chapter contains two running case problems. These cases represent projects that continue to grow throughout a semester using concepts learned in each new chapter. Two cases allow instructors to assign different cases in alternate semesters, or to divide students in a class into two case teams.

- *Program Code*—The downloadable student files provide code for each full program presented in the chapter figures. Providing the code allows students to run it, view the results for themselves, and experiment with multiple input values and changes to the code.

- *Glossary*—A glossary contains definitions for all key terms in the book, presented in alphabetical order.

- *Video lessons*—Each chapter includes three or more video lessons produced by the author. These short videos provide instruction, further explanation, or background about a topic covered in the corresponding chapter. These videos are especially useful for online classes, for student review before exams, and for students who are audio learners.

- *Quality*—Every program example in the book, as well as every exercise, case project, and game solution, was tested by the author and again by a Quality Assurance team using Visual Studio 2015.

Instructor Resources

The following teaching tools are available for download at the Companion Site for this text. Simply search for this text at *sso.cengage.com.* An instructor login is required.

- **Instructor's Manual:** The Instructor's Manual that accompanies this textbook includes additional instructional material to assist in class preparation, including items such as Overviews, Chapter Objectives, Teaching Tips, Quick Quizzes, Class Discussion Topics, Additional Projects, Additional Resources, and Key Terms. A sample syllabus is also available.

- **Test Bank:** Cengage Learning Testing Powered by Cognero is a flexible, online system that allows you to:

  - author, edit, and manage test bank content from multiple Cengage Learning solutions

  - create multiple test versions in an instant

  - deliver tests from your LMS, your classroom, or wherever you want

- **PowerPoint Presentations:** This text provides PowerPoint slides to accompany each chapter. Slides may be used to guide classroom presentations, to make available to students for chapter review, or to print as classroom handouts. Files are provided for every figure in the text. Instructors may use the files to customize PowerPoint slides, illustrate quizzes, or create handouts.

- **Solutions:** Solutions to "You Do It" exercises and all end-of-chapter exercises are available.

Acknowledgments

Thank you to all of the people who make this book a success, including Alyssa Pratt, Senior Content Developer; and Jennifer Feltri-George, Content Project Manager. I want to acknowledge every Cengage Learning Consultant who travels the country guiding instructors in their choices of educational materials.

I am also grateful to the many reviewers who provided helpful comments and encouragement during this book's development, including Tracy Driscoll, Bishop State Community College; Nancy Sanchez, Baylor University; and Mark Shellman, Gaston College.

Thanks, too, to my husband, Geoff, for his constant support and encouragement. Finally, this book is dedicated to the memory of Christopher Cox, especially missed by his parents, Butch and Helen Cox, and his daughter, Amanda Cox.

Joyce Farrell

Read This Before You Begin

To the User of the Data Files

To complete the steps and projects in this book, you need data files that have been created specifically for this book. Your instructor will provide the data files to you. You also can obtain the files electronically from CengageBrain.com. Find the ISBN of your title on the back cover of your book, then enter the ISBN in the search box at the top of the CengageBrain home page. You can find the data files on the product page that opens. Note that you can use a computer in your school lab or your own computer to complete the exercises in this book.

Using Your Own Computer

To use your own computer to complete the steps and exercises, you will need the following:

- *Software*—Microsoft Visual C# 2015, including the Microsoft .NET Framework.

- *Hardware*—Minimum requirements identified by Microsoft are a 1.6 GHz CPU, 1 GB of RAM, 10 GB of available hard disk space, 5400 RPM hard disk drive, and DirectX 9-capable video card that runs at 1024×768 or higher display resolution.

- *Operating system*—Windows 7 or 8.

A First Program Using C#

In this chapter you will:

◎ Learn about programming

◎ Learn about procedural and object-oriented programming

◎ Learn about the features of object-oriented programming languages

◎ Learn about the C# programming language

◎ Write a C# program that produces output

◎ Learn how to select identifiers to use within your programs

◎ Improve programs by adding comments and using the System namespace

◎ Compile and execute a C# program using the command prompt and using Visual Studio

Programming a computer is an interesting, challenging, fun, and sometimes frustrating task. As you learn a programming language, you must be precise and careful as well as creative. Computer programmers can choose from a variety of programming languages, such as Visual Basic, Java, and C++. C# (pronounced "C Sharp") is a newer programming language that offers a wide range of options and features. As you work through this book, you will master many of them, one step at a time. If this is your first programming experience, you will learn new ways to approach and solve problems and to think logically. If you know how to program but are new to C#, you will be impressed by its capabilities.

In this chapter, you will learn about the background of programming that led to the development of C#, and you will write and execute your first C# programs.

Programming

A computer **program** is a set of instructions that tells a computer what to do. Programs are also called **software;** software comes in two broad categories:

- **System software** describes the programs that operate the computer. Examples include operating systems such as Microsoft Windows, Mac OSX, and Linux.

- **Application software** describes the programs that allow users to complete tasks such as creating documents, calculating paychecks, and playing games.

The physical devices that make up a computer system are called **hardware**. Internally, computer hardware is constructed from circuitry that consists of small on/off switches; the most basic circuitry-level language that computers use to control the operation of those switches is called **machine language**. Machine language is expressed as a series of 1s and 0s—1s represent switches that are on, and 0s represent switches that are off. If programmers had to write computer programs using machine language, they would have to keep track of the hundreds of thousands of 1s and 0s involved in programming any worthwhile task. Not only would writing a program be a time-consuming and difficult task, but modifying programs, understanding others' programs, and locating errors within programs all would be cumbersome. Additionally, the number and location of switches vary from computer to computer, which means you would need to customize a machine-language program for every type of machine on which the program had to run.

Fortunately, programming has become easier because of the development of high-level programming languages. A **high-level programming language** allows you to use a limited vocabulary of reasonable keywords. **Keywords** are predefined and reserved identifiers that have special meaning in a language. In other words, high-level language programs contain words such as *read, write,* or *add* instead of the sequence of on/off switches that perform these tasks. High-level languages also allow you to assign reasonable names to areas of computer memory; you can use names such as hoursWorked or payRate, rather than having to remember the memory locations (switch numbers) of those values.

Camel casing, or **lower camel casing**, describes the style of identifiers like `hoursWorked` and `payRate` that appear to have a hump in the middle because they start with a lowercase letter but contain uppercase letters to identify new words. By convention, C# programmers use camel casing when creating variable names. Also, the C# programming language is case sensitive. Therefore, if you create an identifier named `payRate`, you cannot refer to it later using identifiers such as `PayRate` or `payrate`.

Each high-level language has its own **syntax**, or rules of the language. For example, to produce output, you might use the verb *print* in one language and *write* in another. All languages have a specific, limited vocabulary, along with a set of rules for using that vocabulary. Programmers use a computer program called a **compiler** to translate their high-level language statements into machine code. The compiler issues an error message each time a programmer commits a **syntax error**—that is, each time the programmer uses the language incorrectly. Subsequently, the programmer can correct the error and attempt another translation by compiling the program again. The program can be completely translated to machine language only when all syntax errors have been corrected. When you learn a computer programming language such as C#, C++, Visual Basic, or Java, you must learn the vocabulary and syntax rules for that language.

In some languages, such as BASIC, the language translator is called an interpreter. In others, such as assembly language, it is called an assembler. The various language translators operate differently, but the ultimate goal of each is to translate the higher-level language into machine language.

In addition to learning the correct syntax for a particular language, a programmer must understand computer programming logic.

The **logic** behind any program involves executing the various statements and procedures in the correct order to produce the desired results. For example, you might be able to execute perfect individual notes on a musical instrument, but if you do not execute them in the proper order (or execute a B-flat when an F-sharp was expected), no one will enjoy your performance. Similarly, you might be able to use a computer language's syntax correctly but be unable to obtain correct results because the program is not constructed logically. Examples of logical errors include multiplying two values when you should divide them, or attempting to calculate a paycheck before obtaining the appropriate payroll data. The logic used to solve a problem might be identical in two programs, but the programs can be written in different languages, each using different syntax.

Since the early days of computer programming, program errors have been called **bugs**. The term is often said to have originated from an actual moth that was discovered trapped in the circuitry of a computer at Harvard University in 1945. Actually, the term *bug* was in use prior to 1945 to mean trouble with any electrical apparatus; even during Thomas Edison's life, it meant an "industrial defect." In any case, the process of finding and correcting program errors has come to be known as **debugging the program**.

4

TWO TRUTHS & A LIE

Programming

Two of the following statements are true, and one is false. Identify the false statement, and explain why it is false.

1. A high-level programming language allows you to use a vocabulary of reasonable terms such as *read*, *write*, or *add* instead of the sequence of on/off switches that perform these tasks.

2. Each high-level programming language has its own syntax.

3. Programmers use a computer program called a compiler to translate machine code into a high-level language they can understand.

The false statement is #3. Programmers use a compiler to translate their high-level language statements into machine code.

Procedural and Object-Oriented Programming

Two popular approaches to writing computer programs are procedural programming and object-oriented programming.

When you write a **procedural program,** you use your knowledge of a programming language to create and name computer memory locations that can hold values, and you write a series of steps or operations to manipulate those values. For example, a simple payroll program might contain instructions similar to the following:

```
get hoursWorked
pay = hoursWorked * 10.00
output pay
```

Named computer memory locations such as hoursWorked and pay are called **variables** because they hold values that might vary. In programming languages, a variable is referenced by using a one-word name (an **identifier**) with no embedded spaces. For example, the memory location referenced by the name hoursWorked might contain different values at different times for different employees. During the execution of the payroll program, each value stored under the name hoursWorked might have many operations performed on it—for example, reading it from an input device, multiplying it by a pay rate, and printing it on paper.

Examples of procedural programming languages include C and Logo.

For convenience, the individual operations used in a procedural program often are grouped into logical units called **methods**. For example, a series of four or five comparisons and calculations that together determine an employee's withholding tax value might be grouped as a method named CalculateWithholdingTax().

Capitalizing the first letter of all new words in an identifier, even the first one, as in CalculateWithholdingTax(), is a style called **Pascal casing** or **upper camel casing**. Although it is legal to start a method name with a lowercase letter, the convention used in C# is for methods to be named using Pascal casing. This helps distinguish them from variables which conventionally use lower camel casing. Additionally, in C# all method names are followed by a set of parentheses. When this book refers to a method, the name will be followed with parentheses.

A procedural program divides a problem solution into multiple methods, each with a unique name. The program then **calls** or **invokes** the methods to input, manipulate, and output the values stored in those locations. A single procedural program often contains hundreds of variables and thousands of method calls.

Depending on the programming language, methods are sometimes called *procedures, subroutines, or functions*. In C#, the preferred term is *methods*.

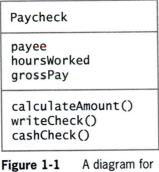

Figure 1-1   A diagram for a Paycheck

Object-oriented programming (OOP) is an extension of procedural programming. OOP uses variables and methods like procedural programs do, but it focuses on objects. An **object** is a concrete entity that has attributes and behaviors. The **attributes of an object** are the features it "has"; the values of an object's attributes constitute the **state of the object**. For example, attributes of a paycheck include its payee and monetary value, and the state of those attributes might be *Alice Nelson* and *$400*. The **behaviors of an object** are the things it "does," or its methods; for example, a paycheck object can be written and cashed, and contains a method to calculate the check amount. Figure 1-1 shows how a programmer might start to visualize a paycheck—thinking about its name, attributes, and behaviors. Beyond a paycheck, object-oriented programmers might design a payroll system by thinking about all the additional objects needed to produce a paycheck, such as employees, time cards, and bank accounts.

Programmers use the term *OO*, pronounced "oh oh," as an abbreviation for *object oriented*. When discussing object-oriented programming, they use *OOP*, which rhymes with *soup*.

Examples of OO languages include C#, Java, Visual Basic, and C++. You can write procedural programs in OO languages, but you cannot write OO programs in procedural languages.

With either approach, procedural or object-oriented, you can produce a correct paycheck, and both techniques employ reusable program modules. The major difference lies in the focus the programmer takes during the earliest planning stages of a project. Taking an **object-oriented approach** to a problem means defining the objects needed to accomplish a task and developing classes that describe the objects so that each object maintains its own data and carries out tasks when another object requests them. The object-oriented approach is said to be "natural"—it is more common to think of a world of objects and the ways they interact than to consider a world of systems, data items, and the logic required to manipulate them.

 Object-oriented programming employs a large vocabulary; you can learn much of this terminology in the chapter called "Using Classes and Objects."

Originally, object-oriented programming was used most frequently for two major types of applications:

- **Computer simulations** are programs that attempt to mimic real-world activities so that their processes can be improved or so that users can better understand how the real-world processes operate.

- **Graphical user interfaces, or GUIs** (pronounced "gooeys") are programs that allow users to interact with a program in a graphical environment, such as by clicking with a mouse or using a touch screen.

Thinking about objects in these two types of applications makes sense. For example, a city might want to develop a program that simulates traffic patterns to better prevent congestion. By creating a model with objects such as cars and pedestrians that contain their own data and rules for behavior, the simulation can be set in motion. For example, each car object has a specific current speed and a procedure for changing that speed. By creating a model of city traffic using objects, a computer can create a simulation of a real city at rush hour.

Creating a GUI environment for users also is a natural use for object orientation. It is easy to think of the components a user manipulates on a computer screen, such as buttons and scroll bars, as similar to real-world objects. Each GUI object contains data— for example, a button on a screen has a specific size and color. Each object also contains behaviors—for example, each button can be clicked and reacts in a specific way when clicked. Some people consider the term *object-oriented programming* to be synonymous with GUI programming, but object-oriented programming means more. Although many GUI programs are object oriented, one does not imply the other. Modern businesses use object-oriented design techniques when developing all sorts of business applications, whether they are GUI applications or not.

> **TWO TRUTHS & A LIE**
>
> ### Procedural and Object-Oriented Programming
>
> 1. Procedural programs use variables and tasks that are grouped into methods or procedures.
>
> 2. Object-oriented programming languages do not support variables or methods; instead they focus on objects.
>
> 3. Object-oriented programs were first used for simulations and GUI programs.
>
> The false statement is #2. Object-oriented programs contain variables and methods just as procedural programs do.

Features of Object-Oriented Programming Languages

For a language to be considered object-oriented, it must support the following features:

- Classes
- Objects
- Encapsulation and interfaces
- Inheritance
- Polymorphism

A **class** describes potential objects, including their attributes and behaviors. A class is similar to a recipe or a blueprint in that it describes what features objects will have and what they will be able to do after they are created. An object is an **instance of a class;** it is one tangible example of a class.

For example, you might create a class named Automobile. Some of an Automobile's attributes are its make, model, year, and purchase price. All Automobiles possess the same attributes, but not the same values, or states, for those attributes. (Programmers also call the values of an object's attributes the **properties** of the object.) When you create specific Automobile objects, each object can hold unique values for the attributes, such as *Ford, Taurus, 2016,* and *$27,000.* Similarly, a Dog has attributes that include its breed, name, age, and vaccination status; the attributes for a particular dog might be *Labrador retriever, Murphy, 7,* and *current.*

When you understand that an object belongs to a specific class, you know a lot about the object. If your friend purchases an Automobile, you know it has *some* model name; if your friend gets a Dog, you know it has *some* breed. You probably don't know the current state of the Automobile's speed or of the Dog's shots, but you do know that those attributes exist for the Automobile and

Dog classes. Similarly, in a GUI operating environment, you expect each window you open to have specific, consistent attributes, such as a menu bar and a title bar, because each window includes these attributes as a member of the general class of GUI windows.

 By convention, programmers using C# begin their class names with an uppercase letter and use a singular noun. Thus, the class that defines the attributes and methods of an automobile would probably be named Automobile, and the class that contains dogs would probably be named Dog. If the class requires two words, programmers conventionally use upper camel casing, as in BankAccount.

Besides attributes, objects possess methods that they use to accomplish tasks, including changing attributes and discovering the values of attributes. Automobiles, for example, have methods for moving forward and backward. They also can be filled with gasoline or be washed; both are methods that change some of an Automobile's attributes. Methods also exist for determining the status of certain attributes, such as the current speed of an Automobile and the number of gallons of gas in its tank. Similarly, a Dog can walk or run, eat, and get a bath, and there are methods for determining whether it needs a walk, food, or a bath. GUI operating system components, such as windows, can be maximized, minimized, and dragged; depending on the component, they can also have their color or font style altered.

Like procedural programs, object-oriented programs have variables (attributes) and procedures (methods), but the attributes and methods are encapsulated into objects that are then used much like real-world objects. **Encapsulation** is the technique of packaging an object's attributes and methods into a cohesive unit that can be used as an undivided entity. Programmers sometimes refer to encapsulation as using a **"black box,"** a device you use without regard for the internal mechanisms. If an object's methods are well written, the user is unaware of the low-level details of how the methods are executed; in such a case, the user must understand only the **interface** or interaction between the method and object. For example, if you can fill your Automobile with gasoline, it is because you understand the interface between the gas pump nozzle and the vehicle's gas tank opening. You don't need to understand how the pump works or where the gas tank is located inside your vehicle. If you can read your speedometer, it does not matter how the display value is calculated. In fact, if someone produces a new, more accurate speedometer and inserts it into your Automobile, you don't have to know or care how it operates, as long as the interface remains the same as the previous one. The same principles apply to well-constructed objects used in object-oriented programs.

Object-oriented programming languages support two other distinguishing features in addition to organizing objects as members of classes. One feature, **inheritance**, provides the ability to extend a class so as to create a more specific class. The more specific class contains all the attributes and methods of the more general class and usually contains new attributes or methods as well. For example, if you have created a Dog class, you might then create a more specific class named ShowDog. Each instance of the ShowDog class would contain, or inherit, all the attributes and methods of a Dog, along with additional methods or attributes. For example, a ShowDog might require an attribute to hold the number of ribbons won and a method for entering a dog show. The advantage of inheritance is that when you need a class such as ShowDog, you often can extend an existing class, thereby saving a lot of time and work.

Object-oriented languages also support **polymorphism**, which is the ability to create methods that act appropriately depending on the context. That is, programs written in object-oriented languages can distinguish between methods with the same name based on the type of object that uses them. For example, you are able to "fill" both a Dog and an Automobile, but you do so by very different means. Similarly, the procedure to "fill" a ShowDog might require different food than that for a "plain" Dog. Older, non-object-oriented languages could not make such distinctions, but object-oriented languages can.

The chapters "Using Classes and Objects" and "Introduction to Inheritance" contain much more information on the features of object-oriented programs.

Watch the video *Object-Oriented Programming*.

TWO TRUTHS & A LIE

Features of Object-Oriented Programming Languages

1. Object-oriented programs contain classes that describe the attributes and methods of objects.

2. Object-oriented programming languages support inheritance, which refers to the packaging of attributes and methods into logical units.

3. Object-oriented programming languages support polymorphism, which is the ability of a method to act appropriately based on the context.

The false statement is #2. Inheritance is the ability to extend classes to make more specific ones. Encapsulation refers to the packaging of attributes and methods.

The C# Programming Language

The **C# programming language** was developed as an object-oriented and component-oriented language. It is part of Microsoft Visual Studio, a package designed for developing applications that run on Windows computers. Unlike other programming languages, C# allows every piece of data to be treated as an object and to consistently employ the principles of object-oriented programming. C# provides constructs for creating components with properties, methods, and events, making it an ideal language for modern programming, where building small, reusable components is more important than building huge, stand-alone applications. You can find Microsoft's C# specifications at *msdn.microsoft.com*. Search for *C# specifications*.

If you have not programmed before, the differences between C# and other languages mean little to you. However, experienced programmers will appreciate the thought that was put into C# features. For example:

- C# contains a GUI interface that makes it similar to Visual Basic, but C# is considered more concise than Visual Basic.

- C# is modeled after the C++ programming language, but is considered easier to learn. Some of the most difficult features to understand in C++ have been eliminated in C#.

Some differences between C# and C++ are that pointers (variables that hold memory addresses) are not used in C# (except in a mode called unsafe, which is rarely used), object destructors and forward declarations are not needed, and using #include files is not necessary. Multiple inheritance, which causes many C++ programming errors, is not allowed in C#.

- C# is very similar to Java, because Java was also based on C++. However, C# is more truly object oriented. Unlike in Java, every piece of data in C# is an object, providing all data with increased functionality.

In Java, simple data types are not objects; therefore, they do not work with built-in methods. Additionally, in Java, data can only be passed to and from methods using a copy; C# omits this limitation. You will learn more in two later chapters: "Introduction to Methods" and "Advanced Method Concepts."

The C# programming language was standardized in 2002 by Ecma International. You can read or download this set of standards at www.ecma-international.org/publications/standards/Ecma-334.htm.

TWO TRUTHS & A LIE

The C# Programming Language

1. The C# programming language was developed as an object-oriented and component-oriented language.

2. C# contains several features that make it similar to other languages such as Java and Visual Basic.

3. C# contains many advanced features, so the C++ programming language was created as a simpler version of the language.

The false statement is 3. C# is modeled after the C++ programming language, but some of the most difficult features to understand in C++ have been eliminated in C#.

Writing a C# Program that Produces Output

At first glance, even the simplest C# program involves a fair amount of confusing syntax. Consider the simple program in Figure 1-2. This program is written on seven lines, and its only task is to display *This is my first C# program* on the screen.

```
class FirstClass
{
    static void Main()
    {
        System.Console.WriteLine("This is my first C# program");
    }
}
```

Figure 1-2   `FirstClass` console application

The statement that does the actual work in this program is in the middle of the figure:

`System.Console.WriteLine("This is my first C# program");`

The statement ends with a semicolon because all C# statements do.

The text `"This is my first C# program"` is a **literal string** of characters—that is, a series of characters that will be used exactly as entered. Any literal string in C# appears between double quotation marks.

The string `"This is my first C# program"` appears within parentheses because the string is an argument to a method, and arguments to methods always appear within parentheses. **Arguments** represent information that a method needs to perform its task. For example, if making an appointment with a dentist's office was a C# method, you would write the following:

`MakeAppointment("September 10", "2 p.m.");`

Accepting and processing a dental appointment is a method that consists of a set of standard procedures. However, each appointment requires different information—the date and time—and this information can be considered the arguments of the `MakeAppointment()` method. If you make an appointment for September 10 at 2 p.m., you expect different results than if you make one for September 9 at 8 a.m. or December 25 at midnight. Likewise, if you pass the argument `"Happy Holidays"` to a method, you will expect different results than if you pass the argument `"This is my first C# program"`.

   Although an argument to a method might be a string, not all arguments are strings. In this book, you will see and write methods that accept many other types of data.

Within the statement `System.Console.WriteLine("This is my first C# program");`, the method to which you are passing the argument string is named `WriteLine()`. The

WriteLine() method displays output on the screen and positions the cursor on the next line, where additional output might be displayed subsequently. The Write() method is very similar to the WriteLine() method. With WriteLine(), the cursor is moved to the following line after the message is displayed. With Write(), the cursor does not advance to a new line; it remains on the same line as the output.

Within the statement System.Console.WriteLine("This is my first C# program");, Console is a class that contains the WriteLine() method. Of course, not all classes have a WriteLine() method (for instance, you can't write a line to a computer's mouse, an Automobile, or a Dog), but the creators of C# assumed that you frequently would want to display output on the screen at your terminal. For this reason, the Console class was created and endowed with the method named WriteLine(). When you use the WriteLine() method, programmers say that you *call* it or *invoke* it. Soon, you will create your own C# classes and endow them with your own callable methods.

Within the statement System.Console.WriteLine("This is my first C# program");, System is a namespace. A **namespace** is a construct that acts like a container to provide a way to group similar classes. To organize your classes, you can (and will) create your own namespaces. The System namespace, which is built into your C# compiler, holds commonly used classes.

An advantage to using Visual Studio is that all of its languages use the same namespaces. In other words, everything you learn about any namespace in C# is knowledge you can transfer to Visual C++ and Visual Basic.

The dots (periods) in the phrase System.Console.WriteLine are used to separate the names of the namespace, class, and method. You will use this same namespace-dot-class-dot-method format repeatedly in your C# programs.

In the FirstClass class in Figure 1-2, the WriteLine() statement appears within a method named Main(). Every executable C# application must contain a Main() method because that is the starting point for every program. As you continue to learn C# from this book, you will write applications that contain additional methods. You will also create classes that are not programs, and so do not need a Main() method.

Every method in C# contains a header and a body. A **method header** includes the method name and information about what will pass into and be returned from a method. A **method body** is contained within a pair of curly braces ({ }) and includes all the instructions executed by the method. The program in Figure 1-2 includes only one statement between the curly braces of the Main() method. Soon, you will write methods with many more statements. In Figure 1-2, the WriteLine() statement within the Main() method is indented within the curly braces. Although the C# compiler does not require such indentation, it is conventional and clearly shows that the WriteLine() statement lies within the Main() method.

For every opening curly brace ({) in a C# program, there must be a corresponding closing curly brace (}). The precise position of the opening and closing curly braces is not important to the compiler. In general, whitespace is optional in C#. **Whitespace** is any combination of spaces, tabs, and carriage returns (blank lines). You use whitespace to organize your program code and make it easier to read; it does not affect your program's execution. Usually, you vertically align each pair of opening and closing curly braces and indent the contents between them, as shown in Figure 1-2.

The method header for the Main() method in Figure 1-2 contains three words. Two of these words are keywords. In this book, C# keywords appear in bold. A complete list of keywords appears in Table 1-1 later in this chapter. In the method header **static void** Main(), the keyword **static** indicates that the Main() method will be executed through a class—not by a variety of objects. It means that you do not need to create an object of type FirstClass to use the Main() method defined within FirstClass. Later in this book, you will create other methods that are nonstatic methods and that are executed by objects.

The second word in the method header in Figure 1-2 is **void**. In English, the word *void* means empty or having no effect. When the keyword **void** is used in the Main() method header, it does not indicate that the Main() method is empty, or that it has no effect, but rather that the method does not return any value when called. You will learn more about methods that return values (and do affect other methods) when you study methods in greater detail.

In the method header, the name of the method is Main(). Main() is not a C# keyword, but all C# applications must include a method named Main(), and most C# applications will have additional methods with other names. Recall that when you execute a C# application, the Main() method always executes first. Classes that contain a Main() method are **application classes**. Applications are executable or **runnable**. Classes that do not contain a Main() method are **non-application classes**, and are not runnable. Non-application classes provide support for other classes.

 Watch the video *The Parts of a C# Program*.

TWO TRUTHS & A LIE

Writing a C# Program that Produces Output

1. Strings are information that methods need to perform their tasks.

2. The WriteLine() method displays output on the screen and positions the cursor on the next line, where additional output might be displayed.

3. Many methods such as WriteLine() have been created for you because the creators of C# assumed you would need them frequently.

The false statement is #1. Strings are literal values represented between quotation marks. Arguments represent information that a method needs to perform its task. Although an argument might be a string, not all arguments are strings.

Selecting Identifiers

Every method that you use within a C# program must be part of a class. To create a class, you use a class header and curly braces in much the same way you use a header and braces for a method within a class. When you write class FirstClass, you are defining a class named FirstClass. A class name does not have to contain the word *Class* as FirstClass does; as a matter of fact, most class names you create will not contain *Class*. You can define a C# class using any identifier you need, as long as it meets the following requirements:

- An identifier must begin with an underscore, the "at" sign (@), or a letter. Letters include foreign-alphabet letters such as Π and Ω, which are contained in the set of characters known as Unicode. You will learn more about Unicode in the next chapter.

- An identifier can contain only letters, digits, underscores, and the @ sign. An identifier cannot contain spaces or any other punctuation or special characters such as #, $, or &.

- An identifier cannot be a C# reserved keyword, such as class or void. Table 1-1 provides a complete list of reserved keywords. Actually, you can use a keyword as an identifier if you precede it with an @ sign, as in @class. An identifier with an @ prefix is a **verbatim identifier**. This feature allows you to use code written in other languages that do not have the same set of reserved keywords. However, when you write original C# programs, you should not use the keywords as identifiers.

abstract	float	return
as	for	sbyte
base	foreach	sealed
bool	goto	short
break	if	sizeof
byte	implicit	stackalloc
case	in	static
catch	int	string
char	interface	struct
checked	internal	switch
class	is	this
const	lock	throw
continue	long	true
decimal	namespace	try
default	new	typeof

Table 1-1 C# reserved keywords *(continues)*

(continued)

delegate	null	uint
do	object	ulong
double	operator	unchecked
else	out	unsafe
enum	override	ushort
event	params	using
explicit	private	virtual
extern	protected	void
false	public	volatile
finally	readonly	while
fixed	ref	

Table 1-1   C# reserved keywords

The following identifiers have special meaning in C# but are not keywords: add, alias, get, global, partial, remove, set, value, where, and yield. For clarity, you should avoid using these words as your own identifiers.

Table 1-2 lists some valid and conventional class names you might use when creating classes in C#. You should follow established conventions for C# so that other programmers can interpret and follow your programs. Table 1-3 lists some class names that are valid, but unconventional; Table 1-4 lists some illegal class names.

Class Name	Description
Employee	Begins with an uppercase letter
FirstClass	Begins with an uppercase letter, contains no spaces, and has an initial uppercase letter that indicates the start of the second word
PushButtonControl	Begins with an uppercase letter, contains no spaces, and has an initial uppercase letter that indicates the start of all subsequent words
Budget2016	Begins with an uppercase letter and contains no spaces

Table 1-2   Some valid and conventional class names in C#

Class Name	Description
employee	Unconventional as a class name because it begins with a lowercase letter
First_Class	Although legal, the underscore is not commonly used to indicate new words in class names
Pushbuttoncontrol	No uppercase characters are used to indicate the start of a new word, making the name difficult to read
BUDGET2016	Unconventional as a class name because it contains all uppercase letters
Void	Although this identifier is legal because it is different from the keyword void, which begins with a lowercase v, the similarity could cause confusion

Table 1-3 Some unconventional (though legal) class names in C#

Class Name	Description
an employee	Space character is illegal
Push Button Control	Space characters are illegal
class	class is a reserved word
2016Budget	Class names cannot begin with a digit
phone#	The # symbol is not allowed; identifiers consist of letters, digits, underscores, or @

Table 1-4 Some illegal class names in C#

In Figure 1-2, the line class FirstClass contains the keyword class, which identifies FirstClass as a class.

The simple program shown in Figure 1-2 has many pieces to remember. For now, you can use the program shown in Figure 1-3 as a shell, where you replace the identifier AnyLegalClassName with any legal class name, and the line /*********/ with any statements that you want to execute.

```
class AnyLegalClassName
{
    static void Main()
    {
        /*********/;
    }
}
```

Figure 1-3   Shell program

Watch the video *C# Identifiers.*

TWO TRUTHS & A LIE

Selecting Identifiers

1. In C#, an identifier must begin with an underscore, the at sign (@), or an uppercase letter.

2. An identifier can contain only letters, digits, underscores, and the @ sign, not special characters such as #, $, or &.

3. An identifier cannot be a C# reserved keyword.

The false statement is #1. In C#, an identifier must begin with an underscore, the @ sign, or a letter. There is no requirement that the initial letter be capitalized, although in C#, it is a convention that the initial letter of a class name is capitalized.

Improving Programs by Adding Comments and Using the System Namespace

As you can see, even the simplest C# program takes several lines of code and contains somewhat perplexing syntax. Large programs that perform many tasks include much more code. As you work through this book, you will discover many ways to improve your ability to handle large programs. Two things you can do immediately are to add program comments and use the System namespace.

Adding Program Comments

As you write longer programs, it becomes increasingly difficult to remember why you included steps and how you intended to use particular variables. **Program comments** are nonexecuting statements that you add to document a program. Programmers use comments to leave notes for themselves and for others who might read their programs.

 As you work through this book, you should add comments as the first few lines of every program file. The comments should contain your name, the date, and the name of the program. Your instructor might want you to include additional comments.

Comments also can be useful when you are developing a program. If a program is not performing as expected, you can **comment out** various statements and subsequently run the program to observe the effect. When you comment out a statement, you turn it into a comment so the compiler will ignore it. This approach helps you pinpoint the location of errant statements in malfunctioning programs.

C# offers three types of comments:

- **Line comments** start with two forward slashes (//) and continue to the end of the current line. Line comments can appear on a line by themselves, or they can occupy part of a line following executable code.

- **Block comments** start with a forward slash and an asterisk (/*) and end with an asterisk and a forward slash (*/). Block comments can appear on a line by themselves, on a line before executable code, or after executable code. When a comment is long, block comments can extend across as many lines as needed.

- C# also supports a special type of comment used to create documentation within a program. These comments, called **XML-documentation format comments**, use a special set of tags within angle brackets (< >). (XML stands for Extensible Markup Language.) You will learn more about this type of comment as you continue your study of C#.

 The forward slash (/) and the backslash (\ ) characters often are confused, but they are distinct characters. You cannot use them interchangeably.

Figure 1-4 shows how comments can be used in code. The program covers 10 lines, yet only seven are part of the executable C# program, including the last two lines, which contain curly braces and are followed by partial-line comments. The only line that actually *does* anything visible when the program runs is the shaded one that displays *Message*.

```
/* This program is written to demonstrate using comments
*/
class ClassWithOneExecutingLine
{
    static void Main()
    {
        // The next line writes the message
        System.Console.WriteLine("Message");
    } // End of Main
} // End of ClassWithOneExecutingLine
```

Figure 1-4   Using comments within a program

Using the System Namespace

A program can contain as many statements as you need. For example, the program in Figure 1-5 produces the three lines of output shown in Figure 1-6. (To get the output, you have to know how to compile and execute the program, which you will learn in the next part of this chapter.) A semicolon separates each program statement.

```
class ThreeLinesOutput
{
    static void Main()
    {
        System.Console.WriteLine("Line one");
        System.Console.WriteLine("Line two");
        System.Console.WriteLine("Line three");
    }
}
```

Figure 1-5   A program that produces three lines of output

Figure 1-6   Output of the ThreeLinesOutput program

 Figure 1-6 shows the output of the ThreeLinesOutput program when it is run in Visual Studio. The prompt to press any key to continue is not part of the program; it is added by Visual Studio, but it does not appear if you run the program from the command prompt.

The program in Figure 1-5 shows a lot of repeated code—the phrase `System.Console.WriteLine` appears three times. When you need to repeatedly use a class from the same namespace, you can shorten the statements you type by adding a clause that indicates a namespace containing the class. You indicate a namespace with a **using clause**, or **using directive**, as shown in the shaded statement in the program in Figure 1-7. If you type `using System;` prior to the class definition, the compiler knows to use the `System` namespace when it encounters the `Console` class. The output of the program in Figure 1-7 is identical to that in Figure 1-5, in which `System` was repeated with each `WriteLine()` statement.

```
using System;
class ThreeLinesOutput
{
    static void Main()
    {
        Console.WriteLine("Line one");
        Console.WriteLine("Line two");
        Console.WriteLine("Line three");
    }
}
```

Figure 1-7   A program that produces three lines of output with a `using System;` clause

Starting with C# 6.0, you can reduce typing in programs even further by inserting `using static System.Console;` at the top of a program. So, In Visual Studio 2015, the program in Figure 1-8 uses only the method name `WriteLine()` in its output statements, and the program works correctly, (You have already seen the word `static` in the `Main()` method header. Recall that `static` means a method is used without creating an object. In Chapter 7, you will learn more about the use of the keyword `static`.) The simpler style shown in Figure 1-8 is the style used for programs in the rest of this book.

```csharp
using static System.Console;
class ThreeLinesOutput
{
    static void Main()
    {
        WriteLine("Line one");
        WriteLine("Line two");
        WriteLine("Line three");
    }
}
```

Figure 1-8   A program that produces three lines of output with a `using static System.Console;` clause

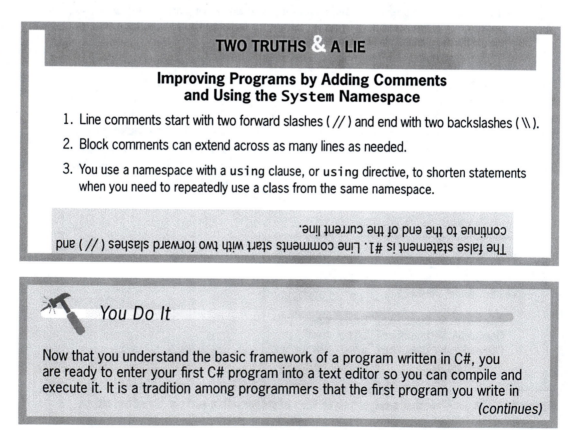

TWO TRUTHS & A LIE

Improving Programs by Adding Comments and Using the System Namespace

1. Line comments start with two forward slashes (//) and end with two backslashes (\\ ).

2. Block comments can extend across as many lines as needed.

3. You use a namespace with a `using` clause, or `using` directive, to shorten statements when you need to repeatedly use a class from the same namespace.

The false statement is #1. Line comments start with two forward slashes (//) and continue to the end of the current line.

You Do It

Now that you understand the basic framework of a program written in C#, you are ready to enter your first C# program into a text editor so you can compile and execute it. It is a tradition among programmers that the first program you write in

(continues)

(continued)

any language produces *Hello, world!* as its output. To create a C# program, you can use any simple text editor, such as Notepad, or the editor that is included as part of Microsoft Visual Studio. There are advantages to using the C# editor to write your programs, but using a plain text editor is simpler when you are getting started.

Entering a Program into an Editor

1. Start any text editor, such as Notepad, and open a new document, if necessary.

2. Type the `using` statement and the header for the class:

```
using static System.Console;
class Hello
```

3. On the next two lines, type the class-opening and class-closing curly braces: `{}`. Some programmers type a closing brace as soon as they type the opening one to guarantee that they always type complete pairs.

4. Between the class braces, insert a new line, type three spaces to indent, and write the `Main()` method header:

```
static void Main()
```

5. On the next two lines, type the opening and closing braces for the `Main()` method, indenting them about three spaces.

6. Between the `Main()` method's braces, insert a new line and type six spaces so the next statement will be indented within the braces. Type the one executing statement in this program:

```
WriteLine("Hello, world!");
```

Your code should look like Figure 1-9.

```
using static System.Console;
class Hello
{
   static void Main()
   {
      WriteLine("Hello, world!");
   }
}
```

Figure 1-9   The Hello class

(continues)

(continued)

7. Choose a location that is meaningful to you to save your program. For example, you might create a folder named C# on your hard drive. Within that folder, you might create a folder named Chapter.01 in which you will store all the examples and exercises in this chapter. If you are working in a school lab, you might be assigned a storage location on your school's server. Save the program as **Hello.cs**. It is important that the file extension be .cs, which stands for *C Sharp*. If the file has a different extension, the compiler for C# will not recognize the program as a C# program.

Many text editors attach their own filename extension (such as .txt or .doc) to a saved file. Double-check your saved file to ensure that it does not have a double extension (as in Hello.cs.txt). If the file has a double extension, rename it. If you use a word-processing program as your editor, select the option to save the file as a plain text file.

Compiling and Executing a C# Program

After you write and save a program, two more steps must be performed before you can view the program output:

1. You must compile the program you wrote (called the **source code**) into **intermediate language (IL)**.

2. The C# **just in time (JIT)** compiler must translate the intermediate code into executable code.

When you compile a C# program, your source code is translated into intermediate language. The JIT compiler converts IL instructions into native code at the last moment, and appropriately for each type of operating system on which the code might eventually be executed. In other words, the same set of IL can be JIT compiled and executed on any supported architecture.

Some developers say that languages like C# are "semi-compiled." That is, instead of being translated immediately from source code to their final executable versions, programs are compiled into an intermediate version that is later translated into the correct executable statements for the environment in which the program is running.

You can write a program using a simple editor such as Notepad and then perform these steps from the command prompt in your system. You also can write a program within the Integrated Development Environment that comes with Visual Studio. Both methods can produce the same output; the one you use is a matter of preference.

- The **command line** is the line on which you type a command in a system that uses a text interface. The **command prompt** is a request for input that appears at the beginning of the command line. In DOS, the command prompt indicates the disk drive and optional path, and ends with >. You might prefer the simplicity of the command line because you do not work with multiple menus and views. Additionally, if you want to pass command-line arguments to a program, you must compile from the command line.

- The **Integrated Development Environment (IDE)** is a programming environment that allows you to issue commands by selecting choices from menus and clicking buttons. Many programmers prefer using the IDE because it provides features such as color-coded keywords and automatic statement completion.

Compiling Code from the Command Prompt

 If you will be using the IDE to write all your programs, you can read this section quickly, and then concentrate on the section titled "Compiling Code Using the Visual Studio IDE."

To compile your source code from the command line, you first locate the developer command prompt. In a Windows 8.1 system, you can swipe from the right, click **Search**, and enter **Developer Command Prompt**. (Depending on your version of Visual Studio, the command prompt might be followed by a year.) If you don't find the command prompt window, you need to obtain and install a copy of Visual Studio. For more information, visit *msdn2.microsoft.com/ en-us/vcsharp.*

In the developer command prompt window, you type **csc**, followed by the name of the file that contains the source code. The command **csc** stands for *C Sharp compiler*. For example, to compile a file named ThreeLinesOutput.cs, you would type the following and then press **Enter**:

```
csc ThreeLinesOutput.cs
```

One of three outcomes is possible:

- You receive an operating system error message such as *Bad command or file name* or *csc is not recognized as an internal or external command, operable program or batch file*. You can recognize operating system messages because they do not start with the name of the program you are trying to compile.

- You receive one or more program language error messages. You can recognize program language error messages because they start with the name of the program followed by a line number and the position where the error was first noticed.

- You receive no error messages (only a copyright statement from Microsoft), indicating that the program has compiled successfully.

What to Do If You Receive an Operating System Error Message at the Command Prompt

If you receive an operating system message such as *csc is not recognized...*, or *Source file... could not be found*, it may mean that:

- You misspelled the command csc.

- You misspelled the filename.

- You forgot to include the extension .cs with the filename.

- You are not within the correct subdirectory or folder on your command line. For example, Figure 1-10 shows the csc command typed in the root directory of the C: drive. If the ThreeLinesOutput.cs file is stored in a folder on the C: drive rather than in the root directory, then the command shown will not work because the C# file cannot be found.

- The C# compiler was not installed properly. If you are working on your own computer, you might need to reinstall C#; if you are working in a school laboratory, you need to notify the system administrator.

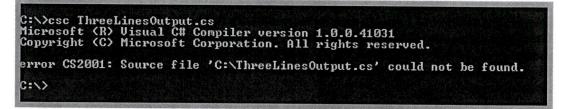

```
C:\>csc ThreeLinesOutput.cs
Microsoft (R) Visual C# Compiler version 1.0.0.41031
Copyright (C) Microsoft Corporation. All rights reserved.

error CS2001: Source file 'C:\ThreeLinesOutput.cs' could not be found.

C:\>
```

Figure 1-10 Attempt to compile a program from the root directory at the command prompt, and error message received

What to Do If You Receive a Programming Language Error Message at the Command Prompt

If you receive a programming language error message, it means that the compiler was installed correctly, but that the source code contains one or more syntax errors. A syntax error occurs when you introduce typing errors into your program. Program error messages start with the program name, followed by parentheses that hold the line number and the position in the line where the compiler noticed the error. For example, in Figure 1-11, an error is found in ThreeLinesOutput.cs in line 8, position 7. In this case, the message is generated because WriteLine is typed as *writeLine* (with a lowercase *w*). The error message is *The name 'writeLine" does not exist in the current context*. If a problem like this occurs, you must reopen the text file that contains the source code, make the necessary corrections, save the file, and compile it again.

24

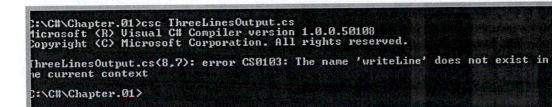

```
C:\C#\Chapter.01>csc ThreeLinesOutput.cs
Microsoft (R) Visual C# Compiler version 1.0.0.50108
Copyright (C) Microsoft Corporation. All rights reserved.

ThreeLinesOutput.cs(8,7): error CS0103: The name 'writeLine' does not exist in t
he current context

C:\C#\Chapter.01>
```

Figure 1-11   Error message generated when WriteLine is mistyped in the ThreeLinesOutput program compiled from the command prompt

The C# compiler issues warnings as well as errors. A warning is less serious than an error; it means that the compiler has determined you have done something unusual, but not illegal. If you have purposely introduced a warning situation to test a program, then you can ignore the warning. Usually, however, you should treat a warning message just as you would an error message and attempt to remedy the situation.

What to Do When the Program Compiles Successfully at the Command Prompt

If you receive no error messages after compiling the code, then the program compiled successfully, and a file with the same name as the source code—but with an .exe extension—is created and saved in the same folder as the program text file. For example, if ThreeLinesOutput.cs compiles successfully, then a file named ThreeLinesOutput.exe is created.

To run the program from the command line, you simply type the program name—for example, *ThreeLinesOutput*. You can also type the full filename, *ThreeLinesOutput.exe*, but it is not necessary to include the extension. The three lines of output, *Line one*, *Line two*, and *Line three*, appear in the command prompt window, and the command prompt is displayed again, awaiting a new command.

Compiling Code Using the Visual Studio IDE

As an alternative to using the command line, you can compile and write your program within the Visual Studio IDE. This approach has several advantages:

- Some of the code you need is already created for you.

- The code is displayed in color, so you can more easily identify parts of your program. Reserved words appear in blue, comments in green, and identifiers in black.

- If error messages appear when you compile your program, you can double-click an error message and the cursor will move to the line of code that contains the error.

- Other debugging tools are available. You will become more familiar with these tools as you develop more sophisticated programs.

If Visual Studio has been installed on your system, you can open it from the **menu bar** which, in the Visual Studio IDE, is the list of choices that runs horizontally across the top of the screen.

Start a new project, designate it to be a Console Project, and give the project a name. Figure 1-12 shows a program and project named ThreeLinesOutput written in the editor of the Visual Studio IDE. Everything in the figure was generated automatically by Visual Studio except for the following:

- The programmer selected the project name.

- The programmer added a `using static System.Console;` statement so that `WriteLine()` could be used without adding `System` and `Console` each time.

- The programmer added the three lines coded in the `Main()` method to produce output.

You can see that the Visual Studio environment looks like a word processor, containing menu options such as File, Edit, and Help, and buttons with icons representing options such as Save Selected Items and Undo. Selecting many of the menu options displays a drop-down list of additional options. Many of the options have shortcut keys that you can use instead of accessing the menus. For example, if you select File from the menu bar, you can see that a shortcut for Save Program.cs is Ctrl + S. You will learn about some of these options later in this chapter and continue to learn about more of them as you work with C# in the IDE.

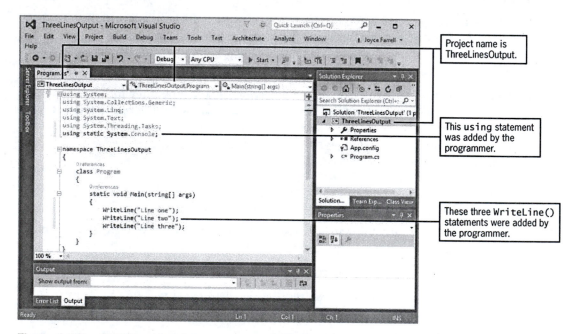

Figure 1-12   The ThreeLinesOutput program as it appears in Visual Studio

In Figure 1-12 you can see two instances of *0 references*, above the class header and the `Main()` method header. This means that neither this class nor method is used by any other method. When you start to write methods in Chapter 7, you will be able to see how many places your methods are referenced.

One way to compile a program from Visual Studio is to select **Build** from the menu bar and then select Build Solution. As an alternative, you can press Ctrl + Shift + B. You can also select **Debug** from the menu bar, and then click **Start Without Debugging**. The advantage of the latter option is that the program will be compiled if there are no syntax errors and then execute so you can see the output.

What to Do If You Receive a Programming Language Error Message in the IDE

If you introduce a syntax error into a program in the IDE, you receive a programming language error message. For example, in Figure 1-13, `WriteLine` is spelled incorrectly because it uses a lowercase *w*. The error message displayed at the bottom is: *'The name 'writeLine' does not exist in the current context'*. (If you cannot read the entire message, you can adjust the size of the window.) The position is given (project, file, and line number), and as an additional visual aid, a wavy underline emphasizes the unrecognized definition. When you fix the problem and compile again, the error message is eliminated.

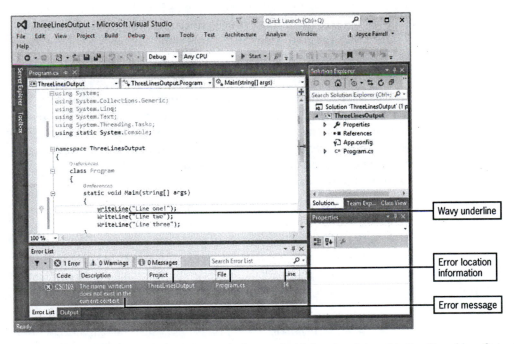

Figure 1-13 Error message generated when `WriteLine` is mistyped in the ThreeLinesOutput program compiled in the IDE

What to Do When the Program Compiles Successfully in the IDE

In Figure 1-13 you can see a code CS0103 next to the generated error message. You can search the web for this code and discover its general meaning. However, usually sufficient explanation is provided in Visual Studio, and a web search is unnecessary.

If you receive no error messages after compiling the code, then the program compiled successfully, and you can run the program. Select **Debug** from the menu bar, and then select **Start Without Debugging**. The output appears, as you saw it in Figure 1-6 earlier in this chapter.

Noticing the Differences Between the Programs in the Text Editor and the IDE

There are a few differences between the ThreeLinesOutput programs in Figures 1-8 and 1-12. Specifically, the Visual Studio version in Figure 1-12 contains the following extra components that are highlighted in Figure 1-14:

- *Five using statements at the top of the file*—Visual Studio automatically provides you with several commonly needed using statements. In this case, you could delete all five statements from the Visual Studio version of the program, and the program would still run correctly. (The only using statement you need to retain is the using static System. Console; statement that allows you to use WriteLine() without qualification.) Conversely, you could add all five additional using statements to the command-line version of the program, and it would also run correctly.

- *A namespace declaration and its opening and closing curly braces*—You already know that C# uses built-in namespaces like System and others that are automatically listed at the top of the Visual Studio version of programs. C# also allows you to create your own namespaces; Visual Studio assumes that you will want to create one using the name you have assigned to the project. In this case, you could remove the namespace declaration from the Visual Studio version of the program, or you could add one to the command-line version of the program. In both cases, the programs would still run correctly.

- *The class name Program*—Visual Studio assumes that you want to avoid confusion by having different names for your namespace and the class contained within it, so it assigns the generic name Program to the class that contains the Main() method. You could change this name to match the namespace identifier, ThreeLinesOutput, or use any other legal identifier, and the program would still work correctly. In the Notepad version of the program, you could change the class name to Program or any other legal identifier, and the program would also work.

- *The words string[] args between the parentheses of the Main() method header.* C# allows a program's Main() method header to be written in several ways. For example, you can include the words string[] args between the method's parentheses, or you can omit the words. The square brackets indicate an array, as you will learn when studying arrays later in this book. In this example, you could write the `Main()` method header with or without the extra code in either the Notepad or Visual Studio version of the program, and the `Main()` method would still work correctly.

In summary, the Visual Studio version of the ThreeLinesOutput program provides everything you need to run the program and saves you as much typing as possible in case you want to include additional options. The command-line and Visual Studio versions of the program function identically.

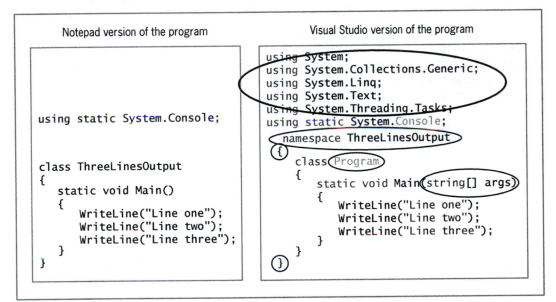

Figure 1-14   Comparing the command line and Visual Studio versions of the ThreeLinesOutput program

Deciding Which Environment to Use

When you write, compile, and execute a C# program, you can use either a text editor and the command line or the Visual Studio IDE. You would never need to use both. You might prefer using an editor with which you are already familiar (such as Notepad) and compiling from the command line because only two files are generated, saving disk space.

On the other hand, the IDE provides many useful features, such as automatic statement completion. For example, if you type *u*, then a list of choices including `using` is displayed and you can click using instead of typing it. Similarly, if you type *using s*, then a list of choices including `static` is displayed

Additionally, in the IDE, words are displayed using different colors based on their category; for example, one color is used for C#-reserved words and a different color for literal strings. It is also easier to correct many errors using the IDE. When compiler errors or warnings are issued, you can double-click the message, and the cursor jumps to the location in the code where the error was detected. Another advantage to learning the IDE is that if you use another programming language in Visual Studio (C++ or Visual Basic), the environment will already be familiar to you.

The C# language works the same way no matter which method you use to compile your programs. Everything you learn in the next chapters about input, output, decision making, loops, and arrays is correct in both environments. You can use just one technique or compile some programs in each environment as the mood strikes you. You can also mix and match techniques if you prefer. For example, you can use an editor you like to compose your programs, then paste them into the IDE to execute them. Although any program can be written using either compilation technique, when you write GUI applications that use existing objects such as buttons and labels, you will find that the extensive amount of code automatically generated by the IDE is very helpful.

 Watch the video Writing and Compiling a Program.

TWO TRUTHS & A LIE

Compiling and Executing a C# Program

1. After you write and save a program, you must compile it into intermediate language and then the C# just in time (JIT) compiler must translate the intermediate code into executable code.

2. You can compile and execute a C# program from the command line or within the Integrated Development Environment (IDE) that comes with Visual Studio.

3. Many programmers prefer to compile their programs from the command line because it provides features such as color-coded keywords and automatic statement completion.

The false statement is #3. Programmers who prefer the command line prefer its simplicity. Programmers who prefer the Visual Studio IDE prefer the color-coded keywords and automatic statement completion.

You Do It

Compiling and Executing a Program from the Command Line

If you do not plan to use the command line to execute programs, you can skip to the next part of this "You Do It" section, called "Compiling and Executing a Program Using the Visual Studio IDE."

1. Go to the command prompt on your system. For example, in Windows 8.1, swipe from the right, click **Search**, start to type **Developer Command Prompt**, and then click it.

2. Change the current directory to the name of the folder that holds your program. You can type `cd\` and then press Enter to return to the root directory. You can then type `cd` to change the path to the one where your program resides. For example, if you stored your program file in a folder named Chapter.01 within a folder named C#, then you can type the following:

    `cd C#\Chapter.01`

    The command `cd` is short for *change directory*.

3. Type the command that compiles your program:

    `csc Hello.cs`

    If you receive no error messages and the prompt returns, it means that the compile operation was successful, that a file named Hello.exe has been created, and that you can execute the program. If you do receive error messages, check every character of the program you typed to make sure it matches Figure 1-9 in the last "You Do It" section. Remember, C# is case sensitive, so all casing must match exactly. When you have corrected the errors, repeat this step to compile the program again.

4. You can verify that a file named Hello.exe was created in these ways:

    - At the command prompt, type **dir** to view a directory of the files stored in the current folder. Both Hello.cs and Hello.exe should appear in the list.

    - Use Windows Explorer to view the contents of the Chapter.01 folder, verifying that two Hello files are listed.

(continues)

(continued)

5. At the command prompt, type **Hello**, which is the name of the program (the name of the executable file), and then press **Enter**. Alternatively, you can type the full filename **Hello.exe**, but typing the .exe extension isn't necessary. The output should look like Figure 1-15.

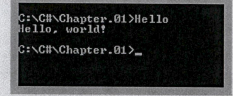
```
C:\C#\Chapter.01>Hello
Hello, world!

C:\C#\Chapter.01>_
```

Figure 1-15   Output of the Hello application

 You can use the /out compiler option between the cs command and the name of the .cs file to indicate the name of the output file. For example, if you type csc /out:Hello.exe Hello.cs, you create an output file named Hello.exe. By default, the name of the output file is the same as the name of the .cs file. Usually, this is your intention, so most often you omit the /out option.

Compiling and Executing a Program Using the Visual Studio IDE

Next, you use the C# compiler environment to compile and execute the same Hello program you ran from the command line.

1. Open **Visual Studio**. If there is a shortcut icon on your desktop, you can double-click it. Alternatively, in Windows 8, you can swipe from the right, click **Search**, start to type **Visual Studio 2015**, and select it. When you see the Start Page, click **New Project**.

2. In the New Project window, click **Visual C#**, and then click **Console Application**. By default, the name for the project is set to *ConsoleApplication1*.

   Change it to **Hello**, and select the path where you want to save the project (see Figure 1-16). Click **OK**. Visual C# creates a new folder for your project named after the project title.

 Students might like to walk through these "You Do It" exercises multiple times for practice. Note that Visual Studio does not allow you to create a project with the same name as one already stored in a folder. When you perform these steps additional times, either delete the first version of the project before you start the next one, store the new version in a different folder, or give the new project a different name.

(continues)

(continued)

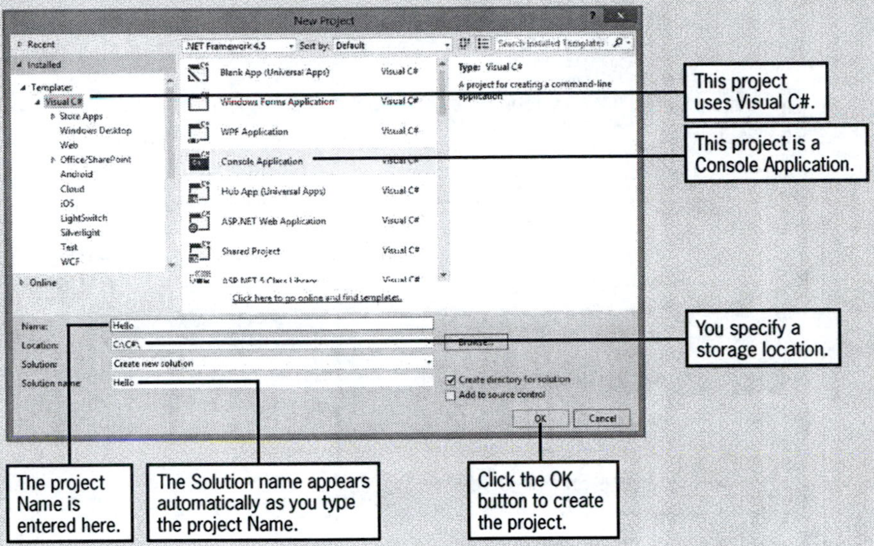

This project uses Visual C#.

This project is a Console Application.

You specify a storage location.

The project Name is entered here.

The Solution name appears automatically as you type the project Name.

Click the OK button to create the project.

Figure 1-16   Starting a new project

3. The Hello application editing window appears. A lot of code is already written for you in this window, including some `using` statements, a namespace named `Hello`, a class named `Program`, and a `Main()` method. To create the Hello program, you need to add only two statements to the prewritten code. Place your cursor after the last using statement, press **Enter** to start a new line, and add an additional using statement:

```
using static System.Console;
```

After the opening brace of the `Main()` method, press **Enter** to start a new line, and add the following statement:

```
WriteLine("Hello, world!");
```

Figure 1-17 shows the editing window after the `using` and `WriteLine()` statements have been added.

(continues)

(continued)

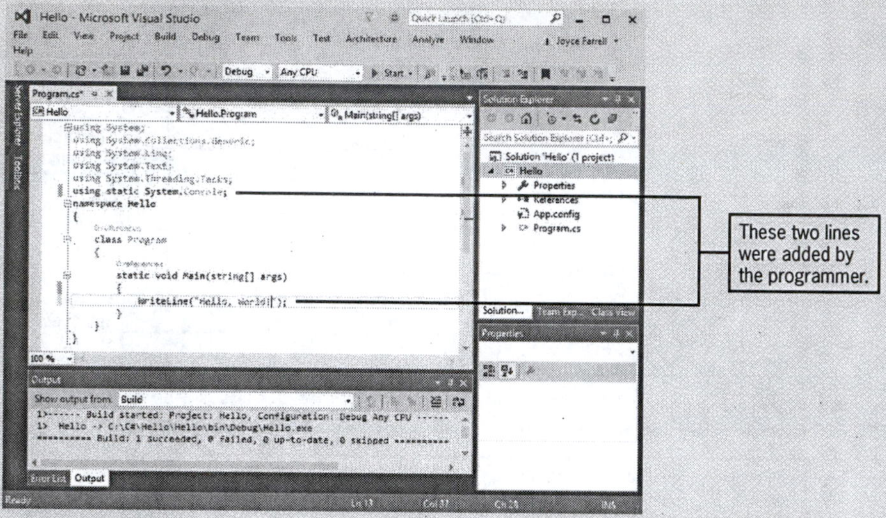

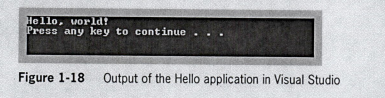

These two lines were added by the programmer.

Figure 1-17   The Hello application editing window after the code has been added

4. Save the project by clicking **File** on the menu bar and then clicking **Save All**, or by clicking the **Save All** button (which shows two disks) on the toolbar, or by typing **Ctrl + Shift + S**.

5. To compile the program, click **Build** on the menu bar, and then click **Build Solution**. You should receive no error messages, and the words *Build succeeded* should appear near the lower-left edge of the window.

6. Click **Debug** on the menu bar, and then click **Start Without Debugging**. Figure 1-18 shows the output; you see *Hello, world!* followed by the message *Press any key to continue*. Press any key to close the output screen.

```
Hello, world!
Press any key to continue . . .
```

Figure 1-18   Output of the Hello application in Visual Studio

(continues)

(continued)

7. Close Visual Studio by clicking **File** on the menu bar and then clicking **Exit**, or by clicking the **Close** box in the upper-right corner of the Visual Studio window.

8. When you create a C# program using an editor such as Notepad and compile it with the `csc` command, only two files are created—Hello.cs and Hello.exe. When you create a C# program using the Visual Studio editor, many additional files are created. You can view their filenames from the command prompt or visually:

   - At the command prompt, type **dir** to view a directory of the files stored in the folder where you saved the project (for example, your Chapter.01 folder). Within the folder, a new folder named Hello has been created. Type the command **cd Hello** to change the current path to include this new folder, then type **dir** again. You see another folder named Hello. Type **cd Hello** again, and **dir** again. You should see several folders and files. (Depending on the version of Visual Studio you are using, your folder configuration might be slightly different.)

   - Use File Explorer to view the contents of the Hello folders within the Chapter.01 folder.

   Regardless of the technique you use to examine the folders, you will find that the innermost Hello folder contains a bin folder, an obj folder, a Properties folder, and additional files. If you explore further, you will find that the bin folder contains Debug and Release folders, which include additional files. Using the Visual Studio editor to compile your programs creates a significant amount of overhead. These additional files become important as you create more sophisticated C# projects.

If you followed the earlier instructions on compiling a program from the command line, and you used the same folder when using the IDE, you will see the additional Hello.cs and Hello.exe files in your folder. These files will have an earlier time stamp than the files you just created. If you were to execute a new program within Visual Studio without saving and executing it from the command line first, you would not see these two additional files.

(continues)

(continued)

Adding Comments to a Program

Comments are nonexecuting statements that help to document a program. In the following steps, you add some comments to the program you just created.

1. If you prefer compiling programs from the command line, then open the **Hello.cs** file in your text editor. If you prefer compiling programs from Visual Studio, then open Visual Studio, click **File**, point to **Open**, click **Project/ Solution**, browse for the correct folder, double-click the **Hello** folder, and then double-click the **Hello** file.

2. Position your cursor at the top of the file, press **Enter** to insert a new line, press the **up** arrow to go to that line, and then type the following comments at the top of the file. Press **Enter** after typing each line. Insert your name and today's date where indicated.

   ```
   //Filename Hello.cs
   //Written by <your name>
   //Written on <today's date>
   ```

3. Scroll to the line that reads `static void Main()`, and press **Enter** to start a new line. Then press the **up** arrow; in the new blank line, aligned with the start of the `Main()` method header, type the following block comment in the program:

   ```
   /* This program demonstrates the use of the WriteLine()
   method to display the message Hello, world!  */
   ```

4. Save the file, replacing the old Hello.cs file with this new, commented version.

5. If you prefer to compile programs from the command line, type `csc Hello.cs` at the command line. When the program compiles successfully, execute it with the command **Hello**. If you prefer compiling and executing programs from Visual Studio, click **Debug**, and then click **Start Without Debugging**. Adding program comments makes no difference in the execution of the program.

6. If you are working from the command line, you can close the command-line window. If you are working from Visual Studio, you can close the output screen and then close Visual Studio.

Chapter Summary

- A computer program is a set of instructions that tell a computer what to do. Programmers write their programs, then use a compiler to translate their high-level language statements into intermediate language and machine code. A program works correctly when both its syntax and logic are correct.

- Procedural programming involves creating computer memory locations, called variables, and sets of operations, called methods. In object-oriented programming, you envision program components as objects that are similar to concrete objects in the real world; then you manipulate the objects to achieve a desired result. OOP techniques were first used for simulations and GUIs.

- Objects are instances of classes and are made up of attributes and methods. Object-oriented programming languages support encapsulation, inheritance, and polymorphism.

- The C# programming language was developed as an object-oriented and component-oriented language. It contains many features similar to those in Visual Basic, Java, and C++.

- To produce a line of console output in a C# program, you must pass a literal string as an argument to the `System.Console.WriteLine()` method. `System` is a namespace and `Console` is a class. Calls to the `WriteLine()` method can appear within the `Main()` method of a class you create.

- You can define a C# class or variable by using any name or identifier that begins with an underscore, a letter, or an @ sign. These names can contain only letters, digits, underscores, and the @ sign, and cannot be C#-reserved keywords.

- You can improve programs by adding comments, which are nonexecuting statements that you add to document a program or to disable statements when you test a program. The three types of comments in C# are line comments that start with two forward slashes (//) and continue to the end of the current line, block comments that start with a forward slash and an asterisk (/*) and end with an asterisk and a forward slash (*/), and XML-documentation comments. You can also improve programs and shorten the statements you type by using a clause that indicates a namespace where your classes can be found.

- To create a C# program, you can use the Microsoft Visual Studio IDE or any text editor, such as Notepad. After you write and save a program, you must compile the source code into intermediate and machine language.

Key Terms

A computer **program** is a set of instructions that tell a computer what to do.

Software is computer programs.

System software describes the programs that operate the computer.

Application software is the programs that allow users to complete tasks.

Hardware comprises all the physical devices associated with a computer.

Machine language is the most basic circuitry-level language.

A **high-level programming language** allows you to use a vocabulary of keywords instead of the sequence of on/off switches that perform these tasks.

Keywords are predefined and reserved identifiers that have special meaning to the compiler.

Camel casing, also called **lower camel casing**, is a style of creating identifiers in which the first letter is not capitalized, but each new word is.

A language's **syntax** is its set of rules.

A **compiler** is a computer program that translates high-level language statements into machine code.

A **syntax error** is an error that occurs when a programming language is used incorrectly.

The **logic** behind any program involves executing the various statements and methods in the correct order to produce the desired results.

Semantic errors are the type of logical errors that occur when you use a correct word in the wrong context, generating incorrect results.

A **bug** is an error in a computer program.

Debugging a program is the process of removing all syntax and logical errors from the program.

A **procedural program** is created by writing a series of steps or operations to manipulate values.

Variables are named computer memory locations that hold values that might vary.

An **identifier** is the name of a program component such as a variable, class, or method.

Pascal casing, also called **upper camel casing**, is a style of creating identifiers in which the first letter of all new words in a name, even the first one, is capitalized.

Methods are compartmentalized, named program units containing instructions that accomplish tasks.

A program **calls** or **invokes** methods.

Object-oriented programming (OOP) is a programming technique that features objects, classes, encapsulation, interfaces, polymorphism, and inheritance.

An **object** is a concrete entity that has attributes and behaviors; an object is an instance of a class.

The **attributes of an object** represent its characteristics.

The **state of an object** is the collective value of all its attributes at any point in time.

The **behaviors of an object** are its methods.

Taking an **object-oriented approach** to a problem means defining the objects needed to accomplish a task and developing classes that describe the objects so each maintains its own data and carries out tasks when another object requests them.

Computer simulations are programs that attempt to mimic real-world activities to foster a better understanding of them.

Graphical User Interfaces, or **GUIs** (pronounced "gooeys"), are program elements that allow users to interact with a program in a graphical environment.

A **class** is a category of objects or a type of object.

An **instance of a class** is an object.

The **properties** of an object are its values.

Encapsulation is the technique of packaging an object's attributes and methods into a cohesive unit that can be used as an undivided entity.

A **black box** is a device you use without regard for the internal mechanisms.

An **interface** is the interaction between a method and an object.

Inheritance is the ability to extend a class so as to create a more specific class that contains all the attributes and methods of a more general class; the extended class usually contains new attributes or methods as well.

Polymorphism is the ability to create methods that act appropriately depending on the context.

The **C# programming language** was developed as an object-oriented and component-oriented language. It exists as part of Visual Studio, a package used for developing applications for the Windows family of operating systems.

A **literal string** of characters is a series of characters enclosed in double quotes that is used exactly as entered.

An **argument** to a method represents information that a method needs to perform its task. An argument is the expression used between parentheses when you call a method.

A **namespace** is a construct that acts like a container to provide a way to group similar classes.

A **method header** includes the method name and information about what will pass into and be returned from a method.

The **method body** of every method is contained within a pair of curly braces ({}) and includes all the instructions executed by the method.

Whitespace is any combination of spaces, tabs, and carriage returns (blank lines). You use whitespace to organize your program code and make it easier to read.

The keyword `static`, when used in a method header, indicates that a method will be executed through a class and not by an object.

The keyword `void`, when used in a method header, indicates that the method does not return any value.

Application classes contain a `Main()` method and are executable programs.

Runnable describes files that are executable.

Non-application classes do not contain a `Main()` method; they provide support for other classes.

A **verbatim identifier** is an identifier with an @ prefix.

Program comments are nonexecuting statements that you add to document a program.

To **comment out** a statement is to make a statement nonexecuting.

Line comments start with two forward slashes (`//`) and continue to the end of the current line. Line comments can appear on a line by themselves or at the end of a line following executable code.

Block comments start with a forward slash and an asterisk (`/*`) and end with an asterisk and a forward slash (`*/`). Block comments can appear on a line by themselves, on a line before executable code, or after executable code. They can also extend across as many lines as needed.

XML-documentation format comments use a special set of tags within angle brackets to create documentation within a program.

A **using clause** or **using directive** declares a namespace.

Source code is the statements you write when you create a program.

Intermediate language (IL) is the language into which source code statements are compiled.

The C# **just in time (JIT)** compiler translates intermediate code into executable code.

The **command line** is the line on which you type a command in a system that uses a text interface.

The **command prompt** is a request for input that appears at the beginning of the command line.

An **Integrated Development Environment (IDE)** is a program development environment that allows you to select options from menus or by clicking buttons. An IDE provides such helpful features as color coding and automatic statement completion.

The **menu bar** in the IDE lies horizontally across the top of the window, and includes submenus that list additional options.

Review Questions

1. Programming languages such as Java and Visual Basic are _____ .

   a. machine languages

   b. low-level languages

   c. high-level languages

   d. uninterpreted languages

2. A program that translates high-level programs into intermediate or machine code is a(n) _____ .

   a. mangler

   b. compiler

   c. analyst

   d. logician

3. The grammar and spelling rules of a programming language constitute its _____ .

   a. logic

   b. variables

   c. syntax

   d. class

4. Variables are _____ .

   a. methods

   b. named memory locations

   c. grammar rules

   d. operations

5. Programs in which you create and use objects that have attributes similar to their real-world counterparts are known as _____ programs.

   a. procedural

   b. logical

   c. authentic

   d. object-oriented

6. Which of the following pairs is an example of a class and an object, in that order? *new book*

   a. Robin and bird

   b. Chair and desk

   c. University and Harvard *Yale*

   d. Oak and tree

7. The technique of packaging an object's attributes into a cohesive unit that can be used as an undivided entity is _____ .

   a. inheritance

   b. encapsulation

   c. polymorphism

   d. interfacing

8. Of the following languages, which is least similar to C#?

   a. Java

   b. Visual Basic

   c. C++

   d. COBOL *machine language*

9. A series of characters that appears within double quotation marks is a(n)____.

    a. method   c. argument

    b. interface   d. literal string

10. The C# method that produces a line of output on the screen and then positions the cursor on the next line is _____ .

    a. `WriteLine()`   c. `DisplayLine()`

    b. `PrintLine()`   d. `OutLine()`

11. Which of the following is a class?

    a. `System`   c. `void`

    b. `Console`   d. `WriteLine()`

12. In C#, a container that groups similar classes is a(n) _____ .

    a. superclass   c. namespace

    b. method   d. identifier

13. Every method in C# contains a _____ .

    a. header and a body   c. variable and a class

    b. header and a footer   d. class and an object

14. Which of the following is a method?

    a. `namespace`   c. `Main()`

    b. `class`   d. `static`

15. Which of the following statements is true?

    a. An identifier must begin with an underscore.

    b. An identifier can contain digits.

    c. An identifier must be no more than 16 characters long.

    d. An identifier can contain only lowercase letters.

16. Which of the following identifiers is not legal in C#?

    a. `per cent increase`   c. `HTML`

    b. `annualReview`   d. `alternativetaxcredit`

17. The text of a program you write is called _____ .

    a. object code   c. machine language

    b. source code   d. executable documentation

18. Programming errors such as using incorrect punctuation or misspelling words are collectively known as _____ errors.

a. syntax

b. logical

c. executable

d. fatal

19. A comment in the form /* this is a comment */ is a(n)____.

a. XML comment

b. block comment

c. executable comment

d. line comment

20. If a programmer inserts using static System.Console; at the top of a C# program, which of the following can the programmer use as an alternative to System.Console.WriteLine("Hello");?

a. System("Hello");

b. WriteLine("Hello");

c. Console.WriteLine ("Hello");

d. Console("Hello");

Exercises

 Programming Exercises

1. Indicate whether each of the following C# programming language identifiers is legal or illegal. If it is legal, indicate whether it is a conventional identifier for a class.

a. paycheck

b. Paycheck

c. Pay check

d. static

e. Void

f. #phone

g. Ay56we

h. Theater_Tickets

i. 102Item

j. heightInInches

k. Zip23891

l. void

2. Name at least three attributes that might be appropriate for each of the following classes:

a. TVShow

b. Party

c. JobApplication

d. CheckingAccount

3. Name at least two classes to which each of these objects might belong:

a. your sister

b. Franklin D. Roosevelt

c. Starbucks

d. Paris

4. Write, compile, and test a program named **PersonalInfo** that displays a person's name, e-mail address, and phone number.

5. Write, compile, and test a program named **Lyrics** that displays at least four lines of your favorite song.

6. Write, compile, and test a program named **Comments** that displays a statement that defines program comments. Include at least one block comment and one line comment in the program.

7. Write, compile, and test a program named **WineGlass** that displays a pattern similar to the following on the screen:

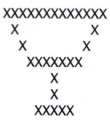

```
XXXXXXXXXXXX
 X          X
  X        X
   XXXXXXX
      X
      X
    XXXXX
```

8. Write a program named **BigLetter** that displays a large letter composed of smaller letters as in the following example:

```
H        H
H        H
H        H
HHHHHHHH
H        H
H        H
H        H
```

9. From 1925 through 1963, Burma Shave advertising signs appeared next to highways all across the United States. There were always four or five signs in a row containing pieces of a rhyme, followed by a final sign that read "Burma Shave." For example, one set of signs that has been preserved by the Smithsonian Institution reads as follows:

    Shaving brushes
    You'll soon see 'em
    On a shelf
    In some museum
    Burma Shave

    Find a classic Burma Shave rhyme on the Web and write a program named **BurmaShave** that displays the rhyme.

Debugging Exercises

1. Each of the following files in the Chapter.01 folder of your downloadable student files has syntax and/or logical errors. In each case, determine the problem and fix the program. After you correct the errors, save each file using the same filename preceded with *Fixed.* For example, DebugOne1.cs will become FixedDebugOne1.cs.

   a. DebugOne1.cs

   b. DebugOne2.cs

   c. DebugOne3.cs

   d. DebugOne4.cs

Case Problems

The case problems in this section introduce two fictional businesses. Throughout this book, you will create increasingly complex classes for these businesses that use the newest concepts you have mastered in each chapter.

1. Greenville County hosts the Greenville Idol competition each summer during the county fair. The talent competition takes place over a 3-day period during which contestants are eliminated following rounds of performances until the year's ultimate winner is chosen. Write a program named **GreenvilleMotto** that displays the competition's motto, which is "The stars shine in Greenville." Create a second program named **GreenvilleMotto2** that displays the motto surrounded by a border composed of asterisks.

2. Marshall's Murals is a company that paints interior and exterior murals for both business and residential customers. Write a program named **MarshallsMotto** that displays the company motto, which is "Make your vision your view." Create a second program named **MarshallsMotto2** that displays the motto surrounded by a border composed of repeated *M*s.

CHAPTER 2

Using Data

In this chapter you will:

- ◎ Learn about declaring variables
- ◎ Display variable values
- ◎ Learn about the integral data types
- ◎ Learn about floating-point data types
- ◎ Use arithmetic operators
- ◎ Learn about the `bool` data type
- ◎ Learn about numeric type conversion
- ◎ Learn about the `char` data type
- ◎ Learn about the `string` data type
- ◎ Define named constants and enumerations
- ◎ Accept console input

In Chapter 1, you learned about programming in general and the C# programming language in particular. You wrote, compiled, and ran a C# program that produced output. In this chapter, you build on your basic C# programming skills by learning how to manipulate data and use data types, variables, and constants. As you will see, using variables to hold data makes computer programs flexible.

Declaring Variables

A data item is **constant** when it cannot be changed after a program is compiled—in other words, when it cannot vary. For example, if you use the number 347 within a C# program, then 347 is a constant, and every time you execute the program, the value 347 will be used. You can refer to the number 347 as a **literal constant**, because its value is taken literally at each use. (A number like 347 is also called an *unnamed constant* because no name is associated with it. Later in this chapter you will learn about named constants.)

On the other hand, when you want a data item's value to be able to change, you can create a variable. A **variable** is a named location in computer memory that can hold different values at different points in time. For example, if you create a variable named heatingBill and include it in a C# program, heatingBill might contain the value 347, or it might contain 200. Different values might be used when the program is executed multiple times, or different values might be used at different times during a single program execution. Because you can use a variable to hold heatingBill within a program used by a utility company's automated billing system, you can write one set of instructions to compute heatingBill, yet use different heatingBill values for thousands of utility customers.

Whether it is a constant or a variable, each data item you use in a C# program has a data type. A **data type** describes the format and size of (amount of memory occupied by) a data item and defines what types of operations can be performed with the item. C# provides for 15 basic, or **intrinsic types**, of data, as shown in Table 2-1. Of these built-in data types, the ones most commonly used are int, double, decimal, char, string, and bool. Each C# intrinsic type is an **alias**, or other name, for a class in the System namespace. (You learned about the System namespace in Chapter 1.) All of the built-in types except object and string are called **simple types**.

The meaning of the largest and smallest values for the numeric types in Table 2-1 is probably clear to you, but some of the other values require explanation.

- The highest char value, 0xFFFF, represents the character in which every bit is turned on. The lowest value, 0x0000, represents the character in which every bit is turned off. Any value that begins with *0x* represents a hexadecimal, or base 16, value.

- For any two strings, the one with the higher Unicode character value in an earlier position is considered higher. (**Unicode** is the system that provides a numeric value for every character. You will learn more about Unicode later in this chapter, and Appendix B contains further information.) For example, "AAB" is higher than "AAA". The string type has no true minimum; however, you can think of the empty string "" as being the lowest.

- Although the bool type has no true maximum or minimum, you can think of true as the highest and false as the lowest.

Type	System Type	Bytes	Description	Largest Value	Smallest Value
Types that hold numbers with no decimal places					
byte	Byte	1	Unsigned byte	255	0
sbyte	Sbyte	1	Signed byte	127	−128
short	Int16	2	Signed short	32,767	−32,768
ushort	UInt16	2	Unsigned short	65,535	0
int	Int32	4	Signed integer	2,147,483,647	−2,147,483,648
uint	UInt32	4	Unsigned integer	4,294,967,295	0
long	Int64	8	Signed long integer	Approximately 9×10^{18}	Approximately -9×10^{18}
ulong	UInt64	8	Unsigned long integer	Approximately 18×10^{18}	0
Types that hold numbers with decimal places					
float	Single	4	Floating-point	Approximately 3.4×10^{38}	Approximately 3.4×10^{38}
double	Double	8	Double-precision floating-point	Approximately 1.8×10^{308}	Approximately 1.8×10^{308}
decimal	Decimal	16	Fixed-precision number	Approximately 7.9×10^{28}	Approximately 7.9×10^{28}
Types that hold other values					
char	Char	2	Unicode character	0xFFFF	0x0000
bool	Boolean	1	Boolean value (true or false)	NA	NA
string	String	NA	Unicode string	NA	NA
object	Object	NA	Any object	NA	NA

Table 2-1 C# data types

You name variables using the same rules for identifiers as you use for class names. A variable name must start with a letter, cannot include embedded spaces, and cannot be a reserved keyword. (Table 1-1 in Chapter 1 lists all the C# keywords.) By convention, each C# variable name starts with a lowercase letter and uses camel casing if it contains multiple words.

You must declare all variables you want to use in a program. A **variable declaration** is the statement that names a variable and reserves storage for it. A declaration includes

- The data type that the variable will store

- The variable's name (its identifier)

- An optional assignment operator and assigned value when you want a variable to contain an initial value

- An ending semicolon

For example, the following statement declares a variable of type int named myAge and assigns it an initial value of 25:

```
int myAge = 25;
```

In other words, the statement reserves four bytes of memory with the name myAge, and the value 25 is stored there. The declaration is a complete statement that ends in a semicolon.

The equal sign (=) is the **assignment operator**; any value to the right of the assignment operator is assigned to the identifier to the left. An assignment made when a variable is declared is an **initialization**; an assignment made later is simply an **assignment**. Thus, the following statement initializes myAge to 25:

```
int myAge = 25;
```

A statement such as the following assigns a new value to the variable:

```
myAge = 42;
```

Notice that the data type is not used again when an assignment is made; it is used only in a declaration.

Also note that the expression 25 = myAge; is illegal because assignment always takes place from right to left. By definition, a literal constant cannot be altered, so it is illegal to place one (such as 25) on the left side of an assignment operator. The assignment operator means "is assigned the value of the following expression." In other words, the statement myAge = 25; can be read as "myAge is assigned the value of the following expression: 25."

Instead of using a type name from the Type column of Table 2-1, you can use the fully qualified type name from the System namespace that is listed in the System Type column. For example, instead of using the type name int, you can use the full name System.Int32. (The number 32 in the name System.Int32 represents the number of bits of storage allowed for the data type. There are eight bits in a byte, and an int occupies four bytes.) It's better to use the shorter alias int, however, for the following reasons:

- The shorter alias is easier to type and read.

- The shorter alias resembles type names used in other languages such as Java and C++.

- Other C# programmers expect the shorter type names.

You can declare a variable without an initialization value, as in the following statement:

```
int myAge;
```

You can make an assignment to an uninitialized variable later in the program, but you cannot use the variable in a calculation or display it until a value has been assigned to it.

You can declare multiple variables of the same type in separate statements. For example, the following statements declare two integer variables:

```
int myAge = 25;
int yourAge = 19;
```

You also can declare multiple variables of the same type in a single statement by using the type once and separating the variable declarations with a comma, as shown in the following statement:

```
int myAge = 25, yourAge = 19;
```

Some programmers prefer to break declarations across multiple lines, as in the following example:

```
int myAge = 25,
    yourAge = 19;
```

When a statement occupies more than one line, it is easier to read if lines after the first one are indented a few spaces. This book follows that convention.

When declaring variables of different types, you must use a separate statement for each type.

  Watch the video *Declaring Variables*.

TWO TRUTHS & A LIE

Declaring Variables

1. A constant value cannot be changed after a program is compiled, but a variable can be changed.

2. A data type describes the format and size of a data item and the types of operations that can be performed with it.

3. A variable declaration requires a data type, name, and assigned value.

The false statement is #3. A variable declaration names a variable and reserves storage for it; it includes the data type that the variable will store and an identifier. An assignment operator and assigned value can be included, but they are not required.

Displaying Variable Values

You can display variable values by using the variable name within a `Write()` or `WriteLine()` method call. For example, Figure 2-1 shows a C# program that displays the value of the variable someMoney. Figure 2-2 shows the output of the program when executed at the command prompt.

```csharp
using static System.Console;
class DisplaySomeMoney
{
    static void Main()
    {
        double someMoney = 39.45;
        WriteLine(someMoney);
    }
}
```

Figure 2-1   Program that displays a variable value

```
C:\CI\Chapter.02>DisplaySomeMoney
39.45

C:\CI\Chapter.02>_
```

Figure 2-2   Output of the `DisplaySomeMoney` program

The output shown in Figure 2-2 is rather stark—just a number with no explanation. The program in Figure 2-3 adds some explanation to the output; the result is shown in Figure 2-4. This program uses the `Write()` method to display the string "The money is $" before displaying the value of someMoney. Because the program uses `Write()` instead of `WriteLine()` for the first output, the second output appears on the same line as the first.

```csharp
using static System.Console;
class DisplaySomeMoney2
{
    static void Main()
    {
        double someMoney = 39.45;
        Write("The money is $");
        WriteLine(someMoney);
    }
}
```

Figure 2-3   Program that displays a string and a variable value

```
C:\CH\Chapter.02>DisplaySomeMoney2
The money is $39.45

C:\CH\Chapter.02>
```

Figure 2-4   Output of the DisplaySomeMoney2 program

If you want to display several strings and several variables, you can end up with quite a few
Write() and WriteLine() statements. To make producing output easier, you can combine
strings and variable values into a single Write() or WriteLine() statement by concatenating
them or by using a format string.

When you **concatenate** a string with another value, you join the values with a plus sign. For
example, the following statement produces the same output as shown in Figure 2-4 but uses
only one WriteLine() statement:

```
WriteLine("The money is $" + someMoney);
```

A **format string** is a string of characters that controls the appearance of output. It optionally
contains fixed text and contains one or more format items or *placeholders* for variable values.
A **place holder** consists of a pair of curly braces containing a number that indicates the desired
variable's position in a list that follows the string. The first position is always position 0.

You can create a formatted string using the String.Format() method that is built into C#. For
example, the following statements create a formatted string and then display it:

```
double someMoney = 39.45;
string mySentence =
    String.Format("The money is ${0} exactly", someMoney);
WriteLine(mySentence);
```

The curly braces that contain a digit create a placeholder {0} into which the value of
someMoney is inserted. Because someMoney is the first variable after the format string (as well
as the only variable in this example), its position is 0. The process of replacing string place
holders with values is often called *string interpolation* or *variable substitution*.

C# also allows you to use a shortcut with the Write() and WriteLine() methods. You can
format a string and output it in one step without declaring a temporary string variable and
without explicitly naming the String.Format() method, as in the following:

```
double someMoney = 39.45;
WriteLine("The money is ${0} exactly", someMoney);
```

For example, the program in Figure 2-5 produces the output shown in Figure 2-6.

```
using static System.Console;
class DisplaySomeMoney3
{
    static void Main()
    {
        double someMoney = 39.45;
        WriteLine("The money is ${0} exactly", someMoney);
    }
}
```

Figure 2-5   Using a format string

Figure 2-6   Output produced using format string

To display two variables within a single call to `Write()` or `WriteLine()`, you can use a statement like the following:

```
WriteLine("The money is {0} and my age is {1}", someMoney, myAge);
```

In this example, the value of someMoney will appear at position 0, and myAge will appear at position 1. The number within any pair of curly braces in a format string must be less than the number of values you list after the format string. In other words, if you list six values to be displayed, valid format position numbers are 0 through 5. You do not have to use the positions in order. You also can display a specific value multiple times. For example, if someMoney has been assigned the value 439.75, the following code produces the output shown in Figure 2-7:

```
WriteLine("I have ${0}. ${0}!! ${0}!!", someMoney);
```

Figure 2-7   Displaying the same value multiple times

The output in Figure 2-7 could be displayed without using a format string, but you would have to name the someMoney variable three separate times as follows:

```
WriteLine("I have $" + someMoney + ". $" + someMoney +
    "!! $" + someMoney + "!!");
```

A new way to display concatenated strings is introduced in C# 6.0. With this method you can use variable names within curly braces that are preceded with a slash. For example, the following code produces the output *Money is 42.56 and age is 29.*

```
double someMoney = 42.56;
int myAge = 29;
WriteLine("Money is \{someMoney} and age is \{myAge}");
```

When you use a series of `WriteLine()` statements to display a list of variable values, the values are not automatically right-aligned as you normally expect numbers to be. For example, the following code produces the unaligned output shown in Figure 2-8:

```
WriteLine("{0}", 4);
WriteLine("{0}", 56);
WriteLine("{0}", 789);
```

```
C:\C#\Chapter.02>CodeForFigure02-08
4
56
789

C:\C#\Chapter.02>
```

Figure 2-8   Displaying values with different numbers of digits without using field sizes

If you use a second number within the curly braces in a format string, you can specify alignment and field size. By default, numbers are right-aligned in their fields. If you use a negative value for the field size in a `Write()` or `WriteLine()` statement, the displayed value will be left-aligned in the field. Most often, you want numbers to be right-aligned and string values to be left-aligned. For example, the following code produces the output shown in Figure 2-9. The output created by each of the first three `WriteLine()` statements is a right-aligned number in a field that is five characters wide, and the output created by each of the last three statements is two left-aligned strings in a field that is eight characters wide.

```
WriteLine("{0, 5}", 4);
WriteLine("{0, 5}", 56);
WriteLine("{0, 5}", 789);
WriteLine("{0, -8}{1, -8}", "Richard", "Lee");
WriteLine("{0, -8}{1, -8}", "Marcia", "Parker");
WriteLine("{0, -8}{1, -8}", "Ed", "Tompkins");
```

```
C:\C#\Chapter.02>CodeForFigure02-09
    4
   56
  789
Richard Lee
Marcia  Parker
Ed      Tompkins

C:\C#\Chapter.02>
```

Figure 2-9   Displaying values with different numbers of digits using field sizes

Format strings can become very long. However, when you include any string value in a program, you cannot extend it across multiple lines by pressing Enter. If you do, you will receive an error message: "Newline in constant". Instead, if you want to break a long string into multiple lines of code, you can concatenate multiple strings into a single entity, as in the following:

```
WriteLine("I have ${0}. " +

    "${0} is a lot. ", someMoney);
```

In the concatenated example, the + could go at the end of the first code line or the beginning of the second one. If the + is placed at the end of the first line, someone reading your code is more likely to notice that the statement is not yet complete. Because of the limitations of this book's page width, you will see examples of concatenation frequently in program code.

TWO TRUTHS & A LIE

Displaying Variable Values

1. Assuming number and answer are legally declared variables with assigned values, then the following statement is valid:

   ```
   WriteLine("{1}{2}", number, answer);
   ```

2. Assuming number and answer are legally declared variables with assigned values, then the following statement is valid:

   ```
   WriteLine("{1}{1}{0}", number, answer);
   ```

3. Assuming number and answer are legally declared variables with assigned values, then the following statement is valid:

   ```
   WriteLine("{0}{1}{1}{0}", number, answer);
   ```

The false statement is #1. When two values are available for display, the position number between any pair of curly braces in the format string must be 0 or 1. If three values were listed after the format string, the position numbers could be any combination of 0, 1, and 2.

Using the Integral Data Types

In C#, nine data types are considered **integral data types**—that is, types that store whole numbers. The nine types are **byte**, **sbyte**, **short**, **ushort**, **int**, **uint**, **long**, **ulong**, and **char**. The first eight always represent whole numbers, and the ninth type, char, is used for characters like *A* or *a*. Actually, you can think of all nine types as numbers because every Unicode character, including the letters of the alphabet and punctuation marks, can be represented as a number. For example, the character *A* is stored within your computer as a 65. Because you more commonly think of the char type as holding alphabetic characters instead of their numeric equivalents, the char type will be discussed in its own section later in this chapter.

The most basic of the other eight integral types is `int`. You use variables of type `int` to store (or hold) **integers**, or whole numbers. An `int` uses four bytes of memory and can hold any whole number value ranging from 2,147,483,647 down to −2,147,483,648. When you type a whole-number constant such as 3 or 589 into a C# program, by default it is an `int`.

If you want to save memory and know you need only a small value, you can use one of the shorter integer types—`byte`, `sbyte` (which stands for signed byte), `short` (short `int`), or `ushort` (unsigned short `int`). For example, a payroll program might contain a variable named `numberOfDependents` that is declared as type `byte`, because `numberOfDependents` will never need to hold a value exceeding 255; for that reason, you can allocate just one byte of storage to hold the value. When you declare variables, you always make a judgment about which type to use. If you use a type that is too large, you waste storage. If you use a type that is too small, your program won't compile. Many programmers simply use `int` for most whole numbers.

Saving memory is seldom an issue for an application that runs on a PC. However, when you write applications for small devices with limited memory, such as smartphones, conserving memory becomes more important.

The word *integer* has only one *r*—at the end. Pronouncing it as "in-ter-ger," with an r in the middle, would mark you as unprofessional.

When you assign a value to any numeric variable, you do not use any commas or other nonnumeric characters such as dollar or percent signs; you type only digits. You can also type a plus or minus sign to indicate a positive or negative integer; a value without a sign is assumed to be positive. For example, to initialize a variable named `annualSalary`, you might write the following without a dollar sign or comma:

```
int annualSalary = 20000;
```

TWO TRUTHS & A LIE

Using the Integral Data Types

1. C# supports nine integral data types, including the most basic one, `int`.

2. Every Unicode character, including the letters of the alphabet and punctuation marks, can be represented as a number.

3. When you assign a value to any numeric variable, it is optional to use commas for values in the thousands.

The false statement is #3. When you assign a value to a numeric variable, you do not use commas, but you can type a plus or minus sign to indicate a positive or negative integer.

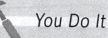

You Do It

Declaring and Using Variables

In the following steps, you write a program that declares several integral variables, assigns values to them, and displays the results.

1. Open a new file. If you are using a simple text editor to write your C# programs, you will save the file as **DemoVariables.cs**. If you are using Visual Studio, select **Console Application**, name the project **DemoVariables**, and delete all the code in the program-editing window before starting.

2. Create the beginning of a program that will demonstrate variable use. Name the class `DemoVariables`, and type the class-opening curly brace.

```
using static System.Console;
class DemoVariables
{
```

3. In the `Main()` method, declare two variables (an integer and an unsigned integer), and assign values to them.

```
static void Main()
{
    int anInt = -123;
    uint anUnsignedInt = 567;
```

4. Add a statement to display the two values.

```
WriteLine("The int is {0} and the unsigned int is {1}.",
    anInt, anUnsignedInt);
```

5. Add two closing curly braces—one that closes the `Main()` method and one that closes the `DemoVariables` class. Align each closing curly brace vertically with the opening brace that is its partner. In other words, the first closing brace aligns with the brace that opens `Main()`, and the second aligns with the brace that opens `DemoVariables`.

6. Save the program, and compile it. If you receive any error messages, correct the errors and compile the program again. When the file is error-free, execute the program. The output should look like Figure 2-10.

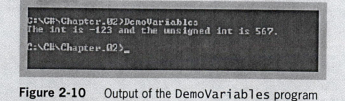

Figure 2-10   Output of the `DemoVariables` program

(continues)

(continued)

7. Experiment with the program by introducing invalid values for the named variables. For example, change the value of `anUnsignedInt` to **–567** by typing a minus sign in front of the constant value. Compile the program. You receive the following error message: *Constant value '–567' cannot be converted to a 'uint'*.

8. Correct the error either by removing the minus sign or by changing the data type of the variable to **int**, and compile the program again. You should not receive any error messages. Remember to save your program file after you make each change and before you compile.

9. Change the value of `anInt` from **–123** to **–123456789000**. When you compile the program, the following error message appears: *Cannot implicitly convert type 'long' to 'int'*.

   The value is a `long` because it is greater than the highest allowed `int` value. Correct the error either by using a lower value or by changing the variable type to `long`, and compile the program again. You should not receive any error messages.

10. Experiment with other changes to the variables. Include some variables of type `short`, `ushort`, `byte`, and `sbyte`, and experiment with their values.

Using Floating-Point Data Types

A **floating-point** number is one that contains decimal positions. Floating-point numbers are described as having varying numbers of significant digits. A value's number of **significant digits** specifies the mathematical accuracy of the value. The concept is often used in rounding. For example, in the statement "The population of New York City is 8,000,000," there is just one significant digit—the 8. The zeros serve as placeholders and are meant to approximate the actual value.

 When numbers are stored in computer memory, using a decimal point that can "float" provides a wider possible range of values. As a very simple example, suppose that the largest number you could store had only two digits with a fixed decimal point between them. Then the positive numbers that could be stored would range from 0.0 to 9.9. However, if the decimal point can float to be first, middle, or last, then the range becomes .00 through 99.

C# supports three floating-point data types: `float`, `double`, and `decimal`.

- A **float** data type can hold as many as seven significant digits of accuracy. For example, a `float` assigned the value 1234.56789 will appear as 1234.568 because it is accurate only to the seventh digit (the third digit to the right of the decimal point).

- A **double** data type can hold 15 or 16 significant digits of accuracy. For example, a `double` given the value 123456789.987654321 will appear as 123456789.987654 because it is accurate to only the fifteenth digit (the sixth digit to the right of the decimal point).

- Compared to floats and doubles, the **decimal** type has a greater precision and a smaller range, which makes it suitable for financial and monetary calculations. A decimal is significant to 28 or 29 digits. As Table 2-1 shows, a decimal cannot hold as large a value as a double can (the highest value is about 10^{28}; the highest value of a double is 10^{308}), but the decimal will be more accurate to more decimal places.

Just as an integer constant is an int by default, a floating-point number constant is a double by default. To explicitly store a constant as a float, you place an *F* after the number, as in the following:

```
float pocketChange = 4.87F;
```

You can use either a lowercase or uppercase *F*. You can also place a *D* (or *d*) after a floating-point value to indicate that it is a double; even without the *D*, however, it will be stored as a double by default. To explicitly store a value as a decimal, use an *M* (or *m*) after the number. (*M* stands for monetary; *D* can't be used for a decimal because it indicates double.)

Because monetary values are extremely important in business applications, many C# developers frequently use the decimal data type. This book most often uses the double type for floating-point values because floating-point numbers are double by default and do not require a modifying letter after the value. However, you should use the data type preferred by your instructor or manager or the type that is most appropriate to your application. Some programmers prefer to use the decimal type for any measurement created by humans (for example, money or test scores) and double for measurements of naturally occurring phenomena (for example, half-lives of elements).

If you store a value that is too large (or too small) in a floating-point variable, you will see output expressed in **scientific notation**. Values expressed in scientific notation include an *E* (for exponent). For example, if you declare float f = 1234567890f;, the value is output as 1.234568E9, meaning that the numeric constant you used is approximately 1.234568 times 10 to the ninth power, or 1.234568 with the decimal point moved nine positions to the right. When the value that follows the *E* is negative, it means the value is very small and the decimal point should move to the left. For example, the value 1.234E–07 represents 0.0000001234.

Formatting Floating-Point Values

By default, C# always displays floating-point numbers in the most concise way possible that maintains the correct value. For example, if you declare a variable and display it as in the following statements, the output will appear as *The amount is 14.*

```
double myMoney = 14.00;
WriteLine("The amount is {0}", myMoney);
```

The two zeros to the right of the decimal point in the assigned value will not appear in the output because they add no mathematical information. To see the decimal places, you can convert the floating-point value to a string using a standard numeric format string.

Standard numeric format strings are strings of characters expressed within double quotation marks that indicate a format for output. They take the form *X0*, where *X* is the format specifier and *0* is the precision specifier. The **format specifier** can be one of nine built-in format characters that define the most commonly used numeric format types. The **precision specifier** controls the number of significant digits or zeros to the right of the decimal point. Table 2-2 lists the nine format specifiers.

Format Character	Description	Default Format (if no precision is given)
C or c	Currency	$XX,XXX.XX
		($XX,XXX.XX)
D or d	Decimal	[–]XXXXXXX
E or e	Scientific	[–]X.XXXXXXE+xxx
	(exponential)	[–]X.XXXXXXe+xxx
		[–]X.XXXXXXE-xxx
		[–]X.XXXXXXe-xxx
F or f	Fixed-point	[–]XXXXXXX.XX
G or g	General	Variable; either with decimal places or scientific
N or n	Number	[–]XX,XXX.XX
P or p	Percent	Represents a numeric value as a percentage
R or r	Round trip	Ensures that numbers converted to strings will have the same values when they are converted back into numbers
X or x	Hexadecimal	Minimum hexadecimal (base 16) representation

Table 2-2 Format specifiers

You can use a format specifier with the ToString() method to convert a number into a string that has the desired format. For example, you can use the *F* format specifier to insert a decimal point to the right of a number that does not contain digits to the right of the decimal point, followed by the number of zeros indicated by the precision specifier. (If no precision specifier is supplied, two zeros are inserted.) For example, the first WriteLine() statement in the following code produces 123.00, and the second produces 123.000:

```
double someMoney = 123;
string moneyString;
moneyString = someMoney.ToString("F");
WriteLine(moneyString);
moneyString = someMoney.ToString("F3");
WriteLine(moneyString);
```

You will learn more about creating and using methods in the chapters "Introduction to Methods" and "Advanced Method Concepts."

You use *C* as the format specifier when you want to represent a number as a currency value. Currency values appear with a dollar sign, appropriate commas, and the desired number of decimal places; negative values appear within parentheses. The integer you use following the *C* indicates the number of decimal places. If you do not provide a value for the number of decimal places, then two digits are shown after the decimal separator by default. For example, the following WriteLine() statement produces $456,789.00:

```
double moneyValue = 456789;
string conversion;
conversion = moneyValue.ToString("C");
WriteLine(conversion);
```

Currency appears with a dollar sign and commas in the English culture. A **culture** is a set of rules that determines how culturally dependent values such as money and dates are formatted. You can change a program's culture by using the CultureInfoClass. The .NET framework supports more than 200 culture settings, such as Japanese, French, Urdu, and Sanskrit.

To display a numeric value as a formatted string, you do not have to create a separate string object. You also can make the conversion in a single statement; for example, the following code displays $12,345.00:

```
double payAmount = 12345;
WriteLine(payAmount.ToString("C"));
```

TWO TRUTHS & A LIE

Using Floating-Point Data Types

1. A floating-point number is one in which the decimal point varies each time you reference it.

2. C# supports three floating-point data types: float, double, and decimal.

3. To explicitly store a constant as a float, you may place an *F* after the number, but to store a constant as a double you need no special designation.

The false statement is #1. A floating-point number is one that contains decimal positions.

Using Arithmetic Operators

Table 2-3 describes the five most commonly used **arithmetic operators**. You use these operators to manipulate values in your programs. The values that operators use in expressions are called **operands**. These arithmetic operators are called **binary operators** because you use two operands with each—one value to the left of the operator and another value to the right of it.

Operator	Description	Example
+	Addition	45 + 2: the result is 47
–	Subtraction	45 – 2: the result is 43
*	Multiplication	45 * 2: the result is 90
/	Division	45 / 2: the result is 22 (not 22.5)
%	Remainder (modulus)	45 % 2: the result is 1 (that is, 45 / 2 = 22 with a remainder of 1)

Table 2-3   Binary arithmetic operators

Unlike some other programming languages, C# does not have an exponential operator. Instead, you can use the built-in method `Math.Pow()` that you will learn about in the chapter "Introduction to Methods."

The operators / and % deserve special consideration. When you divide two numbers and at least one is a floating-point value, the answer is a floating-point value. For example, 45.0 / 2 is 22.5. However, when you divide integers using the / operator, whether they are integer constants or integer variables, the result is an integer; in other words, any fractional part of the result is lost. For example, the result of 45 / 2 is 22, not 22.5.

When you use the remainder operator with two integers, the result is an integer with the value of the remainder after division takes place—so the result of 45 % 2 is 1 because 2 "goes into" 45 twenty-two times with a remainder of 1. Remainder operations should not be performed with floating-point numbers. The results are unpredictable because of the way floating-point numbers are stored in computer memory.

In older languages, such as assembly languages, you had to perform division before you could take a remainder. In C#, performing a division operation is not necessary before using a remainder operation. In other words, a remainder operation can stand alone.

You may hear programmers refer to the remainder operator as the *modulus operator*. Although modulus has a similar meaning to remainder, there are differences.

Even though you define a result variable as a floating-point type, integer division still results in an integer. For example, the statement `double d = 7 / 2;` results in d holding 3, not 3.5, because the expression on the right is evaluated as integer-by-integer division before the assignment takes place. If you want the result to hold 3.5, at least one of the operands in the calculation must be a floating-point number, or else you must perform a cast. You will learn about casting later in this chapter.

When you combine mathematical operations in a single statement, you must understand **operator precedence**, or the rules that determine the order in which parts of a mathematical expression are evaluated. Multiplication, division, and remainder always take place prior to addition or subtraction in an expression. For example, the following expression results in 14:

```
int result = 2 + 3 * 4;
```

The result is 14 because the multiplication operation (3 * 4) occurs before adding 2. You can override normal operator precedence by putting the operation that should be performed first in parentheses. The following statement results in 20 because the addition within parentheses takes place first:

```
int result = (2 + 3) * 4;
```

In this statement, an intermediate result (5) is calculated before it is multiplied by 4.

Operator precedence is also called **order of operation**. A closely linked term is **associativity**, which specifies the order in which a sequence of operations with the same precedence are evaluated. Appendix A describes the precedence and associativity of every C# operator.

You can use parentheses in an arithmetic expression, even if they do not alter the default order of operation. For example, even though multiplication takes place before addition without parentheses, it is perfectly acceptable to add them as follows:

```
weeklyPay = (hours * rate) + bonus;
```

You can use parentheses to make your intentions clear to other programmers who read your programs, which means they do not have to rely on their memory of operator precedence.

In summary, the order of operations for arithmetic operators is:

- *Parentheses.* Evaluate expressions within parentheses first.

- *Multiplication, division, remainder.* Evaluate these operations next from left to right.

- *Addition, subtraction.* Evaluate these operations next from left to right.

Using Shortcut Arithmetic Operators

Increasing the value held in a variable is a common programming task. Assume that you have declared a variable named `counter` that counts the number of times an event has occurred. Each time the event occurs, you want to execute a statement such as the following:

```
counter = counter + 1;
```

This type of statement looks incorrect to an algebra student, but the equal sign (=) is not used to compare values in C#; it is used to assign values. The statement `counter = counter + 1;` says "Take the value of `counter`, add 1 to it, and assign the result to `counter`."

Because increasing the value of a variable is such a common task, C# provides several shortcut ways to count and accumulate. The following two statements are identical in meaning:

```
counter += 1;
counter = counter + 1;
```

The += operator is the **add and assign operator**; it adds the operand on the right to the operand on the left and assigns the result to the operand on the left in one step. For example, if `payRate` is 20, then `payRate += 5` results in `payRate` holding the value 25. Similarly, the following statements both increase `bankBal` by a rate stored in `interestRate`:

```
bankBal +=  bankBal * interestRate;
bankBal = bankBal + bankBal * interestRate;
```

For example, if `bankBal` is 100.00 and `interestRate` is 0.02, then both of the previous statements result in `bankBal` holding 102.00.

Additional shortcut operators in C# are -=,*=, and /=. Each of these operators is used to perform an operation and assign the result in one step. You cannot place spaces between the two characters that compose these operators; spaces preceding or following the operators are optional. Examples in which the shortcut operators are useful follow:

- `balanceDue -= payment` subtracts a payment from `balanceDue` and assigns the result to `balanceDue`.

- `rate *= 100` multiplies `rate` by 100 and assigns the result to `rate`. For example, it converts a fractional value stored in `rate`, such as 0.27, to a whole number, such as 27.

- `payment /= 12` changes a payment value from an annual amount to a monthly amount due.

When you want to increase a variable's value by exactly 1, you can use either of two other shortcut operators—the **prefix increment operator** and the **postfix increment operator**. To use a prefix increment operator, you type two plus signs before the variable name. For example, these statements result in `someValue` holding 7:

```
int someValue = 6;
++someValue;
```

The variable `someValue` holds 1 more than it held before the ++ operator was applied. To use a postfix ++, you type two plus signs just after a variable name. Executing the following statements results in `anotherValue` holding 57:

```
int anotherValue = 56;
anotherValue++;
```

You can use the prefix ++ and postfix ++ with variables but not with constants. An expression such as ++84 is illegal because 84 is constant and must always remain 84. However, you can create a variable as in `int val = 84;`, and then write either ++val or val++ to increase the variable's value to 85.

The prefix and postfix increment operators are **unary operators** because you use them with one operand. Most arithmetic operators, like those used for addition and multiplication, are binary operators that operate on two operands.

When all you want to accomplish is to increase a variable's value by 1, there is no apparent difference between using the prefix and postfix increment operators. However, these operators function differently. When you use the prefix ++, the result is calculated and stored and then the variable is used. For example, in the following code, both b and c end up holding 5. The WriteLine() statement displays "5 5". In this example, 4 is assigned to b, then b becomes 5, and then 5 is assigned to c.

```
b = 4;
c = ++b;
WriteLine("{0} {1}", b, c);
```

In contrast, when you use the postfix ++, the variable is used, and then the result is calculated and stored. For example, in the second line of the following code, 4 is assigned to c; then, *after* the assignment, b is increased and takes the value 5.

```
b = 4;
c = b++;
WriteLine("{0} {1}", b, c);
```

This last WriteLine() statement displays "5 4". In other words, if b = 4, then the value of b++ is also 4, and that value is assigned to c. However, after the 4 is assigned to c, b is increased to 5.

When you need to add 1 to a variable in a stand-alone statement, the results are the same whether you use a prefix or postfix increment operator. However, many programmers routinely use the postfix operator when they could use either operator. This is probably a mistake because the prefix operator is more efficient. You will see an example that proves the superior efficiency of the prefix operator in the chapter "Looping."

A prefix or postfix **decrement operator** (--) reduces a variable's value by 1. For example, if s and t are both assigned the value 34, then the expression --s has the value 33 and the expression t-- has the value 34, but t then becomes 33.

Watch the video *Using Shortcut Arithmetic Operators.*

TWO TRUTHS & A LIE

Using Arithmetic Operators

1. The value of 26 % 4 * 3 is 18.

2. The value of 4 / 3 + 2 is 3.

3. If price is 4 and tax is 5, then the value of price - tax++ is -1.

The false statement is #1. The value of 26 % 4 * 3 is 6. The value of the first part of the expression, 26 % 4, is 2, because 2 is the remainder when 4 is divided into 26. Then 2 * 3 is 6.

You Do It

Performing Arithmetic

In the following steps, you add some arithmetic statements to a program.

1. Open a new C# program file named **DemoVariables2**, and enter the following statements to start a program that demonstrates arithmetic operations:

```
using static System.Console;
class DemoVariables2
{
    static void Main()
    {
```

2. Write a statement that declares seven integer variables. Assign initial values to two of the variables; the values for the other five variables will be calculated. Because all of these variables are the same type, you can use a single statement to declare all seven integers. Recall that to do this, you insert commas between variable names and place a single semicolon at the end. You can place line breaks wherever you want for readability. (Alternatively, you could use as many as seven separate declarations.)

```
int value1 = 43, value2 = 10,
    sum, diff, product, quotient, remainder;
```

3. Write the arithmetic statements that calculate the sum of, difference between, product of, quotient of, and remainder of the two assigned variables.

```
sum = value1 + value2;
diff = value1 - value2;
product = value1 * value2;
quotient = value1 / value2;
remainder = value1 % value2;
```

Instead of declaring the variables sum, diff, product, quotient, and remainder and assigning values later, you could declare and assign all of them at once, as in int sum = value1 + value2;. The only requirement is that value1 and value2 must be assigned values before you can use them in a calculation.

4. Include five WriteLine() statements to display the results.

```
WriteLine("The sum of {0} and {1} is {2}",
    value1, value2, sum);
WriteLine("The difference between {0} and {1}" +
    "is {2}", value1, value2, diff);
WriteLine("The product of {0} and {1} is {2}",
    value1, value2, product);
```

(continues)

(continued)

```
WriteLine("{0} divided by {1} is {2}", value1,
    value2, quotient);
WriteLine("and the remainder is {0}", remainder);
```

5. Add two closing curly braces—one for the Main() method and the other for the DemoVariables2 class.

6. Save the file, compile the program, and execute it. The output should look like Figure 2-11.

```
C:\C#\Chapter.02>DemoVariables2
The sum of 43 and 10 is 53
The difference between 43 and 10 is 33
The product of 43 and 10 is 430
43 divided by 10 is 4
and the remainder is 3

C:\C#\Chapter.02>_
```

Figure 2-11   Output of the DemoVariables2 program

7. Change the values of the value1 and value2 variables, save the program, and compile and run it again. Repeat this process several times. After each execution, analyze the output to make sure you understand the results of the arithmetic operations.

Using the bool Data Type

Boolean logic is based on true-or-false comparisons. An int variable can hold millions of different values at different times, but a **Boolean variable** can hold only one of two values—true or false. You declare a Boolean variable by using type **bool**. The following statements declare and assign appropriate values to two bool variables:

```
bool isItMonday = false;
bool areYouTired = true;
```

If you begin a bool variable name with a form of the verb "to be" or "to do," such as "is" or "are," then you can more easily recognize the identifiers as Boolean variables when you encounter them within your programs.

When you use "Boolean" as an adjective, as in "Boolean variable," you usually begin with an uppercase *B* because the data type is named for Sir George Boole, the founder of symbolic logic, who lived from 1815 to 1864. The C# data type bool, however, begins with a lowercase *b*.

You also can assign values based on the result of comparisons to Boolean variables. A **comparison operator** compares two items; an expression containing a comparison operator has a Boolean value. Table 2-4 describes the six comparison operators that C# supports.

Operator	Description	true Example	false Example
<	Less than	3 < 8	8 < 3
>	Greater than	4 > 2	2 > 4
==	Equal to	7 == 7	3 == 9
<=	Less than or equal to	5 <=5	8 <= 6
>=	Greater than or equal to	7 >= 3	1 >= 2
!=	Not equal to	5 != 6	3 != 3

Table 2-4 Comparison operators

When using any of the operators that require two keystrokes (==, <=, >=, or !=), you cannot place any whitespace between the two symbols.

A frequent mistake among new programmers is attempting to create a Boolean expression for equivalency with a single equal sign. The equivalency operator uses two equal signs. For example, the following assigns either **true** or **false** to **isDiscountProvided**:

```
isDiscountProvided = custStatus == 1;
```

The second operator in the statement (==) compares **custStatus** to 1. The result is then assigned to the variable on the left using the assignment operator (=).

Legal (but somewhat useless) declaration statements might include the following, which compare two values directly:

```
bool isBigger = 6 > 5; // Value stored would be true
bool isSmallerOrEqual = 7 <= 4; // Value stored would be false
```

Using Boolean values is more meaningful when you use variables (that have been assigned values) rather than constants in the comparisons, as in the following examples:

```
bool doesEmployeeReceiveOvertime = hoursWorked > 40;
bool isHighTaxBracket = annualIncome > 100000;
```

In the first statement, the **hoursWorked** variable is compared to a constant value of 40. If the **hoursWorked** variable holds a value less than or equal to 40, then the expression is evaluated as **false**. In the second statement, the **annualIncome** variable value must be greater than 100000 for the expression to be **true**.

Boolean variables become more useful after you learn to make decisions within C# programs in Chapter 4.

When you display a bool variable's value with a call to Write() or WriteLine(), the displayed value is capitalized as True or False. However, the values within programs are lowercase: true or false.

TWO TRUTHS & A LIE

Using the bool Data Type

1. If rate is 7.5 and min is 7, then the value of rate >= min is false.

2. If rate is 7.5 and min is 7, then the value of rate < min is false.

3. If rate is 7.5 and min is 7, then the value of rate == min is false.

The false statement is #1. If rate is 7.5 and min is 7, then the value of rate >= min is true.

You Do It

Working with Boolean Variables

Next, you write a program that demonstrates how Boolean variables operate.

1. Open a new file in your editor, and name it **DemoVariables3.**

2. Enter the following code. In the Main() method, you declare an integer value, then assign different values to a Boolean variable. Notice that when you declare value and isSixMore, you assign types. When you reassign values to these variables later in the program, you do not redeclare them by using a type name. Instead, you simply assign new values to the already declared variables.

```
using static System.Console;
class DemoVariables3
{
    static void Main()
    {
        int value = 4;
        bool isSixMore = 6 > value;
        WriteLine("When value is {0} isSixMore is {1}",
            value, isSixMore);
        value = 35;
        isSixMore = 6 > value;
        WriteLine("When value is {0} isSixMore is {1}",
            value, isSixMore);
    }
}
```

3. Save, compile, and run the program. The output looks like Figure 2-12.

(continues)

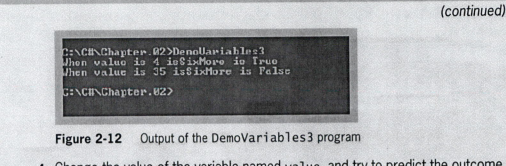

Figure 2-12   Output of the DemoVariables3 program

4. Change the value of the variable named value, and try to predict the outcome.
   Run the program to confirm your prediction.

Understanding Numeric Type Conversion

When you perform arithmetic with variables or constants of the same type, the result of the
arithmetic retains that type. For example, when you divide two ints, the result is an int;
when you subtract two doubles, the result is a double. Often, however, you need to perform
mathematical operations on different types. For example, in the following code, you multiply an
int by a double:

```
int hoursWorked = 36;
double payRate = 12.35;
double grossPay = hoursWorked * payRate;
```

When you perform arithmetic operations with operands of dissimilar types, C# chooses a
unifying type for the result and **implicitly** (or automatically) converts nonconforming operands
to the unifying type, which is the type with the higher **type precedence**. The conversion is
called an **implicit conversion** or an **implicit cast**—the automatic transformation that occurs
when a value is assigned to a type with higher precedence.

The implicit numeric conversions are:

- From sbyte to short, int, long, float, double, or decimal
- From byte to short, ushort, int, uint, long, ulong, float, double, or decimal
- From short to int, long, float, double, or decimal
- From ushort to int, uint, long, ulong, float, double, or decimal
- From int to long, float, double, or decimal
- From uint to long, ulong, float, double, or decimal
- From long to float, double, or decimal
- From ulong to float, double, or decimal
- From char to ushort, int, uint, long, ulong, float, double, or decimal
- From float to double

Implicit conversions occur in simple assignments as well as in calculations. For example, if money is declared as a double, then the following statement implicitly converts the integer 15 to a double:

```
money = 15;
```

Conversions from int, uint, or long to float and from long to double may cause a loss of precision but will never cause a loss of magnitude.

A constant expression of type int, such as 25, can be converted to sbyte, byte, short, ushort, uint, or ulong. For example, sbyte age = 19;, which assigns an int to an sbyte, is legal. However, you must make sure that the assigned value is within the allowed range for the destination type, or the program will not compile.

For example, if you multiply an int and a double, the result is implicitly a double. This requirement means the result must be stored in a double; if you attempt to assign the result to an int, you will receive a compiler error message like the one shown in Figure 2-13.

```
TryingToStoreDoubleInInt.cs(8,17): error CS0266: Cannot implicitly convert type
    'double' to 'int'. An explicit conversion exists (are you missing a
    cast?)

C:\C#\Chapter.02>
```

Figure 2-13   Error message received when trying to compile a program that attempts to store a double in an int

The error message in Figure 2-13 asks "are you missing a cast?" You may **explicitly** (or purposefully) override the unifying type imposed by C# by performing an explicit cast. An **explicit cast** involves placing the desired result type in parentheses followed by the variable or constant to be cast. For example, two explicit casts are performed in the following code:

```
double bankBalance = 191.66;
float weeklyBudget = (float) bankBalance / 4;
   // weeklyBudget is 47.915, one-fourth of bankBalance
int dollars = (int) weeklyBudget;
   // dollars is 47, the integer part of weeklyBudget
```

The value of bankBalance / 4 is implicitly a double because a double divided by an int produces a double. The explicit cast then converts the double result to a float before it is stored in weeklyBudget. Similarly, the float value weeklyBudget is cast to an int before it is stored in dollars (and the decimal-place values are lost).

It is easy to lose data when performing a cast. For example, the largest byte value is 255, and the largest int value is 2,147,483,647, so the following statements produce distorted results because some information is lost during the cast:

- int anOkayInt = 256;
- byte aBadByte = (byte)anOkayInt;

In this example, displaying aBadByte shows 0. If you stored 257 in anOkayInt, the result would appear as 1; if you stored 258, the result would appear as 2; and so on.

Watch the video *Numeric Type Conversion*.

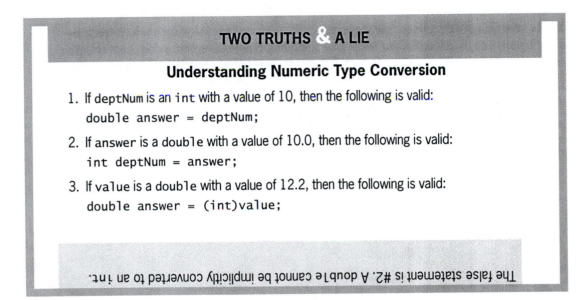

TWO TRUTHS & A LIE

Understanding Numeric Type Conversion

1. If deptNum is an int with a value of 10, then the following is valid:

   double answer = deptNum;

2. If answer is a double with a value of 10.0, then the following is valid:

   int deptNum = answer;

3. If value is a double with a value of 12.2, then the following is valid:

   double answer = (int)value;

The false statement is #2. A double cannot be implicitly converted to an int.

Using the char Data Type

You use the **char** data type to hold any single character. You place constant character values within single quotation marks because the computer stores characters and integers differently. For example, the following statement assigns *D* to initial:

char initial = 'D';

A number can be a character, in which case it must be enclosed in single quotation marks and declared as a char type, as in the following:

char aCharValue = '9';

When you store a digit such as '9' as a character, you cannot use it in ordinary arithmetic statements. If the value of 9 is needed for use in arithmetic, you should store it without quotes as a numeric type, such as int.

A variable of type char can hold only one character, and a literal character is written using single quotation marks. To store a string of characters, such as a person's name, you must use a string; a literal string is written using double quotation marks. You will learn about strings later in this chapter.

You can store any character—including nonprinting characters such as a backspace or a tab—in a char variable. To store these characters, you use two symbols in an **escape sequence**, which always begins with a backslash. The pair of symbols represents a single character. For example, the following code stores a backspace character and a tab character in the char variables aBackspaceChar and aTabChar, respectively:

```
char aBackspaceChar = '\b';
char aTabChar = '\t';
```

In the preceding code, the escape sequence indicates a unique value for each character— a backspace or tab instead of the letter *b* or *t*. Table 2-5 describes some common escape sequences that are used in C#.

Escape Sequence	Character Name
\'	Single quotation mark
\"	Double quotation mark
\\	Backslash
\0	Null
\a	Alert
\b	Backspace
\f	Form feed
\n	Newline
\r	Carriage return
\t	Horizontal tab
\v	Vertical tab

Table 2-5 Common escape sequences

The characters used in C# are represented in Unicode, which is a 16-bit coding scheme for characters. For example, the letter *A* actually is stored in computer memory as a set of 16 zeros and ones—namely, 0000 0000 0100 0001. (The spaces are inserted here after every set of four digits for readability.) Because 16-bit numbers are difficult to read, programmers often use a shorthand notation called **hexadecimal**, or **base 16**. In hexadecimal shorthand, 0000 becomes 0,

0100 becomes 4, and 0001 becomes 1. Thus, the letter *A* is represented in hexadecimal as 0041. You tell the compiler to treat the four-digit hexadecimal 0041 as a single character by preceding it with the \u escape sequence. Therefore, there are two ways to store the character *A*:

```
char letter = 'A';
char letter = '\u0041';
```

For more information about Unicode, see Appendix B.

The second option, using hexadecimal, obviously is more difficult and confusing than the first option, so it is not recommended that you store letters of the alphabet using the hexadecimal method. However, you can produce some interesting values using the Unicode format. For example, letters from foreign alphabets that are not on a standard keyboard (such as letters from Greek, Hebrew, and Chinese alphabets) and other special symbols (foreign currency symbols, mathematical symbols, geometric shapes, and so on) are available in Unicode. You can even output the sound of a beep by displaying the hexadecimal character '\u0007'.

TWO TRUTHS & A LIE

Using the char Data Type

1. The following statement is legal in C#:

   ```
   char department = '5';
   ```

2. The following statement is legal in C#:

   ```
   char department = '\f';
   ```

3. The following statement is legal in C#:

   ```
   char department = '32';
   ```

The false statement is #3. Only a single character can appear between single quotation marks, with the exception of escape sequence characters such as '\t', and '\f'. In these cases, a single character is created using two symbols.

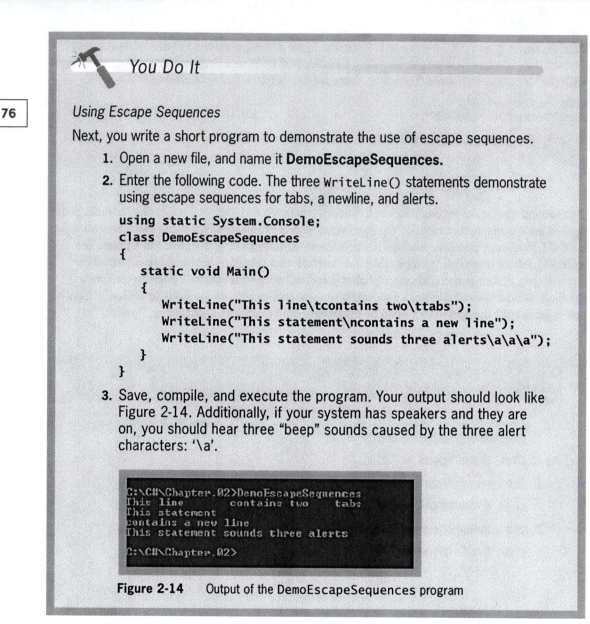

You Do It

Using Escape Sequences

Next, you write a short program to demonstrate the use of escape sequences.

1. Open a new file, and name it **DemoEscapeSequences.**

2. Enter the following code. The three WriteLine() statements demonstrate using escape sequences for tabs, a newline, and alerts.

```
using static System.Console;
class DemoEscapeSequences
{
    static void Main()
    {
        WriteLine("This line\tcontains two\ttabs");
        WriteLine("This statement\ncontains a new line");
        WriteLine("This statement sounds three alerts\a\a\a");
    }
}
```

3. Save, compile, and execute the program. Your output should look like Figure 2-14. Additionally, if your system has speakers and they are on, you should hear three "beep" sounds caused by the three alert characters: '\a'.

```
C:\CH\Chapter.02>DemoEscapeSequences
This line          contains two      tabs
This statement
contains a new line
This statement sounds three alerts

C:\CH\Chapter.02>
```

Figure 2-14   Output of the DemoEscapeSequences program

Using the string Data Type

In C#, you use the **string** data type to hold a series of characters. The value of a **string** is expressed within double quotation marks. For example, the following statement declares a string named firstName and assigns *Jane* to it:

string firstName = "Jane";

You can also initialize a string with a character array. The "Using Arrays" chapter explains more.

You can compare the value of one string to another using the == and != operators in the same ways that you compare numeric or character variables. For example, the program in Figure 2-15 declares three string variables. Figure 2-16 shows the results: strings that contain *Amy* and *Amy* are considered equal, but strings that contain *Amy* and *Matthew* are not.

```
using static System.Console;
class CompareNames1
{
    static void Main()
    {
        string name1 = "Amy";
        string name2 = "Amy";
        string name3 = "Matthew";
        WriteLine("compare {0} to {1}: {2}",
            name1, name2, name1 == name2);
        WriteLine("compare {0} to {1}: {2}",
            name1, name3, name1 == name3);
    }
}
```

Figure 2-15   Program that compares two strings using == operator (not recommended)

```
C:\C#\Chapter.02>CompareNames1
compare Amy to Amy: True
compare Amy to Matthew: False

C:\C#\Chapter.02>
```

Figure 2-16   Output of the CompareNames1 program

In addition to the == comparison operator, you can use several prewritten methods to compare strings. The advantage to using these other methods is that they have standard names; when you use most other C# classes written by others, they will use methods with the same names to compare their objects. You can compare strings with any of the following methods:

- The String class Equals() method requires two string arguments that you place within its parentheses, separated by a comma. As when you use the == operator, the Equals() method returns true or false.

- The String class Compare() method also requires two string arguments, but it returns an integer. When it returns 0, the two strings are equivalent; when it returns a positive number, the first string is greater than the second; and when it returns a negative value, the first string is less than the second. A string is considered equal to, greater than, or less than another string **lexically**, which in the case of letter values means alphabetically. That is, when you compare two strings, you compare each character in turn from left to right. If each Unicode value is the same, then the strings are equivalent. If any corresponding character values are different, the string that has the greater Unicode value earlier in the string is considered greater.

- The CompareTo() method also compares two strings. However, one string is used before the dot and method name, and the second string is placed within the method's parentheses as an argument. Like the Compare() method, the CompareTo() method returns a 0 when the compared strings are equal, a negative number if the first string is less, and a positive number if the second string (the one in parentheses) is less.

Figure 2-17 shows a program that makes several comparisons using the three methods; in each case the method name is shaded. Figure 2-18 shows the program's output.

Methods like Compare() that are not preceded with an object and a dot when they are called are *static methods*. Methods like CompareTo() that are preceded with an object and a dot are nonstatic and are *instance methods*. The "Advanced Method Concepts" chapter explains more.

```
using System;
using static System.Console;
class CompareTwoNames
{
    static void Main()
    {
        string name1 = "Amy";
        string name2 = "Amy";
        string name3 = "Matthew";
        WriteLine("Using Equals() method");
        WriteLine("compare {0} to {1}: {2}",
            name1, name2, String.Equals(name1, name2));
        WriteLine("compare {0} to {1}: {2}",
            name1, name3, String.Equals(name1, name3));
        WriteLine("Using Compare() method");
        WriteLine(" compare {0} to {1}: {2}",
            name1, name2, String.Compare(name1, name2));
        WriteLine("compare {0} to {1}: {2}",
            name1, name3, String.Compare(name1, name3));
        WriteLine("Using CompareTo() method");
        WriteLine("compare {0} to {1}: {2}",
            name1, name2, name1.CompareTo(name2));
        WriteLine("compare {0} to {1}: {2}",
            name1, name3, name1.CompareTo(name3));
    }
}
```

Figure 2-17   Program that compares two strings using three methods

```
C:\C#\Chapter.02>CompareTwoNames
Using Equals() method
   compare Amy to Amy: True
   compare Amy to Matthew: False
Using Compare() method
   compare Amy to Amy: 0
   compare Amy to Matthew: -1
Using CompareTo() method
   compare Amy to Amy: 0
   compare Amy to Matthew: -1

C:\C#\Chapter.02>_
```

Figure 2-18   Output of the `CompareTwoNames` program

In C#, a string is **immutable**. That is, a string's value is not actually modified when you assign a new value to it. For example, when you write `name = "Amy";` followed by `name = "Donald";`, the first literal string of characters, *Amy*, still exists in computer memory, but the `name` variable no longer refers to that string's memory address. Instead, `name` refers to a new address where the characters in *Donald* are stored. The situation is different than with numbers; when you assign a new value to a numeric variable, the value at the named memory address actually changes, erasing the original value.

The comparisons made by the `Equals()`, `Compare()`, and `CompareTo()` methods are case sensitive. In other words, "Amy" does not equal "amy". In Unicode, the decimal value of each uppercase letter is exactly 32 less than its lowercase equivalent. For example, the decimal value of a Unicode 'a' is 97 and the value of 'A' is 65.

You can use the `Length` property of a string to determine its length. For example, suppose you declare a string as follows:

```
string word = "water";
```

The value of `word.Length` is 5. Notice that `Length` is not a method and that it is not followed with parentheses.

The `Substring()` method can be used to extract a portion of a string from a starting point for a specific length. For example, Figure 2-19 shows a string that contains the word *water*. The first character in a string is at position 0, and the last character is at position `Length - 1`. Therefore, after you declare `string word = "water";`, each of the first five expressions in the figure is true. The last expression produces an error message because the combination of the starting position and length attempt to access values outside the range of the string.

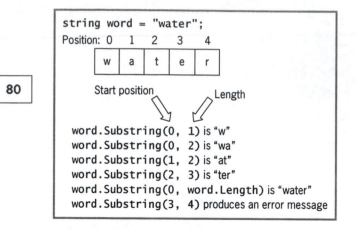

```
string word = "water";
Position: 0   1   2   3   4
         ┌───┬───┬───┬───┬───┐
         │ w │ a │ t │ e │ r │
         └───┴───┴───┴───┴───┘
       Start position        Length

word.Substring(0,  1) is "w"
word.Substring(0,  2) is "wa"
word.Substring(1,  2) is "at"
word.Substring(2,  3) is "ter"
word.Substring(0,  word.Length) is "water"
word.Substring(3,  4) produces an error message
```

Figure 2-19   Using the Substring() method

The StartsWith() method determines whether a string starts with the characters in the string that is used as an argument. For example, if word is "water", the expression word.StartsWith("wa") is true, and the expression word.StartsWith("waet") is false.

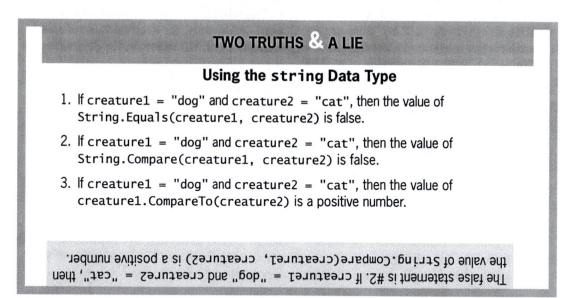

TWO TRUTHS & A LIE

Using the string Data Type

1. If creature1 = "dog" and creature2 = "cat", then the value of String.Equals(creature1, creature2) is false.

2. If creature1 = "dog" and creature2 = "cat", then the value of String.Compare(creature1, creature2) is false.

3. If creature1 = "dog" and creature2 = "cat", then the value of creature1.CompareTo(creature2) is a positive number.

The false statement is #2. If creature1 = "dog" and creature2 = "cat", then the value of String.Compare(creature1, creature2) is a positive number.

Defining Named Constants

By definition, a variable's value can vary or change. Sometimes you want to create a **named constant**, an identifier for a memory location whose contents cannot change. You create a named constant by adding the keyword const before the data type in a declaration. Although there is no requirement to do so, programmers usually name constants using all uppercase letters, inserting underscores for readability. This convention makes constant names stand out so that a reader is less likely to confuse them with variable names. For example, the following declares a constant named TAX_RATE that is initialized to 0.06:

```
const double TAX_RATE = 0.06;
```

You must assign a value to a constant when you create it. You can use a constant just as you would use a variable of the same type—for example, display it or use it in a mathematical equation—but you cannot assign any new value to it.

It's good programming practice to use named constants for any values that should never change; doing so makes your programs clearer. For example, when you declare a constant `const int INCHES_IN_A_FOOT = 12;` within a program, then you can use a statement such as the following:

```
lengthInInches = lengthInFeet * INCHES_IN_A_FOOT;
```

This statement is **self-documenting**; that is, even without a program comment, it is easy for someone reading your program to tell why you performed the calculation in the way you did.

Working with Enumerations

An **enumeration** is a set of constants represented by identifiers. You place an enumeration in a class outside of any methods. Very frequently, programmers place enumerations at the top of a file before any methods. You create an enumeration using the keyword **enum** and an identifier, followed by a comma-separated list of constants between curly braces. By convention, the enumerator identifier begins with an uppercase letter. For example, the following is an enumeration called DayOfWeek:

```
enum DayOfWeek
{
    SUNDAY, MONDAY, TUESDAY, WEDNESDAY,
        THURSDAY, FRIDAY, SATURDAY
}
```

By default, enumeration values are integers. You could also declare an **enum's** type to be **byte**, **sbyte**, **short**, **ushort**, **uint**, **long**, or **ulong** by including a colon and the type after the enumeration name and before the opening curly brace of the assignment list.

Frequently, the identifiers in an enumeration are meant to hold consecutive values. When you do not supply values for the items in an **enum** list, they start with 0 and are automatically increased by 1. For example, in the DayOfWeek enumeration, SUNDAY is 0, MONDAY is 1, and so on.

As is the convention with other constants, you might prefer to name enum constants using all uppercase letters and underscores for readability, as shown in the DayOfWeek enumeration here. This helps distinguish enumeration names from variables. However, the developers of C# frequently violate this convention in both their online documentation and in built-in enumerations in the language. For example, the built-in FontStyle enumeration contains constants with mixed-case names such as Bold and Italic. When you create enumerations, you should follow the convention your instructor or supervisor prefers. Another convention is to use a singular noun or noun phrase as the enum identifier. In other words, DayOfWeek is better than DaysOfWeek.

If you want the first **enum** constant in the list to have a value other than 0, you can assign one, as in the following:

```
enum DayOfWeek
{
    SUNDAY = 1, MONDAY, TUESDAY, WEDNESDAY,
        THURSDAY, FRIDAY, SATURDAY
}
```

In this case, SUNDAY is 1, MONDAY is 2, TUESDAY is 3, and so on.

As another option, you can assign values to each enumeration, as in the following:

```
enum SpeedLimit
{
    SCHOOL_ZONE_SPEED = 20,
    CITY_STREET_SPEED = 30,
    HIGHWAY_SPEED = 55
}
```

The names used within an **enum** must be unique, but the values assigned don't have to be.

When you create an enumeration, you clearly identify what values are valid for an item. You also make your code more self-documenting. You should consider creating an enumeration any time you have a fixed number of integral values allowed for a variable.

As a side benefit, when you use an enum in Visual Studio, Intellisense lists the defined values. Appendix C provides more information on Intellisense.

After you have created an enumeration, you can declare variables of the enumeration type, and you can assign enumeration values to them. For example, you can use the following statements to declare **payrollDay** as data type **DayOfWeek**, and assign a value to it:

```
DayOfWeek payrollDay;
payrollDay = DayOfWeek.TUESDAY;
```

In the chapter "Using Classes and Objects," you will learn to create many additional data types that are more complex than the built-in data types.

You can convert an **enum** value to another data type or an integral type to an **enum** value by using a cast. For example, the following are valid statements:

```
int shipDay;
DayOfWeek deliverDay;
shipDay = (int)DayOfWeek.THURSDAY;
deliverDay = (DayOfWeek)shipDay;
```

Using the preceding example, you can display 5 and *THURSDAY* with the following statements:

```
WriteLine(shipDay);
WriteLine(deliverDay);
```

Creating an enumeration type provides you with several advantages. For example, the DayOfWeek enumeration improves your programs in the following ways:

- If you did not create an enumerated type, you could use another type—for example, ints or strings. The problem is that any value could be assigned to an int or string variable, but only the seven allowed values can be assigned to a DayOfWeek object.

- If you did not create an enumerated type, you could create another type to represent days, but invalid behavior could be applied to the values. For example, if you used integers to represent days, you could multiply or divide two days, which is not logical. Programmers say using **enums** makes the values type-safe. **Type-safe** describes a data type for which only appropriate behaviors are allowed.

- The **enum** constants provide a form of self-documentation. Someone reading your program might misinterpret what 3 means as a day value, but there is less confusion when you use the identifier WEDNESDAY.

> This discussion is meant to be a brief introduction to enumerations. At this point in your study of C#, the advantages to using enumerations are limited. Enumerations are particularly useful with switch statements, which you will learn about in the "Making Decisions" chapter.

TWO TRUTHS & A LIE

Defining Named Constants

1. The following is a valid and conventional C# constant declaration:

   ```
   const string FIRST_HEADING = "Progress Report";
   ```

2. The following is a valid and conventional C# constant declaration:

   ```
   const double COMMISSION_RATE;
   ```

3. By default, enumeration values are integers.

The false statement is #2. A constant must be assigned a value when it is declared.

Accepting Console Input

A program that allows user input is an **interactive program**. You can use the ReadLine() method to create an interactive program that accepts user input from the keyboard. This method accepts all of the characters entered by a user until the user presses Enter.

The characters can be assigned to a `string`. For example, the following statement accepts a user's input and stores it in the variable `myString`:

```
myString = ReadLine();
```

The `Read()` method is similar to the `ReadLine()` method. `Read()` reads just one character from the input stream, whereas `ReadLine()` reads every character in the input stream until the user presses Enter.

> Prior to the release of C# 6.0, the qualified names `Console.ReadLine()` and `Console.Read()` were required. However, just like with `WriteLine()` and `Write()`, you can now include `using static System.Console;` at the top of a file allowing you to use the shorter method names `ReadLine()` and `Read()`.

If you want to use the input value as a type other than `string`, then you must use a conversion method to change the input `string` to the proper type. Two methods are available for converting strings—the `Convert` class and `Parse()` methods.

Using the `Convert` Class

Figure 2-20 shows an interactive program that prompts the user for a price and calculates a 6 percent sales tax. The program displays *Enter the price of an item* on the screen. Such an instruction to the user is a **prompt**. Notice that two using statements appear at the top of the file:

- `using System;` to include the `Convert` class

- `using static System.Console;` to include the `ReadLine()` and `WriteLine()` methods

Notice that the program uses a `Write()` statement for the prompt instead of a `WriteLine()` statement so that the user's input appears on the screen on the same line as the prompt. Also notice that the prompt contains a space just before the closing quote so that the prompt does not crowd the user's input on the screen.

After the prompt appears, the `ReadLine()` statement accepts a string of characters and assigns them to the variable `itemPriceAsString`. Before the tax can be calculated, this value must be converted to a number. This conversion is accomplished using the `Convert` class `ToDouble()` method in the shaded statement. Figure 2-21 shows a typical execution of the program in which the user typed 28.77 as the input value.

```
using System;
using static System.Console;
class InteractiveSalesTax
{
    static void Main()
    {
        const double TAX_RATE = 0.06;
        string itemPriceAsString;
        double itemPrice;
        double total;
        Write("Enter the price of an item >> ");
        itemPriceAsString = ReadLine();
        itemPrice = Convert.ToDouble(itemPriceAsString);
        total = itemPrice * TAX_RATE;
        WriteLine("With a tax rate of {0}, a {1} item " +
            "costs {2} more.", TAX_RATE, itemPrice.ToString("C"),
            total.ToString("C"));
    }
}
```

Figure 2-20 The InteractiveSalesTax program

In the program in Figure 2-20, the angle brackets at the end of the prompt are not required; they are merely cosmetic. You might prefer other punctuation such as a colon, ellipsis, or hyphen to indicate that input is required.

Figure 2-21 Typical execution of the InteractiveSalesTax program

As a shortcut, you can avoid declaring and using the extra `string` variable `itemPriceAsString` in the program in Figure 2-20. Instead, you can accept and convert the input string in one step by nesting the `ReadLine()` and `ToDouble()` method calls, as in the following:

`itemPrice = Convert.ToDouble(ReadLine());`

Table 2-6 shows `Convert` class methods you can use to change `strings` into additional useful data types. The methods use the system types (also called runtime types) in their names. For example, recall from Table 2-1 that the "formal" name for an `int` is `Int32`, so the method you use to convert a `string` to an `int` is named `Convert.ToInt32()`.

Method	Description
ToBoolean()	Converts a specified value to an equivalent Boolean value
ToByte()	Converts a specified value to an 8-bit unsigned integer
ToChar()	Converts a specified value to a Unicode character
ToDecimal()	Converts a specified value to a decimal number
ToDouble()	Converts a specified value to a double-precision floating-point number
ToInt16()	Converts a specified value to a 16-bit signed integer (a short)
ToInt32()	Converts a specified value to a 32-bit signed integer (an int)
ToInt64()	Converts a specified value to a 64-bit signed integer (a long)
ToSByte()	Converts a specified value to an 8-bit signed integer
ToSingle()	Converts a specified value to a single-precision floating-point number
ToString()	Converts the specified value to its equivalent String representation
ToUInt16()	Converts a specified value to a 16-bit unsigned integer
ToUInt32()	Converts a specified value to a 32-bit unsigned integer
ToUInt64()	Converts a specified value to a 64-bit unsigned integer

Table 2-6   Selected Convert class methods

Using the Parse() Methods

As an alternative to the Convert class methods, you can use a Parse() method to convert a string to a number. For example, to convert a string to a double in the InteractiveSalesTax program in Figure 2-20, you can replace the Convert.ToDouble() statement with either of the following Parse() method statements:

```
itemPrice = double.Parse(itemPriceAsString);
itemPrice = Double.Parse(itemPriceAsString);
```

Each of the previous two statements uses a Parse() method defined in the Double class. You can use the system type name Double or its simple type name double. Either version converts the string argument within the parentheses to the correct data type.

Similar methods exist for other data types, such as int.Parse() and boolean.Parse(). For example, either of the following two statements reads an integer and stores it in a variable named score without using a temporary string to hold the input value:

```
score = int.Parse(ReadLine());
score = Int32.Parse(ReadLine());
```

There are some performance differences between the Convert and Parse() techniques, but they are minor and relatively technical. Until you learn more about C#, you should use the method preferred by your instructor or organization.

The term **parse** means to break into component parts. Grammarians talk about "parsing a sentence"— deconstructing it so as to describe its grammatical components. Parsing a string converts it to its numeric equivalent.

TWO TRUTHS & A LIE

Accepting Console Input

1. The following is valid:

   ```
   int age = Convert.ToInt(ReadLine());
   ```

2. The following is valid:

   ```
   double payRate = Convert.ToDouble(ReadLine());
   ```

3. The following is valid:

   ```
   int dependents = int.Parse(ReadLine());
   ```

The false statement is #1. The Convert class method to convert a string to an integer is ToInt32(), not ToInt().

You Do It

Writing a Program that Accepts User Input

In the next steps, you write an interactive program that allows the user to enter two integer values. The program then calculates and displays their sum.

1. Open a new file named **InteractiveAddition**, and type the first few lines needed for the Main() method:

   ```
   using System;
   using static System.Console;
   class InteractiveAddition
   {
       static void Main()
       {
   ```

(continues)

(continued)

2. Add variable declarations for two `strings` that will accept the user's input values. Also, declare three integers for the numeric equivalents of the `string` input values and their sum.

```
string name, firstString, secondString;
int first, second, sum;
```

3. Prompt the user for his or her name, accept it into the `name` string, and then display a personalized greeting to the user, along with the prompt for the first integer value.

```
Write("Enter your name... ");
name = ReadLine();
Write("Hello {0}! Enter the first integer... ", name);
```

4. Accept the user's input as a `string`, and then convert the input `string` to an integer.

```
firstString = ReadLine();
first = Convert.ToInt32(firstString);
```

5. Add statements that prompt for and accept the second `string` and convert it to an integer.

```
Write("Enter the second integer... ");
secondString = ReadLine();
second = Convert.ToInt32(secondString);
```

6. Assign the sum of the two integers to the `sum` variable and display all of the values. Add the closing curly brace for the `Main()` method and the closing curly brace for the class.

```
        sum = first + second;
        WriteLine("{0}, the sum of {1} and {2} is {3}",
            name, first, second, sum);

    }

}
```

7. Save, compile, and run the program. When prompted, supply your name and any integers you want, and confirm that the result appears correctly. Figure 2-22 shows a typical run of the program.

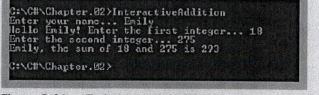

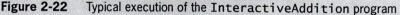

Figure 2-22   Typical execution of the `InteractiveAddition` program

Chapter Summary

- A constant is a data value that cannot be changed after a program is compiled; a value in a variable can change. C# provides for 15 basic built-in types of data. A variable declaration includes a data type, an identifier, an optional assigned value, and a semicolon.

- You can display variable values by using the variable name within a `WriteLine()` or `Write()` method call. To make producing output easier, you can combine strings and variable values into a single `Write()` or `WriteLine()` statement by using a format string.

- C# supports nine integral data types: `byte`, `sbyte`, `short`, `ushort`, `int`, `uint`, `long`, `ulong`, and `char`.

- C# supports three floating-point data types: `float`, `double`, and `decimal`. You can use format and precision specifiers to display floating-point data to a specified number of decimal places.

- You use the binary arithmetic operators +, -, *, /, and % to manipulate values in your programs. Multiplication, division, and remainder always take place prior to addition or subtraction in an expression, unless you use parentheses to override the normal precedence. C# provides several shortcut arithmetic operators, including the binary operators +=, -=, *=, /=, and the unary prefix and postfix increment (++) and decrement (--) operators.

- A `bool` variable can hold only one of two values—true or false. C# supports six comparison operators: >, <, >=, <=, ==, and !=. An expression containing a comparison operator has a Boolean value.

- When you perform arithmetic with variables or constants of the same type, the result of the arithmetic retains that type. When you perform arithmetic operations with operands of different types, C# chooses a unifying type for the result and implicitly converts nonconforming operands to the unifying type. You may explicitly override the unifying type imposed by C# by performing a cast.

- You use the `char` data type to hold any single character. You place constant character values within single quotation marks. You can store any character—including nonprinting characters such as a backspace or a tab—in a `char` variable. To store these characters, you must use an escape sequence, which always begins with a backslash.

- In C#, you use the `string` data type to hold a series of characters. The value of a `string` is expressed within double quotation marks. Although the == and != comparison operators can be used with `string`s that are assigned literal values, you also can use the `Equals()`, `Compare()`, `CompareTo()`, and `Substring()` methods and the `Length` property that belong to the `String` class.

- Named constants are program identifiers whose values cannot change. Conventionally, their identifiers are all uppercase, with underscores inserted for readability. Enumerations are lists of named constants. The constants are integers by default, and frequently the list holds consecutive values.

- You can use the `ReadLine()` method to accept user input. Often you must use a `Convert` class method to change the input string into a usable data type.

Key Terms

Constant describes data items whose values are fixed.

A **literal constant** is a value that is taken literally at each use.

A **variable** is a named location in computer memory that can hold different values at different points in time.

A **data type** describes the format and size of a data item and defines what types of operations can be performed with the item.

Intrinsic types of data are basic types; C# provides 15 intrinsic types.

An **alias** is another name for something.

A **simple type** is one of the following in C#: `byte`, `sbyte`, `short`, `ushort`, `int`, `uint`, `long`, `ulong`, `float`, `double`, `decimal`, `char`, and `bool`.

Unicode is a 16-bit coding scheme for characters.

A **variable declaration** is the statement that names a variable; it includes the data type that the variable will store, an identifier that is the variable's name, an optional assignment operator and assigned value when you want a variable to contain an initial value, and an ending semicolon.

The **assignment operator** is the equal sign (=); any value to the right of the assignment operator is assigned to, or taken on by, the variable to the left.

An **initialization** is an assignment made when a variable is declared.

An **assignment** is a statement that provides a variable with a value.

To **concatenate** a string with another value is to join the two values end to end using a plus sign.

A **format string** is a string of characters that controls the appearance of output.

Integral data types are those that store whole numbers.

The nine integral types are **byte**, **sbyte**, **short**, **ushort**, **int**, **uint**, **long**, **ulong**, and **char**. The first eight always represent whole numbers, and the ninth type, **char**, is used for characters like 'A' or '*a*'.

Integers are whole numbers.

A **floating-point** number is one that contains decimal positions.

Significant digits provide a measure of the mathematical accuracy of a value.

A **float** data type can hold a floating-point number with as many as seven significant digits of accuracy.

A **double** data type can hold a floating-point number with 15 or 16 significant digits of accuracy.

The **decimal** data type is a floating-point type that has a greater precision and a smaller range than a **float** or **double**, which makes it suitable for financial and monetary calculations.

Scientific notation is a means of expressing very large and small numbers using an exponent.

Standard numeric format strings are strings of characters expressed within double quotation marks that indicate a format for output.

The **format specifier** in a format string can be one of nine built-in format characters that define the most commonly used numeric format types.

The **precision specifier** in a format string controls the number of significant digits or zeros to the right of the decimal point.

A C# **culture** is a set of rules that determines how culturally dependent values such as money and dates are formatted.

Arithmetic operators are used to perform arithmetic; they include +, -, *, /, and %.

Operands are the values that operators use in expressions.

Binary operators use two operands—one value to the left of the operator and another value to the right of it.

Operator precedence determines the order in which parts of a mathematical expression are evaluated.

Order of operation is another term for operator precedence.

Associativity specifies the order in which a sequence of operations with the same precedence are evaluated.

The **add and assign operator** (+=) adds the operand on the right to the operand on the left and assigns the result to the operand on the left in one step.

The **prefix increment operator** (++ before a variable) increases the variable's value by 1 and then evaluates it.

The **postfix increment operator** (++ after a variable) evaluates a variable and then adds 1 to it.

Unary operators are operators used with one operand.

The **decrement operator** (--) reduces a variable's value by 1. There is a prefix and a postfix version.

A **Boolean variable** can hold only one of two values—true or false.

The **bool** data type holds a Boolean value.

A **comparison operator** compares two items; an expression containing a comparison operator has a Boolean value.

A **unifying type** is the type chosen for an arithmetic result when operands are of dissimilar types.

Implicitly means automatically.

Type precedence is a hierarchy of data types used to determine the unifying type in arithmetic expressions containing dissimilar data types.

An **implicit conversion** or **implicit cast** is the automatic transformation that occurs when a value is assigned to a type with higher precedence.

Explicitly means purposefully.

An **explicit cast** purposefully assigns a value to a different data type; it involves placing the desired result type in parentheses followed by the variable or constant to be cast.

The **char** data type can hold any single character; a literal character is contained between single quotation marks.

An **escape sequence** is two symbols beginning with a backslash that represent a nonprinting character such as a tab.

Hexadecimal, or **base 16**, is a mathematical system that uses 16 symbols to represent numbers.

The **string** data type is used to hold a series of characters; a literal string is contained between double quotation marks.

Lexically means alphabetically.

Immutable describes unchangeable objects such as **string**s that refer to a new memory location when a new value is assigned.

A **named constant** is an identifier whose value must be assigned upon declaration and whose contents cannot change.

A **self-documenting** program element is one that is self-explanatory.

An **enumeration** is a set of constants represented by identifiers.

Type-safe describes a data type for which only appropriate behaviors are allowed.

An **interactive program** is one that allows user input.

A **prompt** is an instruction to the user to enter data.

To **parse** an item is to break it into component parts.

Review Questions

1. When you use a number such as 45 in a C# program, the number is a
    _____.

    a. literal constant

    b. figurative constant

    c. literal variable

    d. figurative variable

2. A variable declaration must contain all of the following *except* a(n)
    _____.

    a. data type

    b. identifier

    c. assigned value

    d. ending semicolon

3. Which of the following is true of variable declarations?

    a. Two variables of the same type can be declared in the same statement.

    b. Two variables of different types can be declared in the same statement.

    c. Two variables of the same type must be declared in the same statement.

    d. Two variables of the same type cannot coexist in a program.

4. Assume that you have two variables declared as `int var1 = 3;` and `int var2 = 8;`. Which of the following would display 838?

    a. `WriteLine("{0}{1}{2}", var1, var2);`

    b. `WriteLine("{0}{1}{0}", var1, var2);`

    c. `WriteLine("{0}{1}{2}", var2, var1);`

    d. `WriteLine("{0}{1}{0}", var2, var1);`

5. Assume that you have a variable declared as `int var1 = 3;`. Which of the following would display X 3X?

    a. `WriteLine("X{0}X", var1);`

    b. `WriteLine("X{0,2}X", var1);`

    c. `WriteLine("X{2,0}X", var1);`

    d. `WriteLine("X{0}{2}", var1);`

6. Assume that you have a variable declared as `int var1 = 3;`. What is the value of 22 % var1?

    a. 0

    b. 1

    c. 7

    d. 21

7. Assume that you have a variable declared as `int var1 = 3;`. What is the value of `22 / var1`?

    a. 1   c. 7.333

    b. 7   d. 21

8. What is the value of the expression `4 + 2 * 3`?

    a. 0   c. 18

    b. 10   d. 36

9. Assume that you have a variable declared as `int var1 = 3;`. If var2 = ++var1, what is the value of `var2`?

    a. 2   c. 4

    b. 3   d. 5

10. Assume that you have a variable declared as `int var1 = 3;`. If var2 = var1++, what is the value of `var2`?

    a. 2   c. 4

    b. 3   d. 5

11. A variable that can hold the two values `true` and `false` is of type

    _____.

    a. `int`   c. `char`

    b. `bool`   d. `double`

12. Which of the following is *not* a C# comparison operator?

    a. `=>`   c. `==`

    b. `!=`   d. `<`

13. What is the value of the expression `6 >= 7`?

    a. 0   c. true

    b. 1   d. false

14. Which of the following C# types *cannot* contain floating-point numbers?

    a. `float`   c. `decimal`

    b. `double`   d. `int`

15. Assume that you have declared a variable as `double hourly = 13.00;`. What will the statement `WriteLine(hourly);` display?

    a. 13   c. 13.00

    b. 13.0   d. 13.000000

16. Assume that you have declared a variable as `double salary = 45000.00;`. Which of the following will display *$45,000*?

    a. `WriteLine(salary.ToString("c"));`

    b. `WriteLine(salary.ToString("c0"));`

    c. `WriteLine(salary);`

    d. two of these

17. When you perform arithmetic operations with operands of different types, such as adding an `int` and a `float`, _____.

    a. C# chooses a unifying type for the result

    b. you must choose a unifying type for the result

    c. you must provide a cast

    d. you receive an error message

18. Unicode is_____.

    a. an object-oriented language

    b. a subset of the C# language

    c. a 16-bit coding scheme

    d. another term for hexadecimal

19. Which of the following declares a variable that can hold the word *computer*?

    a. `string device = 'computer';`

    b. `string device = "computer";`

    c. `char device = 'computer';`

    d. `char device = "computer";`

20. Which of the following compares two string variables named `string1` and `string2` to determine if their contents are equal?

    a. `string1 = string2`

    b. `string1 == string2`

    c. `Equals.String(string1, string2)`

    d. `two of the above`

Exercises

Programming Exercises

1. What is the numeric value of each of the following expressions, as evaluated by the C# programming language?

   a. 2 + 5 * 3

   b. 9 / 4 + 10

   c. 10 / 3

   d. 21 % 10

   e. (5 − 1) * 3

   f. 37 / 5

   g. 64 % 8

   h. 5 + 2 * 4 − 3 * 4

   i. 3 * (2 + 5) / 5

   j. 28 % 5 − 2

   k. 19 / 2 / 2

   l. 28 / (2 + 4)

2. What is the value of each of the following Boolean expressions?

   a. 5 > 4

   b. 3 <= 3

   c. 2 + 4 > 5

   d. 6 == 7

   e. 2 + 4 <= 6

   f. 3 + 4 == 4 + 3

   g. 1 != 2

   h. 2 != 2

   i. −5 == 7 - 2

   j. 3 + 9 <= 0

3. Choose the best data type for each of the following, so that no memory storage is wasted. Give an example of a typical value that would be held by the variable, and explain why you chose the type you did.

   a. the number of siblings you have

   b. your final grade in this class

   c. the population of Earth

   d. the number of passengers on a bus

   e. one player's score in a Scrabble game

   f. the year a historical event occurred

   g. the number of legs on an animal

   h. one team's score in a Major League Baseball game

4. In this chapter, you learned that although a **double** and a **decimal** both hold floating-point numbers, a **double** can hold a larger value. Write a C# program named **DoubleDecimalTest** that declares and displays two variables—a **double** and a **decimal**. Experiment by assigning the same constant value to each variable

so that the assignment to the **double** is legal but the assignment to the **decimal** is not. In other words, when you leave the **decimal** assignment statement in the program, an error message should be generated that indicates the value is outside the range of the type **decimal**, but when you comment out the **decimal** assignment and its output statement, the program should compile correctly.

5. Write a C# program named **MilesToKilometers** that declares a named constant that holds the number of kilometers in a mile: 1.6. Also declare a variable to represent a distance in miles, and assign a value. Display the distance in both miles and kilometers—for example, *3 miles is 4.8 kilometers*.

6. Convert the **MilesToKilometers** class to an interactive application named **MilesTo-KilometersInteractive**. Instead of assigning a value to the **miles** variable, accept the value from the user as input.

7. Write a C# program named **ProjectedRaises** that includes a named constant representing next year's anticipated 4 percent raise for each employee in a company. Also declare variables to represent the current salaries for three employees. Assign values to the variables, and display, with explanatory text, next year's salary for each employee.

8. Convert the **ProjectedRaises** class to an interactive application named **ProjectedRaisesInteractive**. Instead of assigning values to the salaries, accept them from the user as input.

9. Cramer Car Rental charges $20 per day plus 25 cents per mile. Write a program named **CarRental** that prompts a user for and accepts a number of days and miles driven and displays the total rental fee.

10. Write a program named **HoursAndMinutes** that declares a **minutes** variable to represent minutes worked on a job, and assign a value to it. Display the value in hours and minutes. For example, 197 minutes becomes 3 hours and 17 minutes.

11. Write a program named **Eggs** that declares four variables to hold the number of eggs produced in a month by each of four chickens, and assign a value to each variable. Sum the eggs, then display the total in dozens and eggs. For example, a total of 127 eggs is 10 dozen and 7 eggs.

12. Modify the **Eggs** program to create a new one named **EggsInteractive** that prompts the user for and accepts a number of eggs for each chicken.

13. Write a program named **Dollars** that calculates and displays the conversion of an entered number of dollars into currency denominations—*20s, 10s, 5s,* and *1s*.

14. Write a program named **Tests** that declares five variables to hold scores for five tests you have taken, and assign a value to each variable. Display the average of the test scores to two decimal places.

15. Modify the **Tests** program to create a new one named **TestsInteractive** that accepts five test scores from a user.

16. Write a program named **FahrenheitToCelsius** that accepts a temperature in Fahrenheit from a user and converts it to Celsius by subtracting 32 from the Fahrenheit value and multiplying the result by 5/9. Display both values.

17. Write a program named **Payroll** that prompts the user for a name, Social Security number, hourly pay rate, and number of hours worked. In an attractive format (similar to Figure 2-23), display all the input data as well as the following:

   - gross pay, defined as hourly pay rate times hours worked

   - federal withholding tax, defined as 15 percent of the gross pay

   - state withholding tax, defined as 5 percent of the gross pay

   - net pay, defined as gross pay minus taxes

```
C:\C#\Chapter.02>Payroll
Enter your name: Ruth Roberts
Social Security number: 987-65-4320
Hourly pay rate: 13.50
Hours worked: 36

Payroll Summary for: Ruth Roberts
SSN: 987-65-4320
You worked 36 hours at $13.50 per hour

Gross pay:              $486.00
Federal withholding:     $72.90
State withholding :      $24.30
_____
Net pay:                $388.80

C:\C#\Chapter.02>
```

Figure 2-23   Typical execution of the Payroll program

18. Create an enumeration named Month that holds values for the months of the year, starting with JANUARY equal to 1. Write a program named **MonthNames** that prompts the user for a month integer. Convert the user's entry to a Month value, and display it.

19. Create an enumeration named Planet that holds the names for the eight planets in our solar system, starting with MERCURY and ending with NEPTUNE. Write a program named **Planets** that prompts the user for a numeric position, and display the name of the planet that is in the requested position.

20. Pig Latin is a nonsense language. To create a word in pig Latin, you remove the first letter and then add the first letter and "ay" at the end of the word. For example, "dog" becomes "ogday" and "cat" becomes "atcay." Write a program named **PigLatin** that allows the user to enter a word and displays the pig Latin version.

Debugging Exercises

1. Each of the following files in the Chapter.02 folder of your downloadable student files
   has syntax and/or logical errors. In each case, determine the problem and fix the
   program. After you correct the errors, save each file using the same filename preceded
   with *Fixed*. For example, DebugTwo1.cs will become FixedDebugTwo1.cs.

   a. DebugTwo1.cs
   b. DebugTwo2.cs
   c. DebugTwo3.cs
   d. DebugTwo4.cs

Case Problems

1. In Chapter 1, you created two programs to display the motto for the Greenville Idol
   competition that is held each summer during the Greenville County Fair. Now write a
   program named **GreenvilleRevenue** that prompts a user for the number of contestants
   entered in last year's competition and in this year's competition. Display all the input
   data. Compute and display the revenue expected for this year's competition if each
   contestant pays a $25 entrance fee. Also display a statement that indicates whether this
   year's competition has more contestants than last year's.

2. In Chapter 1, you created two programs to display the motto for Marshall's Murals.
   Now write a program named **MarshallsRevenue** that prompts a user for the number of
   interior and exterior murals scheduled to be painted during the next month. Compute
   the expected revenue for each type of mural. Interior murals cost $500 each, and
   exterior murals cost $750 each. Also display the total expected revenue and a statement
   that indicates whether more interior murals are scheduled than exterior ones.

CHAPTER 3

Using GUI Objects and the Visual Studio IDE

In this chapter you will:

◎ Create a Form in the Visual Studio IDE

◎ Use the Toolbox to add a Button to a Form

◎ Add Labels and TextBoxes to a Form

◎ Name Forms and controls

◎ Correct errors

◎ Decide which interface to use

You have learned to write simple C# programs that accept input from a user at the console and produce output at the command line. The environment the user sees is a program's **interface**; unfortunately, the interfaces in the applications you have written so far look dull. Most modern applications use visually pleasing graphic objects to interact with users. These graphical user interface (GUI) objects include the labels, buttons, and text boxes you manipulate or control with a mouse, touch screen, or keyboard when interacting with Windows-type programs.

In Chapter 1, you learned that when you write a console application, you can use a simple text editor such as Notepad or you can use the Visual Studio integrated development environment (IDE). Technically, you have the same options when you write a GUI program. However, so much code is needed to create even the simplest of GUI programs that it is far more practical to develop the user interface visually in the IDE. This approach allows the IDE to automatically generate much of the code you need to develop appealing GUI programs that are easy to use.

In Visual Studio versions before .NET, C#, C++, and Visual Basic each had its own IDE, so you had to learn about a new environment with each programming language you studied. Now, you can use one IDE to create projects in all the supported languages.

Creating a Form in the IDE

Forms are rectangular GUI objects that provide an interface for collecting, displaying, and delivering information. Although they are not required, forms almost always include **controls**, which are devices such as labels, text boxes, and buttons that users can manipulate to interact with a program. The C# class that creates a form is Form.

To create a Form visually using the IDE, you start Visual Studio, select **New Project**, and then choose **Windows Forms Application**, as shown in Figure 3-1. By default, Visual Studio names your first Forms application *WindowsFormsApplication1*. You can change the name if you want, and you can browse to choose a location to save the application. You should almost always provide a more meaningful name for applications than the default name suggested. Most of the examples in this chapter retain the default names to minimize the number of changes required if you want to replicate the steps on your computer.

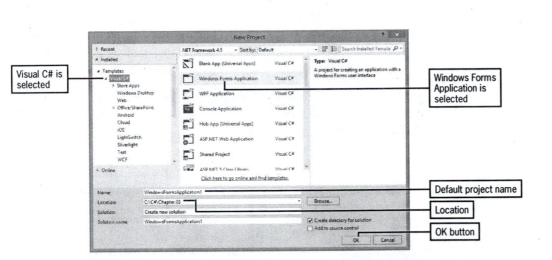

Figure 3-1   Choosing Windows Forms Application in the New Project window

After you click **OK** in the New Project window, you see the IDE main window, as shown in Figure 3-2. The main window contains several smaller windows, each of which can be resized, relocated, or closed. If a window is not currently visible, you can select it from the View menu in the menu bar. Some key features in the IDE follow:

- The *name of the project* shown in three places: on the title bar, and in two locations in the Solution Explorer. In Figure 3-2, the application has the default name WindowsFormsApplication1.

- The *menu bar,* which lies horizontally across the top of the window and includes a File menu from which you open, close, and save projects. It also contains submenus for editing, debugging, and help tasks, among others.

 As you work through any project, you should choose **Save All** frequently. You can select this action from the File menu or click the **Save All** button, which has an icon that looks like two overlapping disks.

- The *Toolbox tab,* which, when opened, provides lists of controls you can drag onto a Form so that you can develop programs visually, using a mouse.

- The *Form Designer,* which appears in the center of the screen. This is where you design applications visually.

- The *Solution Explorer,* for viewing and managing project files and settings.

- The *Properties window,* for configuring properties and events on controls in your user interface. For example, you can use this window to set the Size property of a Button or the Text property of a Form.

- The *Error list,* which displays any warnings and errors that occur when you build or execute a program.

If some of these features are not visible after you start a project in the IDE, you can select them from the View menu.

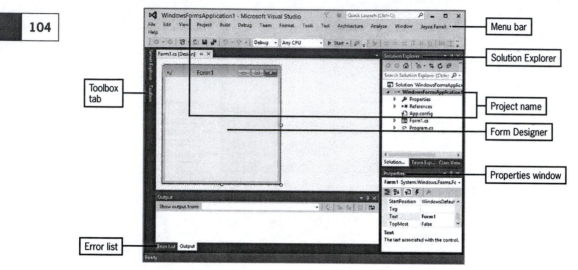

Figure 3-2   The IDE main window

The Solution Explorer file list shows the files that are part of the current project:

- The *Program.cs* file contains the automatically generated Main() method of the application.

- The *Form1.cs* file contains other automatically generated code and is where you write code describing the tasks you will assign to controls in your application.

- To the left of the Form1.cs file, you see a small triangle node. A **node** is an icon that can be used to expand or condense a list or a section of code. In Visual Studio, some nodes appear as triangles, and others appear as small plus or minus signs. When a triangle-shaped node points straight to the right, you see a condensed view. Clicking the triangle reveals hidden items or code—the triangle will point diagonally down and to the right, and you see all the items in the list (or all the hidden code). Clicking the triangle again collapses the list so you can work with a condensed view.

If you expand the Form1.cs node by clicking it, you see the following:

- A file named *Form1.Designer.cs*. The Windows Form Designer automatically writes code in the Designer.cs file; the code created there implements all the actions that are performed when you drag and drop controls from the Toolbox. You should avoid making manual changes to this file because you could easily corrupt a program.

- A file named *Form1* that can hold resources such as images and audio clips; you will add such resources to your programs as you learn more about C#.

When you create a Windows Forms project, Visual C# adds a form to the project and calls it Form1. After you click the Form in the Form Designer area, you can see the name of the form in the following locations as shown in Figure 3-3:

- On the folder tab at the top of the Form Designer area (followed by *[Design]*)

- In the title bar of the form in the Form Designer area

- In the Solution Explorer file list (with a .cs extension)

- At the top of the Properties window indicating that the properties listed are for Form1

- As the contents of the Text property listed within the Properties window

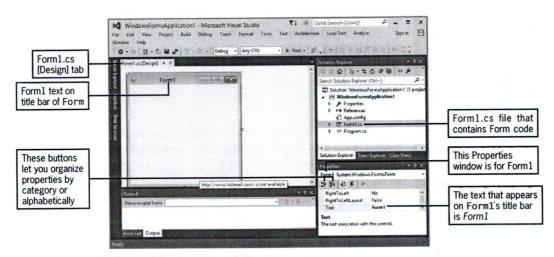

Figure 3-3   Displaying the properties of Form1

You can scroll through a list of properties in the Properties window. For example, Size, Text, and Font are listed. If you click a property, a brief description of it appears at the bottom of the Properties window. For example, Figure 3-3 displays a description of the Text property of Form1.

You can change the appearance, size, color, and window-management features of a Form by setting its properties. The Form class contains approximately 100 properties; Table 3-1 lists a few of the Form features you can change. For example, setting the Text property allows you to specify the caption of the Form in the title bar, and setting the Size, BackColor, and ForeColor allows you to further customize the Form. The two left buttons at the top of the Properties list allow you to organize properties by category or alphabetically. Not every property that can be used with a Form appears in the Properties window in the Visual Studio IDE—only the most frequently used properties are listed.

Property Name	Description
AcceptButton	Gets or sets the button on the form that is clicked when the user presses the Enter key
BackColor	Gets or sets the background color of the Form
CancelButton	Gets or sets the button control that is clicked when the user presses the Esc key
ForeColor	Gets or sets the foreground color of the Form
Name	Gets or sets the name of the Form
Size	Gets or sets the size of the Form
Text	Gets or sets the text associated with the control
Visible	Gets or sets a value indicating whether the control is visible

Table 3-1   Selected properties of Forms

Some of the properties listed in the Properties window have a small plus sign that appears to the left of the property name. This is a node that you can click to expand or condense a property. For example, if you click the Size node, you will see an expanded list that displays the two parts of Size (Width and Height) separately. The node changes to a minus sign, which you can then click to condense the expanded list.

When you sort Properties in alphabetical order in the Properties window, the Name entry is not in alphabetical order—it appears near the top of the list. Name appears in parentheses because the opening parenthesis has a lower value than an *A*, so when the Properties list is sorted in alphabetical order, Name is near the top and easy to find. (An opening parenthesis has a lower Unicode value than any alphabetic letter; Appendix B contains information on Unicode.) For most professional applications, you will want to provide a Form with a reasonable identifier that is more descriptive than Form1.

Do not confuse a Form's Name with its Text property. If you change a Form's Name, you don't notice any difference in the visual design, but all references to the form are changed in the code. Therefore, a Form's Name property is an identifier, and it must follow the rules for variable names. This means, for example, that a Form's Name cannot contain spaces and cannot start with a digit. However, a Form's Text is what appears in its title bar, and it can be any string. For example, in an accounting application, you might name a form BudgetForm but assign *2016 Budget Calculator* as its Text.

In Chapter 2, you learned to enclose a string's contents in quotation marks. Although a Form's Text is a string, you do not type containing quotes when you enter a value for the Text property in the Properties list. However, when you view C# code, you will see quotation marks around the Text value.

 Watch the video *The Visual Studio IDE*.

TWO TRUTHS & A LIE

Creating a Form in the IDE

1. The Visual Studio IDE allows you to use a visual environment for designing Forms.

2. Some key features in Visual C# include the Toolbox, Form Designer, and Solution Explorer.

3. When you create a first Windows Forms project in any folder, Visual C# names the project MyFirstForm by default.

The false statement is #3. When you create a first Windows Forms project in any folder, Visual C# names the project WindowsFormsApplication1 by default.

Using the Toolbox to Add a Button to a Form

When you open the IDE, the left border displays a Toolbox tab. (If you don't see the tab, you can select **View** and then **Toolbox** from the IDE's menu bar.) When you open the Toolbox, a list of tool groups is displayed. The list automatically closes when you move your mouse off the list and click elsewhere, or you can pin the Toolbox to the screen to keep it open by clicking the pushpin icon at the top of the list. When you pin the Toolbox, the Form moves to the right to remain as visible as possible, depending on how you have sized the windows in the IDE. Selecting **All Windows Forms** at the top of the Toolbox displays a complete list of available tools; selecting **Common Controls** displays a smaller list that is a subset of the original one. As shown in Figure 3-4, the Common Controls list contains many controls: the GUI objects a user can click or manipulate. The list includes controls you probably have seen when using Windows applications—for example, Button and CheckBox. You can drag these controls onto the Form. This chapter features only three controls from the Toolbox—Label, Button, and TextBox. You will learn about many of the other controls in the chapter called "Using Controls."

All windows in Visual C# can be made dockable or floating, hidden or visible, or can be moved to new locations. To change the behavior of a window, click the down arrow or pushpin icon on the title bar, and select from the available options. You can customize many aspects of the IDE by clicking the **Tools** menu, then clicking **Options**. To reset the windows to their original states, click **Window** on the main Visual Studio menu bar, and then click **Reset Window Layout**.

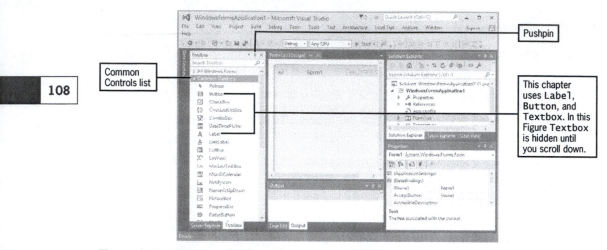

Figure 3-4   The open Toolbox in the IDE

You can drag controls onto a Form where you think they will be most useful or contribute to a pleasing design. After a control is on a Form, you can relocate it by dragging it, or delete the control by selecting it and pressing the **Del** key on your keyboard. You also can delete a control by right-clicking it and selecting the **Delete** option from the menu that appears.

In Figure 3-5, the programmer has dragged a button onto the Form. By default, its Name is button1. (You might guess that if you drag a second Button onto a Form, its Name automatically becomes button2.) In a professional application, you would probably want to change the Name property of the Button to a unique and memorable identifier.

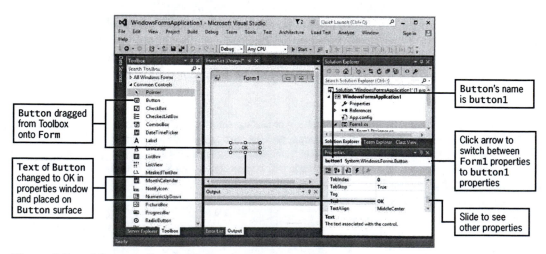

Figure 3-5   A Button dragged onto a Form

In Figure 3-5, the programmer has clicked `button1`, so the Properties window shows the properties for `button1`. (If you click the `Form`, the Properties window changes to show `Form` properties instead of `Button` properties.) The `Text` property of `button1` has been changed to *OK*, and the button on the `Form` has handles that can be used to resize it. You can scroll through the Properties list and examine other properties that can be modified for the `Button`. For example, you can change its `BackColor`, `ForeColor`, `Font`, and `Size`. Table 3-2 describes a few of the properties available for `Button` objects. This chapter discusses only a few properties of each control. You can learn about other properties in the chapter "Using Controls."

Property Name	Description
BackColor	Gets or sets the background color for the control
Enabled	Gets or sets whether the control is enabled
Font	Gets or sets the current font for the control
ForeColor	Gets or sets the foreground color of the control
Name	Gets or sets the name of the control
Size	Gets or sets the size of the control
Text	Gets or sets the text associated with the control
Visible	Gets or sets a value indicating whether the control is visible

Table 3-2 Selected properties of `Buttons`

You can click a control on a `Form` to display its Properties list in the Properties window. Alternatively, you can click the arrow next to the current control name shown at the top of the Properties list and select the desired control to view from a drop-down list. See Figure 3-5.

Adding Functionality to a Button on a Form

Adding functionality to a `Button` is easy when you use the IDE. After you have dragged a `Button` onto a `Form`, you can double-click it to create a method that executes when the user clicks the `Button`. For example, if you have dragged a `Button` onto a `Form` and have not changed its default name from `button1`, code is automatically generated when you double-click the button, as shown in Figure 3-6. (The viewing windows in the figure have been resized by dragging their borders so that you can see more of the code.) You can view the Form Designer again by selecting **View** and then **Designer** from the menu bar. Then, you can revert to the code window by selecting **View** and **Code**. As you create GUI applications, you frequently will switch back and forth between the visual environment and the code. Alternatively, you can use the tabs or press one of the shortcut keys displayed on the drop-down menu to switch the view.

Tabs to switch
between design
and code views

Automatically
generated shell for
button1_Click()
method

Figure 3-6   The automatically generated code after double-clicking `button1`

When you double-click a button to generate a click method, you generate code for the button's default event. Clicking is a button's default event because users typically expect to click a button. As you learn more about C#, you will find that you can write other events for a button. For example, perhaps you want to take a specific action if a user double-clicks or right-clicks a button.

If you scroll through the exposed code, you see many generated statements, some of which are confusing. However, to make a `Button` perform an action, you can ignore most of the statements. You only need to write code between the curly braces of the method with the following header:

```
private void button1_Click(object sender, EventArgs e)
```

Instead of automatically generating the method header that executes when a user clicks a `Button`, you could write it yourself. However, you would have to know more about both methods and event handlers because other code is also automatically written elsewhere in the project that links the `Form`'s button to the method. You will learn about these topics in later chapters.

You have seen the following method header used in console applications:

```
static void Main()
```

The GUI application also contains a `Main()` method that is created automatically; you can see it by opening the Program.cs file that is part of the application.

The button1_Click() method and the Main() method headers both use the void return type, but the methods differ in the following ways:

- The button1_Click() method has a private access specifier. An **access specifier** is a keyword that dictates which types of outside classes can use a method. By default, Visual Studio makes the button1_Click() method private, which limits the ability of other classes to use the method, but you could remove the word private and notice no difference in how the button works. You will learn more about access specifiers later in this book.

- The Main() method is static, whereas the button1_Click() method is not. A static method executes without an object. The button1_Click() method cannot be static because it needs an object, which is the Form in which it is running. The chapter called "Using Classes and Objects" provides more detail about the keyword static.

- The Main() method header shown above contains no parameters between its parentheses, but the button1_Click() method has two parameters, separated with a comma. These represent values about the event (the user clicking the button) that causes execution of the method. When a user interacts with a GUI object, an **event** is generated that causes the program to perform a task. When a user clicks a Button, the action fires a **click event**, which causes the Button's Click() method to execute. This chapter discusses only click events. You can learn about other events in the "Event Handling" chapter.

If you change the Name property of the button1 object in the IDE, the name of its subsequently created Click() method will also change automatically. For example, if you rename button1 to okButton in the Properties list and then double-click it, the name of the generated method is okButton_Click().

If you change a Button's Name from button1 and then place a second button on the Form, the new Button is named button1. If you leave the first Button's default name as button1, then the second Button you place on the Form is named button2, and its default Click() method is named button2_Click(). C# automatically creates a method name for each Button based on its associated object's name. Later in this chapter you will learn what to do if you create the event method first and change the control's name later.

You are not required to create a Click() method for a Button. If, for some reason, you did not want to take any action when a user clicked a Button, you simply would not include the method in your program. Alternatively, you could create an empty method that contains no statements between its curly braces and thus does nothing. However, these choices would be unusual and a poor programming practice—you usually place a Button on a Form because you expect it to be clicked at some point. You will frustrate users if you do not allow your controls to act in expected ways.

You can write any statements you want between the curly braces of the `button1_Click()` method. For example, you can declare variables, perform arithmetic statements, and produce output. You also can include block or line comments. The next sections of this chapter include several statements added to a `Click()` method.

 Watch the video *Creating a Functional Button.*

TWO TRUTHS & A LIE

Using the Toolbox to Add a Button to a Form

1. When a user clicks a `Button`, the action fires a click event that causes the `Button`'s `Click()` method to execute.

2. If a `Button`'s identifier is `reportButton`, then the name of its `Click()` method is `reportButton.Click()`.

3. You can write any statements you want between the curly braces of a `Button`'s `Click()` method.

The false statement is #2. If a Button's identifier is reportButton, then the name of its Click() method is reportButton_Click().

Adding `Label`s and `TextBox`es to a Form

Suppose that you want to create an interactive GUI program that accepts two numbers from a user and outputs their sum when the user clicks a `Button`. To provide prompts for the user and to display output, you can add `Label`s to a `Form`, and to get input from a user, you can provide `TextBox`es.

A **label** is a control that you use to display text to communicate with an application's user; the C# class that creates a label is `Label`. Just like a `Button`, you can drag a `Label` onto a `Form`, as shown in Figure 3-7. By default, the first `Label` you drag onto a `Form` is named `label1`, and the text that appears on the `Label` also is `label1`. You can change its `Text` property to display any string of text; depending on the amount of text you enter, you might need to change the size of the `Label` by dragging its resizing handles or altering its `Size` property. In Figure 3-7, *Enter a number* has been assigned to `label1`'s `Text` property. If you want to create multiple lines of text on a `Label`, click the small, downward-pointing arrow to the right of the `Text` property value to open an editor, and type the needed text in separate lines. You might want a program to start with no text appearing on a label. If so, just delete the entry from the Text property in the Properties list. If you execute a program that starts with a blank label and don't make any changes to its color, the label will be invisible to the user. Note that a label's Text property can be blank, but a Label's Name property cannot.

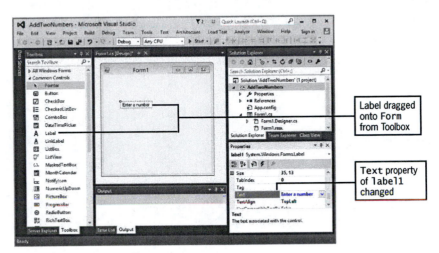

Figure 3-7   A Label on a Form

A **text box** is a GUI control through which a user can enter input data; the C# class is TextBox. Figure 3-8 shows a TextBox on a Form. If the intention is for a user to enter data in a TextBox, you might want to start with its Text property empty, but you are allowed to add text to its Text property if desired.

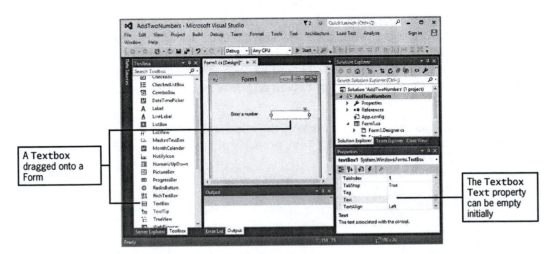

Figure 3-8   A Label and TextBox on a form

Figure 3-9 shows a Form with three Labels, two TextBoxes, and a Button. The third Label has not yet been provided with new text, so it still contains *label3*. You can delete the Text value in the Properties window if you want the Label to be empty at first.

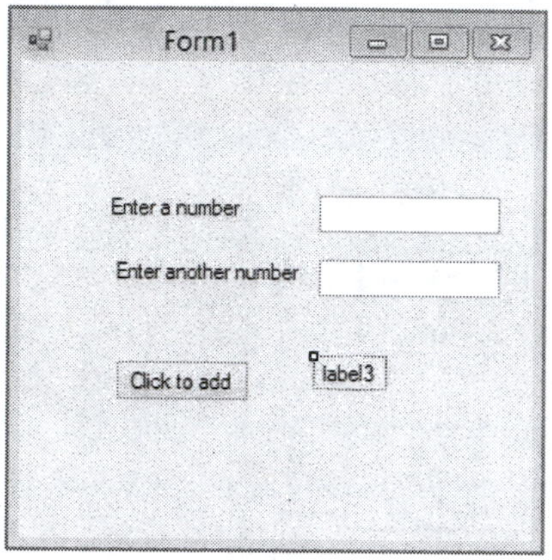

Figure 3-9   A Form with several controls

When a user runs the program that displays the Form in Figure 3-9, the intention is for the user to enter a number in each TextBox. When the user clicks the Button, the sum of the two numbers will be displayed in label3. To sum the numbers, you must write code for the Button. In the Form Designer, you can double-click the Button to expose the prewritten shell of the button1_Click() method.

Figure 3-10 shows the code you can write within the button1_Click() method. The method contains declarations for three integers. When a user types a value into a TextBox in an executing program, it becomes the value for the Text property of the TextBox. Because a user might type any value, the value in a TextBox is a string by default. When you write an application in which the user is supposed to enter a number, you must convert the entered string into a number. You are familiar with this process because it's exactly the same action required when a user enters data in response to a ReadLine() statement in a console application.

The last two statements in the method perform the necessary addition operation and assign a string with the concatenated sum to the Text property of the Label that displays the output.

```
private void button1_Click(object sender, EventArgs e)
{
    int num1;
    int num2;
    int sum;
    num1 = Convert.ToInt32(textBox1.Text);
    num2 = Convert.ToInt32(textBox2.Text);
    sum = num1 + num2;
    label3.Text = "Sum is " + sum;
}
```

Figure 3-10   The button1_Click() method that calculates the sum of the entries in two TextBoxes

You can execute a program from the IDE by selecting **Debug** from the menu bar and then **Start Without Debugging**. (As an alternative, you can hold down the **Ctrl** key and press **F5**.) Figure 3-11 shows how the Form appears when the program executes and the result after the user has entered numbers and clicked the Button. The period during which you design a program is called **design time**. When you execute a program, the stage is called **runtime**.

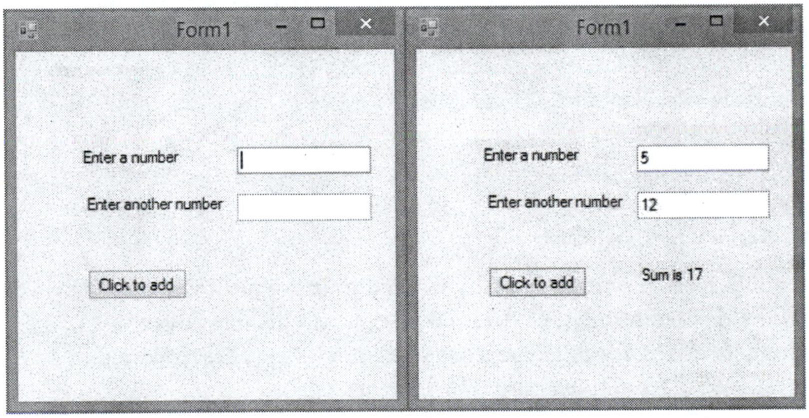

Figure 3-11   The Form when it first appears and after a user has entered two integers and clicked the Button

You can change the values in either or both of the TextBoxes in the Form and click the Button to see a new result. When you finish using the application, you can close it by clicking the **Close** button in the upper-right corner of the Form.

Understanding Focus and Tab Control

When a GUI program displays a Form, one of the components on the Form has focus. The control with **focus** is the one that can receive keyboard input. When a Button has focus, a thin, bright line appears around it to draw your attention, and the Button's associated event executes when you click the button or press the **Enter** key on the keyboard. When a TextBox has focus, a blinking cursor appears inside it.

When an application is running, the user can give focus to a component by clicking it or can switch focus from one component to another using the Tab key. The order in which controls receive focus from successive Tab key presses is their **tab order**. By default, controls are assigned a tab order based on the order in which you place them on a Form when designing a program. The first control you place on a Form has TabIndex 0, the next control has TabIndex 1, and so on. When you start a program, the control with TabIndex 0 automatically has focus. You can check a control's tab order by viewing its TabIndex property in the Properties list of the IDE. If you do not want a control to be part of the tabbing sequence for a Form, you can change its TabStop property from true to false in the Properties list.

You can change a control's TabIndex value by changing the entry next to TabIndex in the Properties list of the IDE. Alternatively, you can select **View** from the menu bar and then select **Tab Order**. You see a representation of the Form with a small blue number next to each control to represent the tab values. To change the focus order for the controls, simply click each control in the desired order. Select **View** and then **Tab Order** again to remove the blue numbers.

 Watch the video *Visual Studio's Automatically Generated Code.*

Formatting Data in GUI Applications

In Chapter 2, you learned about format strings that can be used to make numeric data align appropriately, display the desired number of decimal places, and display dollar signs. For example, the following displays *Total is $4.55* because the double variable myMoney is converted to currency format and placed in position 0 in a string:

```
double myMoney = 4.558;
string mySentence = String.Format("Total is {0}",
    myMoney.ToString("C"));
WriteLine(mySentence);
```

You can use the same String.Format() method to create formatted strings in your GUI applications. For example, suppose you have retrieved a double from a TextBox with a statement similar to the following:

```
double money = Convert.ToDouble(textBox1.Text);
```

You can display the value on a label with explanatory text and as currency with two decimal places with a statement similar to the following:

```
label1.Text = String.Format("The money value is {0}",
    money.ToString("C2"));
```

If necessary, you also can use escape characters in strings that are assigned to controls such as labels. For example, a two-line label might be created using the following code:

```
label1.Text = "Hello\nthere";
```

Changing a Label's Font

The Font property for controls was described briefly in Table 3-2 earlier in this chapter. You will learn more about this property in Chapter 12, but you might want to experiment with it now to align numbers.

When you click any control on a Form and examine its Properties list, you discover that the default font for controls is Microsoft Sans Serif. This font is a **proportional font**, which means that different characters have different pitches or widths. For example, a *w* is wider than an *i*. The opposite of a proportional font is a **fixed-pitch font**, or a **monospaced font**, in which each character has the same width. You might want to use a fixed-pitch font to help align text values on controls. For example, when you stack $11.11 and $88.88 on a Label, you typically want the characters to be an equal width so that the values align.

To change the font for a Label, select the small box with an ellipsis (three dots) to the right of the existing Font name in the Properties list, and select a new Font from the dialog box that opens. For example, Courier New and Consolas are popular fixed-pitch fonts. (You can also change the font style and size if desired.)

TWO TRUTHS & A LIE

Adding Labels and TextBoxes to a Form

1. A Label and a TextBox both have a Text property.

2. When a user types a value on a Label in an executing program, it becomes the value for the Text property of the Label.

3. You can display the value on a Label using a format string.

The false statement is #2. A user does not type on a Label. When a user types a value into a TextBox in an executing program, it becomes the value for the Text property of the TextBox.

Naming Forms and Controls

Usually, you want to provide reasonable Name property values for all the controls you place on a Form. Although any identifier that starts with a letter is legal, note the following conventions:

- Start control names with a lowercase letter, and use camel casing as appropriate.
- Start Form names with an uppercase letter, and use camel casing as appropriate.
- Use the type of object in the name. For example, use names such as okButton, firstValueTextBox, or ArithmeticForm.

 Professional programmers usually do not retain the default names for Forms and controls. An exception is sometimes made for Labels that never change. For example, if three labels provide directions or explanations to the user and are never altered during a program's execution, many programmers would approve of retaining their names as label1, label2, and label3.

Most often, you will want to name controls as soon as you add them to a Form. If you rename a control after you have created an event for it, the program still works, but the name of the control no longer corresponds to its associated method, making the code harder to understand. If you simply change the method name to match the control name, the event code will generate errors. For example, assume that you have created a button named button1 and that you have double-clicked it, creating a method named button1_Click().

Then suppose that you decide to change the Name property of the Button to sumButton. Afterward, when you look at the program code, the Click() method is still named button1_Click(). To fix this, you must refactor the code. **Code refactoring** is the process of changing a program's internal structure without changing the way the program works. To refactor the code after changing the button's name, do the following:

- After you change the name of the control using the Designer, switch to view the code.
- Right-click the name of the method button1_Click().
- From the menu that appears, click **Rename**, as shown in Figure 3-12.

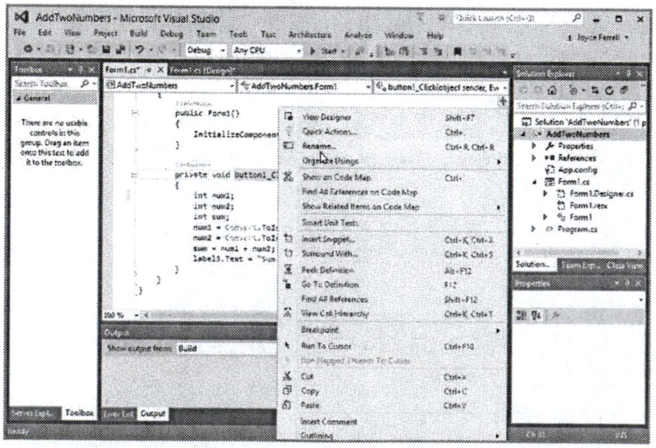

Figure 3-12   Choosing the Rename option for a method

- When you click **Rename**, the `button1_Click` method name is highlighted and a box appears with the heading *Rename button1_Click*, as shown in Figure 3-13.

- Type the new method name (`sumButton_Click`) to replace `button1_Click` in the code.

- When you finish, you can check the Preview changes checkbox if you want to view all the changes before they are applied, although at this point, the changes will not have much meaning for you. Click **Apply** or press **Enter**. A Preview Changes dialog box will highlight the change. You can confirm the change by clicking **Apply**.

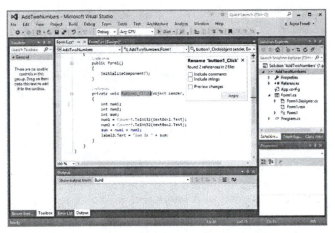

Figure 3-13   Renaming the `button1_Click()` method

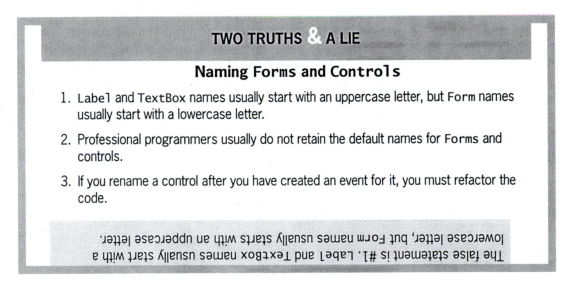

TWO TRUTHS & A LIE

Naming Forms and Controls

1. `Label` and `TextBox` names usually start with an uppercase letter, but `Form` names usually start with a lowercase letter.

2. Professional programmers usually do not retain the default names for `Forms` and controls.

3. If you rename a control after you have created an event for it, you must refactor the code.

The false statement is #1. `Label` and `TextBox` names usually start with a lowercase letter, but `Form` names usually starts with an uppercase letter.

Correcting Errors

Just like in console-based programs, you will often generate syntax errors when you use the visual developer to create GUI applications. If you build or run a program that contains a syntax error, you see *Build failed* in the lower-left corner of the IDE. You also see an error dialog box like the one shown in Figure 3-14. When you are developing a program, you should always click **No** in response to "Would you like to continue and run the last successful build?" Clicking **Yes** will run the previous version of the program you created before inserting the mistake that caused the dialog box to appear. Instead, click **No**, examine the error messages and code, and correct the mistake.

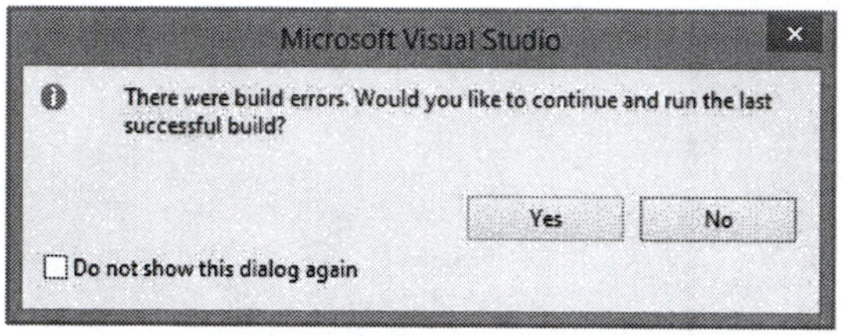

Figure 3-14   Dialog box that appears when an error occurs during compilation

When you select **Build** from the menu bar, two options are Build Solution and Rebuild Solution. The Build Solution option uses only files that have changed since the most recent build, whereas Rebuild Solution works with all the files in a project, regardless of whether they have changed. The Build Solution option is usually sufficient and faster, but if you have made many changes to several parts of a project, you might choose Rebuild Solution to make sure that all files are currently coordinated.

When errors occur, they are shown in the error list at the bottom of the screen. If you do not see error messages, you can click **View** from the IDE's menu bar and then click **Error List**. If the list is partially or completely hidden, you can drag up the divider between the development window and the error list and then click the **Error List** tab. Figure 3-15 shows a single error message, *; expected*, which means *semicolon expected*. The error list also shows the file and line number in which the error occurred. If you double-click the error message, the cursor is placed at the location in the code where the error was found. A wiggly red underline will help you locate the error in the code window. In this case, a semicolon is missing at the end of a statement. You can fix the error and attempt another compilation.

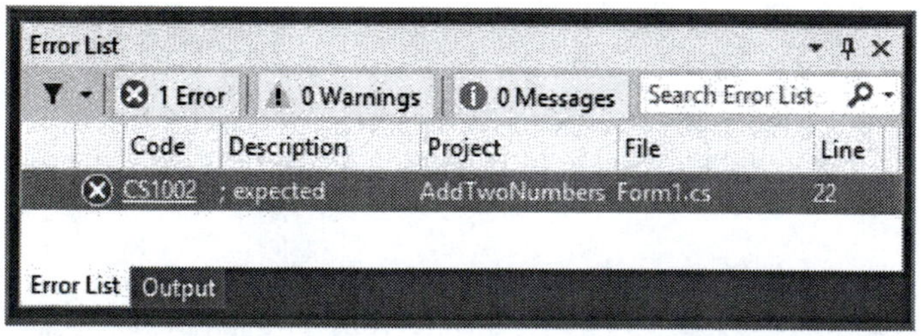

Figure 3-15   The error list

You can add line numbers to your code for reference by selecting **Tools** from Visual Studio's menu bar, then selecting **Options**. Use the triangle-shaped node to expand the Text Editor, and then click the node next to C# from the list that appears. Click **General**, select the **Line numbers** check box, and then click **OK**.

As with console-based programs, GUI applications might compile successfully but contain logical errors. For example, you might type a minus sign instead of a plus sign in the statement that is intended to calculate the sum of two input numbers. You should be prepared to execute a program multiple times and carefully examine the output to discover any logical errors.

Deleting an Unwanted Event-Handling Method

When you are working in the Form Designer in the IDE, it is easy to inadvertently double-click a control and automatically create an event-handling method that you do not want. For example, you might double-click a Label named label1 by mistake and generate a method named label1_Click(). You can leave the automatically created method empty so that no actions result, but in a professional program you typically would not include empty methods. Such empty methods that never execute are known as **orphaned methods**. You should not just delete an orphaned method because, behind the scenes, other code might have been created that refers to the method; if so, the program will not compile. Instead of deleting the method code, you should click the control with the unwanted method so it appears in the Properties window, then click the Events button, which looks like a lightning bolt. Select the event you want to eliminate, and delete the name of the method (see Figure 3-16). This eliminates all the references to the method, and your program can again run successfully.

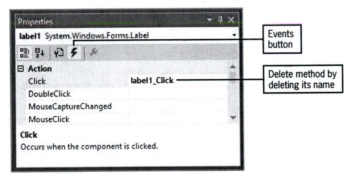

Figure 3-16   Deleting an event from the Properties window

Failing to Close a **Form** Before Attempting to Reexecute a Program

Often you will execute a GUI application and notice something you want to correct in the program. For example, you might want to reword the Text on a Label, or reposition a Button on the Form. In your haste to make the improvement, you might forget to close the application that is still running. If you make a change to the program and then try to rerun it, you get an error message that indicates that changes are not allowed while the program is running. The solution is simply to close the previous execution of the application and then try again.

Using Visual Studio Help

When working with a class that is new to you, such as Button or Form, no book can answer all of your questions. The ultimate authority on C# classes is the Visual Studio Help documentation. You should use this tool often as you continue to learn about C# in particular and the Visual Studio products in general. The Help documentation for Visual Studio is in the MSDN Library, which you can install locally on your own computer. It is also available at http://msdn. microsoft.com. From within Visual Studio, you can click **Help** on the menu bar, and then click **View Help**. You will be taken to the Visual Studio Web site where you can type a topic in the Search box.

TWO TRUTHS & A LIE

Correcting Errors

1. When a program in Visual Studio has a syntax error, you see an error dialog box that asks if you want to continue with the last successful build. You should always respond No.

2. Program errors are harder to locate in the Visual Studio IDE than they are in applications written using a plain text editor.

3. If you inadvertently create a Click() method in Visual Studio, you should not delete its code. You should select the event in the Properties window and delete it there.

The false statement is #2. In the Visual Studio IDE, any displayed syntax errors include the filename, line, position in the line, and project in which the error occurred.

Deciding Which Interface to Use

You have learned to create console applications in which most of the action occurs in a Main() method and the WriteLine() and ReadLine() methods are used for input and output. You also have learned to create GUI applications in which most of the action occurs within an event-handling method such as a Click() method and Labels and TextBoxes are used for input and output. Both types of applications can use declared variables and constants, and, as you will learn in the next few chapters, both types of programs can contain the basic building blocks of applications—decisions, loops, arrays, and calls to other methods. When you want to write a program that displays a greeting or sums some integers, you can do so using either type of interface and employing the same logic to get the same results. So, should you develop programs using a GUI interface or a console interface?

- GUI applications look "snazzier." It is easy to add colors and fonts to them, and they contain controls that a user can manipulate with a mouse or touch screen. Also, users are accustomed to GUI applications from their experiences on the Web. However, GUI programs usually take longer to develop than their console counterparts because you can spend a lot of time setting up the controls, placing them on a **Form**, and adjusting their sizes and relative positions before you write the code that does the actual work of the program. GUI applications created in the IDE also require much more disk space to store.

> Designing aesthetically pleasing, functional, and user-friendly **Forms** is an art; entire books are devoted to the topic.

- Console applications look dull in comparison to GUIs, but they can often be developed more quickly because you do not spend much time setting up objects for a user to manipulate. When you are learning programming concepts like decision making and looping, you might prefer to keep the interface simple so that you can better concentrate on the new logical constructs being presented.

In short, it doesn't matter which interface you use to develop programs while learning the intricacies of the C# programming language. In the following "You Do It" section, you develop an application that is similar to the one you developed at the console in Chapter 1. In the programming exercises at the end of this chapter, you will develop programs that are identical in purpose to programs written using the console in the chapter called "Using Data." Throughout the next several chapters on decisions, looping, and arrays, many concepts will be illustrated in console applications, because the programs are shorter and the development is simpler. However, you also will occasionally see the same concept illustrated in a program that uses a GUI interface, to remind you that the program logic is the same no matter which interface is used. After you complete the chapters "Using Classes and Objects," "Using Controls," and "Handling Events," you will be able to write even more sophisticated GUI applications.

When writing your own programs, you will use the interface you prefer or one that your instructor or boss requires. If time permits, you might even want to develop programs both ways in future chapter exercises.

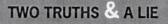

TWO TRUTHS & A LIE

Deciding Which Interface to Use

1. Console applications are used for declaring variables and constants and performing arithmetic, but GUI applications are not.

2. GUI programs usually take longer to develop than their console counterparts because you can spend a lot of time setting up and arranging the controls.

3. Console applications look dull compared to GUI applications, but they can often be developed more quickly because you do not spend much time setting up objects for a user to manipulate.

The false statement is #1. Both console and GUI applications can use declared variables and constants and perform arithmetic.

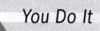 *You Do It*

Working with the Visual Studio IDE

In the next steps, you use the IDE to create a Form with a Button and a Label. Your first console application in Chapter 1's "You Do It" section displayed "Hello, world!" at the command prompt. This application displays "Hello, Visual World!" on a Form.

1. Open Microsoft Visual Studio. You might have a desktop shortcut you can double-click, or in Windows 8.1 you can swipe from the right, click **Search**, type the first few letters of **Visual Studio** in the search box, and then select it from the list of choices. Your steps might differ slightly from the ones listed here if you are using a different version of Visual Studio or a different operating system. If you are using a school network, you might be able to select **Visual Studio** from the school's computing menu.

2. Select **New Project**. Then, in the New Project window, select **Visual C#** and **Windows Forms Application**. (Refer to Figure 3-1.) Instead of using the default project name, use **HelloVisualWorld**, and select a location to store the project. Then click **OK**.

(continues)

(continued)

3. The HelloVisualWorld development environment opens, as shown in Figure 3-17. The text in the title bar of the blank Form contains the default text Form1. If you click the Form, its Properties window appears in the lower-right portion of the screen, and you can see that the Text property for the Form is set to Form1. Take a moment to scroll through the list in the Properties window, examining the values of other properties of the Form. For example, the value of the Size property is 300, 300 by default.

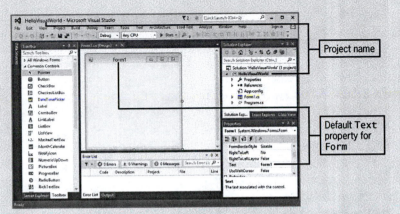

Figure 3-17 The HelloVisualWorld project development environment

 If you do not see the Properties window in the lower-right corner of your screen, click the title bar on the Form. Alternatively, click **View** in the menu bar and click **Properties Window**.

If you do not see the Toolbox shown in Figure 3-17, click the **Toolbox tab** at the left side of the screen, and then click the pushpin near the top to pin the Toolbox to the screen. Alternatively, click **View** from the menu bar and then click **Toolbox**.

 If you do not see the error list at the bottom of the screen, as in Figure 3-17, you can select **View** from the menu bar and then select **Error List**. You might have to drag up the divider that separates the error list from the window above it.

4. In the Properties window, change the Name of the Form to **HelloForm**. (The Name property is under Design if you choose to have the list categorized; if you choose to display it alphabetically, then Name is near the top.) Then change the Text of the Form to **Hello Visual World**. Press **Enter**; the title of the Form in the center of the screen changes to *Hello Visual World*, as shown in Figure 3-18.

(continues)

(continued)

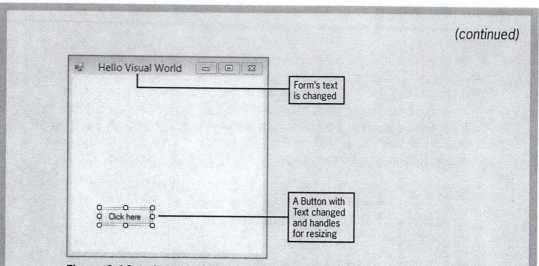

Figure 3-18　A Form with changed Text and a Button

5. Examine the Toolbox on the left side of the screen. Select **Common Controls** if it is not already selected. In the Toolbox, click and hold **Button**. As you move your mouse off the Toolbox and onto the Form, the mouse pointer changes so that it appears to carry a Button. Position your mouse anywhere on the form, then release the mouse button. The Button appears on the Form and contains the text *button1*. When you click the Button, handles appear that you can drag to resize it. When you click off the Button on the Form, the handles disappear. Click the Button to display the properties for button1. Change its Name to **displayOutputButton**, and change its Text property to **Click here**. When you press **Enter** on the keyboard or click anywhere on the Form, the text of the Button on the Form changes to *Click here*. See Figure 3-18.

6. Scroll through the other displayOutputButton properties. For example, examine the Location property. The first value listed for Location indicates horizontal position, and the second value indicates vertical position. Drag the Button across the Form to a new position. Each time you release your mouse button, the value of the Form Button's Location property is updated to reflect the new location. Try to drag the Button to Location 100, 150. Alternatively, delete the contents of the Location property field and type **100, 150**. The Button moves to the requested location on the Form.

7. Save your form by clicking **File** on the menu bar, then clicking **Save All**. Alternatively, you can click the **Save All** button on the toolbar; its icon is two overlapping disks.

(continues)

8. Although your `Form` doesn't do much yet, you can execute the program anyway. Click **Debug** on the menu bar, and then click **Start Without Debugging**. The `Form` appears. You can drag, minimize, and restore it, and you can click its `Button`. The `Button` has not yet been programmed to do anything, but it appears to be pressed when you click it. Click the `Form's` **Close** button to dismiss the `Form`.

9. You can close a project at any time and come back to it later. Exit Visual Studio now by clicking the **Close** button in the upper-right corner of the screen, or by clicking **File** on the menu bar and then clicking **Exit**. If you have made more changes since the last time you saved, you will be prompted to save again. When you choose **Yes**, the program closes.

Providing Functionality for a `Button`

In the next steps, you make the `Button` on the `HelloVisualWorld` Form functional; it will display a message when the user clicks it.

1. Start Visual Studio. Select **File** from the menu, click **Open**, and browse for the **HelloVisualWorld** project. Alternatively, select **File** from the menu, click **Recent Projects and Solutions**, and select the project from the pop-up list.

2. When the `Form` appears, drag a `Label` from the Toolbox to the `Form`. Change its `Name` to **helloLabel** and its `Text` property to **Hello, Visual World!**. If you want your `Form` to match Figure 3-19 exactly, change the `Label's` `Location` property to **90, 75**.

Figure 3-19 The `helloLabel` on the Form

(continues)

(continued)

3. Scroll through the Properties list for the `Label`, and change its `Visible` property from `True` to `False`. You can still see the `Label` in the Designer, but the `Label` will be invisible when you execute the program.

4. Double-click the `Button` on the `Form`. A new window that contains program code is displayed, revealing a newly created `displayOutputButton_Click()` method with no statements. Between the curly braces, type the following statement that causes the `Label` to appear when the user clicks the `Button` on the `Form`:

   `helloLabel.Visible = true;`

5. Save the file, then run the program by clicking **Debug** on the menu bar and clicking **Start Without Debugging**, or by pressing **Ctrl+F5**. When the `Form` appears, click the **Click here** button to reveal the greeting. If you want, experiment with values for some of the `Label` properties, such as `Font`, `BackColor`, and `ForeColor`.

Adding a Second `Button` to a `Form`

In the next steps, you add a second `Button` to the `Form` in the `HelloVisualWorld` project.

1. In the IDE, switch to Design View. Drag a second button onto the `Form` below the first `Button`. Change the new `Button`'s `Name` property to **changeOutputButton** and change its `Text` to **Click me last**.

2. Double-click the `changeOutputButton` to expose the `changeOutputButton_Click()` method.

3. Between the curly braces of the method, add the following code:

   `helloLabel.Text = "Goodbye";`

4. Save the project, then execute the program. Click the `displayOutputButton` to reveal *Hello, Visual World!*. Then click the `changeOutputButton` to reveal *Goodbye*.

5. Execute the program again. This time, click the second `Button` first. No message appears because the `Label` with the message has not been made visible. When you click the `displayOutputButton`, the `Label` becomes visible, but it displays *Goodbye* because the `changeOutputButton`'s `Click()` method has already changed the `Label`'s `Text`.

(continues)

(continued)

6. Return to the Form1.cs [Design] tab. Click the `changeOutputButton`, and change its `Enabled` property to `False`. Now, when the program executes, the user will not be immediately able to click the second `Button`.

7. Double-click the `displayOutputButton`. Add the following statement to the method so that the `changeOutputButton` becomes enabled when the `displayOutputButton` is clicked:

    `changeOutputButton.Enabled = true;`

8. Save the project, then execute the program. When the `Form` appears, the `changeOutputButton` is dimmed and not clickable because it is not enabled. Click the enabled `displayOutputButton` to reveal the *Hello, Visual World!* message and to enable the second `Button`. Then click the `changeOutputButton` to expose the *Goodbye* message.

9. Dismiss the `Form`, and close Visual Studio.

Chapter Summary

- `Forms` are GUI objects that provide an interface for collecting, displaying, and delivering information. They almost always include controls such as labels, text boxes, and buttons that users can manipulate to interact with a program. Every `Form` and control on a `Form` has multiple properties you can set using the IDE.

- The Toolbox displays a list of available controls you can add to a `Form`. The list includes `Button`, `CheckBox`, and `Label`. From the Toolbox, you can drag controls onto a `Form` where they will be most useful. After you have dragged a `Button` onto a `Form`, you can double-click it to create the method that executes when a user clicks the `Button`, and you can write any statements you want between the curly braces of the `Click()` method.

- `Label`s are controls that you use to display text to communicate with an application's user. `TextBox`es are controls through which a user can enter input data in a GUI application. Both have a `Text` property; frequently an application starts with the `Text` empty for `TextBox`es. Because a user might type any value, the value in a `TextBox` is a `string` by default.

- Usually, you want to provide reasonable **Name** property values for all the controls you place on a **Form**. Although any identifier that starts with a letter is legal, by convention you should start control names with a lowercase letter and use camel casing as appropriate, start **Form** names with an uppercase letter and use camel casing as appropriate, and use the type of object in the name.

- If you build or run a program that contains a syntax error, you see *Build failed* in the lower-left corner of the IDE and an error dialog box. An error list shows the filename, line, position in the line, and project for each error. If you double-click an error message, the cursor is placed at the location in the code where the error was found. If you inadvertently create an event-handling method that you do not want, you should eliminate the event using the Properties window in the IDE. If you rename a control after you have created an event for it, you must refactor the code. The ultimate authority on C# classes is the Visual Studio Help documentation.

- Both console and GUI applications can contain variables and constants, decisions, loops, arrays, and calls to other methods. GUI applications look "snazzier," and they contain controls that a user can manipulate with a mouse. However, GUI programs usually take longer to develop than their console counterparts. When writing your own programs, you will use the interface you prefer or one that your instructor or boss requires.

Key Terms

The **interface** is the environment a user sees when a program executes.

Forms are GUI objects that provide an interface for collecting, displaying, and delivering information.

Controls are devices such as labels, text boxes, and buttons that users can manipulate to communicate with a GUI program.

A **node** is an icon that appears beside a list or a section of code and that can be expanded or condensed.

An **access specifier** is a keyword that dictates what outside classes can use a method.

An **event** causes a program to perform a task.

A **click event** is the event generated when a user clicks a control in a GUI program.

A **label** is a control that you use to display text to communicate with an application's user.

A **text box** is a control through which a user can enter input data in a GUI application.

Design time is the period of time during which a programmer designs the interface and writes the code.

Runtime is the period of time during which a program executes.

Focus describes the attribute of a **Form** control that stands out visually from the others and that reacts to keyboard input.

Tab order describes the sequence of controls selected when the user presses the Tab key.

A **proportional font** is one in which different characters have different pitches or widths.

A **fixed-pitch font** is one in which each character occupies the same width.

A **monospaced font** is one in which each character occupies the same width.

Code refactoring is the process of changing a program's internal structure without changing the way the program works.

An **orphaned method** is one that never executes in an application and thus serves no purpose.

Review Questions

1. Which of the following is a GUI object that provides an interface for collecting, displaying, and delivering information and that contains other controls?

   a. `Form`
   b. `Button`
   c. `TextBox`
   d. `Label`

2. In the Visual Studio IDE main window, where does the menu bar lie?

   a. vertically along the left border
   b. vertically along the right border
   c. horizontally across the top of the window
   d. horizontally across the bottom of the window

3. In the IDE, the area where you visually construct a `Form` is the _____ .

   a. Toolbox
   b. Palette
   c. Easel
   d. Form Designer

4. When you create a new Windows Forms project, by default the first `Form` you see is named _____ .

   a. `Form`
   b. `Form1`
   c. `FormA`
   d. `FormAlpha`

5. The `Form` class has _____ properties.

   a. three
   b. ten
   c. about 100
   d. about 1000

6. Which of the following is not a `Form` property?

   a. `BackColor`
   b. `ProjectName`
   c. `Size`
   d. `Text`

7. Which of the following is a legal **Form Name** property?

    a. **Payroll Form**   c. either of the above

    b. **PayrollForm**   d. none of the above

8. Which of the following is a legal **Form Text** property?

    a. **Payroll Form**   c. either of the above

    b. **PayrollForm**   d. none of the above

9. Which of the following does not appear in the IDE's Toolbox list?

    a. **Text**   c. **Label**

    b. **Button**   d. **TextBox**

10. After you have dragged a **Button** onto a **Form** in the IDE, you can double-click it to _____.

    a. delete it

    b. view its properties

    c. create a method that executes when a user clicks the **Button**

    d. execute a method when a user clicks the **Button**

11. The **button1_Click()** method that is generated by the IDE _____.

    a. has a **private** access specifier

    b. is nonstatic

    c. contains parameters between its parentheses

    d. all of the above

12. A(n) _____ is generated when a user interacts with a GUI object.

    a. event   c. method

    b. occasion   d. error

13. If you create a **Button** named **yesButton**, the name of the method that responds to clicks on it is _____.

    a. **button1_Click()**   c. **click_YesButton()**

    b. **yesButton_Method()**   d. **yesButton_Click()**

14. Statements allowed in a **Click()** method include _____.

    a. variable declarations   c. both of the above

    b. arithmetic statements   d. none of the above

15. _____ are controls through which a user can enter input data in a GUI application.

    a. Labels

    b. Tags

    c. Tickets

    d. TextBoxes

16. The value in a TextBox is _____.

    a. an int

    b. a double

    c. a string

    d. It might be any of the above.

17. Which of the following is a legal and conventional name for a TextBox?

    a. Salary TextBox

    b. salaryTextBox

    c. both of the above

    d. none of the above

18. The process of changing a program's internal structure without changing the way the program works is _____.

    a. compiling

    b. debugging

    c. code refactoring

    d. systems analysis

19. If you inadvertently create a Click() method for a control that should not generate a click event, you can successfully eliminate the method by _____.

    a. deleting the method code from the Form1.cs file

    b. eliminating the method from the Events list in the Properties window

    c. adding the method to the Discard window

    d. making the method a comment by placing two forward slashes at the start of each line

20. Of the following, the most significant difference between many console applications and GUI applications is _____.

    a. their appearance

    b. their ability to accept input

    c. their ability to perform calculations

    d. their ability to be created using C#

Exercises

Programming Exercises

1. Write a GUI program named **MilesToKilometersGUI** that allows the user to input a distance in miles and output the value in kilometers. There are 1.6 kilometers in a mile.

The exercises in this section should look familiar to you. Each is similar to an exercise in Chapter 2, where you created solutions using console input and output.

2. Write a GUI program named **ProjectedRaisesGUI** that allows a user to enter an employee's salary. Then display, with explanatory text, next year's salary, which reflects a 4 percent increase.

3. Write a program named **CarRentalInteractiveGUI** that prompts a user for days and miles for a car rental and displays the total rental fee computed as $20 per day plus 25 cents per mile.

4. Write a GUI program named **EggsInteractiveGUI** that allows a user to input the number of eggs produced in a month by each of five chickens. Sum the eggs, then display the total in dozens and eggs. For example, a total of 127 eggs is 10 dozen and 7 eggs. Figure 3-20 shows a typical execution.

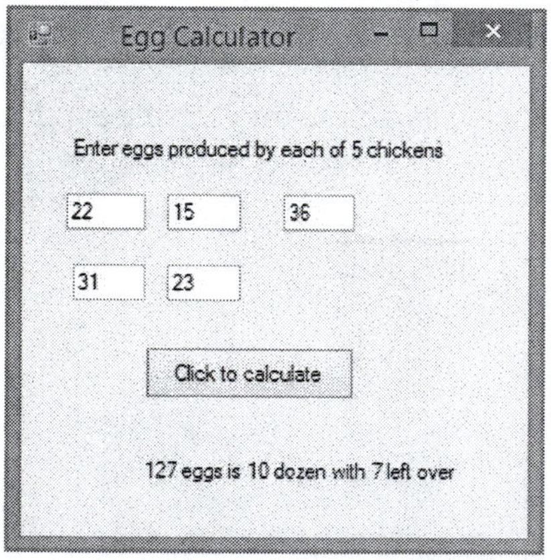

Figure 3-20   An EggsInteractiveGUI application

5. Write a GUI program named **TestsInteractiveGUI** that allows a user to enter scores for five tests he has taken. Display the average of the test scores to two decimal places.

6. Write a GUI program named **PayrollGUI** that prompts the user for a name, Social Security number, hourly pay rate, and number of hours worked. In an attractive format, display all the input data as well as the following:

   - Gross pay, defined as hourly pay rate times hours worked

   - Federal withholding tax, defined as 15 percent of the gross pay

   - State withholding tax, defined as 5 percent of the gross pay

   - Net pay, defined as gross pay minus taxes

7. Create an enumeration named `Month` that holds values for the months of the year, starting with `JANUARY` equal to `1`. (Recall that an enumeration must be placed within a class but outside of any method.) Write a GUI program named **MonthNamesGUI** that prompts the user for a month integer. Convert the user's entry to a `Month` value, and display it.

8. Pig Latin is a nonsense language. To create a word in pig Latin, you remove the first letter and then add the first letter and *ay* at the end of the word. For example, *dog* becomes *ogday*, and *cat* becomes *atcay*. Write a GUI program named **PigLatinGUI** that allows the user to enter a word and displays the pig Latin version.

Debugging Exercises

1. Each of the following projects in the Chapter.03 folder of your downloadable student files has syntax and/or logical errors. In each case, immediately save a copy of the project folder with a new name that begins with *Fixed* before you open the project in Visual Studio. For example, the project folder for DebugThree1 will become FixedDebugThree1. All the files within the folders have already been named with the *Fixed* prefix, so you do not need to provide new filenames for any of the files in the top-level folder. After naming the new folder, open the project, determine the problems, and fix them.

   a. DebugThree1   c. DebugThree3
   b. DebugThree2   d. DebugThree4

Case Problems

1. In Chapter 2, you created a program for the Greenville Idol competition that prompts a user for the number of contestants entered in last year's competition and in this year's competition. The program displays the revenue expected for this year's competition if each contestant pays a $25 entrance fee. The application also displays a statement that indicates whether this year's competition has more contestants than last year's. Now, create an interactive GUI program named **GreenvilleRevenueGUI** that performs all the same tasks.

2. In Chapter 2, you created a program for Marshall's Murals that prompts a user for the number of interior and exterior murals scheduled to be painted during the next month. The program computes the expected revenue for each type of mural when interior murals cost $500 each and exterior murals cost $750 each. The application should display, by mural type, the number of murals ordered, the cost for each type, and a subtotal. The application also displays the total expected revenue and a statement that indicates whether more interior murals are scheduled than exterior ones. Now create an interactive GUI program named **MarshallsRevenueGUI** that performs all the same tasks.

CHAPTER 4

Making Decisions

In this chapter you will:

- ◎ Understand logic-planning tools and decision making
- ◎ Learn how to make decisions using `if` statements
- ◎ Learn how to make decisions using `if-else` statements
- ◎ Use compound expressions in `if` statements
- ◎ Make decisions using `switch` statements
- ◎ Use the conditional operator
- ◎ Use the NOT operator
- ◎ Learn to avoid common errors when making decisions
- ◎ Learn about decision-making issues in GUI programs

Computer programs are powerful because of their ability to make decisions. Programs that decide which travel route will offer the best weather conditions, which Web site will provide the closest match to search criteria, or which recommended medical treatment has the highest probability of success all rely on a program's decision making. In this chapter you will learn to make decisions in C# programs.

Understanding Logic-Planning Tools and Decision Making

When computer programmers write programs, they rarely just sit down at a keyboard and begin typing. Programmers must plan the complex portions of programs. Programmers often use **pseudocode**, a tool that helps them plan a program's logic by writing plain English statements. Using pseudocode requires that you write down the logic of a given task in everyday language and not the syntax used in a programming language. (You learned the difference between *logic* and *syntax* in Chapter 1.) In fact, a task you write in pseudocode does not have to be computer-related. If you have ever written a list of directions to your house—for example, (1) go west on Algonquin Road, (2) turn left on Roselle Road, (3) enter expressway heading east, and so on—you have written pseudocode. A **flowchart** is similar to pseudocode, but you write the steps in diagram form, as a series of shapes connected by arrows or *flowlines*.

Some programmers use a variety of shapes to represent different tasks in their flowcharts, but you can draw simple flowcharts that express very complex situations using just rectangles, diamonds, and connecting flowlines. You can use a rectangle to represent any process or step and a diamond to represent any decision. For example, Figure 4-1 shows a flowchart and pseudocode describing driving directions to a friend's house. Notice how the actions illustrated in the flowchart and the pseudocode statements correspond. Figure 4-1 illustrates a logical structure called a **sequence structure**—one step follows another unconditionally. A sequence structure might contain any number of steps, but one task follows another with no chance to branch away or skip a step.

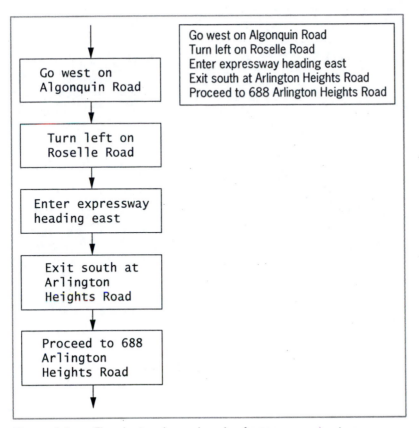

Go west on Algonquin Road
Turn left on Roselle Road
Enter expressway heading east
Exit south at Arlington Heights Road
Proceed to 688 Arlington Heights Road

Figure 4-1   Flowchart and pseudocode of a sequence structure

Sometimes, logical steps do not follow in an unconditional sequence. Instead, some tasks might or might not occur based on decisions you make. To represent a decision, flowchart creators use a diamond shape to hold a question, and they draw paths to alternative courses of action emerging from the corner of the diamond. Figure 4-2 shows a flowchart describing directions in which the execution of some steps depends on a decision.

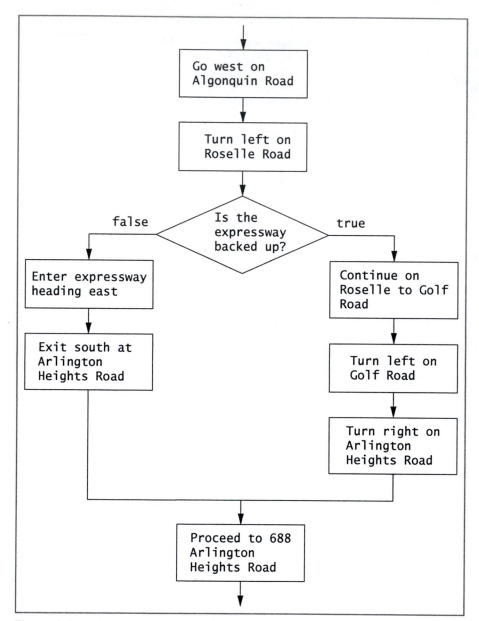

Figure 4-2 Flowchart including a decision structure

Figure 4-2 shows a **decision structure**—one that involves choosing between alternative courses of action based on a value. When reduced to their most basic form, all computer decisions are true-or-false decisions. This is because computer circuitry consists of millions of tiny switches that are either "on" or "off," and the result of every decision sets one of these switches in memory. The values true and false are Boolean values; every computer decision results in a

Boolean value. For example, program code that you write never includes a question like "What number did the user enter?" Instead, the decisions might be: "Did the user enter a 1?" "If not, did the user enter a 2?" "If not, did the user enter a 3?"

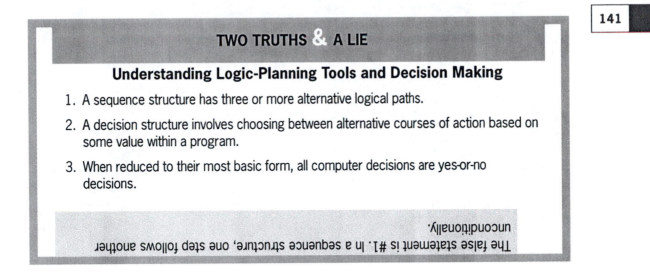

TWO TRUTHS & A LIE

Understanding Logic-Planning Tools and Decision Making

1. A sequence structure has three or more alternative logical paths.

2. A decision structure involves choosing between alternative courses of action based on some value within a program.

3. When reduced to their most basic form, all computer decisions are yes-or-no decisions.

The false statement is #1. In a sequence structure, one step follows another unconditionally.

Making Decisions Using the if Statement

The if and if-else statements are the two most commonly used decision-making statements in C#. You use an **if statement** to make a single-alternative decision. In other words, you use an if statement to determine whether an action will occur. The if statement takes the following form:

```
if(testedExpression)
   statement;
```

In this statement, *testedExpression* represents any C# expression that can be evaluated as true or false, and *statement* represents the action that will take place if the expression evaluates as true. You must place the if statement's evaluated expression between parentheses. You can leave a space between the keyword if and the opening parenthesis if you think that format is easier to read.

Usable expressions in an if statement include Boolean expressions such as amount > 5 and month == "May" as well as the value of bool variables such as isValidIDNumber. If the expression evaluates as true, then the statement executes. Whether the expression evaluates as true or false, the program continues with the next statement following the complete if statement.

You learned about Boolean expressions and the `bool` data type in Chapter 2. Table 2-4 summarizes how comparison operators are used.

In the chapter "Introduction to Methods," you will learn to write methods that return values. A method call that returns a Boolean value also can be used as the tested expression in an `if` statement.

In some programming languages, such as C++, nonzero numbers evaluate as `true` and 0 evaluates as `false`. However, in C#, only Boolean expressions evaluate as `true` and `false`.

For example, the code segment written and diagrammed in Figure 4-3 displays *A* and *B* when `number` holds a value less than 5, but when `number` is 5 or greater, only *B* is displayed. When the tested Boolean expression `number < 5` is `false`, the statement that displays *A* never executes.

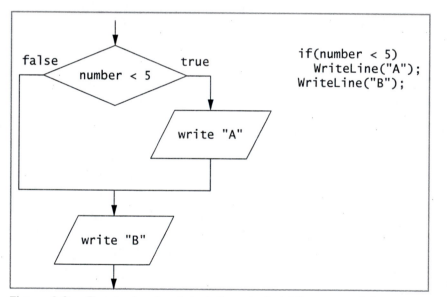

```
if(number < 5)
    WriteLine("A");
WriteLine("B");
```

Figure 4-3   Flowchart and code including a typical `if` statement followed by a separate statement

Although you can create a meaningful flowchart using only rectangles, diamonds, and flowlines, parallelograms have traditionally been used to represent input and output statements, so they are used in Figure 4-3 and in other figures in this chapter.

In the code in Figure 4-3, notice there is no semicolon at the end of the line that contains
if(number < 5). The statement does not end at that point; it ends after WriteLine("A");.
If you incorrectly insert a semicolon at the end of if(number < 5), then the code means,
"If number is less than 5, do nothing; then, no matter what the value of number is, display *A*."
Figure 4-4 shows the flowchart logic that matches the code when a semicolon is incorrectly
placed at the end of the if expression.

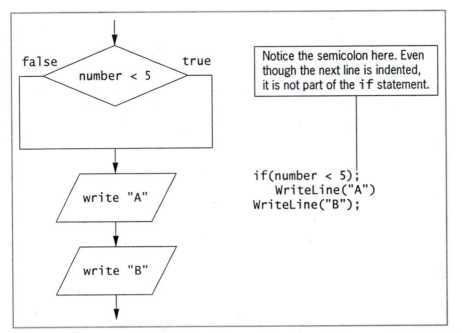

```
if(number < 5);
   WriteLine("A")
WriteLine("B");
```

Notice the semicolon here. Even though the next line is indented, it is not part of the if statement.

Figure 4-4   Flowchart and code including an if statement with a semicolon following the if
expression

Although it is customary, and good style, to indent any statement that executes when an if
Boolean expression evaluates as true, the C# compiler does not pay any attention to the
indentation. Each of the following if statements displays *A* when number is less than 5. The
first shows an if statement written on a single line; the second shows an if statement on two
lines but with no indentation. The third uses conventional indentation. All three examples
execute identically.

```
if(number < 5) WriteLine("A");
if(number < 5)
WriteLine("A");
if(number < 5)
   WriteLine("A");
```

Don't Do It
Although these first two formats work for
if statements, they are not conventional,
and using them makes a program harder
to understand.

When you want to execute two or more statements conditionally, you place the statements within a block. A **block** is a collection of one or more statements contained within a pair of curly braces. For example, the code segment written and diagrammed in Figure 4-5 displays both *C* and *D* when number is less than 5, and it displays neither when number is not less than 5. The if expression that precedes the block is the **control statement** for the decision structure.

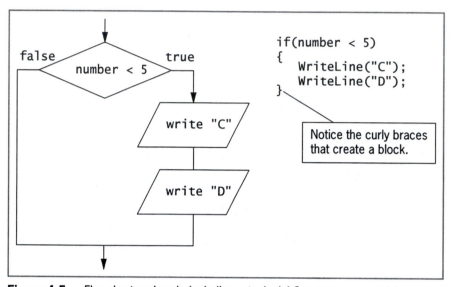

Figure 4-5   Flowchart and code including a typical if statement containing a block

Indenting alone does not cause multiple statements to depend on the evaluation of a Boolean expression following an if control statement. For multiple statements to depend on an if, they must be blocked with braces. For example, Figure 4-6 shows two statements that are indented below an if expression. When you glance at the code, it might first appear that both statements depend on the if; however, only the first one does, as shown in the flowchart, because the statements are not blocked.

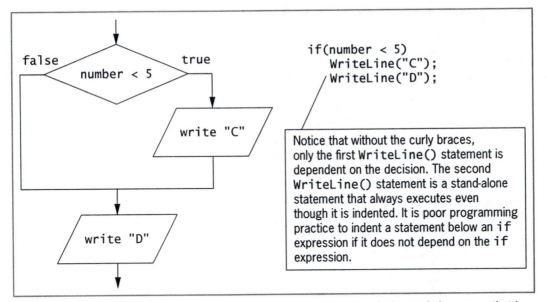

```
if(number < 5)
    WriteLine("C");
    WriteLine("D");
```

Notice that without the curly braces, only the first WriteLine() statement is dependent on the decision. The second WriteLine() statement is a stand-alone statement that always executes even though it is indented. It is poor programming practice to indent a statement below an if expression if it does not depend on the if expression.

Figure 4-6 Flowchart and code including an if statement that is missing curly braces or that has inappropriate indenting

When you create a block using curly braces, you do not have to place multiple statements within it. It is perfectly legal to block a single statement. Blocking a single statement can be a useful technique to help prevent future errors because when a program later is modified to include multiple statements that depend on the if, the braces serve as a reminder to use a block. Creating a block that contains no statements also is legal in C#. You usually do so only when starting to write a program, as a reminder to yourself to add statements later.

 In C#, it is customary to align a block's opening and closing braces. Some programmers prefer to place the opening brace on the same line as the if expression instead of giving the brace its own line. This style is called the K & R style, named for Brian Kernighan and Dennis Ritchie, who wrote the first book on the C programming language.

You can place any number of statements within a block, including other if statements. If a second if statement is the only statement that depends on the first if, then no braces are required. Figure 4-7 shows the logic for a **nested if** statement in which one decision structure is contained within another. With a nested if statement, a second if's Boolean expression is tested only when the first if's Boolean expression evaluates as true.

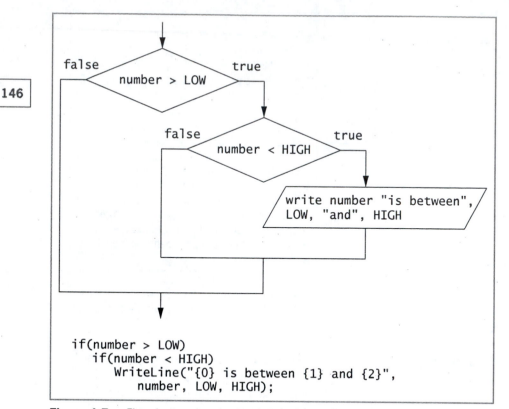

```
if(number > LOW)
    if(number < HIGH)
        WriteLine("{0} is between {1} and {2}",
            number, LOW, HIGH);
```

Figure 4-7   Flowchart and code showing the logic of a nested if

Figure 4-8 shows a program that contains the logic in Figure 4-7. When a user enters a number greater than 5, the first tested expression is **true** and the **if** statement that tests whether the number is less than 10 executes. When the second tested expression also is **true**, the WriteLine() statement executes. If either the first or second tested expression is **false**, no output occurs. Figure 4-9 shows the output after the program is executed three times using three different input values. Notice that when the value input by the user is not between 5 and 10, no output message appears.

```
using System;
using static System.Console;
class NestedDecision
{
    static void Main()
    {
        const int HIGH = 10, LOW = 5;
        string numberString;
        int number;
        Write("Enter an integer ");
        numberString = ReadLine();
        number = Convert.ToInt32(numberString);
        if(number > LOW)
            if(number < HIGH)
                WriteLine("{0} is between {1} and {2}",
                    number, LOW, HIGH);
    }
}
```

Figure 4-8   Program using nested if

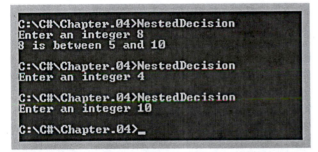

Figure 4-9   Output of three executions of the NestedDecision program

A Note on Equivalency Comparisons

Often, programmers mistakenly use a single equal sign rather than the double equal sign when testing for equivalency. For example, the following expression does not compare number to HIGH:

number = HIGH

Instead, it attempts to assign the value HIGH to the variable number. When an assignment is used between the parentheses in an if statement, as in if(number = HIGH), the assignment is illegal, and the program will not compile.

The only condition under which the assignment operator would work as part of the tested expression in an if statement is when the assignment is made to a bool variable. For example, suppose that a payroll program contains a bool variable named doesEmployeeHaveDependents, and then uses the following statement:

```
if(doesEmployeeHaveDependents = numDependents > 0)...
```

In this case, numDependents would be compared to 0, and the result, true or false, would be assigned to doesEmployeeHaveDependents. Then the decision would be made based on the assigned value. This is not a recommended way to make a comparison because it looks confusing. If your intention was to assign a value to doesEmployeeHaveDependents and to make a decision based on the value, then your intentions would be clearer with the following code:

```
doesEmployeeHaveDependents = numDependents > 0;
if(doesEmployeeHaveDependents)...
```

Notice the difference in the following statement that uses two equal signs within the parentheses in the if statement:

```
if(doesEmployeeHaveDependents == numDependents > 0)...
```

This statement compares doesEmployeeHaveDependents to the result of comparing numDependents to 0 but does not change the value of doesEmployeeHaveDependents.

 One of the many advantages of using the Visual Studio IDE to write programs is that if you use an assignment operator in place of an equivalency operator in a Boolean expression, your mistake will be flagged as an error immediately.

TWO TRUTHS & A LIE

Making Decisions Using the if Statement

1. In C#, you must place an if statement's evaluated expression between parentheses.

2. In C#, for multiple statements to depend on an if, they must be indented.

3. In C#, you can place one if statement within a block that depends on another if statement.

The false statement is #2. Indenting alone does not cause multiple statements to depend on the evaluation of a Boolean expression in an if. For multiple statements to depend on an if, they must be blocked with braces.

Making Decisions Using the `if-else` Statement

Some decisions are **dual-alternative decisions**; they have two possible resulting actions. If you want to perform one action when a Boolean expression evaluates as `true` and an alternate action when it evaluates as `false`, you can use an **if-else statement**. The `if-else` statement takes the following form:

```
if(expression)
    statement1;
else
    statement2;
```

You can code an `if` without an `else`, but it is illegal to code an `else` without an `if`.

Just as you can block several statements so they all execute when an expression within an `if` is `true`, you can block multiple statements after an `else` so that they will all execute when the evaluated expression is `false`. For example, the following code assigns 0 to bonus and also produces a line of output when the Boolean variable `isProjectUnderBudget` is `false`:

```
if(isProjectUnderBudget)
    bonus = 200;
else
{
    bonus = 0;
    WriteLine("Notify contractor");
}
```

Figure 4-10 shows the logic for an `if-else` statement, and Figure 4-11 shows a program that contains the statement. With every execution of the program, one or the other of the two `WriteLine()` statements executes. The indentation shown in the `if-else` example in Figure 4-11 is not required, but it is standard. You vertically align the keyword `if` with the keyword `else`, and then indent the action statements that depend on the evaluation. Figure 4-12 shows two executions of the program.

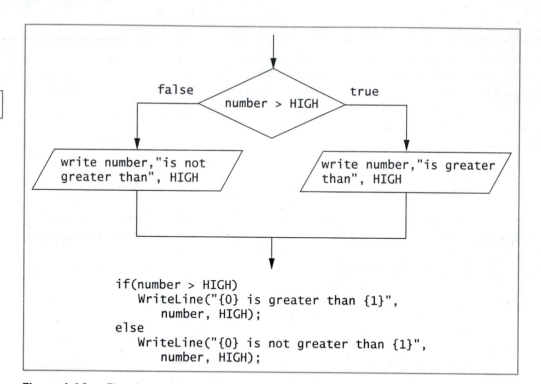

```
if(number > HIGH)
    WriteLine("{0} is greater than {1}",
        number, HIGH);
else
    WriteLine("{0} is not greater than {1}",
        number, HIGH);
```

Figure 4-10   Flowchart and code showing the logic of a dual-alternative if-else statement

```
using System;
using static System.Console;
class IfElseDecision
{
    static void Main()
    {
        const int HIGH = 10;
        string numberString;
        int number;
        Write("Enter an integer ");
        numberString = ReadLine();
        number = Convert.ToInt32(numberString);
        if(number > HIGH)
            WriteLine("{0} is greater than {1}",
                number, HIGH);
        else
            WriteLine("{0} is not greater than {1}",
                number, HIGH);
    }
}
```

Figure 4-11   Program with a dual-alternative if-else statement

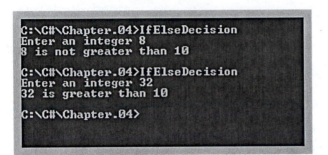

Figure 4-12 Output of two executions of the IfElseDecision program

When if-else statements are nested, each else always is paired with the most recent unpaired if. For example, in the following code, the else is paired with the second if. Correct indentation helps to make this clear.

```
if(saleAmount > 1000)
   if(saleAmount < 2000)
      bonus = 100;
   else
      bonus = 500;
```

In this example, the following bonuses are assigned:

- If saleAmount is between $1000 and $2000, bonus is $100 because both evaluated expressions are true.

- If saleAmount is $2000 or more, bonus is $500 because the first evaluated expression is true and the second one is false.

- If saleAmount is $1000 or less, bonus is unassigned because the first evaluated expression is false and there is no corresponding else.

TWO TRUTHS & A LIE

Making Decisions Using the if-else Statement

1. Dual-alternative decisions have two possible outcomes.

2. In an if-else statement, a semicolon might be the last character typed before the else.

3. When if-else statements are nested, the first if always is paired with the first else.

The false statement is #3. When if-else statements are nested, each else always is paired with the most recent unpaired if.

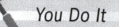

You Do It

Using if-else Statements

In the next steps, you write a program that requires using multiple, nested if-else statements to accomplish its goal—determining whether any of the three integers entered by a user are equal.

1. Open a new file or project named **CompareThreeNumbers,** and write the first lines necessary for the class:

```
using System;
using static System.Console;
class CompareThreeNumbers
{
```

2. Begin a Main() method by declaring a string for input and three integers that will hold the input values.

```
static void Main()
{
    string numberString;
    int num1, num2, num3;
```

3. Add the statements that retrieve the three integers from the user and assign them to the appropriate variables.

```
Write("Enter an integer ");
numberString = ReadLine();
num1 = Convert.ToInt32(numberString);
Write("Enter an integer ");
numberString = ReadLine();
num2 = Convert.ToInt32(numberString);
Write("Enter an integer ");
numberString = ReadLine();
num3 = Convert.ToInt32(numberString);
```

In the chapter "Introduction to Methods," you will learn to write methods, which will allow you to avoid repetitive code like that shown here.

(continues)

(continued)

4. If the first number and the second number are equal, there are two possibilities: either the first is also equal to the third, in which case all three numbers are equal, or the first is not equal to the third, in which case only the first two numbers are equal. Insert the following code:

```
if(num1 == num2)
    if(num1 == num3)
        WriteLine("All three numbers are equal");
    else
        WriteLine("First two are equal");
```

5. If the first two numbers are not equal, but the first and third are equal, display an appropriate message. For clarity, the else should vertically align under the first if statement that compares num1 and num2.

```
else
    if(num1 == num3)
        WriteLine("First and last are equal");
```

6. When num1 and num2 are not equal, and num1 and num3 are not equal, but num2 and num3 are equal, display an appropriate message. For clarity, the else should vertically align under the statement that compares num1 and num3.

```
else
    if(num2 == num3)
        WriteLine("Last two are equal");
```

7. Finally, if none of the pairs (num1 and num2, num1 and num3, or num2 and num3) is equal, display an appropriate message. For clarity, the else should vertically align under the statement that compares num2 and num3.

```
else
    WriteLine("No two numbers are equal");
```

8. Add a closing curly brace for the Main() method and a closing curly brace for the class.

9. Save and compile the program, and then execute it several times, providing different combinations of equal and nonequal integers when prompted. Figure 4-13 shows several executions of the program.

(continues)

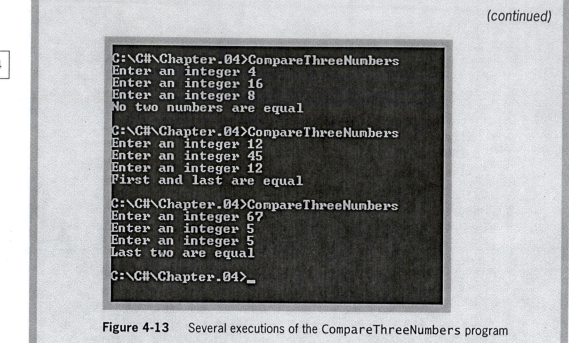

(continued)

```
C:\C#\Chapter.04>CompareThreeNumbers
Enter an integer 4
Enter an integer 16
Enter an integer 8
No two numbers are equal

C:\C#\Chapter.04>CompareThreeNumbers
Enter an integer 12
Enter an integer 45
Enter an integer 12
First and last are equal

C:\C#\Chapter.04>CompareThreeNumbers
Enter an integer 67
Enter an integer 5
Enter an integer 5
Last two are equal

C:\C#\Chapter.04>_
```

Figure 4-13   Several executions of the CompareThreeNumbers program

Using Compound Expressions in if Statements

In many programming situations, you need to make multiple decisions before taking action. No matter how many decisions must be made, you can produce the correct results by using a series of if statements. For convenience and clarity, however, you can combine multiple decisions into a single, compound Boolean expression using a combination of conditional AND and OR operators.

Using the Conditional AND Operator

As an alternative to nested if statements, you can use the **conditional AND operator** (or simply the **AND operator**) to create a compound Boolean expression. The conditional AND operator is written as two ampersands (&&).

A tool that can help you understand the && operator is a truth table. **Truth tables** are diagrams used in mathematics and logic to help describe the truth of an entire expression based on the truth of its parts. Table 4-1 shows a truth table that lists all the possibilities with compound expressions that use && and two operands. For any two expressions x and y, the expression x && y is true only if both x and y are individually true. If either x or y alone is false, or if both are false, then the expression x && y is false.

x	y	x && y
True	True	True
True	False	False
False	True	False
False	False	False

Table 4-1 Truth table for the conditional && operator

For example, the two code samples shown in Figure 4-14 work exactly the same way. The age variable is tested, and if it is greater than or equal to 0 and less than 120, a message is displayed to explain that the value is valid.

```
// using the && operator
if(age >= 0 && age < 120)
    WriteLine("Age is valid");

// using nested ifs
if(age >= 0)
    if(age < 120)
        WriteLine("Age is valid");
```

Figure 4-14   Comparison of the && operator and nested if statements

Using the && operator is never required, because nested if statements achieve the same result, but using the && operator often makes your code more concise, less error-prone, and easier to understand.

It is important to note that when you use the && operator, you must include a complete Boolean expression on each side of the operator. If you want to set a bonus to $400 when saleAmount is both over $1000 and under $5000, the correct statement is as follows:

```
if(saleAmount > 1000 && saleAmount < 5000)
    bonus = 400;
```

The following statement is incorrect and will not compile:

```
if(saleAmount > 1000 && < 5000)
    bonus = 400;
```

Don't Do It
< 5000 is not a Boolean expression because the < operator requires two operands, so this statement is invalid.

For clarity, many programmers prefer to surround each Boolean expression that is part of a compound Boolean expression with its own set of parentheses. For example:

```
if((saleAmount > 1000) && (saleAmount < 5000))
    bonus = 400;
```

In this example, the if clause has a set of parentheses (the first opening parenthesis and the last closing parenthesis), and each Boolean expression that is part of the compound condition has its own set of parentheses. Use this format if it is clearer to you.

The expressions in each part of a compound, conditional Boolean expression are evaluated only as much as necessary to determine whether the entire expression is true or false. This feature is called **short-circuit evaluation**. With the && operator, both Boolean expressions must be true before the action in the statement can occur. If the first expression is false, the second expression is never evaluated, because its value does not matter. For example, if a is not greater than LIMIT in the following if statement, then the evaluation is complete because there is no need to evaluate whether b is greater than LIMIT.

```
if(a > LIMIT && b > LIMIT)
    WriteLine("Both are greater than the limit.");
```

Using the Conditional OR Operator

You can use the **conditional OR operator** (or simply the **OR operator**) when you want some action to occur even if only one of two conditions is true. The OR operator is written as ||. When you use the || operator, only one of the listed conditions must be met for the resulting action to take place. Table 4-2 shows the truth table for the || operator. As you can see, the entire expression x||y is false *only* when x and y each are false individually.

x	y	x||y
True	True	True
True	False	True
False	True	True
False	False	False

Table 4-2   Truth table for the || operator

For example, if you want to display a message indicating an invalid age when the value of an age variable is less than 0 or more than 120, you can use either code sample in Figure 4-15.

 You create the conditional OR operator by using two vertical pipes. On most keyboards, the pipe is found above the backslash key; typing it requires that you also hold down the Shift key.

```
// using the || operator
if(age < 0 || age > 120)
    WriteLine("Age is not valid");

// using nested ifs
if(age < 0)
    WriteLine("Age is not valid");
else
    if(age > 120)
        WriteLine("Age is not valid");
```

Figure 4-15   Comparison of the **||** operator and nested **if** statements

When the **||** operator is used in an **if** statement, only one of the two Boolean expressions in the tested expression needs to be **true** for the resulting action to occur. When the first Boolean expression is **true**, the second expression is never evaluated because it doesn't matter whether the second expression is **true** or **false**. As with the **&&** operator, this feature is called *short-circuit evaluation*.

 Watch the video *Using the AND and OR Operators*.

Using the Logical AND and OR Operators

C# provides two logical operators that you generally do *not* want to use when making comparisons. However, you should learn about them because they might be used in programs written by others, and because you might use one by mistake when you intend to use a conditional operator.

The **Boolean logical AND operator** (**&**) and **Boolean logical inclusive OR operator** (**|**) work just like their **&&** and **||** (*conditional* AND and OR) counterparts, except they do not support short-circuit evaluation. That is, they always evaluate both sides of the expression, no matter what the first evaluation is. This can lead to a **side effect**, or unintended consequence. For example, in the following statement that uses **&&**, if **salesAmountForYear** is not at least 10,000, the first half of the expression is **false**, so the second half of the Boolean expression is never evaluated and **yearsOfService** is not increased.

```
if(salesAmountForYear >= 10000 && ++yearsOfService > 10)
    bonus = 200;
```

On the other hand, when a single **&** is used and **salesAmountForYear** is not at least 10,000, then even though the first half of the expression is **false**, and **bonus** is not set to 200, the second half of the expression is still evaluated, and **yearsOfService** is always increased whether it is more than 10 or not:

```
if(salesAmountForYear >= 10000 & ++yearsOfService > 10)
    bonus = 200;
```

In general, you should avoid writing expressions that contain side effects. If you want `yearsOfService` to increase no matter what the value of `salesAmountForYear` is, then you should increase it in a stand-alone statement. If you want it increased only when the sales amount exceeds 10,000, then you should increase it in a statement that depends on that decision.

The & and | operators are Boolean logical operators when they are placed between Boolean expressions. When the same operators are used between integer expressions, they are **bitwise operators** that are used to manipulate the individual bits of values.

Combining AND and OR Operators

You can combine as many AND and OR operators in an expression as you need. For example, when three conditions must be `true` before performing an action, you can use multiple AND or OR operators in the same expression. For example, in the following statement, all three Boolean variables must be true to produce the output:

```
if(isWeekendDay && isOver80Degrees && isSunny)
    WriteLine("Good day for the beach");
```

In the following statement, only one of the three Boolean variables needs to be true to produce the output:

```
if(isWeekendDay || isHoliday || amSick)
    WriteLine("No work today");
```

When you use a series of only && or only || operators in an expression, they are evaluated from left to right as far as is necessary to determine the value of the entire expression. However, when you combine && and ||operators within the same Boolean expression, they are not necessarily evaluated from left to right. Instead, the && operators take precedence, meaning they are evaluated first. For example, consider a program that determines whether a movie theater patron can purchase a discounted ticket. Assume that discounts are allowed for children (age 12 and younger) and for senior citizens (age 65 and older) who attend G-rated movies. (To keep the comparisons simple, this example assumes that movie ratings are always a single character.) The following code looks reasonable, but it produces incorrect results because the && evaluates before the ||.

```
if(age <= 12 || age >= 65 && rating == 'G')
    WriteLine("Discount applies");
```

For example, suppose that a movie patron is 10 years old and the movie rating is *R*. The patron should not receive a discount (or be allowed to see the movie!). However, within the `if` statement above, the compound expression `age >= 65 && rating == 'G'` evaluates first. It is `false`, so the `if` becomes the equivalent of `if(age <= 12 || false)`. Because `age <= 12` is `true`, the `if` becomes the equivalent of `if(true || false)`, which evaluates as `true`, and the statement *Discount applies* is displayed, which is not the intention for a 10-year-old seeing an R-rated movie.

You can use parentheses to correct the logic and force the expression age <= 12 || age >= 65 to evaluate first, as shown in the following code:

```
if((age <= 12 || age >= 65) && rating == 'G')
    WriteLine("Discount applies");
```

With the added parentheses, both age comparisons are made first. If the age value qualifies a patron for a discount, the expression is evaluated as if(true && rating == 'G'). Then the rating value must also be acceptable for the message to be displayed. Figure 4-16 shows the if statement within a complete program; note that the discount age limits are represented as named constants in the complete program. Figure 4-17 shows the execution before the parentheses were added to the if statement, and Figure 4-18 shows the output after the inclusion of the parentheses.

```
using static System.Console;
class MovieDiscount
{
    static void Main()
    {
        int age = 10;
        char rating = 'R';
        const int CHILD_AGE = 12;
        const int SENIOR_AGE = 65;
        WriteLine("When age is {0} and rating is {1}",
            age, rating);
        if((age <= CHILD_AGE || age >= SENIOR_AGE) && rating == 'G')
            WriteLine("Discount applies");
        else
            WriteLine("Full price");
    }
}
```

Figure 4-16   Movie ticket discount program using parentheses to alter precedence of Boolean evaluations

```
C:\C#\Chapter.04>MovieDiscount
When age is 10 and rating is R
Discount applies

C:\C#\Chapter.04>_
```

Figure 4-17   Incorrect results when MovieDiscount program is executed without added parentheses

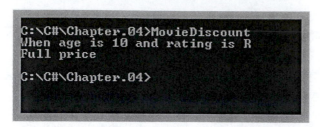

Figure 4-18   Correct results when parentheses are added to MovieDiscount program as shown in Figure 4-16

You can use parentheses for clarity in a Boolean expression, even when they are not required. For example, the following expressions both evaluate a && b first:

```
a && b || c
(a && b) || c
```

If the version with parentheses makes your intentions clearer, you should use it.

In Chapter 2, you learned that parentheses also control arithmetic operator precedence. Appendix A describes the precedence of every C# operator, which is important to understand in complicated expressions. For example, in Appendix A you can see that the arithmetic and relational operators have higher precedence than && and ||.

Watch the video *Combining AND and OR Operations.*

TWO TRUTHS & A LIE

Using Compound Expressions in if Statements

1. If a is true and b and c are false, then the value of b && c || a is true.

2. If d is true and e and f are false, then the value of e || d && f is true.

3. If g is true and h and i are false, then the value of g || h && i is true.

The false statement is #2. If d is true and e and f are false, then the value of e || d && f is false. Because you evaluate && before ||, first d && f is evaluated and found to be false, then e || false is evaluated and found to be false.

You Do It

Using AND and OR Logic

In the next steps, you create an interactive program that allows you to test AND and OR logic for yourself. The program decides whether a delivery charge applies to a shipment. If the customer lives in Zone 1 or Zone 2, then shipping is free, as long as the order contains fewer than 10 boxes. If the customer lives in another zone or if the order is too large, then a delivery charge applies.

1. Open a new file named **DemoORAndAND**, and then enter the first few lines of the program. Define constants for ZONE1, ZONE2, and the LOW_QUANTITY limit as well as variables to hold the customer's input string, which will be converted to the zone and number of boxes in the shipment.

```
using System;
using static System.Console;
class DemoORAndAND
{
    static void Main()
    {
        const int ZONE1 = 1, ZONE2 = 2;
        const int LOW_QUANTITY = 10;
        string inputString;
        int quantity;
        int deliveryZone;
```

2. Enter statements that describe the delivery charge criteria to the user and accept keyboard values for the customer's delivery zone and shipment size.

```
WriteLine("Delivery is free for zone {0} or {1}",
    ZONE1, ZONE2);
WriteLine("when the number of boxes is less than {0}",
    LOW_QUANTITY);
WriteLine("Enter delivery zone ");
inputString = ReadLine();
deliveryZone = Convert.ToInt32(inputString);
WriteLine("Enter the number of boxes in the shipment");
inputString = ReadLine();
quantity = Convert.ToInt32(inputString);
```

(continues)

(continued)

3. Write a compound `if` statement that tests whether the customer lives in Zone 1 or 2 and has a shipment consisting of fewer than 10 boxes. Notice that the first two comparisons joined with the `||` operator are contained in their own set of nested parentheses.

```
if((deliveryZone == ZONE1 || deliveryZone == ZONE2) &&
    quantity < LOW_QUANTITY)
        WriteLine("Delivery is free");
else
    WriteLine("A delivery charge applies");
```

4. Add closing curly braces for the `Main()` method and for the class, and save the program. Compile and execute the program. Enter values for the zone and shipment size. Figure 4-19 shows the output.

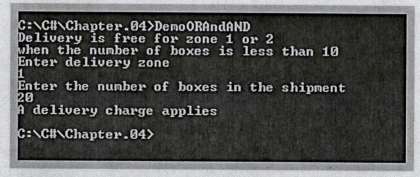

```
C:\C#\Chapter.04>DemoORAndAND
Delivery is free for zone 1 or 2
when the number of boxes is less than 10
Enter delivery zone
1
Enter the number of boxes in the shipment
20
A delivery charge applies

C:\C#\Chapter.04>
```

Figure 4-19   Sample execution of DemoORAndAND program

5. To demonstrate the importance of the nested parentheses in the `if` statement, remove the inner set of parentheses that surround the expression `deliveryZone == ZONE1 || deliveryZone == ZONE2` in the `Main()` method. Save the new version of the program, and compile it. When you execute this version of the program, the output indicates that any delivery to ZONE1 is free, but it should not be. The way the `if` statement is currently constructed, as soon as `deliveryZone == zone1` is `true`, the rest of the Boolean expression is not even evaluated. Reinstate the parentheses, and then save and compile the program. Execute it, and confirm that the output is again correct.

Making Decisions Using the switch Statement

By nesting a series of if and else statements, you can choose from any number of alternatives. For example, suppose that you want to display different strings based on a student's class year. Figure 4-20 shows the logic using nested if statements. The program segment tests the year variable four times and executes one of four statements, or displays an error message.

```
if(year == 1)
   WriteLine("Freshman");
else
   if(year == 2)
      WriteLine("Sophomore");
   else
      if(year == 3)
         WriteLine("Junior");
      else
         if(year == 4)
            WriteLine("Senior");
         else
            WriteLine("Invalid year");
```

Figure 4-20   Executing multiple alternatives using a series of if statements

An alternative to the series of nested if statements in Figure 4-20 is to use the switch structure (see Figure 4-21). The **switch structure** tests a single variable against a series of exact matches. The switch structure is sometimes called the *case structure* or the *switch-case structure*. The switch structure in Figure 4-21 is easier to read and interpret than the series of nested if statements in Figure 4-20. The if statements would become harder to read if additional choices were required and if multiple statements had to execute in each case. These additional choices and statements might also increase the potential to make mistakes.

164

```
switch(year)
{
   case 1:
      WriteLine("Freshman");
      break;
   case 2:
      WriteLine("Sophomore");
      break;
   case 3:
      WriteLine("Junior");
      break;
   case 4:
      WriteLine("Senior");
      break;
   default:
      WriteLine("Invalid year");
      break;
}
```

Figure 4-21 Executing multiple alternatives using a `switch` statement

The `switch` structure uses four new keywords:

- The keyword `switch` starts the structure and is followed immediately by a test expression (called the `switch` *expression*) enclosed in parentheses.

- The keyword `case` is followed by one of the possible values that might equal the `switch` expression. A colon follows the value. The entire expression—for example, `case 1:`—is a case label. A **case label** identifies a course of action in a `switch` structure. Most `switch` structures contain several `case` labels. The value that follows `case` is the **governing type** of the `switch` statement; this value can be `sbyte`, `byte`, `short`, `ushort`, `int`, `uint`, `long`, `ulong`, `char`, `string`, or an `enum` type. You learned about `enum` types in Chapter 2.

- The keyword `break` usually terminates a `switch` structure at the end of each `case`. Although other statements can end a `case`, `break` is the most commonly used.

- The keyword `default` optionally is used prior to any action that should occur if the test expression does not match any `case`.

 Instead of `break`, you can use a `return` statement or a `throw` statement to end a `case`. You learn about `return` statements in the chapter "Introduction to Methods" and `throw` statements in the chapter "Exception Handling."

The switch structure shown in Figure 4-21 begins by evaluating the year variable. If year is equal to any case label value, then the output statement for that case executes. The break statements that follow each output statement cause a bypass of other cases. If year does not contain the same value as any of the case label expressions, then the default statement or statements execute.

You are not required to list the case label values in ascending order, as shown in Figure 4-21, but doing so can make the statement easier for a reader to follow. You can even list the default case first, although usually it is listed last. You receive a compiler error if two or more case label values are the same in a switch statement.

In C#, an error occurs if you reach the end point of the statement list of a case section. For example, the following code is not allowed because when the year value is 1, *Freshman* is displayed, and the code reaches the end of the case. The problem could be fixed by inserting a break statement before case 2.

```
switch(year)
{
    case 1:
        WriteLine("Freshman");
    case 2:
        WriteLine("Sophomore");
        break;
}
```

Don't Do It
This code is invalid because the end of the case is reached after *Freshman* is displayed.

Not allowing code to reach the end of a case is known as the "no fall-through rule." In several other programming languages, such as Java and C++, if you write a case without a break statement, the subsequent cases execute until a break is encountered. For example, in the code above, both *Freshman* and *Sophomore* would be displayed when year is 1. However, falling through to the next case is not allowed in C#.

A switch structure does not need to contain a default case. If the test expression in a switch does not match any of the case label values, and there is no default value, then the program simply continues with the next executable statement. However, it is good programming practice to include a default label in a switch structure; that way, you provide for actions when your data does not match any case.

In C#, it is legal for a case to contain no list of statements. This feature allows you to use multiple labels to govern a list of actions. For example, in the code in Figure 4-22, *Upperclass* is displayed whether the year value is 3 or 4.

```
switch(year)
{
    case 1:
        WriteLine("Freshman");
        break;
    case 2:
        WriteLine("Sophomore");
        break;
    case 3:
    case 4:
        WriteLine("Upperclass");
        break;
    default:
        WriteLine("Invalidyear");
        break;
}
```

Cases 3 and 4 are both "Upperclass".

Figure 4-22   Example `switch` structure using multiple labels to execute a single statement block

Using a `switch` structure is never required; you can always achieve the same results with `if` statements. The `switch` statement is not as flexible as the `if` statement because you can test only one variable, and it must be tested for equality. The `switch` structure is simply a convenience you can use when there are several alternative courses of action depending on a match with a variable. Additionally, it makes sense to use a `switch` only when there are a reasonable number of specific matching values to be tested. For example, if every sale amount from \$1 to \$500 requires a 5 percent commission, it is not reasonable to test every possible dollar amount using the following code:

```
switch(saleAmount)
{
    case 1:
    case 2:
    case 3:
    // ...and so on for several hundred more cases
        commRate = .05;
        break;
```

With 500 different dollar values resulting in the same commission, one test— `if(saleAmount <= 500)`—is far more reasonable than listing 500 separate cases.

Using an Enumeration with a `switch` Statement

Using an enumeration with a `switch` structure can often be convenient. Recall from Chapter 2 that an enumeration allows you to apply values to a list of constants. For example, Figure 4-23 shows a program that uses an enumeration to represent major courses of study at a college. In the enumeration list in Figure 4-23, ACCOUNTING is assigned 1, so the other values in the list are 2, 3, 4, and 5 in order. Suppose that students who are accounting, CIS, or marketing majors are in the business division of the college, and English or math majors are in the humanities division. The program shows how the enumeration values can be used in a **switch** structure. In the program, the user enters an integer. Next, in the shaded **switch** control statement, the input integer is cast to an enumeration value. Then, enumeration values become the governing types for each case. For someone reading the code, the purposes of **enum** values such as ACCOUNTING and CIS are clearer than their integer equivalents would be. Figure 4-24 shows a typical execution of the program.

```
using System;
using static System.Console;
class DivisionBasedOnMajor
{
    enum Major
    {
        ACCOUNTING = 1, CIS, ENGLISH, MATH, MARKETING
    }
    static void Main()
    {
        int major;
        string message;
        Write("Enter major code >> ");
        major = Convert.ToInt32(ReadLine());
        switch((Major)major)
        {
            case Major.ACCOUNTING:
            case Major.CIS:
            case Major.MARKETING:
                message = "Major is in the business division";
                break;
            case Major.ENGLISH:
            case Major.MATH:
                message = "Major is in the humanities division";
                break;
            default:
                message = "Department number is invalid";
                break;
        }
        WriteLine(message);
    }
}
```

Figure 4-23 The DivisionBasedOnMajor class

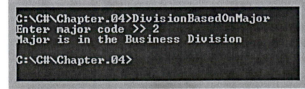

```
C:\C#\Chapter.04>DivisionBasedOnMajor
Enter major code >> 2
Major is in the Business Division

C:\C#\Chapter.04>
```

Figure 4-24 Typical execution of the DivisionBasedOnMajor program

---

TWO TRUTHS & A LIE

Making Decisions Using the `switch` Statement

1. In a `switch` statement, the keyword `case` is followed by one of the possible values that might equal the `switch` expression, and a colon follows the value.

2. The keyword `break` always terminates a `switch` structure at the end of each case.

3. A `switch` statement does not need to contain a `default` case.

The false statement is #2. The keyword `break` typically is used to terminate a `switch` structure at the end of each case, but other statements can end a case.

Using the Conditional Operator

The **conditional operator** is used as an abbreviated version of the `if-else` statement; it requires three expressions separated with a question mark and a colon. Like the `switch` structure, using the conditional operator is never required. Rather, it is simply a convenient shortcut, especially when you want to use the result immediately as an expression. The syntax of the conditional operator is:

```
testExpression ? trueResult : falseResult;
```

Unary operators use one operand; binary operators use two. The conditional operator `?:` is **ternary** because it requires three arguments: a test expression and `true` and `false` result expressions. The conditional operator is the only ternary operator in C#.

The first expression, `testExpression`, is evaluated as `true` or `false`. If it is `true`, then the entire conditional expression takes on the value of the expression before the colon (`trueResult`). If the value of the `testExpression` is `false`, then the entire expression takes on the value of the expression following the colon (`falseResult`). For example, consider the following statement:

```
biggerNum = (a > b) ? a : b;
```

This statement evaluates a > b. If a is greater than b, then the entire conditional expression takes the value of a, which then is assigned to `biggerNum`. If a is not greater than b, then the expression assumes the value of b, and b is assigned to `biggerNum`.

The conditional operator is most often applied when you want to use the result as an expression without creating an intermediate variable. For example, a conditional operator can be used directly in an output statement using either of the following formats:

```
WriteLine((testScore >= 60) ? "Pass" : "Fail");
WriteLine("\{testScore >= 60 ? "Pass" : "Fail"}");
```

In these examples, no variable was created to hold *Pass* or *Fail*. Instead one of the strings was output directly based on the `testScore` comparison. The advantage to the second format (which is new in C# 6.0) is that other variables can easily be included in the same string. For example:

```
WriteLine("\{name}'s status is \{testScore >= 60 ? "Pass" : "Fail"}");
```

If name is *Sally* and `testScore` is *62*, the output would be *Sally's status is Pass*.

Conditional expressions can be more difficult to read than `if-else` statements, but they can be used in places where `if-else` statements cannot, such as in method calls.

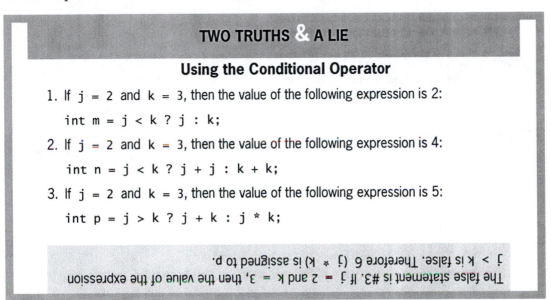

TWO TRUTHS & A LIE

Using the Conditional Operator

1. If `j = 2` and `k = 3`, then the value of the following expression is 2:

   `int m = j < k ? j : k;`

2. If `j = 2` and `k = 3`, then the value of the following expression is 4:

   `int n = j < k ? j + j : k + k;`

3. If `j = 2` and `k = 3`, then the value of the following expression is 5:

   `int p = j > k ? j + k : j * k;`

The false statement is #3. If j = 2 and k = 3, then the value of the expression j > k is false. Therefore 6 (j * k) is assigned to p.

Using the NOT Operator

You use the **NOT operator**, which is written as an exclamation point (!), to negate the result of any Boolean expression. Any expression that evaluates as `true` becomes `false` when preceded by the ! operator, and any `false` expression preceded by the ! operator becomes `true`.

 In Chapter 2 you learned that an exclamation point and equal sign together form the "not equal to" operator. The `!=` operator is a binary operator; it compares two operands. The ! operator is a unary operator; it reverses the meaning of a single Boolean expression.

For example, suppose that a monthly car insurance premium is $200 if the driver is younger than age 26 and $125 if the driver is age 26 or older. Each of the following `if` statements (which have been placed on single lines for convenience) correctly assigns the premium values:

```
if(age < 26) premium = 200; else premium = 125;
if(!(age < 26)) premium = 125; else premium = 200;
if(age >= 26) premium = 125; else premium = 200;
if(!(age>= 26)) premium = 200; else premium = 125;
```

The statements with the ! operator are somewhat more difficult to read, particularly because they require the double set of parentheses, but the result is the same in each case. Using the ! operator is clearer when the value of a Boolean variable is tested. For example, a variable initialized as bool oldEnough = (age >= 25); can become part of the relatively easy-to-read expression if(!oldEnough)... .

The ! operator has higher precedence than the && and || operators. For example, suppose that you have declared two Boolean variables named ageOverMinimum and ticketsUnderMinimum. The following expressions are evaluated in the same way:

```
ageOverMinimum && !ticketsUnderMinimum
ageOverMinimum && (!ticketsUnderMinimum)
```

Augustus de Morgan was a 19th-century mathematician who originally observed the following:

- !(a && b) is equivalent to !a || !b
- !(a || b) is equivalent to !(a && b)

TWO TRUTHS & A LIE

Using the NOT Operator

1. Assume that p, q, and r are all Boolean variables that have been assigned the value true. After the following statement executes, the value of p is still true.

```
p = !q || r;
```

2. Assume that p, q, and r are all Boolean variables that have been assigned the value true. After the following statement executes, the value of p is still true.

```
p = !(!q && !r);
```

3. Assume that p, q and r are all Boolean variables that have been assigned the value true. After the following statement executes, the value of p is still true.

```
p = !(q || !r);
```

The false statement is #3. If p, q, and r are all Boolean variables that have been assigned the value true, then after p = !(q || !r); executes, the value of p is false. First q is evaluated as true, so the entire expression within the parentheses is true. The leading NOT operator reverses that result to false and assigns it to p.

Avoiding Common Errors When Making Decisions

New programmers frequently make errors when they first learn to make decisions. As you have seen, the most frequent errors include the following:

- Using the assignment operator (=) instead of the comparison operator (==) when testing for equality

- Inserting a semicolon after the Boolean expression in an if statement instead of using it after the entire statement is completed

- Failing to block a set of statements with curly braces when several statements depend on the if or the else statement

- Failing to include a complete Boolean expression on each side of an && or || operator in an if statement

In this section, you will learn to avoid other types of errors with if statements. Programmers often make errors at the following times:

- When performing a range check incorrectly or inefficiently

- When using the wrong operator

- When using ! incorrectly

Performing Accurate and Efficient Range Checks

When new programmers must make a range check, they often introduce incorrect or inefficient code into their programs. A **range check** is a series of if statements that determine whether a value falls within a specified range. Consider a situation in which salespeople can receive one of three possible commission rates based on an integer named saleAmount. For example, a sale totaling $1000 or more earns the salesperson an 8 percent commission, a sale totaling $500 through $999 earns 6 percent of the sale amount, and any sale totaling $499 or less earns 5 percent. Using three separate if statements to test single Boolean expressions might result in some incorrect commission assignments. For example, examine the following code:

```
if(saleAmount >= 1000)
    commissionRate = 0.08;
if(saleAmount >= 500)
    commissionRate = 0.06;
if(saleAmount <= 499)
    commissionRate = 0.05;
```

> **Don't Do It**
> Although it was not the programmer's intention, both of the first two if statements are true for any saleAmount greater than or equal to 1000.

Using this code, if saleAmount is $5000, the first if statement executes. The Boolean expression (saleAmount >= 1000) evaluates as true, and 0.08 is correctly assigned to commissionRate. However, the next if expression, (saleAmount >= 500), also evaluates as true, so the commissionRate, which was 0.08, is incorrectly reset to 0.06.

A partial solution to this problem is to add an **else** clause to the statement:

```
if(saleAmount >= 1000)
    commissionRate = 0.08;
else if(saleAmount >= 500)
    commissionRate = 0.06;
else if(saleAmount <= 499)
    commissionRate = 0.05;
```

Don't Do It
If the logic reaches this point, the expression must be true, so it is a waste of time to test this condition.

The last two logical tests in this code are sometimes called else-if statements because each **else** and its subsequent **if** are placed on the same line. When the else-if format is used to test multiple cases, programmers frequently forego the traditional indentation and align each else-if with the others.

With this code, when **saleAmount** is $5000, the expression (**saleAmount >= 1000**) is true and **commissionRate** becomes 0.08; then the entire **if** structure ends. When **saleAmount** is not greater than or equal to $1000 (for example, $800), the first **if** expression is **false** and the **else** statement executes and correctly sets **commissionRate** to 0.06.

This version of the code works, but it is somewhat inefficient because it executes as follows:

- When **saleAmount** is at least $1000, the first Boolean test is **true**, so **commissionRate** is assigned .08 and the **if** structure ends.

- When **saleAmount** is under $1000 but at least $500, the first Boolean test is **false**, but the second one is **true**, so **commissionRate** is assigned .06 and the **if** structure ends.

- The only **saleAmount** values that reach the third Boolean test are under $500, so the next Boolean test, if(**saleAmount <= 499**), is always **true**. When an expression is always **true**, there is no need to evaluate it. In other words, if **saleAmount** is not at least $1000 and is also not at least $500, it must by default be less than or equal to $499.

The improved code is as follows:

```
if(saleAmount >= 1000)
    commissionRate = 0.08;
else if(saleAmount >= 500)
    commissionRate = 0.06;
else
    commissionRate = 0.05;
```

In other words, because this example uses three commission rates, two boundaries should be checked. If there were four rates, there would be three boundaries to check, and so on.

Within a nested **if-else**, processing is most efficient when the first question asked is the one that is most likely to be **true**. In other words, if you know that a large number of **saleAmount** values are over $1000, compare **saleAmount** to that value first. That way, the logic bypasses the rest of the decisions. If, however, you know that most **saleAmounts** are small, processing is most efficient when the first decision is if(**saleAmount < 500**).

Using && and || Appropriately

Beginning programmers often use the **&&** operator when they mean to use **||**, and often use **||** when they should use **&&**. Part of the problem lies in the way we use the English language. For example, your boss might request, "Display an error message when an employee's hourly pay rate is under $5.65 and when an employee's hourly pay rate is over $60." Because your boss used the word *and* in the request, you might be tempted to write a program statement like the following:

```
if(payRate < 5.65 && payRate > 60)
    WriteLine("Error in pay rate");
```

Don't Do It
This expression can never be true.

However, as a single variable, no **payRate** value can ever be both below 5.65 and over 60 at the same time, so the output statement can never execute, no matter what value **payRate** has. In this case, you must write the following statement to display the error message under the correct circumstances:

```
if(payRate < 5.65 || payRate > 60)
    WriteLine("Error in pay rate");
```

Similarly, your boss might request, "Output the names of those employees in departments 1 and 2." Because the boss used the word *and* in the request, you might be tempted to write the following:

```
if(department == 1 && department == 2)
    WriteLine("Name is: {0}", name);
```

Don't Do It
This expression can never be true.

However, the variable **department** can never contain both a 1 and a 2 at the same time, so no employee name will ever be output, no matter what department the employee is in.

The correct statement is:

```
if(department == 1 || department == 2)
    WriteLine("Name is: {0}", name);
```

Using the ! Operator Correctly

Whenever you use negatives, it is easy to make logical mistakes. For example, suppose that your boss says, "Make sure if the sales code is not *A* or *B*, the customer gets a 10 percent discount." You might be tempted to code the following:

```
if(salesCode != 'A' || salesCode != 'B')
    discount = 0.10;
```

Don't Do It
This expression can never be true.

However, this logic will result in every customer receiving the 10 percent discount because every **salesCode** is either not *A* or not *B*. For example, if **salesCode** is *A*, then it is not *B*. The expression **salesCode != 'A' || salesCode != 'B'** is always **true**. The correct statement is either one of the following:

```
if(salesCode != 'A' && salesCode != 'B')
    discount = 0.10;
```

```
if(!(salesCode == 'A' || salesCode == 'B'))
   discount = 0.10;
```

In the first example, if salesCode is not 'A' and it also is not 'B', then the discount is applied correctly. In the second example, if salesCode is 'A' or 'B', the inner Boolean expression is true, and the NOT operator (!) changes the evaluation to false, not applying the discount for *A* or *B* sales. You also could avoid the confusing negative situation by asking questions in a positive way, as in the following:

```
if(salesCode == 'A' || salesCode == 'B')
   discount = 0;
else
   discount = 0.10;
```

Watch the video *Avoiding Common Decision Errors.*

TWO TRUTHS & A LIE

Avoiding Common Errors When Making Decisions

1. If you want to display *OK* when userEntry is 12 and when it is 13, then the following is a usable C# statement:

   ```
   if(userEntry == 12 && userEntry == 13)
      WriteLine("OK");
   ```

2. If you want to display *OK* when userEntry is 20 or when highestScore is at least 70, then the following is a usable C# statement:

   ```
   if(userEntry ==20 || highestScore >= 70)
      WriteLine("OK");
   ```

3. If you want to display *OK* when userEntry is anything other than 99 or 100, then the following is a usable C# statement:

   ```
   if(userEntry != 99 && userEntry != 100)
      WriteLine("OK");
   ```

The false statement is #1. If you want to display *OK* when userEntry is 12 and when it is 13, then you want to display it when it is either 12 or 13 because it cannot be both simultaneously. The expression userEntry == 12 && userEntry == 13 can never be true. The correct Boolean expression is userEntry == 12 || userEntry == 13.

Decision-Making Issues in GUI Programs

Making a decision within a method in a GUI application is no different from making one in a console application; you can use if, if...else, and switch statements in the same ways. For example, Figure 4-25 shows a GUI Form that determines a movie patron discount as described in a program earlier in this chapter. Patrons who are under 12 or over 65 and are seeing a G-rated movie receive a discount, and any other combination pays full price. Figure 4-26 contains the Click() method that makes the discount determination based on age and rating after a user clicks the *Discount?* button. The Boolean expression tested in the if statement in this method is identical to the one in the console version of the program in Figure 4-16.

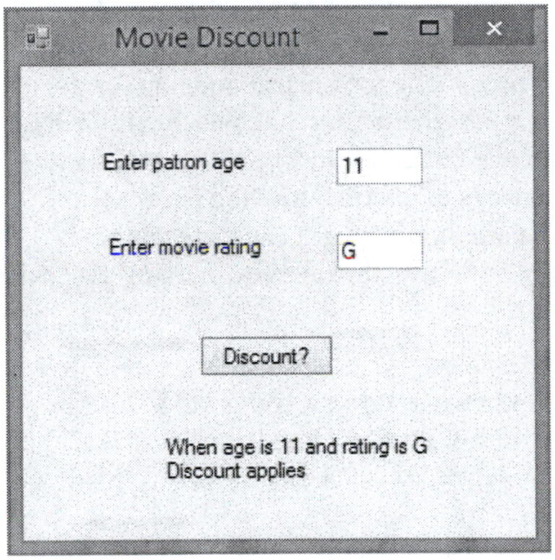

Figure 4-25   The Movie Discount Form

```
private void discountButton_Click(object sender,
   EventArgs e)
{
   int age;
   char rating;
   const int CHILD_AGE = 12;
   const int SENIOR_AGE = 65;
   age = Convert.ToInt32(textBox1.Text);
   rating = Convert.ToChar(textBox2.Text);
   outputLabel.Text = String.Format
      ("When age is {0} and rating is {1}", age, rating);
   if ((age <= CHILD_AGE || age >= SENIOR_AGE) && rating == 'G')
      outputLabel.Text += "\nDiscount applies";
   else
      outputLabel.Text += "\nFull price";
}
```

Figure 4-26   The discountButton_Click() method for the Form in Figure 4-25

Event-driven programs often require fewer coded decisions than console applications. That's because in event-driven programs, some events are determined by the user's actions when the program is running (also called **at runtime**), rather than by the programmer's coding beforehand. You might say that in many situations, a console-based application must act, but an event-driven application has to *react*.

Suppose that you want to write a program in which the user must select whether to receive instructions in English or Spanish. In a console application, you would issue a prompt such as the following:

Which language do you prefer? Enter 1 for English or 2 for Spanish >>

The program would accept the user's entry, make a decision about it, and take appropriate action. However, in a GUI application, you are more likely to place controls on a Form to get a user's response. For example, you might use two Buttons—one for English and one for Spanish. The user clicks a Button, and an appropriate method executes. No decision is written in the program because a different event is fired from each Button, causing execution of a different Click() method. The interactive environment decides which method is called, so the programmer does not have to code a decision. (Of course, you might alternately place a TextBox on a Form and ask a user to enter a 1 or a 2. In that case, the decision-making process would be identical to that in the console-based program.)

An additional benefit to having the user click a button to select an option is that the user cannot enter an invalid value. For example, if the user enters a letter in response to a prompt for an integer, the program will fail unless you write additional code to handle the mistake. However, if the user has a limited selection of buttons to click, no invalid entry can be made.

TWO TRUTHS & A LIE

Decision-Making Issues in GUI Programs

1. Event-driven programs can contain if, if...else, and switch statements.

2. Event-driven programs often require fewer coded decisions than console applications.

3. Event-driven programs usually contain more coded decisions than corresponding console-based applications.

The false statement is #3. Event-driven programs often require fewer coded decisions because user actions, such as clicking a button, are often used to trigger different methods.

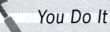

You Do It

Creating a GUI Application That Uses an Enumeration and a switch Structure

In these steps, you create a GUI application for the Chatterbox Diner that allows a user to enter a day and see the special meal offered that day. Creating the program provides experience using an enumeration in a switch structure.

1. Open a new project in Visual Studio, and name it **DailySpecial**.

2. Design a Form like the one in Figure 4-27 that prompts the user for a day number and allows the user to enter it in a TextBox. Name the TextBox **dayBox** and the Button **specialButton**.

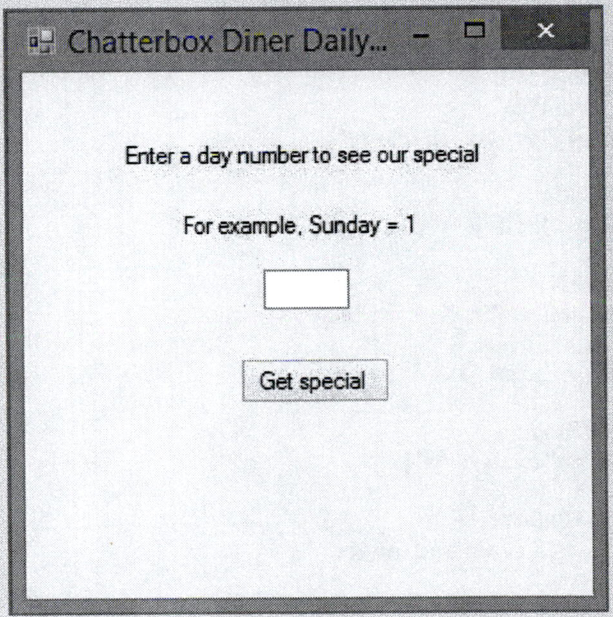

Enter a day number to see our special

For example, Sunday = 1

Get special

Figure 4-27 The Daily Special form

3. Below the Button, add a Label named **outputLabel** and delete its text.

(continues)

(continued)

178

4. Double-click **specialButton** to create a specialButton_Click() method shell. Above the method, add an enumeration for the days of the week as follows:

```
enum Day
{
    SUNDAY = 1, MONDAY, TUESDAY, WEDNESDAY,
        THURSDAY, FRIDAY, SATURDAY
}
```

5. Within the method, declare an integer and accept a value from the TextBox, and then declare a string to hold the daily special.

```
int day = Convert.ToInt32(dayBox.Text);
string special;
```

6. Add a switch structure that lists the daily specials as follows:

```
switch ((Day)day)
{
    case Day.SUNDAY:
        special = "fried chicken";
        break;
    case Day.MONDAY:
        special = "Sorry - closed";
        break;
    case Day.TUESDAY:
    case Day.WEDNESDAY:
    case Day.THURSDAY:
        special = "meat loaf";
        break;
    case Day.FRIDAY:
        special = "fish fry";
        break;
    case Day.SATURDAY:
        special = "liver and onions";
        break;
    default:
        special = "Invalid day";
        break;
}
```

7. Following the completed case structure, assign the result to the Text property of outputLabel:

```
outputLabel.Text = "Today's special is " + special;
```

8. Save, compile, and execute the application. The appropriate special is displayed for each day of the week.

Chapter Summary

- A flowchart is a pictorial tool that helps you understand a program's logic. A decision structure is one that involves choosing between alternative courses of action based on some value within a program.

- The if statement makes a single-alternative decision using the keyword if, followed by parentheses that contain a Boolean expression. When the expression is true, the statement body executes. The body can be a single statement or a block of statements.

- When you make a dual-alternative decision, you can use an if-else statement. You can block multiple statements after an else so they all execute when the evaluated expression is false.

- The conditional AND operator (&&) takes action when two operand Boolean expressions are both true. The conditional OR operator (||) takes action when at least one of two operand Boolean expressions is true. When && and || operators are combined within the same Boolean expression without parentheses, the && operators take precedence, meaning their Boolean values are evaluated first.

- The switch statement tests a single variable against a series of exact matches.

- The conditional operator is used as an abbreviated version of the if-else statement. It requires three expressions separated with a question mark and a colon.

- The NOT operator, which is written as an exclamation point (!), negates the result of any Boolean expression.

- Common errors when making decisions include using the assignment operator instead of the comparison operator, inserting a semicolon after the Boolean expression in an if statement, failing to block a set of statements when they should be blocked, and performing a range check incorrectly or inefficiently.

- Making a decision within a method in a GUI application is no different from making one in a console application; you can use if, if...else, and switch statements in the same ways. However, event-driven programs often require fewer coded decisions than console applications because some events are determined by the user's actions when the program is running, rather than by the programmer's coding beforehand.

Key Terms

Pseudocode is a tool that helps programmers plan a program's logic by writing plain English statements.

A **flowchart** is a tool that helps programmers plan a program's logic by writing program steps in diagram form, as a series of shapes connected by arrows.

A **sequence structure** is a unit of program logic in which one step follows another unconditionally.

A **decision structure** is a unit of program logic that involves choosing between alternative courses of action based on some value.

An **if statement** is used to make a single-alternative decision.

A **block** is a collection of one or more statements contained within a pair of curly braces.

A **control statement** is the part of a structure that determines whether the subsequent block of statements executes.

A **nested if** statement is one in which one decision structure is contained within another.

Dual-alternative decisions have two possible outcomes.

An **if-else statement** performs a dual-alternative decision.

The **conditional AND operator** (or simply the **AND operator**) determines whether two expressions are both **true**; it is written using two ampersands (**&&**).

Truth tables are diagrams used in mathematics and logic to help describe the truth of an entire expression based on the truth of its parts.

Short-circuit evaluation is the C# feature in which parts of an AND or OR expression are evaluated only as far as necessary to determine whether the entire expression is **true** or **false**.

The **conditional OR operator** (or simply the **OR operator**) determines whether at least one of two conditions is **true**; it is written using two pipes (**| |**).

The **Boolean logical AND operator** determines whether two expressions are both **true**; it is written using a single ampersand (**&**). Unlike the conditional AND operator, it does not use short-circuit evaluation.

The **Boolean logical inclusive OR operator** determines whether at least one of two conditions is **true**; it is written using a single pipe (**|**). Unlike the conditional OR operator, it does not use short-circuit evaluation.

A **side effect** is an unintended consequence.

Bitwise operators are used to manipulate the individual bits of values.

The **switch structure** tests a single variable against a series of exact matches.

A **case label** identifies a course of action in a **switch** structure.

The **governing type** of a **switch** statement is established by the **switch** expression and can be **sbyte**, **byte**, **short**, **ushort**, **int**, **uint**, **long**, **ulong**, **char**, **string**, or **enum**.

The **conditional operator** is used as an abbreviated version of the **if-else** statement; it requires three expressions separated by a question mark and a colon.

A **ternary** operator requires three arguments.

The **NOT operator** (!) negates the result of any Boolean expression.

A **range check** is a series of **if** statements that determine whether a value falls within a specified range.

At runtime is a phrase that means *during the time a program is running.*

Review Questions

1. What is the output of the following code segment?

```
int a = 3, b = 4;
if(a == b)
    Write("Black");
    WriteLine("White");
```

   a. Black

   b. White

   c. BlackWhite

   d. nothing

2. What is the output of the following code segment?

```
int a = 3, b = 4;
if(a < b)
{
    Write("Black");
    WriteLine("White");
}
```

   a. Black

   b. White

   c. BlackWhite

   d. nothing

3. What is the output of the following code segment?

```
int a = 3, b = 4;
if(a > b)
    Write("Black");
else
    WriteLine("White");
```

   a. Black

   b. White

   c. BlackWhite

   d. nothing

4. If the following code segment compiles correctly, what do you know about the variable x?

```
if(x) WriteLine("OK");
```

   a. x is an integer variable.

   b. x is a Boolean variable.

   c. x is greater than 0.

   d. none of these

5. What is the output of the following code segment?

```
int c = 6, d = 12;
if(c > d);
    Write("Green");
    WriteLine("Yellow");
```

a. Green

c. GreenYellow

b. Yellow

d. nothing

6. What is the output of the following code segment?

```
int c = 6, d = 12;
if(c < d)
    if(c > 8)
        Write("Green");
    else
        Write("Yellow");
else
    Write("Blue");
```

a. Green

c. Blue

b. Yellow

d. nothing

7. What is the output of the following code segment?

```
int e = 5, f = 10;
if(e < f && f < 0)
    Write("Red");
else
    Write("Orange");
```

a. Red

c. RedOrange

b. Orange

d. nothing

8. What is the output of the following code segment?

```
int e = 5, f = 10;
if(e < f || f < 0)
    Write("Red");
else
    Write("Orange");
```

a. Red

c. RedOrange

b. Orange

d. nothing

9. Which of the following expressions is equivalent to the following code segment?

```
if(g > h)
    if(g < k)
        Write("Brown");
```

   a. `if(g > h && g < k) Write("Brown");`

   b. `if(g > h && < k) Write("Brown");`

   c. `if(g > h || g < k) Write("Brown");`

   d. two of these

183

10. Which of the following expressions assigns `true` to a Boolean variable named `isIDValid` when `idNumber` is both greater than 1000 and less than or equal to 9999, or else is equal to 123456?

   a. `isIDValid = (idNumber > 1000 && idNumber <= 9999 && idNumber == 123456)`

   b. `isIDValid = (idNumber > 1000 && idNumber <= 9999 || idNumber == 123456)`

   c. `isIDValid = ((idNumber > 1000 && idNumber <= 9999) || idNumber == 123456)`

   d. two of these

11. Which of the following expressions is equivalent to `a || b && c || d`?

   a. `a && b || c && d`

   b. `(a || b) && (c || d)`

   c. `a || (b && c) || d`

   d. two of these

12. How many `case` labels would a `switch` statement require to be equivalent to the following `if` statement?

```
if(v == 1)
    WriteLine("one");
else
    WriteLine("two");
```

   a. zero

   b. one

   c. two

   d. impossible to tell

13. Falling through a `switch case` is most often prevented by using the _____ statement.

   a. `break`

   b. `default`

   c. `case`

   d. `end`

14. If the test expression in a `switch` does not match any of the `case` values, and there is no `default` value, then _____.

 a. a compiler error occurs

 b. a runtime error occurs

 c. the program continues with the next executable statement

 d. the expression is incremented and the `case` values are tested again

15. Which of the following is equivalent to the following statement:

```
if(m == 0)
    d = 0;
else
    d = 1;
```

 a. `d = (m == 0) : d = 0, d = 1;`

 b. `m ? (d = 0); (d = 1);`

 c. `m == 0; d = 0; d = 1?`

 d. `d = (m == 0) ? 0 : 1;`

16. Which of the following C# expressions is equivalent to `a < b && b < c`?

 a. `c > b > a`   c. `!(b <= a) && b < c`

 b. `a < b && c >= b`   d. two of these

17. Which of the following C# expressions means, "If `itemNumber` is not 8 or 9, add TAX to `price`"?

 a. `if(itemNumber != 8 || itemNumber != 9)`
    `price = price + TAX;`

 b. `if(itemNumber != 8 && itemNumber != 9)`
    `price = price + TAX;`

 c. `if(itemNumber != 8 && !=         9)`
    `price = price + TAX;`

 d. two of these

18. Which of the following C# expressions means, "If `itemNumber` is 1 or 2 and `quantity` is 12 or more, add TAX to `price`"?

 a. `if(itemNumber = 1 || itemNumber = 2 && quantity >=12)`
    `price = price + TAX;`

 b. `if(itemNumber == 1 || itemNumber == 2 || quantity >=12)`
    `price = price + TAX;`

 c. `if(itemNumber == 1 && itemNumber == 2 && quantity >=12)`
    `price = price + TAX;`

 d. none of these

19. Which of the following C# expressions means, "If itemNumber is 5 and zone is 1 or 3, add TAX to price"?

    a. if(itemNumber == 5 && zone == 1 || zone == 3)
           price = price + TAX;

    b. if(itemNumber == 5 && (zone == 1 || zone == 3))
           price = price + TAX;

    c. if(itemNumber == 5 && (zone ==1 || 3))
           price = price + TAX;

    d. two of these

20. Which of the following C# expressions results in TAX being added to price if the integer itemNumber is not 100?

    a. if(itemNumber != 100)
           price = price + TAX;

    b. if(!(itemNumber == 100))
           price = price + TAX;

    c. if(itemNumber <100 || itemNumber > 100)
           price = price + TAX;

    d. all of these

Exercises

Programming Exercises

1. Write a program named **CheckCredit** that prompts users to enter a purchase price for an item. If the value entered is greater than a credit limit of $5,000, display an error message; otherwise, display *Approved*.

2. Write a program named **Twitter** that accepts a user's message and determines whether it is short enough for a social networking service that does not accept messages of more than 140 characters.

3. Write a program named **Admission** for a college's admissions office. The user enters a numeric high school grade point average (for example, 3.2) and an admission test score. Display the message *Accept* if the student meets either of the following requirements:

    - A grade point average of 3.0 or higher, and an admission test score of at least 60

    - A grade point average of less than 3.0, and an admission test score of at least 80

    - If the student does not meet either of the qualification criteria, display *Reject*.

4. The Saffir-Simpson Hurricane Scale classifies hurricanes into five categories numbered 1 through 5. Write an application named **Hurricane** that outputs a hurricane's category based on the user's input of the wind speed. Category 5 hurricanes have sustained winds of at least 157 miles per hour. The minimum sustained wind speeds for categories 4 through 1 are 130, 111, 96, and 74 miles per hour, respectively. Any storm with winds of less than 74 miles per hour is not a hurricane.

5. Write a program named **CheckMonth** that prompts a user to enter a birth month. If the value entered is greater than 12 or less than 1, display an error message; otherwise, display the valid month with a message such as *3 is a valid month.*

6. Write a program named **CheckMonth2** that prompts a user to enter a birth month and day. Display an error message if the month is invalid (not 1 through 12) or the day is invalid for the month (for example, not between 1 and 31 for January or between 1 and 29 for February). If the month and day are valid, display them with a message.

7. You can create a random number that is at least `min` but less than `max` using the following statements:

```
Random ranNumberGenerator = new Random();
int randomNumber;
randomNumber = ranNumberGenerator.Next(min, max);
```

Write a program named **GuessingGame** that generates a random number between 1 and 10. (In other words, `min` is 1 and `max` is 11.) Ask a user to guess the random number, then display the random number and a message indicating whether the user's guess was too high, too low, or correct.

8. In the game Rock Paper Scissors, two players simultaneously choose one of three options: rock, paper, or scissors. If both players choose the same option, then the result is a tie. However, if they choose differently, the winner is determined as follows:

- Rock beats scissors, because a rock can break a pair of scissors.

- Scissors beats paper, because scissors can cut paper.

- Paper beats rock, because a piece of paper can cover a rock.

Create a game in which the computer randomly chooses rock, paper, or scissors. Let the user enter a character, *r*, *p*, or *s*, each representing one of the three choices. Then, determine the winner. Save the application as **RockPaperScissors.cs**.

9. Create a lottery game application named **Lottery**. Generate three random numbers, each between 1 and 4. Allow the user to guess three numbers. Compare each of the user's guesses to the three random numbers, and display a message that includes the

user's guess, the randomly determined three-digit number, and the amount of money the user has won as follows:

Matching Numbers	Award ($)
Any one matching	10
Two matching	100
Three matching, not in order	1000
Three matching in exact order	10,000
No matches	0

Make certain that your application accommodates repeating digits. For example, if a user guesses 1, 2, and 3, and the randomly generated digits are 1, 1, and 1, do not give the user credit for three correct guesses—just one.

Debugging Exercises

1. Each of the following files in the Chapter.04 folder of your downloadable student files has syntax and/or logical errors. In each case, determine the problem, and fix the program. After you correct the errors, save each file using the same filename preceded with *Fixed*. For example, save DebugFour1.cs as **FixedDebugFour1.cs**.

   a. DebugFour1.cs   c. DebugFour3.cs

   b. DebugFour2.cs   d. DebugFour4.cs

Case Problems

1. In Chapter 2, you created an interactive application named **GreenvilleRevenue**, and in Chapter 3 you created a GUI version of the application named **GreenvilleRevenueGUI**. The programs prompt a user for the number of contestants entered in this year's and last year's Greenville Idol competition, and then they display the revenue expected for this year's competition if each

contestant pays a $25 entrance fee. The programs also display a statement that compares the number of contestants each year. Now, replace that statement with one of the following messages:

- If the competition has more than twice as many contestants as last year, display *The competition is more than twice as big this year!*

- If the competition is bigger than last year's but not more than twice as big, display *The competition is bigger than ever!*

- If the competition is smaller than last year's, display, *A tighter race this year! Come out and cast your vote!*

2. In Chapter 2, you created an interactive application named **MarshallsRevenue**, and in Chapter 3 you created a GUI version of the application named **MarshallsRevenueGUI**. The programs prompt a user for the number of interior and exterior murals scheduled to be painted during the next month by Marshall's Murals. Next, the programs compute the expected revenue for each type of mural when interior murals cost $500 each and exterior murals cost $750 each. The applications also display the total expected revenue and a statement that indicates whether more interior murals are scheduled than exterior ones. Now, modify one or both of the applications to accept a numeric value for the month being scheduled and to modify the pricing as follows:

- Because of uncertain weather conditions, exterior murals cannot be painted in December through February, so change the number of exterior murals to 0 for those months.

- Marshall prefers to paint exterior murals in April, May, September, and October. To encourage business, he charges only $699 for an exterior mural during those months. Murals in other months continue to cost $750.

- Marshall prefers to paint interior murals in July and August, so he charges only $450 for an interior mural during those months. Murals in other months continue to cost $500.

CHAPTER 5

Looping

In this chapter you will:

- ◎ Learn how to create loops using the `while` statement
- ◎ Learn how to create loops using the `for` statement
- ◎ Learn how to create loops using the `do` statement
- ◎ Use nested loops
- ◎ Accumulate totals
- ◎ Understand how to improve loop performance
- ◎ Learn about looping issues in GUI programs

In the previous chapter, you learned how computers make decisions by evaluating Boolean expressions. Looping allows a program to repeat tasks based on the value of a Boolean expression. For example, programs that produce thousands of paychecks or invoices rely on the ability to loop to repeat instructions. Likewise, programs that repeatedly prompt users for a valid credit card number or for the correct answer to a tutorial question run more efficiently with loop structures. In this chapter, you will learn to create loops in C# programs. Computer programs seem smart due to their ability to make decisions; looping makes programs seem powerful.

Creating Loops with the `while` Statement

A **loop** is a structure that allows repeated execution of a block of statements. Within a looping structure, a Boolean expression is evaluated. If it is **true**, a block of statements called the **loop body** executes and the Boolean expression is evaluated again. As long as the expression is **true**, the statements in the loop body continue to execute and the loop-controlling Boolean expression continues to be reevaluated. When the Boolean evaluation is **false**, the loop ends. Figure 5-1 shows a diagram of the logic of a loop. One execution of any loop is called an **iteration**.

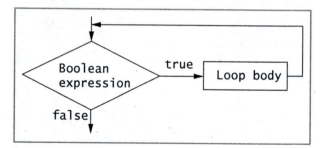

Figure 5-1   Flowchart of a loop structure

You can use a **while loop** to execute a body of statements continuously as long as the loop's test condition continues to be **true**. A while loop consists of the following:

- the keyword while
- a Boolean expression within parentheses
- the loop body

The evaluated Boolean expression in a while statement can be either a single Boolean expression or a compound expression that uses ANDs and ORs. The body can be a single statement or any number of statements surrounded by curly braces.

For example, the following code shows an integer declaration followed by a loop that causes the message *Hello* to display (theoretically) forever because there is no code to end the loop. A loop that never ends is called an **infinite loop**. An infinite loop might not actually execute infinitely. All programs run with the help of computer memory and hardware, both of which have finite capacities, so a program with an infinite loop might eventually fail and end. However, any loop that potentially runs forever is called infinite.

```
int number = 1;
while(number > 0)
    WriteLine("Hello");
```

In this loop, the expression `number > 0` evaluates as `true`, and *Hello* is displayed. The expression `number > 0` evaluates as `true` again, and *Hello* is displayed again. Because the value of `number` is never altered, the loop runs forever, evaluating the same Boolean expression and repeatedly displaying *Hello* as long as computer memory and hardware allow.

 Writing an infinite loop is always a bad idea, although even experienced programmers write them by accident. If you ever find yourself in the midst of an infinite loop in a console application, you can break out by holding down the Ctrl key and pressing the C key or the Break (Pause) key. In a GUI program, you can simply close the `Frame` that is hosting the application.

To make a `while` loop end correctly, three separate actions should occur:

- A variable, the **loop control variable**, is initialized (before entering the loop).

- The loop control variable is tested in the `while` expression.

- The body of the loop must take some action that alters the value of the loop control variable (so that the `while` expression eventually evaluates as `false`).

For example, Figure 5-2 shows the logic for a loop that displays *Hello* four times. The variable `number` is initialized to 1, and a constant, `LIMIT`, is initialized to 5. The variable is less than `LIMIT`, and so the loop body executes. The loop body shown in Figure 5-2 contains two statements. The first displays *Hello*, and the second adds 1 to `number`. The next time `number` is evaluated, its value is 2, which is still less than `LIMIT`, so the loop body executes again. *Hello* displays a third time, and `number` becomes 4; then *Hello* displays a fourth time, and `number` becomes 5. Now when the expression `number < LIMIT` is evaluated, it is `false`, so the loop ends. If there were any subsequent statements following the `while` loop's closing curly brace, they would execute after the loop was finished.

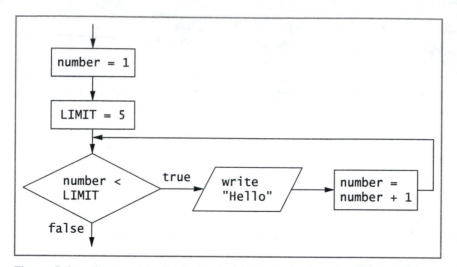

Figure 5-2 Flowchart for the logic of a `while` loop whose body executes four times

Figure 5-3 shows a C# program that uses the same logic as diagrammed in Figure 5-2. After the declarations, the shaded `while` expression compares `number` to `LIMIT`. The two statements that execute each time the Boolean expression is `true` are blocked using a pair of curly braces. Figure 5-4 shows the output.

```
using static System.Console;
class FourHellos
{
    static void Main()
    {
        int number = 1;
        const int LIMIT = 5;
        while(number < LIMIT)
        {
            WriteLine("Hello");
            number = number + 1;
        }
    }
}
```

Figure 5-3 A program that contains a `while` loop whose body executes four times

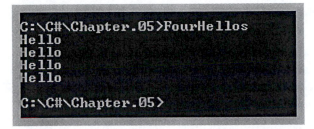

```
C:\C#\Chapter.05>FourHellos
Hello
Hello
Hello
Hello

C:\C#\Chapter.05>
```

Figure 5-4 Output of the FourHellos program

 Recall from Chapter 2 that you also can use a shortcut operator to increase the value of a variable by 1. Instead of number = number + 1, you could achieve the same final result by writing number++, ++number, or number += 1. Because counting is such a common feature of loops, you might want to review the difference between the prefix and postfix increment operators. A video called *Using Shortcut Arithmetic Operators* accompanies Chapter 2.

The curly braces surrounding the body of the while loop in Figure 5-3 are important. If they are omitted, the while loop ends at the end of the statement that displays *Hello*. Without the braces, adding 1 to number would no longer be part of the loop body, so an infinite loop would be created. Even if the statement that increases number was indented under the while statement, it would not be part of the loop without the surrounding curly braces. Figure 5-5 shows the incorrect logic that would result from omitting the curly braces. For clarity, many programmers recommend surrounding a loop body with curly braces even when there is only one statement in the body.

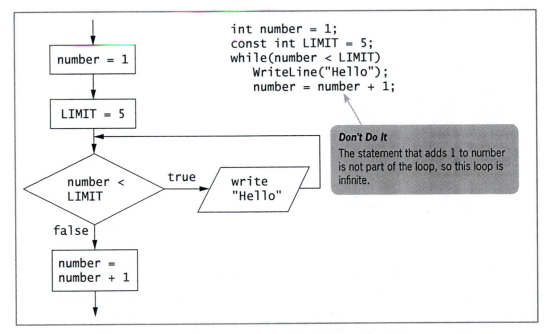

Figure 5-5 Incorrect logic when curly braces are omitted from the loop in the FourHellos program

Because this code contains no curly braces, the while statement ends with the first semicolon, and an infinite loop is created.

Also, if a semicolon is mistakenly placed at the end of the partial statement, as in Figure 5-6, then the loop is also infinite. This loop has an **empty body**, or a body with no statements. In this case, number is initialized to 1, the Boolean expression number < LIMIT evaluates, and because it is true, the loop body is entered. Because the loop body is empty, ending at the semicolon, no action takes place, and the Boolean expression evaluates again. It is still true (nothing has changed), so the empty body is entered again, and the infinite loop continues. The program can never progress to either the statement that displays *Hello* or the statement that increases the value of number. The fact that these two statements are blocked using curly braces has no effect because of the incorrectly placed semicolon.

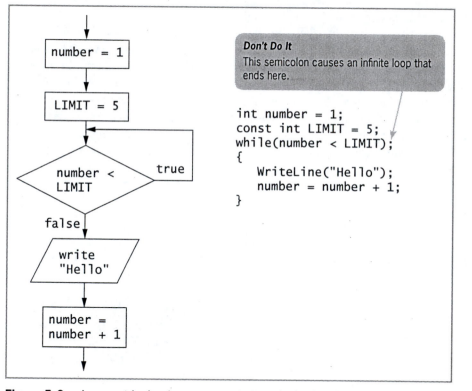

Figure 5-6   Incorrect logic when an unwanted semicolon is mistakenly added to the loop in the FourHellos program

Because this code contains an unwanted semicolon, the loop has an empty body.

Within a correctly functioning loop's body, you can change the value of the loop control variable in a number of ways. Many loop control variable values are altered by **incrementing**, or adding to them, as in Figures 5-2 and 5-3. Other loops are controlled by reducing, or **decrementing**, a variable and testing whether the value remains greater than some benchmark value.

A loop for which the number of iterations is predetermined is called a **definite loop** or **counted loop**. Often, the value of a loop control variable is not altered by arithmetic but instead is altered by user input. For example, perhaps you want to continue performing some task while the user indicates a desire to continue. In that case, you do not know when you write the program whether the loop will be executed two times, 200 times, or not at all. This type of loop is an **indefinite loop**.

Consider a program that displays a bank balance and asks if the user wants to see what the balance will be after one year of interest has accumulated. Each time the user indicates she wants to continue, an increased balance appears. When the user finally indicates she has had enough, the program ends. The program appears in Figure 5-7, and a typical execution appears in Figure 5-8.

```
using System;
using static System.Console;
class LoopingBankBal
{
    static void Main()
    {
        double bankBal = 1000;
        const double INT_RATE = 0.04;
        string inputString;
        char response;
        Write("Do you want to see your balance? Y or N...");
        inputString = ReadLine();
        response = Convert.ToChar(inputString);
        while(response == 'Y')
        {
            WriteLine("Bank balance is {0}",
            bankBal.ToString("C"));
            bankBal = bankBal + bankBal * INT_RATE;
            Write("Do you want to see next year's balance? Y or N...");
            inputString = ReadLine();
            response = Convert.ToChar(inputString);
        }
        WriteLine("Have a nice day!");
    }
}
```

Figure 5-7   The LoopingBankBal program

```
C:\C#\Chapter.05>LoopingBankBal
Do you want to see your balance? Y or N ...Y
Bank balance is $1,000.00
Do you want to see next year's balance? Y or N ...Y
Bank balance is $1,040.00
Do you want to see next year's balance? Y or N ...Y
Bank balance is $1,081.60
Do you want to see next year's balance? Y or N ...N
Have a nice day!

C:\C#\Chapter.05>
```

Figure 5-8   Typical execution of the `LoopingBankBal` program

The program shown in Figure 5-7 continues to display bank balances while the response is *Y*. It could also be written to display while the response is not *N*, as in `while(response != 'N')`.... A value such as `'Y'` or `'N'` that a user must supply to stop a loop is a **sentinel value**.

In the program shown in Figure 5-7, the loop control variable is `response`. It is initialized by the first input and tested with the Boolean expression `response == 'Y'`. If the user types any character other than *Y*, then the loop body never executes; instead, the next statement to execute displays *Have a nice day!*. However, if the user enters *Y*, then all five statements within the loop body execute. The current balance is displayed, and the program increases the balance by the interest rate value; this value will not be displayed unless the user requests another loop repetition. Within the loop, the program prompts the user and reads in a new value for `response`. This input statement is the one that potentially alters the loop control variable. The loop ends with a closing curly brace, and program control returns to the top of the loop, where the Boolean expression is tested again. If the user typed *Y* at the last prompt, then the loop is reentered, and the increased `bankBal` value that was calculated during the last loop cycle is displayed.

In C#, character data is case sensitive. If a program tests `response == 'Y'`, a user response of *y* will result in a `false` evaluation. Beware of the pitfall of writing a loop similar to `while(response != 'Y' ||` `response != 'y')`... to test both for uppercase and lowercase versions of the response. Every character is either not *Y* or not *y*, even *Y* and *y*. A correct loop might begin with the following:

```
while(response != 'Y' && response != 'y')…
```

    Watch the video *Using the `while` Loop*.

TWO TRUTHS & A LIE

Creating Loops with the while Statement

1. To make a while loop that executes correctly, a loop control variable is initialized before entering the loop.

2. To make a while loop that executes correctly, the loop control variable is tested in the while expression.

3. To make a while loop that executes correctly, the body of the while statement must never alter the value of the loop control variable.

The false statement is #3. To make a while loop that executes correctly, the body of the while statement must take some action that alters the value of the loop control variable.

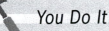 *You Do It*

Using a while Loop

In the next steps, you write a program that continuously prompts the user for a valid ID number until the user enters one. For this application, assume that a valid ID number must be between 1000 and 9999, inclusive.

1. Open a new project named **ValidID**, and enter the beginning of the program by declaring variables for an ID number, the user's input, and constant values for the highest and lowest acceptable ID numbers.

```
using System;
using static System.Console;
class ValidID
{
    static void Main()
    {
        int idNum;
        string input;
        const int LOW = 1000;
        const int HIGH = 9999;
```

(continues)

(continued)

2. Add code to prompt the user for an ID number, and to then convert it to an integer.

```
Write("Enter an ID number: ");
input = ReadLine();
idNum = Convert.ToInt32(input);
```

3. Create a loop that continues while the entered ID number is out of range. While the number is invalid, explain valid ID parameters and reprompt the user, converting the input to an integer.

```
while(idNum < LOW || idNum > HIGH)
{
    WriteLine("{0} is an invalid ID number", idNum);
    Write("ID numbers must be ");
    WriteLine("between {0} and {1} inclusive", LOW, HIGH);
    Write("Enter an ID number: ");
    input = ReadLine();
    idNum = Convert.ToInt32(input);
}
```

4. When the user eventually enters a valid ID number, the loop ends. Display a message, and add closing curly braces for the `Main()` method and for the class.

```
    WriteLine("ID number {0} is valid", idNum);
    }
}
```

5. Save the file, compile the program, and execute it. A typical execution during which the user makes several invalid entries is shown in Figure 5-9.

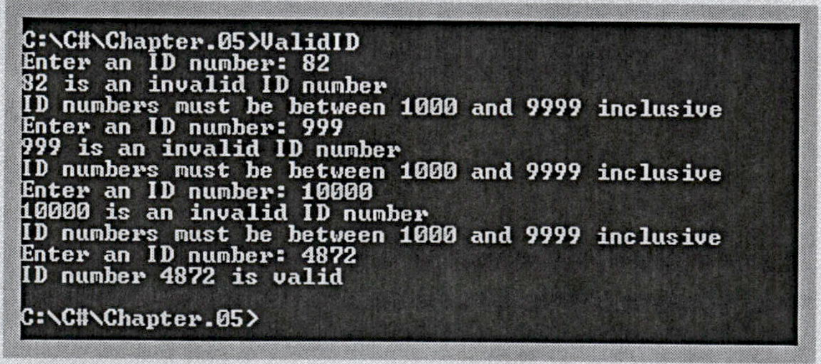

```
C:\C#\Chapter.05>ValidID
Enter an ID number: 82
82 is an invalid ID number
ID numbers must be between 1000 and 9999 inclusive
Enter an ID number: 999
999 is an invalid ID number
ID numbers must be between 1000 and 9999 inclusive
Enter an ID number: 10000
10000 is an invalid ID number
ID numbers must be between 1000 and 9999 inclusive
Enter an ID number: 4872
ID number 4872 is valid

C:\C#\Chapter.05>
```

Figure 5-9   Typical execution of the `ValidID` program

Creating Loops with the for Statement

The LoopingBankBal program in Figure 5-7 contains an indefinite loop because the number of executions is not predetermined; each time the program executes, the user might continue the loop a different number of times. You can use a while loop for either definite or indefinite loops. To write either type of while loop, you initialize a loop control variable, and as long as its test expression is true, you continue to execute the body of the while loop. To avoid an infinite loop, the body of the while loop must contain a statement that alters the loop control variable.

Because you need definite loops (ones with a predefined number of iterations) so frequently when you write programs, C# provides a shorthand way to create such loops. With a **for loop**, you can indicate the starting value for the loop control variable, the test condition that controls loop entry, and the expression that alters the loop control variable, all in one convenient place.

You begin a for statement with the keyword for followed by a set of parentheses. Within the parentheses are three sections separated by exactly two semicolons. The three sections are usually used for:

- Initializing the loop control variable
- Testing the loop control variable
- Updating the loop control variable

As with an if or a while statement, you can use a single statement as the body of a for loop, or you can use a block of statements enclosed in curly braces. The while and for statements shown in Figure 5-10 produce the same output—the integers 1 through 10.

```
// Declare loop control variable and limit
int x;
const int LIMIT = 10;

// Using a while loop to display 1 through 10
x = 1;
while(x <= LIMIT)
{
    WriteLine(x);
    ++x;
}

// Using a for loop to display 1 through 10
for(x = 1; x <= LIMIT; ++x)
    WriteLine(x);
```

Figure 5-10   Displaying integers 1 through 10 with while and for loops

 The amount by which a loop control variable increases or decreases on each cycle through the loop is often called the **step value**. That's because in the BASIC programming language, and its descendent, the Visual Basic language, the keyword STEP is actually used in for loops.

Within the parentheses of the `for` statement shown in Figure 5-10, the initialization section prior to the first semicolon sets a variable named x to 1. The program executes this statement once, no matter how many times the body of the `for` loop eventually executes.

After the initialization expression executes, program control passes to the middle section, or test section, of the `for` statement. If the Boolean expression found there evaluates to `true`, then the body of the `for` loop is entered. In the program segment shown in Figure 5-10, x is initialized to 1, so when x <= LIMIT is tested, it evaluates to `true`, and the loop body outputs the value of x.

After the loop body executes, the final one-third of the `for` expression (the update section that follows the last semicolon) executes, and x increases to 2. Following the third section, program control returns to the second (test) section, where x is compared to LIMIT a second time. Because the value of x is 2, it is still less than or equal to LIMIT, so the body of the `for` loop executes, and the value of x is displayed. Then the third, altering portion of the `for` statement executes again. The variable x increases to 3, and the `for` loop continues.

Eventually, when x is *not* less than or equal to LIMIT (after 1 through 10 have been output), the `for` loop ends, and the program continues with any statements that follow the `for` loop.

Although the three sections of the `for` loop are most commonly used for initializing a variable, testing it, and incrementing it, you can also perform other tasks:

- You can initialize more than one variable by placing commas between separate initializations in the first section of the `for` statement, as in the following:

```
for(g = 0, h = 1; g < 6; ++g)
```

- You can declare a new variable within the `for` statement, as in the following:

```
for(int k = 0; k < 5; ++k)
```

In this example, k is declared to be an `int` and is initialized to 0. This technique is used frequently when the variable exists for no other purpose than to control the loop. When a variable is declared inside a loop, as k is in this example, it can be referenced only for the duration of the loop body; after that, it is **out of scope**, which means it is not usable because it has ceased to exist.

- You can perform more than one test in the middle section of the `for` statement by evaluating compound conditions, as in the following:

```
for(g = 0; g < 3 && h > 1; ++g)
```

- You can perform tasks other than incrementing at the end of the loop's execution, as in the following code that decrements a variable:

```
for(g = 5; g >= 1; --g)
```

- You can perform multiple tasks at the end of the loop's execution by separating the actions with commas, as in the following:

```
for(g = 0; g < 5; ++g, ++h)
```

- You can leave one or more portions of the for expression empty, although the two semicolons are still required as placeholders to separate the three sections. Usually, you want to use all three sections because the function of the loop is clearer to someone reading your program.

Generally, you should use the for loop in the standard manner, which is a shorthand way of initializing, testing, and altering a variable that controls a definite loop. You will learn about a similar loop, the foreach loop, when you study arrays in the next chapter.

Just as with a decision or a while loop, statements in a for loop body can be blocked. For example, the following loop displays *Hello* and *Goodbye* four times each:

```
const int TIMES = 4;
for(int x = 0; x < TIMES; ++x)
{
    WriteLine("Hello");
    WriteLine("Goodbye");
}
```

Without the curly braces in this code, the for loop would end after the statement that displays *Hello*. In other words, *Hello* would be displayed four times, but *Goodbye* would be displayed only once.

 Watch the video *Using the for Loop.*

TWO TRUTHS & A LIE

Creating Loops with the for Statement

1. The following statement displays the numbers 3 through 6:

```
for(int x = 3; x <= 6; ++x)
    WriteLine(x);
```

2. The following statement displays the numbers 4 through 9:

```
for(int x = 3; x < 9; ++x)
    WriteLine(x + 1);
```

3. The following statement displays the numbers 5 through 12:

```
for(int x = 5; x < 12; ++x)
    WriteLine(x);
```

The false statement is #3. That loop displays only the numbers 5 through 11, because when x is 12, the loop body is not entered.

Creating Loops with the do Statement

With each of the loop statements you have learned about so far, the loop body might execute many times, but it is also possible that the loop will not execute at all. For example, recall the bank balance program that displays compound interest, part of which is shown in Figure 5-11. The loop begins at the shaded line by testing the value of `response`. If the user has not entered Y, the loop body never executes. The `while` loop checks a value at the "top" of the loop.

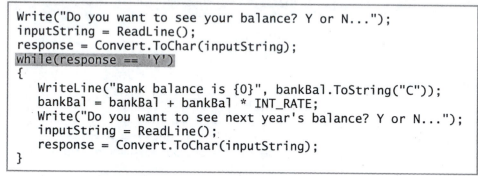

```
Write("Do you want to see your balance? Y or N...");
inputString = ReadLine();
response = Convert.ToChar(inputString);
while(response == 'Y')
{
    WriteLine("Bank balance is {0}", bankBal.ToString("C"));
    bankBal = bankBal + bankBal * INT_RATE;
    Write("Do you want to see next year's balance? Y or N...");
    inputString = ReadLine();
    response = Convert.ToChar(inputString);
}
```

Figure 5-11   Part of the bank balance program using a `while` loop

Sometimes you might need a loop body always to execute at least one time. If so, you can write a loop that checks at the "bottom" of the loop after the first iteration. The **do loop** (also called a **do...while loop**) checks the loop-controlling Boolean expression after one iteration. Figure 5-12 shows a diagram of the structure of a do loop.

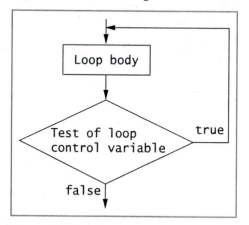

Figure 5-12   Flowchart of a do loop

Figure 5-13 shows the logic and the C# code for a do loop in a bank balance program. The loop starts with the keyword do. The body of the loop follows and is contained within curly braces. Within the loop, the next balance is calculated, and the user is prompted for a response. The Boolean expression that controls loop execution is written using a `while` statement, placed after the loop body. The `bankBal` variable is output the first time before the user has any option of responding. At the end of the loop, the user is prompted, *Do you want to see next year's balance? Y or N...*. Now the user has the option of seeing more balances, but the first view of the balance was unavoidable.

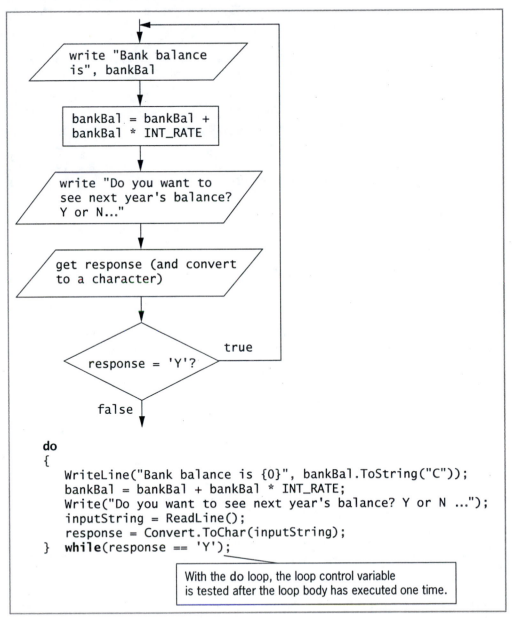

```
do
{
    WriteLine("Bank balance is {0}", bankBal.ToString("C"));
    bankBal = bankBal + bankBal * INT_RATE;
    Write("Do you want to see next year's balance? Y or N ...");
    inputString = ReadLine();
    response = Convert.ToChar(inputString);
} while(response == 'Y');
```

With the do loop, the loop control variable is tested after the loop body has executed one time.

Figure 5-13   Part of the bank balance program using a do loop

In a do loop, as a matter of style, many programmers prefer to align the while expression with the do keyword that starts the loop. Others feel that placing the while expression on its own line increases the chances that readers might misinterpret the line as the start of its own while statement instead of marking the end of a do statement.

You never are required to use a do loop. Within the bank balance example, you could achieve the same results by unconditionally displaying the bank balance once, prompting the user, and then starting a while loop that might not be entered. However, when a task must be performed at least one time, the do loop is convenient.

The while loop and for loop are **pretest loops**—ones in which the loop control variable is tested before the loop body executes. The do loop is a **posttest loop**—one in which the loop control variable is tested after the loop body executes.

TWO TRUTHS & A LIE

Creating Loops with the do Statement

1. The do loop checks the bottom of the loop after one iteration has occurred.

2. The Boolean expression that controls do loop execution is written using a do statement, placed after the loop body.

3. You never are required to use a do loop; you can always substitute one execution of the body statements followed by a while loop.

The false statement is #2. The Boolean expression that controls do loop execution is written using a while statement, placed after the loop body.

Using Nested Loops

Like if statements, loop statements also can be nested. You can place a while loop within a while loop, a for loop within a for loop, a while loop within a for loop, or any other combination. When loops are nested, each pair contains an **inner loop** and an **outer loop**. The inner loop must be entirely contained within the outer loop; loops can never overlap. Figure 5-14 shows a diagram in which the shaded loop is nested within another loop; the shaded area is the inner loop as well as the body of the outer loop.

Suppose you want to display future bank balances for different years at a variety of interest rates. Figure 5-15 shows an application that contains an outer loop controlled by interest rates (starting with the first shaded statement in the figure) and an inner loop controlled by years (starting with the second shaded statement). The application displays annually compounded interest on $1000 at 4 percent, 6 percent, and 8 percent interest rates for one through five years. Figure 5-16 shows the output.

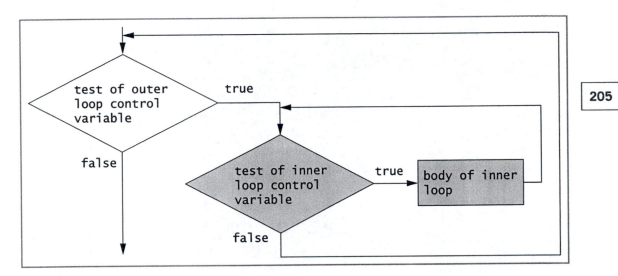

Figure 5-14 Nested loops

```
using static System.Console;
class LoopingBankBal2
{
    static void Main()
    {
        double bankBal;
        double rate;
        int year;
        const double START_BAL = 1000;
        const double START_INT = 0.04;
        const double INT_INCREASE = 0.02;
        const double LAST_INT = 0.08;
        const int END_YEAR = 5;
        for(rate = START_INT; rate <= LAST_INT; rate += INT_INCREASE)
        {
            bankBal = START_BAL;
            WriteLine("Starting bank balance is {0}",
                bankBal.ToString("C"));
            WriteLine(" Interest Rate: {0}", rate.ToString("P"));
            for(year = 1; year <= END_YEAR; ++year)
            {
                bankBal = bankBal + bankBal * rate;
                WriteLine(" After year {0}, bank balance is {1}",
                    year, bankBal.ToString("C"));
            }
        }
    }
}
```

Figure 5-15 The LoopingBankBal2 program

```
C:\C#\Chapter.05>LoopingBankBal2
Starting bank balance is $1,000.00
  Interest Rate: 4.00 %
    After year 1, bank balance is $1,040.00
    After year 2, bank balance is $1,081.60
    After year 3, bank balance is $1,124.86
    After year 4, bank balance is $1,169.86
    After year 5, bank balance is $1,216.65
Starting bank balance is $1,000.00
  Interest Rate: 6.00 %
    After year 1, bank balance is $1,060.00
    After year 2, bank balance is $1,123.60
    After year 3, bank balance is $1,191.02
    After year 4, bank balance is $1,262.48
    After year 5, bank balance is $1,338.23
Starting bank balance is $1,000.00
  Interest Rate: 8.00 %
    After year 1, bank balance is $1,080.00
    After year 2, bank balance is $1,166.40
    After year 3, bank balance is $1,259.71
    After year 4, bank balance is $1,360.49
    After year 5, bank balance is $1,469.33

C:\C#\Chapter.05>
```

Figure 5-16   Output of the LoopingBankBal2 program

When you use a loop within a loop, you should always think of the outer loop as the all-encompassing loop. When you describe the task at hand, you often use the word *each* to refer to the inner loop. For example, if you wanted to output balances for different interest rates each year for 10 years, you could appropriately initialize some constants as follows:

```
const double RATE1 = 0.03;
const double RATE2 = 0.07
const double RATE_INCREASE = 0.01
const int END_YEAR = 10;
```

Then you could use the following nested for loops:

```
for(rate = RATE1; rate <= RATE2; rate += RATE_INCREASE)
   for(year = 1; year <= END_YEAR; ++year)
      WriteLine(bankBal + bankBal * rate);
```

However, if you wanted to display balances for different years for each possible interest rate, you would use the following:

```
for(year = 1; year <= END_YEAR; ++year)
   for(rate = RATE1; rate <= RATE2; rate += RATE_INCREASE)
      WriteLine(bankBal + bankBal * rate);
```

In both of these examples, the same 50 values would be displayed—five different interest rates (from 0.03 through 0.07) for 10 years (1 through 10). However, in the first example, balances for years 1 through 10 would be displayed *within* each interest rate category, and in the second example, each balance for each interest rate would be displayed *within* each year category. In other words, in the first example, the first 10 amounts displayed would all use the first rate of 0.03 for 10 different years, and in the second example, the first five amounts displayed would use different interest values all in the first year.

Watch the video *Using Nested Loops.*

TWO TRUTHS & A LIE

Using Nested Loops

1. The body of the following loop executes six times:

```
for(a = 1; a < 4; ++a)
    for(b = 2; b < 3; ++b)
```

2. The body of the following loop executes four times:

```
for(c = 1; c < 3; ++c)
    for(d = 1; d < 3; ++d)
```

3. The body of the following loop executes 15 times:

```
for(e = 1; e <= 5; ++e)
    for(f = 2; f <= 4; ++f)
```

The false statement is #1. That loop executes only three times. The outer loop executes when a is 1, 2, and 3. The inner loop executes just once for each of those iterations.

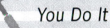 *You Do It*

Using a Nested Loop

In the next steps, you write a program that creates a tipping table that restaurant patrons can use to approximate the correct tip for meals. Prices range from $10 to $100, and tipping percentage rates range from 10 percent to 25 percent. The program uses several loops.

1. Open a new file to start a program named **TippingTable**. It begins by declaring variables to use for the price of a dinner, a tip percentage rate, and the amount of the tip.

```
using static System.Console;
class TippingTable
{
    static void Main()
    {
        double dinnerPrice = 10.00;
        double tipRate;
        double tip;
```

(continues)

(continued)

2. Next, create some constants. Every tip from 10 percent through 25 percent will be computed in 5 percent intervals, so declare those values as LOWRATE, MAXRATE, and TIPSTEP. Tips will be calculated on dinner prices up to $100.00 in $10.00 intervals, so declare those constants, too.

```
const double LOWRATE = 0.10;
const double MAXRATE = 0.25;
const double TIPSTEP = 0.05;
const double MAXDINNER = 100.00;
const double DINNERSTEP = 10.00;
```

3. To create a heading for the table, display *Price*. (For alignment, insert three spaces after the quotes and before the *P* in *Price*.) On the same line, use a loop that displays every tip rate from LOWRATE through MAXRATE in increments of TIPSTEP. In other words, the tip rates are 0.10, 0.15, 0.20, and 0.25. Complete the heading for the table using a WriteLine() statement that advances the cursor to the next line of output and a WriteLine() statement that displays a dashed line.

```
Write("Price");
for(tipRate = LOWRATE; tipRate <= MAXRATE; tipRate += TIPSTEP)
    Write("{0, 8}", tipRate.ToString("F"));
WriteLine();
WriteLine("----------------------------------------");
```

Recall that within a for loop, the expression before the first semicolon executes once, the middle expression is tested, the loop body executes, and then the expression to the right of the second semicolon executes. In other words, TIPSTEP is not added to tipRate until after tipRate is displayed on each cycle through the loop.

As an alternative to typing 40 dashes in the WriteLine() statement, you could use the following loop to display a single dash 40 times. When the 40 dashes were completed, you could use WriteLine() to advance the cursor to a new line.

```
const int NUM_DASHES = 40;
for(int x = 0; x < NUM_DASHES; ++x)
    Write("-");
WriteLine();
```

4. Reset tipRate to 0.10. You must reset the rate because after the last loop, the rate will have been increased to greater than 0.25.

```
tipRate = LOWRATE;
```

5. Create a nested loop that continues while the dinnerPrice remains 100.00 (MAXDINNER) or less. Each iteration of this loop displays one row of the tip table. Within this loop, display the dinnerPrice, then loop to display four tips while the tipRate varies from 0.10 through 0.25. At the end of the

(continues)

(continued)

loop, increase the `dinnerPrice` by 10.00, reset the `tipRate` to 0.10 so it is ready for the next row, and write a new line to advance the cursor.

```
while(dinnerPrice <= MAXDINNER)
{
    Write("{0, 8}", dinnerPrice.ToString("C"));
    while(tipRate <= MAXRATE)
    {
        tip = dinnerPrice * tipRate;
        Write("{0, 8}", tip.ToString("F"));
        tipRate += TIPSTEP;
    }
    dinnerPrice += DINNERSTEP;
    tipRate = LOWRATE;
    WriteLine();
}
```

 Recall that the `{0, 8}` format string in the `Write()` statements displays the first argument in fields that are eight characters wide. You learned about format strings in Chapter 2.

6. Add two closing curly braces—one for the `Main()` method and one for the class.

7. Save the file, compile it, and execute the program. The output looks like Figure 5-17.

```
C:\C#\Chapter.05>TippingTable
   Price      0.10      0.15      0.20      0.25
-------------------------------------------------
$10.00       1.00      1.50      2.00      2.50
$20.00       2.00      3.00      4.00      5.00
$30.00       3.00      4.50      6.00      7.50
$40.00       4.00      6.00      8.00     10.00
$50.00       5.00      7.50     10.00     12.50
$60.00       6.00      9.00     12.00     15.00
$70.00       7.00     10.50     14.00     17.50
$80.00       8.00     12.00     16.00     20.00
$90.00       9.00     13.50     18.00     22.50
$100.00     10.00     15.00     20.00     25.00

C:\C#\Chapter.05>
```

Figure 5-17 Output of the `TippingTable` program

(continues)

(continued)

In the exercises at the end of this chapter, you will be instructed to make an interactive version of the TippingTable program in which many of the values are input by the user instead of being coded into the program as unnamed constants.

You Do It

Using a do Loop

In the next steps, you revise the TippingTable program to use a do loop in place of the while loop.

1. Open the **TippingTable** program, change the class name to **TippingTable2**, and save the file as **TippingTable2**.

2. Cut the while loop clause (while(dinnerPrice <= MAXDINNER)), and replace it with **do**.

3. Paste the while loop clause just after the closing curly brace for the loop and before the final two curly braces in the program, and then add a semicolon.

4. Save, compile, and execute the program. The output is identical to the output in Figure 5-17.

Accumulating Totals

Many computer programs display totals. When you receive a credit card or telephone service bill, you are usually provided with individual transaction details, but you are most interested in the total bill. Similarly, some programs total the number of credit hours generated by college students, the gross payroll for all employees of a company, or the total accounts receivable value for an organization. These totals are **accumulated**—that is, they are summed one at a time in a loop.

Figure 5-18 shows an example of an interactive program that accumulates the user's total purchases. The program prompts the user to enter a purchase price or *0* to quit. While the user continues to enter nonzero values, the amounts are added to a total. With each pass through the loop, the total is recalculated to include the new purchase amount. After the user enters the loop-terminating *0*, the accumulated total can be displayed. Figure 5-19 shows a typical program execution.

```
using System;
using static System.Console;
class TotalPurchase
{
    static void Main()
    {
        double purchase;
        double total = 0;
        string inputString;
        const double QUIT = 0;
        Write("Enter purchase amount >> ");
        inputString = ReadLine();
        purchase = Convert.ToDouble(inputString);
        while(purchase != QUIT)
        {
            total += purchase;
            Write("Enter next purchase amount, or " +
                QUIT + " to quit >> ");
            inputString = ReadLine();
            purchase = Convert.ToDouble(inputString);
        }
        WriteLine("Your total is {0}", total.ToString("C"));
    }
}
```

Figure 5-18   An application that accumulates total purchases entered by the user

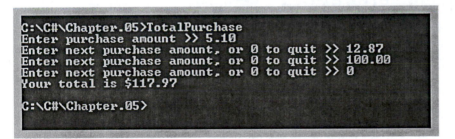

Figure 5-19   Typical execution of the TotalPurchase program

Recall from Chapter 2 that the expression total += purchase uses the shortcut add and assign operator, and that it is equivalent to total = total + purchase. The add and assign operator is frequently used when a running total is kept.

In the application in Figure 5-18, it is very important that the total variable used for accumulation is set to 0 before the loop begins. When it is not, the program will not compile. An unknown, unassigned value is known as **garbage**. The C# compiler prevents you from seeing an incorrect total by requiring you to provide a starting value; C# will not use the garbage value that happens to be stored at an uninitialized memory location.

In the application in Figure 5-18, the total variable must be initialized to 0, but the purchase variable is uninitialized. Many programmers would say it makes no sense to initialize this variable because no matter what starting value you provide, the value can be changed by the first input statement before the variable is ever used. As a matter of style, this book generally does not initialize variables if the initialization value is never used; doing so might mislead you into thinking the starting value had some purpose.

TWO TRUTHS & A LIE

Accumulating Totals

1. When totals are accumulated, 1 is added to a variable that represents the total.

2. A variable used to hold a total must be set to 0 before it is used to accumulate a total.

3. The C# compiler will not allow you to accumulate totals in an uninitialized variable.

The false statement is #1. When totals are accumulated, any value might be added to a variable that represents the total. For example, if you total 10 test scores, then each score is added. If you add only 1 to a total variable on each cycle through a loop, then you are counting rather than accumulating a total.

Improving Loop Performance

Whether you decide to use a while, for, or do loop in an application, you can improve loop performance by doing the following:

- Make sure the loop avoids unnecessary operations.
- Consider the order of evaluation for short-circuit operators.
- Employ loop fusion.
- Use prefix incrementing rather than postfix incrementing.

Avoiding Unnecessary Operations

You can improve loop performance by making sure the loop does not include unnecessary operations or statements. For example, suppose that a loop should execute while x is less than the sum of two integers a and b, and that neither a nor b is altered in the loop body. The loop could be written as:

```
while(x < a + b)
    // loop body
```

If this loop executes 1,000 times, then the expression a + b is calculated 1,000 times. Instead, if you use the following code, the results are the same, but the arithmetic is performed only once:

```
int sum = a + b;
while(x < sum)
    // loop body
```

Of course, if a or b is altered in the loop body, then a new sum must be calculated with every loop iteration. However, if the sum of a and b is fixed prior to the start of the loop, then writing the code the second way is far more efficient.

As another example, suppose you need a temporary variable within a loop to use for some calculation. The loop could be written as follows:

```
while(x < LIMIT)
{
    int tempTotal = a + b;
    // more statements here
}
```

When you declare a variable like tempTotal within a loop, it exists only for the duration of the loop; that is, it exists only until the loop's closing brace. Each time the loop executes, the variable is re-created. A more efficient solution is to declare the variable outside of the loop, as follows:

```
int tempTotal;
while(x < LIMIT)
{
    tempTotal = a + b;
    // more statements here
}
```

It is more efficient to declare this variable outside the loop than to redeclare it on every loop iteration.

Considering the Order of Evaluation of Short-Circuit Operators

In Chapter 4, you learned that the expressions in each part of an AND or OR expression use short-circuit evaluation; that is, they are evaluated only as much as necessary to determine whether the entire expression is true or false. When a loop might execute many times, it becomes increasingly important to consider the number of evaluations that take place.

For example, suppose that a user can request any number of printed copies of a report from 1 to 15, and you want to validate the user's input before proceeding. If you believe that users are far more likely to enter a value that is too high than to enter a negative value, then you want to start a loop that reprompts the user with the following expression:

```
while(requestedNum > 15 || requestedNum < 1)...
```

Because you believe that the first Boolean expression is more likely to be true than the second one, you can eliminate testing the second one on more occasions. The order of the expressions is not very important in a single loop, but if this loop is nested within other loops, then the difference in the number of required tests increases. Similarly, the order of the evaluations in if statements is more important when the if statements are nested within a loop.

Employing Loop Fusion

Loop fusion is the technique of combining two loops into one. For example, suppose that you want to call two methods 100 times each. You can set a constant named TIMES to 100 and use the following code:

```
for(int x = 0; x < TIMES; ++x)
    method1();
for(int x = 0; x < TIMES; ++x)
    method2();
```

However, you can also use the following code:

```
for(int x = 0; x < TIMES; ++x)
{
    method1();
    method2();
}
```

Fusing loops will not work in every situation; sometimes all the activities for method1() must be finished before those in method2() can begin. However, if the two methods do not depend on each other, fusing the loops can improve performance. Performance issues can be crucial when you write programs for small mobile devices such as phones. On the other hand, if saving a few milliseconds ends up making your code harder to understand, you almost always should err in favor of slower but more readable programs.

Using Prefix Incrementing Rather Than Postfix Incrementing

Probably the most common action after the second semicolon in a for statement is to increment the loop control variable. In most textbooks and in many professional programs, the postfix increment operator is used for this purpose, as in the following:

```
for(int x = 0; x < LIMIT; x++)
```

Because incrementing x is a stand-alone statement in the for loop, the result is identical whether you use x++ or ++x. However, using the prefix increment operator produces a faster loop. Consider the test program in Figure 5-20. It uses C#'s Stopwatch class. The statement using System.Diagnostics; is needed for the Stopwatch class. You will better understand how this class works after you read Chapter 9, "Using Classes and Objects," but you can use the class now by making statements similar to the following:

```
Stopwatch sw = Stopwatch.StartNew();
    // Place statements to be timed here
sw.Stop();
```

The first statement creates and starts a Stopwatch object for timing events. The object's name is sw—you can use any legal C# identifier. The last statement stops the Stopwatch.

Subsequently, you can use a statement similar to the following to output the object's elapsed time in milliseconds:

```
WriteLine("Time used: {0} ms", sw.Elapsed.TotalMilliseconds);
```

Figure 5-20 contains a program that uses the `Stopwatch` class to compare loops that use prefix and postfix incrementing. Figure 5-21 shows the output of the program.

```
using System;
using static System.Console;
using System.Diagnostics;
class PrefixPostfixComparison
{
    static void Main()
    {
        int LOOPS = 10000000;
        Stopwatch sw = Stopwatch.StartNew();
        for(int x = 0; x < LOOPS; ++x);
        sw.Stop();
        Stopwatch sw2 = Stopwatch.StartNew();
        for(int x = 0; x < LOOPS; x++);
        sw2.Stop();
        WriteLine("Time with prefix increment: {0} ms",
            sw.Elapsed.TotalMilliseconds);
        WriteLine("Time with postfix increment: {0} ms",
            sw2.Elapsed.TotalMilliseconds);
    }
}
```

Figure 5-20   The `PrefixPostfixComparison` program

```
C:\C#>PrefixPostfixComparison
Time with prefix increment: 45.6296 ms
Time with postfix increment: 49.5856 ms

C:\C#>
```

Figure 5-21   Typical execution of the `PrefixPostfixComparison` program

The program that uses prefix incrementing runs slightly faster than the one that uses postfix incrementing. The difference in duration for the loops is very small, but it would increase if tasks were added to the loop bodies. If you run the PrefixPostfixComparison program multiple times, you will get different results, and occasionally the prefix operator loop might take longer than the postfix loop because other programs are running concurrently on your computer. However, using the prefix operator typically saves a small amount of time. As a professional, you will encounter programmers who insist on using either postfix or prefix increments in their loops. You should follow the conventions established by your organization, but now you have the tools to prove that prefix incrementing is faster.

As you continue to study programming, you will discover many situations in which you can make your programs more efficient. You should always be on the lookout for ways to improve program performance without sacrificing readability.

TWO TRUTHS & A LIE

Improving Loop Performance

1. You can improve loop performance by making sure the loop does not include unnecessary operations or statements.

2. You can improve loop performance by declaring temporary variables outside of a loop instead of continuously redeclaring them.

3. You can improve loop performance by omitting the initialization of the loop control variable.

The false statement is #3. A loop control variable must be initialized for every loop.

Looping Issues in GUI Programs

Using a loop within a method in a GUI application is no different from using one in a console application; you can use while, for, and do statements in the same ways in both types of programs. For example, Figure 5-22 shows a GUI Form that prompts a user to enter a number and then displays *Hello* the corresponding number of times. The image on the left shows the Form when the program starts, and the image on the right shows the output after the user enters a value and clicks the button. Figure 5-23 shows the code in the greetingsButton_Click() method. When a user clicks the greetingsButton, an integer is extracted from the TextBox on the Form. Then a for loop appends *Hello* and a newline character to the Text property of the outputLabel the correct number of times.

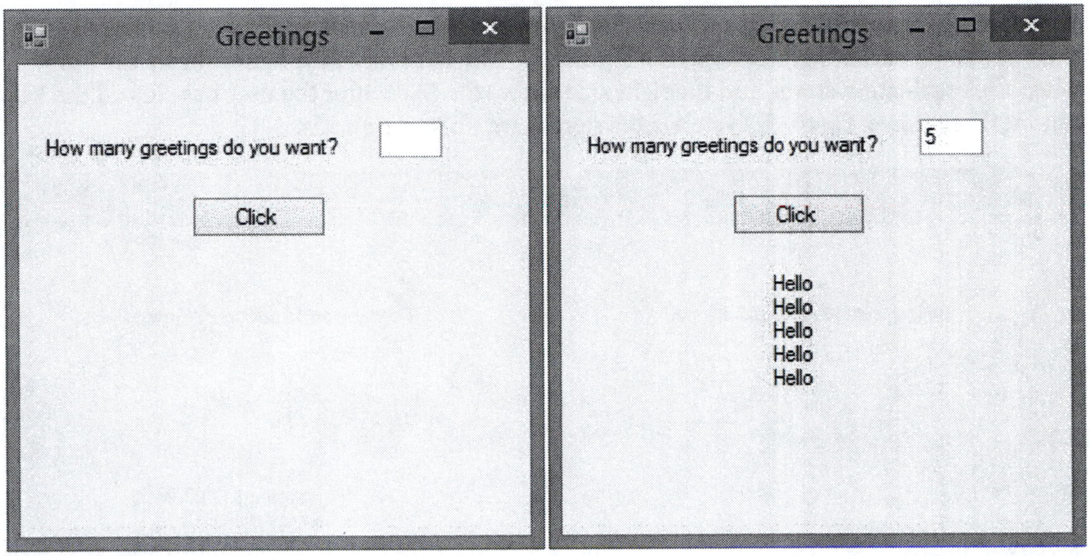

Figure 5-22   The Greetings Form when it starts and after the user enters a number and clicks the button

```
private void greetingsButton_Click(object sender, EventArgs e)
{
    int numGreetings = Convert.ToInt32(greetingsTextBox.Text);
    int count;
    for (count = 0; count < numGreetings; ++count)
        outputLabel.Text += "Hello\n";
}
```

Figure 5-23   The greetingsButton_Click() method in the ManyHellosGUI application

If the user clicked the button in the ManyHellosGUI program again, new instances of *Hello* would be added to the already-displayed ones. If your intention was to only show new *Hellos* then you could add the statement `outputLabel.Text = "";` to the greetingsButtonClick() method before the start of the loop.

Event-driven programs sometimes require fewer coded loops than their counterpart console applications, because in these programs some events are determined by the user's actions when the program is running, rather than by the programmer's coding beforehand. You can write an event-driven program so that an action continues as long as the user continues to make an appropriate selection. Depending on the application, the sentinel value for this sort of implicit loop might occur when the user either clicks a button that indicates *quit* or clicks the close button on the Form that hosts the application.

For example, Figure 5-24 shows a Form that controls a bank balance application similar to the one shown earlier in this chapter in Figure 5-7. The left side of the figure shows the Form when the application starts, and the right side shows the Form after the user has clicked the Yes button three times. Figure 5-25 shows the significant Form class code.

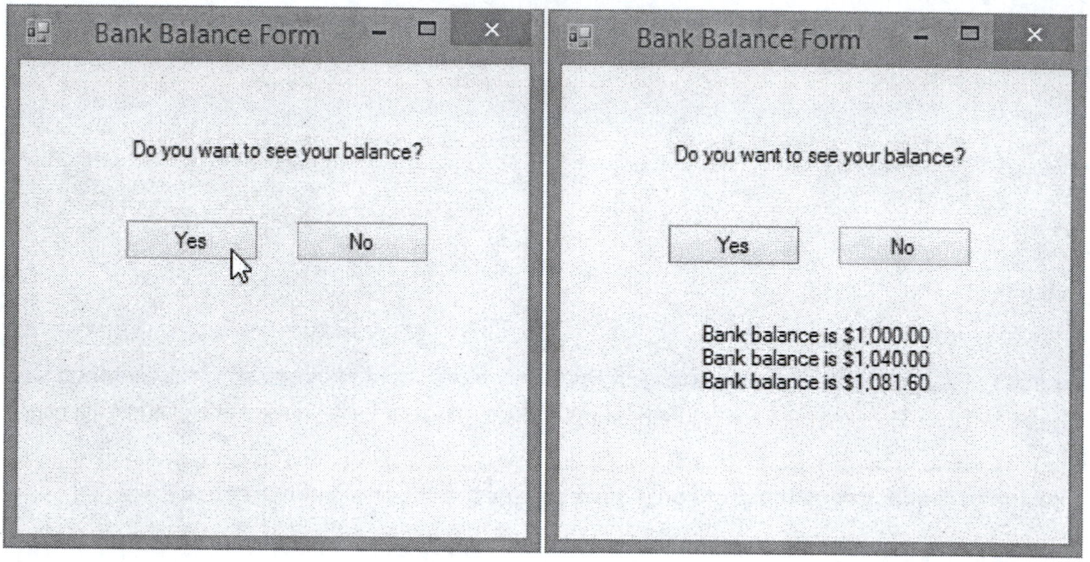

Figure 5-24   The BankBalance Form when it starts and after the user has clicked Yes three times

```
namespace LoopingBankBalGUI
{
   partial class Form1 : Form
   {
      double bankBal = 1000;
      const double INT_RATE = 0.04;
      private void yesButton_Click(object sender, EventArgs e)
      {
         outputLabel.Text += String.Format("Bank balance is {0}\n",
            bankBal.ToString ("C"));
         bankBal = bankBal + bankBal * INT_RATE;
      }
      private void noButton_Click(object sender, EventArgs e)
      {
         outputLabel.Text = "Have a nice day!";
      }
   }
}
```

Figure 5-25   Code for the LoopingBankBalGUI program

In the LoopingBankBalGUI program, you might also choose to disable the *Yes* button or make it invisible so that the user cannot select it again after clicking *No*.

No loop is written in the code in Figure 5-25 because a loop body execution is caused automatically each time a user clicks the *Yes* button on the Form. Whenever yesButton_Click() executes, the Text of the outputLabel is appended to include a new line that displays the bank balance, and then the bank balance is increased by the interest rate. It is important that the bankBal variable is initialized outside the yesButton_Click() method; if it was initialized within the method, the balance would be reset to the original value of $1000 with each new button click. In the application in Figure 5-27, the balances in the outputLabel are replaced with *Have a nice day!* when the user indicates no more balances are needed.

Chapter Summary

- You can use a **while** loop to execute a body of statements continuously while a condition continues to be **true**. A **while** loop consists of the keyword **while**, a Boolean expression within parentheses, and the body of the loop, which can be a single statement or a block of statements surrounded by curly braces.

- A **for** statement includes loop control variable initialization, the test condition that controls loop entry, and the expression that alters the loop control variable. You begin a **for** statement with the keyword **for**, followed by a set of parentheses. Within the parentheses, the initialization, test, and update sections are separated by semicolons.

- The **do** loop checks the loop-controlling Boolean expression at the bottom of the loop after one repetition has occurred.

- You can nest any combination of loops.

- In computer programs, totals frequently are accumulated—that is, summed one at a time in a loop.

- You can improve loop performance by making sure the loop does not include unnecessary operations or statements, considering the order of evaluation for short-circuit operators, using comparisons to zero, employing loop fusion, and using prefix incrementing.

- You can use **while**, **for**, and **do** statements in the same ways in console and GUI programs. However, event-driven programs sometimes require fewer coded loops than console applications because some events are determined by the user's actions when the program is running, rather than by the programmer's coding beforehand.

Key Terms

A **loop** is a structure that allows repeated execution of a block of statements.

A **loop body** is the block of statements executed in a loop.

An **iteration** is one execution of any loop.

A **while loop** executes a body of statements continuously while a test condition continues to be true; it uses the keyword **while**.

An **infinite loop** is one that (theoretically) never ends.

A **loop control variable** determines whether loop execution will continue.

An **empty body** has no statements in it.

Incrementing a variable means adding a value to it. (Specifically, the term often means to add 1 to a variable.)

Decrementing a variable means subtracting a value from it. (Specifically, the term often means to subtract 1 from a variable.)

In a **definite loop**, the number of iterations is predetermined.

A **counted loop** is a definite loop.

An **indefinite loop** is one in which the number of iterations is not predetermined.

A **sentinel value** is one that a user must supply to stop a loop.

A **for loop** contains the starting value for the loop control variable, the test condition that controls loop entry, and the expression that alters the loop control variable, all in one statement.

A **step value** is the amount by which a loop control variable is altered, especially in a **for** loop.

Out of scope describes a program component that is not usable because it has ceased to exist.

The **do loop** (also called a **do...while loop**) checks the loop-controlling Boolean expression at the bottom of the loop after one repetition has occurred.

A **pretest loop** is a loop in which the loop control variable is tested before the loop body executes.

A **posttest loop** is one in which the loop control variable is tested after the loop body executes.

An **inner loop** is the loop in a pair of nested loops that is entirely contained within another loop.

An **outer loop** is the loop in a pair of nested loops that contains another loop.

Accumulated totals are computed by adding values one at a time in a loop.

Garbage is a term used to describe an unknown memory value.

Loop fusion is the technique of combining two loops into one.

Review Questions

1. A structure that allows repeated execution of a block of statements is a(n) _____ .

   a. sequence
   b. selection
   c. loop
   d. array

2. The body of a **while** loop can consist of _____ .

   a. a single statement
   b. a block of statements within curly braces
   c. either a or b
   d. neither a nor b

3. A loop that never ends is called a(n) _____ loop.

   a. **while**
   b. **for**
   c. counted
   d. infinite

4. Which of the following is not required of a loop control variable in a correctly working loop?

   a. It is reset to its initial value before the loop ends.
   b. It is initialized before the loop starts.
   c. It is tested.
   d. It is altered in the loop body.

5. A **while** loop with an empty body contains no _____ .

   a. loop control variable
   b. statements
   c. curly braces
   d. test within the parentheses of the **while** statement

6. A loop for which you do not know the number of iterations when you write it is a(n) _____ .

   a. definite loop
   b. indefinite loop
   c. counted loop
   d. **for** loop

7. What is the major advantage of using a **for** loop instead of a **while** loop?

   a. With a **for** loop, it is impossible to create an infinite loop.

   b. It is the only way to achieve an indefinite loop.

   c. Unlike with a **while** loop, the execution of multiple statements can depend on the test condition.

   d. The loop control variable is initialized, tested, and altered all in one place.

8. A **for** loop statement must contain _____.

   a. two semicolons

   b. three commas

   c. four dots

   d. five pipes

9. In a **for** statement, the section before the first semicolon executes _____.

   a. once

   b. once prior to each loop iteration

   c. once after each loop iteration

   d. one less time than the initial loop control variable value

10. The three sections of the **for** loop are most commonly used for _____ the loop control variable.

    a. testing, outputting, and incrementing

    b. initializing, testing, and incrementing

    c. incrementing, selecting, and testing

    d. initializing, converting, and outputting

11. Which loop is most convenient to use if the loop body must always execute at least once?

    a. a **do** loop

    b. a **while** loop

    c. a **for** loop

    d. an **if** loop

12. The loop control variable is checked at the bottom of which kind of loop?

    a. a **while** loop

    b. a **do** loop

    c. a **for** loop

    d. all of the above

13. A **for** loop is an example of a(n) _____ loop.

    a. untested

    b. pretest

    c. posttest

    d. infinite

14. A `while` loop is an example of a(n) _____ loop.

    a. untested

    c. posttest

    b. pretest

    d. infinite

15. When a loop is placed within another loop, the loops are said to be _____ .

    a. infinite

    c. nested

    b. bubbled

    d. overlapping

16. What does the following code segment display?

```
a = 1;
while (a < 5);
{
    Write("{0} ", a);
    ++a;
}
```

    a. 1 2 3 4

    c. 4

    b. 1

    d. nothing

17. What is the output of the following code segment?

```
s=1;
while(s < 4)
    ++s;
    Write("{0} ", s);
```

    a. 1

    c. 1 2 3 4

    b. 4

    d. 2 3 4

18. What is the output of the following code segment?

```
j = 5;
while(j > 0)
{
    Write("{0} ", j);
    j--;
}
```

    a. 0

    c. 5 4 3 2 1

    b. 5

    d. 5 4 3 2 1 0

19. What does the following code segment display?

```
for(f = 0; f < 3; ++f);
    Write("{0} ", f);
```

    a. 0

    c. 3

    b. 0 1 2

    d. nothing

20. What does the following code segment display?

```
for(t = 0; t < 3; ++t)
    Write("{0} ", t);
```

a. 0   c. 0 1 2

b. 0 1   d. 0 1 2 3

Exercises

Programming Exercises

1. Write an application named **SumFourInts** that allows the user to enter four integers and displays their sum.

2. Write an application named **SumInts** that allows the user to enter any number of integers continuously until the user enters *999*. Display the sum of the values entered, not including 999.

3. Write an application named **EnterLowercaseLetters** that asks the user to type a lowercase letter from the keyboard. If the character entered is a lowercase letter, display *OK*; if it is not a lowercase letter, display an error message. The program continues until the user types an exclamation point.

4. Write an application named **TestScores** that continuously prompts a user for test scores until the user enters a sentinel value. A valid score ranges from 0 through 100. When the user enters a valid score, add it to a total; when the user enters an invalid score, display an error message. Before the program ends, display the number of scores entered and their average.

5. Danielle, Edward, and Francis are three salespeople at Holiday Homes. Write an application named **HomeSales** that prompts the user for a salesperson initial (*D*, *E*, or *F*). Either uppercase or lowercase initials are valid. While the user does not type *Z*, continue by prompting for the amount of a sale. Issue an error message for any invalid initials entered. Keep a running total of the amounts sold by each salesperson. After the user types *Z* or *z* for an initial, display each salesperson's total, a grand total for all sales, and the name of the salesperson with the highest total.

6. Write an application named **DisplayMultiplicationTable** that displays a table of the products of every combination of two integers from 1 through 10.

7. Write an application named **OddNums** that displays all the odd numbers from 1 through 99.

8. Write an application named **MultiplicationTable** that prompts the user for an integer value, for example *7*. Then display the product of every integer from 1 through 10 when multiplied by the entered value. For example, the first three lines of the table might read *1 X 7 = 7, 2 X 7 = 14*, and *3 X 7 = 21*.

9. Write an application named **Sum500** that sums the integers from 1 through 500.

10. Write an application named **Perfect** that displays every perfect number from 1 through 1000. A number is perfect if it equals the sum of all the smaller positive integers that divide evenly into it. For example, 6 is perfect because 1, 2, and 3 divide evenly into it and their sum is 6.

11. In a "You Do It" section of this chapter, you created a tipping table for patrons to use when analyzing their restaurant bills. Now, create a modified program named **TippingTable3** in which each of the following values is obtained from user input:

    - The lowest tipping percentage

    - The highest tipping percentage

    - The lowest possible restaurant bill

    - The highest restaurant bill

12. Write a program named **WebAddress** that asks a user for a business name. Suggest a good Web address by adding *www.* to the front of the name, removing all spaces from the name, and adding *.com* to the end of the name. For example, a good Web address for Acme Plumbing and Supply is *www.AcmePlumbingandSupply.com*.

13. Write a program named **CountVowels** that accepts a phrase from the user and counts the number of vowels in the phrase. For this exercise, count both uppercase and lowercase vowels, but do not consider *y* to be a vowel.

14. In Chapter 4, you created a program that generates a random number, allows a user to guess it, and displays a message indicating whether the guess is too low, too high, or correct. Now, create a modified program called **GuessingGame2** in which the user can continue to enter values until the correct guess is made. After the user guesses correctly, display the number of guesses made.

Recall that you can generate a random number whose value is at least min and less than max using the following statements:

```
Random ranNumber = new Random();
int randomNumber;
randomNumber = ranNumber.Next(min, max);
```

15. Modify the GuessingGame2 program to create a program called **GuessingGame3** in which the player is criticized for making a "dumb" guess. For example, if the player guesses that the random number is 4 and is told that the guess is too low, and then the player subsequently makes a guess lower than 4, display a message that the user should have known not to make such a low guess.

Debugging Exercises

1. Each of the following files in the Chapter.05 folder of your downloadable student files has syntax and/or logical errors. In each case, determine the problem, and fix the program. After you correct the errors, save each file using the same filename preceded with *Fixed*. For example, save DebugFive1.cs as **FixedDebugFive1.cs**.

   a. DebugFive1.cs

   b. DebugFive2.cs

   c. DebugFive3.cs

   d. DebugFive4.cs

Case Problems

1. In Chapter 4, you created an interactive application named **GreenvilleRevenue** that prompts a user for the number of contestants entered in this year's and last year's Greenville Idol competition and displays the revenue expected for this year's competition if each contestant pays a $25 entrance fee. The program also displays one of three appropriate statements specified in the case problem in Chapter 4, based on a comparison between the number of contestants this year and last year. Now, modify the program so that the user must enter a number between 0 and 30, inclusive, for the number of contestants each year. If the user enters an incorrect number, the program prompts for a valid value.

2. In Chapter 4, you created an interactive application named **MarshallsRevenue** that prompts a user for the number of interior and exterior murals scheduled to be painted during a month and computes the expected revenue for each type of mural. The program also prompts the user for the month number and modifies the pricing based on requirements listed in Chapter 4. Now, modify the program so that the user must enter a month value from 1 through 12. If the user enters an incorrect number, the program prompts for a valid value. Also, the user must enter a number between 0 and 30 inclusive for the number of murals of each type; otherwise, the program prompts the user again.

CHAPTER 6

Using Arrays

In this chapter you will:

◎ Declare an array and assign values to array elements

◎ Access array elements

◎ Search an array using a loop

◎ Use the `BinarySearch()`, `Sort()`, and `Reverse()` methods

◎ Use multidimensional arrays

◎ Learn about array issues in GUI programs

Storing values in variables provides programs with flexibility; a program that uses variables to replace constants can manipulate different values each time it executes. When you add loops to your programs, the same variable can hold different values during successive cycles through the loop within the same program execution. Learning to use the data structure known as an array offers further flexibility. Arrays allow you to store multiple values in adjacent memory locations and access them by varying a value that indicates which of the stored values to use. In this chapter, you will learn to create and manage C# arrays.

Declaring an Array and Assigning Values to Array Elements

Sometimes, storing just one value in memory at a time isn't adequate. For example, a sales manager who supervises 20 employees might want to determine whether each employee has produced sales above or below the average amount. When you enter the first employee's sales value into a program, you can't determine whether it is above or below average because you won't know the average until you have entered all 20 values. You might plan to assign 20 sales values to 20 separate variables, each with a unique name, then sum and average them. However, that process is awkward and unwieldy: You need 20 prompts, 20 input statements using 20 separate storage locations (in other words, 20 separate variable names), and 20 addition statements. This method might work for 20 salespeople, but what if you have 30, 40, or 10,000 salespeople?

You could enter data for 20 salespeople using just one variable in 20 successive iterations through a loop that contains one prompt, one input statement, and one addition statement. Unfortunately, when you enter the sales value for the second employee, that data item replaces the value for the first employee, and the first employee's value is no longer available to compare to the average of all 20 values. With this approach, when the data-entry loop finishes, the only sales value left in memory is the last one entered.

The best solution to this problem is to create an array. An **array** is a list of data items that all have the same data type and the same name. Each object in an array is an **array element**. You can distinguish each element from the others in an array with a subscript. A **subscript** (also called an **index**) is an integer that indicates the position of a particular array element. In C#, a subscript is written between square brackets that follow an array name.

You declare an array variable with a data type, a pair of square brackets, and an identifier. For example, to declare an array of **double** values to hold sales values for salespeople, you write the following:

```
double[] sales;
```

In some programming languages, such as C++ and Java, you also can declare an array variable by placing the square brackets after the array name, as in **double sales[];**. This format is illegal in C#.

You can provide any legal identifier you want for an array, but programmers conventionally name arrays like they name variables—starting with a lowercase letter and using uppercase letters to begin subsequent words. Additionally, many programmers observe one of the following conventions to make it more obvious that the name represents a group of items:

- Arrays are often named using a plural noun such as `sales`.

- Arrays are often named by adding a final word that implies a group, such as `salesList`, `salesTable`, or `salesArray`.

After you declare an array variable, you still need to create the actual array because declaring an array and reserving memory space for it are two distinct processes. You can declare an array variable and reserve memory locations for 20 `sales` objects using the following two statements:

```
double[] sales;
sales = new double[20];
```

The keyword new is also known as the **new** *operator*; it is used to create objects. In this case, it creates 20 separate `sales` elements. You also can declare and create an array in one statement, such as the following:

```
double[] sales = new double[20];
```

You can change the size of an array associated with an identifier, if necessary. For example, if you declare `int[] array;`, you can assign five elements later with `array = new int[5];`; later in the program, you might alter the array size to 100 with `array = new int[100];`. Still later, you could alter it again to be either larger or smaller. Most other programming languages do not provide this capability. If you resize an array in C#, the same identifier refers to a new array in memory, and all the values are set to the default value for the data type.

The statement `double[] sales = new double[20];` reserves 20 memory locations. In C#, an array's elements are numbered beginning with 0, so if an array has 20 elements, you can use any subscript from 0 through 19. In other words, the first `sales` array element is `sales[0]`, and the last `sales` element is `sales[19]`. Figure 6-1 shows how the array of 20 sales values appears in computer memory. The figure assumes that the array begins at memory address 20000. When you instantiate an array, you cannot choose its location in memory any more than you can choose the location of any other variable. However, you do know that after the first array element, the subsequent elements will follow immediately. Because a **double** takes eight bytes of storage, each element of a **double** array is stored in succession at an address that is eight bytes higher than the previous one.

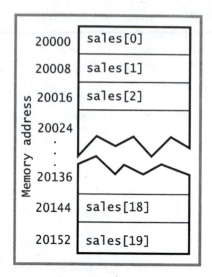

Figure 6-1   An array of 20 sales items in memory

In C#, an array subscript must be an integer. For example, no array contains an element with a subscript of 1.5. A subscript can be an integer constant or variable or an expression that evaluates to an integer. For example, if x and y are integers, and their sum is at least 0 but less than the size of an array named array, then it is legal to refer to the element array[x + y].

Some other languages, such as COBOL, BASIC, and Visual Basic, use parentheses rather than square brackets to refer to individual array elements. By using brackets, the creators of C# made it easier for you to distinguish arrays from methods. Like C#, C++ and Java also use brackets surrounding array subscripts.

A common mistake is to forget that the first element in an array is element 0 (sometimes called the *zeroth element*), especially if you know another programming language in which the first array element is element 1. Making this mistake means you will be "off by one" in your use of any array. If you are "off by one" but still using a valid subscript when accessing an array element, your program will most likely produce incorrect output. If you are "off by one" so that your subscript becomes larger than the highest value allowed, you will cause a program error.

To remember that array elements begin with element 0, it might be helpful to think of the first array element as being "zero elements away from" the beginning of the array, the second element as being "one element away from" the beginning of the array, and so on.

When you work with any individual array element, you treat it no differently than you treat a single variable of the same type. For example, to assign a value to the first element in the sales array, you use a simple assignment statement, such as the following:

```
sales[0] = 2100.00;
```

To output the value of the last sales in a 20-element array, you write:

```
WriteLine(sales[19]);
```

 Watch the video *Searching an Array*.

Initializing an Array

In C#, arrays are objects. When you instantiate an array, you are creating a specific instance of a class that derives from, or builds upon, the built-in class named System.Array. (In the chapter "Introduction to Inheritance," you will learn more about deriving classes.)

When you declare arrays or any other objects, the following default values are assigned to the elements:

- Numeric fields are set to 0.

- Character fields are set to '\u0000' or null. (You learned about escape sequences that start with '\u' in Chapter 2.)

- bool fields are set to false.

You can assign nondefault values to array elements at declaration by including a comma-separated list of values enclosed within curly braces. For example, if you want to create an array named myScores and store five test scores within the array, you can use any of the following declarations:

```
int[] myScores = new int[5] {100, 76, 88, 100, 90};
int[] myScores = new int[] {100, 76, 88, 100, 90};
int[] myScores = {100, 76, 88, 100, 90};
```

The list of values provided for an array is an **initializer list**. When you initialize an array by providing a size and an initializer list, as in the first example, the stated size and number of list elements must match. However, when you initialize an array with values, you are not required to give the array a size, as shown in the second example; in that case, the size is assigned based on the number of values in the initializing list. The third example shows that when you initialize an array, you do not need to use the keyword **new** and repeat the type; instead, memory is assigned based on the stated array type and the length of the list of provided values. Of these three examples, the first is most explicit, but it requires two changes if the number of elements is altered. The third example requires the least typing but might not clarify that a new object is being created. Microsoft's documentation prefers the third example because it is most concise, but you should use the form of array initialization that is clearest to you or that is conventional in your organization.

When you use curly braces at the end of a block of code, you do not follow the closing curly brace with a semicolon. However, when you use curly braces to enclose a list of array values, you must complete the statement with a semicolon.

Programmers who have used other languages such as C++ might expect that when an initialization list is shorter than the number of declared array elements, the "extra" elements will be set to default values. This is not the case in C#; if you declare a size, then you must list a value for each element.

An array of characters can be assigned to a string. For example, you can write the following:

```
char[] arrayOfLetters = {'h', 'e', 'l', 'l', 'o'};
string word = new string(arrayOfLetters);
```

You also can access a single character in a string using a subscript. For example, if you have defined string greeting = "Hello";, then greeting[0] is 'H'. However, a string is not an array of characters, and you cannot assign a character to a portion of a string such as in the invalid assignment word[0] = 'A';.

TWO TRUTHS & A LIE

Declaring an Array and Assigning Values to Array Elements

1. To reserve memory locations for 10 testScores objects, you can use the following statement:

   ```
   int[] testScores = new int[9];
   ```

2. To assign 60 to the last element in a 10-element array named testScores, you can use the following statement:

   ```
   testScores[9] = 60;
   ```

3. The following statement creates an array named testScore and stores four values within the array:

   ```
   int[] testScores = new int [] {90, 85, 76, 92};
   ```

The false statement is #1. To reserve memory locations for 10 testScores objects, you must use 10 within the second set of square braces. The 10 elements will use the subscripts 0 through 9.

Accessing Array Elements

When you declare an array of five integers, such as the following, you often want to perform the same operation on each array element:

```
int[] myScores = {100, 76, 88, 100, 90};
```

To increase each array element by 3, for example, you can write the following five statements:

```
myScores[0] += 3;
myScores[1] += 3;
myScores[2] += 3;
myScores[3] += 3;
myScores[4] += 3;
```

If you treat each array element as an individual entity, declaring an array doesn't offer much of an advantage over declaring individual variables. The power of arrays becomes apparent when you use subscripts that are variables rather than constant values. Then you can use a loop to perform arithmetic on each element in the array. For example, you can use a `while` loop, as follows:

```
int sub = 0;
while(sub < 5)
{
    myScores[sub] += 3;
    ++sub;
}
```

You also can use a `for` loop, as follows:

```
for(int sub = 0; sub < 5; ++sub)
    myScores[sub] += 3;
```

In both examples, the variable `sub` is declared and initialized to 0, then compared to 5. Because it is less than 5, the loop executes, and `myScores[0]` increases by 3. The variable `sub` is incremented and becomes 1, which is still less than 5, so when the loop executes again, `myScores[1]` increases by 3, and so on. If the array had 100 elements, individually increasing the array values by 3 would require 95 additional statements, but the only change required using either loop would be to change the limiting value for `sub` from 5 to 100.

New array users sometimes think there is a permanent connection between a variable used as a subscript and the array with which it is used, but that is not the case. For example, if you vary `sub` from 0 to 10 to fill an array, you do not need to use `sub` later when displaying the array elements—either the same variable or a different variable can be used as a subscript elsewhere in the program.

Using the Length Property

When you work with array elements, you must ensure that the subscript you use remains in the range of 0 through one less than the array's length. If you declare an array with five elements and use a subscript that is negative or more than 4, you will receive the error message *IndexOutOfRangeException* when you run the program. (You will learn about the `IndexOutOfRangeException` in the chapter "Exception Handling.") This message means the index, or subscript, does not hold a value that legally can access an array element. For example, if you declare an array of five integers, you can display them as follows:

```
int[] myScores = {100, 75, 88, 100, 90};
for(int sub = 0; sub < 5; ++sub)
    WriteLine("{0} ", myScores[sub]);
```

If you modify your program to change the size of the array, you must remember to change the comparison in the for loop as well as every other reference to the array size within the program. Many text editors have a "find and replace" feature that lets you change (for example) all of the 5s in a file, either simultaneously or one by one. However, you must be careful not to change 5s that have nothing to do with the array; for example, do not change the 5 in the score 75 inadvertently—it is the second listed value in the myScores array and has nothing to do with the array size.

A better approach is to use a value that is automatically altered when you declare an array. Because every array automatically derives from the class System.Array, you can use the fields and methods that are part of the System.Array class with any array you create. In Chapter 2, you learned that every string has a Length property. Similarly, every array has a Length property that is a member of the System.Array class and that automatically holds an array's length. The Length property is always updated to reflect any changes you make to an array's size. The following segment of code displays *Array size is 5* and subsequently displays the array's contents:

```
int[] myScores = {100, 76, 88, 100, 90};
WriteLine("Array size is {0}", myScores.Length);
for(int x = 0; x < myScores.Length; ++x)
    WriteLine(myScores[x]);
```

 An array's Length is a read-only property—you cannot assign it a new value. It is capitalized, as is the convention with all C# property identifiers. You will create property identifiers for your own classes in the chapter "Using Classes and Objects."

Using foreach

You can easily navigate through arrays using a for or while loop that varies a subscript from 0 through Array.Length - 1. C# also supports a foreach statement that you can use to cycle through every array element without using a subscript. With the foreach statement, you provide a temporary **iteration variable** that automatically holds each array value in turn.

For example, the following code displays each element in the payRate array in sequence:

```
double[] payRate = {6.00, 7.35, 8.12, 12.45, 22.22};
foreach(double money in payRate)
    WriteLine("{0}", money.ToString("C"));
```

The variable money is declared as a double within the foreach statement. During the execution of the loop, money holds each payRate value in turn—first, payRate[0], then payRate[1], and so on. As a simple variable, money does not require a subscript, making it easier to work with.

The foreach statement is used only under certain circumstances:

- You typically use foreach only when you want to access every array element. To access only selected array elements, you must manipulate subscripts using some other technique—for example, using a for loop or while loop.
- The foreach iteration variable is **read-only**—that is, you can access it, but you cannot assign a value to it. If you want to assign a value to array elements, you must use a different type of loop.

TWO TRUTHS & A LIE

Accessing Array Elements

1. Assume you have declared an array of six doubles named balances. The following statement displays all the elements:

```
for(int index = 0; index < 6; ++index)
    WriteLine(balances[index]);
```

2. Assume you have declared an array of eight doubles named prices. The following statement subtracts 2 from each element:

```
for(double pr = 0; pr < 8; ++pr)
    prices[pr] -= 2;
```

3. The following code displays 3:

```
int[] array = {1, 2, 3};
WriteLine(array.Length);
```

The false statement is #2. You can only use an int as the subscript to an array, and this example attempts to use a double.

You Do It

Creating and Using an Array

In the next steps, you create a small array to see how it is used. The array will hold salaries for four categories of employees.

(continues)

(continued)

1. Open a new file, and begin a console-based program named **ArrayDemo1** that demonstrates array use:

```
using static System.Console;
class ArrayDemo1
{
    static void Main()
    {
```

2. Declare and create an array that holds four `double` values by typing:

```
double[] payRate = {6.00, 7.35, 8.12, 12.45};
```

3. To confirm that the four values have been assigned, display them using the following code:

```
for(int x = 0; x < payRate.Length; ++x)
    WriteLine("Pay rate {0} is {1}",
        x, payRate[x].ToString("C"));
```

4. Add the two closing curly braces that end the `Main()` method and the `ArrayDemo1` class.

5. Save the program, and then compile and run it. The output appears in Figure 6-2.

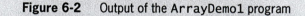

```
C:\C#\Chapter.06>ArrayDemo1
Pay rate 0 is $6.00
Pay rate 1 is $7.35
Pay rate 2 is $8.12
Pay rate 3 is $12.45

C:\C#\Chapter.06>
```

Figure 6-2   Output of the `ArrayDemo1` program

Searching an Array Using a Loop

When you want to determine whether a variable holds one of many possible valid values, one option is to use if statements to compare the variable to valid values. For example, suppose that a company manufactures 10 items. When a customer places an order for an item, you need to determine whether the item number is valid. If valid item numbers are sequential, say 101 through 110, then the following simple if statement that uses an AND operator can verify the order number and set a Boolean field to true:

```
if(itemOrdered >= 101 && itemOrdered <= 110)
    isValidItem = true;
```

If the valid item numbers are nonsequential, however—for example, 101, 108, 201, 213, 266, 304, and so on—you must code the following deeply nested if statement or a lengthy OR comparison to determine the validity of an item number:

```
if(itemOrdered == 101)
    isValidItem = true;
else if(itemOrdered == 108)
    isValidItem = true;
else if(itemOrdered == 201)
    isValidItem = true;
// and so on
```

Instead of creating a long series of if statements, a more elegant solution to determining whether a value is valid is to compare it to a list of values in an array. For example, you can initialize an array with the valid values by using the following statement:

```
int[] validValues = {101, 108, 201, 213, 266, 304, 311,
        409, 411, 412};
```

 You might prefer to declare the validValues array as a constant because, presumably, the valid item numbers should not change during program execution. In C# you must use the keywords static and readonly prior to the constant declaration. To keep these examples simple, all arrays in this chapter are declared as variable arrays.

After the validValues array is declared, you can use either a for loop or a while loop to search whether the itemOrdered variable value matches any of the array entries.

Using a for Loop to Search an Array

One way to determine whether an itemOrdered value equals a value in the validValues array is to use a for statement to loop through the array and set a Boolean variable to true when a match is found:

```
for(int x = 0; x < validValues.Length; ++x)
   if(itemOrdered == validValues[x])
      isValidItem = true;
```

This type of search is called a **sequential search** because each array element is examined in sequence. This simple for loop replaces the long series of if statements. What's more, if a company carries 1000 items instead of 10, then the list of valid items in the array must be altered, but the for statement does not change at all. As an added bonus, if you set up another array as a **parallel array** with the same number of elements and corresponding data, you can use the same subscript to access additional information. For example, if the 10 items your company carries have 10 different prices, then you can set up an array to hold those prices as follows:

```
double[] prices = {0.89, 1.23, 3.50, 0.69...}; // and so on
```

The prices must appear in the same order as their corresponding item numbers in the validValues array. Now the same for loop that finds the valid item number also finds the price, as shown in the program in Figure 6-3. In other words, if the item number is found in the second position in the validValues array, then you can find the correct price in the second position in the prices array. In the program in Figure 6-3, the variable used as a subscript, x, is set to 0 and the Boolean variable isValidItem is false. In the shaded portion of the figure, while the subscript remains smaller than the length of the array of valid item numbers, the subscript is continuously increased so that subsequent array values can be tested. When a match is found between the user's item and an item in the array, isValidItem is set to true and the price of the item is stored in itemPrice. Figure 6-4 shows two typical program executions.

If you initialize parallel arrays, it is convenient to use spacing (as shown in Figure 6-3) so that the corresponding values visually align on the screen or printed page.

Although parallel arrays can be very useful, they also can increase the likelihood of mistakes. Any time you make a change to one array, you must remember to make the corresponding change in its parallel array. As you continue to study C#, you will learn superior ways to correlate data items. For example, in the chapter "Using Classes and Objects," you will learn that you can encapsulate corresponding data items in objects and create arrays of objects.

```
using System;
using static System.Console;
class FindPriceWithForLoop
{
    static void Main()
    {
        int[] validValues = {101,  108,  201,  213,  266,
            304,  311,  409,  411,  412};
        double[] prices =   {0.89, 1.23, 3.50, 0.69, 5.79,
            3.19, 0.99, 0.89, 1.26, 8.00};
        int itemOrdered;
        double itemPrice = 0;
        bool isValidItem = false;
        Write("Please enter an item ");
        itemOrdered = Convert.ToInt32(ReadLine());
        for(int x = 0; x < validValues.Length; ++x)
        {
            if(itemOrdered == validValues[x])
            {
                isValidItem = true;
                itemPrice = prices[x];
            }
        }
        if(isValidItem)
            WriteLine("Price is {0}", itemPrice);
        else
            WriteLine("Sorry - item not found");
    }
}
```

Figure 6-3   The FindPriceWithForLoop program

Figure 6-4   Two typical executions of the FindPriceWithForLoop program

In the fourth statement of the Main() method in Figure 6-3, itemPrice is set to 0. Setting this variable is required because its value is later altered only if an item number match is found in the validValues array. When C# determines that a variable's value is only set depending on an if statement, C# will not allow you to display the variable because the compiler assumes that the if statement's Boolean expression could have been false and the variable might not have been set to a valid value.

Improving a Loop's Efficiency

The code shown in Figure 6-3 can be made more efficient. Currently, the program compares every itemOrdered with each of the 10 validValues. Even when an itemOrdered is equivalent to the first value in the validValues array (101), you always make nine additional cycles through the array comparing all the values. On each of these nine additional iterations, the comparison between itemOrdered and validValues[x] is always false. As soon as a match for an itemOrdered is found, the most efficient action is to break out of the for loop early. An easy way to accomplish this task is to set x to a high value within the block of statements executed when a match is found. Then, after a match, the for loop will not execute again because the limiting comparison (x < validValues.Length) will have been surpassed. Figure 6-5 shows this approach.

```
for(int x = 0; x < validValues.Length; ++x)
{
    if(itemOrdered == validValues[x])
    {
        isValidItem = true;
        itemPrice = prices[x];
        x = validValues.Length;
            // Change x to force break out of loop
            // when you find a match
    }
}
```

Figure 6-5   Loop with forced early exit

In the code segment in Figure 6-5, instead of the statement that sets x to validValues.Length when a match is found, you could remove that statement and change the comparison in the middle section of the for statement to a compound statement, as follows:

```
for(int x = 0; x < validValues.Length && !isValidItem; ++x)...
```

As another alternative, you could remove the statement that sets x to validValues.Length and place a break statement within the loop in its place. A break statement exits the current code block immediately.

If you decide to leave a loop as soon as a match is found, the most efficient strategy is to place the most common items first so they are matched sooner. For example, if item 311 is ordered most often, place 311 first in the validValues array and its price ($0.99) first in the prices array. However, it might be more convenient for people to view the item numbers in ascending numerical order. In many business applications, your first consideration is how easily users can read, understand, and modify your programs. However, in other applications, such as programming for mobile devices, speed and memory considerations are more important. You should follow the recommendations of your instructors or supervisors.

Some programmers disapprove of exiting a for loop early, whether by setting a variable's value or by using a break statement. They argue that programs are easier to debug and maintain if each program segment has only one entry and one exit point. If you (or your instructor) agree with this philosophy, then you can select an approach that uses a while statement, as described next.

Using a while Loop to Search an Array

As an alternative to using a for loop to search an array, you can use a while loop to search for a match. Using this approach, you set a subscript to 0 and, while the itemOrdered is not equal to a value in the array, increase the subscript and keep looking. You search only while the subscript remains lower than the number of elements in the array. If the subscript increases until it matches validValues.Length, then you never found a match in the array. If the loop ends before the subscript reaches validValues.Length, then you found a match, and the correct price can be assigned to the itemPrice variable. Figure 6-6 shows a program that uses this approach.

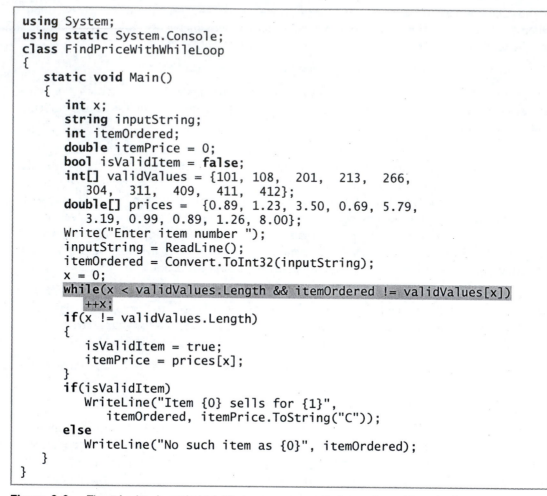

```
using System;
using static System.Console;
class FindPriceWithWhileLoop
{
    static void Main()
    {
        int x;
        string inputString;
        int itemOrdered;
        double itemPrice = 0;
        bool isValidItem = false;
        int[] validValues = {101, 108, 201, 213, 266,
            304, 311, 409, 411, 412};
        double[] prices = {0.89, 1.23, 3.50, 0.69, 5.79,
            3.19, 0.99, 0.89, 1.26, 8.00};
        Write("Enter item number ");
        inputString = ReadLine();
        itemOrdered = Convert.ToInt32(inputString);
        x = 0;
        while(x < validValues.Length && itemOrdered != validValues[x])
            ++x;
        if(x != validValues.Length)
        {
            isValidItem = true;
            itemPrice = prices[x];
        }
        if(isValidItem)
            WriteLine("Item {0} sells for {1}",
                itemOrdered, itemPrice.ToString("C"));
        else
            WriteLine("No such item as {0}", itemOrdered);
    }
}
```

Figure 6-6   The FindPriceWithWhileLoop program that searches with a while loop

In the application in Figure 6-6, the variable used as a subscript, x, is set to 0 and the Boolean variable isValidItem is false. In the shaded portion of the figure, while the subscript remains smaller than the length of the array of valid item numbers, and while the user's requested item does not match a valid item, the subscript is increased so that subsequent array values can be tested. The while loop ends when a match is found or the array tests have been exhausted, whichever comes first. When the loop ends, if x is not equal to the size of the array, then a valid item has been found, and its price can be retrieved from the prices array. Figure 6-7 shows two executions of the program. In the first execution, a match is found; in the second, an invalid item number is entered, so no match is found.

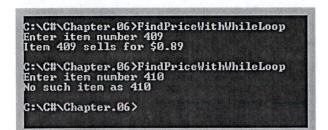

```
C:\C#\Chapter.06>FindPriceWithWhileLoop
Enter item number 409
Item 409 sells for $0.89

C:\C#\Chapter.06>FindPriceWithWhileLoop
Enter item number 410
No such item as 410

C:\C#\Chapter.06>
```

Figure 6-7   Two executions of the `FindPriceWithWhileLoop` application

Watch the video *Searching an Array.*

Searching an Array for a Range Match

Searching an array for an exact match is not always practical. For example, suppose your mail-order company gives customer discounts based on the quantity of items ordered. Perhaps no discount is given for any order of up to a dozen items, but increasing discounts are available for orders of increasing quantities, as shown in Figure 6-8.

Total Quantity Ordered	Discount (%)
1 to 12	None
13 to 49	10
50 to 99	14
100 to 199	18
200 or more	20

Figure 6-8   Discount table for a mail-order company

One awkward, impractical option is to create a single array to store the discount rates. You could use a variable named `numOfItems` as a subscript to the array, but the array would need hundreds of entries, such as the following:

```
double[] discounts = {0, 0, 0, 0, 0, 0, 0, 0, 0, 0,
   0, 0, 0, 0.10, 0.10, 0.10 ...}; // and so on
```

When `numOfItems` is 3, for example, then `discounts[numOfItems]` or `discounts[3]` is 0. When `numOfItems` is 14, then `discounts[numOfItems]` or `discounts[14]` is 0.10. Because a customer might order thousands of items, the array would need to be ridiculously large.

A better option is to create parallel arrays. One array will hold the five discount rates, and the other array will hold five discount range limits. Then you can perform a **range match** by determining the pair of limiting values between which a customer's order falls. The Total Quantity Ordered column in Figure 6-8 shows five ranges. If you use only the first value in each range, then you can create an array that holds five low limits:

```
int[] discountRangeLowLimits = {1, 13, 50, 100, 200};
```

A parallel array will hold the five discount rates:

```
double[] discounts = {0, 0.10, 0.14, 0.18, 0.20};
```

Then, starting at the last discountRangeLowLimits array element, for any numOfItems greater than or equal to discountRangeLowLimits[4], the appropriate discount is discounts[4]. In other words, for any numOfItems less than discountRangeLowLimits[4], you should decrement the subscript and look in a lower range. Figure 6-9 shows the code.

```
// Assume numOfItems is a declared integer for which a user
// has input a value
int[] discountRangeLowLimits = {1, 13,   50,   100,   200};
double[] discounts =           {0, 0.10, 0.14, 0.18, 0.20};
double customerDiscount;
int sub = discountRangeLowLimits.Length - 1;
while(sub >= 0 && numOfItems < discountRangeLowLimits[sub])
   --sub;
customerDiscount = discounts[sub];
```

Figure 6-9   Searching an array of range limits

As an alternate approach to the range-checking logic in Figure 6-9, you can choose to create an array that contains the upper limit of each range, such as the following:

```
int[] discountRangeUpperLimits = {12, 49, 99, 199, 9999999};
```

Then the logic can be written to compare numOfItems to each range limit until the correct range is located, as follows:

```
int sub = 0;
while(sub < discountRangeUpperLimits.Length &&
   numOfItems > discountRangeUpperLimits[sub])
   ++sub;
customerDiscount = discounts[sub];
```

In this example, sub is initialized to 0. While it remains within array bounds, and while numOfItems is more than each upper-range limit, sub is increased. In other words, if numOfItems is 3, the while expression is false on the first loop iteration, the loop ends, sub remains 0, and the customer discount is the first discount. However, if numOfItems is 30, then the while expression is true on the first loop iteration, sub becomes 1, the while expression is `false` on the second iteration, and the second discount is used. In this example, the last `discountRangeUpperLimits` array value is 9999999. This very high value was used with the assumption that no `numOfItems` would ever exceed it, but, because this assumption could possibly be wrong, many programmers prefer to use a range-checking method that uses lower range limits. As with many issues in programming, multiple correct approaches frequently exist for the same problem.

TWO TRUTHS & A LIE

Searching an Array Using a Loop

1. A parallel array has the same number of elements as another array and corresponding data.

2. When you search an array for an exact match in a parallel array, you must perform a loop as many times as there are elements in the arrays.

3. One practical solution to creating an array with which to perform a range check is to design the array to hold the lowest value in each range.

The false statement is #2. When you search an array for an exact match in a parallel array, you can perform a loop as many times as there are elements in the arrays, but once a match is found, the additional loop iterations are unnecessary. Terminating the loop cycles as soon as a match is found is the most efficient approach.

Using the `BinarySearch()`, `Sort()`, and `Reverse()` Methods

You have already learned that every array in C# can use the `Length` property it gets from the `System.Array` class. Additionally, the `System.Array` class contains a variety of useful, built-in methods that can search, sort, and manipulate array elements. (You already have used many built-in C# methods such as `WriteLine()` and `ReadLine()`. You will learn to write your own methods in the next chapter.)

Using the `BinarySearch()` Method

A **binary search** is one in which a sorted list of objects is split in half repeatedly as the search gets closer and closer to a match. Perhaps you have played a guessing game, trying to guess a number from 1 to 100. If you asked, "Is it less than 50?" and continued to narrow your guesses upon hearing each subsequent answer, then you have performed a binary search. In C#, the `BinarySearch()` method finds a requested value in a sorted array.

Figure 6-10 shows a program that declares an array of integer `idNumbers` arranged in ascending order. The program prompts a user for a value, converts it to an integer, and passes the array and the entered value to the `BinarySearch()` method in the shaded statement. The method returns –1 if the value is not found in the array; otherwise, it returns the array position of the sought value. Figure 6-11 shows two executions of this program.

The `BinarySearch()` method takes two arguments—the array name and the value for which to search. In Chapter 1 you learned that arguments represent information that a method needs to perform its task. When methods require multiple arguments, they are separated by commas. For example, when you have used the `WriteLine()` method, you have passed a format string and values to be displayed, all separated by commas.

If you add the statement `using static System.Array;` at the top of a program, then you can use the method name `BinarySearch()` without its class name.

```
using System;
using static System.Console;
class BinarySearchDemo
{
    static void Main()
    {
        int[] idNumbers = {122, 167, 204, 219, 345};
        int x;
        string entryString;
        int entryId;
        Write("Enter an Employee ID ");
        entryString = ReadLine();
        entryId = Convert.ToInt32(entryString);
        x = Array.BinarySearch(idNumbers, entryId);
        if(x < 0)
            WriteLine("ID {0} not found", entryId);
        else
            WriteLine("ID {0} found at position {1} ",
                entryId, x);
    }
}
```

Figure 6-10   The `BinarySearchDemo` program

```
C:\C#\Chapter.06>BinarySearchDemo
Enter an Employee ID 219
ID 219 found at position 3

C:\C#\Chapter.06>BinarySearchDemo
Enter an Employee ID 220
ID 220 not found

C:\C#\Chapter.06>
```

Figure 6-11   Two executions of the `BinarySearchDemo` program

You have sent arguments to methods, as in the following statement:

`Write("Enter an Employee ID ");`

You also have accepted methods' returned values, as in the following statement:

`entryString = ReadLine();`

When you use the `BinarySearch()` method, you both send arguments and receive returned values:

`x = Array.BinarySearch(idNumbers, entryId);`

The statement calls the method that performs the search, returning −1 or the position where `entryId` was found; that value is then stored in `x`. This single line of code is easier to write, less prone to error, and easier to understand than writing a loop to cycle through the `idNumbers` array looking for a match. Still, it is worthwhile to understand how to perform the search without the `BinarySearch()` method, as you learned while studying parallel arrays earlier in this chapter. You will need to use that technique under the following conditions, when the `BinarySearch()` method proves inadequate:

- If your array items are not arranged in ascending order, the `BinarySearch()` method does not work correctly.

- If your array holds duplicate values and you want to find all of them, the `BinarySearch()` method doesn't work—it can return only one value, so it returns the position of the first matching value it finds (which is not necessarily the first instance of the value in the array).

- If you want to find a range match rather than an exact match, the `BinarySearch()` method does not work.

Using the Sort() Method

The Sort() method arranges array items in ascending order. The method works numerically for number types and alphabetically for characters and strings. To use the method, you pass the array name to Array.Sort(), and the element positions within the array are rearranged appropriately. Figure 6-12 shows a program that sorts an array of strings; Figure 6-13 shows its execution.

```csharp
using System;
using static System.Console;
class SortArray
{
    static void Main()
    {
        string[] names = {"Olive", "Patty", "Richard", "Ned", "Mindy"};
        int x;
        Array.Sort(names);
        for(x = 0; x < names.Length; ++x)
            WriteLine(names[x]);
    }
}
```

Figure 6-12   The SortArray program

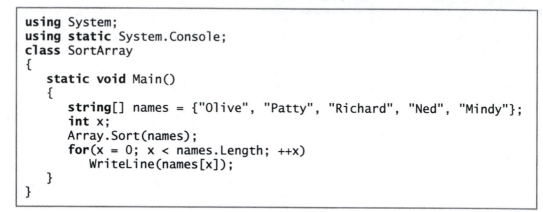

```
C:\C#\Chapter.06>SortArray
Mindy
Ned
Olive
Patty
Richard

C:\C#\Chapter.06>
```

Figure 6-13   Execution of the SortArray program

Because the BinarySearch() method requires that array elements be sorted in order, the Sort() method is often used in conjunction with it.

 The Array.Sort() method provides a good example of encapsulation—you can use the method without understanding how it works internally. The method actually uses an algorithm named *Quicksort*. You will learn how to implement this algorithm yourself as you continue to study programming.

 If you add the statement using static System.Array; at the top of a program, then you can use the method name Sort() without its class name.

Using the Reverse() Method

The Reverse() method reverses the order of items in an array. In other words, for any array, the element that starts in position 0 is relocated to position Length - 1, the element that starts in position 1 is relocated to position Length - 2, and so on until the element that starts in position Length - 1 is relocated to position 0. When you Reverse() an array that contains an odd number of elements, the middle element will remain in its original location. The Reverse() method does not sort array elements; it only rearranges their values to the opposite order.

You call the Reverse() method the same way you call the Sort() method—you simply pass the array name to the method. Figure 6-14 shows a program that uses Reverse() with an array of strings, and Figure 6-15 shows its execution.

```csharp
using System;
using static System.Console;
class ReverseArray
{
    static void Main()
    {
        string[] names = {"Zach", "Rose", "Wendy", "Marcia"};
        int x;
        Array.Reverse(names);
        for(x = 0; x < names.Length; ++x)
            WriteLine(names[x]);
    }
}
```

Figure 6-14 The ReverseArray program

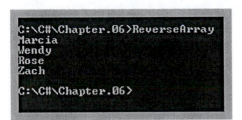

```
C:\C#\Chapter.06>ReverseArray
Marcia
Wendy
Rose
Zach

C:\C#\Chapter.06>
```

Figure 6-15 Execution of the ReverseArray program

TWO TRUTHS & A LIE

Using the BinarySearch(), Sort(), and Reverse() Methods

1. When you use the BinarySearch() method, the searched array items must first be organized in ascending order.

2. The Array.Sort() and Array.Reverse() methods are similar in that both require a single argument.

3. The Array.Sort() and Array.Reverse() methods are different in that one places items in ascending order and the other places them in descending order.

The false statement is #3. The Array.Sort() method places items in ascending order, but the Array.Reverse() method simply reverses the existing order of any array whether it was presorted or not.

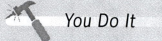

You Do It

Using the Sort() and Reverse() Methods

In the next steps, you create an array of integers and use the Sort() and Reverse() methods to manipulate it.

1. Open a new file and type the beginning of a program named **ArrayDemo2** that includes an array of eight integer test scores, an integer you will use as a subscript, and a string that will hold user-entered data.

```
using System;
using static System.Console;
class ArrayDemo2
{
    static void Main()
    {
        int[] scores = new int[8];
        int x;
        string inputString;
```

(continues)

(continued)

2. Add a loop that prompts the user, accepts a test score, converts the score to an integer, and stores it as the appropriate element of the `scores` array.

```
for(x = 0; x < scores.Length; ++x)
{
   Write("Enter your score on test {0} ", x + 1);
   inputString = ReadLine();
   scores[x] = Convert.ToInt32(inputString);
}
```

The program displays x + 1 with each score[x] because, although array elements are numbered starting with 0, people usually count items starting with 1.

3. Add a statement that creates a dashed line to visually separate the input from the output. Display "Scores in original order:", then use a loop to display each score in a field that is six characters wide.

```
WriteLine("\n--------------------------");
WriteLine("Scores in original order:");
for(x = 0; x < scores.Length; ++x)
   Write("{0, 6}", scores[x]);
```

You learned to set display field sizes when you learned about format strings in Chapter 2.

4. Add another dashed line for visual separation, then pass the `scores` array to the `Array.Sort()` method. Display *Scores in sorted order:*, then use a loop to display each of the newly sorted scores.

```
WriteLine("\n--------------------------");
Array.Sort(scores);
WriteLine("Scores in sorted order:");
for(x = 0; x < scores.Length; ++x)
   Write("{0, 6}", scores[x]);
```

5. Add one more dashed line, reverse the array elements by passing `scores` to the `Array.Reverse()` method, display *Scores in reverse order:*, and show the rearranged scores.

```
WriteLine("\n--------------------------");
Array.Reverse(scores);
WriteLine("Scores in reverse order:");
for(x = 0; x < scores.Length; ++x)
   Write("{0, 6}", scores[x]);
```

(continues)

(continued)

6. Add two closing curly braces—one for the `Main()` method and one for the class.

7. Save the file, and then compile and execute the program. Figure 6-16 shows a typical execution of the program. The user-entered scores are not in order, but after the call to the `Sort()` method, they appear in ascending order. After the call to the `Reverse()` method, they appear in descending order.

```
C:\C#\Chapter.06>ArrayDemo2
Enter your score on test 1 75
Enter your score on test 2 82
Enter your score on test 3 100
Enter your score on test 4 90
Enter your score on test 5 92
Enter your score on test 6 78
Enter your score on test 7 95
Enter your score on test 8 89


Scores in original order:
     75     82    100     90     92     78     95     89
Scores in sorted order:
     75     78     82     89     90     92     95    100
Scores in reverse order:
    100     95     92     90     89     82     78     75
C:\C#\Chapter.06>
```

Figure 6-16   Typical execution of the `ArrayDemo2` program

Using Multidimensional Arrays

When you declare an array such as `double[] sales = new double[20];`, you can envision the declared integers as a column of numbers in memory, as shown at the beginning of this chapter in Figure 6-1. In other words, you can picture the 20 declared numbers stacked one on top of the next. An array that you can picture as a column of values, and whose elements you can access using a single subscript, is a **one-dimensional** or **single-dimensional array**. You can think of the single dimension of a single-dimensional array as the height of the array.

C# also supports **multidimensional arrays**—those that require multiple subscripts to access the array elements. The most commonly used multidimensional arrays are two-dimensional arrays that are rectangular. **Two-dimensional arrays** have two or more columns of values for each row, as shown in Figure 6-17. You can think of the two dimensions of a two-dimensional array as height and width.

sales[0, 0]	sales[0, 1]	sales[0, 2]	sales[0, 3]
sales[1, 0]	sales[1, 1]	sales[1, 2]	sales[1, 3]
sales[2, 0]	sales[2, 1]	sales[2, 2]	sales[2, 3]

Figure 6-17   View of a rectangular, two-dimensional array in memory

The array in Figure 6-17 is a rectangular array. In a **rectangular array**, each row has the same number of columns. You must use two subscripts when you access an element in a two-dimensional array. When mathematicians use a two-dimensional array, they often call it a *matrix* or a *table*; you might have used a two-dimensional array called a spreadsheet. You might want to create a `sales` array with two dimensions, as shown in Figure 6-17, if, for example, each row represented a category of items sold, and each column represented a salesperson who sold them.

When you declare a one-dimensional array, you type a single, empty set of square brackets after the array type, and you use a single subscript in a set of square brackets when reserving memory. To declare a two-dimensional array, you type a comma in the square brackets after the array type, and you use two subscripts, separated by a comma in brackets, when reserving memory. For example, the array in Figure 6-17 can be declared as the following, creating an array named `sales` that holds three rows and four columns:

```
double[ , ] sales = new double[3, 4];
```

When you declare a two-dimensional array, spaces surrounding the comma within the square brackets are optional.

Just as with a one-dimensional array, every element in a two-dimensional array is the same data type. Also, just as with a one-dimensional array if you do not provide values for the elements in a two-dimensional array, the values are set to the default value for the data type (for example, 0 for numeric data). You can assign other values to the array elements later. For example, the following statement assigns the value 14.00 to the element of the `sales` array that is in the first column of the first row:

```
sales[0, 0] = 14.00;
```

Alternatively, you can initialize a two-dimensional array by assigning values when it is created. For example, the following code assigns values to `sales` upon declaration:

```
double[ , ] sales = {{14.00, 15.00, 16.00, 17.00},
                     {21.99, 34.55, 67.88, 31.99},
                     {12.03, 55.55, 32.89, 1.17}};
```

The `sales` array contains three rows and four columns. You contain the entire set of values within a pair of curly braces. The first row of the array holds the four `doubles` 14.00, 15.00, 16.00 and 17.00. Notice that these four values are placed within their own inner set of curly braces to indicate that they constitute one row, or the first row, which is row 0. The row and its curly braces are separated from the next row with a comma. The next four values in their own set of braces make up the second row (row 1), which you reference with the subscript 1, and the last four values constitute the third row (row 2).

When you refer to an element in a two-dimensional array, the first value within the brackets following the array name always refers to the row; the second value, after the comma, refers to the column. As examples, the value of `sales[0, 0]` is 14.00, the value of `sales[0, 1]` is 15.00, the value of `sales[1, 0]` is 21.99, and the value of `sales[2, 3]` is 1.17. You do not need to place each row of values that initializes a two-dimensional array on its own line. However, doing so makes the positions of values easier to understand.

As an example of how useful two-dimensional arrays can be, assume that you own an apartment building with four floors—a basement, which you refer to as floor zero, and three other floors numbered one, two, and three. In addition, each of the floors has studio (with no bedroom), one-, and two-bedroom apartments. The monthly rent for each type of apartment is different, and the rent is higher for apartments with more bedrooms. Figure 6-18 shows the rental amounts.

Floor	Zero Bedrooms	One Bedroom	Two Bedrooms
0	400	450	510
1	500	560	630
2	625	676	740
3	1000	1250	1600

Figure 6-18   Rents charged (in dollars)

To determine a tenant's rent, you need to know two pieces of information about the apartment: the floor and the number of bedrooms. Within a C# program, you can declare an array of rents using the following code:

```
int[ , ] rents = { {400, 450, 510},
                   {500, 560, 630},
                   {625, 676, 740},
                   {1000, 1250, 1600} };
```

If `floor` and `bedrooms` are integers with in-range values, then any tenant's rent can be referred to as `rents[floor, bedrooms]`.

Figure 6-19 shows a complete program that uses a rectangular, two-dimensional array to hold rent values. Figure 6-20 shows a typical execution.

```
using System;
using static System.Console;
class RentFinder
{
    static void Main()
    {
        int[ , ] rents = { {400, 450, 510},
                           {500, 560, 630},
                           {625, 676, 740},
                           {1000, 1250, 1600} };
        int floor;
        int bedrooms;
        string inputString;
        Write("Enter the floor on which you want to live ");
        inputString = ReadLine();
        floor = Convert.ToInt32(inputString);
        Write("Enter the number of bedrooms you need ");
        inputString = ReadLine();
        bedrooms = Convert.ToInt32(inputString);
        WriteLine("The rent is {0}", rents[floor, bedrooms]);
    }
}
```

Figure 6-19   The RentFinder program

```
C:\C#\Chapter.06>RentFinder
Enter the floor on which you want to live 2
Enter the number of bedrooms you need 1
The rent is 676

C:\C#\Chapter.06>
```

Figure 6-20   Typical execution of the RentFinder program

Watch the video *Using a Two-Dimensional Array*.

C# supports arrays with more than two dimensions. For example, as in the program in
Figure 6-19, if you own a multistory apartment building with different numbers of bedrooms
available in apartments on each floor, you can use a two-dimensional array to store the rental
fees. However, if you own several apartment buildings, you might want to employ a third
dimension to store the building number. Suppose you want to store rents for four buildings
that have three floors each and that each hold two types of apartments. Figure 6-21 shows
how you might define such an array.

```
int[ , , ] rents = { { {400, 500}, {450, 550}, {500, 550}},
                     { {510, 610}, {710, 810}, {910, 1010}},
                     { {525, 625}, {725, 825}, {925, 1025}},
                     { {850, 950}, {1050, 1150}, {1250, 1350}}};
```

Figure 6-21   A three-dimensional `array` definition

The empty brackets that follow the data type contain two commas, showing that the array supports three dimensions. A set of curly braces surrounds all the data; the inner curly braces represent the following:

- Four inner sets of braces surround the data for each building—each row of values represents a building (0 through 3).

- Within each row, the three sets of inner braces represent each floor—first a basement, then floor one, and floor two. For example, in building 0, {400, 500} are rents for floor 0, and {450, 550} are rents for floor 1.

- Within each floor, the two braced values represent the bedrooms—first a zero-bedroom apartment and then a one-bedroom apartment. For example, in building 0, floor 0, 400 is the rent for a zero-bedroom apartment, and 500 is the rent for a one-bedroom apartment.

Using the three-dimensional array in Figure 6-21, an expression such as `rents[building, floor, bedrooms]` refers to a specific rent value for a building whose number is stored in the `building` variable and whose floor and bedroom numbers are stored in the `floor` and `bedrooms` variables. Specifically, `rents[3, 1, 0]` refers to a studio (zero-bedroom) apartment on the first floor of building 3 (which is the fourth building). The value of `rents[3, 1, 0]` is $1050 in Figure 6-21. When you are programming in C#, you can use four, five, or more dimensions in an array. As long as you can keep track of the order of the variables needed as subscripts, and as long as you don't exhaust your computer's memory, C# lets you create arrays of any size.

Using Jagged Arrays

C# also supports jagged arrays. A **jagged array** is a one-dimensional array in which each element is another array. The major difference between jagged and rectangular arrays is that in jagged arrays, each row can be a different length.

For example, consider an application in which you want to store train ticket prices for each stop along five different routes. Suppose some of the routes have as many as 10 stops and others have as few as two. Each of the five routes could be represented by a row in a multidimensional array. Then you would have two logical choices for the columns:

- You could create a rectangular, two-dimensional array, allowing 10 columns for each row. In some of the rows, as many as eight of the columns would be empty, because some routes have only two stops.

- You could create a jagged array, allowing a different number of elements for each row. Figure 6-22 shows how you could implement this option.

```
double [][] tickets = {
    new double[] {5.50, 6.75, 7.95, 9.00, 12.00,
        13.00, 14.50, 17.00, 19.00, 20.25},
    new double[] {5.00, 6.00},
    new double[] {7.50, 9.00, 9.95, 12.00, 13.00, 14.00},
    new double[] {3.50, 6.45, 9.95, 10.00, 12.75},
    new double[] {15.00, 16.00} };
```

Figure 6-22   A jagged array

Two square brackets are used following the data type of the array in Figure 6-22. This notation declares a jagged array that is composed of five separate one-dimensional arrays. Within the jagged array, each row needs its own **new** operator and data type. To refer to a jagged array element, you use two sets of brackets after the array name—for example, tickets[route][stop]. In Figure 6-22, the value of tickets[0][0] is 5.50, the value of tickets[0][1] is 6.75, and the value of tickets[0][2] is 7.95. The value of tickets[1][0] is 5.00, and the value of tickets[1][1] is 6.00. Referring to tickets[1][2] is invalid because there is no column 2 in the second row (that is, there are only two stops, not three, on the second train route).

TWO TRUTHS & A LIE

Using Multidimensional Arrays

1. A rectangular array has the same number of columns as rows.

2. The following array contains two rows and three columns:
   ```
   int[ , ] departments = {{12, 54, 16},
                           {22, 44, 47}};
   ```

3. A jagged array is a one-dimensional array in which each element is another array.

The false statement is #1. In a rectangular array, each row has the same number of columns, but the numbers of rows and columns are not required to be the same.

Array Issues in GUI Programs

The major unusual consideration when using an array in a GUI program is that if the array values change based on user input, the array must be stored outside any method that reacts to the user's event. For example, consider an application that accumulates contribution totals for a fund-raising drive competition between four departments in a company. The left side of Figure 6-23 shows a Form into which a user types a department number and a contribution amount. For example, in the figure, the user is adding a $25 contribution for Department 2. The user clicks OK, then enters the next contribution amount. When the user clicks the Done button, a summary of contributions appears, as shown in the right half of Figure 6-23. For example, during program execution, in all $195 in contributions were added for Department 2.

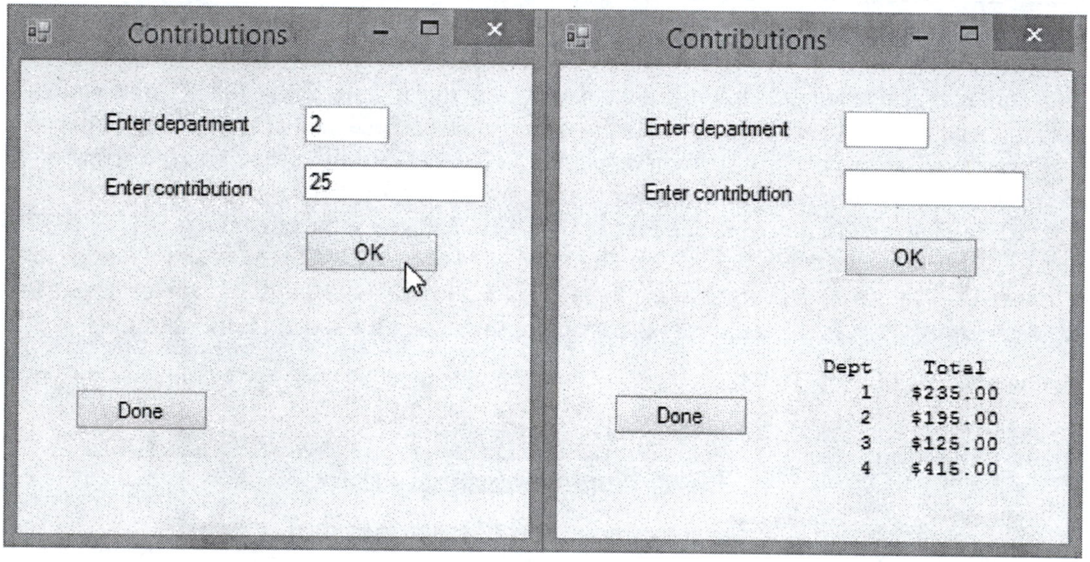

Figure 6-23   The Form for the CountContributions program as the user enters a value and after the user clicks Done

Figure 6-24 shows the code needed to implement the application. An array named total is declared outside of any methods. (See shading.) The okButton_Click() method accepts a department number and contribution amount from the user. It then adds the contribution into the array element that corresponds to the department and clears the text boxes so they are empty prior to the next entry. The total array must be declared outside of the okButton_Click() method; if it was inside the method, it would be redeclared, and all its elements would be reset to 0 with each button click. The doneButton_Click() method displays the array's contents.

```
double[] total = { 0, 0, 0, 0 };
private void okButton_Click(object sender, EventArgs e)
{
    int dept;
    double contribution;
    dept = Convert.ToInt32(deptTextbox.Text);
    contribution = Convert.ToDouble(contributionTextbox.Text);
    --dept;
    total[dept] += contribution;
    deptTextbox.Text = "";
    contributionTextbox.Text = "";
}
private void doneButton_Click(object sender, EventArgs e)
{
    outputLabel.Text = "Dept Total";
    for (int x = 0; x < total.Length; ++x)
        outputLabel.Text +=
            String.Format("\n {0}{1, 10}", x + 1, total[x]. ToString("C"));
}
```

Figure 6-24   Code that declares array and two methods needed for the
CountContributions application

TWO TRUTHS & A LIE

Array Issues in GUI Programs

1. A GUI program can contain declarations for any number of arrays of any data type.

2. If a method reacts to a user-initiated event, it cannot contain an array declaration.

3. If a method reacts to a user-initiated event and the method contains an array declaration, the array will be redeclared with each event occurrence.

The false statement is #2. If a method reacts to a user-initiated event, it can contain an array. The only problem is that the array will be redeclared with each new event, so it cannot store data that must persist over a number of events.

Chapter Summary

- An array is a list of data items, all of which have the same type and the same name but are distinguished from each other using a subscript or index. You declare an array variable by inserting a pair of square brackets after the type and reserve memory for an array by using the keyword **new**. Any array's elements are numbered 0 through one less than the array's length. In C#, arrays are objects that derive from a class named **System.Array**. An array's elements are initialized to default values. To initialize an array to nondefault values, you use a list of values that are separated by commas and enclosed within curly braces.

- Arrays are most powerful when variable subscripts are used to process array elements. Any array subscript must remain in the range of 0 through **Length - 1**. The **Length** property automatically holds an array's length. You can use the **foreach** statement to cycle through every array element without using subscripts.

- When you want to determine whether a variable holds one of many possible valid values, you can compare the variable to a list of values in an array. You can set up a parallel array to access additional information.

- The **BinarySearch()** method finds a requested value in a sorted array. The method returns −1 if the value is not found in the array; otherwise, it returns the array position of the sought value. You cannot use the **BinarySearch()** method if your array items are not arranged in ascending order, if the array holds duplicate values and you want to find all of them, or if you want to find a range match rather than an exact match. The **Sort()** method arranges array items in ascending order. The **Reverse()** method reverses the order of items in an array.

- C# supports multidimensional arrays that require multiple subscripts to access the array elements. The most commonly used multidimensional arrays are two-dimensional arrays that are rectangular. Two-dimensional arrays have two or more columns of values for each row. In a rectangular array, each row has the same number of columns. C# also supports jagged arrays, which are arrays of arrays.

- The major unusual consideration when using an array in a GUI program is that if the array values change based on user input, the array must be stored outside any method that reacts to the user's event.

Key Terms

An **array** is a list of data items that all have the same data type and the same name but are distinguished from each other by a subscript or index.

An **array element** is an individual object within an array.

A **subscript** (also called an **index**) is an integer contained within square brackets that indicates the position of one of an array's elements.

An **initializer list** is the list of values provided for an array.

An **iteration variable** is a temporary location that holds each array value in turn in a `foreach` statement.

Read-only describes a value that can be accessed but not altered.

A **sequential search** is conducted by examining a list in sequence.

A **parallel array** has the same number of elements as another array and corresponding data.

A **range match** determines the pair of limiting values between which a value falls.

A **binary search** is an algorithm that attempts to find an item in a list by splitting the sorted list of objects in half repeatedly as the search gets closer to a match.

A **one-dimensional** or **single-dimensional** array is an array whose elements you can access using a single subscript.

Multidimensional arrays require multiple subscripts to access the array elements.

Two-dimensional arrays have two or more columns of values for each row.

A **rectangular array** is an array in which each row has the same number of columns.

A **jagged array** is a one-dimensional array in which each element is another array.

Review Questions

1. In an array, every element has the same _____ .

   a. subscript

   b. data type

   c. memory location

   d. all of the above

2. The operator used to create objects is _____ .

   a. `=`

   b. `+=`

   c. `new`

   d. `create`

3. Which of the following correctly declares an array of six integers?

   a. `int array[6];`

   b. `int[] array = 6;`

   c. `int[6] array;`

   d. `int[] array = new int[6];`

4. The value placed within square brackets after an array name is
_____ .

a. a subscript

b. an index

c. always an integer

d. all of these

5. If you define an array to contain 10 elements, then the highest array subscript you can use is _____ .

a. 11

b. 10

c. 9

d. 8

6. Initializing an array is _____ in C#.

a. required

b. optional

c. difficult

d. prohibited

7. When you declare an array of six `double` elements but provide no initialization values, the value of the first element is _____ .

a. 0.0

b. 1.0

c. 5.0

d. unknown

8. Which of the following correctly declares an array of four integers?

a. `int[] ages = new int[4] {20, 30, 40, 50};`

b. `int[] ages = new int[] {20, 30, 40, 50};`

c. `int[] ages = {20, 30, 40, 50};`

d. all of these

9. When an `ages` array is correctly initialized using the values `{20, 30, 40, 50}`, as in Question 8, then the value of `ages[1]` is _____ .

a. 0

b. 20

c. 30

d. undefined

10. When an `ages` array is correctly initialized using the values `{20, 30, 40, 50}`, as in Question 8, then the value of `ages[4]` is _____ .

a. 0

b. 4

c. 50

d. undefined

11. When you declare an array as `int[] temperature = {0, 32, 50, 90, 212, 451};`, the value of `temperature.Length` is _____ .

    a. 5

    b. 6

    c. 7

    d. unknown

12. Which of the following doubles every value in a 10-element integer array named `amount`?

    a. `for(int x = 9; x >= 0; --x) amount[x] *= 2;`

    b. `foreach(int number in amount) number *= 2;`

    c. both of these

    d. neither of these

13. Which of the following adds 10 to every value in a 16-element integer array named `points`?

    a. `for(int sub = 0; sub > 16; ++sub) points[sub] += 10;`

    b. `foreach(int sub in points) points += 10;`

    c. both of these

    d. neither of these

14. Two arrays that store related information in corresponding element positions are _____ .

    a. jagged arrays

    b. rectangular arrays

    c. relative arrays

    d. parallel arrays

15. Assume an array is defined as `int[] nums = {2, 3, 4, 5};`. Which of the following would display the values in the array in reverse?

    a. `for(int x = 4; x > 0; --x)`
       `    Write(nums[x]);`

    b. `for(int x = 3; x >= 0; --x)`
       `    Write(nums[x]);`

    c. `for(int x = 3; x > 0; --x)`
       `    Write(nums[x]);`

    d. `for(int x = 4; x >= 0; --x)`
       `    Write(nums[x]);`

16. Assume an array is defined as `int[] nums = {7, 15, 23, 5};`. Which of the following would place the values in the array in descending numeric order?

    a. `Array.Sort(nums);`

    b. `Array.Reverse(nums);`

    c. `Array.Sort(nums); Array.Reverse(nums);`

    d. `Array.Reverse(nums); Array.Sort(nums);`

17. Which of the following traits do the `BinarySearch()` and `Sort()` methods have in common?

    a. Both methods take a single argument that must be an array.

    b. Both methods belong to the `System.Array` class.

    c. The array that each method uses must be in ascending order.

    d. They both operate only arrays made up of numeric data.

18. If you use the `BinarySearch()` method, and the object you seek is not found in the array, _____ .

    a. an error message is displayed

    b. a zero is returned

    c. the value `false` is returned

    d. a negative value is returned

19. The `BinarySearch()` method is inadequate when _____ .

    a. array items are in ascending order

    b. the array holds duplicate values and you want to find them all

    c. you want to find an exact match for a value

    d. array items are not numeric

20. Which of the following declares an integer array that contains eight rows and five columns?

    a. `int[8, 5] num = new int[ , ];`

    b. `int [8][5] num = new int[];`

    c. `int [ , ] num = new int[5, 8];`

    d. `int [ , ] num = new int[8, 5];`

Exercises

 Programming Exercises

For each of the following exercises, you may choose to write a console-based or GUI application, or both.

1. Write a program named **ArrayDemo** that stores an array of eight integers. Until the user enters a sentinel value, allow the user three options: (1) to view the list in order from the first to last position, (2) to view the list in order from the last to first position, or (3) to choose a specific position to view.

2. Write a program named **TemperatureList** that accepts seven int values representing high temperatures for seven consecutive days. Display each of the values along with a message that indicates how far it is from the average.

3. Write a program named **ScoresComparison** that allows a user to input four integer quiz scores ranging from 0 through 100. If no score is lower than any previous score, display a message that congratulates the user on making improvement, and then display the scores in the order they were entered. If every score is lower than the previous one, display the scores in the order they were entered, display an appropriate message about the scores' descent, and then display the scores in the more desirable reverse order. If the scores neither increase nor decrease consistently, display an appropriate message along with the scores.

4. Write a program named **CheckZips** that is used by a package delivery service to check delivery areas. The program contains an array that holds the 10 zip codes of areas to which the company makes deliveries. Prompt a user to enter a zip code, and display a message indicating whether the zip code is in the company's delivery area.

5. Write a program called **DeliveryCharges** for the package delivery service in Exercise 4. The program should again use an array that holds the 10 zip codes of areas to which the company makes deliveries. Create a parallel array containing 10 delivery charges that differ for each zip code. Prompt a user to enter a zip code, and then display either a message indicating the price of delivery to that zip code or a message indicating that the company does not deliver to the requested zip code.

6. The Chat-A-While phone company provides service to six area codes and charges the per-minute rates for phone calls shown in Figure 6-25. Write a program named **ChatAWhile** that stores the area codes and rates in parallel arrays and allows a user to enter an area code and the length of time for a call in minutes, and then display the total cost of the call.

Area Code	Per-Minute Rate ($)
262	0.07
414	0.10
608	0.05
715	0.16
815	0.24
920	0.14

Figure 6-25   Per-minute phone call rates

7. The Whippet Bus Company charges prices for tickets based on distance traveled, as shown in Figure 6-26. Write a program named **WhippetBus** that allows a user to enter a trip distance. The output is the ticket price.

Distance (miles)	Ticket Price ($)
0 – 99	25.00
100 – 299	40.00
300 – 499	55.00
500 and farther	70.00

Figure 6-26   Bus ticket prices

8. Write a program for The Carefree Resort named **ResortPrices** that prompts the user to enter the number of days for a resort stay. Then display the price per night and the total price. Nightly rates are $200 for one or two nights; $180 for three or four nights; $160 for five, six, or seven nights; and $145 for eight nights or more.

9. In Chapter 5, you wrote a **HomeSales** application for three salespeople: Danielle, Edward, and Francis. Now, modify the program to use arrays to store the salesperson names, allowed initials, and accumulated sales values.

10. Create a game similar to Hangman named **GuessAWord** in which a player guesses letters to try to replicate a hidden word. Store at least eight words in an array, and randomly select one to be the hidden word. (The statements needed to generate a random number are shown in the Exercises in the "Decision Making" and "Looping" chapters.) Initially, display the hidden word using asterisks to represent each letter. Allow the user to guess letters to replace the asterisks in the hidden word until the user completes the entire word. If the user guesses a letter that is not in the hidden word, display an appropriate message. If the user guesses a letter that appears multiple times in the hidden word, make sure that each correct letter is placed. Figure 6-27 shows typical games in progress in a console-based application and in a GUI application. In the GUI application, the user

has successfully guessed *e*, and is about to guess *r*. *Hint:* If you create the GUI version of the game, you might want to include a Start button that selects the random word and performs other startup tasks before you reveal the game interface. After the startup tasks are complete, you can remove the Start button from the form.

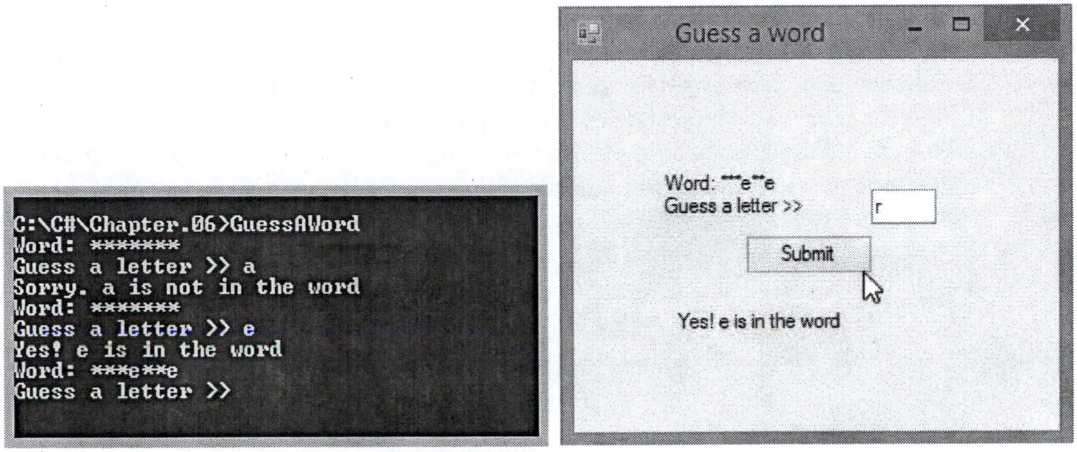

Figure 6-27 Typical executions of console-based and GUI `GuessAWord` programs

Debugging Exercises

1. Each of the following files in the Chapter.06 folder of your downloadable student files has syntax and/or logical errors. In each case, determine the problem, and fix the program. After you correct the errors, save each file using the same filename preceded with *Fixed*. For example, DebugSix01.cs will become FixedDebugSix01.cs.

   a. DebugSix01.cs   c. DebugSix03.cs

   b. DebugSix02.cs   d. DebugSix04.cs

Case Problems

1. In previous chapters, you created applications for the Greenville Idol competition. Now, modify the version of the **GreenvilleRevenue** program created in Chapter 5 so that after the user enters the number of contestants in this year's competition, the user is prompted for the appropriate number of contestant names and a code for each contestant that indicates the type of talent: *S* for singing, *D* for dancing, *M* for playing a musical instrument, or *O* for other. Make sure that all entered codes are valid, and if not, reprompt the user to enter a correct code. After contestant data entry is complete, display a count of each type of talent. Then, continuously prompt the user for a talent code until the user enters a sentinel value. With each code entry, display a list

of the contestants with that code, or display a message that the code is not valid and reprompt the user.

2. In previous chapters, you created applications for Marshall's Murals. Now, modify the version of the **MarshallsRevenue** program created in Chapter 5 so that after mural data entry is complete, the user is prompted for the appropriate number of customer names for both the interior and exterior murals and a code for each that indicates the mural style: *L* for landscape, *S* for seascape, *A* for abstract, *C* for children's, or *O* for other. When a code is invalid, reprompt the user for a valid code continuously. After data entry is complete, display a count of each type of mural. Then, continuously prompt the user for a mural style code until the user enters a sentinel value. With each code entry, display a list of all the customers with that code and whether their mural is interior or exterior. If the requested code is invalid, display an appropriate message and reprompt the user.

CHAPTER 7

Using Methods

In this chapter you will:

- ◎ Learn about methods and implementation hiding
- ◎ Write methods with no parameters and no return value
- ◎ Write methods that require a single argument
- ◎ Write methods that require multiple arguments
- ◎ Write a method that returns a value
- ◎ Pass array values to a method
- ◎ Learn some alternate ways to write a `Main()` method header
- ◎ Learn about issues using methods in GUI programs

In the first chapters of this book, you learned to create C# programs containing `Main()` methods that declare variables, accept input, perform arithmetic, and produce output. You learned to add decisions, loops, and arrays to your programs. As your programs grow in complexity, their `Main()` methods will contain many additional statements. Rather than creating increasingly long `Main()` methods, most programmers prefer to modularize their programs, placing instructions in smaller "packages" called methods. In this chapter, you learn to create many types of C# methods. You will understand how to send data to these methods and receive information back from them.

Understanding Methods and Implementation Hiding

A **method** is an encapsulated series of statements that carry out a task. Any class can contain an unlimited number of methods. So far, you have written console-based applications that contain a `Main()` method but no others. You also have created GUI applications with a `Click()` method. Frequently, the methods you have written have **invoked**, or **called**, other methods; that is, your program used a method's name and the method executed to perform a task for the class. For example, you have created many programs that call the `WriteLine()` and `ReadLine()` methods, and in Chapter 6 you used `BinarySearch()`, `Sort()`, and `Reverse()` methods. These methods are prewritten; you only had to call them to have them work.

For example, consider the simple `HelloClass` program shown in Figure 7-1. The `Main()` method contains a statement that calls the `WriteLine()` method. You can identify method names in a program because they always are followed by a set of parentheses. Depending on the method, there might be an argument within the parentheses. You first encountered the term *argument* in Chapter 1. An argument is the data that appears between the parentheses in a method call. The call to the `WriteLine()` method within the HelloClass program in Figure 7-1 contains the string argument `"Hello"`. Some methods you can invoke don't require any arguments.

Methods are similar to the procedures, functions, and subroutines used in other programming languages.

```
using static System.Console;
class HelloClass
{
    static void Main()
    {
        WriteLine("Hello");
    }
}
```

Figure 7-1   The `HelloClass` program

In the HelloClass program in Figure 7-1, `Main()` is a **calling method**—one that calls another. The `WriteLine()` method is a **called method**.

Understanding Implementation Hiding

When you call the `WriteLine()` method within the HelloClass program in Figure 7-1, you use a method that has already been created for you. Because the creators of C# knew you would often want to write a message to the output screen, they created a method you could call to accomplish that task. This method takes care of all the hardware details of producing a message on the output device; you simply call the method and pass the desired message to it. The `WriteLine()` method provides an example of **implementation hiding**, which means keeping the details of a method's operations hidden. For example, when you make a dental appointment, you do not need to know how the appointment is actually recorded at the dental office—perhaps it is written in a book, marked on a large chalkboard, or entered into a computerized database. The implementation details are of no concern to you as a client, and if the dental office changes its methods from one year to the next, the change does not affect your use of the appointment-making method. Your only concern is the way you interact with the dental office, not how the office tracks appointments. In the same way that you are a client of the dental practice, a method that uses another is a **client** of that method.

Hidden implementation methods often are said to exist in a black box. A **black box** is any device you can use without knowing how it works internally. The same is true with well-written program methods; the invoking program or method must know the name of the method it is using and what type of information to send it, but the program does not need to know how the method works. Later, you might substitute a new, improved method for the old one, and if the user's means of accessing the method does not change, you won't need to make any changes in programs that invoke the method. The creators of C# were able to anticipate many of the methods that would be necessary for your programs; you will continue to use many of these methods throughout this book. However, your programs often will require custom methods that the creators of C# could not have expected. In this chapter, you will learn to write your own custom methods.

To more easily incorporate methods into a program, it is common practice to store methods (or groups of associated methods) in their own classes and files. Then you can add the methods into any application that uses them. The resulting compound program is called a **multifile assembly**. As you learn more about C#, you might prefer to take this approach with your own programs. For simplicity, most example methods in this book are contained in the same file as any other methods that use them.

TWO TRUTHS & A LIE

Understanding Methods and Implementation Hiding

1. A method is an encapsulated series of statements that carry out a task.

2. Any class can contain an unlimited number of methods.

3. All the methods that will be used by your programs have been written for you and stored in files.

The false statement is #3. As you write programs, you will want to write many of your own custom methods.

Writing Methods with No Parameters and No Return Value

The output of the program in Figure 7-1 is simply the word *Hello*. Suppose you want to add three more lines of output to display a standard welcoming message when users execute your program. Of course, you can add three new WriteLine() statements to the existing program, but you also can create a method to display the three new lines.

Creating a method instead of adding three lines to the existing program is useful for two major reasons:

- If you add a method call instead of three new lines, the Main() method will remain short and easy to follow. The Main() method will contain just one new statement that calls a method rather than three separate WriteLine() statements.

- More importantly, a method is easily *reusable*. After you create the welcoming method, you can use it in any program, and you can allow other programmers to use it in their programs. In other words, you do the work once, and then you can use the method many times.

 When you place code in a callable method instead of repeating the same code at several points in a program, you are avoiding **code bloat**—a colorful term that describes unnecessarily long or repetitive statements.

Figure 7-2 shows the parts of a C# method. A method must include:

- A **method declaration**, which is also known as a **method header** or **method definition**
- An opening curly brace
- A method body, which is a block of statements that carry out the method's work
- A closing curly brace

The method declaration defines the rules for using the method. It contains:

- Optional declared accessibility
- An optional static modifier
- The return type for the method
- The method name, or identifier
- An opening parenthesis
- An optional list of method parameters (separated with commas if there is more than one parameter)
- A closing parenthesis

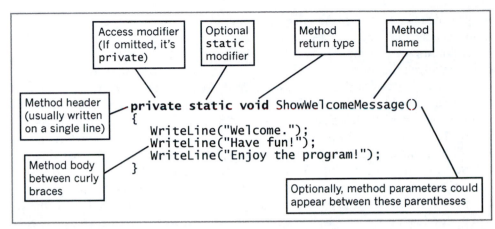

Figure 7-2   The ShowWelcomeMessage() method

An Introduction to Accessibility

The optional declared **accessibility** for a method sets limits as to how other methods can use your method; accessibility can be any of the levels described in Table 7-1. The two levels you will use most frequently, `public` and `private` access, are shaded in the table. You will learn about protected access and what it means to derive types in the chapter "Introduction to Inheritance."

- **Public access** is established by including a `public` modifier in the member declaration. This modifier allows access to the method from other classes.

- **Private access** is established by including a `private` modifier in the member declaration or by omitting any accessibility modifier. This modifier limits method access to the class that contains the method.

Declared accessibility	Can methods contained in the same class access this method?	Can derived classes access this method?	Can assemblies or projects that contain this class access this method?	Can any class access this method?
`public`	Yes	Yes	Yes	Yes
`protected internal`	Yes	Yes	Yes	No
`protected`	Yes	Yes	No	No
`internal`	Yes	No	Yes	No
`private`	Yes	No	No	No

Table 7-1   Summary of method accessibility

If you do not provide an accessibility modifier for a method, it is private by default. The Main() method headers that you have seen in all of the examples in this book have no access modifier, so they are private. You could explicitly add the keyword private to the method headers in any of the programs you have seen so far in this book, and you would notice no difference in execution: The methods still would be private. Actually, you could also substitute the public keyword in the Main() method headers without noticing any execution differences either—it's just that with that modification, other classes could have called the public Main() methods by using the appropriate class name and a dot before the method name. When you use a method's complete name, including its class, you are using its **fully qualified** name. In Chapter 1, you learned that you can use the fully qualified method call Console.WriteLine() to produce output. When you include either using System; or using static System.Console; at the top of a program, then you do not need to use the fully qualified method name. Either way, because the classes you write can use the Console class method WriteLine(), you know the method must not be private.

In Chapter 3, you learned to create simple GUI applications, and you learned how to automatically generate a Click() method for a button; the generated method header started with the keyword private. For example, a private method named button1_Click() cannot be used by any other class. If you changed the method's access specifier to public, it could be used by another class, but you probably would have no reason to do so. As you study C#, you will learn how to decide which access modifier to choose for each method you write. For now, unless you want a method to be accessible by outside classes, you should use the private access modifier with the method. This book uses no modifiers with Main() methods because Visual Studio does not create them in its automatically generated code, but this book uses appropriate access modifiers with other methods.

An Introduction to the Optional static Modifier

You can declare a method to be **static** or **nonstatic**. If you use the keyword modifier static, you indicate that a method can be called without referring to an object. Instead, you refer only to the class. For example, if MethodS() is static and MethodN() is nonstatic, the following statements describe typical method calls:

```
someClass.MethodS();
someObject.MethodN();
```

You won't create objects until Chapter 9, so this chapter will use only nonstatic methods.

A nonstatic method might be called with or without its class name. For example, if you have a class named PayrollApplication that contains a static method named DeductUnionDues(), you can call the method in two ways:

- If you call the method from a method in a different class, you use the class name, a dot, and the method name, as in the following:

    PayrollApplication.DeductUnionDues();

- If you call the method from another method in the same class, you *can* use the class name as a prefix as shown above, but this approach is neither required nor conventional. Within a method in the PayrollApplication class, you can simply write the following abbreviated method call:

    DeductUnionDues();

If you do not indicate that a method is static, it is nonstatic by default and can be used only in conjunction with an object. When you begin to create your own classes in the chapter "Using Classes and Objects," you will write many nonstatic methods, and your understanding of the terms *static* and *nonstatic* will become clearer. As you work through this chapter, you will learn why each method is created to be static or nonstatic. Do not worry if you do not completely understand this chapter's references to nonstatic methods that require an object—the concept is explored in Chapter 9.

An Introduction to Return Types

Every method has a **return type**, indicating what kind of value the method will return to any other method that calls it. If a method does not return a value, its return type is void. A method's return type is known more succinctly as a **method's type**. Later in this chapter, you will create methods with return types such as int or double that return values of the corresponding type; such methods can be called *value-returning methods*. For now, the methods discussed are void methods that do not return a value.

When a method's return type is void, most C# programmers do not end the method with a return statement. However, you can end a void method with the following statement that indicates nothing is returned:

return;

Understanding the Method Identifier

Every method has a name that must be a legal C# identifier; that is, it must not contain spaces and must begin with a letter of the alphabet or an underscore. By convention, many programmers start method names with a verb because methods cause actions. Examples of conventional method names include DeductTax() and DisplayNetPay().

Every method name is followed by a set of parentheses. Sometimes these parentheses contain parameters, but in the simplest methods, the parentheses are empty. A **parameter to a method** is a variable that holds data passed to a method when it is called. The terms *argument* and *parameter* are closely related. An argument is data in a method call, and a parameter is in the method header—it receives an argument's value when the method executes.

The parentheses that follow a method name in its header can hold one parameter or multiple parameters separated with commas. The contents within the parentheses are known as the **parameter list**.

Placing a Method in a Class

In summary, the first methods you write in console applications will be `private`, `static`, and `void` and will have empty parameter lists. That means they won't be called from other classes, they won't require an object reference, they will not return any value to their calling method, and they will not accept any data from the outside. Therefore, you can write the `ShowWelcomeMessage()` method as it is shown in Figure 7-2. According to its declaration, the method is `private` and `static`. It returns nothing, so the return type is void. Its identifier is `ShowWelcomeMessage`, and it receives nothing, so its parameter list is empty. The method body, consisting of three `WriteLine()` statements, appears within curly braces that follow the header.

By convention, programmers indent the statements in a method body, which makes the method header and its braces stand out. When you write a method using the Visual Studio editor, the method statements are indented for you automatically. You can place as many statements as you want within a method body.

You also can place a method within a class in which other methods will use it, but you cannot place a method within any other method. Figure 7-3 shows the two locations where you can place the `ShowWelcomeMessage()` method within the class named `HelloClass`—before the `Main()` method header or after the `Main()` method's closing brace but before the closing curly brace for the class.

```
using static System.Console;
class HelloClass
{
    // The ShowWelcomeMessage() method could go here
    static void Main()
    {
        WriteLine("Hello");
    }
    // Alternatively, the ShowWelcomeMessage() method could go here
    // But it cannot go in both places; it can appear only once
}
```

Figure 7-3   Placement of a method

To make the `Main()` method call the `ShowWelcomeMessage()` method, you simply use the `ShowWelcomeMessage()` method's name as a statement within the body of the `Main()` method. Figure 7-4 shows the complete program with the method call shaded, and Figure 7-5 shows the output.

```
using static System.Console;
class HelloClass
{
    static void Main()
    {
        ShowWelcomeMessage();
        WriteLine("Hello");
    }
    private static void ShowWelcomeMessage()
    {
        WriteLine("Welcome.");
        WriteLine("Have fun!");
        WriteLine("Enjoy the program!");
    }
}
```

Figure 7-4   The `HelloClass` program with `Main()` method calling the `ShowWelcomeMessage()` method

```
C:\C#\Chapter.07>HelloClass
Welcome.
Have fun!
Enjoy the program!
Hello

C:\C#\Chapter.07>
```

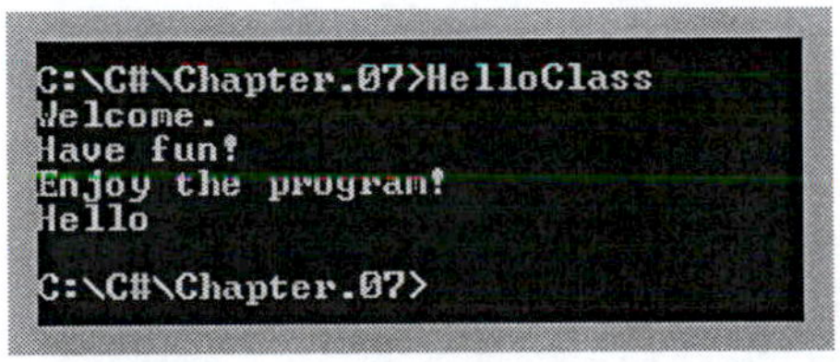

Figure 7-5   Output of the `HelloClass` program

The `ShowWelcomeMessage()` method in the `HelloClass` class is `static`, and therefore it is called from the `Main()` method without an object reference (that is, without an object name and a dot before the method name. It also resides in the same class as the `Main()` method, so it can be called without using its class name.

When the `Main()` method executes, it calls the `ShowWelcomeMessage()` method, so the three lines that make up the welcome message appear first in the output in Figure 7-5. Then, after the method is done, the `Main()` method displays *Hello*.

Each of two different classes can have its own method named `ShowWelcomeMessage()`. Such a method in the second class would be entirely distinct from the identically named method in the first class. The complete name of this method is `HelloClass.ShowWelcomeMessage()`, but you do not need to use the complete name when calling the method within the same class.

If another class named `SomeOtherClass` had a *public* static method with the same name, you could call the method from `HelloClass` using the following statement:

`SomeOtherClass.ShowWelcomeMessage();`

Declaring Variables and Constants in a Method

You can write any statements you need within a method, including variable and constant declarations. When a variable or constant is declared within a method, it is known only from that point to the end of the method; programmers say the variable or constant is in scope until the end of its method. A program element's **scope** is the segment of code in which it can be used. Programmers also say that the variable is **local** to the method, meaning it can be used anywhere in the method after the point of declaration.

A locally declared variable is not known to other methods or usable in them, and if another method contains a variable with the same name, the two variables are completely distinct. For example, Figure 7-6 shows a program containing two methods—Main() and MethodWithItsOwnA()—that each declare a variable named a. The variable in each method is completely distinct from the other and holds its own value, as shown in Figure 7-7. If you declared a variable named b in the Main() method and then tried to use b in MethodWithItsOwnA(), you would generate a compiler error. If you declared a variable named c in MethodWithItsOwnA() and tried to use it in Main(), you would generate another compiler error.

```
using static System.Console;
class LocalVariableDemo
{
   static void Main()
   {
      int a = 12;
      WriteLine("In Main() a is {0}", a);
      MethodWithItsOwnA();
      WriteLine("In Main() a is {0}", a);
   }
   private static void MethodWithItsOwnA()
   {
      int a = 354;
      WriteLine("In method a is {0}", a);
   }
}
```

Figure 7-6   The LocalVariableDemo program

```
C:\C#\Chapter.07>LocalVariableDemo
In Main() a is 12
In method a is 354
In Main() a is 12

C:\C#\Chapter.07>_
```

Figure 7-7   Execution of the LocalVariableDemo program

 Watch the video *Using Methods*.

TWO TRUTHS & A LIE

Writing Methods with No Parameters and No Return Value

1. A method header must contain declared accessibility.

2. A method header must contain a return type.

3. A method header must contain an identifier.

The false statement is #1. Declaring accessibility in a method header is optional. If you do not use an access modifier, the method is private by default.

You Do It

Calling a Method

In this section, you write a program in which a `Main()` method calls another method that displays a company's logo.

1. Open a new program named **DemoLogo**, and enter the statement that allows the program to use `System.Console` methods without qualifying them. Then type the class header for the `DemoLogo` class and the class-opening curly brace.

```
using static System.Console;
class DemoLogo
{
```

2. Type the `Main()` method for the `DemoLogo` class. This method displays a line, then calls the `DisplayCompanyLogo()` method.

```
static void Main()
{
    Write("Our company is ");
    DisplayCompanyLogo();
}
```

(continues)

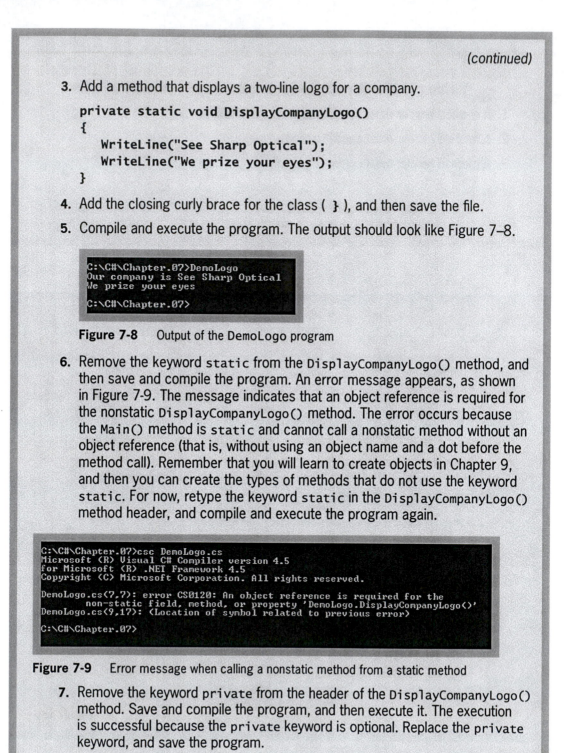

(continued)

3. Add a method that displays a two-line logo for a company.

```
private static void DisplayCompanyLogo()
{
    WriteLine("See Sharp Optical");
    WriteLine("We prize your eyes");
}
```

4. Add the closing curly brace for the class (}), and then save the file.

5. Compile and execute the program. The output should look like Figure 7–8.

```
C:\C#\Chapter.07>DemoLogo
Our company is See Sharp Optical
We prize your eyes

C:\C#\Chapter.07>
```

Figure 7-8   Output of the DemoLogo program

6. Remove the keyword `static` from the `DisplayCompanyLogo()` method, and then save and compile the program. An error message appears, as shown in Figure 7-9. The message indicates that an object reference is required for the nonstatic `DisplayCompanyLogo()` method. The error occurs because the `Main()` method is `static` and cannot call a nonstatic method without an object reference (that is, without using an object name and a dot before the method call). Remember that you will learn to create objects in Chapter 9, and then you can create the types of methods that do not use the keyword `static`. For now, retype the keyword `static` in the `DisplayCompanyLogo()` method header, and compile and execute the program again.

```
C:\C#\Chapter.07>csc DemoLogo.cs
Microsoft (R) Visual C# Compiler version 4.5
for Microsoft (R) .NET Framework 4.5
Copyright (C) Microsoft Corporation. All rights reserved.

DemoLogo.cs(7,7): error CS0120: An object reference is required for the
      non-static field, method, or property 'DemoLogo.DisplayCompanyLogo()'
DemoLogo.cs(9,17): (Location of symbol related to previous error)

C:\C#\Chapter.07>
```

Figure 7-9   Error message when calling a nonstatic method from a static method

7. Remove the keyword `private` from the header of the `DisplayCompanyLogo()` method. Save and compile the program, and then execute it. The execution is successful because the `private` keyword is optional. Replace the `private` keyword, and save the program.

Writing Methods That Require a Single Argument

Some methods require additional information. If a method could not receive arguments, then you would have to write an infinite number of methods to cover every possible situation. For example, when you make a dental appointment, you do not need to employ a different method for every date of the year at every possible time of day. Rather, you can supply the date and time as information to the method, and no matter what date and time you supply, the method is carried out correctly. If you design a method to compute an employee's paycheck, it makes sense that you can write a method named ComputePaycheck() and supply it with an hourly pay rate rather than having to develop methods with names like ComputePaycheckAtEightDollarsAnHour(), ComputePaycheckAtNineDollarsAnHour(), and so on.

You already have used methods to which you supplied a wide variety of parameters. At any call, the WriteLine() method can receive any one of an infinite number of strings as a parameter—"Hello", "Goodbye", and so on. No matter what message you send to the WriteLine() method, the message is displayed correctly.

When you write the declaration for a method that accepts a parameter, you need to include the following items within the method declaration parentheses:

- The data type of the parameter
- A local identifier (name) for the parameter

For example, consider a method named DisplaySalesTax(), which computes and displays a tax as 7 percent of a selling price. The method header for a usable DisplaySalesTax() method could be the following:

```
static void DisplaySalesTax(double saleAmount)
```

You can think of the parentheses in a method declaration as a funnel into the method—data parameters listed there are "dropping in" to the method.

The parameter double saleAmount within the parentheses indicates that the DisplaySalesTax() method will receive a value of type double. Within the method, the value will be known as saleAmount. Figure 7-10 shows a complete method.

```
private static void DisplaySalesTax(double saleAmount)
{
    double tax;
    const double RATE = 0.07;
    tax = saleAmount * RATE;
    WriteLine("The tax on {0} is {1}",
        saleAmount, tax.ToString("C"));
}
```

Figure 7-10   The DisplaySalesTax() method

Within the DisplaySalesTax() method, you must use the format string and ToString() method if you want figures to display to exactly two decimal positions. You learned how to display values to a fixed number of decimal places in Chapter 2; recall that using the fixed format with no number defaults to two decimal places.

You create the DisplaySalesTax() method as a void method (one that has a void return type) because you do not need it to return any value to any method that uses it—its only function is to receive the saleAmount value, multiply it by 0.07, and then display the result. You create it as a static method because you do not want to create an object with which to use it; you want the static Main() method to be able to call it directly.

Within a program, you can call the DisplaySalesTax() method by using the method's name and, within parentheses, an argument that is either a constant value or a variable. Thus, both of the following calls to the DisplaySalesTax() method invoke it correctly:

```
double myPurchase = 12.99;
DisplaySalesTax(12.99);
DisplaySalesTax(myPurchase);
```

You can call the DisplaySalesTax() method any number of times, with a different constant or variable argument each time. The value of each of these arguments becomes known as saleAmount within the method. Interestingly, if the argument in the method call is a variable, it might possess the same identifier as saleAmount or a different one, such as myPurchase. The identifier saleAmount is simply the name the value "goes by" while being used within the method, no matter what name it goes by in the calling program. That is, the variable saleAmount is a local variable to the DisplaySalesTax() method, as are variables and constants declared within a method. The variable saleAmount is also an example of a **formal parameter**, a parameter within a method header that accepts a value. In contrast, arguments within a method *call* often are referred to as **actual parameters**. For example, in the method calling statement DisplaySalesTax(myPurchase);, myPurchase is an actual parameter.

The variable saleAmount is a formal parameter, and it also is an example of a *value parameter*, or a *parameter* that receives a copy of the value passed to it. You will learn more about value parameters and other types of parameters in the next chapter.

The DisplaySalesTax() method employs implementation hiding. That is, if a programmer changes the way in which the tax value is calculated—for example, by coding one of the following—programs that use the DisplaySalesTax() method will not be affected and will not need to be modified:

```
tax = saleAmount * 7 / 100;
tax = 0.07 * saleAmount;
tax = RATE * saleAmount;
```

No matter how the tax is calculated, a calling program passes a value into the DisplaySalesTax() method, and a calculated result appears on the screen.

Figure 7-11 shows a complete program called UseTaxMethod. It uses the DisplaySalesTax() method twice, first with a variable argument, and then with a constant argument. The program's output appears in Figure 7-12.

```
using static System.Console;
class UseTaxMethod
{
    static void Main()
    {
        double myPurchase = 12.99;
        DisplaySalesTax(myPurchase);
        DisplaySalesTax(35.67);
    }
    private static void DisplaySalesTax(double saleAmount)
    {
        double tax;
        const double RATE = 0.07;
        tax = saleAmount * RATE;
        WriteLine("The tax on {0} is {1}",
            saleAmount.ToString("C"), tax.ToString("C"));
    }
}
```

Figure 7-11   Complete program using the DisplaySalesTax() method two times

```
C:\C#\Chapter.07>UseTaxMethod
The tax on $12.99 is $0.91
The tax on $35.67 is $2.50

C:\C#\Chapter.07>
```

Figure 7-12   Output of the UseTaxMethod program

An argument type in a method call can match the method's parameter type exactly, but it can use a different data type if the argument can be converted automatically to the parameter type. Recall from Chapter 2 that C# supports the following automatic conversions:

- From sbyte to short, int, long, float, double, or decimal
- From byte to short, ushort, int, uint, long, ulong, float, double, or decimal
- From short to int, long, float, double, or decimal
- From ushort to int, uint, long, ulong, float, double, or decimal
- From int to long, float, double, or decimal
- From uint to long, ulong, float, double, or decimal
- From long to float, double, or decimal
- From ulong to float, double, or decimal

- From char to ushort, int, uint, long, ulong, float, double, or decimal

- From float to double

As an example, a method with the header private static void DisplaySalesTax(double saleAmount) can work with the following method call that uses an integer argument because integers are promoted automatically to doubles:

DisplaySalesTax(100);

Now that you have seen how to write methods that accept an argument, you might guess that when you write WriteLine("Hello");, the header for the called method is similar to public static void WriteLine(string s). You might not know the parameter name the creators of C# have chosen, but you do know the method's return type, name, and parameter type. (If you use the IntelliSense feature of Visual Studio, you can discover the parameter name. See Appendix C for more details.)

Watch the video *Arguments and Parameters*.

TWO TRUTHS & A LIE

Writing Methods That Require a Single Argument

1. When you write the declaration for a method that accepts a parameter, you need to include the parameter's data type within the method header.

2. When you write the declaration for a method that accepts a parameter, you need to include the identifier of the argument that will be sent to the method within the method header.

3. When you write the declaration for a method that accepts a parameter, you need to include a local identifier for the parameter within the method header.

The false statement is #2. When you write the definition for a method, you include the data type and a local parameter name within the parentheses of the method header, but you do not include the name of any argument that will be sent from a calling method. After all, the method might be invoked any number of times with any number of different arguments.

Writing Methods That Require Multiple Arguments

You can pass multiple arguments to a method by listing the arguments within the call to the method and separating them with commas. For example, rather than creating a DisplaySalesTax() method that multiplies an amount by 0.07, you might prefer to create a more flexible method to which you can pass two values—the value on which the tax is calculated and the tax percentage by which it should be multiplied. Figure 7-13 shows a method that uses two parameters.

```
private static void DisplaySalesTax(double saleAmount, double taxRate)
{
    double tax;
    tax = saleAmount * taxRate;
    WriteLine("The tax on {0} at {1} is {2}",
        saleAmount.ToString("C"), taxRate.ToString("P"),
        tax.ToString("C"));

}
```

Figure 7-13   The `DisplaySalesTax()` method that accepts two parameters

In Figure 7-13, two parameters (`saleAmount` and `taxRate`) appear within the parentheses in the method header. A comma separates the parameters, and each parameter requires its own named type (in this case, both parameters are of type `double`) and an identifier. A declaration for a method that receives two or more arguments must list the type for each parameter separately, even if the parameters have the *same* type.

When you pass values to the method in a statement such as `DisplaySalesTax(myPurchase, localRate);`, the first value passed will be referenced as `saleAmount` within the method, and the second value passed will be referenced as `taxRate`. Therefore, it is very important that arguments be passed to a method in the correct order. The following call results in output stating that *The tax on $200.00 at 10.00% is $20.00*:

`DisplaySalesTax(200.00, 0.10);`

However, the following call results in output stating that *The tax on $0.10 at 10.00% is $20.00*, which is clearly incorrect.

`DisplaySalesTax(0.10, 200.00);`

You can write a method to take any number of parameters in any order. When you call the method, however, the arguments you send to it must match (in both number and type) the parameters listed in the method declaration, with the following exceptions:

- The type of an argument does not need to match the parameter list exactly if the argument can be promoted to the parameter type. For example, an `int` argument can be passed to a `double` parameter.

- The number of arguments does not need to match the number in the parameter list when you use *default arguments*. You will learn about default arguments in Chapter 8.

Thus, a method to compute and display an automobile salesperson's commission might require arguments such as a string for the salesperson's name, an integer value of a sold car, a `double` percentage commission rate, and a character code for the vehicle type. The correct method will execute only when all arguments of the correct types are sent in the correct order.

TWO TRUTHS & A LIE

Writing Methods That Require Multiple Arguments

1. The following is a usable C# method header:

   private static void MyMethod(double amt, sum)

2. The following is a usable C# method header:

   private static void MyMethod2(int x, double y)

3. The following is a usable C# method header:

   static void MyMethod3(int id, string name, double rate)

The false statement is #1. In a method header, each parameter must have a data type, even if the data types for all the parameters are the same. The header in #3 does not contain an accessibility indicator, but that is optional.

Writing a Method That Returns a Value

A method can return, at most, one value to a method that calls it. The return type for a method can be any type used in the C# programming language, which includes the basic built-in types int, double, char, and so on. You can also use a class type as the return type for a method, including any type built into the C# language. For example, you have used a return value from the ReadLine() method when writing a statement such as inputString = ReadLine();. Because the ReadLine() method call can be assigned to a string, its return type is string. You will learn to create your own types in Chapter 9, and these might also be returned from a method. Of course, a method also can return nothing, in which case the return type is void.

For example, suppose that you want to create a method to accept the hours an employee worked and the hourly pay rate, and to return a calculated gross pay value. The header for this method could be:

private static double CalcPay(double hours, double rate)

Figure 7-14 shows this method.

```
private static double CalcPay(double hours, double rate)
{
   double gross;
   gross = hours * rate;
   return gross;
}
```

Figure 7-14   The CalcPay() method

Notice the **return** statement, which is the last statement within the **CalcPay()** method. A **return statement** causes a value to be sent back to the calling method; in the **CalcPay()** method, the value stored in **gross** is sent back to any method that calls the **CalcPay()** method. Also notice the type **double** that precedes the method name in the method header. The data type used in a method's **return** statement must be the same as the return type declared in the method's header, or the program will not compile.

287

If a method returns a value and you call the method, you typically will want to use the returned value, although you are not required to use it. For example, when you invoke the **CalcPay()** method, you might want to assign the value to a **double** variable named **grossPay**, as in the following statement:

```
grossPay = CalcPay(myHours, myRate);
```

The **CalcPay()** method returns a **double**, so it is appropriate to assign the returned value to a **double** variable. Figure 7-15 shows a program that uses the **CalcPay()** method in the shaded statement, and Figure 7-16 shows the output.

```
using static System.Console;
class UseCalcPay
{
    static void Main()
    {
        double myHours = 37.5;
        double myRate = 12.75;
        double grossPay;
        grossPay = CalcPay(myHours, myRate);
        WriteLine("I worked {0} hours at {1} per hour",
            myHours, myRate);
        WriteLine("My gross pay is {0}", grossPay.ToString("C"));
    }
    private static double CalcPay(double hours, double rate)
    {
        double gross;
        gross = hours * rate;
        return gross;
    }
}
```

Figure 7-15 Program using the **CalcPay()** method

```
C:\C#\Chapter.07>UseCalcPay
I worked 37.5 hours at 12.75 per hour
My gross pay is $478.13

C:\C#\Chapter.07>
```

Figure 7-16 Output of the UseCalcPay program

Instead of storing a method's returned value in a variable, you can use it directly, as in statements that produce output or perform arithmetic such as the following:

```
WriteLine("My gross pay is {0}",
    CalcPay(myHours, myRate).ToString("C"));
double tax = CalcPay(myHours, myRate) * TAX_RATE;
```

In the first statement, the call to the CalcPay() method is made within the WriteLine() method call. In the second, CalcPay()'s returned value is used in an arithmetic statement. Because CalcPay() returns a double, you can use the method call CalcPay() in the same way you would use any double value. The method call CalcPay() has a double data type in the same way a double variable does.

As an additional example, suppose that you have a method named GetPrice() that accepts an item number and returns its price. The header is as follows:

```
private static double GetPrice(int itemNumber)
```

Further suppose that you want to ask the user to enter an item number from the keyboard so you can pass it to the GetPrice() method. You can get the value from the user, store it in a string, convert the string to an integer, pass the integer to the GetPrice() method, and store the returned value in a variable named price in four or five separate statements. Or you can write the following:

```
price = GetPrice(Convert.ToInt32(ReadLine()));
```

This statement contains a method call to ReadLine() within a method call to Convert.ToInt32(), within a method call to GetPrice(). When method calls are placed inside other method calls, the calls are **nested method calls**. When you write a statement with three nested method calls like the previous statement, the innermost method executes first. Its return value is then used as an argument to the intermediate method, and its return value is used as an argument to the outer method. There is no limit to how "deep" you can go with nested method calls.

The system keeps track of where to return after a method call in an area of memory called the *stack*. Another area of memory called the *heap* is where memory can be allocated while a program is executing.

Writing a Method That Returns a Boolean Value

When a method returns a value that is type bool, the method call can be used anywhere you can use a Boolean expression. For example, suppose you have written a method named isPreferredCustomer() that returns a Boolean value indicating whether a customer is a preferred customer who qualifies for a discount. Then you can write an if statement such as the following:

```
if(isPreferredCustomer())
    price = price - DISCOUNT;
```

In Chapter 4 you learned about side effects and how they affect compound Boolean expressions. When you use Boolean methods, you must be especially careful not to cause unintended side effects. For example, consider the following `if` statement, in which the intention is to set a delivery fee to 0 if both the `isPreferredCustomer()` and `isLocalCustomer()` methods return true:

```
if(isPreferredCustomer() && isLocalCustomer())
    deliveryFee = 0;
```

If the `isLocalCustomer()` method should perform some desired task—for example, displaying a message about the customer's status or applying a local customer discount to the price—then you might not achieve the desired results. Because of short-circuit evaluation, if the `isPreferredCustomer()` method returns `false`, the `isLocalCustomer()` method never executes. If that is your intention, then using methods in this way is fine, but always consider any unintended side effects.

Analyzing a Built-In Method

C# provides you with many prewritten methods such as `WriteLine()` and `ReadLine()`. In Chapter 2, you learned about C#'s arithmetic operators, such as + and *, and you learned that C# provides no exponential operator. Instead, to raise a number to a power, you can use the built-in `Pow()` method. For example, to raise 2 to the third power (2 * 2 * 2) and store the answer in the variable `result`, you can write a program that includes the following statement:

```
double result = Math.Pow(2.0, 3.0);
```

From this statement, you know the following about the `Pow()` method:

- It is in the `Math` class because the class name and a dot precede the method call.

- It is `public` because you can write a program that uses it.

- It is `static` because it is used with its class name and a dot, without any object.

- It accepts two `double` parameters.

- It returns a `double` or a type that can be promoted automatically to a `double` (such as an `int`) because its answer is stored in a `double`.

Although you know many facts about the `Pow()` method, you do not know how its instructions are carried out internally. In good object-oriented style, its implementation is hidden.

TWO TRUTHS & A LIE

Writing a Method That Returns a Value

1. A method can return, at most, one value to a method that calls it.

2. The data type used in a method's `return` statement must be the same as the return type declared in the method's header.

3. If a method returns a value and you call the method, you must store the value in a variable that has the same data type as the method's parameter.

The false statement is #3. If a method returns a value and you call the method, you typically will want to use the returned value, but you are not required to use it. Furthermore, if you do assign the returned value to a storage variable, that variable does not have to match any parameter's value. Instead, the storage variable needs to be capable of accepting the method's returned type.

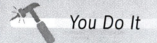

You Do It

Writing a Method That Receives Parameters and Returns a Value

Next, you write a method named `CalcPhoneCallPrice()` that both receives parameters and returns a value. The purpose of the method is to accept the length of a phone call in minutes and the rate charged per minute and to then calculate the price of a call, assuming each call includes a 25-cent connection charge in addition to the per-minute charge. After writing the `CalcPhoneCallPrice()` method, you write a `Main()` method that calls the `CalcPhoneCallPrice()` method using four different sets of data as arguments.

1. Start a program named **PhoneCall** by typing a `using` statement, class header, and opening brace:

```
using static System.Console;
class PhoneCall
{
```

(continues)

(continued)

2. Type the following `CalcPhoneCallPrice()` method. The method is declared as `static` because it will be called by a `static` `Main()` method without creating an object. The method receives an integer and a `double` as parameters. The fee for a call is calculated as 0.25 plus the minutes times the rate per minute. The method returns the phone call fee to the calling method.

```
private static double CalcPhoneCallPrice(int minutes,
    double rate)
{
    const double BASE_FEE = 0.25;
    double callFee;
    callFee = BASE_FEE + minutes * rate;
    return callFee;
}
```

3. Add the `Main()` method header for the `PhoneCall` class. Begin the method by declaring two arrays; one contains two call lengths, and the other contains two rates. You will use all the possible combinations of call lengths and rates to test the `CalcPhoneCallPrice()` method. Also, declare a `double` named `priceOfCall` that will hold the result of a calculated call price.

```
static void Main()
{
    int[] callLengths = {2, 5};
    double[] rates = {0.03, 0.12};
    double priceOfCall;
```

4. Add a statement that displays column headings under which you can list combinations of call lengths, rates, and prices. The three column headings are right-aligned, each in a field 10 characters wide.

```
WriteLine("{0, 10}{1, 10}{2, 10}",
    "Minutes", "Rate", "Price");
```

(continues)

(continued)

5. Add a pair of nested loops that pass each `callLength` and each `rate` to the `CalcPhoneCallPrice()` method in turn. As each pair is passed, the result is stored in the `priceOfCall` variable, and the details are displayed. Using the nested loops allows you to pass each combination of call time and rate so that multiple possibilities for the values can be tested conveniently.

```
for(int x = 0; x < callLengths.Length; ++x)
    for(int y = 0; y < rates.Length; ++y)
    {
        priceOfCall = CalcPhoneCallPrice(callLengths[x],
            rates[y]);
        WriteLine("{0, 10}{1, 10}{2, 10}",
            callLengths[x], rates[y], priceOfCall.ToString("C"));
    }
```

6. Add a closing curly brace for the `Main()` method and another for the `PhoneCall` class.

7. Save the file, and then compile and run the program. The output looks like Figure 7-17. It shows how a single method can produce a variety of results when you use different values for the arguments.

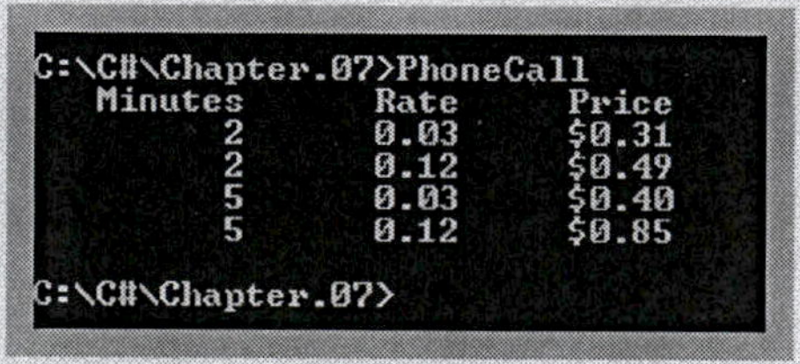

```
C:\C#\Chapter.07>PhoneCall
  Minutes       Rate      Price
        2       0.03      $0.31
        2       0.12      $0.49
        5       0.03      $0.40
        5       0.12      $0.85

C:\C#\Chapter.07>
```

Figure 7-17   Output of the PhoneCall program

Passing Array Values to a Method

Passing an array element to a method and passing an array to a method require different approaches.

Passing a Single Array Element to a Method

In the chapter "Using Arrays," you learned that you can declare an array to create a list of elements, and that you can use any individual array element in the same manner as you would use any single variable of the same type. That is, suppose you declare an integer array as follows:

```
int[] someNums = new int[12];
```

You can subsequently output someNums[0] or add 1 to someNums[1], just as you would for any integer. Similarly, you can pass a single array element to a method in exactly the same manner as you would pass a variable.

Consider the program shown in Figure 7-18. This program creates and uses an array of four integers. Figure 7-19 shows the program's execution.

```
using static System.Console;
class PassArrayElement
{
   static void Main()
   {
      int[] someNums = {10, 12, 22, 35};
      int x;
      Write("\nAt beginning of Main() method...");
      for(x = 0; x < someNums.Length; ++x)
         Write("{0,6}", someNums[x]);
      WriteLine();
      for(x = 0; x < someNums.Length; ++x)
         MethodGetsOneInt(someNums[x]);
      Write("At end of Main() method..........");
      for(x = 0; x < someNums.Length; ++x)
         Write("{0,6}", someNums[x]);
   }
   private static void MethodGetsOneInt(int oneVal)
   {
      Write("In MethodGetsOneInt() {0}", oneVal);
      oneVal = 999;
      WriteLine("     After change {0}", oneVal);
   }
}
```

Figure 7-18   The PassArrayElement program

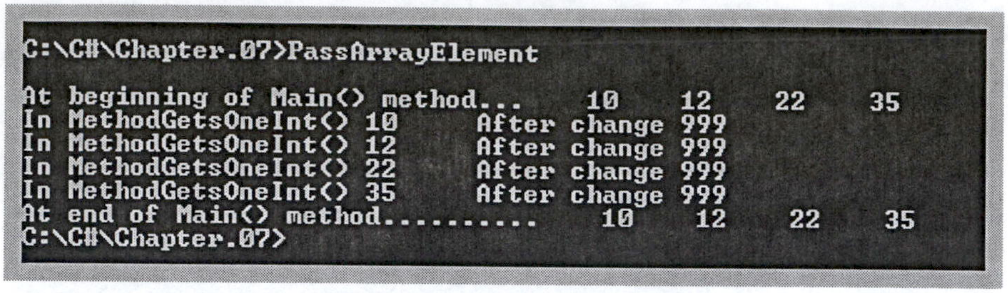

```
C:\C#\Chapter.07>PassArrayElement

At beginning of Main() method...      10      12      22      35
In MethodGetsOneInt() 10      After change 999
In MethodGetsOneInt() 12      After change 999
In MethodGetsOneInt() 22      After change 999
In MethodGetsOneInt() 35      After change 999
At end of Main() method...........      10      12      22      35
C:\C#\Chapter.07>
```

Figure 7-19   Output of the `PassArrayElement` program

As you can see in Figure 7-19, the program displays the four original values, then passes each to the `MethodGetsOneInt()` method, where it is displayed and then changed to 999. After the method executes four times, the `Main()` method displays the four values again, showing that they are unchanged by the assignments within `MethodGetsOneInt()`. The `oneVal` variable is local to the `MethodGetsOneInt()` method; therefore, any changes to variables passed into the method are not permanent and are not reflected in the array declared in the `Main()` program. Each time the `MethodGetsOneInt()` method executes, its `oneVal` parameter holds only a copy of the array element passed into the method, and the `oneVal` variable exists only while the `MethodGetsOneInt()` method is executing.

Passing an Array to a Method

Instead of passing a single array element to a method, you can pass an entire array. You indicate that a method parameter must be an array by placing square brackets after the data type in the method's parameter list. When you pass an array to a method, changes you make to array elements within the method are reflected in the original array that was sent to the method. Arrays, like all objects but unlike built-in types such as `double` and `int`, are **passed by reference**. That is, when a simple built-in type is passed to a method, the method receives a copy of the value at a new memory address, but when an array is passed to a method, the method receives the actual memory address of the array and has access to the actual values in the array elements. You already have seen that methods can alter arrays passed to them. When you use the `Sort()` and `Reverse()` methods, the methods change the array parameter contents.

The program shown in Figure 7-20 creates an array of four integers. After the integers are displayed, the entire array is passed to a method named `MethodGetsArray()` in the shaded statement. Within the method header, the parameter is declared as an array by using square brackets after the parameter data type. Within the method, the numbers are output, which shows that they retain their values from `Main()` upon entering the method, but then the value 888 is assigned to each number. Even though `MethodGetsArray()` is a `void` method (meaning that nothing is returned to the `Main()` method), when the program displays the array for the second time within the `Main()` method, all of the values have been changed to 888, as you can see in Figure 7-21. Because arrays are passed by reference, the `MethodGetsArray()` method "knows" the address of the array declared in `Main()` and makes its changes directly to the original array that was declared in the `Main()` method.

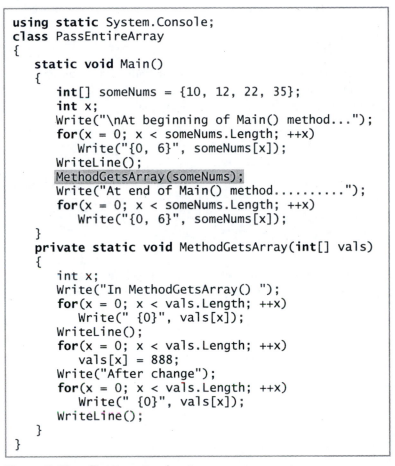

```
using static System.Console;
class PassEntireArray
{
    static void Main()
    {
        int[] someNums = {10, 12, 22, 35};
        int x;
        Write("\nAt beginning of Main() method...");
        for(x = 0; x < someNums.Length; ++x)
            Write("{0, 6}", someNums[x]);
        WriteLine();
        MethodGetsArray(someNums);
        Write("At end of Main() method..........");
        for(x = 0; x < someNums.Length; ++x)
            Write("{0, 6}", someNums[x]);
    }
    private static void MethodGetsArray(int[] vals)
    {
        int x;
        Write("In MethodGetsArray() ");
        for(x = 0; x < vals.Length; ++x)
            Write(" {0}", vals[x]);
        WriteLine();
        for(x = 0; x < vals.Length; ++x)
            vals[x] = 888;
        Write("After change");
        for(x = 0; x < vals.Length; ++x)
            Write(" {0}", vals[x]);
        WriteLine();
    }
}
```

Figure 7-20   The PassEntireArray program

```
C:\C#\Chapter.07>PassEntireArray

At beginning of Main() method...      10     12     22     35
In MethodGetsArray()  10 12 22 35
After change 888 888 888 888
At end of Main() method..........    888    888    888    888
C:\C#\Chapter.07>_
```

Figure 7-21   Output of the PassEntireArray program

Notice that you do not insert a number within the square brackets of the array definition in the method parameter list. Inserting a number causes a compiler error. It makes sense that the brackets are empty because a method that receives an array gets its starting address, not a number of elements.

You can create and pass an unnamed array to a method in a single step. For example, you can write the following:

```
MethodThatAcceptsArray(new int[] {45, 67, 89});
```

You can pass a multidimensional array to a method by indicating the appropriate number of dimensions after the data type in the method header. For example, the following method headers accept two-dimensional arrays of `int`s and `double`s, respectively:

```
private static void displayScores(int[ , ] scoresArray)
private static boolean areAllPricesHigh(double[ , ] prices)
```

With jagged arrays, you can insert the appropriate number of square brackets after the data type in the method header. For example, the following method headers accept jagged arrays of `int`s and `double`s, respectively:

```
private static void displayIDs(int[][] idArray)
private static double computeTotal(double[][] prices)
```

With methods that accept multidimensional arrays as parameters (whether jagged or not), notice that the brackets that define the array in each method header are empty. Like any other array passed to a method, inserting numbers into the brackets for a jagged array is not necessary because each passed array name is a starting memory address. The way you manipulate subscripts within the method determines how rows and columns are accessed.

The size of each dimension of a multidimensional array can be accessed using the `GetLength()` method. For example, `scoresArray.GetLength(0)` returns the value of the first dimension of `scoresArray`.

Watch the video *Passing Arrays to Methods*.

TWO TRUTHS & A LIE

Passing Array Values to a Method

1. You indicate that a method parameter can be an array element by placing a data type and identifier in the method's parameter list.

2. You indicate that a method parameter must be an array by placing parentheses after the data type in the method's parameter list.

3. Arrays are passed by reference; that is, the method receives the actual memory address of the array and has access to the actual values in the array elements.

The false statement is #2. You indicate that a method parameter must be an array by placing square brackets after the data type in the method's parameter list.

Alternate Ways to Write a Main() Method Header

Throughout this book, you have written Main() methods with the following header:

```
static void Main()
```

Using the return type void and listing nothing between the parentheses that follow Main is just one way to write a Main() method header in a program. However, it is the first way listed in the C# documentation, and it is the convention used in this book. This section describes alternatives because you might see different Main() method headers in other books or in programs written by others.

Writing a Main() Method with a Parameter List

An alternate way to write a Main() method header is as follows:

```
static void Main(string[] args)
```

The phrase string[] args is a parameter to the Main() method. The variable args represents an array of strings that you can pass to Main(). Although you can use any identifier, args is conventional. In particular, Java programmers might prefer the C# version of Main() that includes the string[] args parameter because their convention is to write main methods with the same parameter.

Use this format for the Main() method header if you need to access command-line arguments passed in to your application. For example, the program in Figure 7-22 displays an args array that is a parameter to its Main() method. Figure 7-23 shows how a program might be executed from the command line using arguments to Main().

```
using static System.Console;
class DisplayArgs
{
    static void Main(string[] args)
    {
        for(int x = 0; x < args.Length; ++x)
            WriteLine("Argument {0} is {1}", x, args[x]);
    }
}
```

Figure 7-22 A Main() method with a string[] args parameter

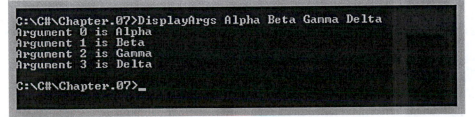

```
C:\C#\Chapter.07>DisplayArgs Alpha Beta Gamma Delta
Argument 0 is Alpha
Argument 1 is Beta
Argument 2 is Gamma
Argument 3 is Delta

C:\C#\Chapter.07>_
```

Figure 7-23 Executing the DisplayArgs program with arguments

Even if you do not need access to command-line arguments, you can still use the version of the Main() method header that references them. You should use this version if your instructor or supervisor indicates you should follow this convention.

Writing a Main() Method with an Integer Return Type

Some programmers prefer to write Main() method headers that have a return type of int instead of void. If you use this form, the last statement in the Main() method must be a return statement that returns an integer. By convention, a return value of 0 means that an application ended without error. The value might be used by your operating system or another program that uses your program. In particular, C++ programmers might prefer the version of Main() that returns an int because conventionally they write their main methods with an int return type.

Even if you do not need to use a return value from a Main() method, you can still use the version of the Main() method header that includes a return value. You should use this version if your instructor or supervisor indicates you should follow this convention.

Writing a Main() Method with public Access

Some programmers prefer to write Main() method headers with public access rather than private, which is the default access when no specifier is listed. In particular, Java programmers might prefer using public because the style is conventional for them. If a class's Main() method is public, it can be called from another class by using its fully qualified name. Because you rarely want to do this, C# programmers often omit the Main() method's access specifier, making it private.

TWO TRUTHS & A LIE

Alternate Ways to Write a Main() Method Header

1. In C#, a Main() method header can be written public static void Main().

2. In C#, a Main() method header can be written static void Main(string[] args).

3. In C#, a Main() method header can be written static int main(string args).

The false statement is #3. In C#, a Main() method header can be written as shown in either of the first two examples. Statement #3 is wrong because Main() must be capitalized, and string must be followed by a pair of square brackets.

Issues Using Methods in GUI Programs

You can call methods from other methods in a GUI application in the same way you can in a console application. Some special considerations when creating GUI applications include the following:

- Understanding methods that are automatically generated in the visual environment

- Appreciating scope in a GUI program

- Creating methods to be nonstatic when associated with a Form

Understanding Methods That Are Automatically Generated in the Visual Environment

When you create GUI applications using the IDE, many methods are generated automatically. For example, when you place a Button named okButton on a Form in the IDE and double-click it, a method is generated with the following header:

```
private void okButton_Click(object sender, EventArgs e)
```

The method is private, which means it can be used only within its class, and it is void, meaning it does not return a value. You could change the access specifier to public and the method would still work, but usually you would have no reason to make such a change. If you change the return type (void), the program will not compile.

The format of the method name okButton_Click() is conventional for automatically created event handling methods. The name includes the control name, an underscore, and the event that causes the method to execute—in this case, a Click event. Although the C# convention is to begin method names with an uppercase letter, event-handling method names like okButton_Click() begin with a lowercase letter to echo the format of the control's name.

The parameters received by the okButton_Click() method arrive automatically when a user clicks the okButton. The parameter sender is the object that generated the event that caused the method to execute, and the parameter e contains information about the type of event. Figure 7-24 shows a Click() method in a GUI application that displays the ToString() values of these two parameters.

```
private void okButton_Click(object sender, EventArgs e)
{
    label1.Text = sender.ToString();
    label2.Text = e.ToString();
}
```

Figure 7-24   The okButton_Click() method in the ClickParameterInfo program

Figure 7-25 shows the output after the button is clicked. The object that generated the event is the button that contains the text *OK*, and the type of event was generated by a mouse. You have seen many Click() methods in earlier chapters that had the same parameters, but you did not use them. As with any other method, you never are required to use the parameters passed in.

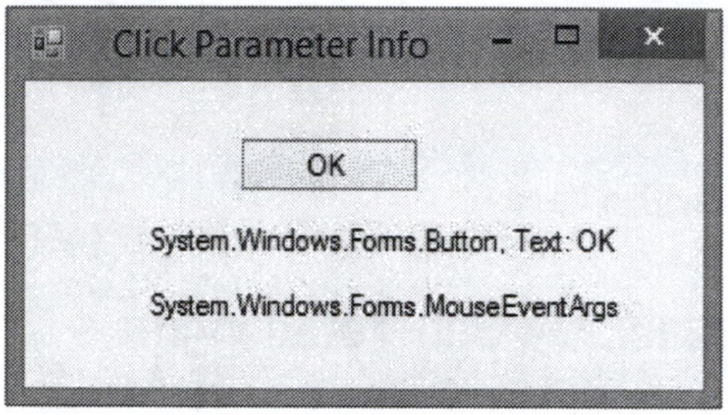

Figure 7-25   Output generated by the okButton_Click() method in Figure 7-24

Appreciating Scope in a GUI Program

When you create event-handling methods in a GUI application, you must constantly be aware of which variables and constants are needed by multiple methods. When you declare a variable or constant within a method, it is local to that method. If a variable or constant is needed by multiple event-handling methods—for example, by two different Click() methods—then the variables or constants in question must be defined outside the methods (but within the Form class) so that both Click() methods have access to them. When you write other methods, you can decide what arguments to pass in, but automatically generated event-handling methods have predefined sets of parameters, so you cannot be as flexible in using them as you can with other methods you write. In Chapter 9, "Using Classes and Objects," you see many examples of variables declared within a class but outside methods; such variables are called *fields*.

Creating Methods to be Nonstatic When Associated with a Form

In Chapter 1, you learned that the keyword static is used with Main() methods in console applications because the method is associated with its containing class and not with an object. When you create a GUI application and generate a method, such as a Click() method associated with a Button on a Form, the keyword static does not appear in the method header because the method is associated with an object—the Form from which the method-invoking events are sent. When you execute a GUI program using a Form, the program creates a Form object, and the methods associated with it are nonstatic. In the chapter "Using Classes and Objects," you will learn much more about the differences between static and nonstatic methods. For now, omit the word static when you create methods that are intended to be called by other nonstatic methods in your GUI applications. For example, if you create a Click() method that responds to button clicks, it will be nonstatic by default because it is associated with an object that is a Form.

TWO TRUTHS & A LIE

Issues Using Methods in GUI Programs

1. An advantage to using the IDE to create GUI programs is that many methods you need are generated automatically.

2. As with any other methods, when you create a `Click()` method associated with a button in a GUI application, you do not need to reference the parameters within the method body.

3. If you want a `Click()` method to add two variables, you must pass them in as parameters.

The false statement is #3. Automatically generated event-handling methods have predefined sets of parameters, so you cannot be as flexible in using them as you can with other methods you write. Typically the variables used in a `Click()` method would be defined outside the method but inside the `Form` class where the `Click()` method resides.

Chapter Summary

- A method is a series of statements that carry out a task. Any class can contain an unlimited number of methods. Object-oriented programs hide their methods' implementations.

- You write methods to make programs easier to understand and so that you can easily reuse them. In C#, a method must include a method declaration, an opening curly brace, a method body, and a closing curly brace. The method declaration defines the rules for using the method; it contains an optional declared accessibility, an optional **static** modifier, a return type for the method, an identifier, and an optional list of method parameters between parentheses.

- Some method calls require arguments. The items received by a method are parameters. When you write the declaration for a method that can receive a parameter, you need to include the type of parameter and a local identifier for it within the method declaration parentheses. A variable declared in a method header is a formal parameter, and an argument within a method call is an actual parameter.

- You can pass multiple arguments to a method by listing the arguments within the parentheses in the call to the method and separating them with commas. You can write a method to take any number of parameters. When you call the method, the arguments you send to it must match in both number and type (allowing for type conversion) with the nondefault parameters listed in the method declaration.

- The return type for a method defines the type of value sent back to the calling method. It can be any type used in the C# programming language, which includes the basic built-in types `int`, `double`, `char`, and so on, as well as class types (including class types you create). A method also can return nothing, in which case the return type is `void`.

- You can pass an array as a parameter to a method. You indicate that a method parameter is an array by placing square brackets after the data type in the method's parameter list. Arrays, like all objects but unlike built-in types, are passed by reference; that is, the method receives the actual memory address of the array and has access to the actual values in the array elements.

- You might see different `Main()` method headers in other books or in programs written by others. Some programmers include an array of strings as a parameter to `Main()`, some programmers return an `int` from the `Main()` method, and some programmers give `Main()` methods public access.

- Special considerations exist for methods when you create GUI applications. You must understand the automatically generated methods in the visual environment, appreciate the differences in scope in GUI programs, and understand that many methods must be nonstatic when associated with a `Form`.

Key Terms

A **method** is an encapsulated series of statements that carry out a task.

Invoked and **called** describe what one method has done to execute another.

A **calling method** calls another method.

A **called method** is invoked by another method.

Implementation hiding means keeping the details of a method's operations hidden.

A **client** is a method that uses another method.

A **black box** is any device you can use without knowing how it works internally.

A **multifile assembly** is a group of files containing methods that work together to create an application.

Code bloat describes unnecessarily long or repetitive program statements.

A **method declaration** is a **method header** or **method definition**.

A **method body** is a block of statements that carry out a method's work.

Accessibility for a method is a declaration that sets limits as to whether and how other methods can use it.

Public access is a level of method accessibility that allows unlimited access to a method by any class.

Private access is a level of method accessibility that limits method access to the containing class.

A **fully qualified** name is one that includes the class name.

A **static** method is called without an object reference. It can be called from any class using its class name, a dot, and the method name. Within its own class, a static method can be called by just using its name.

A **nonstatic** method call requires an object reference.

A **return type** indicates what kind of value a method will return to any other method that calls it.

A **method's type** is its return type.

A **parameter to a method** is a variable that holds data passed to a method when it is called.

A **parameter list** consists of the data types and parameter names that appear between parentheses in a method header. The list might hold only one item or multiple items separated with commas.

A variable's **scope** is the segment of program code where it can be used.

A **local** variable is one that is declared in the current method.

A **formal parameter** is a parameter within a method header that accepts a value.

Actual parameters are arguments within a method call.

A **return statement** causes a value to be sent back from a method to its calling method.

Nested method calls are method calls placed inside other method calls.

Passed by reference describes the state of an argument passed to a method when the method receives its memory address.

Review Questions

1. At most, a class can contain _____ method(s).

   a. 0

   b. 1

   c. 2

   d. any number of

2. Which of the following is a good reason for creating methods within a program?

   a. Methods are easily reusable.

   b. Because all methods must be stored in the same class, they are easy to find.

   c. The `Main()` method becomes more detailed.

   d. All of these are true.

3. In C#, a method must include all of the following *except* a _____.

    a. return type   c. body

    b. access modifier   d. closing curly brace

4. A method declaration might contain _____.

    a. declared accessibility   c. multiple return types

    b. a nonstatic modifier   d. parameters separated by dots

5. Every method declaration must contain _____.

    a. a statement of purpose   c. the **static** modifier

    b. declared accessibility   d. a return type

6. If you want to create a method that other methods in other classes can access without limitations, you declare the method to be _____.

    a. unlimited   c. shared

    b. public   d. unrestricted

7. If you use the keyword modifier **static** in a method header, you indicate that the method _____.

    a. cannot be copied

    b. can be called only once

    c. cannot require parameters

    d. is called without an object reference

8. A method's type is also its _____.

    a. return type   c. parameter type

    b. accessibility   d. scope

9   When you use a method, you do not need to know how it operates internally. This feature is called _____.

    a. scope management   c. implementation hiding

    b. selective ignorance   d. privacy

10. When you write the method declaration for a method that can receive a parameter, you need to include all of the following items *except* _____.

    a. a pair of parentheses   c. a local name for the parameter

    b. the type of the parameter   d. an initial value for the parameter

11. Suppose you have declared a variable as `int myAge = 21;`.
    Which of the following is a legal call to a method with the declaration

    `private static void AMethod(int num)`?

    a. `AMethod(int 55);`   c. `AMethod(int myAge);`

    b. `AMethod(myAge);`   d. `AMethod();`

12. Suppose you have declared a method named
    `private static void CalculatePay(double rate)`. When a method calls
    the `CalculatePay()` method, the calling method _____.

    a. must contain a declared **double** named **rate**

    b. might contain a declared **double** named **rate**

    c. cannot contain a declared **double** named **rate**

    d. cannot contain any declared **double** variables

13. In the method call `PrintTheData(double salary);`, `salary` is the
    _____ parameter.

    a. formal   c. proposed

    b. actual   d. preferred

14. A program contains the method call `PrintTheData(salary);`. In the method
    definition, the name of the formal parameter must be _____.

    a. `salary`

    b. any legal identifier other than `salary`

    c. any legal identifier

    d. omitted

15. What is a correct declaration for a method that receives two **double** arguments,
    calculates and displays the difference between them, and returns nothing?

    a. `private static void CalcDifference(double price1, price2)`

    b. `private static void CalcDifference(double price1, double price2)`

    c. Both of these are correct.

    d. None of these are correct.

16. What is a correct declaration for a method that receives two **double** arguments and sums them but does not return anything?

    a. `private static void CalcSum(double firstValue, double secondValue)`

    b. `private static void CalcSum(double price1, double price2)`

    c. Both of these are correct.

    d. None of these are correct.

17. A method is declared as `private static double CalcPay(int hoursWorked)`. Suppose you write a `Main()` method in the same class that contains the declarations `int hours = 35;` and `double pay;`. Which of the following represents a correct way to call the `CalcPay()` method from the `Main()` method?

    a. `hours = CalcPay();`

    b. `hours = Main.CalcPay();`

    c. `pay = CalcPay(hoursWorked);`

    d. `pay = CalcPay(hours);`

18. Suppose the value of `isRateOK()` is `true`, and the value of `isQuantityOK()` is `false`. When you evaluate the expression `isRateOK() || isQuantityOK()`, which of the following is true?

    a. Only the method `isRateOK()` executes.

    b. Only the method `isQuantityOK()` executes.

    c. Both methods execute.

    d. Neither method executes.

19. Suppose the value of `isRateOK()` is `true`, and the value of `isQuantityOK()` is `false`. When you evaluate the expression `isRateOK() && isQuantityOK()`, which of the following is true?

    a. Only the method `isRateOK()` executes.

    b. Only the method `isQuantityOK()` executes.

    c. Both methods execute.

    d. Neither method executes.

20. When an array is passed to a method, the method has access to the array's memory address. This means an array is passed by _____.

    a. reference

    b. value

    c. alias

    d. orientation

Exercises

Programming Exercises

1. Create a C# statement that uses each of the following built-in methods you have used in previous chapters, then make an intelligent guess about the return type and parameter list for the method used in each statement you created.

   a. `Console.WriteLine()`   d. `Convert.ToInt32()`

   b. `String.Equals()`   e. `Convert.ToChar()`

   c. `String.Compare()`   f. `Array.Sort()`

2. Create a program named **SalesLetter** whose `Main()` method uses several `WriteLine()` calls to display a sales letter to prospective clients for a business of your choice. Display your contact information at least three times in the letter. The contact information should contain at least three lines with data such as land line phone number, cell number, email address, and so on. Each time you want to display the contact information, call a method named `DisplayContactInfo()`.

3. Create a program named **PaintingEstimate** whose `Main()` method prompts a user for length and width of a room in feet. Create a method that accepts the values and then computes the cost of painting the room, assuming the room is rectangular and has four full walls and 9-foot ceilings. The price of the job is $6 per square foot. Return the price to the `Main()` method, and display it.

4. Create an application named **ConvertQuartsToLiters** whose `Main()` method prompts a user for a number of quarts, passes the value to a method that converts the value to liters, and then returns the value to the `Main()` method where it is displayed. A quart is 0.966353 liters.

5. Create a program named **FortuneTeller** whose `Main()` method contains an array of at least six strings with fortune-telling phrases such as *I see a tall, dark stranger in your future*. The program randomly selects two different fortunes and passes them to a method that displays them.

6. Create an application named **Multiplication** whose `Main()` method asks the user to input an integer and then calls a method named `DisplayMultiplicationTable()`, which displays the results of multiplying the integer by each of the numbers 2 through 10.

7. In Chapter 4, you wrote a program named **Admission** for a college admissions office in which the user enters a numeric high school grade point average and an admission test score. The program displays *Accept* or *Reject* based on those values. Now, create a modified program named **AdmissionModularized** in which the grade point average and test score are passed to a method that returns a string containing *Accept* or *Reject*.

8. Write a program named **CountVowelsModularized** that passes a string to a method that returns the number of vowels in the string.

9. Create an application named **Desks** that computes the price of a desk and whose `Main()` method calls the following methods:

    - A method to accept the number of drawers in the desk as input from the keyboard. This method returns the number of drawers to the `Main()` method.

    - A method to accept as input and return the type of wood, *m* for mahogany, *o* for oak, or *p* for pine.

    - A method that accepts the number of drawers and wood type, and calculates the cost of the desk based on the following:

    - Pine desks are $100.

    - Oak desks are $140.

    - All other woods are $180.

    - A $30 surcharge is added for each drawer.

    - This method returns the cost to the `Main()` method.

    - A method to display all the details and the final price.

10. Create a program named **FlexibleArrayMethod** that declares at least three integer arrays of different sizes. In turn, pass each array to a method that displays all the integers in each array and their sum.

Debugging Exercises

1. Each of the following files in the Chapter.07 folder of your downloadable student files has syntax and/or logical errors. In each case, determine the problem, and fix the program. After you correct the errors, save each file using the same filename preceded with *Fixed*. For example, DebugSeven1.cs will become FixedDebugSeven1.cs.

    a. DebugSeven1.cs
    b. DebugSeven2.cs

    c. DebugSeven3.cs
    d. DebugSeven4.cs

Case Problems

1. In Chapter 6, you continued to modify the **GreenvilleRevenue** program. Now, modify the program so that the major functions appear in the following individual methods:

   - A method that gets and returns a valid number of contestants and is called twice—once for last year's number of contestants and once for this year's value

   - A method that accepts the number of contestants this year and last year and displays one of the three messages that describes the relationship between the two contestant values

   - A method that fills the array of competitors and their talent codes

   - A method that continuously prompts for talent codes and displays contestants with the corresponding talent until a sentinel value is entered

2. In previous chapters, you continued to modify the **MarshallsRevenue** program. Now, modify the program so that the major functions appear in the following individual methods:

   - A method that prompts for and returns the month

   - A method that prompts for and returns the number of murals scheduled and is called twice—once for interior murals and once for exterior murals

   - A method that accepts the number of interior and exterior murals scheduled, accepts the month they are scheduled, displays the interior and exterior prices, and then returns the total expected revenue

   - A method that fills an array with customer names and mural codes and is called twice—once to fill the array of interior murals and once to fill the array of exterior murals

   - A method that continuously prompts for mural codes and displays jobs of the corresponding type until a sentinel value is entered

Advanced Method Concepts

In the last chapter you learned to call methods, pass arguments to them, and receive values from them. In this chapter you will expand your method-handling skills to include more sophisticated techniques, including using reference, output, and optional parameters and overloading methods. Understanding how to manipulate methods is crucial when you are working on large, professional, real-world projects. With methods, you can more easily coordinate your work with that of other programmers.

Understanding Parameter Types

In C#, an argument can be passed to a method's parameter by value or by reference. In the previous chapter, you passed arguments of simple data types (like `int` and `double`) by value, and you passed arrays by reference. Parameters also can be classified as mandatory or optional. When you use a **mandatory parameter**, an argument for it is required in every method call. An **optional parameter** to a method is one for which a default value is automatically supplied if you do not explicitly send one as an argument. All the methods that you have seen with simple and array parameters have used mandatory parameters.

Mandatory parameters also include:

- Reference parameters
- Output parameters
- Parameter arrays

C# includes only one type of optional parameter:

- Value parameters, when they are declared *with* default values

Using Mandatory Value Parameters

So far, all of the method parameters you have created have been mandatory, and all except arrays have been value parameters. When you use a **value parameter** in a method header, you indicate the parameter's type and name, and the method receives a copy of the value passed to it. A variable that is used as an argument to a method with a value parameter must have a value assigned to it. If it does not, the program will not compile.

The value of a method's value parameter is stored at a different memory address than the variable used as the argument in the method call. In other words, the actual parameter (the argument in the calling method) and the formal parameter (the parameter in the method header) refer to two separate memory locations, and the called method receives a copy of the sent value. Changes to value parameters never affect the original arguments in calling methods.

 A popular advertising campaign declares, "What happens in Vegas, stays in Vegas." The same is true of value parameters within a method—changes to them do not persist outside the method.

Figure 8-1 shows a program that declares a variable named x; the figure assumes that x is stored at memory address 2000. The value 4 is assigned to x and then displayed. Then x is passed to a method that accepts a value parameter. The method declares its own local parameter named x, which receives the value 4. This local variable is at a different memory address; for example, assume that it is 8800. The method assigns a new value, 777, to the local variable and displays it. When control returns to the Main() method, the value of x is accessed from memory location 2000 and remains 4.

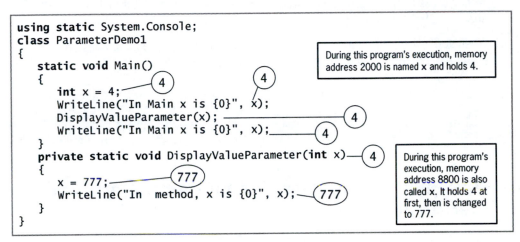

```
using static System.Console;
class ParameterDemo1
{
    static void Main()
    {
        int x = 4;
        WriteLine("In Main x is {0}", x);
        DisplayValueParameter(x);
        WriteLine("In Main x is {0}", x);
    }
    private static void DisplayValueParameter(int x)
    {
        x = 777;
        WriteLine("In  method, x is {0}", x);
    }
}
```

During this program's execution, memory address 2000 is named x and holds 4.

During this program's execution, memory address 8800 is also called x. It holds 4 at first, then is changed to 777.

Figure 8-1   Program calling a method with a value parameter

Changing the value of x within the DisplayValueParameter() method has no effect on x in the Main() method. Even though both methods contain a variable named x, they represent two separate variables, each with its own memory location. Programmers say that a value parameter is used for "in" parameter passing—values for "in" parameters go into a method, but modifications to them do not come "out." In the program in Figure 8-1, it makes no difference whether you use the name x as the Main() method's actual parameter or use some other name. In either case, the parameter received by the DisplayValueParameter() method occupies a separate memory location. Figure 8-2 shows the output of the program in Figure 8-1.

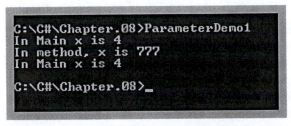

```
C:\C#\Chapter.08>ParameterDemo1
In Main x is 4
In method, x is 777
In Main x is 4

C:\C#\Chapter.08>
```

Figure 8-2   Output of the ParameterDemo1 program

> ## TWO TRUTHS & A LIE
>
> ### Understanding Parameter Types
>
> 1. When you call a method that has a mandatory parameter, you must send an argument.
>
> 2. When you call a method that has an optional parameter, you do not have to send an argument, but you can.
>
> 3. When you call a method with a mandatory value parameter, you must pass an argument, but if it is a variable, you do not have to have initialized it.
>
> The false statement is #3. A mandatory value parameter must receive an initialized argument.

Using Reference Parameters, Output Parameters, and Parameter Arrays

On occasion, you might want a method to be able to alter a value you pass to it. In that case, you can use a reference parameter, an output parameter, or a parameter array. Each **reference parameter**, **output parameter**, and **parameter array** represents a memory address that is passed to a method, allowing the method to alter the original variable. Reference parameters, output parameters, and parameter arrays differ as follows:

- When you declare a reference parameter in a method header, the argument used to call the method must have been assigned a value.

- When you declare an output parameter, the argument used in the call need not contain an original, assigned value. However, an output parameter must be assigned a value before the method ends.

- When you declare a parameter array, the argument used in the call need not contain any original, assigned values, and the parameter array need not be assigned any values within the method.

Reference parameters, output parameters, and parameter arrays do not occupy their own memory locations. Rather, they act as aliases, or pseudonyms (other names), for the same memory location occupied by the values passed to them. You use the keyword ref as a modifier to indicate a reference parameter, the keyword out as a modifier to indicate an output parameter, and the keyword params to indicate a parameter array.

Using an alias for a variable is similar to using an alias for a person. Jane Doe might be known as "Ms. Doe" at work but "Sissy" at home. Both names refer to the same person.

Using a `ref` Parameter

Figure 8-3 shows a `Main()` method that calls a `DisplayReferenceParameter()` method. The `Main()` method declares and initializes a variable, displays its value, and then passes the variable to the method. The modifier `ref` precedes both the variable name in the method call and the parameter declaration in the method header. The method's parameter `number` refers to the memory address of `x`, making `number` an alias for `x`. When `DisplayReferenceParameter()` changes the value of `number`, the change persists in the `x` variable within `Main()`. Figure 8-4 shows the output of the program.

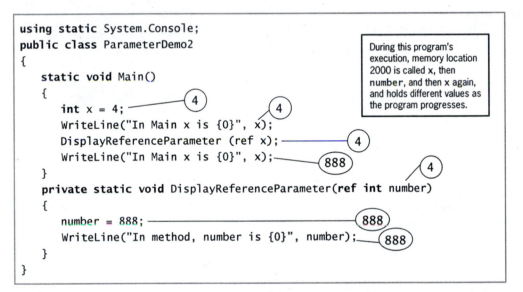

Figure 8-3 Program calling a method with a reference parameter

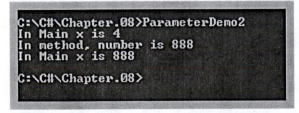

Figure 8-4 Output of the ParameterDemo2 program

In the header for the `DisplayReferenceParameter()` method, it makes no difference whether you use the same name as the `Main()` method's passed variable (x) or some other name, such as `number`. In either case, the passed and received variables occupy the same memory location—the address of one is the address of the other.

Using an `out` Parameter

When you use a reference parameter, any passed variable must have an assigned value. Using an output parameter is convenient when the passed variable doesn't have a value yet. For example, the program in Figure 8-5 uses `InputMethod()` to obtain values for two parameters. The arguments that are sent in the shaded statement get their values from the called method, so it makes sense to provide them with no values going in. Instead, they acquire values in the method and retain the values coming out. Figure 8-6 shows a typical execution of the program.

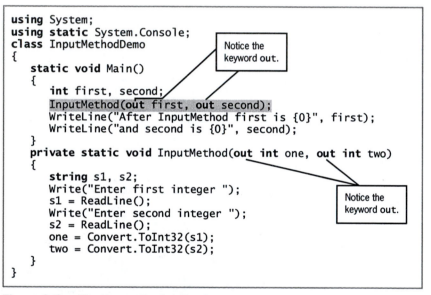

```
using System;
using static System.Console;
class InputMethodDemo                    Notice the
{                                        keyword out.
    static void Main()
    {
        int first, second;
        InputMethod(out first, out second);
        WriteLine("After InputMethod first is {0}", first);
        WriteLine("and second is {0}", second);
    }
    private static void InputMethod(out int one, out int two)
    {
        string s1, s2;
        Write("Enter first integer ");
        s1 = ReadLine();                      Notice the
        Write("Enter second integer ");       keyword out.
        s2 = ReadLine();
        one = Convert.ToInt32(s1);
        two = Convert.ToInt32(s2);
    }
}
```

Figure 8-5   The `InputMethodDemo` program

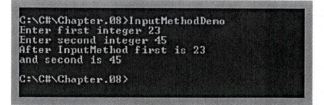

```
C:\C#\Chapter.08>InputMethodDemo
Enter first integer 23
Enter second integer 45
After InputMethod first is 23
and second is 45

C:\C#\Chapter.08>
```

Figure 8-6   Output of the `InputMethodDemo` program

It might be helpful to remember:

- If you will always have an initial value, use `ref`.

- If you do not have an initial value or you do not know whether you will have an initial value, use `out`. (For example, in an interactive program, a user might not provide a value for a variable, so you don't know whether the variable has an initial value.)

In summary, when you need a method to share a single value from a calling method, you have two options:

- Use a return type. You can send an argument to a method that accepts a value parameter, alter the local version of the variable within the method, return the altered value, and assign the return value to the original variable back in the calling method. The drawback to this approach is that a method can have only a single return type and can return only one value at most.

- Pass by reference. You can send an argument to a method that accepts a reference or output parameter and alter the value at the original memory location within the method. A major advantage to using reference or output parameters exists when you want a method to change multiple variables. A method can have only a single return type and can return only one value at most, but by using reference or output parameters to a method, you can change multiple values. However, a major disadvantage to using reference and output parameters is that they allow multiple methods to have access to the same data, weakening the "black box" paradigm that is so important to object-oriented methodology. You should never use `ref` or `out` parameters to avoid having to return a value, but you should understand them so you can use them if required.

Watch the video *Using `ref` and `out` Parameters*.

As with simple parameters, you can use `out` or `ref` when passing an array to a method. You do so when you want to declare the array in the calling method, but use the `new` operator to allocate memory for it in the called method.

Using a Built-in Method That Has an `out` Parameter

In Chapter 2, you learned two ways to convert a string to a number—you can use a `Convert` class method or a `Parse()` method. For example, each of the following statements accepts a string and converts it to an integer named `score`:

```
int score = Convert.ToInt32(ReadLine());
int score = int.Parse(ReadLine());
```

With either of these statements, if the value accepted by `ReadLine()` cannot be converted to an integer (for example, because it contains a decimal point or an alphabetic character), the program abruptly stops running. Consider the simple program in Figure 8-7. The program prompts the user for a score and displays it. Figure 8-8 shows two executions of the program. In the first execution, the user enters a valid integer and everything goes smoothly. In the second execution, the user enters alphabetic characters, the program stops, and a series of error messages is displayed.

```
using static System.Console;
class ConversionWithParse
{
    static void Main()
    {
        string entryString;
        int score;
        Write("Enter your test score >> ");
        entryString = ReadLine();
        score = int.Parse(entryString);
        WriteLine("You entered {0}", score);
    }
}
```

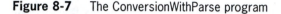

Figure 8-7   The ConversionWithParse program

Figure 8-8   Two typical executions of the ConversionWithParse program

The messages in Figure 8-8 indicate that the program contains an unhandled exception because *Input string was not in a correct format.* An exception is a program error; you will learn much more about exceptions in Chapter 11, "Exception Handling." For now, however, you can handle data conversion exceptions by the TryParse() method. Unlike the Parse() method, TryParse() accepts an out parameter. The TryParse() method converts a string to the correct data type and stores the result in a passed variable if possible. If conversion is not possible, the method assigns 0 to the variable.

Figure 8-9 contains a program that uses the int.TryParse() method to convert entryString to an integer that is assigned to score. The only differences from the program in Figure 8-7 are the shaded change to the class name and the shaded call to the int.TryParse() method.

The TryParse() method accepts two parameters: the string to be converted and the variable where the result is stored. The keyword out is required with the second parameter because the method receives its address and changes the value. Figure 8-10 shows two typical executions of the ConversionWithTryParse program. When the user's input cannot be converted correctly, the out parameter is assigned 0. Whether or not the user's input is in the correct format, the program continues and displays output instead of error messages.

```
using static System.Console;
class ConversionWithTryParse
{
    static void Main()
    {
        string entryString;
        int score;
        Write("Enter your test score >> ");
        entryString = ReadLine();
        int.TryParse(entryString, out score);
        WriteLine("You entered {0}", score);
    }
}
```

Figure 8-9   The ConversionWithTryParse program

```
C:\C#\Chapter.08>ConversionWithTryParse
Enter your test score >> 100
You entered 100

C:\C#\Chapter.08>ConversionWithTryParse
Enter your test score >> perfect
You entered 0

C:\C#\Chapter.08>
```

Figure 8-10   Two typical executions of the ConversionWithTryParse program

The TryParse() method requires the receiving variable to be an out parameter for two reasons:

- The argument does not have an assigned value in the calling method.

- The method returns a Boolean value that indicates whether the conversion was successful and so cannot return the score value too.

Suppose that you do not want a score to be assigned 0 if the conversion fails, because 0 is a legitimate score. Instead, you want to assign a −1 if the conversion fails. In that case you can use a statement similar to the following:

```
if(!int.TryParse(entryString, out score))
    score = -1;
```

In this example, if `entryString`'s conversion is successful, `score` holds the converted value; otherwise, `score` holds −1.

As another example, you might consider code that includes a loop that continues until the entered value is in the correct format, such as the following:

```
Write("Enter your test score >> ");
entryString = ReadLine();
while(!int.TryParse(entryString, out score))
{
    WriteLine("Input data was not formatted correctly");
    Write("Please enter score again >> ");
    entryString = ReadLine();
}
```

In this example, the loop continues until the `TryParse()` method returns `true`.

C# also provides `char.TryParse()`, `double.TryParse()`, and `decimal.TryParse()` methods that work in the same way—each converts a first parameter string and assigns its value to the second parameter variable, returning `true` or `false` based on the success of the conversion.

Using Parameter Arrays

When you don't know how many arguments of the same data type might eventually be sent to a method, you can declare a parameter array—a local array declared within the method header using the keyword `params`. Such a method accepts any number of elements that are all the same data type.

For example, a method with the following header accepts an array of strings:

```
private static void DisplayStrings(params string[] people)
```

In the call to this method, you can use any number of strings as actual parameters; within the method, they will be treated as an array.

When a method header uses the `params` keyword, the following two restrictions apply:

- Only one `params` keyword is permitted in a method declaration.
- If a method declares multiple parameters, the `params`-qualified parameter must be the last one in the list.

Figure 8-11 shows a program that calls `DisplayStrings()` three times—once with one string argument, once with three string arguments, and once with an array of strings. In each case, the method works correctly, treating the passed strings as an array and displaying them appropriately. Figure 8-12 shows the output.

```
using static System.Console;
class ParamsDemo
{
    static void Main()
    {
        string[] names = {"Mark", "Paulette", "Carol", "James"};
        DisplayStrings("Ginger");
        DisplayStrings("George", "Maria", "Thomas");
        DisplayStrings(names);
    }
    private static void DisplayStrings(params string[] people)
    {
        foreach(string person in people)
            Write("{0} ", person);
        WriteLine("\n--------------");
    }
}
```

Figure 8-11 The ParamsDemo program

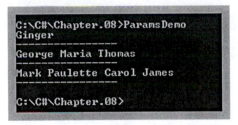

Figure 8-12 Output of the ParamsDemo program

You could create an even more flexible method by using a method header such as
Display(params Object[] things). Then the passed parameters could be any type—
strings, integers, other classes, and so on. The method could be implemented as follows:

```
private static void Display(params Object[] things)
{
    foreach(Object obj in things)
        Write("{0} ", obj);
    WriteLine("\n-------------");
}
```

All data types are Objects; you will learn more about the Object class in the chapters
"Using Classes and Objects" and "Introduction to Inheritance."

322

TWO TRUTHS & A LIE

Using Reference Parameters, Output Parameters, and Parameter Arrays

1. Both reference and output parameters represent memory addresses that are passed to a method, allowing the method to alter the original variables.

2. When you declare a reference parameter in a method header, the parameter must not have been assigned a value.

3. When you use an output parameter, it need not contain an original, assigned value when the method is called, but it must receive a value before the method ends.

The false statement is #2. When you declare a reference parameter in a method header, the parameter must have been assigned a value.

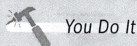

You Do It

Using Reference Parameters

You use reference parameters when you want a method to have access to the memory address of arguments in a calling method. For example, suppose that you have two values and you want to exchange them (or swap them), making each equal to the value of the other. Because you want to change two values, a method that accepts copies of arguments will not work—a method can return one value at most. Therefore, you can use reference parameters to provide your method with the actual addresses of the values you want to change.

1. Open your editor and begin a program named **SwapProgram** as follows:

```
using static System.Console;
class SwapProgram
{
    static void Main()
    {
```

2. Declare two integers, and display their values. Call the Swap() method, and pass in the addresses of the two variables to swap. Because the parameters already have assigned values, and because you want to alter those values

(continues)

(continued)

in `Main()`, you can use reference parameters. After the method call, display the two values again. Add the closing curly brace for the `Main()` method.

```
int first = 34, second = 712;
Write("Before swap first is {0}", first);
WriteLine(" and second is {0}", second);
Swap(ref first, ref second);
Write("After swap first is {0}", first);
WriteLine(" and second is {0}", second);
}
```

3. Create the `Swap()` method as shown. You can swap two values by storing the first value in a temporary variable, then assigning the second value to the first variable. At this point, both variables hold the value originally held by the second variable. When you assign the temporary variable's value to the second variable, the two values are reversed.

```
private static void Swap(ref int one, ref int two)
{
    int temp;
    temp = one;
    one = two;
    two = temp;
}
```

4. Add the closing curly brace for the class. Save the program, and then compile and execute it. Figure 8-13 shows the output.

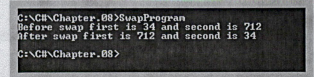

```
C:\C#\Chapter.08>SwapProgram
Before swap first is 34 and second is 712
After swap first is 712 and second is 34

C:\C#\Chapter.08>
```

Figure 8-13   Output of the SwapProgram program

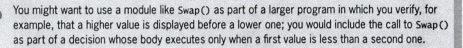

You might want to use a module like `Swap()` as part of a larger program in which you verify, for example, that a higher value is displayed before a lower one; you would include the call to `Swap()` as part of a decision whose body executes only when a first value is less than a second one.

Overloading Methods

Overloading involves the ability to write multiple versions of a method using the same method name. When you make a purchase at a store, you might use one of a variety of "pay" methods they accept, for example, cash, a credit card, or a check. The "pay" method works differently depending on the type of currency sent to it, but all of the transactions are called "pay." When you overload a C# method, you write multiple method implementations with the same name but different parameter lists. A method's name and parameter list constitute the method's **signature**.

In this book you have seen the WriteLine() method used with a string parameter and a numeric parameter. You can also use it with no parameter to output a blank line. You have also seen the method used with several parameters when you have used a format string along with several variables. Therefore, you know WriteLine() is an overloaded method.

Some C# operators are overloaded. For example, a + between two numeric values indicates addition, but a single + to the left of a value means the value is positive. The + sign has different meanings based on the operands used with it. In the chapter "Using Classes and Objects," you will learn how to overload operators to make them mean what you want with your own classes.

The compiler understands which method to use based on the arguments you use in a method call. For example, suppose that you create a method to display a string surrounded by a border. The method receives a string and uses the string Length property to determine how many asterisks to use to construct a border around the string. Figure 8-14 shows a program that contains the method.

```
using static System.Console;
class BorderDemo1
{
   static void Main()
   {
      DisplayWithBorder("Ed");
      DisplayWithBorder("Theodore");
      DisplayWithBorder("Jennifer Ann");
   }
   private static void DisplayWithBorder(string word)
   {
      const int EXTRA_STARS = 4;
      const string SYMBOL = "*";
      int size = word.Length + EXTRA_STARS;
      int x;
      for(x = 0; x < size; ++x)
         Write(SYMBOL);
      WriteLine();
      WriteLine(SYMBOL + " " + word + " " + SYMBOL);
      for(x = 0; x < size; ++x)
         Write(SYMBOL);
      WriteLine("\n\n");
   }
}
```

Figure 8-14   The BorderDemo1 program

When the `Main()` method calls the `DisplayWithBorder()` method in the program in Figure 8-14 and passes a `string` value, the method calculates a size as the length of the string plus 4, and then draws that many symbols on a single line. The method then displays a symbol, a space, the string, another space, and another symbol on the next line.

Figure 8-15   Output of the BorderDemo1 program

Suppose that you are so pleased with the output of the `DisplayWithBorder()` method that you want to use something similar to display your company's weekly sales goal figure. The problem is that the weekly sales goal amount is stored as an integer, and so it cannot be passed to the existing method. You can take one of several approaches:

- You can convert the integer sales goal to a `string` and use the existing method. This is an acceptable approach, but it requires that you remember to write an extra step in any program in which you display an integer using the border.

- You can create a new method with a unique name such as `DisplayWithBorderUsingInt()` and use it to accept an integer parameter. The drawback to this approach is that you must remember different method names when you use different data types.

- You can overload the `DisplayWithBorder()` method. Overloading methods involves writing multiple methods with the same name but with different parameter types. For example, in addition to the `DisplayWithBorder()` method shown in Figure 8-14, you could use the method shown in Figure 8-16.

```
private static void DisplayWithBorder(int number)
{
    const int EXTRA_STARS = 4;
    const string SYMBOL = "*";
    int size = EXTRA_STARS + 1;
    int leftOver = number;
    int x;
    while(leftOver >= 10)
    {
        leftOver = leftOver / 10;
        ++size;
    }
    for(x = 0; x < size; ++x)
        Write(SYMBOL);
    WriteLine();
    WriteLine(SYMBOL + " " + number + " " + SYMBOL);
    for(x = 0; x < size; ++x)
        Write(SYMBOL);
    WriteLine("\n\n");
}
```

Figure 8-16   The DisplayWithBorder() method with an integer parameter

In the version of the DisplayWithBorder() method in Figure 8-16, the parameter is an int. To determine how many asterisks to display, the method initializes size to the number of extra stars in the display (in this case 4), plus one more. It then determines the number of asterisks to display in the border by repeatedly dividing the parameter by 10 and adding the result to size. For example, when the argument to the method is 456, leftOver is initialized to 456. Because it is at least 10, it is divided by 10, giving 45, and size is increased from 5 to 6. Then 45 is divided by 10, giving 4, and size is increased to 7. Because 4 is not at least 10, the loop ends, and the program has determined that the top and bottom borders of the box surrounding 456 require seven stars each. The rest of the method executes like the original version that accepts a string parameter.

The DisplayWithBorder() method does not quite work correctly if a negative integer is passed to it because the negative sign occupies an additional display space. To rectify the problem, you could modify the method to add an extra symbol to the border when a negative argument is passed in, or you could force all negative numbers to be their positive equivalent.

If both versions of DisplayWithBorder() are included in a program and you call the method using a string, as in DisplayWithBorder("Ed"), the first version of the method shown in Figure 8-14 executes. If you use an integer as the argument in the call to DisplayWithBorder(), as in DisplayWithBorder(456), then the method shown in Figure 8-16 executes. Figure 8-17 shows a program that demonstrates several method calls, and Figure 8-18 shows the output.

```
using static System.Console;
class BorderDemo2
{
    static void Main()
    {
        DisplayWithBorder("Ed");
        DisplayWithBorder(3);
        DisplayWithBorder(456);
        DisplayWithBorder(897654);
        DisplayWithBorder("Veronica");
    }
    private static void DisplayWithBorder(string word)
    {
        const int EXTRA_STARS = 4;
        const string SYMBOL = '*';
        int size = word.Length + EXTRA_STARS;
        int x;
        for(x = 0; x < size; ++x)
            Write(SYMBOL);
        WriteLine();
        WriteLine(SYMBOL + " " + word + " " + SYMBOL);
        for(x = 0; x < size; ++x)
            Write(SYMBOL);
        WriteLine("\n\n");
    }
    private static void DisplayWithBorder(int number)
    {
        const int EXTRA_STARS = 4;
        const string SYMBOL = "*";
        int size = EXTRA_STARS + 1;
        int leftOver = number;
        int x;
        while(leftOver >= 10)
        {
            leftOver = leftOver / 10;
            ++size;
        }
        for(x = 0; x < size; ++x)
            Write(SYMBOL);
        WriteLine();
        WriteLine(SYMBOL + " " + number + " " + SYMBOL);
        for(x = 0; x < size; ++x)
            Write(SYMBOL);
        WriteLine("\n\n");
    }
}
```

Figure 8-17   The BorderDemo2 program

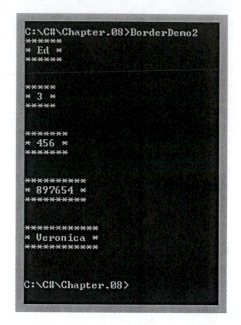

```
C:\C#\Chapter.08>BorderDemo2
******
* Ed *
******

*****
* 3 *
*****

*******
* 456 *
*******

**********
* 897654 *
**********

************
* Veronica *
************

C:\C#\Chapter.08>
```

Figure 8-18   Output of the BorderDemo2 program

Methods are overloaded correctly when they have the same identifier but their parameter lists are different. Parameter lists differ when the number and order of types within the lists are unique. For example, you could write several methods with the same identifier, and one method could accept an int, another two ints, and another three ints. A fourth method could accept an int followed by a double, and another could accept a double followed by an int. Yet another version could accept no parameters. The parameter identifiers in overloaded methods do not matter, and neither do the return types of the methods. The only two requirements to overload methods are the same identifier and different parameter lists.

Instead of overloading methods, you can choose to use methods with different names to accept the diverse data types, and you can place a decision within your program to determine which version of the method to call. However, it is more convenient to use one method name and then let the compiler determine which method to use. Overloading a method also makes it more convenient for other programmers to use your method in the future. Usually you do not create overloaded methods so that a single program can use all the versions. More often, you create overloaded methods so different programs can use the version most appropriate to the task at hand. Frequently, you create overloaded methods in your classes not because you need them immediately, but because you know client programs might need multiple versions in the future, and it is easier for programmers to remember one reasonable name for tasks that are functionally identical except for parameter types.

Understanding Overload Resolution

When a method call *could* execute multiple overloaded method versions, C# determines which method to execute using a process called **overload resolution**. For example, suppose that you create a method with the following declaration:

```
private static void MyMethod(double d)
```

You can call this method using a `double` argument, as in the following:

```
MyMethod(2.5);
```

You can also call this method using an `int` argument, as in the following:

```
MyMethod(4);
```

The call that uses the `int` argument works because an `int` can automatically be promoted to a `double`. In Chapter 2 you learned that when an `int` is promoted to a `double`, the process is called an *implicit conversion* or *implicit cast*.

Suppose that you create overloaded methods with the following declarations:

```
private static void MyMethod(double d)
private static void MyMethod(int i)
```

If you then call `MyMethod()` using an integer argument, both methods are **applicable methods**. That means either method on its own could accept a call that uses an `int`. However, if both methods exist in the same class (making them overloaded), the second version will execute because it is a better match for the method call. The rules that determine which method version to call are known as **betterness rules**.

Betterness rules are similar to the implicit conversion rules you learned in Chapter 2. For example, although an `int` could be accepted by a method that accepts an `int`, a `float`, or a `double`, an `int` is the best match. If no method version with an `int` parameter exists, then a `float` is a better match than a `double`. Table 8-1 shows the betterness rules for several data types.

Data Type	Conversions Are Better in This Order
byte	short, ushort, int, uint, long, ulong, float, double, decimal
sbyte	short, int, long, float, double, decimal
short	int, long, float, double, decimal
ushort	int, uint, long, ulong, float, double, decimal
int	long, float, double, decimal
uint	long, ulong, float, double, decimal
long	float, double, decimal
ulong	float, double, decimal
float	double
char	ushort, int, uint, long, ulong, float, double, decimal

Table 8-1 Betterness rules for data type conversion

Discovering Built-In Overloaded Methods

When you use the IDE to create programs, Visual Studio's IntelliSense features provide information about methods you are using. For example, Figure 8-19 shows the IDE just after the programmer has typed the opening parenthesis to the `Convert.ToInt32()` method. Notice the drop-down list that indicates `Convert.ToInt32(bool value)` is just 1 of 19 overloaded versions of the method. You can click the nodes to scroll through the rest of the list and see that other versions accept `bool`, `byte`, `char`, and so on. When retrieving an entry from a `TextBox` on a `Form`, your intention is to use the `Convert.ToInt32(string value)` version of the method, but many overloaded versions are available for your convenience. C# could have included multiple methods with different names such as `ConvertBool.ToInt32()` and `ConvertString.ToInt32()`, but having a single method with the name `Convert.ToInt32()` that takes many different argument types makes it easier for you to remember the method name and to use it. As you work with the IDE, you will examine many such methods.

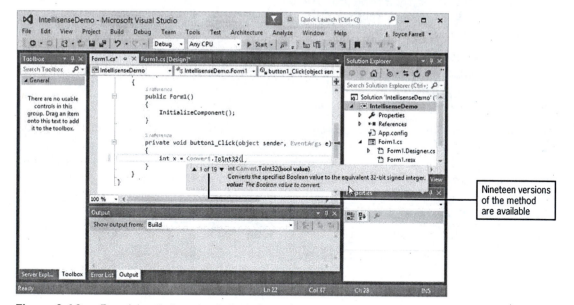

Figure 8-19   Examining the overloaded versions of `Convert.ToInt32()`

TWO TRUTHS & A LIE

Overloading Methods

1. The following methods are overloaded:

   ```
   private static void MethodA(int a)
   private static void MethodA(double b)
   ```

2. The following methods are overloaded:

   ```
   private static void MethodC(int c)
   private static void MethodD(int c)
   ```

3. The following methods are overloaded:

   ```
   private static void MethodE(int e)
   private static void MethodE(int e, int f)
   ```

The false answer is #2. Overloaded methods must have the same name but different parameter lists.

You Do It

Overloading Methods

In the next steps, you overload methods that correctly triple a parameter that might be an integer or a string.

1. Start a new program named **OverloadedTriples**, and create a method that triples and displays an integer parameter as follows:

   ```
   private static void Triple(int num)
   {
       const int MULT_FACTOR = 3;
       WriteLine("{0} times {1} is {2}\n",
           num, MULT_FACTOR, num * MULT_FACTOR);
   }
   ```

2. Create a second method with the same name that takes a string parameter. Assume you want to define tripling a message as displaying it three times, separated by tabs.

   ```
   private static void Triple(string message)
   {
       WriteLine("{0}\t{0}\t{0}\n", message);
   }
   ```

(continues)

(continued)

3. Position your cursor at the top of the file, and add a `using` statement, class header, and opening curly brace so the overloaded `Triple()` methods will be contained in a class named `OverloadedTriples`.

```
using static System.Console;
class OverloadedTriples
{
```

4. Position your cursor at the bottom of the file, and add the closing curly brace for the `OverloadedTriples` class.

5. Position your cursor after the opening curly brace for the class. On a new line, insert a `Main()` method that declares an integer and a string and, in turn, passes each to the appropriate `Triple()` method. Notice that as you type the parenthesis after the `Triple()` method, the IDE displays your two overloaded `Triple()` methods.

```
static void Main()
{
    int num = 20;
    string message = "Go team!";
    Triple(num);
    Triple(message);
}
```

6. Save the file, and then compile and execute the program. Figure 8-20 shows the output. Even though the same method name is used in the two method calls, the appropriate overloaded method executes each time.

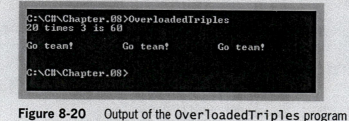

```
C:\C#\Chapter.08>OverloadedTriples
20 times 3 is 60

Go team!        Go team!        Go team!


C:\C#\Chapter.08>
```

Figure 8-20   Output of the `OverloadedTriples` program

Avoiding Ambiguous Methods

When you overload a method, you run the risk of creating **ambiguous** methods—a situation in which the compiler cannot determine which method to use. Every time you call a method, the compiler decides whether a suitable method exists; if so, the method executes, and if not, you receive an error message.

For example, suppose that you write two versions of a simple method, as in the program in Figure 8-21. The class contains two versions of a method named `SimpleMethod()`—one that takes a `double` and an `int`, and one that takes an `int` and a `double`.

```
using static System.Console;
class AmbiguousMethods
{
    static void Main()
    {
        int iNum = 20;
        double dNum = 4.5;
        SimpleMethod(iNum, dNum); // calls first version
        SimpleMethod(dNum, iNum); // calls second version
        SimpleMethod(iNum, iNum); // error! Call is ambiguous.
    }
    private static void SimpleMethod(int i, double d)
    {
        WriteLine("Method receives int and double");
    }
    private static void SimpleMethod(double d, int i)
    {
        WriteLine("Method receives double and int");
    }
}
```

Figure 8-21   Program containing an ambiguous method call

In the `Main()` method in Figure 8-21, a call to `SimpleMethod()` with an integer argument first and a `double` argument second executes the first version of the method, and a call to `SimpleMethod()` with a `double` argument first and an integer argument second executes the second version of the method. With each of these calls, the compiler can find an exact match for the arguments you send. However, if you call `SimpleMethod()` using two integer arguments, as in the shaded statement, an ambiguous situation arises because there is no exact match for the method call. Because the first integer could be promoted to a `double` (matching the second version of the overloaded method), or the second integer could be promoted to a `double` (matching the first version), the compiler does not know which version of `SimpleMethod()` to use, and the program will not compile or execute. Figure 8-22 shows the error message that is generated.

```
C:\C#\Chapter.08>csc Ambiguousmethods.cs
Microsoft (R) Visual C# 2010 Compiler version 4.0.21006.1
Copyright (C) Microsoft Corporation. All rights reserved.

AmbiguousMethods.cs(10,7): error CS0121: The call is ambiguous between the
        following methods or properties: 'AmbiguousMethods.SimpleMethod(int,
        double)' and 'AmbiguousMethods.SimpleMethod(double, int)'

C:\C#\Chapter.08>
```

Figure 8-22   Error message generated by an ambiguous method call

An overloaded method is not ambiguous on its own—it becomes ambiguous only if you create an ambiguous situation. A program with potentially ambiguous methods will run without problems if you make no ambiguous method calls. For example, if you remove the shaded statement from Figure 8-21 that calls `SimpleMethod()` using two integer arguments, the program compiles and executes.

If you remove one of the versions of `SimpleMethod()` from the program in Figure 8-21, then the method call that uses two integer arguments would work, because one of the integers could be promoted to a `double`. However, then one of the other method calls would fail.

Methods can be overloaded correctly by providing different parameter lists for methods with the same name. Methods with identical names that have identical parameter lists but different return types are not overloaded—they are illegal. For example, the following two methods cannot coexist within a class:

```
private static int AMethod(int x)
private static void AMethod(int x)
```

The compiler determines which of several versions of a method to call based on parameter lists. When the method call `AMethod(17);` is made, the compiler will not know which method to execute because both possibilities take an integer argument. Similarly, the following method could not coexist with either of the previous versions:

```
private static void AMethod(int someNumber)
```

Even though this method uses a different local identifier for the parameter, its parameter list— a single integer—is still the same to the compiler.

  Watch the video *Overloading Methods*.

TWO TRUTHS & A LIE

Avoiding Ambiguous Methods

1. The following methods are potentially ambiguous:

   ```
   private static int Method1(int g)
   private static int Method1(int g, int h)
   ```

2. The following methods are potentially ambiguous:

   ```
   private static double Method2(int j)
   private static void Method2(int k)
   ```

3. The following methods are potentially ambiguous:

   ```
   private static void Method3(string m)
   private static string Method3(string n)
   ```

The false answer is #1. Those methods are not ambiguous because they have different parameter lists. Their matching return types do not cause ambiguity.

Using Optional Parameters

Sometimes it is useful to create a method that allows one or more arguments to be omitted from the method call. An optional parameter is not required; if you don't send a value as an argument, a default value is automatically supplied. You make a parameter optional by providing a value for it in the method declaration. Only value parameters can be given default values; those that use `ref`, `out`, and `params` cannot have default values. Any optional parameters in a parameter list must appear to the right of the mandatory parameters.

For example, suppose that you write a method that calculates either the area of a square or the volume of a cube, depending on whether two or three arguments are sent to it. Figure 8-23 shows such a method; notice the shaded default value provided for the third parameter. When you want a cube's volume, you can pass three arguments to the method: length, width, and height. When you want a square's area, you pass only two parameters, and a default value of 1 is used for the height. In this example, the height is a default parameter and is optional; the length and width, which are not provided with default values, are mandatory parameters. That is, at least two arguments must be sent to the

DisplaySize() method, but three *can* be sent. In the program in Figure 8-23, calling DisplaySize(4, 6) has the same effect as calling DisplaySize(4, 6, 1). Figure 8-24 shows the execution of the OptionalParameterDemo program.

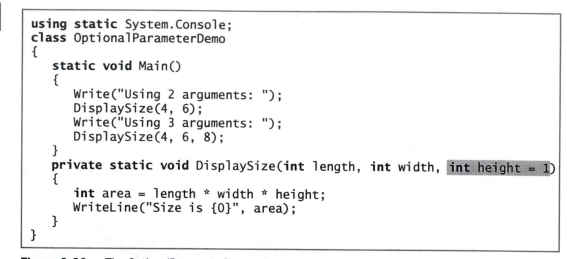

```
using static System.Console;
class OptionalParameterDemo
{
    static void Main()
    {
        Write("Using 2 arguments: ");
        DisplaySize(4, 6);
        Write("Using 3 arguments: ");
        DisplaySize(4, 6, 8);
    }
    private static void DisplaySize(int length, int width, int height = 1)
    {
        int area = length * width * height;
        WriteLine("Size is {0}", area);
    }
}
```

Figure 8-23   The OptionalParameterDemo class

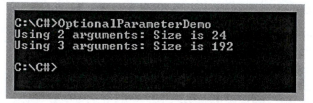

```
C:\C#>OptionalParameterDemo
Using 2 arguments: Size is 24
Using 3 arguments: Size is 192

C:\C#>
```

Figure 8-24   Execution of the OptionalParameterDemo program

If you assign a default value to any variable in a method's parameter list, then all parameters to the right of that parameter must also have default values. Table 8-2 shows some examples of valid and invalid method declarations.

Method Declaration	Explanation
`private static void M1(int a, int b, int c, int d = 10)`	Valid. The first three parameters are mandatory and the last one is optional.
`private static void M2(int a, int b = 3, int c)`	Invalid. Because b has a default value, c must also have one.
`private static void M3(int a = 3, int b = 4, int c = 5)`	Valid. All parameters are optional.
`private static void M4(int a, int b, int c)`	Valid. All parameters are mandatory.
`private static void M5(int a = 4, int b, int c = 8)`	Invalid. Because a has a default value, both b and c must have default values.

Table 8-2 Examples of valid and invalid optional parameter method declarations

When you call a method that contains default parameters, you can always choose to provide a value for every parameter. However, if you omit an argument when you call a method that has default parameters, then you must do one of the following:

- You must leave out all unnamed arguments to the right of the last argument you use.
- You can name arguments.

Leaving Out Unnamed Arguments

When calling a method with optional parameters (and using unnamed arguments), you must leave out any arguments to the right of the last one used. In other words, once an argument is left out, you must leave out all the arguments that would otherwise follow.

For example, assume you have declared a method as follows:

```
private static void Method1(int a, char b, int c = 22, double d = 33.2)
```

Table 8-3 shows some legal and illegal calls to this method.

Call to Method1()	Explanation
Method1(1, 'A', 3, 4.4);	Valid. The four arguments are assigned to the four parameters.
Method1(1, 'K', 9);	Valid. The three arguments are assigned to a, b, and c in the method, and the default value of 33.2 is used for d.
Method1(5, 'D');	Valid. The two arguments are assigned to a and b in the method, and the default values of 22 and 33.2 are used for c and d, respectively.
Method1(1);	Invalid. Method1() requires at least two arguments for the first two parameters.
Method1();	Invalid. Method1() requires at least two arguments for the first two parameters.
Method1(3, 18.5);	Invalid. The first argument, 3, can be assigned to a, but the second argument must be type char.
Method1(4, 'R', 55.5);	Invalid. The first argument, 4, can be assigned to a, and the second argument, 'R', can be assigned to b, but the third argument must be type int. When arguments are unnamed, you cannot "skip" parameter c, use its default value, and assign 55.5 to parameter d.

Table 8-3   Examples of legal and illegal calls to Method1()

Using Named Arguments

You can leave out optional arguments in a method call if you pass the remaining arguments by name. A **named argument** is a method argument that is preceded with the name of the called method's parameter to which it will be assigned. Named arguments can appear in any order, but they must appear after all the unnamed arguments have been listed. Each unnamed argument is also known as a **positional argument**. You name an argument using its parameter name and a colon before the value.

In Chapter 7, you learned that if you use the IntelliSense feature of Visual Studio, you can discover a method's parameter names. See Appendix C for more details.

For example, assume you have declared a method as follows:

```
private static void Method2(int a, char b, int c = 22, double d = 33.2)
```

Table 8-4 shows some legal and illegal calls to this method.

Call to Method2()	Explanation
Method2(1, 'A');	Valid. The two arguments are assigned to a and b in the method, and the default values of 22 and 33.2 are used for c and d, respectively.
Method2(2, 'E', 3);	Valid. The three arguments are assigned to a, b, and c. The default value 33.2 is used for d.
Method2(2, 'E', c : 3);	Valid. This call is identical to the one above.
Method2(1, 'K', d : 88.8);	Valid. The first two arguments are assigned to a and b. The default value 22 is used for c. The named value 88.8 is used for d.
Method2(d : 2.1, b : 'A', c : 88, a: 12);	Valid. All the arguments are assigned to parameters whether they are listed in order or not.
Method2(5, 'S', d : 7.4, c: 9);	Valid. The first two arguments are assigned to a and b. Even though the values for c and d are not listed in order, they are assigned correctly.
Method2(d : 11.1, 6, 'P');	Invalid. This call contains an unnamed argument after the first named argument. Named arguments must appear after all unnamed arguments.

Table 8-4   Examples of legal and illegal calls to Method2()

Advantages to Using Named Arguments

Optional parameters can provide a convenient shortcut to writing multiple overloaded versions of a method. For example, suppose that you want to create a method that adds your signature to business letters. Usually, you want the signature to be *Sincerely, James O'Hara*. However, occasionally you want to change the name to a more casual *Jim*. You could write two method versions, as shown on the top in Figure 8-25, or you could write one version, as shown on the bottom. With both versions, you can call Closing() with or without an argument. The version with the optional parameter is less work when you write the method. It is also less work if you later want to modify the method—for example, to change *Sincerely* to *Best wishes* or some other closing.

```
// Overloaded implementations of Closing()
private static void Closing()
{
    WriteLine("Sincerely,");
    WriteLine("James O'Hara");
}
private static void Closing(string name)
{
    WriteLine("Sincerely,");
    WriteLine(name);
}

// Single implementation of Closing() with optional parameter
private static void Closing(string name = "James O'Hara")
{
    WriteLine("Sincerely,");
    WriteLine(name);
}
```

Figure 8-25   Two ways to implement `Closing()` to accept a name parameter or not

Another advantage to using named parameters is to make your programs more self-documenting. Programs that are **self-documenting** provide built-in explanations that make the code clearer to readers and therefore easier for others to modify in the future. For example, suppose that you encounter the following method call:

```
DisplayEmployeeData(empNumber, true);
```

From the method call, it is not clear what **true** means. Perhaps it means that only certain parts of the record should be displayed, or that the employee is a current employee, or that the employee's salary should be hidden from view. The following method call makes your intentions clearer:

```
DisplayEmployeeData(empNumber, shouldHideSalary : true);
```

Of course, a program comment adjacent to the statement could also provide clarity.

Disadvantages to Using Named Arguments

A major disadvantage to using named arguments is that the calling method becomes linked to details within the method. When the calling method must know parameter names within the called method, an important principle of programming—method implementation hiding—is compromised. If the parameter name in the called method is changed in the future, the client method also will have to change.

Suppose that a payroll program contains two methods used in paycheck calculations. The first method, shown in Figure 8-26, accepts three parameters—hours, rate, and bonus. A gross pay value is calculated by multiplying hours by rate, and a bonus value is assigned based on the number of hours worked. The second method sums its gross and bonus parameters. The intention is that an employee who works 40 hours at $10 per hour receives $400 gross pay, plus a $100 bonus, for a total of $500.

```
private static double ComputeGross(double hours, double rate,
   out double bonus)
{
   double gross = hours * rate;
   if (hours >= 40)
      bonus = 100;
   else
      bonus = 50;
   return gross;
}
private static double ComputeTotalPay(double gross, double bonus)
{
   double total = gross + bonus;
   return total;
}
```

Figure 8-26   Two payroll program methods

Figure 8-27 shows the Main() method of a program that assigns 40 to hours and 10.00 to rate. Then, the method calls the ComputeTotalPay() method by passing it the result of ComputeGross() and the value of bonus that is set within ComputeGross(). Figure 8-28 shows that the employee's total pay is correctly calculated as $500.

```
static void Main()
{
   double hours = 40;
   double rate = 10.00;
   double bonus = 0;
   double totalPay;
   totalPay = ComputeTotalPay(ComputeGross(hours, rate, out bonus),
      bonus);
   WriteLine("Total pay is {0}", totalPay);
}
```

Figure 8-27   A Main() method that calls ComputeTotalPay() using positional arguments

```
C:\C#\Chapter.08>Payroll1
Total pay is 500

C:\C#\Chapter.08>
```


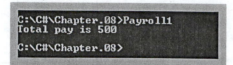

Figure 8-28 Execution of the `Main()` method in Figure 8-27

A possible disadvantage to using named arguments occurs when a named parameter value is an expression instead of a constant. Figure 8-29 shows a `Main()` method that calls `ComputeTotalPay()` using named arguments. The only difference from the program in Figure 8-27 is the shaded method call that uses named arguments. In this case, when `ComputeTotalPay()` is called, first 0 is sent to `bonus`, and then `ComputeGross()` is called to assign a value to `gross`. However, the bonus alteration in `ComputeGross()` is too late because `bonus` has already been assigned. The program output is incorrect, as shown in Figure 8-30.

```
static void Main()
{
   double hours = 40;
   double rate = 10.00;
   double bonus = 0;
   double totalPay;
   totalPay = ComputeTotalPay(bonus: bonus,
      gross: ComputeGross(hours, rate, out bonus));
   WriteLine("Total pay is {0}", totalPay);
}
```

Figure 8-29 A `Main()` method that calls `ComputeTotalPay()` using named arguments

```
C:\C#\Chapter.08>Payroll2
Total pay is 400

C:\C#\Chapter.08>
```

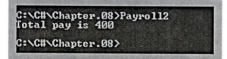

Figure 8-30 Execution of the `Main()` method in Figure 8-29

In Chapter 4, you learned that when you combine operands in a Boolean expression using && or ||, you risk side effects because of short-circuit evaluation. The situation with named arguments is similar. When a named argument is an expression, there can be unintended consequences.

Overload Resolution with Named and Optional Arguments

Named and optional arguments affect overload resolution. The rules for betterness on argument conversions are applied only for arguments that are given explicitly; in other words, omitted optional arguments are ignored for betterness purposes. For example, suppose that you have the following methods:

```
private static void AMethod(int a, double b = 2.2)
private static void AMethod(int a, char b = 'H')
```

Both are applicable methods when a call is made using an integer argument; in other words, if either method existed alone, the call AMethod(12) would work. When the two methods coexist, however, neither is "better." Because C# cannot determine which one is better, the code will not compile.

If two signatures are equally good, the one that does not omit optional parameters is considered better. For example, suppose that you have two methods as follows:

```
private static void BMethod(int a)
private static void BMethod(int a, char b = 'B')
```

If either method existed alone, the call BMethod(12) would work, but when the two coexist, the first version is better because no optional parameters are omitted in the call.

Watch the video *Using Optional Method Parameters*.

TWO TRUTHS & A LIE

Using Optional Parameters

1. An optional parameter to a method is one for which an argument can be a value parameter, a ref parameter, or an out parameter.

2. You make a parameter optional by providing a value for it in the method declaration.

3. If you assign a default value to any variable in a method's parameter list, then all parameters to the right of that parameter must also have default values.

The false statement is #1. An optional parameter to a method is one for which a default value is automatically supplied if you do not explicitly send one as an argument. Only value parameters can be optional.

Chapter Summary

- Method parameters can be mandatory or optional. Mandatory parameters include value parameters without default values, reference parameters, output parameters, and parameter arrays. A value parameter can be optional if it is supplied with a default value.

- When you overload a C# method, you write multiple methods with a shared name but different parameter lists. The compiler understands your meaning based on the combination of arguments you use with the method. When a method call could execute multiple overloaded method versions, C# determines which method to execute using a process called *overload resolution*.

- When you overload a method, you run the risk of creating an ambiguous situation—one in which the compiler cannot determine which method to use. Methods can be overloaded correctly by providing different parameter lists for methods with the same name.

- An optional parameter to a method is a value parameter for which a default value is automatically supplied if you do not explicitly send one as an argument. You make a parameter optional by providing a value for it in the method declaration. When calling a method with optional parameters, you must leave out all unnamed arguments to the right of the last one used, or you can name arguments.

Key Terms

Mandatory parameters are method parameters for which an argument is required in every method call.

An **optional parameter** to a method is one for which a default value is automatically supplied if you do not explicitly send one as an argument; a parameter is optional when it is given a value in the method declaration.

A **value parameter** in a method header receives a copy of the value passed to it.

A **reference parameter** in a method header receives the parameter's address; a variable sent to a reference parameter is required to have been assigned a value before it is used in the method call.

An **output parameter** in a method header receives the parameter's address; a variable sent to an output parameter is not required to have been assigned a value before it is used in the method call.

A **parameter array** is a local array declared within a method header that can accept any number of elements of the same data type.

Overloading involves the ability to write multiple versions of a method using the same method name but different parameter lists.

A method's **signature** is composed of its name and parameter list.

Overload resolution is the process of determining which of multiple applicable methods is the best match for a method call.

Applicable methods are all the methods that could be used by a method call.

Betterness rules are the rules that determine the best overloaded method to execute based on the arguments in a method call.

Ambiguous methods are overloaded methods from which the compiler cannot determine which one to use.

A **named argument** is a method argument that is preceded with the name of the called method's parameter to which it will be assigned.

A **positional argument** is an unnamed method argument that is assigned to a parameter list based on its position in the method call.

Self-documenting describes programs that provide built-in explanations to make the code clearer to readers and therefore easier for others to modify in the future.

Review Questions

1. A mandatory parameter _____.

    a. is any argument sent to a method

    b. is preceded by the keyword `man`

    c. requires an argument to be sent from a method call

    d. All of the above are true.

2. Which is *not* a type of method parameter in C#?

    a. value

    b. reference

    c. forensic

    d. output

3. Which type of method parameter receives the address of the variable passed in?

    a. a value parameter

    b. a reference parameter

    c. an output parameter

    d. two of the above

4. When you declare a value parameter, you precede its name with _____.

    a. nothing

    b. a data type

    c. the keyword `val` and a data type

    d. the keyword `ref` and its data type

5. Assume that you declare a variable as `int x = 100;` and correctly pass it to a method with the declaration `private static void IncreaseValue(ref int x)`. There is a single statement within the `IncreaseValue()` method: `x = x + 25;`. Back in the `Main()` method, after the method call, what is the value of x?

    a. 100

    b. 125

    c. It is impossible to tell.

    d. The program will not run.

6. Assume that you declare a variable as `int x = 100;` and correctly pass it to a method with the declaration `private static void IncreaseValue(int x)`. There is a single statement within the `IncreaseValue()` method: `x = x + 25;`. Back in the `Main()` method, after the method call, what is the value of x?

    a. 100

    b. 125

    c. It is impossible to tell.

    d. The program will not run.

7. Which of the following is a difference between a reference parameter and an output parameter?

    a. A reference parameter receives a memory address; an output parameter does not.

    b. A reference parameter occupies a unique memory address; an output parameter does not.

    c. A reference parameter requires an initial value; an output parameter does not.

    d. A reference parameter does not require an initial value; an output parameter does.

8. A parameter array _____.

    a. is declared using the keyword `params`

    b. can accept any number of arguments of the same data type

    c. Both of these are true.

    d. Neither of these is true.

9. Assume that you have declared a method with the following header:
    `private static void DisplayScores(params int[] scores)` Which of the following method calls is valid?

    a. `DisplayScores(20);`

    b. `DisplayScores(20, 33);`

    c. `DisplayScores(20, 30, 90);`

    d. All of the above are valid.

10. Correctly overloaded methods must have the same _____.

    a. return type

    b. identifier

    c. parameter list

    d. All of the above.

11. Methods are ambiguous when they _____.

    a. are overloaded

    b. are written in a confusing manner

    c. are indistinguishable to the compiler

    d. have the same parameter type as their return type

12. Which of the following pairs of method declarations represent correctly overloaded methods?

    a. `private static void MethodA(int a)`
          `private static void MethodA(int b, double c)`

    b. `private static void MethodB(double d)`
          `private static void MethodB()`

    c. `private static double MethodC(int e)`
          `private static double MethodD(int f)`

    d. Two of these are correctly overloaded methods.

13. Which of the following pairs of method declarations represent correctly overloaded methods?

    a. `private static void Method(int a)`
          `private static void Method(int b)`

    b. `private static void Method(double d)`
          `private static int Method()`

    c. `private static double Method(int e)`
          `private static int Method(int f)`

    d. Two of these are correctly overloaded methods.

14. The process of determining which overloaded version of a method to execute is overload _____.

    a. confusion   c. revolution

    b. infusion   d. resolution

15. When one of a method's parameters is optional, it means that _____.

    a. no arguments are required in a call to the method

    b. a default value will be assigned to the parameter if no argument is sent for it

    c. a default value will override any argument value sent to it

    d. you are not required to use the parameter within the method body

16. Which of the following is an illegal method declaration?

    a. `private static void CreateStatement(int acctNum, double balance = 0.0)`

    b. `private static void CreateStatement(int acctNum = 0, double balance)`

    c. `private static void CreateStatement(int acctNum = 0, double balance = 0)`

    d. All of these are legal.

17. Assume you have declared a method as follows:
    `private static double ComputeBill(int acct, double price, double discount = 0)`
    Which of the following is a legal method call?

    a. `ComputeBill();`

    b. `ComputeBill(1001);`

    c. `ComputeBill(1001, 200.00);`

    d. None of the above is legal.

18. Assume you have declared a method as follows:
    `private static double CalculateDiscount(int acct = 0, double price = 0, double discount = 0)`
    Which of the following is a legal method call?

    a. `CalculateDiscount();`

    b. `CalculateDiscount(200.00);`

    c. `CalculateDiscount(3000.00, 0.02);`

    d. None of the above is legal.

19. Assume you have declared a method as follows:
    `private static double DisplayData(string name = "XX", double amount = 10.0)`
    Which of the following is an illegal method call?

    a. `DisplayData(name : "Albert");`

    b. `DisplayData(amount : 200, name : "Albert");`

    c. `DisplayData(amount : 900.00);`

    d. All of these are legal.

20. Suppose that you have declared an integer array named **scores**, and you make the following method call:
    ```
    TotalScores(scores, num : 1);
    ```
    Of the following overloaded method definitions, which would execute?

    a. `private static void TotalScores(int[] scores)`

    b. `private static void TotalScores(int[] scores, int num)`

    c. `private static void TotalScores(int[] scores, int num = 10, int code = 10)`

    d. The program would not compile.

Exercises

Programming Exercises

1. Unless otherwise indicated, for each of the following programming exercises, you may choose to write a console-based or GUI application, or both.

    a. Create a program named **Reverse3** whose **Main()** method declares three integers named **firstInt**, **middleInt**, and **lastInt**. Assign values to the variables, display them, and then pass them to a method that accepts them as reference variables, places the first value in the **lastInt** variable, and places the last value in the **firstInt** variable. In the **Main()** method, display the three variables again, demonstrating that their positions have been reversed.

    b. Create a new program named **Reverse4**, which contains a method that reverses the positions of four variables. Write a **Main()** method that demonstrates the method works correctly.

2. Create a program named **IntegerFacts** whose **Main()** method declares an array of 20 integers. Call a method to interactively fill the array with any number of values up to 20 or until a sentinel value is entered. If an entry is not an integer, reprompt the user. Call a second method that accepts **out** parameters for the highest value in the array, lowest value in the array, sum of the values in the array, and arithmetic average. In the **Main()** method, display all the statistics.

3. Create a program for The Cactus Cantina named **FoodOrder** that accepts a user's choice from the options in the accompanying table. Allow the user to enter either an integer item number or a string description. Pass the user's entry to one of two overloaded **GetDetails()** methods, and then display a returned string with all the

order details. The method version that accepts an integer looks up the description and price; the version that accepts a string description looks up the item number and price. The methods return an appropriate message if the item is not found.

Item number	Description	Price
20	Enchilada	2.95
23	Burrito	1.95
25	Taco	2.25
31	Tostada	3.10

4. Create a program named **Auction** that allows a user to enter an amount bid on an online auction item. Include three overloaded methods that accept an int, double, or string bid. Each method should display the bid and indicate whether it is over the minimum acceptable bid of $10. If the bid is a string, accept it only if one of the following is true: it is numeric and preceded with a dollar sign, or it is numeric and followed by the word *dollars*. Otherwise, display a message that indicates the format was incorrect.

5. Create a program named **BonusCalculation** that includes two overloaded methods—one that accepts a salary and a bonus expressed as doubles (for example, 600.00 and 0.10, where 0.10 represents a 10 percent bonus), and one that accepts a salary as a double and a bonus an integer (for example, 600.00 and 50, where 50 represents a $50 bonus). Each method displays the salary, the bonus in dollars, and the total. Include a Main() method that demonstrates each method.

6. Write a program named **InputMethodDemo2** that eliminates the repetitive code in the InputMethod() in the InputMethodDemo program in Figure 8-5. Rewrite the program so the InputMethod() contains only two statements:

```
one = DataEntry("first");
two = DataEntry("second");
```

7. Write a program named **Averages** that includes a method that accepts any number of numeric parameters, displays them, and displays their average. Demonstrate that the method works correctly when passed one, two, or three numbers, or an array of numbers.

8. Write a program named **Desks2** that modifies the Desks program you created in Chapter 7 so that all the methods are void methods and receive ref or out parameters as appropriate.

9. Write a program named **SortWords** that includes a method that accepts any number of words and sorts them in alphabetical order. Demonstrate that the program works correctly when the method is called with one, two, five, and ten words.

10. Write a program named **Movie** that contains a method that accepts and displays two parameters: a string name of a movie and an integer running time in minutes. Provide a default value for the minutes so that if you call the method without an integer argument, `minutes` is set to 90. Write a `Main()` method that proves you can call the movie method with only a `string` argument as well as with a `string` and an integer.

11. In the card game War, a deck of playing cards is divided between two players. Each player exposes a card; the player whose card has the higher value wins possession of both exposed cards. Create a console-based computerized game of War named **WarCardGame** in which a standard 52-card deck is randomly divided between two players, one of which is the computer. Reveal one card for the computer and one card for the player at a time. Award two points for the player whose card has the higher value. (For this game the king is the highest card, followed by the queen and jack, then the numbers 10 down to 2, and finally the ace.) If the computer and player expose cards with equal values in the same turn, award one point to each. At the end of the game, all 52 cards should have been played only once, and the sum of the player's and computer's score will be 52.

   a. Use an array of 52 integers to store unique values for each card. Write a method named `FillDeck()` that places 52 unique values into this array. Write another method named `SelectCard()` that you call twice on each deal to select a unique card for each player, with no repetition of cards in 26 deals. (To pause the play between each dealt hand, use a call to `ReadLine()`.)

   The left side of Figure 8-31 shows the start of a typical program execution. (*Caution*: This is a difficult exercise!)

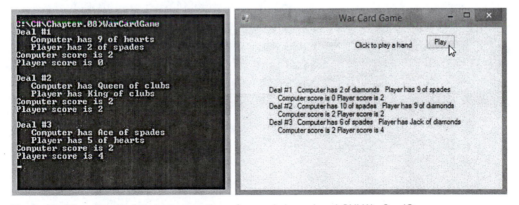

Figure 8-31   Start of typical execution of console-based and GUI WarCardGame programs

b. Create a GUI version of the War card game described in Exercise 11a, and name it **WarCardGameGUI**. Let the user click a button to deal the cards, then make that button invisible and expose a Play button. Each time the user clicks Play, a pair of cards is revealed. To keep the **Frame** size reasonable, you might want to erase the output label's contents every four hands or so. The right side of Figure 8-31 shows a typical game in progress.

Debugging Exercises

1. Each of the following files in the Chapter.08 folder of your downloadable student files has syntax and/or logical errors. In each case, determine the problem, and fix the program. After you correct the errors, save each file using the same filename preceded with *Fixed*. For example, DebugEight1.cs will become FixedDebugEight1.cs.

   a. DebugEight1.cs

   b. DebugEight2.cs

   c. DebugEight3.cs

   d. DebugEight4.cs

Case Problems

1. In Chapter 7, you modified the **GreenvilleRevenue** program to include a number of methods. Now modify every data entry statement to use a **TryParse()** method to ensure that each piece of data is the correct type. Any invalid user entries should generate an appropriate message, and the user should be required to reenter the data.

2. In Chapter 7, you modified the **MarshallsRevenue** program to include a number of methods. Now modify every data entry statement to use a **TryParse()** method to ensure that each piece of data is the correct type. Any invalid user entries should generate an appropriate message, and the user should be required to reenter the data.

CHAPTER 9

Using Classes and Objects

In this chapter you will:

- ◎ Learn about class concepts
- ◎ Create classes from which objects can be instantiated
- ◎ Create objects
- ◎ Create properties, including auto-implemented properties
- ◎ Learn more about using `public` and `private` access modifiers
- ◎ Learn about the `this` reference
- ◎ Write and use constructors
- ◎ Use object initializers
- ◎ Overload operators
- ◎ Declare object arrays and use methods with them
- ◎ Write destructors
- ◎ Understand GUI application objects

Much of your understanding of the world comes from your ability to categorize objects and events into classes. As a young child, you learned the concept of *animal* long before you knew the word. Your first encounter with an animal might have been with the family dog, a neighbor's cat, or a goat at a petting zoo. As you developed speech, you might have used the same term for all of these creatures, gleefully shouting, "Doggie!" as your parents pointed out cows, horses, and sheep in picture books or along the roadside on drives in the country. As you grew more sophisticated, you learned to distinguish dogs from cows; still later, you learned to distinguish breeds. Your understanding of the class *animal* helps you see the similarities between dogs and cows, and your understanding of the class *dog* helps you see the similarities between a Great Dane and a Chihuahua. Understanding classes gives you a framework for categorizing new experiences. You might not know the term *okapi*, but when you learn it's an animal rather than a food or piece of clothing, you begin to develop a concept of what an okapi might be like.

Classes are also the basic building blocks of object-oriented programming. You already understand that differences exist among the `Double`, `Int32`, and `Float` classes, yet you also know that items belonging to these classes possess similarities—they are all data types, you can perform arithmetic with all of them, they all can be converted to strings, and so on. Understanding classes enables you to see similarities in objects and increases your understanding of the programming process. In this chapter, you will discover how C# handles classes, learn to create your own classes, and learn to construct objects that are members of those classes.

Understanding Class Concepts

When you write programs in C#, you create two types of classes:

- *Classes that are only application programs with a* `Main()` *method.* These classes can contain other methods that the `Main()` method calls. You have been creating these classes throughout this book.

- *Classes from which you instantiate objects.* To **instantiate** an object is to create a tangible example. An object is an **instantiation** of a class or an **instance** of a class. A class that is created to be a model for object instantiations can contain a `Main()` method, but it is not required. This chapter explores the nuances of such classes.

When you think in an object-oriented manner, things are objects, and every object is an instance or example of a class. You can think of any inanimate physical item as an object—your desk, your computer, and your house are all called *objects* in everyday conversation. You can think of living things as objects, too—your houseplant, your pet fish, and your sister are objects. Events also are objects—for example, the stock purchase you made, the mortgage closing you attended, or a graduation party in your honor.

Every object is an instance of a more general class. Your desk is a specific instance of the class that includes all desks, and your pet fish is an instance of the class that contains all fish. In part, the concept of a class is useful because it provides you with knowledge about objects.

Objects receive their attributes from classes; so, for example, if you invite me to a graduation party, I automatically know many things about the object. I assume that there will be a starting time, a number of guests, and some refreshments. I understand your party because of my previous knowledge of the Party class. I don't necessarily know the number of guests or the date or time of this particular party, but I understand that because all parties have a date and time, then this one must as well. Similarly, even though every stock purchase is unique, each must have a dollar amount and a number of shares. All objects have predictable attributes because they are instances of certain classes.

The data components of a class that differ for each object are stored in **instance variables**. Instance variables also are called **fields** to help distinguish them from other variables you might use. In Chapter 1, you learned that the data field values of an object are also called its *attributes* and that the set of attributes is known as an object's *state*. For example, the current state of a particular party is 8 p.m. and Friday; the state of a particular stock purchase is $10 and five shares.

In addition to their attributes, objects have methods associated with them, and every object that is an instance of the same class possesses the same methods. Methods associated with objects are **instance methods**. For example, two Party objects might possess the identifiers myGraduationParty and yourAnniversaryParty that both have access to an IssueInvitations() method. The method might operate in the same way for both Party objects, but use data appropriate to the specific object. When you program in C#, you frequently create classes from which objects will be instantiated (or other programmers create them for you). You also write applications to use the objects, along with their data and methods. Often, you will write programs that use classes created by others; similarly, you might create a class that other programmers will use to instantiate objects within their own programs. A program or class that instantiates objects of another prewritten class is a **class client** or **class user**.

TWO TRUTHS & A LIE

Understanding Class Concepts

1. C# classes always contain a Main() method.

2. An object is an instantiation of a class.

3. The data components of a class often are its instance variables.

The false statement is #1. C# applications always contain a Main() method, but some classes do not if they are not meant to be run as programs.

Creating a Class from Which Objects Can Be Instantiated

When you create a class, you must assign a name to it and determine what data and methods will be part of the class. For example, suppose that you decide to create a class named Employee. One instance variable of Employee might be an employee number, and one necessary method might display a welcome message to new employees. To begin, you create a **class header** or **class definition** that starts the class. It contains three parts:

1. An optional access modifier

2. The keyword class

3. Any legal identifier you choose for the name of your class; because each class represents a type of object, class names are usually singular nouns.

You will learn about other optional components that can be added to a class definition as you continue to study C#.

For example, one usable header for an Employee class is internal class Employee. The keyword internal is an example of a **class access modifier**. You can declare a class using any of the modifiers in Table 9-1.

Class Access Modifier	Description
public	Access to the class is not limited.
protected	Access to the class is limited to the class and to any classes derived from the class. (You will learn about deriving classes in the chapter *Introduction to Inheritance*.)
internal	Access is limited to the assembly to which the class belongs. (An **assembly** is a group of code modules compiled together to create an executable program. The .exe files you create after compiling a C# program are assemblies.)
private	Access is limited to another class to which the class belongs. In other words, a class should be private if it is contained within another class, and the containing class is the only one that should have access to it.

Table 9-1   Class access modifiers

If you do not explicitly include an access specifier, class access is internal by default. Because most classes you create will have internal access, typing an access specifier is often unnecessary. (When you declare a class using a namespace, you only can declare it to be public or internal.)

In addition to the class header, classes you create must have a class body enclosed between curly braces. Figure 9-1 shows a shell for an Employee class.

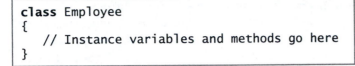

```
class Employee
{
    // Instance variables and methods go here
}
```

Figure 9-1 Employee class shell

Creating Instance Variables and Methods

When you create a class, you define both its attributes and its methods. You declare the class's instance variables within the curly braces using the same syntax you use to declare other variables—you provide a type and an identifier. For example, within the Employee class, you can declare an integer ID number, and when you create Employee objects, each will have its own idNumber. You can define the ID number simply as int idNumber;. However, programmers frequently include an access modifier for each field in a class and declare the idNumber as private int idNumber;. Figure 9-2 shows an Employee class that contains the private idNumber field.

```
class Employee
{
    private int idNumber;
}
```

Figure 9-2 Employee class containing idNumber field

The allowable field modifiers are new, public, protected, internal, private, static, readonly, and volatile. If you do not provide an access specifier for a field, its access is private and nonstatic by default, which means that no other class can access the field's values, and only nonstatic methods of the same class will be allowed to set, get, or otherwise use the private field directly. Using private fields within classes is an example of **information hiding**, a feature found in all object-oriented languages.

You see cases of information hiding in real-life objects every day. For instance, you cannot see into your automobile's gas tank to determine how full it is. Instead, you use a gauge on the dashboard to provide you with the necessary information. Similarly, data fields are frequently private in object-oriented programming, but their contents are accessed through public methods. The private data of a class should be changed or manipulated only by its own methods, not by methods that belong to other classes. A benefit of making data items private is the ability to control their values. A method that sets a variable's value can use decisions to ensure that the value falls within a specified range. For example, perhaps an Employee's salary should not be below the federal minimum wage, or perhaps a department number should not be negative or greater than 10.

In contrast to a class's private data fields, most instance methods are not usually private; they are public. The resulting private data/public method arrangement provides a means to control outside access to your data—only a class's nonprivate methods can be used to access a class's `private` data. The situation is similar to having a "public" receptionist who controls the messages passed in and out of your private office. The way in which the nonprivate methods are written controls how you will use the `private` data.

For example, an `Employee` class that contains an `idNumber` might need a method to display the employee's welcoming message to company clients. A reasonable name for this method is `WelcomeMessage()`, and its declaration is `public void WelcomeMessage()`, because it will have `public` access and return nothing. Figure 9-3 shows the `Employee` class with the addition of the `WelcomeMessage()` method.

```
class Employee
{
    private int idNumber;
    public void WelcomeMessage()
    {
        WriteLine("Welcome from Employee #{0}", idNumber);
        WriteLine("How can I help you?");
    }
}
```

Figure 9-3   Employee class with `idNumber` field and `WelcomeMessage()` method

Notice that the `WelcomeMessage()` method does not employ the `static` modifier, unlike many other methods you have created. The keyword `static` is used for classwide methods but not for instance methods that "belong" to objects. If you are creating a program with a `Main()` method that you will execute to perform some task, then many of your methods will be `static`. You call `static` methods from `Main()` without creating an object. (If the method is in a different class, you use the class name, a dot, and the method call.) However, if you are creating a class from which objects will be instantiated, most methods will probably be nonstatic, as you will be associating the methods with individual objects and their data. (You use an object name, a dot, and the method call.) Each time the `WelcomeMessage()` instance method is used in the class in Figure 9-3, it will display an `idNumber` for a specific object. In other words, the method will work appropriately for each object instance, so it is not static.

In Chapter 7, you learned that when you create a `Form`, you sometimes include nonstatic variable declarations outside of any methods—for example, if two `Click()` methods must access the same data. Now you can understand that such variables are nonstatic because they are associated with an object—the `Form` that is being defined.

The `Employee` class in Figure 9-3 is not a program that will run; it contains no `Main()` method. Rather, it simply describes what `Employee` objects will have (an `idNumber`) and be able to do (display a greeting) when you write a program that contains one or more `Employee` objects.

A class can contain fields that are objects of other classes. For example, you might create a class named Date that contains a month, day, and year and add two Date fields to an Employee class to hold the Employee's birth date and hire date. You might also create a BusinessOffice class and declare Employee objects within it. Using an object within another object is known as **composition**. The relationship created is also called a **has-a relationship** because one object "has an" instance of another.

Watch the video *Creating a Class*.

TWO TRUTHS & A LIE

Creating a Class from Which Objects Can Be Instantiated

1. A class header always contains the keyword class.

2. When you create a class, you define both its attributes and its methods.

3. Most fields and methods defined in a class are private.

The false statement is #3. Most fields in a class are private, but most methods are public.

Creating Objects

Declaring a class does not create any actual objects. A class is just an abstract description of what an object will be like if any objects are ever actually instantiated. Just as you might understand all the characteristics of an item you intend to manufacture long before the first item rolls off the assembly line, you can create a class with fields and methods before you instantiate any objects that are occurrences of that class. You can think of a class declaration as similar to a blueprint for building a new house or a recipe for baking a cake. In other words, it is a plan that exists before any objects are created.

Defining an object is similar to defining a simple variable that is a built-in data type; in each case, you use a data type and an identifier. For example, you might define an integer as int someValue;, and you might define an Employee as Employee myAssistant;, where myAssistant could be any legal identifier you choose to represent an Employee.

Every object name is a reference—that is, it holds a computer memory location where the fields for the object reside. The memory location holds the values for the object.

When you declare an integer as int myInteger;, you notify the compiler that an integer named myInteger will exist, and computer memory automatically is reserved for it at the same time— the exact amount of computer memory depends on the declared data type. When you declare the myAssistant instance of the Employee class, you are notifying the compiler that you will use the identifier myAssistant. However, you are not yet setting aside computer memory in which the Employee named myAssistant can be stored—that is done only for the built-in, predefined types. To allocate the needed memory for the object, you must use the new operator. You used the new operator earlier in this book when you learned to set aside memory for an array.

Defining an Employee object named myAssistant requires two steps—you must declare a reference to the object and then you must use the statement that actually sets aside enough memory to hold myAssistant:

```
Employee myAssistant;
myAssistant = new Employee();
```

You also can declare and reserve memory for myAssistant in one statement, as in the following:

```
Employee myAssistant = new Employee();
```

In this statement, Employee is the object's type (as well as its class), and myAssistant is the name of the object. The equal sign is the assignment operator, so a value is being assigned to myAssistant. The new operator is allocating a new, unused portion of computer memory for myAssistant. The value being assigned to myAssistant is a memory address at which the object created by the Employee() constructor will be located. You need not be concerned with the actual memory address—when you refer to myAssistant, the compiler will locate it at the appropriate address for you.

Because the identifiers for objects are references to their memory addresses, you can call any class a **reference type**—in other words, a type that refers to a specific memory location. A reference type is a type that holds an address, as opposed to the predefined types such as int, double, and char, which are **value types** and hold a value as opposed to its address. (In Chapter 2, you learned about enumerations; they are value types too.) In programming circles, you might hear debate about whether everything in C# is an object. Although some disagree, the general consensus is that value types like int and double are not objects; only reference types are. Further confusing the issue, a value type can easily be converted to an Object with a statement such as Object myObject = myInteger;. The action that takes place in such an implicit conversion is known as *boxing*.

In C#, you can create a struct which is similar to a class in that it can contain field and methods but is a value type rather than a reference type. See the C# documentation for further details.

You also can use the new operator for simple data types. For example, to declare an integer variable x, you can write the following:

```
int x = new int();
```

However, programmers usually use the simpler form:

```
int x;
```

With the first form, x is initialized to 0. With the second form, x holds no usable starting value.

In the statement Employee myAssistant = new Employee();, the last portion of the statement after the new operator, Employee(), looks suspiciously like a method name with its parentheses. In fact, it is the name of a method that constructs an Employee object. Employee() is a *constructor*. You will write your own constructors later in this chapter. For now, note that when you don't write a constructor for a class, C# writes one for you, and the name of the constructor is always the same as the name of the class whose objects it constructs.

 Later in this chapter you will learn that the automatically generated constructor for a class is a *default constructor*, which means it takes no parameters. Programmers sometimes erroneously equate the terms *automatically generated* and *default*. The automatically created constructor for a class is an *example* of a default constructor, but you also can explicitly create your own default constructor.

After an object has been instantiated, its nonstatic public members can be accessed using the object's identifier, a dot, and the nonstatic public member's identifier. For example, if you declare an Employee named myAssistant, you can access myAssistant's WelcomeMessage() method with the following statement:

myAssistant.WelcomeMessage();

An object such as myAssistant that uses an instance method is an **invoking object**. The statement myAssistant.WelcomeMessage(); would be illegal if WelcomeMessage() was a static method. The method can be used appropriately with each unique Employee object only because it is nonstatic.

A program that declares myAssistant cannot access myAssistant's idNumber directly; the only way a program can access the private data is by using one of the object's public methods. Because the WelcomeMessage() method is part of the same class as idNumber, and because WelcomeMessage() is public, a client method (for example, a Main() method in a program) can use the method. Figure 9-4 shows a class named CreateEmployee whose Main() method declares an Employee and displays the Employee's welcome message. Figure 9-5 shows the execution of the program.

```
using static System;
class CreateEmployee
{
    static void Main()
    {
        Employee myAssistant = new Employee();
        myAssistant.WelcomeMessage();
    }
}
```

Figure 9-4   The CreateEmployee program

Figure 9-5   Output of the CreateEmployee program

In the output in Figure 9-5, the Employee's ID number is 0. By default, all unassigned numeric fields in an object are initialized to 0. When you compile the program in Figure 9-4, you receive a warning message:

```
Field 'Employee.idNumber' is never assigned to, and will always have its
default value 0.
```

Of course, usually you want to provide a different value for each Employee's idNumber field. One way to provide values for object fields is to create *properties*, which you will do later in this chapter.

Passing Objects to Methods

A class represents a data type, and you can pass objects to methods just as you can pass variables that are simple data types. For example, the program in Figure 9-6 shows how string and Employee objects can be passed to a DisplayEmployeeData() method. Each Employee is assigned to the emp parameter within the method. Figure 9-7 shows the program's output.

```csharp
using static System.Console;
class CreateTwoEmployees
{
    static void Main()
    {
        Employee aWorker = new Employee();
        Employee anotherWorker = new Employee();
        DisplayEmployeeData("First", aWorker);
        DisplayEmployeeData("Second", anotherWorker);
    }
    static void DisplayEmployeeData(string order, Employee emp)
    {
        WriteLine("\n{0} employee's message:", order);
        emp.WelcomeMessage();
    }
}
```

Figure 9-6   The CreateTwoEmployees program

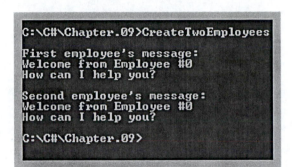

Figure 9-7   Output of the CreateTwoEmployees program

When you pass an object to a method, you pass a reference. Therefore, any change made to an object parameter in a method also affects the object used as an argument in the calling method.

In Figure 9-6, the DisplayEmployeeData() method is **internal** by default. Because the method accepts an Employee parameter, it must be no more accessible than the Employee class, which is also **internal**. This restriction preserves the security provided for the Employee class's nonpublic members. The program would also work if you made both the DisplayEmployeeData() method and the Employee class **public**.

TWO TRUTHS & A LIE

Creating Objects

1. Declaring a class creates one object of a new data type.

2. After you declare a class, you must use the new operator to allocate memory for an object of that class and to instantiate it.

3. After an object has been instantiated, its public members can be accessed using the object's identifier, a dot, and a method call.

The false statement is #1. Declaring a class does not create any actual objects; the declaration describes only what an object of that class will be.

Creating Properties

Frequently, methods you call with an object are used to alter the states of its fields. For example, you might want to set or change the date or time of a party. In the Employee class, you could write a method such as SetIdNumber() to set an employee's idNumber field as follows:

```
public void SetIdNumber(int number)
{
    idNumber = number;
}
```

Then, after you instantiate an Employee object named myAssistant, you could call the method with a statement like the following:

```
myAssistant.SetIdNumber(785);
```

Although this technique would work, and might be used in other programming languages, C# programmers more often create properties to perform similar tasks. A **property** is a member of a class that provides access to a field of a class; properties define how fields will be set and retrieved. C# programmers refer to properties as "smart fields" because they provide a combination of the best features of private fields and public methods:

- Like public methods, they protect private data from outside access.

- Like fields, their names are used in the same way simple variable names are used. When you create properties, the syntax in your client programs becomes more natural and easier to understand.

Properties have **accessors** that specify the statements that execute when a class's fields are accessed. Specifically, properties contain **set accessors** for setting an object's fields and **get accessors** for retrieving the stored values. Figure 9-8 shows an Employee class in which a property named IdNumber has been defined in the shaded area.

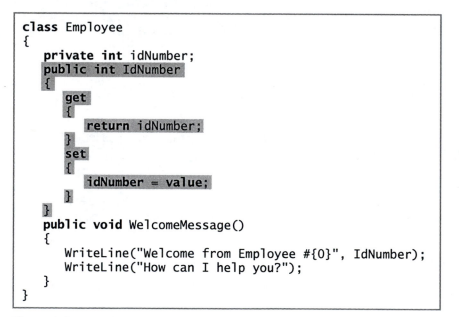

```
class Employee
{
    private int idNumber;
    public int IdNumber
    {
        get
        {
            return idNumber;
        }
        set
        {
            idNumber = value;
        }
    }
    public void WelcomeMessage()
    {
        WriteLine("Welcome from Employee #{0}", IdNumber);
        WriteLine("How can I help you?");
    }
}
```

Figure 9-8   Employee class with defined property

A property declaration resembles a variable declaration; it contains an access modifier, a data type, and an identifier. It also resembles a method in that it is followed by curly braces that contain statements. By convention, a property identifier is the same as the field it manipulates, except the first letter is capitalized. The field that supports a property is its **backing field**. Be careful with capitalization of properties. For example, within a get accessor for IdNumber, if you return the property (IdNumber) instead of the backing field (idNumber), you initiate an infinite loop—the property continuously accesses itself.

The IdNumber property in Figure 9-8 contains both get and set accessors defined between curly braces; a property declaration can contain a get accessor, a set accessor, or both. When a property has a set accessor, programmers say the property can be "written to." When it has a get accessor, programmers say the property can be "read from." When a property has only a get accessor (and not a set accessor), it is a **readonly property**. In C#, the get and set accessors often are called the **getter** and the **setter**, respectively.

In the WelcomeMessage() method in Figure 9-8, the IdNumber property is displayed. Alternatively, this method could continue to use the idNumber field (as in Figure 9-3) because the method is a member of the same class as the field. Programmers are divided on whether a method of a class should use a field or a property to access its own methods. One popular position is that if get and set accessors are well designed, they should be used everywhere, even within the class. Sometimes, you want a field to be readonly, so you do not create a set accessor. In such a case, you can use the field (with the lowercase initial by convention) within class methods.

Throughout this book you have seen keywords displayed in boldface in the program figures. The words get, set, and value are not C# keywords—for example, you could declare a variable named get within a C# program. However, within a property, get, set, and value have special meanings and are not allowed to be declared as identifiers there. In the Visual Studio Integrated Development Environment, these three words appear in blue within properties, but in black elsewhere. Identifiers that act like keywords in specific circumstances are **contextual keywords**. C# has six contextual keywords: get, set, value, partial, where, and yield.

Each accessor in a property looks like a method, except no parentheses are included in the identifier. A set accessor acts like a method that accepts a parameter and assigns it to a variable. However, it is not a method and you do not use parentheses with it. A get accessor returns the value of the field associated with the property, but you do not code a return type; the return type of a get accessor is implicitly the type of the property in which it is contained.

When you use set and get accessors in a method, you do not use the words *set* or *get*. Instead, to set a value, you use the assignment operator (=), and to get a value, you simply use the property name. For example, if you declare an Employee named myChef, you can assign an IdNumber as simply as you would a variable, as in the following:

```
Employee myChef = new Employee();
myChef.IdNumber = 2345;
```

In the second statement, the `IdNumber` property is set to 2345. The value to the right of the equal sign is sent to the `set` accessor as an implicit parameter named value. (An **implicit parameter** is one that is undeclared and that gets its value automatically.) In the statement myChef.IdNumber = 2345;, the constant 2345 is sent to the `set` accessor, where it becomes the value of `value`. Within the `set` accessor, value is assigned to the field `idNumber`. The `idNumber` field could not have been set directly from `Main()` because it is private; however, the `IdNumber` property can be set through its `set` accessor because the property is `public`.

Writing a `get` accessor allows you to use a property like you would a simple variable. For example, a declared `Employee`'s ID number can be displayed with the following:

```
WriteLine("ID number is {0}", myChef.IdNumber);
```

The expression myChef.idNumber (using the field name that starts with a lowercase *i*) would not be allowed in a client program because `idNumber` is `private`; however, the `public get` accessor of the property allows myChef.IdNumber to be displayed. Figure 9-9 shows a complete application that uses the `Employee` class with accessors defined in Figure 9-8. Figure 9-10 shows the output.

```
using static System.Console;
class CreateEmployee2
{
    static void Main()
    {
        Employee myChef = new Employee();
        myChef.IdNumber = 2345;
        WriteLine("ID number is {0}", myChef.IdNumber);
        myChef.WelcomeMessage();
    }
}
```

Figure 9-9   The CreateEmployee2 application that uses the `Employee` class containing a property

```
C:\C#\Chapter.09>CreateEmployee2
ID number is 2345
Welcome from Employee #2345
How can I help you?

C:\C#\Chapter.09>
```

Figure 9-10   Output of the CreateEmployee2 application

At this point, declaring get and set accessors that do nothing except retrieve a value from a field or assign a value to one might seem like a lot of work for very little payoff. After all, if a field was public instead of private, you would just use it directly and avoid the work of creating the property. However, it is conventional (and consistent with object-oriented principles) to make a class's fields private and allow accessors to manipulate them only as you deem appropriate. Keeping data hidden is an important feature of object-oriented programming, as is controlling how data values are set and used. Additionally, you can customize accessors to suit the restrictions you want to impose on how some fields are retrieved and accessed. For example, you could write a set accessor that restricts ID numbers within the Employee class as follows:

```
set
{
    if(value < 500)
        idNumber = value;
    else
        idNumber = 500;
}
```

This set accessor would ensure that an Employee idNumber would never be greater than 500. If clients had direct access to a private idNumber field, you could not control what values could be assigned there, but when you write a custom set accessor for your class, you gain full control over the allowed data values.

A minor inconvenience when using properties is that a property cannot be passed to a method as a ref or out parameter. For example, if IdNumber is an Employee property and myChef is an Employee object, the following statement does not compile:

```
int.TryParse(ReadLine(), out myChef.IdNumber);
```

Instead, to use TryParse() to interactively get an IdNumber value, you must use a temporary variable, as in the following example:

```
int temp;
int.TryParse(ReadLine(), out temp);
myChef.IdNumber = temp;
```

Using Auto-Implemented Properties

Although you can include any number of custom statements within the get and set accessors in a property, the most frequent scenario is that a set accessor simply assigns a value to the appropriate field, and the get accessor simply returns the field value. Because the code in get and set accessors frequently is standard as well as brief, programmers sometimes take one of several shorthand approaches to writing properties.

For example, instead of writing an `IdNumber` property using 11 code lines as in Figure 9-8, a programmer might write the property on five lines, as follows:

```
public int IdNumber
{
    get{return idNumber;}
    set{idNumber = value;}
}
```

This format does not eliminate any of the characters in the original version of the property; it eliminates only some of the white space, placing each accessor on a single line.

Other programmers choose an even more condensed form and write the entire property on one line as:

```
public int IdNumber {get{return idNumber;} set{idNumber = value;}}
```

An even more concise format was introduced in C# 3.0. In this and newer versions of C#, you can write a property as follows:

```
public int IdNumber {get; set;}
```

A property written in this format is an **auto-implemented property**. The property's implementation (its set of working statements) is created for you automatically with the assumptions that the `set` accessor should simply assign a value to the appropriate field, and the `get` accessor should simply return the field. You cannot use an auto-implemented property if you need to include customized statements within one of your accessors (such as placing restrictions on an assigned value), and you can declare an auto-implemented property only when you use both `get` and `set`. Auto-implemented properties are sometimes called **automatic properties**.

When you create an auto-implemented property, you should not declare the backing field that corresponds to the property. The corresponding backing field is generated by the compiler and has an internal name that would not match the field's name if you had coded the field yourself. If you also declare a field for the property and do not refer to it explicitly, you will receive a warning that your field is never used because your field and the property's field refer to separate memory addresses. You can avoid the warning by using the declared field, but that can lead to potential confusion and errors. For example, Figure 9-11 shows an `Employee` class in which no specialized code is needed for the properties associated with the ID number and salary. In this class, the fields are not declared explicitly; only auto-implemented properties are declared. The figure also contains a short program that uses the class, and Figure 9-12 shows the output. Auto-implemented properties provide a convenient shortcut when you need both `get` and `set` abilities without specialized statements.

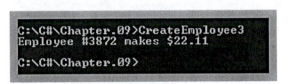

```
using static System.Console;
class CreateEmployee3
{
    static void Main()
    {
        Employee aWorker = new Employee();
        aWorker.IdNumber = 3872;
        aWorker.Salary = 22.11;
        WriteLine("Employee #{0} makes {1}",
            aWorker.IdNumber, aWorker.Salary.ToString("C"));
    }
}
class Employee
{
    public int IdNumber {get; set;}
    public double Salary {get; set;}
}
```

Figure 9-11 An Employee class with no declared fields and auto-implemented properties, and a program that uses them

```
C:\C#\Chapter.09>CreateEmployee3
Employee #3872 makes $22.11

C:\C#\Chapter.09>
```

Figure 9-12 Output of the CreateEmployee3 application

If you want to create a read-only property using auto-implemented accessors, you can make the set accessor private, as in the following:

```
public int IdNumber {get; private set;}
```

Using this technique, the IdNumber property cannot be set by any statement in another class. However, it could be assigned a value by methods within its own class. You also might want to create a property that outside classes could set but not retrieve, as follows:

```
public int IdNumber {private get; set;}
```

  Watch the video *Creating Properties*.

TWO TRUTHS & A LIE

Creating Properties

1. A property is a member of a class that defines how fields will be set and retrieved.

2. Properties contain `set` accessors for retrieving an object's fields and `get` accessors for setting the stored values.

3. You can create auto-implemented properties when you want a field's `set` accessor simply to assign a value to the appropriate field, and a field's `get` accessor simply to return the field value.

The false statement is #2. Properties contain `set` accessors for setting an object's fields and `get` accessors for retrieving the stored values.

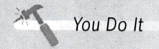

You Do It

Creating a Class and Objects

In this section, you create a `Student` class and instantiate objects from it. This class contains an ID number, last name, and grade point average for the Student. It also contains properties that get and set each of these fields. You also pass each `Student` object to a method.

1. Start a new project by declaring a `Student` class. Insert an opening curly brace, and declare three `private` fields that will hold an ID number, last name, and grade point average, as follows:

```
class Student
{
    private int idNumber;
    private string lastName;
    private double gradePointAverage;
```

2. Add two constants that represent the highest and lowest possible values for a grade point average.

```
public const double HIGHEST_GPA = 4.0;
public const double LOWEST_GPA = 0.0;
```

(continues)

(continued)

3. Add two properties that get and set `idNumber` and `lastName`. By convention, properties have an identifier that is the same as the field they service, except they start with a capital letter.

```
public int IdNumber
{
    get
    {
        return idNumber;
    }
    set
    {
        idNumber = value;
    }
}
public string LastName
{
    get
    {
        return lastName;
    }
    set
    {
        lastName = value;
    }
}
```

4. Add the following `set` accessor in the property for the `gradePointAverage` field. It sets limits on the value assigned, assigning 0 if the value is out of range.

```
public double GradePointAverage
{
    get
    {
        return gradePointAverage;
    }
    set
    {
        if(value >= LOWEST_GPA && value <= HIGHEST_GPA)
            gradePointAverage = value;
        else
            gradePointAverage = LOWEST_GPA;
    }
}
```

(continues)

(continued)

5. Add a closing curly brace for the class. Save the file as **CreateStudents.cs**.

6. At the top of the file, begin a program that creates two `Student` objects, assigns some values, and displays the `Student`s.

```
using System;
using static System.Console;
class CreateStudents
{
```

7. Add a `Main()` method that declares two `Student`s. Assign field values, including one "illegal" value—a grade point average that is too high.

```
static void Main()
{
    Student first = new Student();
    Student second = new Student();
    first.IdNumber = 123;
    first.LastName = "Anderson";
    first.GradePointAverage = 3.5;
    second.IdNumber = 789;
    second.LastName = "Daniels";
    second.GradePointAverage = 4.1;
```

8. Instead of creating similar `WriteLine()` statements to display the two `Student`s, call a method with each `Student`. You will create the method to accept a `Student` argument in the next step. Add a closing curly brace for the `Main()` method.

```
    Display(first);
    Display(second);
}
```

9. Write the `Display()` method so that the passed-in `Student`'s `IdNumber`, `LastName`, and `GradePointAverage` are displayed and aligned. Add a closing curly brace for the class.

```
static void Display(Student stu)
{
    WriteLine("{0, 5} {1, -10}{2, 6}", stu.IdNumber,
        stu.LastName, stu.GradePointAverage.ToString("F1"));
}
}
```

Recall that field contents are left-aligned when you use a minus sign before the field size. Also recall that the "F1" argument to the `ToString()` method causes the value to be displayed to one decimal place.

(continues)

(continued)

10. Save the file, and then compile and execute the program. Figure 9-13 shows the output. Each Student has unique data values and uses the same Display() method. Notice how the second Student's grade point average was forced to 0 by the set accessor in the property for the field.

```
C:\C#\Chapter.09>CreateStudents
   123   Anderson        3.5
   789   Daniels         0.0

C:\C#\Chapter.09>_
```

Figure 9-13   Output of the CreateStudents program

Using Auto-Implemented Properties

When a property's get accessor simply returns the corresponding field's value, and its set accessor simply assigns a value to the appropriate field, you can reduce the code in your classes by using auto-implemented properties. In the **Student** class, both IdNumber and LastName are candidates for this shortcut, so you can replace the full versions of these properties with their auto-implemented versions. The GradePointAverage property cannot take advantage of auto-implementation because additional code is required for the property to fulfill its intended function.

1. Open the file that contains the Student class if it is not still open on your screen. Remove the properties for IdNumber and LastName and replace them with these auto-implemented versions:

   ```
   public int IdNumber {get; set;}
   public string LastName {get; set;}
   ```

2. Remove the declarations for the fields idNumber and lastName.

3. Save the file, and then recompile and execute it. The output is the same as when the program used the original version of the Student class in Figure 9-13.

More About public and private Access Modifiers

Most of the time, a class's data fields are private and its methods are public. This technique ensures that data will be used and changed only in the ways provided in your accessors. Novice programmers might make a data field public to avoid having to create a property containing get and set accessors. However, doing so violates a basic principle of object-oriented programming. Data should be hidden when at all possible, and access to it should be controlled by well-designed accessors.

Although private fields and public methods and accessors are the norm, occasionally you need to create public fields or private methods. Consider the Carpet class shown in Figure 9-14. Although it contains several private data fields, this class also contains one public constant field (shaded). Following the three public property declarations, one private method is defined (also shaded).

374

```
class Carpet
{
    public const string MOTTO = "Our carpets are quality-made";
    private int length;
    private int width;
    private int area;
    public int Length
    {
        get
        {
            return length;
        }
        set
        {
            length = value;
            CalcArea();
        }
    }
    public int Width
    {
        get
        {
            return width;
        }
        set
        {
            width = value;
            CalcArea();
        }
    }
    public int Area
    {
        get
        {
            return area;
        }
    }
    private void CalcArea()
    {
        area = Length * Width;
    }
}
```

Figure 9-14   The Carpet class

When you create `Carpet` objects from the class in Figure 9-14, each `Carpet` will have its own `length`, `width`, and `area`, but all `Carpet` objects will have the same `MOTTO`. The field `MOTTO` is preceded by the keyword `const`, meaning `MOTTO` is constant. That is, no program can change its value. Making a constant `public` does not violate information hiding in the way that making an object's data fields `public` would, because programs that use this class cannot change the constant's value.

When you define a named constant within a class, it is always `static`, even though you cannot use the keyword `static` as a modifier. In other words, the field belongs to the entire class, not to any particular instance of the class. When you create a `static` field, only one copy is stored for the entire class, no matter how many objects you instantiate. When you use a constant field in a client class, you use the class name and a dot rather than an object name, as in `Carpet.MOTTO`. Some built-in C# classes contain useful named constants, such as `Math.PI`, which contains the value of pi. You do not create a `Math` object to use `PI`; therefore, you know it is `static`.

 Throughout this book, you have been using `static` to describe the `Main()` method of a class. You do not need to create an object of any class that contains a `Main()` method to be able to use `Main()`.

Figure 9-15 shows a program that instantiates and uses a `Carpet` object, and Figure 9-16 shows the results when the program executes. Notice that, although the output statements require an object to use the `Width`, `Length`, and `Area` properties, `MOTTO` is referenced using the class name only.

```
using static System.Console;
class TestCarpet
{
    static void Main()
    {
        Carpet aRug = new Carpet();
        aRug.Width = 12;
        aRug.Length = 14;
        Write("The {0} X {1} carpet ", aRug.Width, aRug.Length);
        WriteLine("has an area of {0}", aRug.Area);
        WriteLine("Our motto is: {0}", Carpet.MOTTO);
    }
}
```

Figure 9-15   The `TestCarpet` class

```
C:\C#\Chapter.09>TestCarpet
The 12 X 14 carpet has an area of 168
Our motto is: Our carpets are quality-made

C:\C#\Chapter.09>
```

Figure 9-16   Output of the TestCarpet program

The Carpet class contains one private method named CalcArea(). As you examine the code in the TestCarpet class in Figure 9-15, notice that Width and Length are set using an assignment operator but Area is not. The TestCarpet class can make assignments to Width and Length because these properties are public. However, you would not want a client program to assign a value to Area because the assigned value might not agree with the Width and Length values. Therefore, the Area property is a read-only property—it does not contain a set accessor, and no assignments by clients are allowed. Instead, whenever the Width or Length properties are changed, the private CalcArea() method is called from the accessor. The CalcArea() method is defined as private because there is no reason for a client class like TestCarpet to call CalcArea(). Programmers probably create private methods more frequently than they create public data fields. Some programmers feel that the best style is to use public methods that are nothing but a list of method calls with descriptive names. Then, the methods that actually do the work are all private.

TWO TRUTHS & A LIE

More About public and private Access Modifiers

1. Good object-oriented techniques require that data should usually be hidden and access to it should be controlled by well-designed accessors.

2. Although private fields, methods, and accessors are the norm, occasionally you need to create public versions of them.

3. When you define a named constant within a class, it is always static; that is, the field belongs to the entire class, not to any particular instance of the class.

The false statement is #2. Although private fields and public methods and accessors are the norm, occasionally you need to create public fields or private methods.

Understanding the this Reference

When you create a class, only one copy of the class code is stored in computer memory. However, you might eventually create thousands of objects from the class. When you create each object, you provide storage for each of the object's instance variables. For example, Figure 9-17 shows part of a Book class that contains three fields, a property for the title field, and an advertising message method. When you declare several Book objects, as in the following statements, each Book object requires separate memory locations for its title, numPages, and price:

```
Book myBook = new Book();
Book yourBook = new Book();
```

```
class Book
{
    private string title;
    private int numPages;
    private double price;
    public string Title
    {
        get
        {
            return title;
        }
        set
        {
            title = value;
        }
    }
    public void AdvertisingMessage()
    {
        WriteLine("Buy it now: {0}", Title);
    }
}
```

Figure 9-17   Partially developed Book class

 When you compile the Book class, you receive warnings that the numPages and price fields are never used. The omission was purposeful for this demonstration program.

In this example, storing a single Book object requires allocating storage space for three separate fields; the storage requirements for Book objects used by a library or retail bookstore would be far more considerable, but necessary—each Book must be able to "hold" its own data, including publisher, date published, author, ISBN, and so on. Each nonstatic field is called an *instance variable* precisely because separate values are stored for each instance. In addition to its fields, if each Book object also required its own copy of each property and method contained in the class, the storage requirements would multiply. It makes sense that each Book needs space to store its unique title and other data, but because every Book uses the same methods, storing multiple copies of methods is wasteful and unnecessary.

Fortunately, each Book object does not need to store its own copy of each property and method. Whether you make the method call myBook.AdvertisingMessage() or yourBook.AdvertisingMessage(), you access the same AdvertisingMessage() method. However, there must be a difference between the two method calls, because each displays a different title in its message. The difference lies in an implicit, or invisible, reference that is passed to every instance method and property accessor. The implicitly passed reference is the **this reference**, which is the address of the invoking object. When you call the method myBook.AdvertisingMessage(), you automatically pass the this reference to the method so that it knows which instance of Book to use. Only nonstatic methods receive a this reference. The this reference is aptly named. When you execute a nonstatic method such as myBook.AdvertisingMessage(), you might ask yourself which object's data will be used in the method. The answer is "*This* object's (myBook's) data."

You can explicitly refer to the this reference within an instance method or property, as shown in Figure 9-18. When you refer to Title (or title) within a Book class method or accessor, you are referring to the title field of "this" Book—the Book whose name you used in the method call, perhaps myBook or yourBook. Using the shaded keywords in Figure 9-18 is not required; the version of the methods shown in Figure 9-17 (where this was implied but not written explicitly) works just as well. Figure 9-19 shows an application that uses the Book class, and Figure 9-20 shows the output.

```
class Book
{
    private string title;
    private int numPages;
    private double price;
    public string Title
    {
        get
        {
            return this.title;
        }
        set
        {
            this.title = value;
        }
    }
    public void AdvertisingMessage()
    {
        WriteLine("Buy it now: {0}", this.Title);
    }
}
```

Figure 9-18   The Book class with methods explicitly using this references

```
using static System;
class CreateTwoBooks
{
    static void Main()
    {
        Book myBook = new Book();
        Book yourBook = new Book();
        myBook.Title = "Silas Marner";
        yourBook.Title = "The Time Traveler's Wife";
        myBook.AdvertisingMessage();
        yourBook.AdvertisingMessage();
    }
}
```

Figure 9-19   Program that declares two Book objects

Figure 9-20   Output of the CreateTwoBooks program

The Book class in Figure 9-18 worked without adding the explicit references to this. However, you should be aware that the this reference is always there, working behind the scenes, even if you do not code it. Sometimes, you may want to include the this reference within a method for clarity, so the reader has no doubt when you are referring to an instance variable.

On occasion, you might need to explicitly code the this reference. For example, consider the abbreviated Book class in Figure 9-21. The programmer has chosen the same identifier for a field and a parameter to a method that uses the field. To distinguish between the two, the field must be referenced as this.price within the method that has a parameter with the same name. All references to price (without using this) in the SetPriceAndTax() method in Figure 9-21 are references to the local parameter. If the method included the statement price = price;, the parameter's value would be assigned to itself and the class's field would never be set.

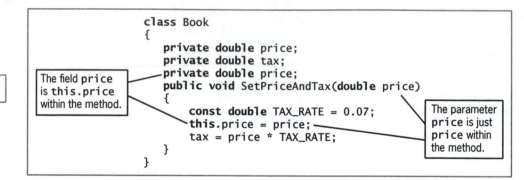

Figure 9-21 Book class that must explicitly use the this reference

 Watch the video Understanding the *this* Reference.

TWO TRUTHS & A LIE

Understanding the this Reference

1. An implicit, or invisible, this reference is passed to every instance method and property accessor in a class; instance methods and properties are nonstatic.

2. You can explicitly refer to the this reference within an instance method or property.

3. Although the this reference exists in every instance method, it is invisible, so you can never refer to it within a method.

The false statement is #3. Sometimes, you may want to include the this reference within a method for clarity, so the reader has no doubt when you are referring to an instance variable.

Understanding Constructors

When you create a class such as Employee and instantiate an object with a statement such as Employee aWorker = new Employee();, you are actually calling a method named Employee() that is provided by C#. A **constructor** is a method that instantiates (creates an instance of) an object. If you do not write a constructor for a class, then each class you create is automatically supplied with a public constructor with no parameters. A constructor without parameters is a class's **default constructor**. (The term *default constructor* is not just used for a class's automatically supplied constructor; it is used for any constructor that takes no parameters. You will learn to create constructors with parameters in the next section.)

The automatically created constructor named Employee() establishes one Employee with the identifier aWorker, and provides the following initial values to the Employee's data fields:

- Numeric fields are set to 0 (zero).

- Character fields are set to '\0'.

- Boolean fields are set to false.

- References, such as string fields or any other object fields, are set to null (or empty).

The value of an object initialized with a default constructor is known as the **default value of the object**. If you do not want all of an Employee's fields to hold default values, or if you want to perform additional tasks when you create an Employee, you can write your own constructor to replace the automatically supplied version. Any constructor you write must have the same name as its class, and constructors cannot have a return type. For example, if you create an Employee class that contains a Salary property, and you want every new Employee object to have a salary of 300.00, you could write the constructor for the Employee class as follows:

```
Employee()
{
    Salary = 300.00;
}
```

Assuming a Salary property has been defined for the salary field, any instantiated Employee will have a default salary value of 300.00.

You can write any statement in a constructor. For example, you can perform arithmetic or display a message. However, the most common constructor task is to initialize fields. If you create a class in which one or more fields are never assigned a value, the compiler will issue a warning that the fields in question will hold default values.

Passing Parameters to Constructors

You can create a constructor to ensure that all objects of a class are initialized with the same values in their data fields. Alternatively, you might create objects initialized with unique field values by writing constructors to which you pass one or more parameters. You then can use the parameter values to set properties or fields for individual object instantiations.

For example, consider an Employee class with two data fields, a constructor, and an auto-implemented property, as shown in Figure 9-22. Its constructor assigns 9.99 to each potentially instantiated Employee's PayRate. Any time an Employee object is created using a statement such as Employee partTimeWorker = new Employee();, even if no other data-assigning methods are ever used, you are ensured that the Employee's PayRate holds a default value.

```
class Employee
{
    private int idNumber;
    private string name;
    public Employee()
    {
        PayRate = 9.99;
    }
    public double PayRate {get; set;}
    // Other class members can go here
}
```

Figure 9-22 Employee class with a parameterless constructor

The constructor in Figure 9-22 is a **parameterless constructor**—one that takes no arguments. In other words, it is a default constructor. As an alternative, you might choose to create Employees with a different initial pay rate value for each Employee. To accomplish this task, you can pass a pay rate to the constructor. Figure 9-23 shows an Employee constructor that receives a parameter. A value is passed to the constructor using a statement such as the following:

```
Employee partTimeWorker = new Employee(12.50);
```

When the constructor executes, the double used as the actual parameter within the method call is passed to Employee() and assigned to the Employee's PayRate.

```
public Employee(double rate)
{
    PayRate = rate;
}
```

Figure 9-23 Employee constructor with parameter

Overloading Constructors

C# automatically provides a default constructor for your classes. As soon as you create your own constructor, whether it has parameters or not, you no longer have access to the automatically created version. However, if you want a class to have both parameter and parameterless versions of a constructor, you can create them. Like any other C# methods, constructors can be overloaded. You can write as many constructors for a class as you want, as long as their parameter lists do not cause ambiguity. A class can contain only one parameterless constructor: the default constructor, which can be the automatically provided one or one that you write. If you wrote multiple parameterless constructors, they would be ambiguous. If you create any number of constructors but do not create a parameterless version, then the class does not have a default constructor.

For example, the Employee class in Figure 9-24 contains four constructors. The Main() method within the CreateSomeEmployees class in Figure 9-25 shows how different types of Employees might be instantiated. Notice that one version of the Employee constructor—the one that supports a character parameter—doesn't even use the parameter; sometimes you might create a constructor with a specific parameter type simply to force that constructor to be the version that executes. The output of the CreateSomeEmployees program is shown in Figure 9-26.

```
class Employee
{
    public int IdNumber {get; set;}

    public double Salary {get; set;}
    public Employee()          This parameterless constructor
    {                          is the class's default constructor.
        IdNumber = 999;
        Salary = 0;
    }
    public Employee(int empId)
    {
        IdNumber = empId;
        Salary = 0;
    }
    public Employee(int empId, double sal)
    {
        IdNumber = empId;
        Salary = sal;
    }
    public Employee(char code)
    {
        IdNumber = 111;
        Salary = 100000;
    }
}
```

Figure 9-24   Employee class with four constructors

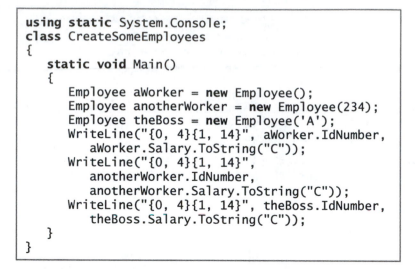

```
using static System.Console;
class CreateSomeEmployees
{
    static void Main()
    {
        Employee aWorker = new Employee();
        Employee anotherWorker = new Employee(234);
        Employee theBoss = new Employee('A');
        WriteLine("{0, 4}{1, 14}", aWorker.IdNumber,
            aWorker.Salary.ToString("C"));
        WriteLine("{0, 4}{1, 14}",
            anotherWorker.IdNumber,
            anotherWorker.Salary.ToString("C"));
        WriteLine("{0, 4}{1, 14}", theBoss.IdNumber,
            theBoss.Salary.ToString("C"));
    }
}
```

Figure 9-25   The CreateSomeEmployees program

```
C:\C#\Chapter.09>CreateSomeEmployees
 999          $0.00
 234          $0.00
 111    $100,000.00

C:\C#\Chapter.09>
```

Figure 9-26   Output of the CreateSomeEmployees program

Most likely, a single application would not use all four constructors of the Employee class. More likely, each application that uses the class would use only one or two constructors. You create a class with multiple constructors to provide flexibility for your clients. For example, some clients might choose to construct Employee objects with just ID numbers, and others might prefer to construct them with ID numbers and salaries.

Using Constructor Initializers

The Employee class in Figure 9-24 contains four constructors, and each constructor initializes the same two fields. In a fully developed class used by a company, many more fields would be initialized, creating a lot of duplicated code. Besides the original extra work of writing the repetitive statements in these constructors, even more work will be required when the class is modified in the future. For example, if your organization institutes a new employee ID number format that requires a specific number of digits, then each constructor will have to be modified, requiring extra work. In addition, one or more of the constructor versions that must be modified might be overlooked, introducing errors into the programs that are clients of the class.

As an alternative to repeating code in the constructors, you can use a constructor initializer. A **constructor initializer** is a clause that indicates another instance of a class constructor should be executed before any statements in the current constructor body. Figure 9-27 shows a new version of the Employee class using constructor initializers in three of the four overloaded constructor versions.

```
class Employee
{
    public int IdNumber {get; set;}
    public double Salary {get; set;}
    public Employee() : this(999, 0)
    {
    }
    public Employee(int empId) : this(empId, 0)
    {
    }
    public Employee(int empId, double sal)
    {
        IdNumber = empId;
        Salary = sal;
    }
    public Employee(char code) : this(111, 100000)
    {
    }
}
```

Figure 9-27 Employee class with constructor initializers

In the three shaded clauses in Figure 9-27, the this reference is used to mean "the constructor for this object being constructed." For example, when a client calls the parameterless Employee constructor, 999 and 0 are passed to the two-parameter constructor. There, they become empId and sal, parameters that are assigned to the IdNumber and Salary properties. If statements were written within the parameterless constructor, they would then execute; however, in this class, additional statements are not necessary. Similarly, if a client uses the constructor version that accepts only an ID number, that parameter and a 0 for salary are passed to the two-parameter constructor. The only time just one version of the constructor executes is when a client uses both an ID number and a salary as constructor arguments. In the future, if additional statements need to be added to the class (for example, a decision that ensures an ID number was at least five digits at construction), the decision would be added only to the two-parameter version of the constructor, and all the other versions could use it.

Using the `readonly` Modifier in a Constructor

You have already learned that when you use the `const` modifier with a variable, you must assign a value at declaration and the value cannot be changed. The `readonly` modifier is similar to `const` in that it is used to assign a constant value that cannot be changed, but when you use `readonly` with a field you can assign a value either at declaration or within a constructor. This means that different constructor versions can assign different values to a `readonly` field. A `const` field must be assigned its value when a program is compiled, but a `readonly` field can be assigned a value when initialized or at runtime. For example, a `readonly` field's value might be retrieved from user input or from the operating system.

Figure 9-28 shows a program with an `Employee` class with an `idNumber` field that has been declared `readonly`. (See the first shaded statement.) The `Main()` program can send different values to the constructor to assign to `idNumber`, but after construction, `idNumber` cannot be changed. The second shaded statement causes a compiler error.

```
class EmployeesReadOnlyDemo
{
    static void Main()
    {
        Employee myAssistant = new Employee(1234);
        Employee myDriver = new Employee(2345);
        myAssistant.IdNumber = 3456;
    }
}
class Employee
{
    private readonly int idNumber;
    public Employee(int id)
    {
        idNumber = id;
    }
    public int IdNumber
    {
        get
        {
            return idNumber;
        }
        set
        {                                    Don't Do It
        {                                    The idNumber field cannot be
            idNumber = value;                assigned a value after construction.
        }                                    This statement generates an error.
    }
}
```

Figure 9-28   Employee class with a `readonly` field

TWO TRUTHS & A LIE

Understanding Constructors

1. Every class you create is automatically supplied with a public constructor with no parameters.

2. If you write a constructor for a class, you do not have a default constructor for the class.

3. Any constructor you write must have the same name as its class, and constructors cannot have a return type.

The false statement is #2. If you write a parameterless constructor for a class, it becomes the default constructor, and you lose the automatically supplied version. If you write only constructors that require parameters, then the class no longer contains a default constructor.

You Do It

Adding Overloaded Constructors to a Class

In these steps, you add overloaded constructors to the Student class.

1. Open the file that contains the Student class if it is not still open on your screen. Just before the closing curly brace for the Student class, add the following constructor. It takes three parameters and assigns them to the appropriate fields:

```
public Student(int id, string name, double gpa)
{
    IdNumber = id;
    LastName = name;
    GradePointAverage = gpa;
}
```

2. Add a second parameterless constructor. It calls the first constructor, passing 0 for the ID number, "XXX" for the name, and 0.0 for the grade point average. Its body is empty.

```
public Student() : this(0, "XXX", 0.0)
{
}
```

(continues)

(continued)

3. Change the name of the CreateStudents class to **CreateStudents2**.

4. After the existing declarations of the Student objects, add two more declarations. With one, use three arguments, but with the other, do not use any.

   ```
   Student third = new Student(456, "Marco", 2.4);
   Student fourth = new Student();
   ```

5. At the end of the Main() method, just after the two existing calls to the Display() method, add two more calls using the new objects:

   ```
   Display(third);
   Display(fourth);
   ```

6. Save the file, and then compile and execute it. The output looks like Figure 9-29. All four objects are displayed. The first two have had values assigned to them after declaration, but the third and fourth ones obtained their values from their constructors.

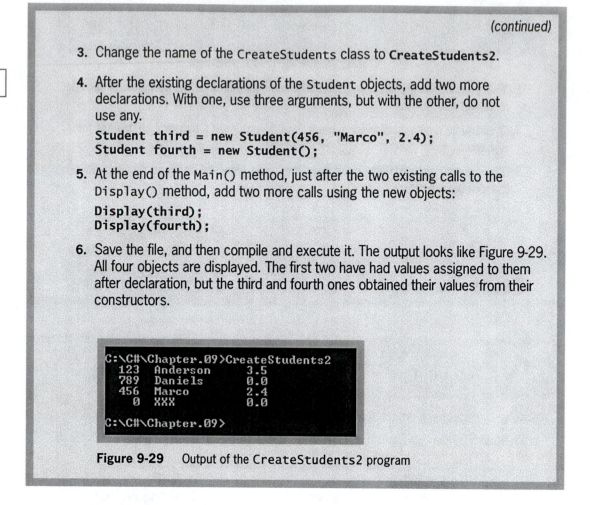

```
C:\C#\Chapter.09>CreateStudents2
  123   Anderson      3.5
  789   Daniels       0.0
  456   Marco         2.4
    0   XXX           0.0

C:\C#\Chapter.09>
```

Figure 9-29   Output of the CreateStudents2 program

Using Object Initializers

An **object initializer** allows you to assign values to any accessible members or properties of a class at the time of instantiation without calling a constructor with parameters. For example, assuming an Employee class has been created with a public IdNumber property and a parameterless constructor, you can write an object initializer in either of the following ways, with or without parentheses:

```
Employee aWorker = new Employee{IdNumber = 101};
Employee aWorker = new Employee(){IdNumber = 101};
```

In either of these statements, 101 is assigned to the aWorker object's IdNumber property. The assignment is made within a pair of curly braces; using parentheses with the constructor name is optional. When either of these statements execute, the parameterless, default constructor for the class is executed first, and then the object initializer assignment is made.

For example, Figure 9-30 shows an Employee class that contains properties for IdNumber and Salary and a default constructor that assigns a value to Salary. For demonstration purposes, the constructor displays the current object's ID number and salary. The figure also shows a program that instantiates one Employee object and displays its value, and Figure 9-31 shows the output. When the object is created in the shaded statement, the constructor executes, assigns 99.99 to Salary, and displays the first line of output, showing IdNumber is still 0. After the object is constructed in the Main() method, the next output line is displayed, showing that the assignment of the ID number occurred after construction.

```
using static System.Console;
class DemoObjectInitializer
{
   static void Main()
   {
      Employee aWorker = new Employee {IdNumber = 101};
      WriteLine("Employee #{0} exists. Salary is {1}.",
         aWorker.IdNumber, aWorker.Salary);
   }
}
class Employee
{
   public int IdNumber {get; set;}
   public double Salary {get; set;}
   public Employee()
   {
      Salary = 99.99;
      WriteLine("Employee #{0} created. Salary is {1}.",
         IdNumber, Salary);
   }
}
```

Figure 9-30   The DemoObjectInitializer program

```
C:\C#\Chapter.09>DemoObjectInitializer
Employee #0 created. Salary is 99.99.
Employee #101 exists. Salary is 99.99.

C:\C#\Chapter.09>
```

Figure 9-31   Output of the DemoObjectInitializer program

To use object initializers, a class must have a default constructor. That is, you either must not create any constructors or you must create one that requires no parameters.

Multiple assignments can be made with an object initializer by separating them with commas, as in the following:

```
Employee myAssistant = new Employee {IdNumber = 202, Salary = 25.00};
```

This single code line has the same results as the following three statements:

```
Employee myAssistant = new Employee();
myAssistant.IdNumber = 202;
myAssistant.Salary = 25.00;
```

Using object initializers allows you to create multiple objects with different initial assignments without having to provide multiple constructors to cover every possible situation. Additionally, using object initializers allows you to create objects with different starting values for different properties of the same data type. For example, consider a class like the Box class in Figure 9-32 that contains multiple properties of the same type. The constructor sets the Height, Width, and Depth properties to 1. You could write a constructor that accepts a single integer parameter to be assigned to Height (using the default value 1 for the other dimensions), but then you could not write an additional overloaded constructor that accepts a single integer parameter to be assigned to Width because the constructors would be ambiguous. However, by using object initializers, you can create objects to which you assign the properties you want. Figure 9-33 shows a program that declares three Box objects, each with a different assigned dimension, and Figure 9-34 shows the output, which demonstrates that each property was assigned appropriately.

```
class Box
{
    public int Height {get; set;}
    public int Width {get; set;}
    public int Depth {get; set;}
    public Box()
    {
        Height = 1;
        Width = 1;
        Depth = 1;
    }
}
```

Figure 9-32   The Box class

```
using static System.Console;
class DemoObjectInitializer2
{
   static void Main()
   {
      Box box1 = new Box {Height = 3};
      Box box2 = new Box {Width = 15};
      Box box3 = new Box {Depth = 268};
      DisplayDimensions(1, box1);
      DisplayDimensions(2, box2);
      DisplayDimensions(3, box3);
   }
   static void DisplayDimensions(int num, Box box)
   {
      WriteLine("Box {0}: Height: {1} Width: {2} Depth: {3}",
         num, box.Height, box.Width, box.Depth);
   }
}
```

Figure 9-33   The DemoObjectInitializer2 program

```
C:\C#\Chapter.09>DemoObjectInitializer2
Box 1: Height: 3 Width: 1 Depth: 1
Box 2: Height: 1 Width: 15 Depth: 1
Box 3: Height: 1 Width: 1 Depth: 268

C:\C#\Chapter.09>
```

Figure 9-34   Output of the DemoObjectInitializer2 program

TWO TRUTHS & A LIE

Using Object Initializers

Assume that a working program contains the following object initializer:

Invoice oneBill = new Invoice{Amount = 0};

1. You know that the Invoice class contains a default constructor.

2. You know that an Invoice object could be constructed without using a parameter.

3. You know that the Invoice class contains a single property.

The false statement is #3. The Invoice class might have any number of properties. However, only one is being initialized in this statement.

Overloading Operators

C# operators are the symbols you use to perform operations on objects. You have used many operators, including arithmetic operators (such as + and -) and logical operators (such as == and <). Separate actions can result from what seems to be the same operation or command. This occurs frequently in all computer programming languages, not just object-oriented languages. For example, in most programming languages and applications such as spreadsheets and databases, the + operator has a variety of meanings. A few of them include:

- Alone before a value (called *unary form*), + indicates a positive value, as in the expression +7.

- Between two integers (called *binary form*), + indicates integer addition, as in the expression 5 + 9.

- Between two floating-point numbers (also called binary form), + indicates floating-point addition, as in the expression 6.4 + 2.1.

- Between two strings, + indicates concatenation, as in the expression "Hello," + "there".

Expressing a value as positive is a different operation from using the + operator to perform arithmetic or concatenate strings, so + is overloaded several times in that it can take one or two arguments and have a different meaning in each case. It also can take different operand types—you use a + to add two ints, two doubles, an int and a double, and a variety of other combinations. Each use results in different actions behind the scenes.

Just as it is convenient to use a + between both integers and doubles to add them, it also can be convenient to use a + between objects, such as Employees or Books, to add them. To be able to use arithmetic symbols with your own objects, you must overload the symbols.

C# operators are classified as unary or binary, depending on whether they take one or two arguments, respectively. The rules for overloading are shown in the following list.

- The overloadable unary operators are:
- + - ! ~ ++ -- true false
- The overloadable binary operators are:
- + - * / % & | ^ == != > < >= <=
- You cannot overload the following operators:
- = && || ?? ?: checked unchecked new typeof as is
- You cannot overload an operator for a built-in data type. For example, you cannot change the meaning of + between two ints.

- When a binary operator is overloaded and it has a corresponding assignment operator, it is also overloaded. For example, if you overload +, then += is automatically overloaded too.

- Some operators must be overloaded in pairs. For example, when you overload ==, you also must overload !=, and when you overload >, you also must overload <.

 When you overload ==, you also receive warnings about methods in the Object class. You will learn about this class in the chapter "Introduction to Inheritance"; you should not attempt to overload == until you have studied that chapter.

You have used many, but not all, of the operators listed above. If you want to include an overloaded operator in a class, you must decide what the operator will mean in your class. When you do, you write statements in a method to carry out your meaning. The method has a return type and arguments just like other methods, but its identifier is required to be named operator followed by the operator being overloaded—for example, operator+() or operator*().

For example, suppose that you create a Book class in which each object has a title, number of pages, and a price. Further assume that, as a publisher, you have decided to "add" Books together. That is, you want to take two existing Books and combine them into one. Assume that you want the new Book to have the following characteristics:

- The new title is a combination of the old titles, joined by the word "and."

- The number of pages in the new book is equal to the sum of the pages in the original Books.

- Instead of charging twice as much for a new Book, you have decided to charge the price of the more expensive of the two original Books, plus $10.

A different publisher might have decided that "adding Books" means something different—for example, an added Book might have a fixed new price of $29.99. The statements you write in your operator+() method depend on how you define adding for your class. You could write an ordinary method to perform these tasks, but you could also overload the + operator to mean "add two Books." Figure 9-35 shows a Book class that has properties for each field and a shaded operator+() method.

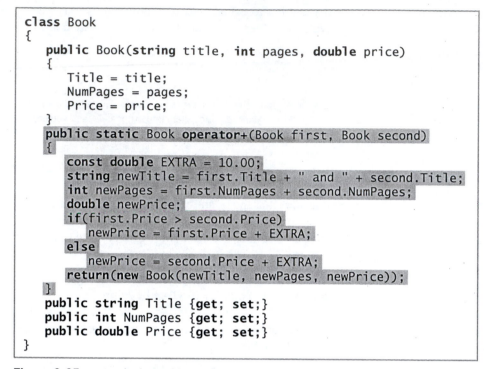

```
class Book
{
    public Book(string title, int pages, double price)
    {
        Title = title;
        NumPages = pages;
        Price = price;
    }
    public static Book operator+(Book first, Book second)
    {
        const double EXTRA = 10.00;
        string newTitle = first.Title + " and " + second.Title;
        int newPages = first.NumPages + second.NumPages;
        double newPrice;
        if(first.Price > second.Price)
            newPrice = first.Price + EXTRA;
        else
            newPrice = second.Price + EXTRA;
        return(new Book(newTitle, newPages, newPrice));
    }
    public string Title {get; set;}
    public int NumPages {get; set;}
    public double Price {get; set;}
}
```

Figure 9-35   Book class with overloaded + operator

The operator+() method in Figure 9-35 is declared to be public (so that class clients can use it) and static (which is required). The method is static because it does not receive a this reference to any object; instead, the two objects to be added are both parameters to the method.

The return type is Book because the addition of two Books is defined to be a new Book with different values from either of the originals. You could overload the + operator so that when two Books are added they return some other type, but it is most common to make the addition of two objects result in an "answer" of the same type.

The two parameters in the operator+() method in the Book class are both Books. Therefore, when you eventually call this method, the data types on both sides of the + sign will be Books. For example, you could write other methods that add a Book and an Employee, or a Book and a double.

Within the operator+() method, the statements perform the following tasks:

- A constant is declared to hold the extra price used in creating a new Book from two existing ones.

- A new string is created and assigned the first parameter Book's title, plus the string " and ", plus the second parameter Book's title.

- A new integer is declared and assigned the sum of the number of pages in each of the parameter Books.

- A new **double** is declared and assigned the value of the more expensive original Book plus $10.00.

- Within the **return** statement, a new anonymous Book is created (an anonymous object is one without an identifier) using the new title, page number, and price and is returned to the calling method. (Instead of an anonymous Book, it would have been perfectly acceptable to use two statements—the first one creating a named Book with the same arguments, and the second one returning the named Book.)

Figure 9-36 shows a client program that can use the + operator in the Book class. It first declares three Books; then, in the shaded statement, it adds two Books together and assigns the result to the third. When **book1** and **book2** are added, the **operator+()** method is called. The returned Book is assigned to book3, which is then displayed. Figure 9-37 shows the results.

```
using static System.Console;
class AddBooks
{
    static void Main()
    {
        Book book1 = new Book("Silas Marner", 350, 15.95);
        Book book2 = new Book("Moby Dick", 250, 16.00);
        Book book3;
        book3 = book1 + book2;
        WriteLine("The new book is \"{0}\"", book3.Title);
        WriteLine("It has {0} pages and costs {1}",
            book3.NumPages, book3.Price.ToString("C"));
    }
}
```

Figure 9-36   The AddBooks program

```
C:\C#\Chapter.09>AddBooks
The new book is "Silas Marner and Moby Dick"
It has 600 pages and costs $26.00

C:\C#\Chapter.09>
```

Figure 9-37   Output of the AddBooks program

In the Book class, it took many statements to overload the operator; however, in the client class, just typing a + between objects allows a programmer to use the objects and operator intuitively. You could write any statements you wanted within the operator method. However, for clarity, you should write statements that intuitively have the same meaning as the common use of the operator. For example, although you could overload the `operator*()` method to display a Book's title and price instead of performing multiplication, it would be a bad programming technique.

Because each addition operation returns a Book, it is possible to chain addition in a statement such as `collection = book1 + book2 + book3;`, assuming that all the variables have been declared to be Book objects. In this example, book1 and book2 would be added, returning a temporary Book. Then the temporary Book and book3 would be added, returning a different temporary Book that would be assigned to `collection`.

When you overload an operator, at least one argument to the method must be a member of the containing class. In other words, within the Book class, you can overload `operator*()` to multiply a Book by an integer, but you cannot overload `operator*()` to multiply a `double` by an integer.

When you overload a unary operator, the method takes a single argument. For example, suppose that you want to use a negative sign with a Book to make its price negative. You could use the operator in a statement such as the following:

`returnedBook = -purchasedBook;`

The `operator-()` method header might appear as follows:

`public static Book operator-(Book aBook)`

In this example, the minus sign is understood to cause unary negation instead of binary subtraction because the method accepts only one parameter, which is a Book. The method also returns a Book, which is an altered version of the parameter. Figure 9-38 shows a method that overloads the minus sign for a Book object. The method accepts a Book parameter, changes the price to its negative value, and returns the altered Book object to the calling method.

```
public static Book operator-(Book aBook)
{
    aBook.Price = -aBookPrice;
    return aBook;
}
```

Figure 9-38   An `operator-()` method for a Book

In some other languages, notably C++, you can write two methods to overload ++ and -- differently as prefix and postfix operators. However, when you overload either the ++ or -- operator in C#, the operator can be used either before or after the object, but the same method executes either way.

Watch the video *Overloading Operators*.

TWO TRUTHS & A LIE

Overloading Operators

1. All C# operators can be overloaded.

2. You cannot overload an operator for a built-in data type.

3. Some operators must be overloaded in pairs.

The false statement is #1. You cannot overload the following operators: = && ||
?? ?: checked unchecked new typeof as is

Declaring an Array of Objects

Just as you can declare arrays of integers or doubles, you can declare arrays that hold elements of any type, including objects. Remember that object names are references. When you create an array from a value type, such as int or char, the array holds the actual values. When you create an array from a reference type, such as a class you create, the array holds the memory addresses of the objects. In other words, the array "refers to" the objects instead of containing the objects.

You can create an array of references to seven Employee objects as follows:

```
Employee[] empArray = new Employee[7];
```

This statement reserves enough computer memory for the references to seven Employee objects named empArray[0] through empArray[6]. It does not actually construct those Employees; all the references are initialized to null. To create objects to fill the array, you must call the Employee() constructor seven times.

If the Employee class contains a default constructor, you can use the following loop to call the constructor seven times:

```
for(int x = 0; x < empArray.Length; ++x)
    empArray[x] = new Employee();
```

As x varies from 0 through 6, each of the seven empArray objects is constructed.

If you want to use a nondefault constructor, you must provide appropriate arguments. For example, if the Employee class contains a constructor with an int parameter, you can write the following to fill three of the seven array elements:

```
Employee[] empArray = {new Employee(123),
    new Employee(234), new Employee(345)};
```

To use a method that belongs to an object that is part of an array, you insert the appropriate subscript notation after the array name and before the dot-method. For example, to set all seven `Employee IdNumber` properties to 999, you can write the following:

```
for(int x = 0; x < empArray.Length; ++x)
    empArray[x].IdNumber = 999;
```

Using the `Sort()` and `BinarySearch()` Methods with Arrays of Objects

In the chapter "Using Arrays," you learned about using the `System.Array` class's built-in `BinarySearch()` and `Sort()` methods with simple data types such as `int`, `double`, and `string`. The `Sort()` method accepts an array parameter and arranges its elements in descending order. The `BinarySearch()` method accepts a sorted array and a value that it attempts to match in the array.

A complication arises when you consider searching or sorting arrays of objects you create. When you create and sort an array of simple data items, there is only one type of value to consider, and the order is based on the Unicode value of that item. The classes that support simple data items each contain a method named `CompareTo()`, which provides the details of how the basic data types compare to each other. In other words, they define comparisons such as "2 is more than 1" and "B is more than A." The `Sort()` and `BinarySearch()` methods use the `CompareTo()` method for the current type of data being sorted. In other words, `Sort()` uses the `Int32` version of `CompareTo()` when sorting integers and the `Char` version of `CompareTo()` when sorting characters.

You learned about the built-in data type class names in Chapter 2; they are summarized in Table 2-1.

You have been using the `String` class (and its `string` alias) throughout this book. The class also contains a `CompareTo()` method that you first used in Chapter 2.

When you create a class in which comparisons will be made between objects, you must tell the compiler which field to use when making those comparisons. For example, you logically might sort an organization's `Employee` objects by ID number, salary, department number, last name, hire date, or any field contained in the class. To tell C# which field to use for placing `Employee` objects in order, you must create an interface.

An **abstract method** has no method statements; an interface contains abstract methods. In the next chapter, you learn more about abstract methods. For now, understand that an **interface** is a data type, like a class, except it is a collection of empty, abstract methods (and perhaps other members) that can be used by any class, as long as the class provides definitions to override the interface's do-nothing method definitions. Unlike a class, an interface cannot contain instance fields, and you cannot create objects from it.

A class that implements an interface must override the interface's methods. When a method **overrides** another, it takes precedence over the method, and is used instead of the original version. In other words, the methods in an interface are empty, and any class that uses them must contain a new version that provides the details and is used instead. Interfaces define named behaviors that classes must implement, so that all classes can use the same method names but use them appropriately for the class. In this way, interfaces provide for polymorphism—the ability of different objects to use the same method names but act appropriately based on the context.

 When a method overrides another, it has the same signature as the method it overrides. When methods are overloaded, they have different signatures. You will learn more about overriding methods and abstract methods and classes in the next chapter.

C# supports many interfaces. You can identify an interface name by its initial letter *I*. For example, C# contains an `IComparable` interface, which contains the definition for the `CompareTo()` method that compares one object to another and returns an integer. Figure 9-39 shows the definition of `IComparable`. The `CompareTo()` method accepts a parameter `Object` but does not contain any statements; you must provide an implementation for this method in classes you create if you want the objects to be comparable. That is, the `CompareTo()` method is abstract and you must determine the meanings of *greater than*, *less than*, and *equal to* for the class.

```
interface IComparable
{
    int CompareTo(Object o);
}
```

Figure 9-39   The `IComparable` interface

When you create a class whose instances will likely be compared by clients:

- You must include a single colon and the interface name `IComparable` after the class name.
- You must write a method that contains the following header:

```
int IComparable.CompareTo(Object o)
```

 `Object` is a class—the most generic of all classes. Every `Employee` object you create is not only an `Employee` but also an `Object`. By using the type `Object` as a parameter, the `CompareTo()` method can accept anything. You will learn more about the `Object` class in the next chapter.

To work correctly in methods such as BinarySearch() and Sort(), the CompareTo() method you create for your class must return an integer value. Table 9-2 shows the return values that every version of CompareTo() should provide.

Return Value	Meaning
Negative	This instance is less than the compared object.
Zero	This instance is equal to the compared object.
Positive	This instance is greater than the compared object.

Table 9-2   Return values of IComparable.CompareTo() method

When you create a class that contains an IComparable.CompareTo() method, the method is an instance method and receives a this reference to the object used to call it. A second object is passed to the method; within the method, you first must convert, or cast, the passed object to the same type as the calling object's class and then compare the corresponding fields you want from the this object and the passed object. For example, Figure 9-40 shows an Employee class that contains a shaded CompareTo() method and compares Employee objects based on the contents of their idNumber fields.

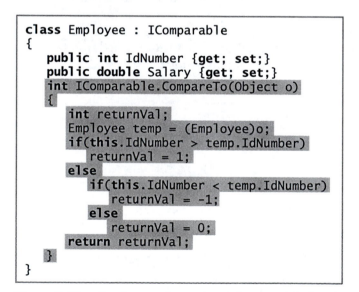

```
class Employee : IComparable
{
    public int IdNumber {get; set;}
    public double Salary {get; set;}
    int IComparable.CompareTo(Object o)
    {
        int returnVal;
        Employee temp = (Employee)o;
        if(this.IdNumber > temp.IdNumber)
            returnVal = 1;
        else
            if(this.IdNumber < temp.IdNumber)
                returnVal = -1;
            else
                returnVal = 0;
        return returnVal;
    }
}
```

Figure 9-40   Employee class using IComparable interface

The Employee class in Figure 9-40 uses a colon and IComparable in its class header to indicate an interface. The shaded method is an instance method; that is, it "belongs" to an Employee object.

When another Employee is passed in as Object o, it is cast as an Employee and stored in the temp variable. The idNumber values of the this Employee and the passed Employee are compared, and one of three integer values is returned.

For example, if you declare two Employee objects named worker1 and worker2, you can use the following statement:

```
int answer = worker1.CompareTo(worker2);
```

Within the CompareTo() method in the Employee class, worker1 would be "this" Employee—the controlling Employee in the method (the invoking Employee object). The temp Employee would be worker2. If, for example, worker1 had a higher ID number than worker2, the value of answer would be 1.

Figure 9-41 shows a program that uses the Employee class. The program declares an array of five Employee objects with different ID numbers and all with salaries of 0; the ID numbers are purposely out of order to demonstrate that the Sort() method works correctly. The program also declares a seekEmp object with an ID number of 222. The program sorts the array, displays the sorted elements, then finds the array element that matches the seekEmp object. Figure 9-42 shows the program execution.

```
using System;
using static System.Console;
class ComparableEmployeeArray
{
    static void Main()
    {
        Employee[] empArray = new Employee[5];
        int x;
        for(x = 0; x < empArray.Length; ++x)
            empArray[x] = new Employee();
        empArray[0].IdNumber = 333;
        empArray[1].IdNumber = 444;
        empArray[2].IdNumber = 555;
        empArray[3].IdNumber = 111;
        empArray[4].IdNumber = 222;
        Employee seekEmp = new Employee();
        seekEmp.IdNumber = 222;
        Array.Sort(empArray);
        WriteLine("Sorted employees:");
        for(x = 0; x < empArray.Length; ++x)
            WriteLine("Employee #{0}: {1} {2}", x,
                empArray[x].IdNumber, empArray[x].Salary.ToString("C"));
        x = Array.BinarySearch(empArray, seekEmp);
        WriteLine("Employee #{0} was found at position {1}",
            seekEmp.IdNumber, x);
    }
}
```

Figure 9-41   The ComparableEmployeeArray program

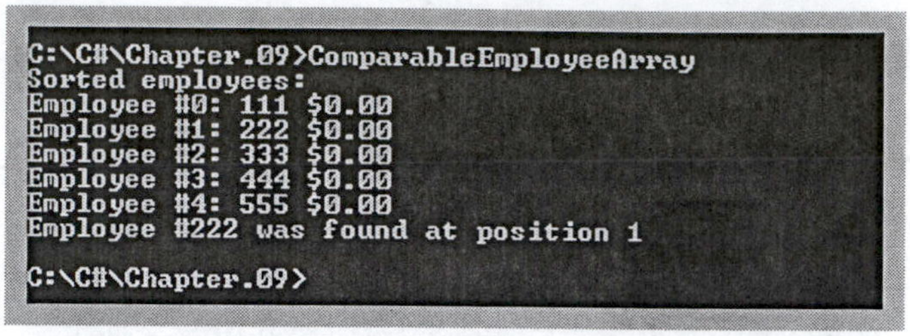

```
C:\C#\Chapter.09>ComparableEmployeeArray
Sorted employees:
Employee #0: 111 $0.00
Employee #1: 222 $0.00
Employee #2: 333 $0.00
Employee #3: 444 $0.00
Employee #4: 555 $0.00
Employee #222 was found at position 1

C:\C#\Chapter.09>
```

Figure 9-42　Output of the `ComparableEmployeeArray` program

Notice that the `seekEmp` object matches the `Employee` in the second array position based on the `idNumber` only—not the `salary`—because the `CompareTo()` method in the `Employee` class uses only `idNumber` values and not salaries to make comparisons. You *could* have written code that requires both the `idNumber` and salary values to match before returning a positive number.

TWO TRUTHS & A LIE

Declaring an Array of Objects

Assume that a working program contains the following array declaration:

```
BankAccount[] acctArray = new BankAccount[500];
```

1. This statement reserves enough computer memory for 500 `BankAccount` objects.

2. This statement constructs 500 `BankAccount` objects.

3. The valid subscripts for `acctArray` are 0 through 499.

The false statement is #2. This statement reserves space for 500 BankAccount objects but does not actually construct those objects; to do so, you must call the constructor 500 times.

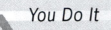

You Do It

Creating an Array of Objects

In the next steps, you create an array of Student objects. You prompt the user for data to fill the array, and you sort the array by student ID number before displaying all the data.

1. Open the **CreateStudents2** program and immediately save it as **CreateStudents3**. Change the class name to **CreateStudents3**.

2. Delete all the existing statements in the Main() method, leaving the opening and closing curly braces. Between the braces, declare an array of eight Student objects. Also declare a variable to use as an array subscript and declare three variables that will temporarily hold a user's input data before Student objects are constructed.

```
Student[] students = new Student[8];
int x;
int id;
string name;
double gpa;
```

3. In a loop, call a GetData() method (which you will write shortly). Send the method out arguments so that you can retrieve values for variables that will hold an ID number, name, and grade point average. Then, in turn, send these three values to the Student constructor for each of the eight Student objects.

```
for(x = 0; x < students.Length; ++x)
{
   GetData(out id, out name, out gpa);
   students[x] = new Student(id, name, gpa);
}
```

4. Call the Array.Sort() method, sending it the student array. Then, one object at a time in a loop, call the Display() method that you wrote in the last set of steps.

```
Array.Sort(students);
WriteLine("Sorted List:");
for(x = 0; x < students.Length; ++x)
   Display(students[x]);
```

(continues)

(continued)

5. Write the `GetData()` method. Its parameters are `out` parameters so that their values will be known to the calling method. The method simply prompts the user for each data item, reads it, and converts it to the appropriate type, if necessary.

```
static void GetData(out int id, out string name,
   out double gpa)
{
   string inString;
   Write("Please enter student ID number >> ");
   inString = ReadLine();
   int.TryParse(inString, out id);
   Write("Please enter last name for student {0} >> ",
      id);
   name = ReadLine();
   Write("Please enter grade point average >> ");
   inString = ReadLine();
   double.TryParse(inString, out gpa);
}
```

6. After the header for the `Student` class, add a colon and **`IComparable`** so that objects of the class can be sorted:

   `class Student : IComparable`

7. Just before the closing curly brace for the `Student` class, add the `IComparable.CompareTo()` method that is required for the objects of the class to be sortable. The method will sort `Student` objects based on their ID numbers, so it returns 1, −1, or 0 based on `IdNumber` property comparisons. The method accepts an object that is cast to a `Student` object. If the `IdNumber` of the controlling `Student` object is greater than the argument's `IdNumber`, then the return value is set to 1. If the `IdNumber` of the controlling `Student` object is less than the argument's `IdNumber`, then the return value is −1. Otherwise, the return value is 0.

```
int IComparable.CompareTo(Object o)
{
   int returnVal;
   Student temp = (Student)o;
   if(this.IdNumber > temp.IdNumber)
      returnVal = 1;
   else
      if(this.IdNumber < temp.IdNumber)
         returnVal = -1;
      else
         returnVal = 0;
   return returnVal;
}
```

(continues)

(continued)

8. Save the file, and then compile and execute it. When prompted, enter any student IDs, names, and grade point averages you choose. The objects will be sorted and displayed in `idNumber` order. Figure 9-43 shows a typical execution.

```
C:\C#\Chapter.09>CreateStudents3
Please enter student ID number >> 912
Please enter last name for student 912 >> Harris
Please enter grade point average >> 3.4
Please enter student ID number >> 634
Please enter last name for student 634 >> Lewis
Please enter grade point average >> 2.2
Please enter student ID number >> 610
Please enter last name for student 610 >> Johnson
Please enter grade point average >> 2.6
Please enter student ID number >> 377
Please enter last name for student 377 >> Lee
Please enter grade point average >> 4.0
Please enter student ID number >> 391
Please enter last name for student 391 >> Young
Please enter grade point average >> 3.9
Please enter student ID number >> 215
Please enter last name for student 215 >> Jenks
Please enter grade point average >> 3.8
Please enter student ID number >> 185
Please enter last name for student 185 >> Bower
Please enter grade point average >> 2.3
Please enter student ID number >> 478
Please enter last name for student 478 >> Cooper
Please enter grade point average >> 2.6
Sorted List:
   185   Bower         2.3
   215   Jenks         3.8
   377   Lee           4.0
   391   Young         3.9
   478   Cooper        2.6
   610   Johnson       2.6
   634   Lewis         2.2
   912   Harris        3.4

C:\C#\Chapter.09>_
```

Figure 9-43   Typical execution of the `CreateStudents3` program

Understanding Destructors

A **destructor** contains the actions you require when an instance of a class is destroyed. Most often, an instance of a class is destroyed when it goes out of scope. As with constructors, if you do not explicitly create a destructor for a class, C# automatically provides one.

To explicitly declare a destructor, you use an identifier that consists of a tilde (~) followed by the class name. You cannot provide any arguments when you call a destructor; it must have an empty parameter list. As a consequence, destructors cannot be overloaded; a class can have one destructor at most. Like a constructor, a destructor has no return type.

Figure 9-44 shows an `Employee` class that contains only one field (`idNumber`), a property, a constructor, and a (shaded) destructor. When you execute the `Main()` method in the `DemoEmployeeDestructor` class in Figure 9-45, you instantiate two `Employee` objects, each with its own `idNumber` value. When the `Main()` method ends, the two `Employee` objects go out of scope, and the destructor for each object is called. Figure 9-46 shows the output.

```
class Employee
{
    public int idNumber {get; set;}
    public Employee(int empID)
    {
        IdNumber = empID;
        WriteLine("Employee object {0} created", IdNumber);
    }
    ~Employee()
    {
        WriteLine("Employee object {0} destroyed!", IdNumber);
    }
}
```

Figure 9-44   Employee class with destructor

```
using static System.Console;
class DemoEmployeeDestructor
{
    static void Main()
    {
        Employee aWorker = new Employee(101);
        Employee anotherWorker = new Employee(202);
    }
}
```

Figure 9-45   The DemoEmployeeDestructor program

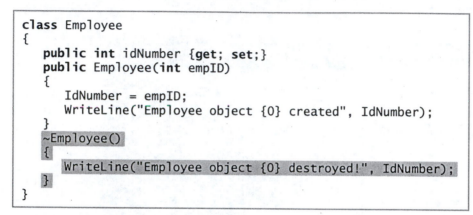

```
C:\C#\Chapter.09>DemoEmployeeDestructor
Employee object 101 created
Employee object 202 created
Employee object 202 destroyed!
Employee object 101 destroyed!

C:\C#\Chapter.09>
```

Figure 9-46   Output of DemoEmployeeDestructor program

The program in Figure 9-44 never explicitly calls the Employee class destructor, yet you can see from the output that the destructor executes twice. Destructors are invoked automatically; you cannot explicitly call one. Interestingly, the last object created is the first object destroyed; the same relationship would hold true no matter how many objects the program instantiated.

An instance of a class becomes eligible for destruction when it is no longer possible for any code to use it—that is, when it goes out of scope. The actual execution of an object's destructor might occur at any time after the object becomes eligible for destruction.

For now, you have little reason to create a destructor except to demonstrate how it is called automatically. Later, when you write more sophisticated C# programs that work with files, databases, or large quantities of computer memory, you might want to perform specific cleanup or close-down tasks when an object goes out of scope. Then you will place appropriate instructions within a destructor.

TWO TRUTHS & A LIE

Understanding Destructors

1. To explicitly declare a destructor, you use an identifier that consists of a tilde (~) followed by the class name.

2. You cannot provide any parameters to a destructor; it must have an empty argument list.

3. The return type for a destructor is always void.

The false statement is #3. Like a constructor, a destructor has no return type.

Understanding GUI Application Objects

The objects you have been using in GUI applications, such as Forms, Buttons, and Labels, are objects just like others you have studied in this chapter. That is, they encapsulate properties and methods. When you start a Windows Forms application in the IDE and drag a Button onto a Form, a statement is automatically created to instantiate a Button object.

Figure 9-47 shows a new GUI application that a programmer started simply by dragging one Button onto a Form.

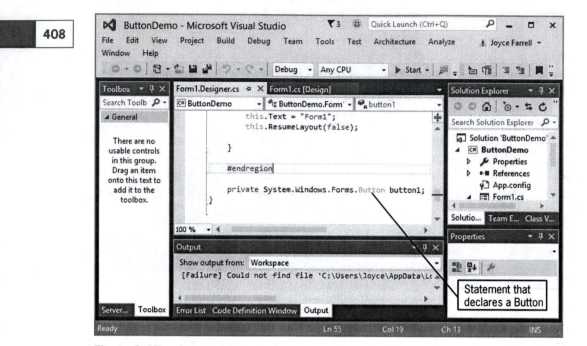

Figure 9-47   A Button on a Form

If you click on Form1.Designer.cs in the Solution Explorer and scroll down, you can display the code where the **Button** is declared. See Figure 9-48.

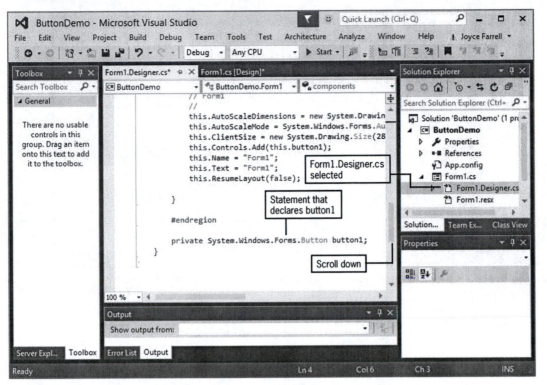

Figure 9-48 The automatically generated statement that declares button1

If you right-click **button1** in the code and select Find All References from the menu that appears, a list of every reference to **button1** in the project is displayed in the Find Symbol Results area at the bottom of the IDE. (You might need to resize the window to see the references clearly.) You can double-click each entry in the list in turn to locate all the places where code has been generated for **button1**. For example, several instances of **button1** are in a method named **InitializeComponent()**, as shown in Figure 9-49. The first reference to **button1** calls its constructor. You can also see how the **Button's Name**, **Location**, **Size**, and other properties are set. You could have written these statements yourself, especially now that you know more about objects and how they are constructed, but it is easier to develop an application visually by dragging a **Button** onto a **Form** and allowing the IDE to create these statements for you.

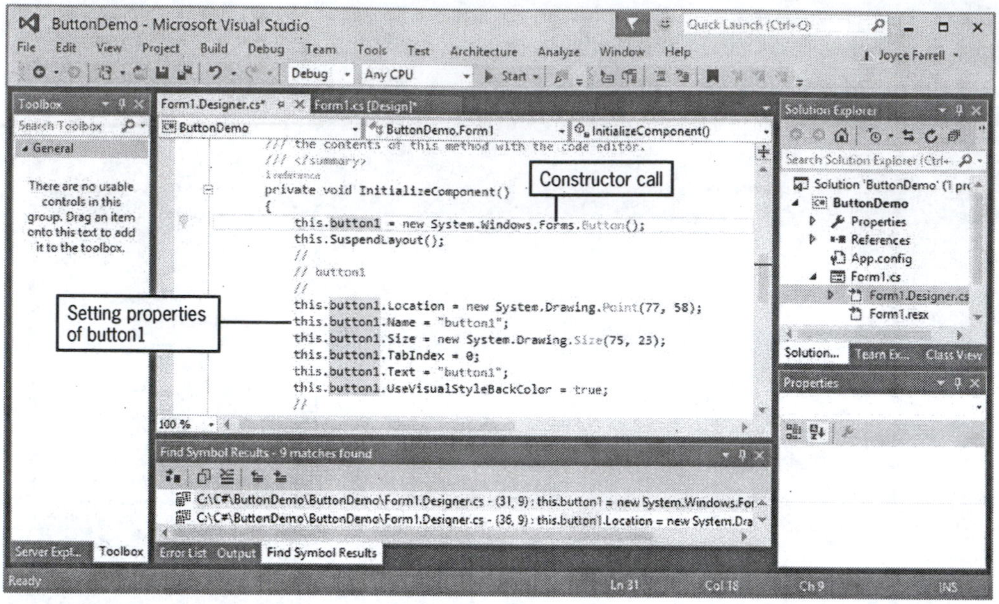

Figure 9-49   Some automatically generated `button1` references in the IDE

In Figure 9-49, the `this` reference preceding each occurrence of `button1` refers to the class (`Form1`) that contains these statements.

> Now that you understand how to create properties in your own classes, you can understand the properties of GUI objects and how they were created for your use.

Chapter Summary

- Application classes contain a `Main()` method. You also can create classes from which you instantiate objects; these classes need not have a `Main()` method. The data components of a class are its instance variables (or fields) and methods. A program or class that instantiates objects of another prewritten class is a class client or class user.

- When you create a class, you must assign a name to it and determine what data and methods will be part of the class. A class header or class definition contains an optional access modifier, the keyword `class`, and an identifier. A class body is enclosed between curly braces. When you create a class, you usually declare instance variables to be `private` and instance methods to be `public`.

- When you create an object that is an instance of a class, you supply a type and an identifier, and you allocate computer memory for that object using the **new** operator. After an object has been instantiated, its **public** methods can be accessed using the object's identifier, a dot, and a method call. You can pass objects to methods just as you can pass simple data types.

- A property is a member of a class that provides access to a field. Properties have **set** accessors for setting an object's fields and **get** accessors for retrieving the stored values. As a shortcut, you can create an auto-implemented property when a field's **set** accessor should simply assign a value to the appropriate field, and when its **get** accessor should simply return the field.

- In most classes, fields are **private** and methods are **public**. This technique ensures that data will be used and changed only in the ways provided in the class's accessors. Occasionally, however, you need to create **public** fields or **private** methods.

- The **this** reference is passed to every instance method and property accessor in a class. You can explicitly refer to the **this** reference within an instance method or property, but usually you are not required to do so.

- A constructor is a method that instantiates an object. If you do not write a constructor, then each class is automatically supplied with a **public** constructor with no parameters. You can write your own constructor to replace the automatically supplied version. Any constructor you write must have the same name as its class, and constructors cannot have a return type. You can overload constructors and pass arguments to a constructor.

- An object initializer allows you to assign values to any accessible members or properties of a class at the time of instantiation without calling a constructor with parameters. Using object initializers allows you to create multiple objects with different initial assignments without having to provide multiple constructors to cover every possible situation. Additionally, using object initializers allows you to create objects with different starting values for different properties of the same data type.

- You can overload an operator by writing a method whose identifier is **operator**, followed by the operator being overloaded—for example, **operator+()** or **operator*()**. When you overload an operator, you should write statements that intuitively have the same meaning as the common use of the operator.

- You can declare arrays of references to objects. After doing so, you must call a constructor to instantiate each object. To use a method that belongs to an object that is part of an array, you insert the appropriate subscript notation after the array name and before the dot-method. The **IComparable** interface contains the definition for the **CompareTo()** method; you override this method to tell the compiler how to compare objects.

- A destructor contains the actions you require when an instance of a class is destroyed. If you do not explicitly create a destructor for a class, C# automatically provides one. To explicitly declare a destructor, you use an identifier that consists of a tilde (~) followed by the class name. You cannot provide any parameters to a destructor; a class can have one destructor at most.

- GUI objects such as `Forms`, `Buttons`, and `Labels` are typical C# objects that encapsulate properties and methods. When you start a Windows Forms application and drag a component onto a `Form`, statements are automatically created by the IDE to instantiate the object and assign values to some of its properties.

Key Terms

To **instantiate** an object is to create it.

An **instantiation** of a class is a created object.

An **instance** of a class is one object, or one instantiation.

The **instance variables** of a class are the data components that exist separately for each instantiation.

Fields are instance variables within a class.

Instance methods are methods that are used with object instantiations.

A **class client** or **class user** is a program or class that instantiates objects of another prewritten class.

A **class header** or **class definition** describes a class; it contains an optional access modifier, the keyword `class`, and any legal identifier for the name of the class.

A **class access modifier** describes access to a class.

The **public** class access modifier means access to the class is not limited.

The **protected** class access modifier means access to the class is limited to the class and to any classes derived from the class.

The **internal** class access modifier means access is limited to the assembly to which the class belongs.

The **private** class access modifier means access is limited to another class to which the class belongs. In other words, a class can be `private` if it is contained within another class, and only the containing class should have access to the `private` class.

An **assembly** is a group of code modules compiled together to create an executable program.

Information hiding is a feature found in all object-oriented languages, in which a class's data is private and changed or manipulated only by its own methods.

Composition is the technique of using an object within another object.

A **has-a relationship** is the relationship created using composition, so-called because one class "has an" instance of another.

A **reference type** is a type that holds a memory address.

Value types hold a value; they include predefined types such as `int`, `double`, and `char`.

An **invoking object** is an object that calls an instance method.

A **property** is a member of a class that provides access to a field of a class; properties define how fields will be set and retrieved.

Accessors in properties specify how a class's fields are accessed.

The **set accessors** of a class allow assignment of values to fields using a property name.

The **get accessors** of a class allow retrieval of a field value by using a property name.

A **backing field** is a field that has a property coded for it.

A **read-only property** has only a get accessor, and not a set accessor.

The **getter** is another term for a class property's get accessor.

The **setter** is another term for a class property's set accessor.

Contextual keywords are identifiers that act like keywords in specific circumstances.

An **implicit parameter** is undeclared and gets its value automatically.

An **auto-implemented property** is one in which the code within the accessors is created automatically. The only action in the set accessor is to assign a value to the associated field, and the only action in the get accessor is to return the associated field value.

Automatic properties are auto-implemented properties.

The **this reference** is the reference to an object that is implicitly passed to an instance method of its class.

A **constructor** is a method that instantiates (creates an instance of) an object.

A **default constructor** is a parameterless constructor.

The **default value of an object** is the value initialized with a default constructor.

A **parameterless constructor** is one that takes no arguments.

A **constructor initializer** is a clause that indicates another instance of a class constructor should be executed before any statements in the current constructor body.

An **object initializer** allows you to assign values to any accessible members or properties of a class at the time of instantiation without calling a constructor with parameters.

An **abstract method** has no method statements.

An **interface** is a collection of abstract methods (and perhaps other members) that can be used by any class, as long as the class provides a definition to override the interface's do-nothing, or abstract, method definitions.

To **override** a method is to take precedence over another method version.

A **destructor** contains the actions required when an instance of a class is destroyed.

Review Questions

1. An object is a(n) _____ of a class.

   a. child

   b. institution

   c. instantiation

   d. relative

414

2. A class header or class definition can contain all of the following *except* _____.

   a. an optional access modifier

   b. the keyword `class`

   c. an identifier

   d. initial field values

3. Most fields in a class are created with the _____ modifier.

   a. `public`

   b. `protected`

   c. `new`

   d. `private`

4. Most methods in a class are created with the _____ modifier.

   a. `public`

   b. `protected`

   c. `new`

   d. `private`

5. Instance methods that belong to individual objects are _____ `static` methods.

   a. always

   b. usually

   c. occasionally

   d. never

6. To allocate memory for an object instantiation, you must use the _____ operator.

   a. `mem`

   b. `alloc`

   c. `new`

   d. `instant`

7. Assume that you have created a class named `MyClass`. The header of the `MyClass` constructor can be _____.

   a. `public void MyClass()`

   b. `public MyClassConstructor()`

   c. Either of these can be the constructor header.

   d. Neither of these can be the constructor header.

8. Assume that you have created a class named `MyClass`. The header of the `MyClass` constructor can be _____.

   a. `public MyClass()`

   b. `public MyClass (double d)`

   c. Either of these can be the constructor header.

   d. Neither of these can be the constructor header.

9. Assume that you have created a class named `DemoCar`. Within the `Main()` method of this class, you instantiate a `Car` object named `myCar` and the following statement executes correctly:

   ```
   WriteLine("The Car gets {0} miles per gallon",
       myCar.ComputeMpg());
   ```

   Within the `Car` class, the `ComputeMpg()` method can be _____.

   a. **public** and **static**

   b. **public** and nonstatic

   c. **private** and **static**

   d. **private** and nonstatic

10. Assume that you have created a class named `TermPaper` that contains a character field named `letterGrade`. You also have created a property for the field. Which of the following cannot be true?

    a. The property name is `letterGrade`.

    b. The property is read-only.

    c. The property contains a `set` accessor that does not allow a grade lower than 'C'.

    d. The property does not contain a `get` accessor.

11. A `this` reference is _____.

    a. implicitly passed to nonstatic methods

    b. implicitly passed to `static` methods

    c. explicitly passed to nonstatic methods

    d. explicitly passed to `static` methods

12. When you use an instance variable within a class's nonstatic methods, you _____ explicitly refer to the method's `this` reference.

    a. must

    b. can

    c. cannot

    d. should (even though it is not required)

13. A class's default constructor _____.

    a.　sets numeric fields to 0

    b.　is parameterless

    c.　both of these

    d.　none of these

14. Assume that you have created a class named `Chair` with a constructor defined as `Chair(int height)`. Which of the following overloaded constructors could coexist with the `Chair` constructor without ambiguity?

    a.　`Chair(int legs)`

    b.　`Chair(int height, int legs)`

    c.　both of these

    d.　none of these

15. Which of the following statements correctly instantiates a `House` object if the `House` class contains a single constructor with the declaration `House(int bedrooms, double price)`?

    a.　`House myHouse = new House();`

    b.　`House myHouse = new House(3, 125000.00);`

    c.　`House myHouse = House(4, 200000.00);`

    d.　two of these

16. You explicitly call a destructor _____.

    a.　when you are finished using an object

    b.　when an object goes out of scope

    c.　when a class is destroyed

    d.　You cannot explicitly call a destructor.

17. In a program that creates five object instances of a class, the constructor executes _____ time(s) and the destructor executes _____ time(s).

    a.　one; one

    b.　one; five

    c.　five; one

    d.　five; five

18. Suppose that you declare a class named **Furniture** that contains a **string** field named **woodType** and a conventionally named property with a **get** accessor. When you declare an array of 200 **Furniture** objects named **myChairs**, which of the following accesses the last **Furniture** object's wood type?

    a. Furniture.Get(woodType[199])

    b. myChairs[199].WoodType()

    c. myChairs.WoodType[199]

    d. myChairs[199].WoodType

19. A collection of methods that can be used by any class, as long as the class provides a definition to override the collection's abstract definitions, is _____.

    a. a superclass

    b. a polymorph

    c. a perimeter

    d. an interface

20. When you create a class and want to include the capability to compare its objects so they can use the **Array.Sort()** or **Array.BinarySearch()** method, you must _____.

    a. include at least one numeric field within the class

    b. write a **CompareTo()** method for the class

    c. be careful not to override the existing **IComparable.CompareTo()** method

    d. Two of these are true.

Exercises

 Programming Exercises

For each of the following programming exercises, you may choose to write a console-based or GUI application, or both.

1. Create an application named **TestHockeyPlayer** that instantiates and displays a **HockeyPlayer** object. The **HockeyPlayer** class contains fields for a player's name (a string), jersey number (an integer), and goals scored (an integer).

2. Create an application named **TestClassifiedAd** that instantiates and displays a ClassifiedAd object. A ClassifiedAd has fields for a category (for example, *Used Cars*), a number of words, and a price. Include properties that contain get and set accessors for the category and number of words, but only a get accessor for the price. The price is calculated at nine cents per word.

3. Create an application named **SalesTransactionDemo** that declares several SalesTransaction objects and displays their values and their sum. The SalesTransaction class contains fields for a salesperson name, sales amount, and commission and a readonly field that stores the commission rate. Include three constructors for the class. One constructor accepts values for the name, sales amount, and rate, and when the sales value is set, the constructor computes the commission as sales value times commission rate. The second constructor accepts a name and sales amount, but sets the commission rate to 0. The third constructor accepts a name and sets all the other fields to 0. An overloaded + operator adds the sales values for two SalesTransaction objects.

4. Create a program named **TilingDemo** that instantiates an array of 10 Room objects and demonstrates its methods. The Room constructor requires parameters for length and width fields; use a variety of values when constructing the objects. The Room class also contains a field for floor area of the Room and number of boxes of tile needed to tile the room. Both of these values are computed by calling private methods. A room requires one box of tile for every 12 full square feet plus a box for any partial square footage over 12, plus one extra box for waste from irregular cuts. In other words, a 122 square foot room requires 12 boxes—10 boxes for the first 120 square feet, 1 box for the 2 extra square feet over 120, and 1 box for waste. Include read-only properties to get a Room's values.

5. Create an application named **CarDemo** that declares at least two Car objects and demonstrates how they can be incremented using an overloaded ++ operator. Create a Car class that contains a model and a value for miles per gallon. Include two overloaded constructors. One accepts parameters for the model and miles per gallon; the other accepts a model and sets the miles per gallon to 20. Overload a ++ operator that increases the miles per gallon value by 1. The CarDemo application creates at least one Car using each constructor and displays the Car values both before and after incrementation.

6. a. Create a program named **TaxPayerDemo** that declares an array of 10 Taxpayer objects. Prompt the user for data for each object and display the 10 objects. Data fields for Taxpayer objects include the Social Security number (use a string for the type, but do not use dashes within the Social Security number), the yearly gross income, and the income tax owed. Include a property with get and set accessors for the first two data fields, but make the tax owed a read-only property.

The tax should be calculated whenever the income is set. Assume that the tax rate is 15 percent for incomes under $30,000 and 28 percent for incomes that are $30,000 or higher.

b. Create a program named **TaxpayerDemo2** so that after the 10 Taxpayer objects are displayed, they are sorted in order by the amount of tax owed and displayed again. Modify the Taxpayer class so its objects are comparable to each other based on tax owed.

7. Create an application named **ShirtDemo** that declares several Shirt objects and includes a display method to which you can pass different numbers of Shirt objects in successive method calls. The Shirt class contains auto-implemented properties for a material, color, and size.

8. Create a program named **ConferencesDemo** for a hotel that hosts business conferences. Allows a user to enter data about five Conference objects and then displays them in order of attendance from smallest to largest. The Conference class contains fields for the Conference group name, starting date (as a string), and number of attendees. Include properties for each field. Also, include an IComparable.CompareTo() method so that Conference objects can be sorted.

9. a. Create a program named **RelativesList** that declares an array of at least 12 Relative objects and prompts the user to enter data about them. The Relative class includes auto-implemented properties for the Relative's name, relationship to you (for example, *aunt*), and three integers that together represent the Relative's birthday—month, day, and year. Display the Relative objects in alphabetical order by first name.

   b. Create a **RelativesBirthday** program that modifies the RelativeList program so that after the alphabetical list is displayed, the program prompts the user for a specific Relative's name and the program returns the Relative's relationship and birthday. Display an appropriate message if the relative requested by the user is not found.

10. a. Write a program named **DemoJobs** for Harold's Home Services. The program should instantiate several Job objects and demonstrate their methods. The Job class contains four data fields—description (for example, "wash windows"), time in hours to complete (for example, 3.5), per-hour rate charged (for example, $25.00), and total fee (hourly rate times hours). Include properties to get and set each field except the total fee—that field will be read-only, and its value is calculated each time either the hourly fee or the number of hours is set. Overload the + operator so that two Jobs can be added. The sum of two Jobs is a new Job containing the descriptions of both original Jobs (joined by *and*), the sum of the time in hours for the original Jobs, and the average of the hourly rate for the original Jobs.

b. Harold has realized that his method for computing the fee for combined jobs is not fair. For example, consider the following:

- His fee for painting a house is $100 per hour. If a job takes 10 hours, he earns $1000.

- His fee for dog walking is $10 per hour. If a job takes 1 hour, he earns $10.

- If he combines the two jobs and works a total of 11 hours, he earns only the average rate of $55 per hour, or $605.

Devise an improved, weighted method for calculating Harold's fees for combined Jobs and include it in the overloaded operator+() method. Write a program named **DemoJobs2** that demonstrates all the methods in the class work correctly.

11. a. Write a **FractionDemo** program that instantiates several Fraction objects and demonstrates that their methods work correctly. Create a Fraction class with fields that hold a whole number, a numerator, and a denominator. In addition:

- Create properties for each field. The set accessor for the denominator should not allow a 0 value; the value defaults to 1.

- Add three constructors. One takes three parameters for a whole number, numerator, and denominator. Another accepts two parameters for the numerator and denominator; when this constructor is used, the whole number value is 0. The last constructor is parameterless; it sets the whole number and numerator to 0 and the denominator to 1. (After construction, Fractions do not have to be reduced to proper form. For example, even though 3/9 could be reduced to 1/3, your constructors do not have to perform this task.)

- Add a Reduce() method that reduces a Fraction if it is in improper form. For example, 2/4 should be reduced to 1/2.

- Add an operator+() method that adds two Fractions. To add two fractions, first eliminate any whole number part of the value. For example, 2 1/4 becomes 9/4 and 1 3/5 becomes 8/5. Find a common denominator and convert the fractions to it. For example, when adding 9/4 and 8/5, you can convert them to 45/20 and 32/20. Then you can add the numerators, giving 77/20. Finally, call the Reduce() method to reduce the result, restoring any whole number value so the fractional part of the number is less than 1. For example, 77/20 becomes 3 17/20.

- Include a function that returns a string that contains a Fraction in the usual display format—the whole number, a space, the numerator, a slash (/), and a denominator. When the whole number is 0, just the Fraction part of the value should be displayed (for example, 1/2 instead of 0 1/2). If the numerator is 0, just the whole number should be displayed (for example, 2 instead of 2 0/3).

b. Add an **operator*()** method to the **Fraction** class created in Exercise 11a so that it correctly multiplies two **Fraction**s. The result should be in proper, reduced format. Demonstrate that the method works correctly in a program named **FractionDemo2**.

c. Write a program named **FractionDemo3** that includes an array of four **Fraction**s. Prompt the user for values for each. Display every possible combination of addition results and every possible combination of multiplication results for each **Fraction** pair (that is, each type will have 16 results).

Debugging Exercises

1. Each of the following files in the Chapter.09 folder of your downloadable student files has syntax and/or logical errors. In each case, determine the problem and fix the program. After you correct the errors, save each file using the same filename preceded with *Fixed*. For example, DebugNine1.cs will become FixedDebugNine1.cs.

    a. DebugNine1.cs

    b. DebugNine2.cs

    c. DebugNine3.cs

    d. DebugNine4.cs

Case Problems

1. In previous chapters, you have created programs for the Greenville Idol competition. Now create a **Contestant** class with the following characteristics:

    *   The **Contestant** class contains public static arrays that hold talent codes and descriptions. Recall that the talent categories are *Singing, Dancing, Musical instrument,* and *Other.*

    *   The class contains an auto-implemented property that holds a contestant's name.

    *   The class contains fields for a talent code and description. The **set** accessor for the code assigns a code only if it is valid. Otherwise, it assigns *I* for *Invalid*. The talent description is a read-only property that is assigned a value when the code is set.

Modify the **GreenvilleRevenue** program so that it uses the `Contestant` class and performs the following tasks:

- The program prompts the user for the number of contestants in this year's competition; the number must be between 0 and 30. The program continues to prompt the user until a valid value is entered.

- The expected revenue is calculated and displayed. The revenue is $25 per contestant.

- The program prompts the user for names and talent codes for each contestant entered. Along with the prompt for a talent code, display a list of the valid categories.

- After data entry is complete, the program displays the valid talent categories and then continuously prompts the user for talent codes and displays the names of all contestants in the category. Appropriate messages are displayed if the entered code is not a character or a valid code.

2. In previous chapters, you have created programs for Marshall's Murals. Now create a `Mural` class with the following characteristics:

- The `Mural` class contains public static arrays that hold mural codes and descriptions. Recall that the mural categories are *Landscape, Seascape, Abstract, Children's*, and *Other*.

- The class contains an auto-implemented property that holds a mural customer's name.

- The class contains fields for a mural code and description. The `set` accessor for the code assigns a code only if it is valid. Otherwise, it assigns *I* for *Invalid*. The mural description is a read-only property that is assigned a value when the code is set.

Modify the **MarshallsRevenue** program so that it uses the Mural class and performs the following tasks:

- The program prompts the user for the month, the number of interior murals scheduled, and the number of exterior murals scheduled. In each case, the program continues to prompt the user until valid entries are made.

- The expected revenue is calculated and displayed. Recall that exterior murals cannot be painted in December through February. Also recall that exterior murals are $750 in all months except April, May, September, and October, when they are $699. Interior murals are $500 except during July and August, when they are $450.

- The program prompts the user for names and mural codes for interior and exterior murals. Along with the prompt for a mural code, display a list of the valid categories.

- After data entry is complete, the program displays the valid mural categories and then continuously prompts the user for codes and displays the names of all customers ordering murals in the category. Appropriate messages are displayed if the entered code is not a character or a valid code.

CHAPTER 10

Introduction to Inheritance

In this chapter you will:

- ◎ Learn about inheritance
- ◎ Extend classes
- ◎ Use the `protected` access specifier
- ◎ Override base class members
- ◎ Understand how a derived class object "is an" instance of the base class
- ◎ Learn about the `Object` class
- ◎ Work with base class constructors
- ◎ Create and use abstract classes
- ◎ Create and use interfaces
- ◎ Use extension methods
- ◎ Recognize inheritance in GUI applications and understand the benefits of inheritance

Understanding classes helps you organize objects. Understanding inheritance helps you organize them more precisely. If you have never heard of a *Braford*, for example, you would have a hard time forming a picture of one in your mind. When you learn that a Braford is an animal, you gain some understanding of what it must be like. That understanding grows when you learn it is a mammal, and the understanding is almost complete when you learn it is a cow. When you learn that a Braford is a cow, you understand it has many characteristics that are common to all cows. To identify a Braford, you must learn only relatively minor details—its color or markings, for example. Most of a Braford's characteristics, however, derive from its membership in a particular hierarchy of classes: animal, mammal, and cow.

All object-oriented programming languages make use of inheritance for the same reasons—to organize the objects used by programs, and to make new objects easier to understand based on your knowledge of their inherited traits. In this chapter, you will learn to make use of inheritance with your C# objects.

Understanding Inheritance

Inheritance is the principle that you can apply your knowledge of a general category to more specific objects. You are familiar with the concept of inheritance from all sorts of situations. When you use the term *inheritance*, you might think of genetic inheritance. You know from biology that your blood type and eye color are the products of inherited genes. You can say that many other facts about you (your attributes) are inherited. Similarly, you often can attribute your behaviors to inheritance; for example, the way you handle money might be similar to the way your grandmother handles it, and your gait might be the same as your father's—so your methods are inherited, too.

You also might choose to own plants and animals based on their inherited attributes. You plant impatiens next to your house because they thrive in the shade; you adopt a poodle because you know poodles don't shed. Every plant and pet has slightly different characteristics, but within a species, you can count on many consistent inherited attributes and behaviors. In other words, you can reuse the knowledge you gain about general categories and apply it to more specific categories. Similarly, the classes you create in object-oriented programming languages can inherit data and methods from existing classes. When you create a class by making it inherit from another class, you are provided with data fields and methods automatically; you can reuse fields and methods that are already written and tested.

You already know how to create classes and how to instantiate objects from those classes. For example, consider the `Employee` class in Figure 10-1. The class contains two data fields, `idNum` and `salary`, as well as properties that contain accessors for each field and a method that creates an `Employee` greeting.

```
class Employee
{
    private int idNum;
    private double salary;
    public int IdNum
    {
        get
        {
            return idNum;
        }
        set
        {
            idNum = value;
        }
    }
    public double Salary
    {
        get
        {
            return salary;
        }
        set
        {
            salary = value;
        }
    }
    public string GetGreeting()
    {
        string greeting = "Hello. I am employee #" + IdNum;
        return greeting;
    }
}
```

Figure 10-1   The Employee class

After you create the Employee class, you can create specific Employee objects, as in the following:

```
Employee receptionist = new Employee();
Employee deliveryPerson = new Employee();
```

These Employee objects can eventually possess different numbers and salaries, but because they are Employee objects, you know that each possesses *some* ID number and salary.

Suppose that you hire a new type of Employee who earns a commission as well as a salary. You can create a class with a name such as CommissionEmployee, and provide this class with three fields (idNum, salary, and commissionRate), three properties (with accessors to get and set each of the three fields), and a greeting method. However, this work would duplicate much of the work that you already have done for the Employee class. The wise and efficient alternative is to create the class CommissionEmployee so it inherits all the attributes and methods of Employee. Then, you can add just the single field and property with two accessors that are additions within CommissionEmployee objects. Figure 10-2 depicts these relationships.

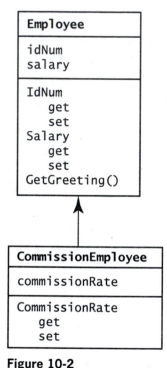

Figure 10-2
CommissionEmployee inherits from Employee

In class diagrams, the convention is to provide three sections for the class name, its data, and its methods, respectively. The upward-pointing arrow between the classes in Figure 10-2 indicates that the class on the bottom inherits from the one on the top. Using an arrow in this way is conventional in **Unified Modeling Language (UML) diagrams**, which are graphical tools that programmers and analysts use to describe systems.

When you use inheritance to create the CommissionEmployee class, you acquire the following benefits:

- You save time, because you need not re-create the Employee fields, properties, and methods.

- You reduce the chance of errors, because the Employee properties and methods have already been used and tested.

- You make it easier for anyone who has used the Employee class to understand the CommissionEmployee class because such users can concentrate on the new features only.

The ability to use inheritance makes programs easier to write, easier to understand, and less prone to errors. Imagine that besides CommissionEmployee, you want to create several other specific Employee classes (perhaps PartTimeEmployee, including a field for hours worked, or DismissedEmployee, including a reason for dismissal). By using inheritance, you can develop each new class correctly and more quickly.

In part, the concept of class inheritance is useful because it makes class code reusable and development faster. However, you do not use inheritance simply to save work. When properly used, inheritance always involves a general-to-specific relationship.

Understanding Inheritance Terminology

A class that is used as a basis for inheritance, like `Employee`, is called a **base class**. When you create a class that inherits from a base class (such as `CommissionEmployee`), it is a **derived class** or **extended class**. When presented with two classes that have a parent-child relationship, you can tell which class is the base class and which is the derived class by using the two classes in a sentence with the phrase "is a." A derived class always "is a" case or instance of the more general base class. For example, a `Tree` class may be a base class to an `Evergreen` class. Every `Evergreen` "is a" `Tree`; however, it is not true that every `Tree` is an `Evergreen`. Thus, `Tree` is the base class, and `Evergreen` is the derived class. Similarly, a `CommissionEmployee` "is an" `Employee`—not always the other way around—so `Employee` is the base class and `CommissionEmployee` is derived.

You can use the terms **superclass** and **subclass** as synonyms for base class and derived class. Thus, `Evergreen` can be called a subclass of the `Tree` superclass. You also can use the terms **parent class** and **child class**. A `CommissionEmployee` is a child to the `Employee` parent. Use the pair of terms with which you are most comfortable; all of these terms will be used interchangeably in this book.

As an alternative way to discover which of two classes is the base class and which is the derived class, you can try saying the two class names together (although this technique might not work with every superclass-subclass pair). When people say their names together in the English language, they state the more specific name before the all-encompassing family name, such as *Ginny Kroening*. Similarly, with classes, the order that "makes more sense" is the child-parent order. Thus, because *Evergreen Tree* makes more sense than *Tree Evergreen*, you can deduce that `Evergreen` is the child class. It also is convenient to think of a derived class as building upon its base class by providing the "adjectives" or additional descriptive terms for the "noun." Frequently, the names of derived classes are formed in this way, as in `CommissionEmployee`.

Finally, you usually can distinguish base classes from their derived classes by size. A derived class is larger than a base class, in the sense that it usually has additional fields and methods. A derived class description may look small, but any subclass contains all the fields and methods of its superclass as well as its own more specific fields and methods. Do not think of a subclass as a "subset" of another class—in other words, possessing only parts of its superclass. In fact, a derived class contains everything in the superclass, plus any new attributes and methods.

A derived class can be further extended. In other words, a subclass can have a child of its own. For example, after you create a `Tree` class and derive `Evergreen`, you might derive a `Spruce` class from `Evergreen`. Similarly, a `Poodle` class might derive from `Dog`, `Dog` from

DomesticPet, and DomesticPet from Animal. The entire list of parent classes from which a child class is derived constitutes the **ancestors** of the subclass.

After you create the Spruce class, you might be ready to create Spruce objects. For example, you might create theTreeInMyBackYard, or you might create an array of 1000 Spruce objects for a tree farm. Similarly, one Poodle object might be myPetDogFifi.

Inheritance is **transitive**, which means a child inherits all the members of all its ancestors. In other words, when you declare a Spruce object, it contains all the attributes and methods of both an Evergreen and a Tree. As you work with C#, you will encounter many examples of such transitive chains of inheritance.

When you create your own transitive inheritance chains, you want to place fields and methods at their most general level. In other words, a method named Grow() rightfully belongs in a Tree class, whereas LeavesTurnColor() does not, because the method applies to only some of the Tree child classes. Similarly, a LeavesTurnColor() method would be better located in a Deciduous class than separately within the Oak or Maple child class.

TWO TRUTHS & A LIE

Understanding Inheritance

1. When you use inheritance to create a class, you save time because you can copy and paste fields, properties, and methods that have already been created for the original class.

2. When you use inheritance to create a class, you reduce the chance of errors because the original class's properties and methods have already been used and tested.

3. When you use inheritance to create a class, you make it easier for anyone who has used the original class to understand the new class because such users can concentrate on the new features.

The false statement is #1. When you use inheritance to create a class, you save time because you need not re-create fields, properties, and methods that have already been created for the original class. You do not copy these class members; you inherit them.

Extending Classes

When you create a class that is an extension or child of another class, you use a single colon between the derived class name and its base class name. For example, the following class header creates a subclass-superclass relationship between CommissionEmployee and Employee.

```
class CommissionEmployee : Employee
```

Each CommissionEmployee object automatically contains the fields and methods of the base class; you then can add new fields and methods to the new derived class. Figure 10-3 shows a CommissionEmployee class.

```
class CommissionEmployee : Employee
{
    private double commissionRate;
    public double CommissionRate
    {
        get
        {
            return commissionRate;
        }
        set
        {
            commissionRate = value;
        }
    }
}
```

Figure 10-3 The CommissionEmployee class

Although you see only one field defined in the CommissionEmployee class in Figure 10-3, it contains three fields: idNum and salary, inherited from Employee, and commissionRate, which is defined within the CommissionEmployee class. Similarly, the CommissionEmployee class contains three properties and a method—two properties and the method are inherited from Employee, and one property is defined within CommissionEmployee itself. When you write a program that instantiates an object using the following statement, then you can use any of the next statements to set field values for the salesperson:

```
CommissionEmployee salesperson = new CommissionEmployee();
salesperson.IdNum = 234;
salesperson.Salary = Convert.ToDouble(ReadLine());
salesperson.CommissionRate = 0.07;
```

The salesperson object has access to all three set accessors (two from its parent and one from its own class) because it is both a CommissionEmployee and an Employee. Similarly, the object has access to three get accessors and the GetGreeting() method. Figure 10-4 shows a

Main() method that declares Employee and CommissionEmployee objects and shows all the properties and methods that can be used with each. Figure 10-5 shows the program output.

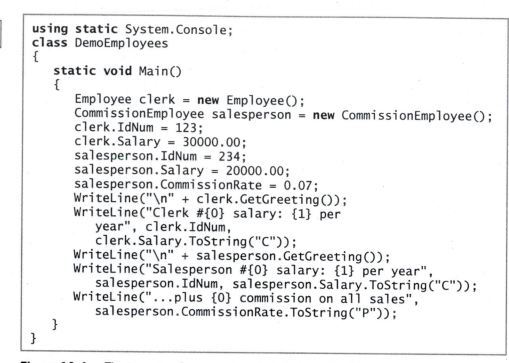

```
using static System.Console;
class DemoEmployees
{
    static void Main()
    {
        Employee clerk = new Employee();
        CommissionEmployee salesperson = new CommissionEmployee();
        clerk.IdNum = 123;
        clerk.Salary = 30000.00;
        salesperson.IdNum = 234;
        salesperson.Salary = 20000.00;
        salesperson.CommissionRate = 0.07;
        WriteLine("\n" + clerk.GetGreeting());
        WriteLine("Clerk #{0} salary: {1} per
            year", clerk.IdNum,
            clerk.Salary.ToString("C"));
        WriteLine("\n" + salesperson.GetGreeting());
        WriteLine("Salesperson #{0} salary: {1} per year",
            salesperson.IdNum, salesperson.Salary.ToString("C"));
        WriteLine("...plus {0} commission on all sales",
            salesperson.CommissionRate.ToString("P"));
    }
}
```

Figure 10-4   The DemoEmployees class that declares Employee and CommissionEmployee objects

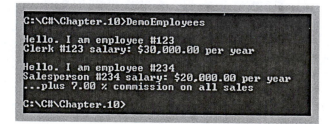

Figure 10-5   Output of the DemoEmployees program

Inheritance works only in one direction: A child inherits from a parent—not the other way around. If a program instantiates an Employee object as in the following statement, the Employee object does *not* have access to the CommissionEmployee properties or methods.

```
Employee clerk = new Employee();
clerk.CommissionRate = 0.1;
```

> **Don't Do It**
> This statement is invalid—Employee objects don't have a CommissionRate.

Employee is the parent class, and clerk is an object of the parent class. It makes sense that a parent class object does not have access to its child's data and methods. When you create the parent class, you do not know how many future child classes might be created, or what their data or methods might look like. In addition, child classes are more specific. A HeartSurgeon class and an Obstetrician class are children of a Doctor class. You do not expect all members of the general parent class Doctor to have the HeartSurgeon's RepairValve() method or the Obstetrician's DeliverBaby() method. However, HeartSurgeon and Obstetrician objects have access to the more general Doctor methods TakeBloodPressure() and BillPatients(). As with doctors, it is convenient to think of derived classes as *specialists*. That is, their fields and methods are more specialized than those of the base class.

 Watch the video *Inheritance*.

TWO TRUTHS & A LIE

Extending Classes

1. The following class header indicates that Dog is a subclass of Pet:
   public class Pet : Dog

2. If class X has four fields and class Y derives from it, then class Y also contains at least four fields.

3. Inheritance works only in one direction: A child inherits from a parent—not the other way around.

The false statement is #1. The following class header indicates that Dog is a subclass of Pet:
public class Dog : Pet

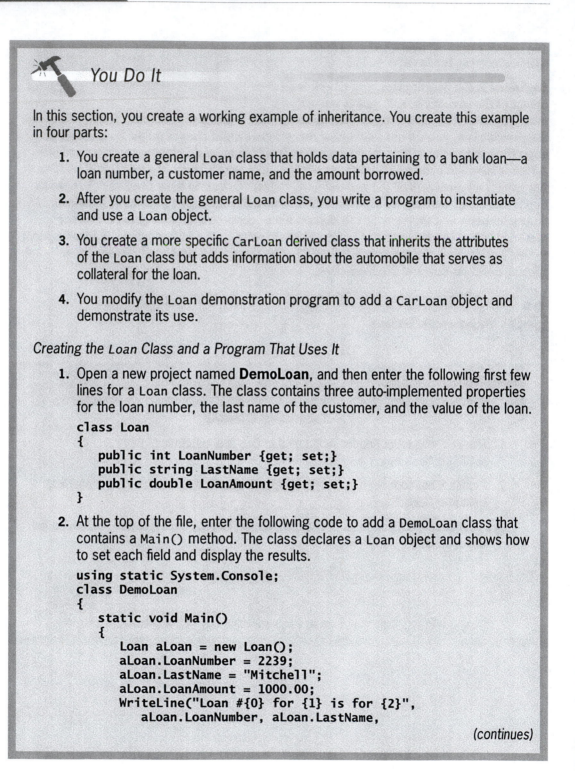

You Do It

In this section, you create a working example of inheritance. You create this example in four parts:

1. You create a general Loan class that holds data pertaining to a bank loan—a loan number, a customer name, and the amount borrowed.

2. After you create the general Loan class, you write a program to instantiate and use a Loan object.

3. You create a more specific CarLoan derived class that inherits the attributes of the Loan class but adds information about the automobile that serves as collateral for the loan.

4. You modify the Loan demonstration program to add a CarLoan object and demonstrate its use.

Creating the Loan Class and a Program That Uses It

1. Open a new project named **DemoLoan**, and then enter the following first few lines for a Loan class. The class contains three auto-implemented properties for the loan number, the last name of the customer, and the value of the loan.

```
class Loan
{
    public int LoanNumber {get; set;}
    public string LastName {get; set;}
    public double LoanAmount {get; set;}
}
```

2. At the top of the file, enter the following code to add a DemoLoan class that contains a Main() method. The class declares a Loan object and shows how to set each field and display the results.

```
using static System.Console;
class DemoLoan
{
    static void Main()
    {
        Loan aLoan = new Loan();
        aLoan.LoanNumber = 2239;
        aLoan.LastName = "Mitchell";
        aLoan.LoanAmount = 1000.00;
        WriteLine("Loan #{0} for {1} is for {2}",
            aLoan.LoanNumber, aLoan.LastName,
```

(continues)

(continued)

```
                  aLoan.LoanAmount.ToString("C2"));
      }
  }
```

433

3. Save the file, and then compile and execute the program. The output looks like Figure 10-6. There is nothing unusual about this class or how it operates; it is similar to many you saw in the last chapter before you learned about inheritance.

```
C:\C#\Chapter.10>DemoLoan
Loan #2239 for Mitchell is for $1,000.00

C:\C#\Chapter.10>
```

Figure 10-6   Output of the DemoLoan program

Extending a Class

Next, you create a class named CarLoan. A CarLoan "is a" type of Loan. As such, it has all the attributes of a Loan, but it also has the year and make of the car that the customer is using as collateral for the loan. Therefore, CarLoan is a subclass of Loan.

1. Save the DemoLoan file as **DemoCarLoan**. Change the **DemoLoan** class name to **DemoCarLoan**. Begin the definition of the CarLoan class after the closing curly brace for the Loan class. CarLoan extends Loan and contains two properties that hold the year and make of the car.

```
class CarLoan : Loan
{
    public int Year {get; set;}
    public string Make {get; set;}
}
```

2. Within the Main() method of the DemoCarLoan class, just after the declaration of the Loan object, declare a CarLoan as follows:

```
CarLoan aCarLoan = new CarLoan();
```

3. After the three property assignments for the Loan object, insert five assignment statements for the CarLoan object.

```
aCarLoan.LoanNumber = 3358;
aCarLoan.LastName = "Jansen";
aCarLoan.LoanAmount = 20000.00;
```

(continues)

434

(continued)

```
aCarLoan.Make = "Ford";
aCarLoan.Year = 2005;
```

4. Following the `WriteLine()` statement that displays the `Loan` object data, insert two `WriteLine()` statements that display the `CarLoan` object's data.

```
WriteLine("Loan #{0} for {1} is for {2}",
    aCarLoan.LoanNumber, aCarLoan.LastName,
    aCarLoan.LoanAmount.ToString("C2"));
WriteLine("    Loan #{0} is for a {1} {2}",
    aCarLoan.LoanNumber, aCarLoan.Year,
    aCarLoan.Make);
```

5. Save the program, and then compile and execute it. The output looks like Figure 10-7. The `CarLoan` object correctly uses its own fields and properties as well as those of the parent `Loan` class.

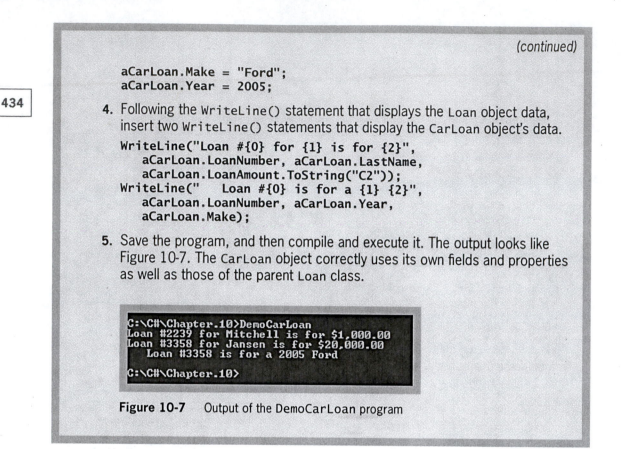

```
C:\C#\Chapter.10>DemoCarLoan
Loan #2239 for Mitchell is for $1,000.00
Loan #3358 for Jansen is for $20,000.00
    Loan #3358 is for a 2005 Ford

C:\C#\Chapter.10>
```

Figure 10-7 Output of the DemoCarLoan program

Using the protected Access Specifier

The `Employee` class in Figure 10-1 is a typical C# class in that its data fields are `private` and its properties and methods are `public`. In the chapter "Using Classes and Objects," you learned that this scheme provides for information hiding—protecting your `private` data from alteration by methods outside the data's own class. When a program is a client of the `Employee` class (that is, it instantiates an `Employee` object), the client cannot alter the data in any `private` field directly. For example, when you write a `Main()` method that creates an `Employee` named `clerk`, you cannot change the `Employee`'s `idNum` or `salary` directly using a statement such as `clerk.idNum = 2222;`. Instead, you must use the `public IdNum` property to set the `idNum` field of the `clerk` object.

When you use information hiding, you are assured that your data will be altered only by the properties and methods you choose and only in ways that you can control. If outside classes could alter an `Employee`'s `private` fields, then the fields could be assigned values that the `Employee` class couldn't control. In such a case, the principle of information hiding would be destroyed, causing the behavior of the object to be unpredictable.

Any derived class you create, such as CommissionEmployee, inherits all the data and methods of its base class. However, even though a child of Employee has idNum and salary fields, the CommissionEmployee methods cannot alter or use those private fields directly. If a new class could simply extend your Employee class and "get to" its data fields without "going through the proper channels," then information hiding would not be operating.

On some occasions, you do want to access parent class data from a child class. For example, suppose that the Employee class Salary property set accessor has been written so that no Employee's salary is ever set to less than 15000, as follows:

```
set
{
    double MINIMUM = 15000;
    if(value < MINIMUM)
        salary = MINIMUM;
    else
        salary = value;
}
```

Also assume that a CommissionEmployee draws commission only and no regular salary; that is, when you set a CommissionEmployee's commissionRate field, the salary should become 0. You would write the CommissionEmployee class CommissionRate property set accessor as follows:

```
set
{
    commissionRate = value;
    Salary = 0;
}
```

Using this implementation, when you create a CommissionEmployee object and set its CommissionRate, 0 is sent to the set accessor for the Employee class Salary property. Because the value of the salary is less than 15000, the salary is forced to 15000 in the Employee class set accessor, even though you want it to be 0.

A possible alternative would be to rewrite the set accessor for the CommissionRate property in the CommissionEmployee class using the field salary instead of the property Salary, as follows:

```
set
{
    commissionRate = value;
    salary = 0;
}
```

In this set accessor, you bypass the parent class's Salary set accessor and directly use the salary field. However, when you include this accessor in a program and compile it, you receive an error message: *Employee.salary is inaccessible due to its protection level.* In other words, Employee.salary is private, and no other class can access it, even a child class of Employee.

So, in summary:

- Using the `public set` accessor in the parent class does not work because of the minimum salary requirement.

- Using the `private` field in the parent class does not work because it is inaccessible.

- Making the parent class field `public` would work, but doing so would violate the principle of information hiding.

Fortunately, there is a fourth option. The solution is to create the `salary` field with **protected access**, which provides you with an intermediate level of security between `public` and `private` access. A `protected` data field or method can be used within its own class or in any classes extended from that class, but it cannot be used by "outside" classes. In other words, `protected` members can be used "within the family"—by a class and its descendents.

Some sources say that `private`, `public`, and `protected` are *access specifiers*, while other class designations, such as `static`, are *access modifiers*. However, Microsoft developers, who created C#, use the terms interchangeably in their documentation.

Figure 10-8 shows how you can declare `salary` as `protected` within the `Employee` class so that it becomes legal to access it directly within the `CommissionRate set` accessor of the `CommissionEmployee` derived class. Figure 10-9 shows a program that instantiates a `CommissionEmployee` object, and Figure 10-10 shows the output. Notice that the `CommissionEmployee`'s salary initially is set to 20000 in the program, but the salary becomes 0 when the `CommissionRate` is set later.

```
class Employee
{
    private int idNum;
    protected double salary;
    public int IdNum
    {
        get
        {
            return idNum;
        }
        set
        {
            idNum = value;
        }
    }
}
```

Figure 10-8   The Employee class with a `protected` field and the CommissionEmployee class *(continues)*

(continued)

```
    public double Salary
    {
      get
      {
        return salary;
      }
      set
      {
        double MINIMUM = 15000;
        if(value < MINIMUM)
            salary = MINIMUM;
        else
            salary = value;
      }
    }
    public string GetGreeting()
    {
      string greeting = "Hello. I am employee #" + IdNum;
      return greeting;
    }
}
class CommissionEmployee : Employee
{
    private double commissionRate;
    public double CommissionRate
    {
      get
      {
        return commissionRate;
      }
      set
      {
        commissionRate = value;
        salary = 0;
      }
    }
}
```

The protected salary field is accessible in the child class.

Figure 10-8   The Employee class with a protected field and the CommissionEmployee class

```
using static System.Console;
class DemoSalesperson
{
    static void Main()
    {
        CommissionEmployee salesperson = new CommissionEmployee();
        salesperson.IdNum = 345;
        salesperson.Salary = 20000;
        salesperson.CommissionRate = 0.07;
        WriteLine("Salesperson #{0} makes {1} per year",
            salesperson.IdNum, salesperson.Salary.ToString("C"));
        WriteLine("...plus {0} commission on all sales",
            salesperson.CommissionRate.ToString("P"));
    }
}
```

Figure 10-9 The DemoSalesperson program

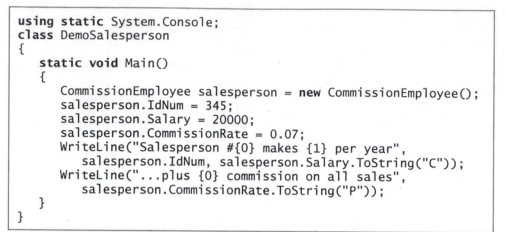

Figure 10-10 Output of the DemoSalesperson program

 If you set the salesperson's CommissionRate first in the DemoSalesperson program, then set Salary to a nonzero value, salary will not be reduced to 0. If your intention is to always create CommissionEmployees with salaries of 0, then the Salary property should also be overridden in the derived class.

Using the **protected** access specifier for a field can be convenient, and it also slightly improves program performance by using a field directly instead of "going through" property accessors. Also, using the **protected** access specifier is occasionally necessary. However, **protected** data members should be used sparingly. Whenever possible, the principle of information hiding should be observed, and even child classes should have to go through accessors to "get to" their parent's private data. When child classes are allowed direct access to a parent's fields, the likelihood of future errors increases. Classes that depend on field names from parent classes are said to be **fragile** because they are prone to errors—that is, they are easy to "break."

TWO TRUTHS & A LIE

Using the protected Access Specifier

1. A child class does not contain the private members of its parent.

2. A child class cannot use the private members of its parent.

3. A child class can use the protected members of its parent, but outside classes cannot.

The false statement is #1. A child class contains the private members of its parent, but cannot use them directly.

Overriding Base Class Members

When you create a derived class by extending an existing class, the new derived class contains properties and methods that were defined in the original base class. Sometimes, the superclass features are not entirely appropriate for the subclass objects. Using the same method or property name to indicate different implementations is called polymorphism. The word *polymorphism* means "many forms"—in programming, it means that many forms of action take place, even though you use the same method name. The specific method executed depends on the object.

You first learned the term *polymorphism* in Chapter 1.

Everyday cases provide many examples of polymorphism:

- Although both are musical instruments and have a Play() method, a guitar is played differently than a drum.

- Although both are vehicles and have an Operate() method, a bicycle is operated differently than a truck.

- Although both are schools and have a SatisfyGraduationRequirements() method, a preschool's requirements are different from those of a college.

You understand each of these methods based on the context in which it is used. In a similar way, C# understands your use of the same method name based on the type of object associated with it.

For example, suppose that you have created a Student class as shown in Figure 10-11. Students have names, credits for which they are enrolled, and tuition amounts. You can set a Student's name and credits by using the set accessors in the Name and Credits properties, but you cannot set a Student's tuition directly because there is no set accessor for the Tuition property. Instead, tuition is calculated based on a standard RATE (of $55.75) for each credit that the Student takes.

 In Figure 10-11, the Student fields that hold credits and tuition are declared as protected because a child class will use them.

```
class Student
{
   private const double RATE = 55.75;
   private string name;
   protected int credits;
   protected double tuition;
   public string Name
   {
      get
      {
         return name;
      }
      set
      {
         name = value;
      }
   }
   public virtual int Credits
   {
      get
      {
         return credits;
      }
      set
      {
         credits = value;
         tuition = credits * RATE;
      }
   }
   public double Tuition
   {
      get
      {
         return tuition;
      }
   }
}
```

Figure 10-11   The Student class

In Figure 10-11, `Credits` is declared to be virtual (see shading). A **virtual method** (or property) is one that can be overridden by a method with the same signature in a child class. In Chapter 9, you learned that when a method overrides another, it takes precedence over the method.

Suppose that you derive a subclass from `Student` called `ScholarshipStudent`, as shown in Figure 10-12. A `ScholarshipStudent` has a `name`, `credits`, and `tuition`, but the tuition is not calculated in the same way as it is for a `Student`; instead, `tuition` for a `ScholarshipStudent` should be set to 0. You want to use the `Credits` property to set a `ScholarshipStudent`'s `credits`, but you want the property to behave differently than the parent class `Student`'s `Credits` property. As a child of `Student`, a `ScholarshipStudent` possesses all the attributes, properties, and methods of a `Student`, but its `Credits` property behaves differently.

```
class ScholarshipStudent : Student
{
    public override int Credits
    {
        set
        {
            credits = value;
            tuition = 0;
        }
    }
}
```

Figure 10-12   The `ScholarshipStudent` class

In C#, you can use either `new` or `override` when defining a derived class member that has the same name as a base class member, but you cannot use both together. When you write a statement such as `ScholarshipStudent s1 = new ScholarshipStudent();`, you won't notice the difference. However, if you use `new` when defining the derived class `Credits` property and write a statement such as `Student s2 = new ScholarshipStudent();` (using `Student` as the type), then `s2.Credits` accesses the base class property. On the other hand, if you use `override` when defining `Credits` in the derived class, then `s2.Credits` uses the derived class property.

In the child `ScholarshipStudent` class in Figure 10-12, the `Credits` property is declared with the `override` modifier (see shading) because it has the same header (that is, the same signature—the same name and parameter list) as a property in its parent class. The `Credits` property overrides and **hides** its counterpart in the parent class. (You could do the same thing with methods.) If you omit `override`, the program will still operate correctly, but you will receive a warning that you are hiding an inherited member with the same name in the base class. Using the keyword `override` eliminates the warning and makes your intentions clear. When you use the `Name` property with a `ScholarshipStudent` object, a program uses the parent class property `Name`; it is not hidden. However, when you use `Credits` to set a value for a `ScholarshipStudent` object, the program uses the new, overriding property from its own class.

If `credits` and `tuition` had been declared as `private` within the `Student` class, then `ScholarshipStudent` would not be able to use them.

442

You are not required to override a virtual method or property in a derived class; a derived class can simply use the base class version. A base class member that is not hidden by the derived class is **visible** in the derived class.

Figure 10-13 shows a program that uses `Student` and `ScholarshipStudent` objects. Even though each object assigns the `Credits` property with the same number of credit hours (in the two shaded statements), the calculated `tuition` values are different because each object uses a different version of the `Credits` property. Figure 10-14 shows the execution of the program.

```
using static System.Console;
class DemoStudents
{
    static void Main()
    {
        Student payingStudent = new Student();
        ScholarshipStudent freeStudent = new ScholarshipStudent();
        payingStudent.Name = "Megan";
        payingStudent.Credits = 15;
        freeStudent.Name = "Luke";
        freeStudent.Credits = 15;
        WriteLine("{0}'s tuition is {1}",
            payingStudent.Name, payingStudent.Tuition.ToString("C"));
        WriteLine("{0}'s tuition is {1}",
            freeStudent.Name, freeStudent.Tuition.ToString("C"));
    }
}
```

Figure 10-13   The DemoStudents program

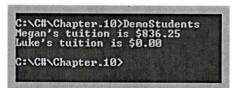
```
C:\C#\Chapter.10>DemoStudents
Megan's tuition is $836.25
Luke's tuition is $0.00

C:\C#\Chapter.10>
```

Figure 10-14   Output of the DemoStudents program

If a base class and a derived class have methods with the same names but different parameter lists, then the derived class method does not override the base class method; instead, it *overloads* the base class method. For example, if a base class contains a method with the header `public void Display()`, and its child contains a method with the header `public void Display(string s)`, then the child class would have access to both methods. (You learned about overloading methods in the chapter "Advanced Method Concepts.")

Accessing Base Class Methods and Properties from a Derived Class

When a derived class contains a method or property that overrides a parent class method or property, you might have occasion to use the parent class version within the subclass. If so, you can use the keyword `base` to access the parent class method or property.

For example, recall the `GetGreeting()` method that appears in the `Employee` class in Figure 10-8. If its child, `CommissionEmployee`, also contains a `GetGreeting()` method, as shown in Figure 10-15, then within the `CommissionEmployee` class you can call `base.GetGreeting()` to access the base class version of the method. Figure 10-16 shows an application that uses the method with a `CommissionEmployee` object. Figure 10-17 shows the output.

```csharp
class CommissionEmployee : Employee
{
    private double commissionRate;
    public double CommissionRate
    {
        get
        {
            return commissionRate;
        }
        set
        {
            commissionRate = value;
            salary = 0;
        }
    }
    new public string GetGreeting()
    {
        string greeting = base.GetGreeting();
        greeting += "\nI work on commission.";
        return greeting;
    }
}
```

Figure 10-15   The `CommissionEmployee` class with a `GetGreeting()` method

444

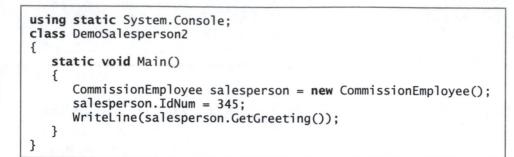

```
using static System.Console;
class DemoSalesperson2
{
    static void Main()
    {
        CommissionEmployee salesperson = new CommissionEmployee();
        salesperson.IdNum = 345;
        WriteLine(salesperson.GetGreeting());
    }
}
```

Figure 10-16   The DemoSalesperson2 program

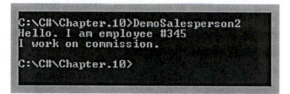

```
C:\C#\Chapter.10>DemoSalesperson2
Hello. I am employee #345
I work on commission.

C:\C#\Chapter.10>
```

Figure 10-17   Output of the DemoSalesperson2 program

In Figure 10-15, the child class, the GetGreeting() method uses the keyword new in its header to eliminate a compiler warning. Then, within the method, the parent's version of the GetGreeting() method is called. The returned string is stored in the greeting variable, and then an "I work on commission." statement is added to it before the complete message is returned to the calling program. By overriding the base class method in the child class, the duplicate typing to create the first part of the message is eliminated. Additionally, if the first part of the message is altered in the future, it will be altered in only one place—in the base class.

Watch the video *Handling Methods and Inheritance*.

TWO TRUTHS & A LIE

Overriding Base Class Members

1. When you override a parent class method in a child class, the methods have the same name.

2. When you override a parent class method in a child class, the methods have the same parameter list.

3. When you override a parent class method in a child class and then use the child class method, the parent class method executes first, followed by the child class method.

The false statement is #3. When you override a parent class method in a child class and then use the child class method, the child class method executes instead of the parent class version.

 You Do It

In the previous sections, you created Loan and CarLoan classes and objects. Suppose that the bank adopts new rules as follows:

- No regular loan will be made for less than $5000.
- No car loan will be made for any car older than model year 2006.
- Although Loans might have larger loan numbers, CarLoans will have loan numbers that are no more than three digits. If a larger loan number is provided, the program will use only the last three digits for the loan number.

Using Base Class Members in a Derived Class

1. Open the DemoCarLoan file, and immediately save it as **DemoCarLoan2**. Also change the class name from DemoCarLoan to **DemoCarLoan2**.

2. Within the Loan class, add a new constant that represents the minimum loan value:

```
public const double MINIMUM_LOAN = 5000;
```

(continues)

(continued)

3. Add a field for the `loanAmount` because the `LoanAmount` property, which was previously an auto-implemented property, will need to use it:

```
protected double loanAmount;
```

The field is protected so that `CarLoan` objects will be able to access it as well as `Loan` objects.

4. Replace the auto-implemented property for `LoanAmount` in the `Loan` class with `get` and `set` accessors as follows. This change ensures that no loan is made for less than the minimum allowed value.

```
public double LoanAmount
{
    set
    {
        if(value < MINIMUM_LOAN)
            loanAmount = MINIMUM_LOAN;
        else
            loanAmount = value;
    }
    get
    {
        return loanAmount;
    }
}
```

5. Within the `CarLoan` class, add two new constants to hold the earliest year for which car loans will be given and the lowest allowed loan number:

```
private const int EARLIEST_YEAR = 2006;
private const int LOWEST_INVALID_NUM = 1000;
```

6. Also within the `CarLoan` class, add a field for the year of the car, and replace the existing auto-implemented `Year` property with one that contains coded `get` and `set` accessors. The `Year` property `set` accessor not only sets the year field, it sets `loanAmount` to 0 when a car's year is less than 2006.

```
private int year;
public int Year
{
    set
    {
        if(value < EARLIEST_YEAR)
        {
            year = value;
            loanAmount = 0;
        }
```

(continues)

(continued)

```
        else
            year = value;
    }
    get
    {
        return year;
    }
}
```

If `loanAmount` were `private` in the parent `Loan` class, you would not be able to set its value in the child `CarLoan` class, as you do here. You could use the `public` property `LoanAmount` to set the value, but the parent class `set` accessor would force the value to 5000.

7. Suppose that unique rules apply for issuing loan numbers for cars. Within the `CarLoan` class, just before the closing curly brace, change the inherited `LoanNumber` property to accommodate the new rules. If a car loan number is three digits or fewer, pass it on to the base class property. If not, obtain the last three digits by calculating the remainder when the loan number is divided by 1000, and pass the new number to the base class property. Add the following property after the definition of the `Make` property.

```
public new int LoanNumber
{
    get
    {
        return base.LoanNumber;
    }
    set
    {
        if(value < LOWEST_INVALID_NUM)
            base.LoanNumber = value;
        else
            base.LoanNumber = value % LOWEST_INVALID_NUM;
    }
}
```

If you did not use the keyword `base` to access the `LoanNumber` property within the `CarLoan` class, you would be telling this version of the `LoanNumber` property to call itself. Although the program would compile, it would run continuously in an infinite loop until it ran out of memory and issued an error message.

(continues)

(continued)

A method that calls itself is a **recursive** method. Recursive methods are sometimes useful, but they require specialized code to avoid infinite loops and are not appropriate in this case.

8. Save the file. Compile it, and correct any errors. When you execute the program, the output looks like Figure 10-18. Compare the output to Figure 10-7. Notice that the $1000 bank loan has been forced to $5000. Also notice that the car loan number has been shortened to three digits and the value of the loan is $0 because of the age of the car.

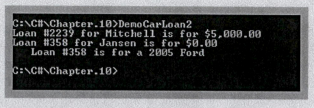

```
C:\C#\Chapter.10>DemoCarLoan2
Loan #2239 for Mitchell is for $5,000.00
Loan #358 for Jansen is for $0.00
    Loan #358 is for a 2005 Ford

C:\C#\Chapter.10>
```

Figure 10-18   Output of the `DemoCarLoan2` program

9. Change the assigned values within the `DemoCarLoan2` class to combinations of early and late years and valid and invalid loan numbers. After each change, save the program, compile and execute it, and confirm that the program operates as expected.

Understanding Implicit Reference Conversions

Every derived object "is a" specific instance of both the derived class and the base class. In other words, myCar "is a" Car as well as a `Vehicle`, and myDog "is a" Dog as well as a `Mammal`. You can assign a derived class object to an object of any of its superclass types. When you do, C# makes an **implicit conversion** from derived class to base class.

You have already learned that C# also makes implicit conversions when casting one data type to another. For example, in the statement `double money = 10;`, the integer value 10 is implicitly converted (or cast) to a `double`. When a derived class object is assigned to its ancestor's data type, the conversion can more specifically be called an **implicit reference conversion**. This term is more accurate because it emphasizes the difference between numerical conversions and reference objects. When you assign a derived class object to a base class type, the object is treated as though it had only the characteristics defined in the base class and not those added in the child class definition.

For example, when a CommissionEmployee class inherits from Employee, an object of either type can be passed to a method that accepts an Employee parameter. In Figure 10-19, an Employee is passed to DisplayGreeting() in the first shaded statement, and a CommissionEmployee is passed in the second shaded statement. Each is referred to as emp within the method, and each is used correctly, as shown in Figure 10-20.

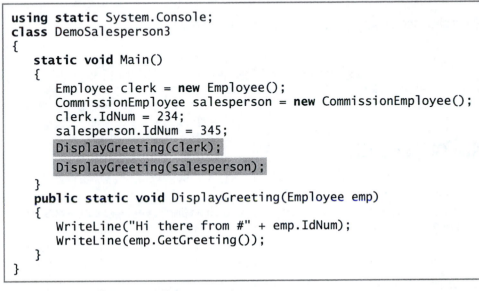

```
using static System.Console;
class DemoSalesperson3
{
    static void Main()
    {
        Employee clerk = new Employee();
        CommissionEmployee salesperson = new CommissionEmployee();
        clerk.IdNum = 234;
        salesperson.IdNum = 345;
        DisplayGreeting(clerk);
        DisplayGreeting(salesperson);
    }
    public static void DisplayGreeting(Employee emp)
    {
        WriteLine("Hi there from #" + emp.IdNum);
        WriteLine(emp.GetGreeting());
    }
}
```

Figure 10-19   The DemoSalesperson3 program

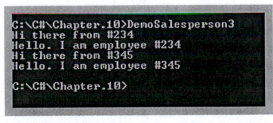

Figure 10-20   Output of the DemoSalesperson3 program

450

TWO TRUTHS & A LIE

Understanding Implicit Reference Conversions

1. You can assign a derived class object to an object of any of its superclass types.

2. You can assign a base class object to an object of any of its derived types.

3. An implicit conversion from one type to another is an automatic conversion.

The false statement is #2. You can assign a derived class object to an object of any of its superclass types but not the other way around.

Using the `Object` Class

Every class you create in C# derives from a single class named `System.Object`. In other words, the **object** (or `Object`) class type in the `System` namespace is the ultimate base class, or **root class**, for all other types. When you create a class such as `Employee`, you usually use the header `class Employee`, which implicitly, or automatically, descends from the `Object` class. Alternatively, you could use the header `class Employee : Object` to explicitly show the name of the base class, but it would be extremely unusual to see such a format in a C# program.

The keyword `object` is an alias for the `System.Object` class. You can use the lowercase and uppercase versions of the class interchangeably. The fact that `object` is an alias for `System.Object` should not surprise you. You already know, for example, that `int` is an alias for `Int32` and that `double` is an alias for `Double`.

Because every class descends from `Object`, every object "is an" `Object`. As proof, you can write a method that accepts an argument of type `Object`, and it will accept arguments of any type. Figure 10-21 shows a program that declares three objects using classes created earlier in this chapter—a `Student`, a `ScholarshipStudent`, and an `Employee`. Even though these types possess different attributes and methods (and one type, `Employee`, has nothing in common with the other two), each type can serve as an argument to the `DisplayObjectMessage()` because each type "is an" `Object`. Figure 10-22 shows the execution of the program.

```
using System;
using static System.Console;
class DiverseObjects
{
    static void Main()
    {
        Student payingStudent = new Student();
```

Figure 10-21 The `DiverseObjects` program *(continues)*

(continued)

```
        ScholarshipStudent freeStudent = new ScholarshipStudent();
        Employee clerk = new Employee();
        Write("Using Student: ");
        DisplayObjectMessage(payingStudent);
        Write("Using ScholarshipStudent: ");
        DisplayObjectMessage(freeStudent);
        Write("Using Employee: ");
        DisplayObjectMessage(clerk);
    }
    public static void DisplayObjectMessage(Object o)
    {
        WriteLine("Method successfully called");
    }
}
```

Figure 10-21　The DiverseObjects program

```
C:\C#\Chapter.10>DiverseObjects
Using Student: Method successfully called
Using ScholarshipStudent: Method successfully called
Using Employee: Method successfully called

C:\C#\Chapter.10>
```

Figure 10-22　Output of the DiverseObjects program

When you create any child class, it inherits all the methods of all of its ancestors. Because all classes inherit from the Object class, all classes inherit the Object class methods. The Object class contains a constructor, a destructor, and four public instance methods, as summarized in Table 10-1.

Method	Explanation
Equals()	Determines whether two Object instances are equal
GetHashCode()	Gets a unique code for each object; useful in certain sorting and data management tasks
GetType()	Returns the type, or class, of an object
ToString()	Returns a String that represents the object

Table 10-1　The four public instance methods of the Object class

The Object class contains other nonpublic and noninstance (static) methods in addition to the four methods listed in Table 10-1. The C# documentation provides more details on these methods.

Using the Object Class's GetType() Method

The GetType() method returns an object's type, or class. For example, if you have created an Employee object named someWorker, then the following statement displays *Employee*:

```
WriteLine(someWorker.GetType());
```

If an object's class is defined in a namespace, then GetType() returns a string composed of the namespace, a dot, and the class name.

Using the Object Class's ToString() Method

The Object class methods are not very useful as they stand. For example, when you use the Object class's ToString() method with an object you create, it simply returns a string that holds the name of the class, just as GetType() does. That is, if someWorker is an Employee, then the following statement displays *Employee*:

```
WriteLine(someWorker.ToString());
```

When you create a class such as Employee, you often want to override the Object class's ToString() method with your own, more useful version—perhaps one that returns an Employee's ID number, name, or combination of the two. Of course, you could create a differently named method to do the same thing—perhaps GetEmployeeIdentification() or ConvertEmployeeToString(). However, by naming your class method ToString(), you make the class easier for others to understand and use. Programmers know the ToString() method works with every object; when they use it with your objects, you can provide a useful set of information. A class's ToString() method is often a useful debugging aid.

For example, you might create an Employee class ToString() method, as shown in Figure 10-23. This method assumes that IdNum and Name are Employee properties with get accessors. The returned string will have a value such as *Employee: 234 Johnson*.

```
public override string ToString()
{
    return(getType() + ": " + IdNum + " " + Name);
}
```

Figure 10-23　An Employee class ToString() method

You have been using an overloaded version of the ToString() method since Chapter 2. There, you learned that you can format numeric output when you pass a string such as "F3" or "C2" to the ToString() method.

Using the Object Class's Equals() Method

The Equals() method compares objects for reference equality. **Reference equality** occurs when two reference type objects refer to the same object. The Equals() method returns true if two Objects have the same memory address—that is, if one object is a reference to the other and both are literally the same object. For example, you might write the following:

```
if(oneObject.Equals(anotherObject))...
```

Like the ToString() method, this method might not be useful to you in its original form. For example, you might prefer to think of two Employee objects at unique memory addresses as equal if their ID numbers or first and last names are equal. You might want to override the Equals() method for any class you create if you anticipate that class clients will want to compare objects based on any of their field values.

If you overload the Equals() method, it should meet the following requirements by convention:

- Its header should be as follows (you can use any identifier for the Object parameter):

  ```
  public override bool Equals(Object o)
  ```

- It should return false if the argument is null.

- It should return true if an object is compared to itself.

- It should return true only if both of the following are true:

  ```
  oneObject.Equals(anotherObject)
  anotherObject.Equals(oneObject)
  ```

- If oneObject.Equals(anotherObject) returns true and oneObject.Equals(aThirdObject) returns true, then anotherObject.Equals(aThirdObject) should also be true.

 You first used the Equals() method to compare String objects in Chapter 2. When you use Equals() with Strings, you use the String class's Equals() method that compares String contents as opposed to String addresses. In other words, the Object class's Equals() method has already been overridden in the String class.

When you create an Equals() method to override the one in the Object class, the parameter must be an Object. For example, if you consider Employee objects equal when their IdNum properties are equal, then an Employee class Equals() method might be created as follows:

```
public override bool Equals(Object e)
{
    bool isEqual;
    Employee temp = (Employee)e;
    if(IdNum == temp.IdNum)
        isEqual = true;
    else
        isEqual = false;
    return isEqual;
}
```

In the shaded statement in the method, the Object parameter is cast to an Employee so the Employee's IdNum can be compared. If you did not perform the cast and tried to make the comparison with e.IdNum, the method would not compile because an Object does not have an IdNum property.

An even better alternative is to ensure that compared objects are the same type before making any other decisions. For example, the Equals() method in Figure 10-24 uses the GetType() method with both the this object and the parameter before proceeding. If compared objects are not the same type, then the Equals() method should return false.

```
public override bool Equals(Object e)
{
    bool isEqual = true;
    if(this.GetType() != e.GetType())
        isEqual = false;
    else
    {
        Employee temp = (Employee)e;
        if(IdNum == temp.IdNum)
            isEqual = true;
        else
            isEqual = false;
    }
    return isEqual;
}
```

Figure 10-24   An Equals() method for the Employee class

Using the Object Class's GetHashCode() Method

When you override the Equals() method, you should also override the GetHashCode() method, because Equals() uses GetHashCode(), and two objects considered equal should have the same hash code. A **hash code** is a number that should uniquely identify an object; you might use hash codes in some advanced C# applications. For example, Figure 10-25 shows an application that declares two Employees from a class in which the GetHashCode() method has not been overridden. The output in Figure 10-26 shows a unique number for each object. (The number, however, is meaningless to you.) If you choose to override the GetHashCode() method, you should write this method so it returns a unique integer for every object—an Employee ID number, for example.

A hash code is sometimes called a *fingerprint* for an object because it uniquely identifies the object. In C#, the default implementation of the GetHashCode() method does not guarantee unique return values for different objects. However, if GetHashCode() is explicitly implemented in a derived class, it must return a unique hash code.

In cooking, hash is a dish that is created by combining ingredients. The term hash code derives from the fact that the code is sometimes created by mixing some of an object's data.

```
using static System.Console;
class TestHashCode
{
    static void Main()
    {
        Employee first = new Employee();
        Employee second = new Employee();
        WriteLine(first.GetHashCode());
        WriteLine(second.GetHashCode());
    }
}
```

Figure 10-25   The TestHashCode program

Figure 10-26   Output of the TestHashCode program

Although you can write an Equals() method for a class without overriding GetHashCode(), you receive a warning message. Additionally, if you overload == or != for a class, you will receive warning messages if you do not also override both the Equals() and GetHashCode() methods.

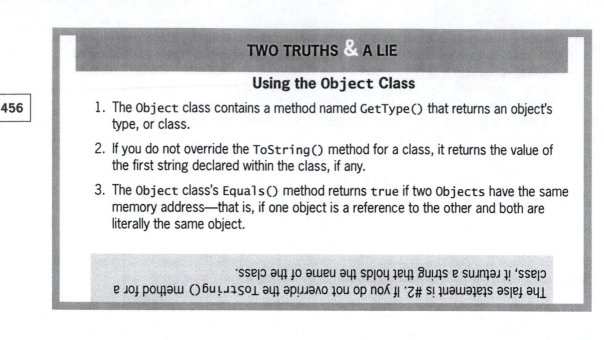

TWO TRUTHS & A LIE

Using the Object Class

1. The Object class contains a method named GetType() that returns an object's type, or class.

2. If you do not override the ToString() method for a class, it returns the value of the first string declared within the class, if any.

3. The Object class's Equals() method returns true if two Objects have the same memory address—that is, if one object is a reference to the other and both are literally the same object.

The false statement is #2. If you do not override the ToString() method for a class, it returns a string that holds the name of the class.

Working with Base Class Constructors

When you create any object, you call a constructor that has the same name as the class itself. Consider the following example:

```
SomeClass anObject = new SomeClass();
```

When you instantiate an object that is a member of a derived class, the constructor for the base class executes first, and then the derived class constructor executes. In other words, when you create any object, you always implicitly call the Object constructor because all classes are derived from Object. So, when you create a base class and a derived class, and instantiate a derived class object, you call three constructors: one from the Object class, one from the base class, and one from the derived class.

In the examples of inheritance you have seen so far in this chapter, each class contained default constructors, so their execution was transparent. However, you should realize that when you create a subclass instance, both the base and derived constructors execute. For example, consider the abbreviated Employee and CommissionEmployee classes in Figure 10-27. Employee contains just two fields and a constructor; CommissionEmployee descends from Employee and contains a constructor as well. The DemoSalesperson4 program in Figure 10-28 contains just one statement; it instantiates a CommissionEmployee. The output in Figure 10-29 shows that this one statement causes both constructors to execute.

```
class Employee
{
    private int idNum;
    protected double salary;
    public Employee()
    {
        WriteLine("Employee constructed");
    }
}
class CommissionEmployee : Employee
{
    private double commissionRate;
    public CommissionEmployee()
    {
        WriteLine("CommissionEmployee constructed");
    }
}
```

Figure 10-27   The Employee and CommissionEmployee classes with parameterless constructors

```
using static System.Console;
class DemoSalesperson4
{
    static void Main()
    {
        CommissionEmployee salesperson = new CommissionEmployee();
    }
}
```

Figure 10-28   The DemoSalesperson4 program

```
C:\C#\Chapter.10>DemoSalesperson4
Employee constructed
CommissionEmployee constructed

C:\C#\Chapter.10>
```

Figure 10-29   Output of the DemoSalesperson4 program

Of course, most constructors perform many more tasks than displaying a message to inform you that they exist. When constructors initialize variables, you usually want the base class constructor to initialize the data fields that originate in the base class. The derived class constructor needs to initialize only the data fields that are specific to the derived class.

457

Using Base Class Constructors That Require Arguments

When you create a class and do not provide a constructor, C# automatically supplies one that never requires arguments. When you write your own constructor for a class, you replace the automatically supplied version. Depending on your needs, the constructor you create for a class might require arguments. When you use a class as a base class and the class only has constructors that require arguments, you must make sure that any derived classes provide arguments so that one of the base class constructors can execute.

When all base class constructors require arguments, you must include a constructor for each derived class you create. Your derived class constructor can contain any number of statements; however, within the header of the constructor, you must provide values for any arguments required by the base class constructor that you use. Even if you have no other reason for creating a derived class constructor, you must write the derived class constructor so it can call its parent's constructor.

The header for a derived class constructor that calls a base class constructor includes a colon, the keyword base, and a list of arguments within parentheses. The keyword base always refers to the superclass of the class in which you use it. Although it seems that you should be able to use the base class constructor name to call the base class constructor, C# does not allow you to do so—you must use the keyword base.

For example, if you create an Employee class with a constructor that requires two arguments— an integer and a string—and you create a CommissionEmployee class that is a subclass of Employee, then the following code shows a valid constructor for CommissionEmployee:

```
public CommissionEmployee() : base(1234, "XXXX")
{
    // Other statements can go here
}
```

In this example, the CommissionEmployee constructor requires no arguments for its own execution, but it passes two arguments to its base class constructor. Every CommissionEmployee instantiation passes *1234* and *XXXX* to the Employee constructor. A different CommissionEmployee constructor might accept arguments; then it could pass the appropriate arguments on to the base class constructor, as in the following example:

```
public CommissionEmployee(int id, string name) : base(id, name)
{
    // Other statements can go here
}
```

Yet another CommissionEmployee constructor might require that some arguments be passed to the base class constructor and that some be used within CommissionEmployee. Consider the following example:

```
public CommissionEmployee(int id, string name, double rate) :
    base(id, name) // two parameters passed to base constructor
{
```

```
        CommissionRate = rate;
        // rate is used within child constructor
        // Other statements can go here
}
```

 Watch the video *Constructors and Inheritance*.

TWO TRUTHS & A LIE

Working with Base Class Constructors

1. When you create any derived class object, the base class constructor executes first, followed by the derived class constructor.

2. When a base class constructor requires arguments, you must include a constructor for each derived class you create.

3. When a derived class's constructor requires arguments, all of the arguments must be passed to the base class constructor.

The false statement is #3. When a derived class's constructor requires arguments, all of the arguments might be needed in the derived class, or perhaps all must be passed to the base class constructor. It also might be possible that some arguments are passed to the base class constructor and others are used within the derived class constructor.

You Do It

Adding Constructors to Base and Derived Classes

When a base class contains only constructors that require parameters, then any derived classes must provide for the base class constructor. In the next steps, you add constructors to the Loan and CarLoan classes and demonstrate that they work as expected.

1. Open the DemoCarLoan2 program, and change the class name to **DemoCarLoan3**. Save the file as **DemoCarLoan3**.

(continues)

(continued)

2. In the Loan class, just after the declaration of the loanAmount field, add a constructor that requires values for all the Loan's properties:

```
public Loan(int num, string name, double amount)
{
    LoanNumber = num;
    LastName = name;
    LoanAmount = amount;
}
```

3. In the CarLoan class, just after the declaration of the year field, add a constructor that takes five parameters. It passes three of the parameters to the base class constructor and uses the other two to assign values to the properties that are unique to the child class.

```
public CarLoan(int num, string name, double amount,
    int year, string make) : base(num, name, amount)
{
    Year = year;
    Make = make;
}
```

4. In the Main() method of the DemoCarLoan3 class, remove the existing declarations for aLoan and aCarLoan, and replace them with two declarations that use the arguments passed to the constructors.

```
Loan aLoan = new Loan(333, "Hanson", 7000.00);
CarLoan aCarLoan = new CarLoan(444, "Carlisle",
    30000.00, 2011, "BMW");
```

5. Remove the eight statements that assigned values to Loan and CarLoan, but retain the WriteLine() statements that display the values.

6. Save the program, and then compile and execute it. The output looks like Figure 10-30. Both constructors work as expected. The CarLoan constructor has called its parent's constructor to set the necessary fields before executing its own unique statements.

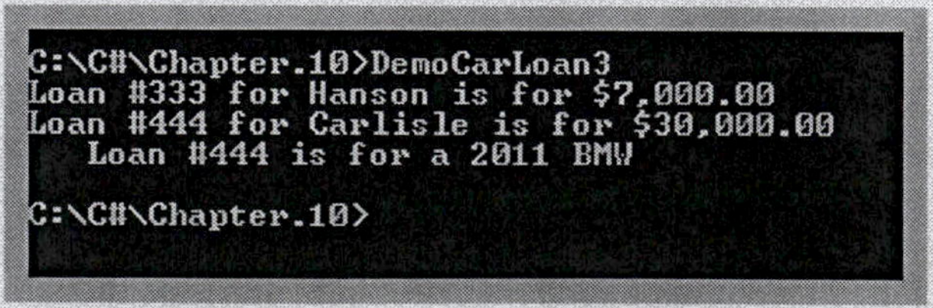

```
C:\C#\Chapter.10>DemoCarLoan3
Loan #333 for Hanson is for $7,000.00
Loan #444 for Carlisle is for $30,000.00
    Loan #444 is for a 2011 BMW

C:\C#\Chapter.10>
```

Figure 10-30   Output of the DemoCarLoan3 program

Creating and Using Abstract Classes

Creating classes can become easier after you understand the concept of inheritance. When you create a child class, it inherits all the general attributes you need; you must create only the new, more specific attributes required by the child class. For example, a `Painter` and a `Sculptor` are more specific than an `Artist`. They inherit all the general attributes of `Artists`, but you must add the attributes and methods that are specific to `Painter` and `Sculptor`.

Another way to think about a superclass is to notice that it contains the features shared by its subclasses. The derived classes are more specific examples of the base class type; they add features to the shared, general features. Conversely, when you examine a derived class, you notice that its parent is more general.

Sometimes you create a parent class to be so general that you never intend to create any specific instances of the class. For example, you might never create "just" an `Artist`; each `Artist` is more specifically a `Painter`, `Sculptor`, `Illustrator`, and so on. A class that is used to instantiate objects is a **concrete class.** A class that you create only to extend from, but not to instantiate from, is an abstract class. An **abstract class** is one from which you cannot create concrete objects but from which you can inherit. You use the keyword `abstract` when you declare an abstract class. If you attempt to instantiate an object from an abstract class, you will receive a compiler error message.

Abstract classes are like regular classes in that they can contain data fields and methods. The difference is that you cannot create instances of abstract classes by using the **new** operator. Rather, you create abstract classes simply to provide a base class from which other objects may be derived.

Abstract classes usually contain abstract methods, and they also can contain nonabstract methods. However, they are not required to contain any methods. Recall from Chapter 9 that an abstract method has no statements. Any class derived from a class that contains an abstract method must override the abstract method by providing a body (an implementation) for it. (Alternatively, the derived class can declare the method to be abstract; in that case, the derived class's children must implement the method.) You can create an `abstract` class with no `abstract` methods, but you cannot create an `abstract` method outside of an `abstract` class.

 A method that is declared `virtual` is not required to be overridden in a child class, but a method declared `abstract` must be overridden.

When you create an abstract method, you provide the keyword `abstract` and the intended method type, name, and parameters, but you do not provide statements within the method; you do not even supply curly braces. When you create a derived class that inherits an abstract method from a parent, you must use the keyword **override** in the method header and provide the actions, or implementation, for the inherited method within the derived class. In other words, you are required to code a derived class method to override any empty base class methods that are inherited.

For example, suppose that you want to create classes to represent different animals. You can create a generic, abstract class named Animal so you can provide generic data fields, such as the animal's name, only once. An Animal is generic, but each specific Animal, such as Dog or Cat, makes a unique sound. If you code an abstract Speak() method in the abstract Animal class, then you require all future Animal derived classes to override the Speak() method and provide an implementation that is specific to the derived class. Figure 10-31 shows an abstract Animal class that contains a data field for the name, a constructor that assigns a name, a Name property, and an abstract Speak() method.

```
abstract class Animal
{
    private string name;
    public Animal(string name)
    {
        this.name = name;
    }
    public string Name
    {
        get
        {
            return name;
        }
    }
    public abstract string Speak();
}
```

Figure 10-31   The Animal class

The Animal class in Figure 10-31 is declared to be abstract. (The keyword is shaded.) You cannot place a statement such as Animal myPet = new Animal("Murphy"); within a program, because the program will not compile. Because Animal is an abstract class, no Animal objects can exist.

You create an abstract class like Animal so that you can extend it. For example, you can create Dog and Cat classes as shown in Figure 10-32. Because the Animal class contains a constructor that requires a string argument, both Dog and Cat must contain constructors that provide string arguments for their base class.

```
class Dog : Animal
{
    public Dog(string name) : base(name)
    {
    }
    public override string Speak()
    {
        return "woof";
    }
}
class Cat : Animal
{
    public Cat(string name) : base(name)
    {
    }
    public override string Speak()
    {
        return "meow";
    }
}
```

Figure 10-32   The Dog and Cat classes

 If a method that should be overridden in a child class has its own implementation, you declare the base class method to be virtual. If it does not have its own implementation, you declare the base class and the method to be abstract.

The Dog and Cat constructors perform no tasks other than passing out the name to the Animal constructor. The overriding Speak() methods within Dog and Cat are required because the abstract parent Animal class contains an abstract Speak() method. The keyword override (shaded) is required in each Speak() method header. You can code any statements you want within the Dog and Cat class Speak() methods, but the methods must exist.

Figure 10-33 shows a program that implements Dog and Cat objects. Figure 10-34 shows the output, in which Speak() operates correctly for each animal type.

```
using static System.Console;
class DemoAnimals
{
    static void Main()
    {
        Dog spot = new Dog("Spot");
        Cat puff = new Cat("Puff");
        WriteLine(spot.Name + " says " + spot.Speak());
        WriteLine(puff.Name + " says " + puff.Speak());
    }
}
```

Figure 10-33   The DemoAnimals program

Figure 10-34   Output of the DemoAnimals program

Figure 10-35 shows an alternate way to create the DemoAnimals program. In this version the Dog and Cat objects are passed to a method that accepts an Animal parameter. The output is the same as in Figure 10-34. The Name property and Speak() method operate polymorphically, acting appropriately for each object type.

```
using static System.Console;
class DemoAnimals2
{
    static void Main()
    {
        Dog spot = new Dog("Spot");
        Cat puff = new Cat("Puff");
        DisplayAnimal(spot);
        DisplayAnimal(puff);
    }
    public static void DisplayAnimal(Animal creature)
    {
        WriteLine(creature.Name + " says " + creature.Speak());
    }
}
```

Figure 10-35   The DemoAnimals2 program

TWO TRUTHS & A LIE

Creating and Using Abstract Classes

1. An abstract class is one from which you cannot create concrete objects.

2. Unlike regular classes, abstract classes cannot contain methods.

3. When a base class contains an abstract method, the descendents of the base class must override the abstract method or declare the overriding method to be abstract.

The false statement is #2. Abstract classes are like regular classes in that they can contain data fields and methods. The difference is that you cannot create instances of abstract classes by using the new operator. Rather, you create abstract classes simply to provide a base class from which other objects may be derived.

Creating and Using Interfaces

Some object-oriented programming languages, notably C++, allow a subclass to inherit from more than one parent class. For example, you might create an Employee class that contains data fields pertaining to each employee in your organization. You also might create a Product class that holds information about each product your organization manufactures. When you create a Patent class for each product for which your company holds a patent, you might want to include product information as well as information about the employee who was responsible for the invention. In this situation, it would be convenient to inherit fields and methods from both the Product and Employee classes. The ability to inherit from more than one class is called **multiple inheritance**.

Multiple inheritance is a difficult concept, and programmers encounter many problems when they use it. For example, variables and methods in the parent classes may have identical names, creating a conflict when the child class uses one of the names. Additionally, as you already have learned, a child class constructor must call its parent class constructor. When two or more parents exist, this becomes a more complicated task: To which class should base refer when a child class has multiple parents?

For all of these reasons, multiple inheritance is prohibited in C#. However, C# does provide an alternative to multiple inheritance, known as an interface. Much like an abstract class, an **interface** is a collection of methods (and perhaps other members) that can be used by any class as long as the class provides a definition to override the interface's abstract definitions. Within an abstract class, some methods can be abstract, while others need not be. Within an interface, all methods are abstract.

You first learned about interfaces in the chapter "Using Classes and Objects" when you used the IComparable interface.

You create an interface much as you create an abstract class definition, except that you use the keyword `interface` instead of `abstract class`. For example, suppose that you create an IWorkable interface as shown in Figure 10-36. For simplicity, the IWorkable interface contains a single method named Work().

Although not required, in C# it is customary to start interface names with an uppercase *I*. Other languages follow different conventions. Interface names frequently end with *able*.

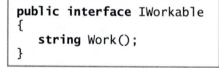

```
public interface IWorkable
{
    string Work();
}
```

Figure 10-36   The IWorkable interface

When any class implements IWorkable, it must also include a Work() method that returns a string. Figure 10-37 shows two classes that implement IWorkable: the Employee class and the Animal class. Because each implements IWorkable, each must declare a Work() method. The Employee class implements Work() to return the *I do my job* string. The abstract Animal class defines Work() as an abstract method, meaning that descendents of Animal must implement Work(). Figure 10-37 also shows two child classes of Animal: Dog and Cat. Note how Work() is defined differently for each.

```
class Employee : IWorkable
{
    public Employee(string name)
    {
        Name = name;
    }
    public string Name {get; set;}
    public string Work()
    {
        return "I do my job";
    }
}
abstract class Animal : IWorkable
{
    public Animal(string name)
    {
        Name = name;
    }
    public string Name {get; set;}
    public abstract string Work();
}
class Dog : Animal
{
    public Dog(string name) : base(name)
    {
    }
    public override string Work()
    {
        return "I watch the house";
    }
}
class Cat : Animal
{
    public Cat(string name) : base(name)
    {
    }
    public override string Work()
    {
        return "I catch mice";
    }
}
```

Figure 10-37   The Employee, Animal, Cat, and Dog classes with the IWorkable interface

When you create a program that instantiates an Employee, a Dog, or a Cat, as in the DemoWorking program in Figure 10-38, each object type knows how to "Work()" appropriately. Figure 10-39 shows the output.

```
using static System.Console;
class DemoWorking
{
    static void Main()
    {
        Employee bob = new Employee("Bob");
        Dog spot = new Dog("Spot");
        Cat puff = new Cat("Puff");
        WriteLine(bob.Name + " says " + bob.Work());
        WriteLine(spot.Name + " says " + spot.Work());
        WriteLine(puff.Name + " says " + puff.Work());
    }
}
```

Figure 10-38   The DemoWorking program

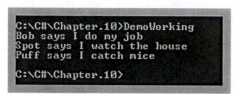

```
C:\C#\Chapter.10>DemoWorking
Bob says I do my job
Spot says I watch the house
Puff says I catch mice

C:\C#\Chapter.10>
```

Figure 10-39   Output of the DemoWorking program

Abstract classes and interfaces are similar in that you cannot instantiate concrete objects from either one. Abstract classes differ from interfaces in that abstract classes can contain nonabstract methods, but all methods within an interface must be abstract. A class can inherit from only one base class (whether abstract or not), but it can implement any number of interfaces. For example, if you want to create a Child that inherits from a Parent class and implements two interfaces, IWorkable and IPlayable, you would define the class name and list the base class and interfaces separated by commas:

`class Child : Parent, IWorkable, IPlayable`

You implement an existing interface because you want a class to be able to use a method that already exists in other applications. For example, suppose that you have created a Payroll application that uses the Work() method in the interface class. Also suppose that you create a new class named BusDriver. If BusDriver implements the IWorkable interface, then BusDriver objects can be used by the existing Payroll program. As another example, suppose that you have written a game program that uses an IAttackable interface with methods that determine how and when an object can attack. When you create new classes such as MarsAlien, Vampire, and CivilWarSoldier, and each implements the IAttackable interface, you must define how each one attacks and how each type of object can be added to the game. If you use these IAttackable classes, you are guaranteed that they can all determine how and when to attack.

 You can think of an interface as a contract. A class that implements an interface must abide by the rules of the contract.

Beginning programmers sometimes find it difficult to decide when to create an abstract base class and when to create an interface. You can follow these guidelines:

- Typically, you create an abstract class when you want to provide some data or methods that derived classes can inherit, but you want the subclasses to override some specific methods that you declare to be abstract.

- You create an interface when you want derived classes to override every method.

In other words, you inherit from an abstract base class when the class you want to create "is a" subtype, and you use an interface when the class you want to create will act like the interface.

Interfaces provide you with a way to exhibit polymorphic behavior. If diverse classes implement the same interface in unique ways, then you can treat each class type in the same way using the same language. When various classes use the same interface, you know the names of the methods that are available with those classes, and C# classes adopt a more uniform functionality; this consistency helps you to understand new classes you encounter more easily. If you know, for example, the method names contained in the IWorkable interface, and you see that a class implements IWorkable, you have a head start in understanding how the class functions.

 Now that you understand how to construct your own interfaces, you will benefit from rereading the section describing the IComparable interface in the chapter "Using Classes and Objects."

TWO TRUTHS & A LIE

Creating and Using Interfaces

1. An interface is a collection of methods (and perhaps other members) that can be used by any class as long as the class provides a definition to override the interface's abstract definitions.

2. Abstract classes and interfaces differ in that all methods in abstract classes must be abstract, but interfaces can contain nonabstract methods.

3. A class can inherit from only one base class, but it can implement any number of interfaces.

The false statement is #2. Abstract classes and interfaces are similar in that you cannot instantiate concrete objects from either one. However, they differ in that abstract classes can contain nonabstract methods, but all methods within an interface must be abstract.

Using Extension Methods

When you write a C# program, sometimes you might wish a class had an additional method that would be useful to you. If you created the original class, you have two options:

- You could revise the existing class, including the new useful method.

- You could derive a child class from the existing class and provide it with a new method.

Sometimes, however, classes you use were created by others, and you might not be allowed to either revise or extend them. Of course, you could create an entirely new class that includes your new method, but that would duplicate a lot of the work already done when the first class was created. In these cases, the best option is to write an extension method. **Extension methods** are methods you can write to add to any type. Extension methods were introduced in C# 3.0.

 Programmers sometimes define classes as sealed within the class header, as in sealed class InventoryItem. A **sealed class** cannot be extended. For example, the built-in String class is a sealed class.

For example, you have used the prewritten Int32 class throughout this book to declare integers. Suppose that you work for a company that frequently uses customer account numbers, and that the company has decided to add an extra digit to each account number. For simplicity, assume that all account numbers are two digits and that the new, third digit should be the rightmost digit in the sum of the first two digits. You could handle this problem by creating a class named

AccountNumber, including a method to produce the extra digit, and redefining every instance of a customer's account number in your applications as an AccountNumber object. However, if you already have many applications that define the account number as an integer, you might prefer to create an extension method that extends the Int32 class.

In Chapter 2 you learned that each C# intrinsic type, such as int, is an alias for a class in the System namespace, such as Int32.

When organizations append extra digits to account numbers, the extra digits are called check digits. *Check digits* help assure that all the digits in account numbers and other numbers are entered correctly. Check digits are calculated using different formulas. If a digit used to calculate the check digit is incorrect, then the resulting check digit is probably incorrect as well.

Figure 10-40 contains a method that extends the Int32 class. The first parameter in an extension method specifies the type extended and must begin with the keyword this. For example, the first (and in this case, only) parameter in the AddCheckDigit() method is this int num, as shown in the shaded portion of the figure. Within the AddCheckDigit() method in Figure 10-40, the first digit is extracted from the two-digit account number by dividing by 10 and taking the resulting whole number, and the second digit is extracted by taking the remainder. Those two digits are added, and the last digit of that sum is returned from the method. For example, if 49 is passed into the method, first becomes 4, second becomes 9, and third becomes the last digit of 13, or 3. Then the original number (49) is multiplied by 10 and added to the third digit, resulting in 493.

```
public static int AddCheckDigit(this int num)
{
    int first = num / 10;
    int second = num % 10;
    int third = (first + second) % 10;
    int result = num * 10 + third;
    return result;
}
```

Figure 10-40   The AddCheckDigit() extension method

An extension method must be static and must be stored in a static class. For example, the DemoExtensionMethod program in Figure 10-41 shows an application that is declared static in the shaded portion of the class header and uses the extension method in the second shaded statement. The static method AddCheckDigit() is used as if it were an instance method of the Int32 class; in other words, it is attached to an Int32 object with a dot, just as instance methods are when used with objects. No arguments are passed to the AddCheckDigit() method explicitly from the DemoExtensionMethod class. The parameter in the method is implied, just as these references are always implied in instance methods. Figure 10-42 shows the execution of the program.

```
using static System.Console;
static class DemoExtensionMethod
{
    static void Main()
    {
        int acctNum = 49;
        int revisedAcctNum = acctNum.AddCheckDigit();
        WriteLine("Original account number was {0}", acctNum);
        WriteLine("Revised account number is {0}", revisedAcctNum);
    }
    public static int AddCheckDigit(this int num)
    {
        int first = num / 10;
        int second = num % 10;
        int third = (first + second) % 10;
        int result = num * 10 + third;
        return result;
    }
}
```

Figure 10-41   The DemoExtensionMethod application

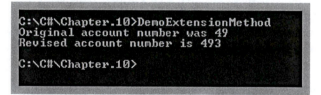

```
C:\C#\Chapter.10>DemoExtensionMethod
Original account number was 49
Revised account number is 493

C:\C#\Chapter.10>
```

Figure 10-42   Execution of the DemoExtensionMethod application

You can create extension methods for your own classes in the same way one was created for the Int32 class in this example. Just like other outside methods, and unlike ordinary class instance methods, extension methods cannot access any private members of classes they extend. Furthermore, if a class contains an instance method with the same signature as an extension method, the instance method takes priority and will be the one that executes.

TWO TRUTHS & A LIE

Using Extension Methods

1. The first parameter in an extension method specifies the type extended and must be preceded by the keyword `this`.

2. Extension methods must be static methods.

3. When you write an extension method, it must be stored within the class to which it refers, along with the class's other instance methods.

The false statement is #3. Although you use an extension method like an instance method, any extension method you write must be stored in a static class.

Recognizing Inheritance in GUI Applications and Recapping the Benefits of Inheritance

When you create a Windows Forms application using Visual Studio's IDE, you automatically use inheritance. Every `Form` you create is a descendent of the `Form` class. Figure 10-43 shows a just-started project in which the programmer has double-clicked the automatically generated `Form` to expose the code. You can see that the automatically generated `Form1` class extends `Form`.

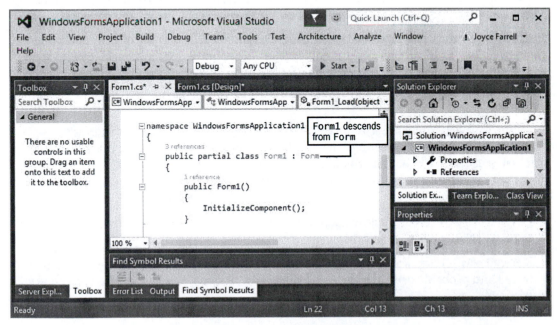

Figure 10-43   Automatically generated `Form` code in the IDE

The `Form` class descends from the `Object` class like all other C# classes but not directly. It is six generations removed from the `Object` class in the following line of descent:

- `Object`
- `MarshalByRefObject`
- `Component`
- `Control`
- `ScrollableControl`
- `ContainerControl`
- `Form`

Other GUI objects such as `Labels` and `Buttons` follow similar lengthy ancestry lines. You might guess that certain universal properties of GUI controls such as `Text` and `Visible` are inherited from ancestors. You will learn more about these hierarchies in the chapter "Using Controls," but even though you have worked with only a few controls so far, you can understand the benefits inheritance provides.

When an automobile company designs a new car model, it does not build every component from scratch. The car might include a new feature—for example, some model contained the first air bag—but many of a new car's features are simply modifications of existing features. The manufacturer might create a larger gas tank or a more comfortable seat, but these new features still possess many of the properties of their predecessors from older models. Most features of new car models are not even modified; instead, existing components, such as air filters and windshield wipers, are included on the new model without any changes.

Similarly, you can create many computer programs more easily if many of their components are used either "as is" or with slight modifications. Inheritance does not enable you to write any programs that you could not write if inheritance did not exist; you *could* create every part of a program from scratch, but reusing existing classes and interfaces makes your job easier.

You already have used many "as is" classes, such as `Console`, `Int32`, and `String`. Using these classes made it easier to write programs than if you had to invent the classes yourself. Now that you have learned about inheritance, you can extend existing classes as well as just use them. When you create a useful, extendable base class, you and other future programmers gain several advantages:

- Derived class creators save development time because much of the code that is needed for the class already has been written.

- Derived class creators save testing time because the base class code already has been tested and probably used in a variety of situations. In other words, the base class code is reliable.

- Programmers who create or use new derived classes already understand how the base class works, so the time it takes to learn the new class features is reduced.

- When you create a derived class in C#, the base class source code is not changed. Thus, the base class maintains its integrity.

Classes that are not intended to be instantiated and that contain only `static` members are declared as `static` classes. You cannot extend `static` classes. For example, `System.Console` is a static class.

When you think about classes, you need to think about the commonalities between them, and then you can create base classes from which to inherit. You might even be rewarded professionally when you see your own superclasses extended by others in the future.

TWO TRUTHS & A LIE

Recognizing Inheritance in GUI Applications and Recapping the Benefits of Inheritance

1. Inheritance enables you to create powerful computer programs more easily.

2. Without inheritance, you *could* create every part of a program from scratch, but reusing existing classes and interfaces makes your job easier.

3. Inheritance is frequently inefficient because base class code is seldom reliable when extended to a derived class.

The false statement is #3. Derived class creators save testing time because the base class code already has been tested and probably used in a variety of situations. In other words, the base class code is reliable.

Chapter Summary

- The classes you create in object-oriented programming languages can inherit data and methods from existing classes. The ability to use inheritance makes programs easier to write, easier to understand, and less prone to errors. A class that is used as a basis for inheritance is called a base class, superclass, or parent class. When you create a class that inherits from a base class, it is called a derived class, extended class, subclass, or child class.

- When you create a class that is an extension or child of another class, you use a single colon between the derived class name and its base class name. The child class inherits all the methods, properties, and fields of its parent. Inheritance works only in one direction—a child inherits from a parent, but not the other way around.

- If you could use private data outside of its class, the principle of information hiding would be destroyed. However, when you must access parent class data from a derived class, you declare parent class fields using the keyword **protected**, which provides you with an intermediate level of security between **public** and **private** access.

- When you declare a child class method with the same name and parameter list as a method within its parent class, you override the parent class method and allow your class objects to exhibit polymorphic behavior. You can use the keyword **new** or **override** with the derived class method. When a derived class overrides a parent class member but you want to access the parent class version, you can use the keyword **base**.

- Every derived class object "is a" specific instance of both the derived class and the base class. Therefore, you can assign a derived class object to an object of any of its base class types. When you do so, C# makes an implicit conversion from derived class to base class.

- Every class you create in C# derives from a single class named **System.Object**. Because all classes inherit from the **Object** class, all classes inherit the four **Object** class **public** instance methods: **Equals()**, **GetHashCode()**, **GetType()**, and **ToString()**.

- When you instantiate an object that is a member of a subclass, the base class constructor executes first, and then the derived class constructor executes.

- An abstract class is one from which you cannot create concrete objects but from which you can inherit. Usually, abstract classes contain abstract methods; an abstract method has no method statements. Any class derived from a class that contains an abstract method must override the abstract method by providing a body (an implementation) for it.

- An interface provides an alternative to multiple inheritance. Much like an abstract class, an interface is a collection of methods (and perhaps other members) that can be used by any class as long as the class provides a definition to override the interface's abstract definitions. Within an abstract class, some methods can be abstract, while others need not be. Within an interface, all methods are abstract. A class can inherit from only one abstract base class, but it can implement any number of interfaces.

- Extension methods are methods you can write to add to any type. They are static methods, but they operate like instance methods. Their parameter lists begin with the keyword `this` and the data type being extended.

- GUI objects such as buttons and forms descend from several ancestors. You can create many computer programs more easily using inheritance because it saves development and testing time.

Key Terms

Inheritance is the application of your knowledge of a general category to more specific objects.

Unified Modeling Language (UML) diagrams are graphical tools that programmers and analysts use to describe systems.

A **base class** is a class that is used as a basis for inheritance.

A **derived class** or **extended class** is one that has inherited from a base class.

A **superclass** is a base class.

A **subclass** is a derived class.

A **parent class** is a base class.

A **child class** is a derived class.

The **ancestors** of a derived class are all the superclasses from which the subclass is derived.

Transitive describes the feature of inheritance in which a child inherits all the members of all its ancestors.

Protected access provides an intermediate level of security between public and private access; a `protected` data field or method can be used within its own class or in any classes extended from that class, but it cannot be used by "outside" classes.

Fragile describes classes that depend on field names from parent classes because they are prone to errors—that is, they are easy to "break."

A **virtual method** is one whose behavior is determined by the implementation in a child class.

To **hide** a parent class member is to override it in a derived class.

Visible describes a base class member that is not hidden by a derived class.

Recursive describes a method that calls itself.

An **implicit conversion** occurs when a type is automatically converted to another upon assignment.

An **implicit reference conversion** occurs when a derived class object is assigned to its ancestor's data type.

The **object** (or **Object**) class type in the **System** namespace is the root base class for all other types.

A **root class** is the first base class in a hierarchal ancestry tree.

Reference equality occurs when two reference type objects refer to the same object.

A **hash code** is a number that should uniquely identify an object.

A **concrete class** is a nonabstract class from which objects can be instantiated.

An **abstract class** is one from which you cannot create concrete objects but from which you can inherit.

The keyword **override** is used in method headers when you create a derived class that inherits an abstract method from a parent.

Multiple inheritance is the ability to inherit from more than one class.

An **interface** is a collection of abstract methods (and perhaps other members) that can be used by any class as long as the class provides a definition to override the interface's abstract definitions.

Extension methods are static methods that act like instance methods. You can write extension methods to add to any type.

A **sealed class** cannot be extended.

Review Questions

1. Specific types of objects assume features of more general classes through _____ .

   a. polymorphism

   b. encapsulation

   c. inheritance

   d. structure

2. Which of the following is *not* a benefit of using inheritance when creating a new class?

   a. You save time, because you need not create fields and methods that already exist in a parent class.

   b. You reduce the chance of errors, because the parent class methods have already been used and tested.

   c. You make it easier for anyone who has used the parent class to understand the new class because the programmer can concentrate on the new features.

   d. You save computer memory because when you create objects of the new class, storage is not required for parent class fields.

3. A child class is also called a(n) _____ .

   a. extended class   c. superclass

   b. base class   d. delineated class

4. Assuming that the following classes are well named, which of the following is a parent class of **House**?

   a. **Apartment**   c. **Victorian**

   b. **Building**   d. **myHouse**

5. A derived class usually contains _____ than its parent.

   a. more fields and methods

   b. the same number of fields but fewer methods

   c. fewer fields but more methods

   d. fewer fields and methods

6. When you create a class that is an extension or child of another class, you use a(n) _____ between the derived class name and its base class name.

   a. ampersand   c. dot

   b. colon   d. hyphen

7. A base class named **Garden** contains a private field **width** and a property **public int Width** that contains **get** and **set** accessors. A child class named **VegetableGarden** does not contain a **Width** property. When you write a class in which you declare an object as follows, what statement can you use to access the **VegetableGarden**'s **width**?

   VegetableGarden myGarden = new VegetableGarden();

   a. **myGarden.Width**

   b. **myGarden.base.Width**

   c. **VegetableGarden.Width**

   d. You cannot use **Width** with a **VegetableGarden** object.

8. When a parent class contains a **private** data field, the field is _____ the child class.

   a. hidden in   c. directly accessible in

   b. not a member of   d. **public** in

9. When a base class and a derived class contain a method with the same name and parameter list, and you call the method using a derived class object, _____ .

   a. you receive an error message

   b. the base class version overrides the derived class version

   c. the derived class version overrides the base class version

   d. both method versions execute

10. Which of the following is an English-language form of polymorphism?

    a. seeing a therapist and seeing the point

    b. moving friends with a compelling story and moving friends to a new apartment

    c. both of these

    d. neither of these

11. When base and derived classes contain a method with the same name and parameter list, you can use the base class method within the derived class by using the keyword _____ before the method name.

    a. new   c. base

    b. override   d. super

12. In a program that declares a derived class object, you _____ assign it to an object of its base class type.

    a. can   c. must

    b. cannot   d. should not

13. The root base class for all other class types is _____ .

    a. Base   c. Parent

    b. Super   d. Object

14. All of the following are Object class methods *except* _____ .

    a. ToString()   c. Print()

    b. Equals()   d. GetHashCode()

15. When you create any derived class object, _____ .

    a. the base class and derived class constructors execute simultaneously

    b. the base class constructor must execute first, and then the derived class constructor executes

    c. the derived class constructor must execute first, and then the base class constructor executes

    d. neither the base class constructor nor the derived class constructor executes

16. When a base class constructor requires arguments, then each derived class _____ .

    a. must include a constructor

    b. must include a constructor that requires arguments

    c. must include two or more constructors

    d. must not include a constructor

17. When you create an abstract class, _____ .

    a. you can inherit from it

    b. you can create concrete objects from it

    c. Both of these are true.

    d. None of these is true.

18. When you create an abstract method, you provide _____ .

    a. the keyword `abstract`

    b. curly braces

    c. method statements

    d. all of these

19. Within an interface, _____ .

    a. no methods can be `abstract`

    b. some methods might be `abstract`

    c. some, but not all, methods must be `abstract`

    d. all methods must be `abstract`

20. Abstract classes and interfaces are similar in that _____ .

   a. you can instantiate concrete objects from both

   b. you cannot instantiate concrete objects from either one

   c. all methods in both must be **abstract**

   d. neither can contain nonabstract methods

Exercises

Programming Exercises

1. Create an application class named **LetterDemo** that instantiates objects of two classes named **Letter** and **CertifiedLetter** and that demonstrates all their methods. The classes are used by a company to keep track of letters they mail to clients. The **Letter** class includes auto-implemented properties for the name of the recipient and the date mailed. Also, include a **ToString()** method that overrides the **Object** class's **ToString()** method and returns a string that contains the name of the class (using **GetType()**) and the **Letter**'s data field values. Create a child class named **CertifiedLetter** that includes an auto-implemented property that holds a tracking number for the letter.

2. Create an application class named **PhotoDemo** that demonstrates the methods of three related classes for a company that develops photographs. Create a class named **Photo** that includes fields for width and height in inches and properties for each field. Include a **protected** price field, and set it to $3.99 for an 8-inch by 10-inch photo, $5.99 for a 10-inch by 12-inch photo, and $9.99 for any other size (because custom cutting is required). The price field requires a **get** accessor but no **set** accessor. Also include a **ToString()** method that returns a string constructed from the return value of the object's **GetType()** method and the values of the fields. Derive two subclasses—**MattedPhoto** and **FramedPhoto**. The **MattedPhoto** class includes a string field to hold a color, and the **FramedPhoto** class includes two string fields that hold the frame's material (such as *silver*) and style (such as *modern*). The price for a **MattedPhoto** increases by $10 over its base cost, and the price for a **FramedPhoto** increases by $25 over its base cost. Each subclass should include a **ToString()** method that overrides the parent class version.

3. a. Create an application named **OrderDemo** that declares and uses **Order** objects. The **Order** class performs order processing of a single item that sells for $19.95 each. The class has four variable fields that hold an order number, customer name, quantity ordered, and total price. Create a constructor that requires parameters for all the fields except total price. Include **public get** and **set** accessors for each field except the total price field; that field is calculated as quantity ordered times

unit price (19.95) whenever the quantity is set, so it needs only a `get` accessor. Also create the following for the class:

- An `Equals()` method that determines two `Orders` are equal if they have the same order number
- A `GetHashCode()` method that returns the order number
- A `ToString()` method that returns a string containing all order information

The OrderDemo application declares a few `Order` objects and sets their values. Make sure to create at least two orders with the same order number. Display the string from the `ToString()` method for each order. Write a method that compares two orders at a time and displays a message if they are equal. Send the `Orders` you created to the method two at a time and display the results.

b. Using the `Order` class you created in Exercise 3a, write a new application named **OrderDemo2** that creates an array of five `Orders`. Prompt the user for values for each `Order`. Do not allow duplicate order numbers; force the user to reenter the order when a duplicate order number is entered. When five valid orders have been entered, display them all, plus a total of all orders.

c. Create a `ShippedOrder` class that derives from `Order`. A `ShippedOrder` has a $4.00 shipping fee (no matter how many items are ordered). Override any methods in the parent class as necessary. Write a new application named **OrderDemo3** that creates an array of five `ShippedOrders`. Prompt the user for values for each, and do not allow duplicate order numbers—force the user to reenter the order when a duplicate order number is entered. When five valid orders have been entered, display them all, plus a total of all orders.

d. Make any necessary modifications to the `ShippedOrder` class so that it can be sorted by order number. Modify the `OrderDemo3` application so the displayed orders have been sorted. Save the application as **OrderDemo4**.

4. Create an application named **PackageDemo** that declares and demonstrates objects of the `Package` class and its descendents. The `Package` class includes auto-implemented properties for an ID number, recipient's name, and weight in ounces. The class also contains a delivery price field that is set when the weight is set as $5 for the first 32 ounces and 12 cents per ounce for every ounce over 32. b. Create a child class named `InsuredPackage`, which includes a field for the package's value. Override the method that sets a `Package`'s delivery price to include insurance, which is $1 for packages valued up to $20 and $2.50 for packages valued $20 or more.

5. a. Create an application named **AutomobileDemo** that prompts a user for data for eight `Automobile` objects. The `Automobile` class includes auto-implemented properties for ID number, make, year, and price. Override the `ToString()` method to return all the details for a `Automobile`. During data entry, reprompt the user if any ID number is a duplicate. Sort the objects in ID number order, and display all their data as well as a total of all their prices.

b. Using the `Automobile` class as a base, derive a `FinancedAutomobile` class that contains all the data of an `Automobile`, plus fields to hold the amount financed and interest rate. Override the parent class `ToString()` method to include the child class's additional data. Create a program named **AutomobileDemo2** that contains an array of four `FinancedAutomobile` objects. Prompt the user for all the necessary data, and do not allow duplicate ID numbers and do not allow the amount financed to be greater than the price of the automobile. Sort all the records in ID number order and display them with a total price for all `FinancedAutomobiles` and a total amount financed.

c. Write an application named **AutomobileDemo3** that uses an extension method for the `FinancedAutomobile` class. The method computes and returns a `FinancedAutomobile`'s monthly payment due (1/24 of the amount financed). The application should allow the user to enter data for four objects and then display all the data for each.

6. Create an application named **ShapesDemo** that creates several objects that descend from an abstract class called `GeometricFigure`. Each `GeometricFigure` includes a height, a width, and an area. Provide `get` and `set` accessors for each field except area; the area is computed and is read only. Include an abstract method called `ComputeArea()` that computes the area of the `GeometricFigure`. Create three additional classes:

   - A `Rectangle` is a `GeometricFigure` whose area is determined by multiplying width by height.

   - A `Square` is a `Rectangle` in which the width and height are the same. Provide a constructor that accepts both height and width, forcing them to be equal if they are not. Provide a second constructor that accepts just one dimension and uses it for both height and width. The `Square` class uses the `Rectangle`'s `ComputeArea()` method.

   - A `Triangle` is a `GeometricFigure` whose area is determined by multiplying the width by half the height.

   In the `ShapesDemo` class, after each object is created, pass it to a method that accepts a `GeometricFigure` argument in which the figure's data is displayed. Change some dimensions of some of the figures, and pass each to the display method again.

7. Create an application named **RecoveringDemo** that declares objects of three types: `Patient`, `Upholsterer`, and `FootballPlayer`. Create an interface named `IRecoverable` that contains a single method named `Recover()`. Create the classes named `Patient`, `Upholsterer`, and `FootballPlayer` so that each implements `IRecoverable`. Create each class's `Recover()` method to display an appropriate message. For example, the `Patient`'s `Recover()` method might display "I am getting better."

8. Create an application named **TurningDemo** that creates instances of four classes: `Page`, `Corner`, `Pancake`, and `Leaf`. Create an interface named `ITurnable` that contains a single method named `Turn()`. The classes named `Page`, `Corner`,

Pancake, and Leaf implement ITurnable. Create each class's Turn() method to display an appropriate message. For example, the Page's Turn() method might display "You turn a page in a book."

9. Write a program named **SalespersonDemo** that instantiates objects using classes named RealEstateSalesperson and GirlScout. Demonstrate that each object can use a SalesSpeech() method appropriately. Also, use a MakeSale() method two or three times with each object, and display the final contents of each object's data fields. First, create an abstract class named Salesperson. Fields include first and last names; the Salesperson constructor requires both these values. Include properties for the fields. Include a method that returns a string that holds the Salesperson's full name—the first and last names separated by a space. Then perform the following tasks:

- Create two child classes of Salesperson: RealEstateSalesperson and GirlScout. The RealEstateSalesperson class contains fields for total value sold in dollars and total commission earned (both of which are initialized to 0),and a commission rate field required by the class constructor. The GirlScout class includes a field to hold the number of boxes of cookies sold, which is initialized to 0. Include properties for every field.

- Create an interface named ISellable that contains two methods: SalesSpeech() and MakeSale(). In each RealEstateSalesperson and GirlScout class, implement SalesSpeech() to display an appropriate one- or two-sentence sales speech that the objects of the class could use.

In the RealEstateSalesperson class, implement the MakeSale() method to accept an integer dollar value for a house, add the value to the RealEstateSalesperson's total value sold, and compute the total commission earned. In the GirlScout class, implement the MakeSale() method to accept an integer representing the number of boxes of cookies sold and add it to the total field.

Debugging Exercises

1. Each of the following files in the Chapter.10 folder of your downloadable student files has syntax and/or logical errors. In each case, determine the problem and fix the program. After you correct the errors, save each file using the same filename preceded with *Fixed*. For example, DebugTen01.cs will become FixedDebugTen01.cs.

   a. DebugTen01.cs

   b. DebugTen02.cs

   c. DebugTen03.cs

   d. DebugTen04.cs

Case Problems

1. In Chapter 9, you created a **Contestant** class for the Greenville Idol competition. The class includes a contestant's name, talent code, and talent description. The competition has become so popular that separate contests with differing entry fees have been established for children, teenagers, and adults. Modify the **Contestant** class to contain a field that holds the entry fee for each category, and add **get** and **set** accessors.

    Extend the **Contestant** class to create three subclasses: **ChildContestant**, **TeenContestant**, and **AdultContestant**. Child contestants are 12 years old and younger, and their entry fee is $15. Teen contestants are between 13 and 17 years old, inclusive, and their entry fee is $20. Adult contestants are 18 years old and older, and their entry fee is $30. In each subclass, set the entry fee field to the correct value, and override the **ToString()** method to return a string that includes all the contestant data, including the age category and the entry fee.

    Modify the **GreenvilleRevenue** program so that it performs the following tasks:

    *   The program prompts the user for the number of contestants in this year's competition, which must be between 0 and 30. The program continues to prompt the user until a valid value is entered.

    *   The program prompts the user for names, ages, and talent codes for the contestants entered. Along with the prompt for a talent code, display a list of valid categories. Based on the age entered for each contestant, create an object of the correct type (adult, teen, or child), and store it in an array of **Contestant** objects.

    *   After data entry is complete, display the total expected revenue, which is the sum of the entry fees for the contestants.

    *   After data entry is complete, display the valid talent categories and then continuously prompt the user for talent codes, and display all the data for all the contestants in each category. Display an appropriate message if the entered code is not a character or a valid code.

2. In Chapter 9, you created a **Mural** class for Marshall's Murals. The class holds a customer's name, a mural code, and a description. Now, add a field to the **Mural** class that holds a price. Extend the **Mural** class to create subclasses named **InteriorMural** and **ExteriorMural**, and place statements that determine a mural's price within these classes. (A mural's price depends on the month, as described in the case problem in Chapter 9.) Also create **ToString()** methods for these subclasses that return a string containing all the pertinent data for a mural.

Modify the **Marshalls**Revenue program so that it performs the following tasks:

- The program prompts the user for the month, the number of interior murals scheduled, and the number of exterior murals scheduled. In each case, the program continues to prompt the user until valid entries are made.

- The program prompts the user for customer names and mural codes for interior and exterior murals. Along with the prompt for a mural code, display a list of valid categories.

- After data entry is complete, display the total revenue of interior murals, exterior murals, and all murals.

- After data entry is complete, the program displays the valid mural categories and then continuously prompts the user for codes and uses the `ToString()` method to display all the details for the murals in each category. Appropriate messages are displayed if the entered code is not a character or a valid code.

CHAPTER 11

Exception Handling

In this chapter you will:

◎ Learn about exceptions, the Exception class, and generating SystemExceptions

◎ Compare traditional and object-oriented error-handling methods

◎ Use the Exception class's ToString() method and Message property

◎ Catch multiple exceptions

◎ Examine the structure of the TryParse() methods

◎ Use the finally block

◎ Handle exceptions thrown from outside methods

◎ Trace Exception objects through the call stack

◎ Create your own Exception classes

◎ Rethrow Exceptions

While visiting Web sites, you have probably seen an unexpected and cryptic message that announces an error and then shuts down your browser immediately. Perhaps something similar has happened to you while using a piece of application software. Certainly, if you have worked your way through all of the programming exercises in this book, you have encountered such errors while running your own programs. A program that just stops is aggravating, especially when you lose data, and the error message seems to indicate that the program "knows" what is causing the problem. You might grumble, "If the program knows what is wrong, why doesn't it just fix the problem?" In this chapter, you will learn how to handle these unexpected error conditions so your programs can be more user-friendly than those that simply shut down in the face of errors.

Understanding Exceptions

An **exception** is any error condition or unexpected behavior in an executing program. Exceptions are caused by errors in program logic or insufficient system resources. The programs you write can generate many types of potential exceptions, including when:

- Your program asks for user input, but the user enters invalid data.

- The program attempts to divide an integer by zero.

- You attempt to access an array with a subscript that is too large or too small.

- You calculate a value that is too large for the answer's variable type.

These errors are called exceptions because presumably they are not usual occurrences; they are "exceptional." The object-oriented techniques used to manage such errors make up the group of methods known as **exception handling**. If you do not handle an exception, the running program terminates abruptly.

Managing exceptions involves an oxymoron; you must expect the unexpected.

Errors you discover when compiling a program are not exceptions; they are compiler errors. Only execution-time (also called *runtime*) errors are called exceptions.

In C#, all exceptions are objects that are instances of the Exception class or one of its derived classes. An exception condition generates an object that encapsulates information about the error. Like all other classes in the C# programming language, the Exception class is a descendent of the Object class. The Exception class has several descendent classes of its own, many with unusual names such as CodeDomSerializerException, SUDSParserException, and SoapException. Others have names that are more easily understood, such as IOException (for input and output errors), InvalidPrinterException (for when a user requests an invalid printer), and PathTooLongException (used when the path to a file contains more characters than a system allows). C# has more than 100 defined Exception subclasses; Table 11-1 lists just a few to give you an idea of the wide variety of circumstances they cover.

Class	Description
System.ArgumentException	Thrown when one of the arguments provided to a method is not valid
System.ArithmeticException	Thrown for errors in an arithmetic, casting, or conversion operation
System.ArrayTypeMismatchException	Thrown when an attempt is made to store an element of the wrong type within an array
System.Data.OperationAbortedException	Thrown when an ongoing operation is aborted by the user
System.Drawing.Printing.InvalidPrinterException	Thrown when you try to access a printer using printer settings that are not valid
System.FormatException	Thrown when the format of an argument does not meet the parameter specifications of the invoked method
System.IndexOutOfRangeException	Thrown when an attempt is made to access an element of an array with an index that is outside the bounds of the array; this class cannot be inherited
System.InvalidCastException	Thrown for an invalid casting or explicit conversion
System.InvalidOperationException	Thrown when a method call is invalid for the object's current state
System.IO.InvalidDataException	Thrown when a data stream is in an invalid format
System.IO.IOException	Thrown when an I/O error occurs
System.MemberAccessException	Thrown when an attempt to access a class member fails
System.NotImplementedException	Thrown when a requested method or operation is not implemented
System.NullReferenceException	Thrown when there is an attempt to dereference a null object reference
System.OperationCanceledException	Thrown in a thread upon cancellation of an operation that the thread was executing
System.OutOfMemoryException	Thrown when there is not enough memory to continue the execution of a program
System.RankException	Thrown when an array with the wrong number of dimensions is passed to a method
System.StackOverflowException	Thrown when the execution stack overflows because it contains too many nested method calls; this class cannot be inherited

Table 11-1   Selected C# Exception subclasses

Table 11-1 uses the term *thrown*, which is explained later in this chapter.

Most exceptions you will use derive from three classes:

- The predefined Common Language Runtime exception classes derived from `SystemException`

- The user-defined application exception classes you derive from `ApplicationException`

- The `Exception` class, which is the parent of `SystemException` and `ApplicationException`

Microsoft previously advised that you should create your own custom exceptions from the `ApplicationException` class. They have revised their thinking and now advise that you should use the `Exception` class as a base because in practice, they have not found the previous approach to be of significant value. For updates, visit *http://msdn.microsoft.com*.

Purposely Generating a `SystemException`

You can deliberately generate a `SystemException` by forcing a program to contain an error. As an example, in every programming language, it is illegal to divide an integer by zero because the operation is mathematically undefined. Consider the simple `MilesPerGallon` program in Figure 11-1, which prompts a user for two values and divides the first by the second. If the user enters nonzero integers, the program runs correctly and without incident. However, if the user enters 0 when prompted to enter gallons, division by 0 takes place, and an error is generated. Figure 11-2 shows two executions of the program.

When you divide a floating-point value by 0 in C#, no exception occurs. Instead, C# assigns the special value `Infinity` to the result. Because `float`s and `double`s are imprecise, dividing them by 0.000000. . . to an infinite number of decimal places approaches infinity mathematically.

```
using System;
using static System.Console;
class MilesPerGallon
{
    static void Main()
    {
        int milesDriven;
        int gallonsOfGas;
        int mpg;
        Write("Enter miles driven ");
        milesDriven = Convert.ToInt32(ReadLine());
        Write("Enter gallons of gas purchased ");
        gallonsOfGas = Convert.ToInt32(ReadLine());
        mpg = milesDriven / gallonsOfGas;
        WriteLine("You got {0} miles per gallon", mpg);
    }
}
```

Figure 11-1   The MilesPerGallon program

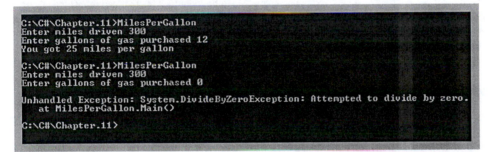

```
C:\C#\Chapter.11>MilesPerGallon
Enter miles driven 300
Enter gallons of gas purchased 12
You got 25 miles per gallon

C:\C#\Chapter.11>MilesPerGallon
Enter miles driven 300
Enter gallons of gas purchased 0

Unhandled Exception: System.DivideByZeroException: Attempted to divide by zero.
    at MilesPerGallon.Main()

C:\C#\Chapter.11>
```

Figure 11-2   Two executions of the MilesPerGallon program

When the user enters a 0 for gallons in the MilesPerGallon program, a dialog box reports that the application has stopped working and needs to close. Because this error is intentional for demonstration purposes, you can ignore the message by clicking the Close program button in the lower-right corner of the dialog box.

In the first execution of the MilesPerGallon program in Figure 11-2, the user entered two usable integers, and division was carried out successfully. However, in the second execution, the user entered 0 for gallons of gas, and the error message indicates that an unhandled exception named System.DivideByZeroException was created. The message gives further information ("Attempted to divide by zero.") and shows the method where the exception occurred—in MilesPerGallon.Main().

The DivideByZeroException object was generated automatically by C#. It is an instance of the DivideByZeroException class that has four ancestors. It is a child of the ArithmeticException class, which descends from the SystemException class. The SystemException class derives from the Exception class, which is a child of the Object class.

494

Just because an exception occurs and an Exception object is created, you don't necessarily have to deal with it. In the MilesPerGallon class, you simply let the offending program terminate; that's why the error message in Figure 11-2 indicates that the Exception is "Unhandled." However, the termination of the program is abrupt and unforgiving. When a program divides two numbers, or performs some other trivial task like playing a game, the user might be annoyed if the program ends abruptly. If the program is used for air-traffic control or to monitor a patient's vital statistics during surgery, an abrupt conclusion could be disastrous. With exception handling, a program can continue after dealing with a problem. This is especially important in mission-critical applications. The term **mission critical** refers to any process that is crucial to an organization. Object-oriented error-handling techniques provide more elegant solutions than simply shutting down.

Programs that can handle exceptions appropriately are said to be more fault tolerant and robust than those that do not. **Fault-tolerant** applications are designed so that they continue to operate, possibly at a reduced level, when some part of the system fails. **Robustness** represents the degree to which a system is resilient to stress, maintaining correct functioning.

Watch the video *System Exceptions*.

TWO TRUTHS & A LIE

Understanding Exceptions

1. An exception is any error condition or unexpected behavior in an executing program.

2. In C#, all exceptions are objects that are members of the Exception class or one of its derived classes.

3. In C#, when an exception occurs and an Exception object is created, you must employ a specific set of exception-handling techniques in order to manage the problem.

The false statement is #3. Just because an exception occurs and an Exception object is created, you don't necessarily have to deal with it.

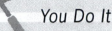 *You Do It*

Purposely Causing Exceptions

C# generates SystemExceptions automatically under many circumstances. In the next steps, you purposely generate a SystemException by executing a program that provides multiple opportunities for Exceptions.

1. Start a new project named **ExceptionsOnPurpose**, and type the following program, which allows you to generate several different Exceptions.

```
using System;
using static System.Console;
class ExceptionsOnPurpose
{
    static void Main()
    {
        int answer;
        int result;
        int zero = 0;
        Write("Enter an integer >> ");
        answer = Convert.ToInt32(ReadLine());
        result = answer / zero;
        WriteLine("The answer is " + answer);
    }
}
```

2. You cannot divide by the unnamed constant 0 (by changing the dividing statement to result = answer /0;), nor can you change the variable zero to a named constant (by inserting const at the start of the int zero declaration). If you made either of these changes, the program would not compile because the compiler can determine that division by zero will occur. Using a variable zero instead of either an unnamed or named constant, however, the compiler "trusts" that a legitimate value will be provided for the variable before division occurs (although in this case, the trust is not warranted). Save the program, and compile it.

3. Execute the program several times using different input values, and observe the results. Two windows appear with each execution. The first reports that Windows is collecting more information about the problem. This window is soon replaced with the one shown in Figure 11-3, which repeats that

(continues)

496

(continued)

ExceptionsOnPurpose.exe has stopped working. You would never write a program that purposely divides by zero; you do so here to demonstrate C#'s exception-generating capabilities. If you were executing a professional application, you might be notified of a solution. Because you created this exception on purpose, just click the **Close program** button.

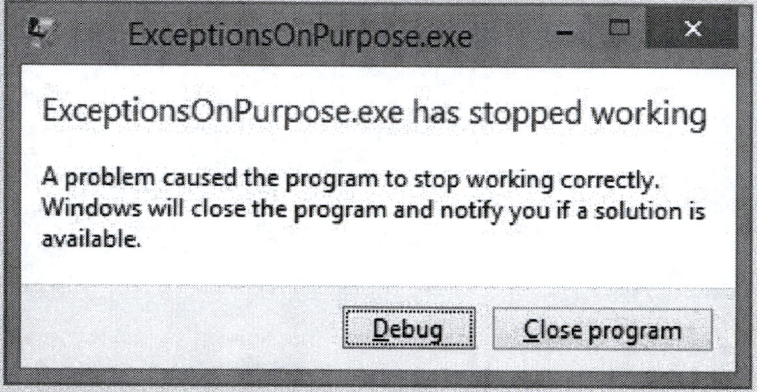

Figure 11-3   The error report window generated by an unhandled exception

Figure 11-4 shows three executions of the program during which the user typed the following:

- **seven**—This generates a System.FormatException, which occurs when the program tries to convert the input value to an integer, because letters are not allowed in integers.

- **7.7**—This also generates a System.FormatException because the decimal point is not allowed in an integer.

- **7**—This does not generate a System.FormatException but instead causes a System.DivideByZeroException when the result is calculated.

(continues)

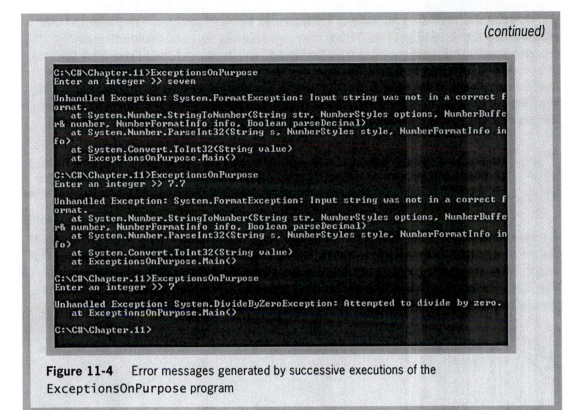

(continued)

```
C:\C#\Chapter.11>ExceptionsOnPurpose
Enter an integer >> seven

Unhandled Exception: System.FormatException: Input string was not in a correct f
ormat.
   at System.Number.StringToNumber(String str, NumberStyles options, NumberBuffe
r& number, NumberFormatInfo info, Boolean parseDecimal)
   at System.Number.ParseInt32(String s, NumberStyles style, NumberFormatInfo in
fo)
   at System.Convert.ToInt32(String value)
   at ExceptionsOnPurpose.Main()

C:\C#\Chapter.11>ExceptionsOnPurpose
Enter an integer >> 7.7

Unhandled Exception: System.FormatException: Input string was not in a correct f
ormat.
   at System.Number.StringToNumber(String str, NumberStyles options, NumberBuffe
r& number, NumberFormatInfo info, Boolean parseDecimal)
   at System.Number.ParseInt32(String s, NumberStyles style, NumberFormatInfo in
fo)
   at System.Convert.ToInt32(String value)
   at ExceptionsOnPurpose.Main()

C:\C#\Chapter.11>ExceptionsOnPurpose
Enter an integer >> 7

Unhandled Exception: System.DivideByZeroException: Attempted to divide by zero.
   at ExceptionsOnPurpose.Main()

C:\C#\Chapter.11>
```

Figure 11-4 Error messages generated by successive executions of the
ExceptionsOnPurpose program

497

Comparing Traditional and Object-Oriented Error-Handling Methods

Programmers had to deal with error conditions long before object-oriented methods were conceived. For example, dividing by zero is an avoidable error for which programmers always have had to plan. If you simply check a variable's value with an `if` statement before attempting to divide it into another number, you can prevent the creation of an `Exception` object. For example, the following code uses a traditional `if` statement to check a variable to prevent division by zero.

```
if(gallonsOfGas != 0)
   mpg = milesDriven / gallonsOfGas;
else
   mpg = 0;
```

This code successfully prevents division by zero, but it does not really "handle an exception" because no `Exception` class object is created. The example code illustrates a perfectly legal and reasonable method of preventing division by zero, and it represents the most efficient method of handling the error if you think it will be a frequent problem. Because a program

498

that contains this code does not have to instantiate an Exception object every time the user enters a 0 for the value of gallonsOfGas, the program saves time and computer memory. (Programmers say this program has little "overhead.") On the other hand, if you think dividing by zero will be infrequent—that is, the *exception* to the rule—then the decision will execute many times when it is not needed. In other words, if a user enters 0 for gallonsOfGas in only one case out of 1,000, then the if statement is executed unnecessarily 999 times. In that case, it is more efficient to eliminate the if test and instantiate an Exception object when needed.

The creators of C# define "infrequent" as an event that happens less than 30 percent of the time. That is, if you think an error will occur in less than 30 percent of all program executions, create an exception; if you think the error will occur more often, use traditional error checking. Of course, your boss or instructor might prefer a different percentage to use as a guideline.

Another advantage to using exception handling instead of decision making to control errors is that when a program's main logic is interrupted by a series of if statements and decisions that might detect errors, the program can become more complicated and difficult to understand. The object-oriented approach to error handling separates a program's main tasks from code that deals with rare exceptions.

Programmers use the phrase *sunny day case* to describe a scenario in which everything goes well and no errors occur.

Understanding Object-Oriented Exception-Handling Methods

Object-oriented exception handling uses three unique terms: *try*, *throw*, and *catch*.

- You "try" a procedure that may not complete correctly.
- A method that detects an error condition "throws" an exception.
- The block of code that processes the error "catches" the exception.

When you write a block of code in which something can go wrong, you can place the code in a **try block**, which consists of the following elements:

- The keyword try
- A pair of curly braces containing statements that might cause exceptions

You must code at least one catch block or finally block immediately following a try block. (You will learn about finally blocks later in this chapter.) Each **catch block** can "catch" one type of exception—that is, an Exception object or an object of one of its child classes. Programmers sometimes refer to a catch block as a *catch clause*. You can create a catch block by typing the following elements:

- The keyword catch

- Parentheses containing an Exception type and, optionally, a name for an instance of the Exception type
- A pair of curly braces containing statements that deal with the error condition

You also can create a catch block omitting the parentheses and Exception type. If you do, the catch block will execute when any Exception type is thrown. In other words catch and catch(Exception) are both correct ways to start a catch block to catch all Exceptions when you do not want to name the Exception object because you do not care about displaying its details.

Figure 11-5 shows the general format of a try…catch pair. The placeholder XxxException in the catch block represents the Exception class or any of its more specific subclasses. The placeholder XxxException is the data type of the anExceptionInstance object. A catch block looks a lot like a method named catch(), which takes an argument that is an instance of XxxException. However, it is not a method; you cannot call it directly. A method can accept multiple arguments, but a catch block can catch only one object, and, unlike a method, a catch block has no return type.

As XxxException implies, Exception classes typically are created using Exception as the second half of the name, as in SystemException and ApplicationException. The compiler does not require this naming convention, but the convention does make Exception descendents easier to identify.

```
try
{
    // Any number of statements;
    // some might cause an exception
}
catch(XxxException anExceptionInstance)
{
    // Do something about it
}
// Statements here execute whether there was an exception or not
```

Figure 11-5   General form of a try…catch pair

You can place any number of statements in a try block, including those you know will never throw an exception. However, if any one of the statements you place within a try block does throw an exception, then the statements in the catch block that catches the exception will execute. If no exception occurs within the try block, then the catch block does not execute. Either way, the statements following the catch block execute normally.

For example, Figure 11-6 contains a program in which the statements that prompt for, accept, and use gallonsOfGas are encased in a try block. (The three variable declarations are made before the try block by convention. In this case, mpg must be declared outside the try block to be recognized in the program's final output statement.) Figure 11-7 shows two executions of the program. In the first execution, a usable value is entered for gallonsOfGas, and the program operates normally, bypassing the catch block. In the second execution, however, the user enters 0 for gallonsOfGas. When division is attempted, an Exception object is automatically created and thrown. The catch block catches the Exception, where it becomes known as e. (The shaded arrow in Figure 11-6 extends from where the exception is created and thrown to where it is caught.) The statements in the catch block set mpg to 0 and display a message. Whether the catch block executes or not, the final WriteLine() statement that follows the catch block's closing curly brace executes.

```csharp
using System;
using static System.Console;
class MilesPerGallon2
{
    static void Main( )
    {
        int milesDriven;
        int gallonsOfGas;
        int mpg;
        try
        {
            Write("Enter miles driven ");
            milesDriven = Convert.ToInt32(ReadLine( ));
            Write("Enter gallons of gas purchased ");
            gallonsOfGas = Convert.ToInt32(ReadLine( ));
            mpg = milesDriven / gallonsOfGas;
        }

        catch(Exception e)
        {
            mpg = 0;
            WriteLine("You attempted to divide by zero!");
        }
        WriteLine("You got {0} miles per gallon", mpg);
    }
}
```

Figure 11-6   The MilesPerGallon2 program

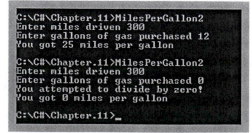

Figure 11-7   Two executions of the MilesPerGallon2 program

When you compile the program in Figure 11-6, you receive a warning that e is declared but never used. You can declare a variable to hold the thrown Exception object, but you do not want to use it in this example, so you can safely ignore the warning. If you do not want to use the caught Exception object within a catch block, then you do not have to provide an instance name for it. For example, in Figure 11-6, the catch clause could begin as follows:

```
catch(Exception)
```

In later examples in this chapter, the Exception object will be used to provide information. In those cases, it is required to have an identifier.

In the MilesPerGallon2 program, you could catch a more specific DivideByZeroException object instead of catching an Exception object. You will employ this technique later in the chapter. If you are working on a professional project, Microsoft recommends that you never use the general Exception class in a catch block because doing so can hide problems.

In the application in Figure 11-6, the source of the exception and the catch block reside in the same method. Later in this chapter, you will learn that exceptions and their corresponding catch blocks frequently reside in separate methods.

Watch the video *Throwing and Catching Exceptions*.

TWO TRUTHS & A LIE

Comparing Traditional and Object-Oriented Error-Handling Methods

1. Before object-oriented methods were conceived, programmers had no way of handling unexpected conditions.

2. Using object-oriented techniques, when you write a block of code in which something can go wrong, you can place the code in a try block.

3. If a catch block executes, then an Exception must have been thrown.

The false statement is #1. Programmers had to deal with error conditions long before object-oriented methods were conceived. They typically used decision-making techniques to check for errors.

Using the Exception Class's ToString() Method and Message Property

When the MilesPerGallon2 program displays the error message ("You attempted to divide by zero!"), you actually cannot confirm from the message that division by zero was the source of the error. In reality, any Exception type generated within the try block of the program would be caught by the catch block in the method because the argument in the catch block is a general Exception, which is the parent class to all the Exception subtypes.

Instead of writing your own message, you can use the ToString() method that every Exception object inherits from the Object class. The Exception class overrides ToString() to provide a descriptive error message so a user can receive precise information about the nature of any Exception that is thrown. For example, Figure 11-8 shows a MilesPerGallon3 program. The shaded areas show the only changes from the MilesPerGallon2 program: the name of the class and the message that is displayed when an Exception is thrown. In this example, the ToString() method is used with the caught Exception e. Figure 11-9 shows an execution of the program in which the user enters 0 for gallonsOfGas. You can see in the output that the type of Exception caught is a System.DivideByZeroException.

You learned about overriding the Object class ToString() method in the chapter "Introduction to Inheritance."

```
using System;
using static System.Console;
class MilesPerGallon3
{
    static void Main()
    {
        int milesDriven;
        int gallonsOfGas;
        int mpg;
        try
        {
            Write("Enter miles driven ");
            milesDriven = Convert.ToInt32(ReadLine());
            Write("Enter gallons of gas purchased ");
            gallonsOfGas = Convert.ToInt32(ReadLine());
            mpg = milesDriven / gallonsOfGas;
        }
```

Figure 11-8   The MilesPerGallon3 program (continues)

(continued)

```
        catch(Exception e)
        {
            mpg = 0;
            WriteLine(e.ToString());
        }
        WriteLine("You got {0} miles per gallon", mpg);
    }
}
```

Figure 11-8   The MilesPerGallon3 program

```
C:\C#\Chapter.11>MilesPerGallon3
Enter miles driven 300
Enter gallons of gas purchased 0
System.DivideByZeroException: Attempted to divide by zero.
   at MilesPerGallon3.Main()
You got 0 miles per gallon

C:\C#\Chapter.11>
```

Figure 11-9   Execution of the MilesPerGallon3 program

The error message displayed in Figure 11-9 (*System.DivideByZeroException: Attempted to divide by zero.*) is the same message that appeared in Figure 11-2 when you provided no exception handling. Therefore, you can assume that the operating system most likely uses the same ToString() method you can use when displaying information about an Exception object. In the program in which you provided no exception handling, execution simply stopped; in this one, execution continues, and the final output statement is displayed whether the user's input was usable or not. Programmers would say this new version of the program ends more "elegantly."

The Exception class also contains a read-only property named Message that contains useful information about an Exception object. For example, the program in Figure 11-10 contains just two shaded changes from the MilesPerGallon3 program: the class name and the use of the Message property in the statement that displays the error message in the catch block. The program produces the output shown in Figure 11-11. The value of e.Message is a string that is identical to the second part of the value returned by the ToString() method. You can guess that the DivideByZeroException class's ToString() method used in MilesPerGallon3 constructs its string from two parts: the return value of the getType() method (that indicates the name of the class) and the return value from the Message property.

504

```
using System;
using static System.Console;
class MilesPerGallon4
{
    static void Main()
    {
        int milesDriven;
        int gallonsOfGas;
        int mpg;
        try
        {
            Write("Enter miles driven ");
            milesDriven = Convert.ToInt32(ReadLine());
            Write("Enter gallons of gas purchased ");
            gallonsOfGas = Convert.ToInt32(ReadLine());
            mpg = milesDriven / gallonsOfGas;
        }
        catch(Exception e)
        {
            mpg = 0;
            WriteLine(e.Message);
        }
        WriteLine("You got {0} miles per gallon", mpg);
    }
}
```

Figure 11-10   The MilesPerGallon4 program

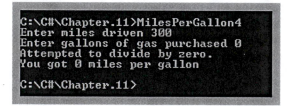

Figure 11-11   Execution of the MilesPerGallon4 program

TWO TRUTHS & A LIE

Using the Exception Class's ToString() Method and Message Property

1. Any Exception type generated within a try block in a program will be caught by a catch block that has an Exception type argument.

2. The Exception class overrides the Object class Description() method to provide a descriptive error message so a user can receive precise information about the nature of any Exception object that is thrown.

3. The Exception class contains a property named Message that contains useful information about an Exception.

The false statement is #2. The Exception class overrides the Object class ToString() method to provide a descriptive error message so a user can receive precise information about the nature of any Exception that is thrown.

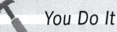

You Do It

Handling Exceptions

You can handle exceptions by placing them in a try block and then catching any exceptions that are thrown from it.

1. Open the **ExceptionsOnPurpose** program if it is not still open. Change the class name to **ExceptionsOnPurpose2**, and immediately save the project as **ExceptionsOnPurpose2**.

2. In the Main() method, after the three variable declarations, enclose the next three statements in a try block as follows:

```
try
{
    Write("Enter an integer >> ");
    answer = Convert.ToInt32(ReadLine());
    result = answer / zero;
}
```

3. Following the try block (but before the WriteLine() statement that displays answer), add a catch block that catches any thrown Exception object and displays its Message property:

(continues)

(continued)

```
catch(Exception e)
{
    WriteLine(e.Message);
}
```

4. Save the program, and compile it. You should receive a compiler error indicating that `answer` is an unassigned local variable. This error occurs at the last line of the program where `answer` is displayed. In the first version of this program, no such message appeared. However, now that the assignment to `answer` is within the `try` block, the compiler understands that an exception might be thrown, terminating the block before a valid value is assigned to `answer`. To eliminate this problem, initialize `answer` at its declaration:

```
int answer = 0;
```

5. Compile and execute the program again. Figure 11-12 shows three executions. The values typed by the user are the same as in Figure 11-4 in the previous "You Do It" section. However, the results are different in several significant ways:

- No error message window appears (as in Figure 11-3).

- The error messages displayed are cleaner and "friendlier" than the automatically generated versions in Figure 11-4.

- The program ends normally in each case, with the `answer` value displayed in a user-friendly manner.

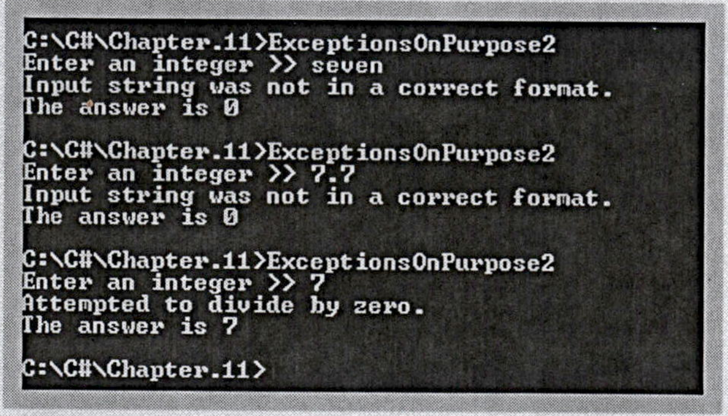

```
C:\C#\Chapter.11>ExceptionsOnPurpose2
Enter an integer >> seven
Input string was not in a correct format.
The answer is 0

C:\C#\Chapter.11>ExceptionsOnPurpose2
Enter an integer >> 7.7
Input string was not in a correct format.
The answer is 0

C:\C#\Chapter.11>ExceptionsOnPurpose2
Enter an integer >> 7
Attempted to divide by zero.
The answer is 7

C:\C#\Chapter.11>
```

Figure 11-12   Error messages generated by successive executions of the `ExceptionsOnPurpose2` program

Catching Multiple Exceptions

You can place as many statements as you need within a try block, and you can include as many catch blocks as you want to handle different Exception types. When a try block contains more than one statement, only the first error-generating statement throws an exception. As soon as the exception occurs, the logic transfers to the catch block, which leaves the rest of the statements in the try block unexecuted.

 The set of catch blocks following a try block should cover all possible exceptions that the code in the try block might encounter. Assuming there is at least one catch block, if an exception is thrown without a matching catch block, the program will terminate abruptly. (It's okay if there are no catch blocks at all if there is a finally block, as you will see shortly.)

When an Exception object is thrown and multiple catch blocks are present, the catch blocks are examined in sequence until a match is found. The matching catch block then executes, and each remaining catch block is bypassed.

For example, consider the program in Figure 11-13. The Main() method in the TwoErrors class potentially throws two types of Exceptions—a DivideByZeroException and an IndexOutOfRangeException. (An IndexOutOfRangeException occurs when an array subscript is not within the allowed range. In the TwoErrors program, the array has only three elements, but 13 is used as a subscript.)

```
using System;
using static System.Console;
class TwoErrors
{
    static void Main( )
    {
        int num = 13, denom = 0, result;
        int[ ] array = {22, 33, 44};
        try
        {
            result = num / denom;
            result = array[num];
        }
        catch(DivideByZeroException error)
        {
            WriteLine("In first catch block: ");
            WriteLine(error.Message);
        }
        catch(IndexOutOfRangeException error)
        {
            WriteLine("In second catch block: ");
            WriteLine(error.Message);
        }
    }
}
```

Figure 11-13   The TwoErrors program with two catch blocks

The TwoErrors class declares three integers and an integer array with three elements. In the Main() method, the try block executes, and at the first statement within the try block, an exception occurs because the denom in the division problem is zero. The try block is abandoned, and control transfers to the first catch block. Integer division by zero causes a DivideByZeroException, and because the first catch block receives that type of Exception, the message *In first catch block* appears along with the Message value of the Exception object. In this example, the second try statement is never attempted, and the second catch block is skipped. Figure 11-14 shows the output.

```
C:\C#\Chapter.11>TwoErrors
In first catch block:
Attempted to divide by zero.

C:\C#\Chapter.11>
```

Figure 11-14   Output of the TwoErrors program

If you reverse the two statements within the try block in the TwoErrors program, the process changes. If you use the try block in Figure 11-15, division by zero does not take place because the invalid array access throws an exception first.

```csharp
using System;
using static System.Console;
class TwoErrors2
{
    static void Main( )
    {
        int num = 13, denom = 0, result;
        int[ ] array = {22, 33, 44};
        try
        {
            result = array[num];
            result = num / denom;
        }
        catch(DivideByZeroException error)
        {
            WriteLine("In first catch block: ");
            WriteLine(error.Message);
        }
        catch(IndexOutOfRangeException error)
        {
            WriteLine("In second catch block: ");
            WriteLine(error.Message);
        }
    }
}
```

Figure 11-15   The TwoErrors2 program

The first statement within the `try` block in Figure 11-15 attempts to access element 13 of a three-element array, so the program throws an `IndexOutOfRangeException`. The `try` block is abandoned, and the first `catch` block is examined and found unsuitable because the `Exception` object is of the wrong type—it is not a `DivideByZeroException` object. The program logic proceeds to the second `catch` block, whose `IndexOutOfRangeException` argument type is a match for the thrown `Exception` type. The message *In second catch block* and the `Exception`'s `Message` value are therefore displayed. Figure 11-16 shows the output.

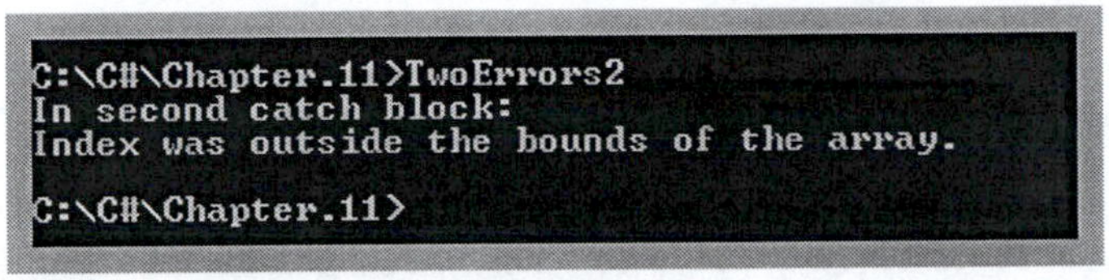

```
C:\C#\Chapter.11>TwoErrors2
In second catch block:
Index was outside the bounds of the array.

C:\C#\Chapter.11>
```

Figure 11-16   Output of the TwoErrors2 program

Sometimes you want to execute the same code, no matter which `Exception` type occurs. For example, in each version of the `TwoErrors` program, each of the two `catch` blocks displays a unique message. Instead, you might want both the `DivideByZeroException` catch block and the `IndexOutOfRangeException` catch block to use the thrown `Exception`'s `Message` field. Because `DivideByZeroException` and `IndexOutOfRangeException` both are subclasses of `Exception`, you can rewrite the `TwoErrors` class as shown in Figure 11-17 and include only one `Exception` catch block that catches any type of `Exception`.

```csharp
using System;
using static System.Console;
class TwoErrors3
{
    static void Main()
    {
        int num = 13, denom = 0, result;
        int[] array = {22, 33, 44};
        try
        {
            result = array[num];
            result = num / denom;
        }
        catch(Exception error)
        {
            WriteLine(error.Message);
        }
    }
}
```

Figure 11-17   The TwoErrors3 class with one `catch` block

As an alternative to using a single catch block for multiple Exception types that require the same action, as in Figure 11-17, you could create the class to have separate catch blocks, each of which calls the same error-handling method.

The catch block in Figure 11-17 accepts a more generic Exception type than might be thrown by either statement in the try block, so the generic catch block can act as a "catch-all" block. That is, when either a division arithmetic error or an array error occurs, the thrown error is "promoted" to an Exception error in the catch block. Through inheritance, DivideByZeroExceptions and IndexOutOfRangeExceptions are Exceptions.

As stated earlier, Microsoft recommends that a catch block should not handle general Exceptions. They say that if you cannot predict all possible causes of an exception, you should allow the application to terminate instead of handling the exception. Otherwise, it is easier for malicious code to exploit the resulting application state. However, many professional programmers disagree with this policy.

Although a block of code can throw any number of exceptions, many developers believe that it is poor style for a block or method to throw more than three or four types. If it does, one of the following conditions might be true:

- Perhaps the code block or method is trying to accomplish too many diverse tasks and should be broken up into smaller blocks or methods.

- Perhaps the Exception types thrown are too specific and should be generalized, as they are in the TwoErrors3 program in Figure 11-17.

When you list multiple catch blocks following a try block, you must be careful that some catch blocks don't become unreachable. **Unreachable** blocks contain statements that can never execute under any circumstances because the program logic "can't get there." Programmers also call unreachable code **dead code**.

For example, if successive catch blocks catch an Exception followed by a DivideByZeroException, then even DivideByZeroExceptions will be caught by the Exception catch. The second, DivideByZeroException catch block is unreachable because the more general Exception catch block is in its way, and therefore the class will not compile.

TWO TRUTHS & A LIE

Catching Multiple Exceptions

1. If you try more than one statement in a block, each error-generating statement throws an `Exception`.

2. You can write `catch` blocks that catch multiple `Exception` types.

3. When you list multiple `catch` blocks following a `try` block, you must be careful that some `catch` blocks don't become unreachable.

The false statement is #1. If you try more than one statement in a block, only the first error-generating statement throws an `Exception`.

You Do It

Catching Multiple Exception Types

In this section, you instigate multiple outcomes by providing multiple `catch` blocks for code in a `try` block.

1. Open the **ExceptionsOnPurpose2** program if it is not still open. Change the class name to **ExceptionsOnPurpose3**, and immediately save the project as **ExceptionsOnPurpose3**.

2. Replace the existing generic `catch` block with two `catch` blocks. (The statement that displays the answer still follows these `catch` blocks.) The first catches any `FormatException` and displays a short message. The second catches a `DivideByZeroException` and displays a much longer message.

```
catch(FormatException e)
{
   WriteLine("You did not enter an integer");
}
catch(DivideByZeroException e)
{
   WriteLine("This is not your fault.");
   WriteLine("You entered the integer correctly.");
   WriteLine("The program divides by zero.");
}
```

(continues)

(continued)

3. Save the program and compile it. When you execute the program and enter a value that is not an integer, the first `catch` block executes. When you enter an integer so that the program can proceed to the statement that divides by 0, the second `catch` block executes. Figure 11-18 shows two typical executions of the program.

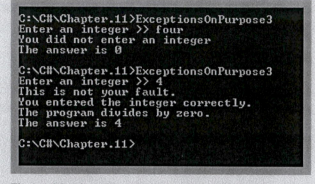

```
C:\C#\Chapter.11>ExceptionsOnPurpose3
Enter an integer >> four
You did not enter an integer
The answer is 0

C:\C#\Chapter.11>ExceptionsOnPurpose3
Enter an integer >> 4
This is not your fault.
You entered the integer correctly.
The program divides by zero.
The answer is 4

C:\C#\Chapter.11>
```

Figure 11-18   Error messages generated by successive executions of the ExceptionsOnPurpose3 program

Examining the Structure of the `TryParse()` Methods

In Chapter 8, you learned about the `TryParse()` methods that you can use to convert string data to another data type, such as `int`, `double`, or `bool`, without fear of generating an exception. A typical `TryParse()` statement might be as follows:

```
if(!int.TryParse(inputString, out number))
    number = DEFAULT_VALUE;
```

This statement uses the `int` version of the `TryParse()` method. The first argument is the string that you want to convert to a number, and the second argument is an `out` parameter that receives the result if the conversion is successful or 0 if it is not. Each of the `TryParse()` methods returns a Boolean value that indicates whether the conversion was successful. In the preceding example, the variable `number` is assigned a constant `DEFAULT_VALUE` if the method returns `false`—that is, if `inputString` is not an integer.

Suppose that no `TryParse()` method existed to convert a string to an integer safely. Using what you have learned so far in this chapter, you could now write your own method. The method handles the exception it might generate so that when a client uses the method, the client doesn't have to be concerned with exception handling. Figure 11-19 shows a usable method.

```
public static bool TryParse(string inputString, out int number)
{
    bool wasSuccessful = true;
    try
    {
        number = Convert.ToInt32(inputString);
    }
    catch(FormatException e)
    {
        wasSuccessful = false;
        number = 0;
    }
    return wasSuccessful;
}
```

Figure 11-19   A possible TryParse() method version

The TryParse() method in Figure 11-19 is public so that other classes can use it and static so that no object of its class needs to be instantiated. The method accepts a string and an out parameter that can hold the string's converted value. A bool variable named wasSuccessful is set to true, and then conversion is attempted. If the Convert.ToInt32() method works correctly, the variable number accepts the converted value. However, if a FormatException object is thrown, wasSuccessful is set to false and 0 is assigned to number. Whether an exception is thrown or not, the value of wasSuccessful is returned.

The creators of C# wrote code similar to that in Figure 11-19 when they created the TryParse() method for the Integer class. They may have included some differences— for example, they probably gave their variables different identifiers, and they might have reversed the positions of the statements in the catch block that set the Boolean value and the integer value, but the basic structure of the method must be similar. If no TryParse() method existed, you could write one for yourself, but the method is a convenience that already exists. As you continue to study programming, you might develop a method that would be convenient for others, and you might be rewarded in seeing your method used by other developers.

 Your downloadable Student Data Files contain a program named TestTryParse.cs that can be used to test the TryParse() method.

TWO TRUTHS & A LIE

Examining the Structure of the TryParse() Methods

1. The TryParse() method uses an out parameter.

2. The TryParse() method employs exception handling.

3. The TryParse() method must be used within a try block.

The false statement is #3. The TryParse() method contains a try block, but you don't need to use the method in a try block because it handles its own exception.

Using the `finally` Block

When you have actions to perform at the end of a try...catch sequence, you can use a **finally block**, which executes whether or not the try block identifies any exceptions. Typically, you use the finally block to perform clean-up tasks that must occur, regardless of whether any errors occurred or were caught. Figure 11-20 shows the format of a try...catch sequence that uses a finally block.

```
try
{
    // Statements that might cause an Exception
}
catch(SomeException anExceptionInstance)
{
    // What to do about it
}
finally
{
    // Statements here execute
    // whether an Exception occurred or not
}
```

Figure 11-20 General form of a try...catch block with a finally block

At first glance, it seems as though the finally block serves no purpose. When a try block works without error, control passes to the statements that come after the catch block. Additionally, if the try code fails and throws an Exception object that is caught, then the catch block executes, and control again passes to any statements that are coded after the catch block. Therefore, it seems as though the statements after the catch block always execute, so there is no need to place any statements within a special **finally** block. However, statements after the **catch** block might never execute for at least two reasons:

- An **Exception** for which you did not plan might occur, terminating the program.
- The **try** or **catch** block might contain a statement that terminates the application.

You can terminate an application with a statement such as Environment.Exit(0);. The Environment.Exit() method is part of the System namespace. It terminates a program and passes the argument (which can be any integer) to the operating system. You also might exit a catch block with a break statement or a return statement. You encountered break statements when you learned about the switch statement, and you learned about return statements when you studied methods.

The possibility exists that a **try** block might throw an **Exception** for which you did not provide a **catch**. After all, exceptions occur all the time without your handling them, as you saw in the first MilesPerGallon program at the beginning of this chapter. In the case of an unhandled exception, program execution stops immediately, sending the error to the operating system for handling and abandoning the current method. Likewise, if the **try** block contains an exit statement, execution stops immediately. When you include a **finally** block, you are assured that its enclosed statements will execute before the program is abandoned, even if the method concludes prematurely.

For example, the **finally** block is used frequently with file input and output to ensure that open files are closed. You will learn more about writing to and reading from data files in a later chapter. For now, however, consider the format shown in Figure 11-21, which represents part of the logic for a typical file-handling program. The **catch** block was written to catch an **IOException**, which is the type of **Exception** automatically generated if there is a problem opening a file, reading data from a file, or writing to a file.

```
try
{
    // Open the file
    // Read the file
    // Place the file data in an array
    // Calculate an average from the data
    // Display the average
}
catch(IOException e)
{
    // Issue an error message
    // Exit
}
finally
{
    // If the file is open, close it
}
```

Figure 11-21   Format of code that tries reading a file and handles an exception

516

The pseudocode in Figure 11-21 handles any file problems using the catch block. However, because the application uses an array (see the statement *Place the file data in an array*) and performs division (see the comment *Calculate an average...*), an uncaught exception could occur even though the file opened successfully. In such an event, you would want to close the file before proceeding. By using the finally block, you ensure that the file is closed, because the code in the finally block executes before the uncaught exception returns control to the operating system. The code in the finally block executes no matter which of the following outcomes of the try block occurs:

- The try ends normally.

- The try ends abnormally, and the catch executes.

- The try ends abnormally, and the catch does not execute. For example, an exception in the try block might cause the method to end prematurely—perhaps the array is not large enough to hold the data, or calculating the average results in division by 0. These exceptions do not allow the try block to finish, nor do they cause the catch block to execute because the catch block catches only IOExceptions.

- The try ends abnormally, the catch executes, but then the catch ends abnormally because an uncaught exception occurs.

If an application might throw several types of exceptions, you can try some code, catch the possible exception, try some more code, catch the possible exception, and so on. Usually, however, the superior approach is to try all the statements that might throw exceptions, then include all the needed catch blocks and an optional finally block. This is the approach shown in Figure 11-21, and it usually results in logic that is easier to follow.

You often can avoid using a finally block, but you would need repetitious code. For example, instead of using the finally block in the pseudocode in Figure 11-21, you could insert the statement *If the file is open, close it* as both the last statement in the try block and the second-to-last statement in the catch block, just before the program exits. However, writing code just once in a finally block is clearer and less prone to error.

Java, Visual Basic, and C++ provide try and catch blocks. Java and Visual Basic also provide a finally block, but C++ does not.

Many well-designed programs with one or more try blocks do not include catch blocks; instead, they contain only try-finally pairs. The finally block is used to release resources that other applications might be waiting for, such as database connections.

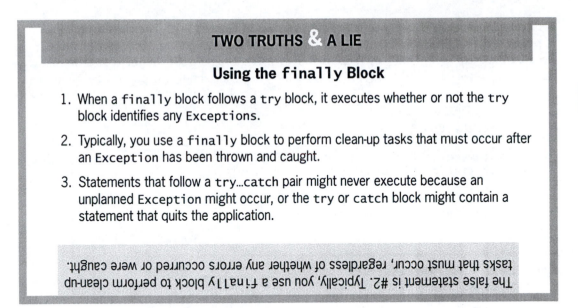

TWO TRUTHS & A LIE

Using the `finally` Block

1. When a `finally` block follows a `try` block, it executes whether or not the `try` block identifies any `Exceptions`.

2. Typically, you use a `finally` block to perform clean-up tasks that must occur after an `Exception` has been thrown and caught.

3. Statements that follow a `try`...`catch` pair might never execute because an unplanned `Exception` might occur, or the `try` or `catch` block might contain a statement that quits the application.

The false statement is #2. Typically, you use a `finally` block to perform clean-up tasks that must occur, regardless of whether any errors occurred or were caught.

Handling Exceptions Thrown from Outside Methods

An advantage of using object-oriented exception-handling techniques is the ability to deal with exceptions appropriately as you decide how to handle them. When methods from other classes throw exceptions, the methods don't have to catch them; instead, your calling program can catch them, and you can decide what to do.

For example, suppose that you prompt a user to enter a value at the console and then call the `Convert.ToInt32()` method to convert the input to an integer with a statement such as the following:

```
int answer = Convert.ToInt32(ReadLine());
```

If the user enters a noninteger value, a `FormatException` is generated from the `Convert.ToInt32()` method, but it is not caught and handled there. Instead, your program can catch the exception, and you can take appropriate action for your specific application. For example, you might want to force the user to reenter a value, but a different program might force the value to a default value or display an error message and terminate the program. This flexibility is an advantage when you need to create specific reactions to thrown exceptions. In many cases, you want a method to check for errors, but you do not want to require the method to handle an error if it finds one. Just as a police officer can deal with a speeding driver differently depending on circumstances, you can react to exceptions specifically for your current purposes.

When you design classes containing methods that have statements that might throw exceptions, you most frequently should create the methods so they throw the `Exception` object but do not handle it. Handling an exception usually should be left to the client—the program that uses your class—so the exception can be handled in an appropriate way for the application.

For example, consider the very brief PriceList class in Figure 11-22. The class contains a list of prices and a single method that displays one price based on a parameter subscript value. Because the DisplayPrice() method uses an array, an IndexOutOfRangeException might be thrown. However, the DisplayPrice() method does not handle the potential exception.

```
class PriceList
{
   private static double[] price = {15.99, 27.88, 34.56, 45.89};
   public static void DisplayPrice(int item)
   {
      WriteLine("The price is " +
         price[item].ToString("C"));
   }
}
```

Figure 11-22   The PriceList class

Figure 11-23 shows an application that uses the DisplayPrice() method. It calls the method in a try block and handles an IndexOutOfRangeException by displaying a price of $0. Figure 11-24 shows the output when a user enters an invalid item number.

```
using System;
using static System.Console;
class PriceListApplication1
{
   static void Main()
   {
      int item;
      try
      {
         Write("Enter an item number >> ");
         item = Convert.ToInt32(ReadLine());
         PriceList.DisplayPrice(item);
      }
      catch(IndexOutOfRangeException e)
      {
         WriteLine(e.Message + " The price is $0");
      }
   }
}
```

Figure 11-23   The PriceListApplication1 program

Figure 11-24 Output of the `PriceListApplication1` program when a user enters an invalid item number

Figure 11-25 shows a different application that uses the same `PriceList` class but handles the exception differently. In this case, the programmer wanted the user to keep responding until a correct entry was made. If an `IndexOutOfRangeException` is thrown from the `try` block, the `try` block is abandoned, `isGoodItem` is not set to `true`, and the `catch` block executes. Because `isGoodItem` remains `false`, the `while` loop continues to execute. Only when the first three statements in the `try` block are successful does the last statement execute, changing `isGoodItem` to `true` and ending the loop repetitions. Because the `DisplayPrice()` method in the `PriceList` class was written to throw an `Exception` but not handle it, the programmer of `PriceListApplication2` could handle the `Exception` in a totally different manner from the way it was handled in `PriceListApplication1`. Figure 11-26 shows a typical execution of this program.

```csharp
using System;
using static System.Console;
class PriceListApplication2
{
    static void Main()
    {
        int item = 0;
        bool isGoodItem = false;
        while(!isGoodItem)
        {
            try
            {
                Write("Enter an item number >> ");
                item = Convert.ToInt32(ReadLine());
                PriceList.DisplayPrice(item);
                isGoodItem = true;
            }
```

Figure 11-25 The `PriceListApplication2` program *(continues)*

(continued)

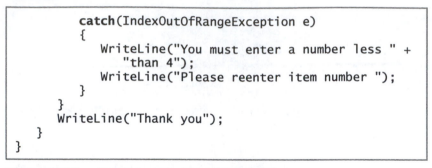

```
        catch(IndexOutOfRangeException e)
        {
            WriteLine("You must enter a number less " +
                "than 4");
            WriteLine("Please reenter item number ");
        }
    }
    WriteLine("Thank you");
    }
}
```

Figure 11-25   The PriceListApplication2 program

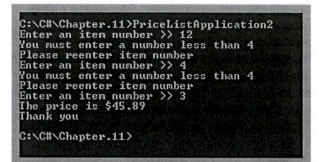

Figure 11-26   Output of the PriceListApplication2 program when a user enters an invalid item number several times

---

TWO TRUTHS & A LIE

Handling Exceptions Thrown from Outside Methods

1. When methods from other classes throw exceptions, the methods don't have to catch them; instead, your calling program can catch them, and you can decide what to do.

2. Often, you don't want a called method to handle its own exception; in many cases, you want the calling program to hande any exception in the way most appropriate for the application.

3. When you design classes containing methods that have statements that might throw exceptions, you almost always should make sure your class handles each exception appropriately.

The false statement is #3. When you design classes containing methods that have statements that might throw Exceptions, you most frequently should create the methods so they throw the exception but do not handle it.

Tracing Exception Objects Through the Call Stack

When one method calls another, the computer's operating system must keep track of where the method call came from, and program control must return to the calling method when the called method is complete. For example, if MethodA() calls MethodB(), the operating system has to "remember" to return to MethodA() when MethodB() ends. Similarly, if MethodB() calls MethodC(), then while MethodC() is executing, the computer needs to "remember" that it will return to MethodB() and eventually to MethodA(). The memory location where the computer stores the list of locations to which the system must return is known as the **call stack**.

If a method throws an exception and does not catch it, then the exception is thrown to the next method "up" the call stack; in other words, it is thrown to the method that called the offending method. Consider this sequence of events:

- MethodA() calls MethodB().

- MethodB() calls MethodC().

- MethodC() throws an Exception.

- C# looks first for a catch block in MethodC().

- If none exists, then C# looks for the same thing in MethodB().

- If MethodB() does not have a catch block for the Exception, then C# looks to MethodA().

- If MethodA() doesn't catch the Exception, then the program terminates, and the operating system displays an error message.

This system of passing an exception through the chain of calling methods is called **propagating the exception**. It has great advantages because it allows your methods to handle exceptions more appropriately. However, a program that uses several classes makes it difficult for the programmer to locate the original source of an exception.

You already have used the Message property to obtain information about an Exception object. The StackTrace property is another useful Exception property. When you catch an Exception, you can display the value of StackTrace to provide a list of methods in the call stack so you can determine the location where the Exception object was created.

The StackTrace property can be a useful debugging tool. When your program stops abruptly, it is helpful to discover the method in which the exception occurred. Often, you do not want to display a StackTrace property in a finished program; the typical user has no interest in the cryptic messages that would appear. However, while you are developing a program, using StackTrace can help you diagnose problems.

A Case Study: Using StackTrace

As an example of when StackTrace can be useful, consider the Tax class in Figure 11-27. Suppose that your company has created or purchased this class to make it easy to calculate tax rates on products sold. For simplicity, assume that only two tax rates are in effect—6 percent for sales of $20 or less and 7 percent for sales over $20. The Tax class would be useful for anyone who wrote a program involving product sales, except for one flaw: in the shaded statement, the subscript is erroneously set to 2 instead of 1 for the higher tax rate. If this subscript is used with the taxRate array in the next statement, it will be out of bounds.

522

```
class Tax
{
    private static double[] taxRate = {0.06, 0.07};
    private static double CUTOFF = 20.00;
    public static double DetermineTaxRate(double price)
    {
        int subscript;
        double rate;
        if(price <= CUTOFF)
            subscript = 0;
        else
            subscript = 2;
        rate = taxRate[subscript];
        return rate;
    }
}
```

Don't Do It
This mistake is intentional.

Figure 11-27   The Tax class

Assume that your company has also created a revised PriceList class, as shown in Figure 11-28. This class is similar to the one in Figure 11-22, except that it includes a tax calculation and calls the DetermineTaxRate() method in the shaded statement.

```
class PriceList
{
    private static double[] price = {15.99, 27.88, 34.56, 45.89};
    public static void DisplayPrice(int item)
    {
        double tax;
        double total;
        double pr;
        pr = price[item];
        tax = pr * Tax.DetermineTaxRate(pr);
        total = pr + tax;
        WriteLine("The total price is " + total.ToString("C"));
    }
}
```

Figure 11-28   The PriceList class that includes a call to the Tax class method

Suppose that you write the application shown in Figure 11-29. Your application is similar to the price list applications created earlier in this chapter, including a call to `PriceList.DisplayPrice()`. As in `PriceListApplication1` and `PriceListApplication2`, your new program tries the data entry and display statement and then catches an exception. When you run the program using what you know to be a good item number, as in Figure 11-30, you are surprised to see the shaded "Error!" message you have coded in the `catch` block. In the earlier examples that used `PriceList.DisplayPrice()`, using an item number 1 would have resulted in a successful program execution.

```
using System;
using static System.Console;
class PriceListApplication3
{
    static void Main()
    {
        int item;
        try
        {
            Write("Enter an item number >> ");
            item = Convert.ToInt32(ReadLine());
            PriceList.DisplayPrice(item);
        }
        catch(Exception e)
        {
            WriteLine("Error!");
        }
    }
}
```

Figure 11-29   The PriceListApplication3 class

When you compile the program in Figure 11-29, you receive a warning that variable e is declared but never used. If you omit the name e from the catch block, the application will execute identically without displaying a warning.

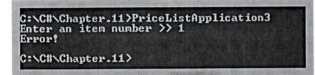

```
C:\C#\Chapter.11>PriceListApplication3
Enter an item number >> 1
Error!

C:\C#\Chapter.11>
```

Figure 11-30   Execution of the PriceListApplication3 program when a user enters 1 for the item number

To attempt to discover what caused the *Error!* message, you can replace the statement that writes it as follows:

```
WriteLine(e.Message);
```

 When the statement to display e.Message is added to the price list program, a warning that e is never used no longer appears when the program is compiled.

However, when you execute the program to display e.Message, you receive the output in Figure 11-31, indicating that the index is out of the bounds of the array. You are puzzled because you know 1 is a valid item number for the price array, and it should not be considered out of bounds.

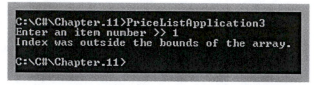

```
C:\C#\Chapter.11>PriceListApplication3
Enter an item number >> 1
Index was outside the bounds of the array.

C:\C#\Chapter.11>
```

Figure 11-31 Execution of the modified price list application in which e.Message is displayed in the catch block

Finally, you decide to replace the WriteLine() argument in the catch block statement with a StackTrace call, as follows:

```
WriteLine(e.StackTrace);
```

The output is shown in Figure 11-32. You can see from the list of methods that the error in your application came from Tax.DetermineTaxRate(), which was called by PriceList.DisplayPrice(), which was called by Main(). Notice that the last method executed is the first one dislayed in the list. Before using StackTrace, you might have not even considered that the Tax class could have been the source of the problem. If you work in a small organization, you can look at the code yourself and fix it. If you work in a larger organization or you purchased the class from an outside vendor, you can contact the programmer who created the class for assistance.

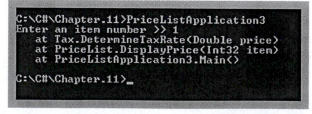

```
C:\C#\Chapter.11>PriceListApplication3
Enter an item number >> 1
   at Tax.DetermineTaxRate(Double price)
   at PriceList.DisplayPrice(Int32 item)
   at PriceListApplication3.Main()

C:\C#\Chapter.11>
```

Figure 11-32 Execution of the modified price list application in which e.StackTrace is displayed in the catch block

The classes in this example were small to help you easily follow the discussion. However, a real-world application might have many more classes that contain many more methods, and so using StackTrace would become increasingly beneficial. In a large system of programs, you might find it useful to locate StackTrace calls strategically throughout the programs while testing them and then remove them or comment them out when the programs are complete.

525

 Watch the video *Tracing Exceptions Through the Call Stack*.

TWO TRUTHS & A LIE

Tracing Exception Objects Through the Call Stack

1. The memory location where the computer stores the list of locations to which the system must return after a series of method calls is known as the stack trace.

2. If a method throws an exception and does not catch it, then the exception is thrown to the method that called the offending method.

3. When you catch an Exception object, you can output the value of StackTrace to display a list of methods in the call stack so you can determine the location of the error.

The false statement is #1. The memory location where the computer stores the list of locations to which the system must return after a series of method calls is known as the call stack.

Creating Your Own Exception Classes

C# provides more than 100 categories of Exceptions that you can throw in your programs. However, C#'s creators could not predict every condition that might be an exception in the programs you write. For example, you might want to declare an Exception when your bank balance is negative or when an outside party attempts to access your e-mail account. Most organizations have specific rules for exceptional data, such as "an employee number must not exceed three digits" or "an hourly salary must not be less than the legal minimum wage." Of course, you can handle these potential error situations with if statements, but you also can create your own Exception subclasses.

To create your own Exception type from which you can instantiate throwable objects, you can extend the ApplicationException class, which is a subclass of Exception, or you can extend Exception. As you saw earlier in the chapter, Microsoft's advice on this matter has changed over time. Although you might see extensions of ApplicationException in classes written by others, the current advice is simply to derive your own classes from Exception. Either approach will produce workable programs.

Figure 11-33 shows a NegativeBalanceException class that extends Exception. This class passes an appropriate string message to its parent's constructor. If you create an Exception object and display its Message property, you will see the message *Error in the application.* When the NegativeBalanceException constructor passes the string *Bank balance is negative.* to its parent's constructor, the Message property will hold this more descriptive message. The C# documentation recommends that you create all Exception subclass messages to be grammatically correct, complete sentences ending in a period.

```
class NegativeBalanceException : Exception
{
    private static string msg = "Bank balance is negative. ";
    public NegativeBalanceException() : base(msg)
    {
    }
}
```

Figure 11-33   The NegativeBalanceException class

When you create a BankAccount class like the one shown in Figure 11-34, you can create the Balance property set accessor to throw a NegativeBalanceException when a client attempts to set the balance to be negative.

 Instead of creating the nbe object in the Balance property in Figure 11-34, you could code the following statement, which creates and throws an anonymous NegativeBalanceException in a single step: throw(new NegativeBalanceException());

Figure 11-35 shows a program that attempts to set a BankAccount balance to a negative value in the shaded statement. When the BankAccount class's Balance set accessor throws the NegativeBalanceException, the catch block in the TryBankAccount program executes, displaying both the NegativeBalanceException Message and the value of StackTrace. Figure 11-36 shows the output.

526

```
class BankAccount
{
   private double balance;
   public int AccountNum {get; set;}
   public double Balance
   {
      get
      {
         return balance;
      }
      set
      {
         if(value <0)
         {
            NegativeBalanceException nbe =
               new NegativeBalanceException();
            throw(nbe);
         }
         balance = value;
      }
   }
}
```

Figure 11-34 The BankAccount class

```
using System;
using static System.Console;
class TryBankAccount
{
   static void Main()
   {
      BankAccount acct = new BankAccount();
      try
      {
         acct.AccountNum = 1234;
         acct.Balance = -1000;
      }
      catch(NegativeBalanceException e)
      {
         WriteLine(e.Message);
         WriteLine(e.StackTrace);
      }
   }
}
```

Figure 11-35 The TryBankAccount program

```
C:\C#\Chapter.11>TryBankAccount
Bank balance is negative.
   at BankAccount.set_Balance(Double value)
   at TryBankAccount.Main()

C:\C#\Chapter.11>
```

Figure 11-36 Output of the TryBankAccount program

In the error message in Figure 11-36, notice that the set accessor for the Balance property is known internally as set_Balance. You can guess that the set accessor for the AccountNum property is known as set_AccountNum.

The StackTrace begins at the point where an Exception is thrown, not where it is instantiated. This consideration makes a difference when you create an Exception in a class and throw it from multiple methods.

Exceptions can be particularly useful when you throw them from constructors. Constructors do not have a return type, so they have no other way to send information back to a calling method.

In C#, you can't throw an object unless it is an Exception or a descendent of the Exception class. In other words, you cannot throw a double or a BankAccount. However, you can throw any type of Exception at any time, not just Exceptions of your own creation. For example, within any program you can code any of the following:

```
throw(new ApplicationException());
throw(new IndexOutOfRangeException());
throw(new Exception());
```

Of course, you should throw appropriate Exception types. In other words, you should not throw an IndexOutOfRangeException when you encounter division by 0 or data of an incorrect type; you should use it only when an index (subscript) is too high or too low. However, if a built-in Exception type is appropriate and suits your needs, you should use it. You should not create an excessive number of special Exception types for your classes, especially if the C# development environment already contains an Exception type that accurately describes the error. Extra Exception types add a level of complexity for other programmers who will use your classes. Nevertheless, when appropriate, creating a specialized Exception class is an elegant way for you to take care of error situations. Exceptions allow you to separate your error code from the usual, nonexceptional sequence of events and allow for errors to be passed up the stack and traced.

TWO TRUTHS & A LIE

Creating Your Own Exception Classes

1. To create your own Exception types whose objects you can throw, you can extend the ApplicationException class or the Exception class.

2. In C#, you can throw any object that you create if it is appropriate for the application.

3. You can throw any type of Exception at any time—both those that are already created as part of C# and those of your own creation.

The false statement is #2. In C#, you can't throw an object unless it is an Exception or a descendent of the Exception class.

Rethrowing an Exception

When you write a method that catches an exception, your method does not have to handle it. Instead, you might choose to **rethrow the exception** to the method that called your method. Then you can let the calling method handle the problem.

Within a catch block, you can rethrow an unnamed exception that was caught by using the keyword throw with no object after it. For example, Figure 11-37 shows a class that contains four methods. In this program, the following sequence of events takes place:

1. The Main() method calls MethodA().

2. MethodA() calls MethodB().

3. MethodB() calls MethodC().

4. MethodC() throws an Exception.

5. When MethodB() catches the Exception, it does not handle the Exception; instead, it throws the Exception back to MethodA().

6. MethodA() catches the Exception but does not handle it either. Instead, MethodA() throws the Exception back to the Main() method.

7. The Exception is caught in the Main() method, where the message that was created in MethodC() is finally displayed.

Figure 11-38 shows the execution of the program.

```
using System;
using static System.Console;
class ReThrowDemo
{
    static void Main()
    {
        try
        {
            WriteLine("Trying in Main() method");
            MethodA();
        }
        catch(Exception ae)
        {
        WriteLine("Caught in Main() method --\n {0}",
            ae.Message);
        }
        WriteLine("Main() method is done");
    }
    private static void MethodA()
    {
        try
        {
            WriteLine("Trying in method A");
            MethodB();
        }
        catch(Exception)
        {
            WriteLine("Caught in method A");
            throw;
        }
    }
    private static void MethodB()
    {
        try
        {
            WriteLine("Trying in method B");
            MethodC();
        }
        catch(Exception)
        {
            WriteLine("Caught in method B");
            throw;
        }
    }
    private static void MethodC()
    {
        WriteLine("In method C");
        throw(new Exception("This came from method C"));
    }
}
```

Figure 11-37   The ReThrowDemo program

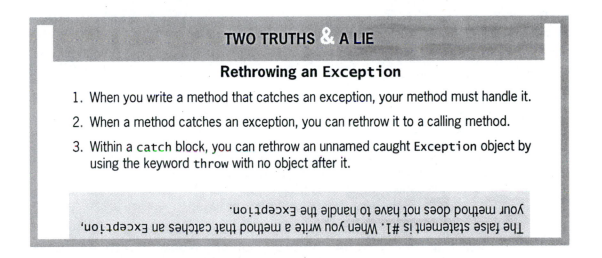

Figure 11-38 Execution of the ReThrowDemo program

If you name the Exception argument in a catch block (for example, catch(Exception e)), then you should use that identifier when you use a throw statement in the block (for example, throw e;).

TWO TRUTHS & A LIE

Rethrowing an Exception

1. When you write a method that catches an exception, your method must handle it.

2. When a method catches an exception, you can rethrow it to a calling method.

3. Within a catch block, you can rethrow an unnamed caught Exception object by using the keyword throw with no object after it.

The false statement is #1. When you write a method that catches an Exception, your method does not have to handle the Exception.

Chapter Summary

- An exception is any error condition or unexpected behavior in an executing program. In C#, all exceptions are objects that are instances of the Exception class or one of its derived classes. Most exceptions you will use are derived from three classes: SystemException, ApplicationException, and their parent Exception. You can purposely generate a SystemException by forcing a program to contain an error. Although you are not required to handle exceptions, you can use object-oriented techniques to provide elegant error-handling solutions.

- When you think an error will occur frequently, the most efficient approach is to handle the error in the traditional way, with `if` statements. If an error will occur infrequently, instantiating an `Exception` object when needed is more efficient. In object-oriented terminology, you "try" a procedure that may not complete correctly. A method that detects an error condition or exception "throws" an exception, and the block of code that processes the error "catches" the exception. You must include at least one `catch` block or `finally` block immediately following a `try` block.

- Every `Exception` object contains a `ToString()` method and a `Message` property that contains useful information about the `Exception`.

- You can place as many statements as you need within a `try` block, and you can catch as many different exceptions as you want. If you try more than one statement, only the first error-generating statement throws an exception. When multiple `catch` blocks are present, they are examined in sequence until a match is found for the `Exception` type that occurred. When you list multiple `catch` blocks after a `try` block, you must be careful about their order, or some `catch` blocks might become unreachable.

- The `TryParse()` methods that you can use to convert strings to other data types without causing exceptions use exception-handling techniques internally.

- A `finally` block performs actions at the end of a `try`...`catch` sequence, whether an exception was thrown or not.

- Exceptions do not have to be caught by the methods that generate them. Instead, a program that calls a method that throws an exception can catch and handle it. Often, this approach produces the best software design.

- If a method throws an exception and does not catch it, then the `Exception` object is thrown to the calling method. When you catch an `Exception` object, you can display the value of the `StackTrace` property, which provides a list of methods in the call stack, allowing you to determine the location where the error occurred.

- To create your own `Exception` classes from which you create throwable objects, you can extend the `ApplicationException` class or the `Exception` class. The current advice is to extend `Exception`.

- When you write a method that catches an exception, your method does not have to handle it. Instead, you might choose to rethrow the exception to the method that called your method and let that method handle it.

Key Terms

An **exception** is any error condition or unexpected behavior in an executing program.

Exception handling is the set of object-oriented techniques used to manage unexpected errors in an executing program.

Mission critical describes any process that is crucial to an organization.

Fault-tolerant applications are designed so that they continue to operate, possibly at a reduced level, when some part of the system fails.

Robustness represents the degree to which a system is resilient to stress, maintaining correct functioning even in the presence of errors.

A **try block** contains code that might create exceptions you want to handle.

A **catch block** can catch one type of `Exception`.

Unreachable blocks contain statements that can never execute under any circumstances because the program logic "can't get there."

Dead code is unreachable code.

A **finally block** can follow a `try` block; code within a `finally` block executes whether the `try` block identifies any `Exceptions` or not.

The **call stack** is the memory location where the computer stores the list of locations to which the system must return after method calls.

Propagating an exception is the act of transmitting it unchanged through the call stack.

To **rethrow an exception** is to throw a caught exception to a calling method instead of handling it within the method that generated it.

Review Questions

1. Any error condition or unexpected behavior in an executing program is known as an _____.

   a. exception   c. exclusion

   b. anomaly   d. omission

2. Which of the following is *not* treated as a C# `Exception`?

   a. Your program asks the user to input a number, but the user enters a character.

   b. You attempt to execute a C# program, but the C# compiler has not been installed.

   c. You attempt to access an array with a subscript that is too large.

   d. You calculate a value that is too large for the answer's variable type.

3. Most exceptions you will use derive from three classes: _____.

   a. `Object`, `ObjectException`, and `ObjectApplicationException`

   b. `Exception`, `SystemException`, and `ApplicationException`

   c. `FormatException`, `ApplicationException`, and `IOException`

   d. `SystemException`, `IOException`, and `FormatException`

4. **Exception** objects can be _____.

    a. generated automatically by C#   c. both of these

    b. created by a program   d. none of these

5. When a program creates an **Exception** object, you _____.

    a. must handle it

    b. can handle it

    c. must not handle it

    d. none of these; programs cannot create **Exceptions**

6. If you do not use object-oriented techniques, _____.

    a. there are no error situations

    b. you cannot manage error situations

    c. you can manage error situations but with great difficulty

    d. you can manage error situations

7. In object-oriented terminology, you _____ a procedure that may not complete correctly.

    a. circumvent   c. catch

    b. attempt   d. try

8. In object-oriented terminology, a method that detects an error condition _____ an exception.

    a. throws   c. tries

    b. catches   d. unearths

9. When you write a block of code in which something can go wrong, and you want to throw an exception if it does, you place the code in a _____ block.

    a. **catch**   c. **system**

    b. **blind**   d. **try**

10. A **catch** block executes when its **try** block _____.

    a. completes   c. throws an **Exception** of an acceptable type

    b. throws any **Exception** object   d. completes without throwing anything

11. Which of the following `catch` blocks will catch any `Exception` object?

   a. `catch(Any e) {}`

   b. `catch(Exception e) {}`

   c. `catch(e) {}`

   d. All of the above will catch any `Exception`.

12. Which of the following is valid within a `catch` block with the header `catch(Exception error)`?

   a. `WriteLine(error.ToString());`

   b. `WriteLine(error.Message);`

   c. `return(error.ToString());`

   d. two of these

13. You can place _____ statement(s) within a `try` block.

   a. zero   c. two

   b. one   d. any number of

14. How many `catch` blocks might follow a `try` block within the same method?

   a. only one

   b. any number as long as it is greater than zero

   c. any number as long as it is greater than one

   d. any number, including zero or one

15. Consider the following `try` block. If `x` is 15, what is the value of `a` when this code completes?

```
try
{
    a = 99;
    if(x > 10)
        throw(new Exception());
    a = 0;
    ++a;
}
```

   a. 0   c. 99

   b. 1   d. undefined

536

16. Consider the following **catch** blocks. The variable **b** has been initialized to 0. If a **DivideByZeroException** occurs in a **try** block just before this **catch** block, what is the value of **b** when this code completes?

```
catch(DivideByZeroException e)
{
    ++b;
}
catch(Exception e)
{
    ++b;
}
```

a. 0

b. 1

c. 2

d. 3

17. Consider the following **catch** blocks. The variable **c** has been initialized to 0. If an **IndexOutOfRangeException** occurs in a **try** block just before this **catch** block, what is the value of **c** when this code completes?

```
catch(IndexOutOfRangeException e)
{
    ++c;
}
catch(Exception e)
{
    ++c;
}
finally
{
    ++c;
}
```

a. 0

b. 1

c. 2

d. 3

18. If your program throws an **IndexOutOfRangeException**, and the only available **catch** block catches an **Exception**, _____.

a. an **IndexOutOfRangeException catch** block is generated automatically

b. the **Exception catch** block executes

c. the **Exception catch** block is bypassed

d. the **IndexOutOfRangeException** is thrown to the operating system

19. When you design your own classes that might cause exceptions, and other classes will use your classes as clients, you should usually create your methods to _____.

    a. neither throw nor handle exceptions

    b. throw exceptions but not handle them

    c. handle exceptions but not throw them

    d. both throw and handle exceptions

20. When you create an **Exception** subclass of your own, you should extend the _____ class.

    a. `SystemException`

    b. `PersonalException`

    c. `OverloadedException`

    d. `Exception`

Exercises

Programming Exercises

1. Write a program named **SubscriptExceptionTest** in which you declare an array of 20 **doubles** and store values in the array. Write a **try** block in which you place a loop that prompts the user for a subscript value and displays the value stored in the corresponding array position. Create a **catch** block that catches any **IndexOutOfRangeException** and displays an appropriate error message.

2. **ArgumentException** is an existing class that derives from **Exception**; you use it when one or more of a method's arguments do not fall within an expected range. Create an application for Merrydale Mortgage Company named **MortgageApplication** containing variables that can hold an applicant's name and credit score. Within the class, create a method that accepts a parameter for the credit score and returns **true** or **false**, indicating whether the applicant is eligible for a mortgage. If the score is not between 300 and 850, it is invalid, and the method should throw an **ArgumentException**. An application is accepted when the credit score is valid and at least 650. In the **Main()** method, continuously prompt the user for appplicant data, pass it to the method, and then display a message indicating whether the applicant is accepted, rejected, or has an invalid score.

3. Create a program named **FindSquareRoot** that finds the square root of a user's input value. The Math class contains a static method named Sqrt() that accepts a double and returns the parameter's square root. If the user's entry cannot be converted to a double, display an appropriate message, and set the square root value to 0. Otherwise, test the input number's value. If it is negative, throw a new ApplicationException to which you pass the message "Number can't be negative." and again set sqrt to 0. If the input value is a double and not negative, pass it to the Math.Sqrt() method, and display the returned value.

4. a. Create a program named **OrderExceptionDemo** that attempts to create several valid and invalid Order objects. Immediately after each instantiation attempt, handle any thrown exceptions by displaying an error message. Create an Order class with three fields for an item number, quantity, and day ordered. The Order constructor requires values for each field. Upon construction, throw an ArgumentException if the item number is less than 100 or more than 999, or if the quantity ordered is less than 1 or more than 12, or the day ordered is not between 1 and 31, inclusive. Display the data if the instantiation is successful.

   b. Add get properties for each field in the Order class. Then, write an application named **OrderExceptionDemo2** that creates an array of five Orders. Prompt the user for values for each field; if the user enters improper or invalid data for any field, set item number, quantity, and day all to 0. (You will have to modify the Order constructor so that an object with all default values is legal.) At the end of the program, display all the records.

5. a. Create a program named **BookExceptionDemo** for the Peterman Publishing Company. Create a BookException class that is instantiated when a Book's price exceeds 10 cents per page and whose constructor requires three arguments for title, price, and number of pages. Create an error message that is passed to the Exception class constructor for the Message property when a Book does not meet the price-to-pages ratio. For example, an error message might be:

   For Goodnight Moon, ratio is invalid.

   ...Price is $12.99 for 25 pages.

   b. Create a Book class that contains fields for title, author, price, and number of pages. Include properties for each field. Throw a BookException if a client program tries to construct a Book object for which the price is more than 10 cents per page. Create a program that creates at least four Book objects—some where the ratio is acceptable, and others where it is not. Catch any thrown exceptions, and display the BookException Message.

   c. Using the Book class, write an application named **BookExceptionDemo2** that creates an array of five Books. Prompt the user for values for each Book. To handle any exceptions that are thrown because of improper or invalid data entered by the user, set the Book's price to the maximum of 10 cents per page. At the end of the program, display all the entered, and possibly corrected, records.

6. Create a GUI application named **ExceptionHandlingDemoGUI** that prompts a user to enter an integer. When the user clicks a button, try to convert the user's entry to an integer using the `Convert.ToInt32()` method, and display a message indicating whether the user was successful.

7. In Chapter 6, you created a game named `GuessAWord` in which a player guesses letters to try to replicate a hidden word. Now create a modified version of the program named **GuessAWordWithExceptionHandling** that throws and catches an exception when the user enters a guess that is not a letter of the alphabet. Create a `NonLetterException` class that descends from `Exception`. The `Message string` for your new class should indicate the nonletter character that caused the `Exception`'s creation. When a `NonLetterException` is thrown and caught, the message should be displayed.

Debugging Exercises

1. Each of the following files in the Chapter.11 folder of your downloadable student files has syntax and/or logical errors. In each case, determine the problem and fix the program. After you correct the errors, save each file using the same filename preceded with *Fixed*. For example, DebugEleven1.cs will become FixedDebugEleven1.cs.

    a. DebugEleven1.cs

    b. DebugEleven2.cs

    c. DebugEleven3.cs

    d. DebugEleven4.cs

Case Problems

1. Modify the **GreenvilleRevenue** program created in the previous chapter so that it performs the following tasks:

    - The program prompts the user for the number of contestants in this year's competition; the number must be between 0 and 30. Use exception-handling techniques to ensure a valid value.

    - The program prompts the user for talent codes. Use exception-handling techniques to ensure a valid code.

    - After data entry is complete, the program prompts the user for codes so the user can view lists of appropriate contestants. Use exception-handling techniques for the code verification.

2. Modify the **MarshallsRevenue** program created in the previous chapter so that it performs the following tasks:

- Modify the program to use exception-handling techniques to ensure valid values for the month, the number of interior murals scheduled, and the number of exterior murals scheduled. In each case, the program continues to prompt the user until valid entries are made.

- Modify the program to use exception-handling techniques to ensure valid mural codes for the scheduled jobs.

- After data entry is complete, the program continuously prompts the user for codes and displays associated jobs. Use exception-handling techniques to verify valid codes.

CHAPTER 12

Using Controls

In this chapter you will:

- ◎ Learn about `Controls`
- ◎ Examine the IDE's automatically generated code
- ◎ Set a `Control`'s Font
- ◎ Create a `Form` that contains `LinkLabel`s
- ◎ Add color to a `Form`
- ◎ Add `CheckBox` and `RadioButton` objects to a `Form`
- ◎ Add a `PictureBox` to a `Form`
- ◎ Add `ListBox`, `ComboBox`, and `CheckedListBox` items to a `Form`
- ◎ Add a `MonthCalendar` and `DateTimePicker` to a `Form`
- ◎ Work with a `Form`'s layout
- ◎ Add a `MenuStrip` to a `Form`
- ◎ Learn to use other controls

Throughout this book, you have created both console and GUI applications. Your GUI applications have used only a few Controls—Forms, Labels, TextBoxes, and Buttons. **Graphical control elements** are the components through which a user interacts with a GUI program. (Since Chapter 3, you have used the simpler name *controls* for these objects.)

> If you have been creating mostly console applications while learning the concepts in this book, you might want to review the chapter "Using GUI Objects and the Visual Studio IDE." That chapter provides instruction in the basic procedures used to create GUI applications and describes Visual Studio Help.

When using programs or visiting Internet sites, you have encountered and used many other interactive controls such as scroll bars, check boxes, and radio buttons. C# has many classes that represent these GUI objects, and the Visual Studio IDE makes it easy to add them to your programs. (Controls are also often called **widgets**.) In this chapter, you will learn to incorporate some of the most common and useful widgets into your programs. Additionally, you will see how these components work in general so you can use other controls that are not covered in this book or that become available to programmers in future releases of C#.

> GUI components are referred to as *widgets*, which some sources claim is a combination of the terms *window* and *gadgets*. Originally, *widget* comes from the 1924 play "Beggar on Horseback," by George Kaufman and Marc Connelly. In the play, a young composer gets engaged to the daughter of a rich businessman and foresees spending his life doing pointless work in a bureaucratic big business that manufactures widgets, which represent a useless item whose purpose is never explained.

Understanding Controls

When you design a Form, you can place Buttons and other controls on the Form surface. In C#, the Control class provides the definitions for these GUI objects. Control objects such as Forms and Buttons, like all other objects in C#, ultimately derive from the Object class. Figure 12-1 shows where the Control class fits into the inheritance hierarchy.

```
System.Object
    System.MarshalByRefObject
        System.ComponentModel.Component
            System.Windows.Forms.Control
                26 Derived classes
```

Figure 12-1   The Control class inheritance hierarchy

Figure 12-1 shows that all Controls are Objects, of course. They are also all MarshalByRefObjects. (A MarshalByRefObject is one you can instantiate on a remote computer so that you can manipulate a reference to the object rather than a local copy of the object.) Controls also descend from Component. (The Component class provides containment and cleanup for other objects—inheriting from `Component` allows `Controls` to be contained in objects such as `Forms` and provides for disposal of `Controls` when they are destroyed. The `Control` class adds visual representation to `Components`.) The `Control` class implements very basic functionality required by classes that define the GUI objects the user sees on the screen. This class handles user input through the keyboard, pointing devices, and touch screens as well as message routing and security. It defines the bounds of a `Control` by determining its position and size.

Table 12-1 shows the 26 direct descendents of `Control` and some commonly used descendents of those classes. It does not show all the descendents that exist; rather, it shows only the descendents covered previously or in this chapter. For example, the `ButtonBase` class is the parent of `Button`, a class you have used throughout this book. In this chapter, you will use two other `ButtonBase` children—`CheckBox` and `RadioButton`. This chapter cannot cover every `Control` that has been invented; however, after you learn to use some `Controls`, you will find that others work in much the same way. You also can read more about them in the Visual Studio Help documentation.

Class	Commonly used descendents
`Microsoft.WindowsCE.Forms.DocumentList`	
`System.Windows.Forms.AxHost`	
`System.Windows.Forms.ButtonBase`	Button, CheckBox, RadioButton
`System.Windows.Forms.DataGrid`	
`System.Windows.Forms.DataGridView`	
`System.Windows.Forms.DateTimePicker`	
`System.Windows.Forms.GroupBox`	
`System.Windows.Forms.Integration.ElementHost`	
`System.Windows.Forms.Label`	LinkLabel
`System.Windows.Forms.ListControl`	ListBox, ComboBox, CheckedListBox
`System.Windows.Forms.ListView`	
`System.Windows.Forms.MdiClient`	
`System.Windows.Forms.MonthCalendar`	
`System.Windows.Forms.PictureBox`	

Table 12-1 Classes derived from `System.Windows.Forms.Control` (continues)

(continued)

Class	Commonly used descendents
System.Windows.Forms.PrintPreviewControl	
System.Windows.Forms.ProgressBar	
System.Windows.Forms.ScrollableControl	
System.Windows.Forms.ScrollBar	
System.Windows.Forms.Splitter	
System.Windows.Forms.StatusBar	
System.Windows.Forms.TabControl	
System.Windows.Forms.TextBoxBase	TextBox
System.Windows.Forms.ToolBar	
System.Windows.Forms.TrackBar	
System.Windows.Forms.TreeView	
System.Windows.Forms.WebBrowserBase	

Table 12-1 Classes derived from System.Windows.Forms.Control

Because Controls are all relatives, they share many of the same attributes. Each Control has more than 80 public properties and 20 protected properties. For example, each Control has a Font and a ForeColor that dictate how its text is displayed, and each Control has a Width and Height. Table 12-2 shows just some of the public properties associated with Controls in general; reading through them will give you an idea of the Control attributes that you can change.

Property	Description
AllowDrop	Gets or sets a value indicating whether the control can accept data that the user drags onto it
Anchor	Gets or sets the edges of the container to which a control is bound and determines how a control is resized with its parent
BackColor	Gets or sets the background color for the control
BackgroundImage	Gets or sets the background image displayed in the control

Table 12-2 Selected public Control properties *(continues)*

(continued)

Property	Description
Bottom	Gets the distance, in pixels, between the bottom edge of the control and the top edge of its container's client area
Bounds	Gets or sets the size and location of the control, including its nonclient elements, in pixels, relative to the parent control
CanFocus	Gets a value indicating whether the control can receive focus
CanSelect	Gets a value indicating whether the control can be selected
Capture	Gets or sets a value indicating whether the control has captured the mouse
Container	Gets the IContainer that contains the Component (inherited from Component)
ContainsFocus	Gets a value indicating whether the control or one of its child controls currently has the input focus
Cursor	Gets or sets the cursor that is displayed when the mouse pointer is over the control
Disposing	Gets a value indicating whether the base Control class is in the process of disposing
Dock	Gets or sets which control borders are docked to their parent control and determines how a control is resized with its parent
Enabled	Gets or sets a value indicating whether the control can respond to user interaction
Focused	Gets a value indicating whether the control has input focus
Font	Gets or sets the font of the text displayed by the control
ForeColor	Gets or sets the foreground color of the control
HasChildren	Gets a value indicating whether the control contains one or more child controls
Height	Gets or sets the height of the control
IsDisposed	Gets a value indicating whether the control has been disposed of
Left	Gets or sets the distance, in pixels, between the left edge of the control and the left edge of its container's client area
Location	Gets or sets the coordinates of the upper-left corner of the control relative to the upper-left corner of its container
Margin	Gets or sets the space between controls

Table 12-2   Selected public Control properties *(continues)*

(continued)

Property	Description
ModifierKeys	Gets a value indicating which of the modifier keys (Shift, Ctrl, and Alt) is in a pressed state
MouseButtons	Gets a value indicating which of the mouse buttons is in a pressed state
MousePosition	Gets the position of the mouse cursor in screen coordinates
Name	Gets or sets the name of the control
Parent	Gets or sets the parent container of the control
Right	Gets the distance, in pixels, between the right edge of the control and the left edge of its container's client area
Size	Gets or sets the height and width of the control
TabIndex	Gets or sets the tab order of the control within its container
TabStop	Gets or sets a value indicating whether the user can give focus to the control using the Tab key
Text	Gets or sets the text associated with this control
Top	Gets or sets the distance, in pixels, between the top edge of the control and the top edge of its container's client area
TopLevelControl	Gets the parent control that is not parented by another Windows Forms control; typically, this is the outermost Form in which the control is contained
Visible	Gets or sets a value indicating whether the control and all its parent controls are displayed
Width	Gets or sets the width of the control

Table 12-2 Selected public Control properties

The description of each property in Table 12-2 indicates whether the property is read-only; such properties only get values and do not set them.

You have altered Label, TextBox, and Button properties such as Text and Visible using the Properties window in Visual Studio. All the other Controls you learn about in this chapter can be manipulated in the same way.

A project can contain multiple Forms, each with its own Controls. You will learn how to add more Forms to a project in the "You Do It" exercises later in this chapter.

TWO TRUTHS & A LIE

Understanding Controls

1. The Control class implements basic functionality required by GUI objects that a user sees on the screen.

2. Most Controls have Font and ForeColor properties.

3. Every Control has Width and Height properties.

The false statement is #2. Every Control has Font and ForeColor properties.

Examining the IDE's Automatically Generated Code

Figure 12-2 shows a Form created in the IDE. The following actions have been performed:

1. A new Windows Forms project has been started and given the name FormWithALabelAndAButton.

2. A Label has been dragged onto Form1. Using the Properties window in the IDE, the Label's Text property has been changed to *Click the button*, and its Font has been changed to Georgia, Bold, and size 16. Its Name has not been changed from the default name label1.

3. A Button has been dragged onto Form1. The Button's Text property has been changed to *OK*, and its Name has been changed from the default Name button1 to okButton.

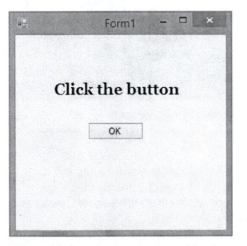

Figure 12-2 A Form generated by the FormWithALabelAndAButton program

As you drag controls in the Form Designer or change properties in the Properties Window, Visual Studio automatically generates code in the file named Form1.Designer.cs. When you open the Form1.Designer.cs file in Visual Studio, you can look for the method named InitializeComponent(), and you can see two lines of code generated within it near the bottom as follows:

```
private System.Windows.Forms.Label
label1;
private System.Windows.Forms.Button
okButton;
```

If you were to continue to drag additional components onto the Form, more declarations would be generated.

The following lines appear just before the method header for the InitializeComponent() method:

```
#region Windows Form Designer generated code

/// <summary>
/// Required method for Designer support - do not modify
/// the contents of this method with the code editor.
/// </summary>
```

Within the InitializeComponent() method, you can see automatically-generated statements that set the properties of the label, the button, and the form itself as partially shown in Figure 12-3. In the code in the figure, every instance of this means "this Form".

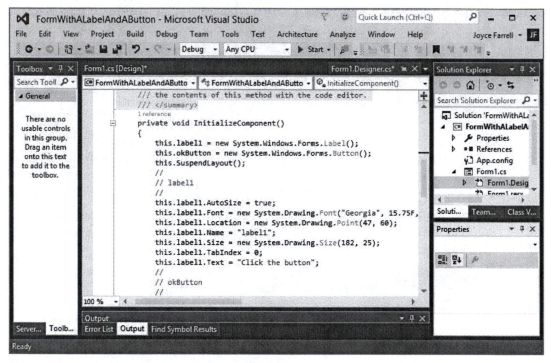

Figure 12-3 Some of the code in the InitializeComponent() method for FormWithALabelAndAButton

So much code is automatically generated by Visual Studio that it can be hard to find what you want. To locate a line of code, click Edit on the menu bar in the IDE, click Find and Replace, click Quick Find, type a key phrase to search for. Make sure that the drop down box correctly identifies the area in which you want to search—for example, the current selection or the current document.

Do not be intimidated by the amount of code automatically generated by the IDE. Based on what you have learned so far in this book, you can easily make sense of most of it.

- After the `InitializeComponent()` method header and opening brace, the next two statements call the constructor for each control that the programmer dragged onto the `Form`:

```
this.label1 = new System.Windows.Forms.Label();
this.okButton = new System.Windows.Forms.Button();
```

These statements create the actual objects.

- The next statement is a method call as follows:

```
this.SuspendLayout();
```

`SuspendLayout()` is a method that prevents conflicts when you are placing `Controls` on a form. Its counterparts, `ResumeLayout()` and `PerformLayout()`, appear at the bottom of the method. If you remove these method calls from small applications, you won't notice the difference. However, in large applications, suspending the layout logic while you adjust the appearance of components improves performance.

- Comments that start with forward slashes serve to separate the `label1` code from other code in the method. Following the `label1` comment lines, seven statements set properties of the `Label` as follows:

```
this.label1.AutoSize = true;
this.label1.Font = new System.Drawing.Font("Georgia",
    15.75F, System.Drawing.FontStyle.Bold,
    System.Drawing.GraphicsUnit.Point, ((byte)(0)));
this.label1.Location = new System.Drawing.Point(47, 60);
this.label1.Name = "label1";
this.label1.Size = new System.Drawing.Size(182, 25);
this.label1.TabIndex = 0;
this.label1.Text = "Click the button";
```

You can see that the `Font`, `Location`, `Name`, `Size`, and `Text` have been assigned values based on the programmer's choices in the IDE. The `TabIndex` for `label1` is 0 by default; `TabIndex` values determine the order in which `Controls` receive focus when the user presses the Tab key. This property is typically more useful for selectable items like `Buttons`.

- If you return to the visual designer and make changes to the form or its components, for example by relocating the label, when you next view the code, it will have been updated accordingly.

- Although not completely visible in Figure 12-3, the next set of statements defines the properties of the `Button` on the `Form`. The `TabIndex` for the `Button` is set to 1 because it was dragged onto the `Form` after the `Label`. Additional `Controls` would receive consecutive `TabIndex` values.

```
this.okButton.Location = new System.Drawing.Point(98, 117);
this.okButton.Name = "okButton";
this.okButton.Size = new System.Drawing.Size(75, 23);
this.okButton.TabIndex = 1;
this.okButton.Text = "OK";
this.okButton.UseVisualStyleBackColor = true;
```

- The `InitializeComponent()` method ends with statements that set the properties of the Form, such as its drawing size and text, and that add the `Label` and `Button` to the `Form`:

```
// Form1
//
this.AutoScaleDimensions = new System.Drawing.SizeF(6F, 13F);
this.AutoScaleMode = System.Windows.Forms.AutoScaleMode.Font;
this.ClientSize = new System.Drawing.Size(284, 262);
this.Controls.Add(this.okButton);
this.Controls.Add(this.label1);
this.Name = "Form1";
this.Text = "Form1";
this.ResumeLayout(false);
this.PerformLayout();
```

Although the property settings for the `Label` and `Button` include identifiers for the `Controls` (for example, `this.label1.Name` or `this.okButton.Text`), the property settings for the `Form` itself use only the reference `this`. That's because the statements are part of the `Form1` class.

In this chapter, you will learn about several additional `Controls`. When designing a `Form`, you should use the drag-and-drop design features in the IDE to place components and use the Properties window in the IDE to set properties instead of typing statements in the code editor. However, this chapter also teaches you about the code behind these actions so you can troubleshoot problems in projects and write usable statements when necessary.

Watch the video *Examining the IDE Code.*

TWO TRUTHS & A LIE

Examining the IDE's Automatically Generated Code

1. By using the Form Designer and the Properties window, you save time and eliminate many chances for error.

2. When you use the Form Designer to drag a `Label` onto a `Form`, no constructor call is needed for the `Label`.

3. You can use the Properties Window to set properties for a `Label` such as `Font`, `Location`, `Size`, and `Text`.

The false statement is #2. When you use the Form Designer to drag a `Label` onto a `Form`, you do not have to write a constructor call, but one is generated for you.

Setting a Control's Font

You use the Font class to change the appearance of printed text on your Forms. When designing a Label, Button, or other Control on a Form, it is easiest to select a Font from the Properties list. After you place a Control on a Form in the IDE, you can select the ellipsis (three dots) that follows the current Font property name in the Properties list. (See Figure 12-4.) This selection displays a Font window in which you can choose a Font name, size, style, and other effects. (See Figure 12-5.)

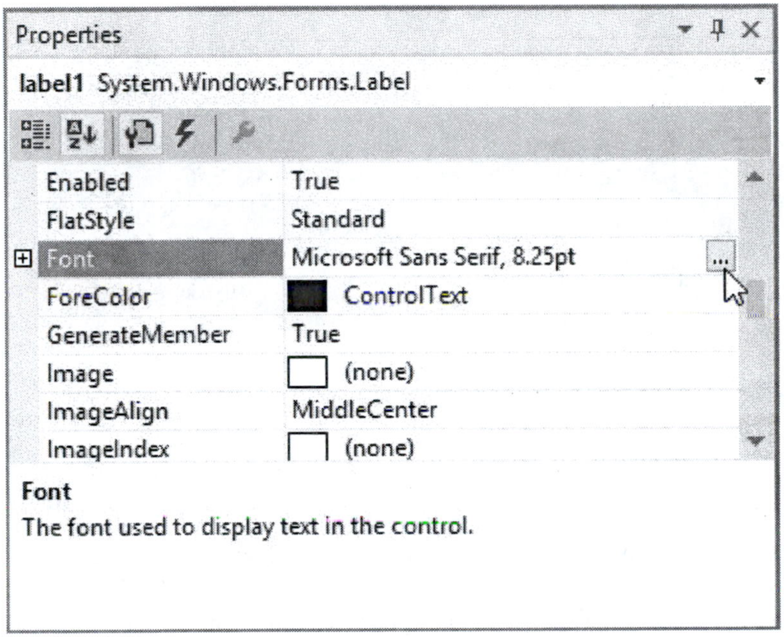

Figure 12-4   Clicking the ellipsis following the Font property

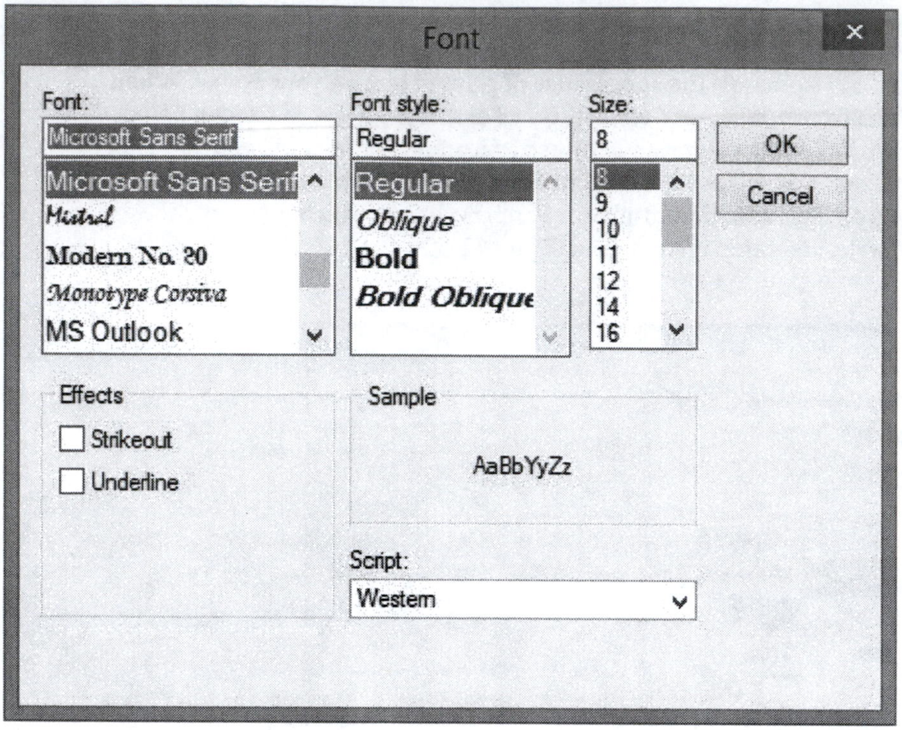

Figure 12-5 The Font window

However, if you wanted to change a Font later in a program—for example, after a user clicks a button—you might want to create your own instance of the Font class. As another example, suppose you want to create multiple controls that use the same Font. In that case, it makes sense to declare a named instance of the Font class. For example, you can declare the following Font:

```
System.Drawing.Font bigFont = new
    System.Drawing.Font("Courier New", 16.5f);
```

This version of the Font constructor requires two arguments—a string and a float. The string you pass to the Font constructor is the name of the font. If you use a font name that does not exist in your system, the font defaults to Microsoft Sans Serif. The second value is a float that represents the font size. Notice that you must use an *F* (or an *f*) following the Font size value constant when it contains a decimal point to ensure that the constant will be recognized as a float and not a double. (If you use an int as the font size, you do not need the *f* because the int will automatically be cast to a float.) An alternative would be to instantiate a float constant or variable and use its name as an argument to the Font constructor.

In Chapter 2, you learned to use an *f* following a floating-point constant to indicate the `float` type. Recall that a numeric constant with a decimal point is a `double` by default.

After a `Font` object named `bigFont` is instantiated, you can code statements similar to the following:

```
this.label1.Font = bigFont;
this.okButton.Font = bigFont;
```

If you want to change the properties of several objects at once in the IDE, you can drag your mouse around them to create a temporary group and then change the property for all of them with one entry in the Properties list.

The `Font` class includes a number of overloaded constructors. For example, you also can create a `Font` using three arguments, adding a `FontStyle`, as in the following declaration:

```
Font aFancyFont = new Font("Arial", 24, FontStyle.Italic);
```

Table 12-3 lists the available `FontStyles`. You can combine multiple styles using the pipe (|), which is also called the *logical OR operator* or the *bitwise OR operator*. (You first learned about this operator in Chapter 4.) The word *or* indicates that bits are turned on in the result when either of the operands contains an on-bit in a given position. For example, the following code creates a `Font` that is bold and underlined because the bits that indicate bold and underlined are both turned on in the result:

```
Font boldAndUnderlined = new Font("Helvetica",
    10, FontStyle.Bold | FontStyle.Underline);
```

Member Name	Description
Bold	Bold text
Italic	Italic text
Regular	Normal text
Strikeout	Text with a line through the middle
Underline	Underlined text

Table 12-3   `FontStyle` enumeration

Instead of instantiating a named Font object, you can create and assign an anonymous Font in one step. In other words, an identifier is not provided for the Font, as in this example:

```
this.label1.Font = new
    System.Drawing.Font("Courier New", 12.5F);
```

If you don't provide an identifier for a Font, you can't reuse it. You will have to create it again to use it with additional Controls.

TWO TRUTHS & A LIE

Setting a Control's Font

1. You use the Font class to change the appearance of printed text on Controls in your Forms.

2. When designing a Control on a Form, you must select a Font from the Properties list in the IDE.

3. The Font class includes several overloaded constructors.

The false statement is #2. When designing a Control on a Form, a default font is selected. If you want to change the font, it is easiest to select a font from the Properties list, but you also can create your own instance of the Font class.

Using a LinkLabel

A **link label** is a control with a label that provides the user a way to link to other sources, such as Web pages or files. The C# class that creates a link label is LinkLabel; it is a child of Label. Table 12-4 summarizes the properties and lists the default event method for a LinkLabel. The **default event** for a Control is:

- The method whose shell is automatically created when you double-click the Control while designing a project in the IDE

- The method that you are most likely to alter when you use the Control

- The event that users most likely expect to generate when they encounter the Control in a working application

With many Controls, including a LinkLabel, a mouse click by the user triggers the default event. When designing a program, you can double-click a Control in the IDE to generate the default method shell, and then write any necessary statements within the shell.

Property or Method	Description
ActiveLinkColor	The color of the link when it is clicked
LinkColor	The original color of links before they have been visited; usually blue by default
LinkVisited	If true, the link's color is changed to the VisitedLinkColor
VisitedLinkColor	The color of a link after it has been visited; usually purple by default
LinkClicked()	Default event that is generated when the link is clicked by the user

Table 12-4   Commonly used LinkLabel properties and default event

The default event for many Controls, such as Buttons and LinkLabels, occurs when the user clicks the Control. However, the default event for a Form is the Load() method. In other words, if you double-click a Form in the IDE, you generate this method. In it, you can place statements that execute as soon as a Form is loaded.

When you create a LinkLabel, it appears as underlined text. The text is blue by default, but you can change the color in the LinkLabel Properties list in the IDE. When you pass the mouse pointer over a LinkLabel, the pointer changes to a hand; you have seen similar behavior while using hyperlinks in Web pages. When a user clicks a LinkLabel, it generates a click event, just as clicking a Button does. When a click event is fired from a LinkLabel, a LinkClicked() method is executed, similar to how clicking a Button can execute a Click() method.

You can create a program so that a user generates an event by clicking many types of objects. For example, for a Label named label1, you could write statements in a label1_Click() method. However, users do not usually expect to click Labels; they do expect to click LinkLabels.

When you double-click a Label (as well as most other controls), the automatically generated method name ends with Click(), but when you double-click a LinkLabel, the corresponding method ends with Clicked().

Figure 12-6 shows a Form onto which two LinkLabels have been dragged from the Toolbox in the IDE. The default Frame size has been reduced, and the Text properties of the LinkLabels have been changed to *Course Technology Website* and *Read Our Policy.*

555

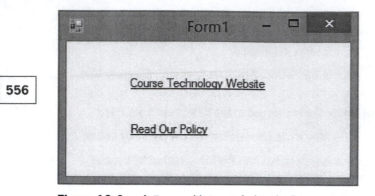

Figure 12-6 A Form with two `LinkLabel`s

If you double-click a `LinkLabel` in the IDE, a method shell is created for you in the format `xxx_LinkClicked()`, where xxx is the value of the `Name` property assigned to the `LinkLabel`. (This corresponds to what happens when you double-click a `Button` in the IDE.) For example, Figure 12-7 shows the two generated methods for the `Form` in Figure 12-6 when the default `LinkLabel` identifiers `linkLabel1` and `linkLabel2` are used. In Figure 12-7, all the code was automatically generated except for the two shaded statements. The programmer added those lines to indicate which actions should occur when a user clicks the corresponding `LinkLabel` in a running application.

```csharp
public partial class Form1 : Form
{
    public Form1()
    {
        InitializeComponent();
    }
    private void linkLabel1_LinkClicked(object sender,
        LinkLabelLinkClickedEventArgs e)
    {
        System.Diagnostics.Process.Start("IExplore",
            "http://www.course.com");
    }
    private void linkLabel2_LinkClicked(object sender,
        LinkLabelLinkClickedEventArgs e)
    {
        System.Diagnostics.Process.Start
            (@"C:\C#\Chapter.12\Policy.txt");
    }
}
```

Figure 12-7 Two `LinkClicked()` methods

If you add using `System.Diagnostics`; at the top of your file, you can eliminate the references in Figure 12-7 and refer to the process simply as `Process.Start`.

In each of the LinkClicked() methods in Figure 12-7, the programmer has added a call to System.Diagnostics.Process.Start(). This method allows you to run other programs within an application. The Start() method has two overloaded versions:

- When you use one string argument, you provide the name of the file to be opened.
- When you use two arguments, you provide the name of an application and its needed arguments.

In the linkLabel1_LinkClicked() method, the two arguments open Internet Explorer ("IExplore") and pass it the address of the Course Technology Web site. If an Internet connection is active, control transfers to the Web site.

In the linkLabel2_LinkClicked() method, only one argument is provided. It opens a file stored on the local disk. The default application opens based on the file's application type, which is determined by its file extension. For example, Notepad is the default application for a file with a .txt extension. Alternatively, you could code the following, which explicitly names Notepad as the application:

```
System.Diagnostics.Process.Start("Notepad",
    @"C:\C#\Chapter.12\Policy.txt");
```

In the linkLabel2_LinkClicked() method, an at sign (@) appears in front of the filename to be opened. This symbol indicates that all characters in the string should be interpreted literally. Therefore, the backslashes in the path are not interpreted as escape sequence characters.

The LinkVisited property can be set to true when you determine that a user has clicked a link, as shown in the shaded statement in Figure 12-8. This setting indicates that the link should be displayed in a different color so the user can see the link has been visited. By default, the visited link color is purple, but you can change this setting in the Properties list for the LinkLabel.

```
private void linkLabel1_LinkClicked(object sender,
    LinkLabelLinkClickedEventArgs e)
{
    System.Diagnostics.Process.Start("IExplore",
        "http://www.course.com");
    linkLabel1.LinkVisited = true;
}
```

Figure 12-8   Setting the LinkVisited property

TWO TRUTHS & A LIE

Using a LinkLabel

1. A LinkLabel is a child class of Label, and it provides the additional capability to link the user to other sources.

2. The default event for a Control is the method whose shell is automatically created when you double-click the Control while designing a project in the IDE. Users most likely expect to generate this event when they encounter the Control in a working application.

3. When you create a LinkLabel, it appears as italicized underlined text, and when you pass the mouse pointer over a LinkLabel, the pointer changes to an hourglass.

The false statement is #3. When you create a LinkLabel, it appears as underlined text, and when you pass the mouse pointer over a LinkLabel, the pointer changes to a hand.

Adding Color to a Form

The Color class contains a wide variety of predefined Colors that you can use with your Controls (see Table 12-5).

 C# also allows you to create custom colors. If no color in Table 12-5 suits your needs, search for *custom color* in Visual Studio Help to obtain more information.

AliceBlue	DeepPink	Lime	RosyBrown
AntiqueWhite	DeepSkyBlue	LimeGreen	RoyalBlue
Aqua	DimGray	Linen	SaddleBrown
Aquamarine	DodgerBlue	Magenta	Salmon
Azure	Firebrick	Maroon	SandyBrown
Beige	FloralWhite	MediumAquamarine	SeaGreen
Bisque	ForestGreen	MediumBlue	SeaShell
Black	Fuchsia	MediumOrchid	Sienna

Table 12-5 Color properties *(continues)*

(continued)

BlanchedAlmond	Gainsboro	MediumPurple	Silver
Blue	GhostWhite	MediumSeaGreen	SkyBlue
BlueViolet	Gold	MediumSlateBlue	SlateBlue
Brown	Goldenrod	MediumSpringGreen	SlateGray
BurlyWood	Gray	MediumTurquoise	Snow
CadetBlue	Green	MediumVioletRed	SpringGreen
Chartreuse	GreenYellow	MidnightBlue	SteelBlue
Chocolate	Honeydew	MintCream	Tan
Coral	HotPink	MistyRose	Teal
CornflowerBlue	IndianRed	Moccasin	Thistle
Cornsilk	Indigo	NavajoWhite	Tomato
Crimson	Ivory	Navy	Transparent
Cyan	Khaki	OldLace	Turquoise
DarkBlue	Lavender	Olive	Violet
DarkCyan	LavenderBlush	OliveDrab	Wheat
DarkGoldenrod	LawnGreen	Orange	White
DarkGray	LemonChiffon	OrangeRed	WhiteSmoke
DarkGreen	LightBlue	Orchid	Yellow
DarkKhaki	LightCoral	PaleGoldenrod	YellowGreen
DarkMagenta	LightCyan	PaleGreen	
DarkOliveGreen	LightGoldenrodYellow	PaleTurquoise	
DarkOrange	LightGray	PaleVioletRed	
DarkOrchid	LightGreen	PapayaWhip	
DarkRed	LightPink	PeachPuff	
DarkSalmon	LightSalmon	Peru	
DarkSeaGreen	LightSeaGreen	Pink	
DarkSlateBlue	LightSkyBlue	Plum	
DarkSlateGray	LightSlateGray	PowderBlue	
DarkTurquoise	LightSteelBlue	Purple	
DarkViolet	LightYellow	Red	

Table 12-5 Color properties

When you are designing a Form, you can choose colors from a list next to the BackColor and ForeColor properties in the IDE's Properties list. The statements created will be similar to the following:

```
this.label1.BackColor = System.Drawing.Color.Blue;
this.label1.ForeColor = System.Drawing.Color.Gold;
```

If you add using System.Drawing; at the top of your file, you can eliminate the references in the preceding lines and refer to the colors simply as Color.Blue and Color.Gold.

For professional-looking results when you prepare a resume or most other business documents, experts recommend that you use only one or two fonts and colors, even though your word-processing program allows many such selections. The same is true when you design GUI applications. Although many fonts and colors are available, you probably should stick with just a few choices in a single project.

TWO TRUTHS & A LIE

Adding Color to a Form

1. Because the choice of colors in C# is limited, you are required to create custom colors for many GUI applications.

2. When you are designing a Form, color choices appear in a list next to the BackColor and ForeColor properties in the IDE's Properties list.

3. The complete name of the color pink in C# is System.Drawing.Color.Pink.

The false statement is #1. The Color class contains a wide variety of predefined colors that you can use with your Controls.

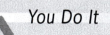 *You Do It*

Adding Labels to a Form and Changing Their Properties

In the next steps, you begin to create an application for Bailey's Bed and Breakfast. The main Form allows the user to select one of two suites and discover the amenities and price associated with each choice. You will start by placing two Labels on a Form and setting several of their properties.

(continues)

(continued)

The screen images in the next steps represent a typical Visual Studio environment. Based on the version of Visual Studio you are using and the options selected during your installation, your screen might look different.

1. Open Microsoft Visual Studio. Select **New Project** and **Windows Forms Application**. Near the bottom of the New Project window, click in the **Name** text box, and replace the default name with **BedAndBreakfast**. Make sure that the Location field contains the folder where you want to store the project. See Figure 12-9.

		New Project		? ✕
▷ Recent		.NET Framework 4.5 ▾ Sort by: Default ▾	⊞ ☰ Search Installed Te 🔎 ▾	
▲ Installed		🗔 Blank App (Universal Apps)	Visual C#	**Type:** Visual C#
▲ Templates				A project for creating an application with a Windows Forms user interface
▲ Visual C#		🗔 Windows Forms Application	Visual C#	
▷ Store Apps				⎡ Windows Forms ⎤
Windows Desktop		🗔 WPF Application	Visual C#	⎣ Application selected ⎦
Web				
▷ Office/SharePoint		🗔 Console Application	Visual C#	
Android				
Cloud		🗔 Hub App (Universal Apps)	Visual C#	
▷ Online				
		Click here to go online and find templates.		

Name: BedAndBreakfast ───────   ⎡ Project Name entered ⎤

Location: C:\C#\Chapter.12\   ▾   Browse...

Solution: Create new solution   ▾

Solution name: BedAndBreakfast   ☑ Create directory for solution
     ☐ Add to source control

     OK   Cancel

Figure 12-9   The New Project window for the BedAndBreakfast application

2. Click **OK**. The design screen opens. The blank Form in the center of the screen has an empty title bar. Click the Form. The lower-right corner of the screen contains a Properties window that lists the Form's properties. (If you do not see the Properties window, you can click **View** on the menu bar, and then click **Properties Window**.) In the Properties list, click the **Name** property and change the Name of the Form to **BaileysForm**. Click the **Text** property and change it to **Bailey's Bed and Breakfast**.

(continues)

(continued)

3. From the Toolbox at the left of the screen, drag a Label onto the Form. Change the Name of label1 to **welcomeLabel** and change the Text property to **Welcome to Bailey's**. Drag and resize the Label so it is close to the position of the Label in Figure 12-10. (If you prefer to set the Label's Location property manually in the Properties list, the Location should be **60, 30**.)

If you do not see the Toolbox, click the **Toolbox tab** at the left side of the screen and pin it to the screen by clicking the pushpin. Alternatively, you can select **View** from the menu bar, and then click **Toolbox**.

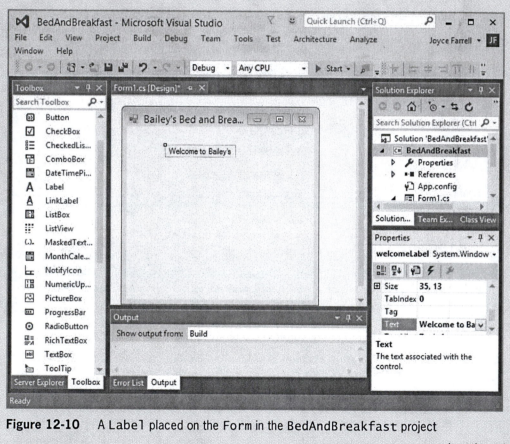

Figure 12-10   A Label placed on the Form in the BedAndBreakfast project

(continues)

(continued)

4. Locate the Font property in the Properties list. Currently, it lists the default font: Microsoft Sans Serif, 8.25 pt. Notice the ellipsis (three dots) at the right of the Font property name. (You might have to click in the Property to see the button.) Click the ellipsis to display the Font dialog box. Make selections to change the font to **Microsoft Sans Serif**, **18 point**, and **Bold**. Click **OK**. When you enlarge the Font for the Label, it is too close to the right edge of the Form. Drag the Label to change its Location property to approximately **20, 30**, or type the new Location value in the Properties window.

5. Drag a second Label onto the Form beneath the first one, and then set its Name property to rateLabel and its Text property to **Check our rates**. Change its Location to approximately **80, 80** and its Font to **Microsoft Sans Serif**, **12 point**, **Regular**.

6. Save the project, click **Debug** on the menu bar, and click **Start Without Debugging**, or use the shortcut keys listed in the menu. The Form appears, as shown in Figure 12-11.

Figure 12-11   The BedAndBreakfast Form with two Labels

7. Dismiss the Form by clicking the **Close** button in its upper-right corner.

(continues)

564

(continued)

Examining the Code Generated by the IDE

In the next steps, you examine the code generated by the IDE for the following reasons:

- To gain an understanding of the types of statements created by the IDE.

- To lose any intimidation you might have about the code that is generated. You will recognize many of the C# statements from what you have already learned in this book.

1. In the Solution Explorer at the right side of the screen, double-click **Form1.Designer.cs**. Scroll down until you can view the statements similar to those shown in Figure 12-12. (You can drag the bottom and side borders of the code window to expose more of the code, or you can scroll to see all of it.) You should be able to view statements that assign values to the properties of the components that you dragged into the Form.

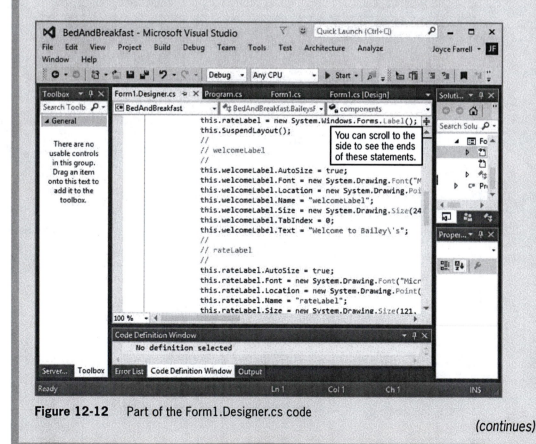

Figure 12-12   Part of the Form1.Designer.cs code

(continues)

(continued)

2. Next, change the BackColor property of the Bailey's Bed and Breakfast Form. Click the **Form1.cs[Design]** tab and click the **Form**, or click the list box of components at the top of the Properties window and select **BaileysForm**. In the Properties list, click the **BackColor** property and click its down arrow to see its list of choices. Choose the **Custom** tab and select **Yellow** in the third row of available colors. Click the **Form**, notice the color change, and then view the code in the Form1.Designer.cs file. Locate the statement that changes the BackColor of the Form to Yellow. As you continue to design Forms, periodically check the code to confirm your changes and better learn C#.

3. Save the project.

4. If you want to take a break at this point, close Visual Studio. You return to this project in the "You Do It" section at the end of this chapter.

Using CheckBox and RadioButton Objects

A **checkbox** is a control that is a small rectangle that indicates whether a user has chosen an option. The C# class that allows you to create a checkbox is CheckBox. When a form contains multiple checkboxes, the user can select any number of them. When options are grouped so that only one can be checked at a time and selecting one deselects the others, they are called **radio buttons**. (You might also hear the term *option buttons*.) The C# class that creates a radio button is RadioButton. Like Button, both CheckBox and RadioButton descend from ButtonBase.

Table 12-6 contains commonly used CheckBox and RadioButton properties and the default event for which a method shell is generated when you double-click a CheckBox or RadioButton in the IDE.

Property or Method	Description
Checked	Indicates whether the CheckBox or RadioButton is checked
Text	The text displayed to the right of the CheckBox or RadioButton
CheckedChanged()	Default event that is generated when the Checked property changes

Table 12-6 Commonly used CheckBox and RadioButton properties and default event

If you precede a letter with an ampersand (&) in the Text property value of a ButtonBase object, that letter acts as an access key. An **access key** provides a shortcut way to make a selection using the keyboard. For example, if a Button's text is defined as &Press, then typing Alt+P has the same effect as clicking the Button. Access keys are also called *hot keys*.

You can place multiple groups of RadioButtons on a Form by using a GroupBox or Panel. You will learn more about GroupBoxes and Panels later in this chapter.

Figure 12-13 shows an example of a Form with which a user can select pizza otions. It contains several Labels, four CheckBox objects, and three RadioButton objects. It makes sense for the pizza topping choices to be displayed using CheckBoxes because a user might select multiple toppings. However, options for delivery, pick-up, and dining in the restaurant are mutually exclusive, so they are presented using RadioButton objects.

![Pizza Order Form showing Select toppings checkboxes (Onions, Green pepper, Pepperoni, Sausage) and Dining options radio buttons (Pick-up, Delivery, Dine in)]

Figure 12-13   A Form with Labels, CheckBoxes, and RadioButtons

When you add CheckBox and RadioButton objects to a form, they automatically are named using the same conventions you have seen with Buttons and Labels. That is, the first CheckBox without an explicitly assigned name is checkBox1 by default, the second is named checkBox2, and so on. Using the Properties list, you can assign more meaningful names such as sausageCheckBox and pepperoniCheckBox. Naming objects appropriately makes your code more understandable to others, and makes your programming job easier.

Both CheckBox and RadioButton objects have a Checked property whose value is true or false. For example, if you create a CheckBox named sausageCheckBox and you want to add $1.00 to a pizzaPrice value when the user checks the box, you can write the following:

```
if(sausageCheckBox.Checked)
   pizzaPrice = pizzaPrice + 1.00;
```

The Checked property is a read/write property. That is, you can assign a value to it as well as access its value.

The default method that executes when a user clicks either a CheckBox or RadioButton is xxx_CheckedChanged(), where xxx represents the name of the invoking object. For example, suppose that the total price of a pizza should be altered based on a user's CheckBox selections. In this example, the base price for a pizza is $12.00, and $1.25 is added for each selected topping. You can declare constants for the BASE_PRICE and TOPPING_PRICE of a pizza and declare a variable that is initialized to the pizza base price as follows:

```
private const double BASE_PRICE = 12.00;
private const double TOPPING_PRICE = 1.25;
private double price = BASE_PRICE;
```

These declarations typically are placed in a Form's .cs file in the Form1 class, above both the constructor and other methods. Figure 12-14 shows the code you would add to the Form.cs file for the application. The sausageCheckBox_CheckedChanged() method changes the pizza price. The method shell was created by double-clicking the sausageCheckBox on the form; the statements within the method were written by a programmer. If a change occurs because the sausageCheckBox was checked, then the TOPPING_PRICE is added to the price. If the change to the checkBox was to uncheck it, the TOPPING_PRICE is subtracted from the price. Either way, the Text property of a Label named outputLabel is changed to reflect the new price.

```
private void sausageCheckBox_CheckedChanged(object sender, EventArgs e)
{
    if (sausageCheckBox.Checked)
        price += TOPPING_PRICE;
    else
        price -= TOPPING_PRICE;
    outputLabel.Text = "Total is " + price.ToString("C");
}
```

Figure 12-14   The sausageCheckBox_CheckedChanged() method

In a similar fashion, you can add appropriate code for RadioButton objects. For example, assume that a $2.00 delivery charge is in effect, but there is no extra charge for customers who pick up a pizza or dine in. The code for deliverRadioButton_CheckedChanged() appears in Figure 12-15. When the user selects the deliverRadioButton, $2.00 is added to the total. When the user selects either of the other RadioButtons, the deliverRadioButton becomes unchecked and the $2.00 charge is removed from the total. Figure 12-16 shows a typical execution of the PizzaOrder program after it is complete.

```
private void deliverRadioButton_CheckedChanged(object sender, EventArgs e)
{
    const double DELIVERY_CHARGE = 2.00;
    if (deliverRadioButton.Checked)
        price += DELIVERY_CHARGE;
    else
        price -= DELIVERY_CHARGE;
    outputLabel.Text = "Total is " + price.ToString("C");
}
```

568

Figure 12-15   The deliverRadioButton_CheckedChanged() method

The entire pizza-order application can be found in the downloadable student files.

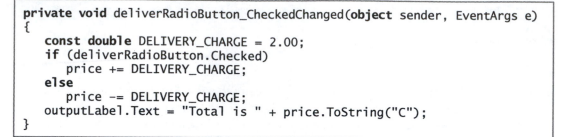

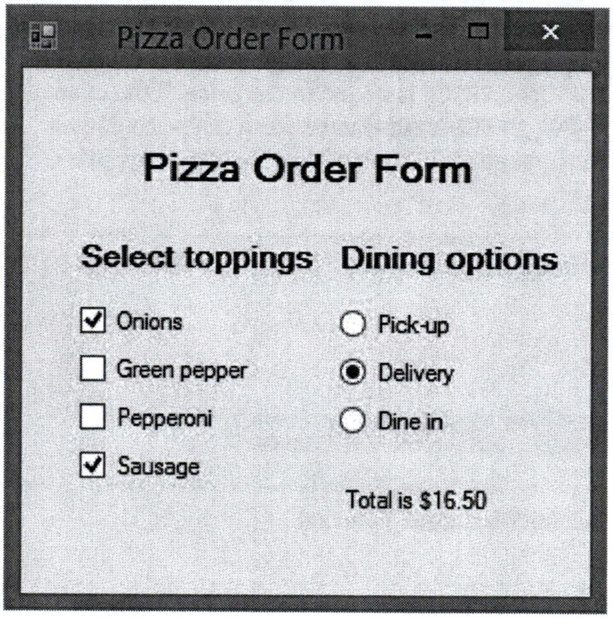

When an application starts, sometimes you want a specific CheckBox or RadioButton to be selected by default. If so, you can set the Control's Checked property to true in the Properties list in the IDE.

Watch the video *CheckBoxes and RadioButtons*.

Figure 12-16   Typical execution of the PizzaOrder program

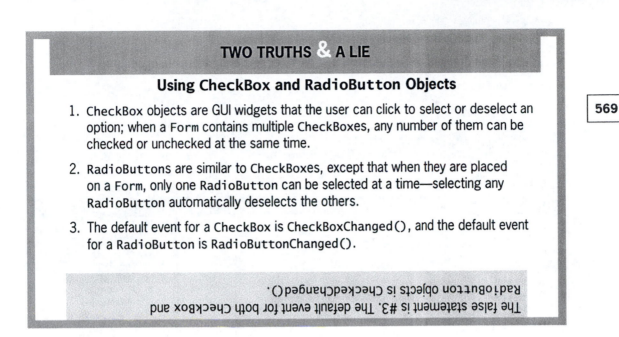

TWO TRUTHS & A LIE

Using CheckBox and RadioButton Objects

1. CheckBox objects are GUI widgets that the user can click to select or deselect an option; when a Form contains multiple CheckBoxes, any number of them can be checked or unchecked at the same time.

2. RadioButtons are similar to CheckBoxes, except that when they are placed on a Form, only one RadioButton can be selected at a time—selecting any RadioButton automatically deselects the others.

3. The default event for a CheckBox is CheckBoxChanged(), and the default event for a RadioButton is RadioButtonChanged().

The false statement is #3. The default event for both CheckBox and RadioButton objects is CheckedChanged().

Adding a PictureBox to a Form

A **picture box** is a GUI element you use to display graphics. In C#, a PictureBox object can display graphics from a bitmap, icon, JPEG, GIF, or other image file type. Just as with a Button or a Label, you can easily drag a PictureBox Control onto a Form in the Visual Studio IDE. Table 12-7 shows the common properties and default event for a PictureBox.

Property or Method	Description
Image	Sets the image that appears in the PictureBox
SizeMode	Controls the size and position of the image in the PictureBox; values are Normal, StretchImage (which resizes the image to fit the PictureBox), AutoSize (which resizes the PictureBox to fit the image), and CenterImage (which centers the image in the PictureBox)
Click()	Default event that is generated when the user clicks the PictureBox

Table 12-7   Commonly used PictureBox properties and default event

Figure 12-17 shows a new project in the IDE. The following tasks have been completed:

- A project was started.
- The Form Text property was changed to *Save Money*.

- The Form BackColor property was changed to White.

- A Label was dragged onto the Form, and its Text and Font were changed.

- A PictureBox was dragged onto the Form.

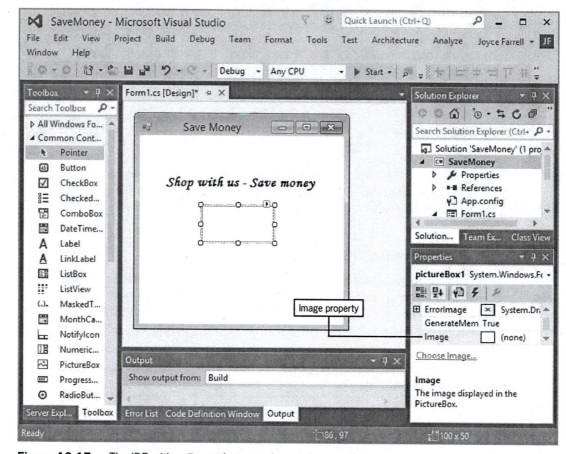

Figure 12-17 The IDE with a Form that contains a PictureBox

In Figure 12-17, in the Properties list at the right of the screen, the Image property is set to *(none)*. If you click the value, a button with an ellipsis appears. If you click it, a Select Resource window appears, as shown on the left in Figure 12-18. When you click the Import button, you can browse for stored images. When you select one, you see a preview in the Select Resource window, as shown on the right in Figure 12-18.

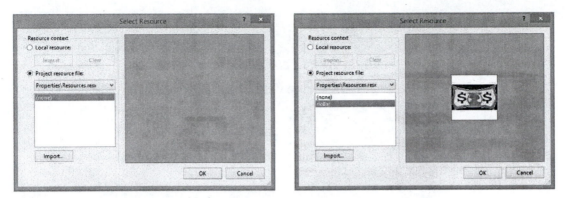

Figure 12-18   The Select Resource window before and after an image is selected

After you click OK, the image appears in the PictureBox, as in Figure 12-19. (You can resize the PictureBox in the IDE so the image displays completely.)

Figure 12-19   The SaveMoney Frame with an inserted image

If you examine the generated code, you can find the statements that instantiate a PictureBox (named pictureBox1 by default) and statements that set its properties, such as Size and Location.

571

TWO TRUTHS & A LIE

Adding a PictureBox to a Form

1. A PictureBox is a Control in which you can display graphics from a bitmap, icon, JPEG, GIF, or other image file type.

2. The default event for a PictureBox is LoadImage().

3. The Image property of a PictureBox holds the name of a file where a picture is stored.

The false statement is #2. The default event for a PictureBox is Click().

Adding ListBox, CheckedListBox, and ComboBox Controls to a Form

ListBox, CheckedListBox, and ComboBox objects all allow users to select choices from a list. The three classes descend from ListControl. Of course, they are also Controls and so inherit properties such as Text and BackColor from the Control class. Other properties are more specific to list-type objects. Table 12-8 describes some commonly used ListBox properties.

Property or Method	Description
Items	The collection of items in the ListBox; frequently, these are strings, but they can also be other types of objects
MultiColumn	Indicates whether display can be in multiple columns
SelectedIndex	Returns the index of the selected item. If no item has been selected, the value is –1. Otherwise, it is a value from 0 through $n - 1$, where n is the number of items in the ListBox.
SelectedIndices	Returns a collection of all the selected indices (when SelectionMode is more than One)
SelectedItem	Returns a reference to the selected item
SelectedItems	Returns a collection of the selected items (when SelectionMode is more than One)
SelectionMode	Determines how many items can be selected (see Table 12-9)
Sorted	Sorts the items when set to true
SelectedIndexChanged()	Default event that is generated when the selected index changes

Table 12-8   Commonly used ListBox properties and default event

A **list box** displays a list of items from which the user can select by clicking. Figure 12-20 shows a typical `ListBox` on a `Form`. After you drag a `ListBox` onto a `Form`, you can select its `Items` property and type a list into a String Collection Editor, as shown on the left in Figure 12-20.

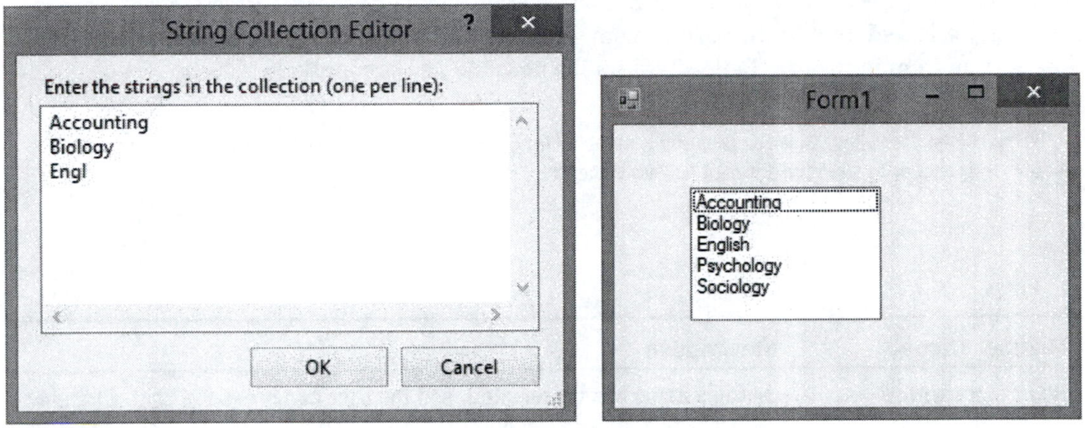

Figure 12-20 The String Collection Editor while filling a `ListBox` and the completed `ListBox` on a `Form`

Assuming the `Name` property of the `ListBox` is `majorListBox`, the following code is generated in the `InitializeComponent()` method when you fill the String Collection Editor with the strings in Figure 12-20:

```
this.majorListBox.Items.AddRange(new object[] {
    "Accounting",
    "Biology",
    "English",
    "Psychology",
    "Sociology" });
```

Objects added to a `ListBox` are not required to be strings. For example, you could add a collection of `Employee` or `Student` objects. The value returned by each added object's `ToString()` method is displayed in the `ListBox`. After the user selects an object, you can cast the `ListBox`'s `SelectedItem` to the appropriate type and access the object's other properties. The Chapter.12 folder of your student files contains a project named `AddRangeObjectsDemo` that illustrates this technique.

With a `ListBox`, you allow the user to make a single selection or multiple selections by setting the `SelectionMode` property appropriately. For example, when the `SelectionMode` property is set to `One`, the user can make only a single selection from the `ListBox`. When the `SelectionMode` is set to `MultiExtended`, pressing Shift and clicking the mouse or pressing Shift and one of the arrow keys (up, down, left, or right) extends the selection to span from the previously selected item to the current item. Pressing Ctrl and clicking the mouse selects or deselects an item in the list. Table 12-9 lists the possible `SelectionMode` values.

When the `SelectionMode` property is set to `SelectionMode.MultiSimple`, click the mouse or press the spacebar to select or deselect an item in the list.

Member Name	Description
MultiExtended	Multiple items can be selected, and the user can press the Shift, Ctrl, and arrow keys to make selections.
MultiSimple	Multiple items can be selected.
None	No items can be selected.
One	Only one item can be selected.

Table 12-9 `SelectionMode` enumeration list

For example, within a `Form`'s `Load()` method (the one that executes when a `Form` is first loaded), you could add the following:

```
this.majorListBox.SelectionMode =
    System.Windows.Forms.SelectionMode.MultiExtended;
```

As the example in Figure 12-21 shows, when you size a `ListBox` so that all the items cannot be displayed at the same time, a scroll bar is provided automatically on the side. The `ListBox` also provides the Boolean `MultiColumn` property, which you can set to display items in columns instead of a straight vertical list. This approach allows the control to display more items and can eliminate the need for the user to scroll down to an item. See Figure 12-22 which shows a multi-column list box to which eight strings have been added.

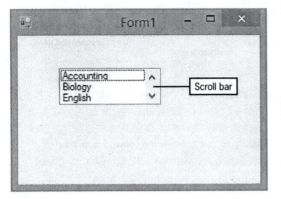

Figure 12-21 A ListBox with a scroll bar

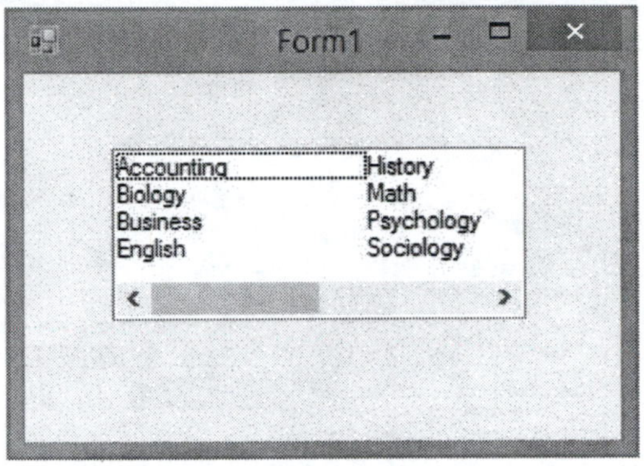

Figure 12-22 A multicolumn ListBox

The SelectedItem property of a ListBox contains a reference to the item a user has selected. For example, you can modify a Label's Text property in the majorListBox_SelectedIndexChanged() method with a statement such as the following, which appends the SelectedItem value to a label. Figure 12-23 shows a tyical result.

```
private void majorListBox_SelectedIndexChanged
    (object sender, EventArgs e)
{
    majorLabel.Text = "You selected " + majorListBox.SelectedItem;
}
```

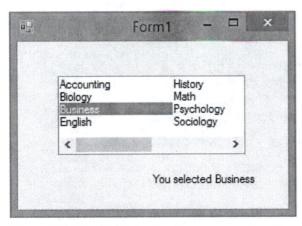

Figure 12-23 The ListBoxDemo application after a user has chosen *Business*

The Items.Count property of a ListBox object holds the number of items in the ListBox. The GetSelected() method accepts an integer argument representing the position of an item in the list. The method returns **true** if an item is selected and **false** if it is not. Therefore, code like the following could be used to count the number of selections a user makes from majorListBox:

```
int count = 0;
for(int x = 0; x < majorListBox.Items.Count; ++x)
    if(majorListBox.GetSelected(x))
        ++count;
```

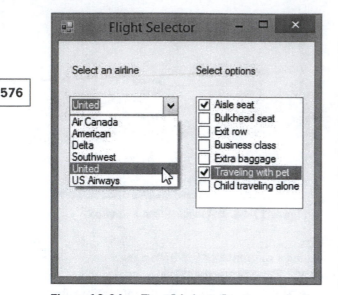

Figure 12-24 The FlightSelector application after the user has made some selections

Recall that the first position in an array is position 0. The same is true in a ListBox.

Alternatively, you can use a ListBox's SelectedItems property; it contains the items selected in a list. The following code assigns the number of selections a user makes from the majorListBox to count:

```
count = majorListBox.SelectedItems.
Count;
```

The SetSelected() method can be used to set a ListBox item to be automatically selected. For example, the following statement causes the first item in majorListBox to be selected:

```
majorListBox.SetSelected(0, true);
```

A **combo box** is a combination of a list box and and an editing control that allows a user to select from the list or to enter new text. The C# class is ComboBox, and the default ComboBox displays an editing area with a hidden list box. The application in Figure 12-24 contains a ComboBox for selecting an airline. A CheckedListBox is also similar to a ListBox, with check boxes appearing to the left of each desired item. The application in Figure 12-24 uses a CheckedListBox for flight options.

TWO TRUTHS & A LIE

Adding ListBox, CheckedListBox, and ComboBox Controls to a Form

1. With a ListBox Control, the user can select only one option at a time.

2. A ComboBox is similar to a ListBox, except that it displays an additional editing control that allows users to select from the list or to enter new text.

3. A CheckedListBox is similar to a ListBox, with check boxes appearing to the left of each desired item.

The false statement is #1. With a ListBox, you allow the user to make a single selection or multiple selections by setting the SelectionMode property appropriately.

Adding MonthCalendar and DateTimePicker Controls to a Form

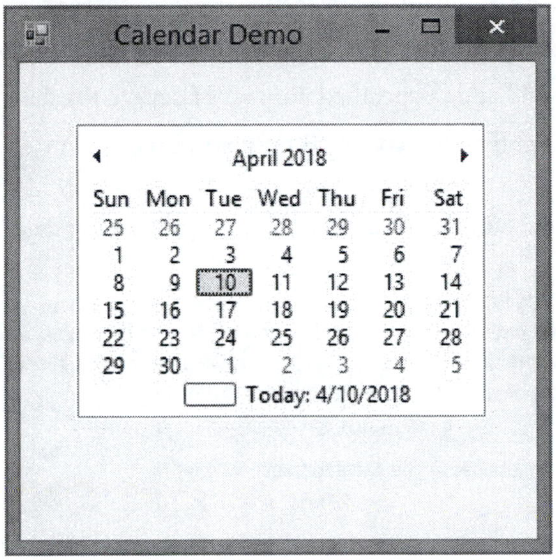

Figure 12-25   Typical execution of the MonthCalendarDemo application at startup

The MonthCalendar and DateTimePicker Controls allow you to retrieve date and time information. Figure 12-25 shows a MonthCalendar that has been placed on a Form. The current date is contained in a rectangle by default. When the user clicks a different date, it is shaded. Controls at the top of the calendar allow the user to go forward or back one month at a time, or the user can also move to a specific month or year by clicking the month and year title at the top of the calendar and then making a new month and year selection. Table 12-10 describes common MonthCalendar properties and the default event.

Property or Method	Description
MaxDate	Sets the last day that can be selected (the default is 12/31/9998)
MaxSelectionCount	Sets the maximum number of dates that can be selected at once (the default is 7)
MinDate	Sets the first day that can be selected (the default is 1/1/1753)
MonthlyBoldedDates	An array of dates that appear in boldface in the calendar (for example, holidays)
SelectionEnd	The last of a range of dates selected by the user
SelectionRange	The dates selected by the user
SelectionStart	The first of a range of dates selected by the user
ShowToday	If true, the date is displayed in text at the bottom of the calendar
ShowTodayCircle	If true, today's date is circled (the "circle" appears as a square)
DateChanged()	Default event that is generated when the user selects a date

Table 12-10   Commonly used MonthCalendar properties and default event

Several useful methods can be applied to the SelectionStart and SelectionEnd properties of MonthCalendar, including the following:

- ToShortDateString(), which displays the date in the format of 2/16/2016

- ToLongDateString(), which displays the date in the format of Sunday, February 16, 2016

- AddDays(), which takes a double argument and adds a specified number of days to the date

- AddMonths(), which takes an int argument and adds a specified number of months to the date

- AddYears(), which takes an int argument and adds a specified number of years to the date

The format in which dates are displayed depends on the operating system's regional settings. For example, using United Kingdom settings, the short string format would use the day first, followed by the month, as in 16/02/2016. The examples in the list above assume United States settings. To change your regional setting in Windows, you can go to Control Panel, click Region, and choose a region from the drop down list.

The AddDays() method accepts a double argument because you can add fractional days to SelectionStart and SelectionEnd.

SelectionStart and SelectionEnd are structures of the DateTime type. The chapter "Files and Streams" contains additional information about using DateTime objects to determine when files were created, modified, or accessed.

Many business and financial applications use AddDays(), AddMonths(), and AddYears() to calculate dates for events, such as payment for a bill (perhaps due in 10 days from an order) or scheduling a salesperson's callback to a customer (perhaps two months after initial contact). The default event for MonthCalendar is DateChanged(). For example, Figure 12-26 shows a method that executes when the user clicks a MonthCalendar named calendar. Ten days are added to a selected date and the result is displayed on a Label that has been named messageLabel. Figure 12-27 shows the output when the user selects May 29, 2018. The date that is 10 days in the future is correctly calculated as June 8.

```
private void calendar_DateChanged(object sender, DateRangeEventArgs e)
{
   const int DAYS_TO_ADD = 10;
   messageLabel.Text = "Date " + DAYS_TO_ADD +
      " days after selection is " +
      calendar.SelectionStart.AddDays(DAYS_TO_ADD).ToShortDateString();
}
```

Figure 12-26 The calendar_DateChanged() method

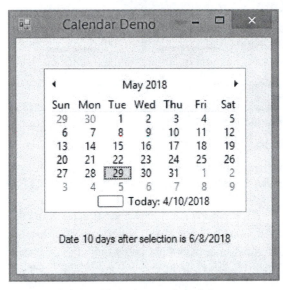

In Chapter 14, you will learn to use DateTime objects to hold data about dates and times.

Figure 12-27 Typical execution of the MonthCalendarDemo program

If you set the MinDate value to the MonthCalendar's TodayDate property, the user cannot select a date before the date you select. For example, you cannot make appointments or schedule deliveries in the past, so you might code the following in a form's Load() method:

```
calendar1.MinDate =
calendar1.TodayDate;
```

Conversely, you might want to prevent users from selecting a date in the future—for example, if the user is entering his birth date, it cannot be in the future. In that case, you could code a statement similar to the following:

```
calendar1.MaxDate = calendar1.TodayDate;
```

The DateTimePicker Control displays a month calendar when the down arrow is selected. This feature can be especially useful if you do not have much space available on a Form. Figure 12-28 shows a DateTimePicker before and after the user clicks the down arrow.

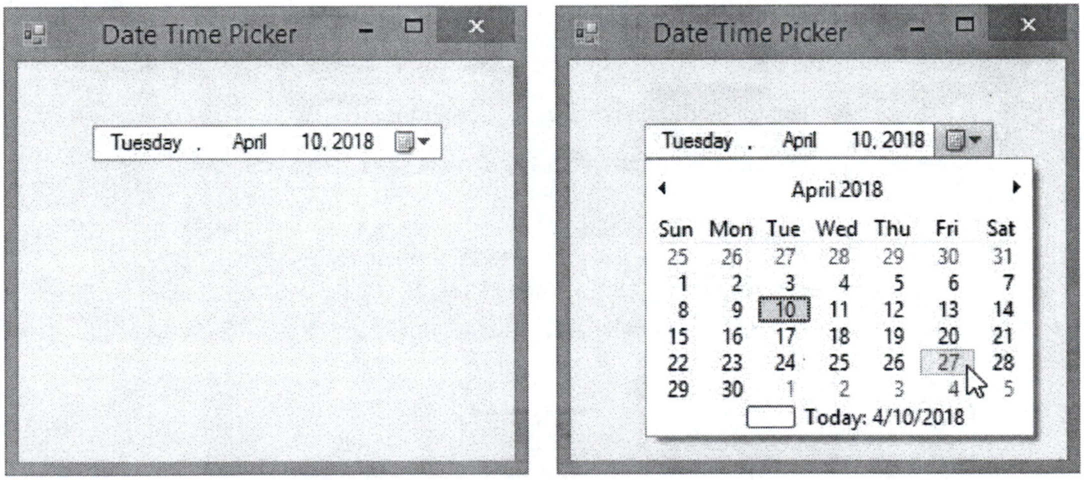

Figure 12-28 The DateTimePicker Control

When you use the `CustomFormat` property, the date displayed in a `DateTimePicker` Control is more customizable than the one in a `MonthCalendar`. Table 12-11 describes some commonly used `DateTimePicker` properties and the default event.

Property or Method	Description
CalendarForeColor	Sets the calendar text color
CalendarMonthBackground	Sets the calendar background color
CustomFormat	A string value that uses codes to set a custom date and time format. For example, to display the date and time as 02/16/2011 12:00 PM - Wednesday, set this property to "MM'/'dd'/'yyyy hh':'mm tt - dddd". See the C# documentation for a complete set of format string characters.
Format	Sets the format for the date or time. Options are Long (for example, Wednesday, February 16, 2011), Short (2/16/2011), and Time (for example, 3:15:01 PM). You can also create a CustomFormat.
Value	The data selected by the user
ValueChanged()	Default event that is generated when the Value property changes

Table 12-11 Commonly used `DateTimePicker` properties and default event

TWO TRUTHS & A LIE

Adding MonthCalendar and DateTimePicker Controls to a Form

1. The `MonthCalendar` and `DateTimePicker` Controls allow you to retrieve date and time information.

2. The default event for `MonthCalendar` is `DateChanged()`.

3. The `DateTimePicker` Control displays a small clock when you click it.

The false statement is #3. The DateTimePicker Control displays a month calendar when the down arrow is selected.

Working with a Form's Layout

When you place Controls on a Form in the IDE, you can drag them to any location to achieve the effect you want.

When you drag multiple Controls onto a Form, blue **snap lines** appear and help you align new Controls with others already in place. Figure 12-29 shows two snap lines that you can use to align a second label below the first one. Snap lines also appear when you place a control closer to the edge of a container than is recommended.

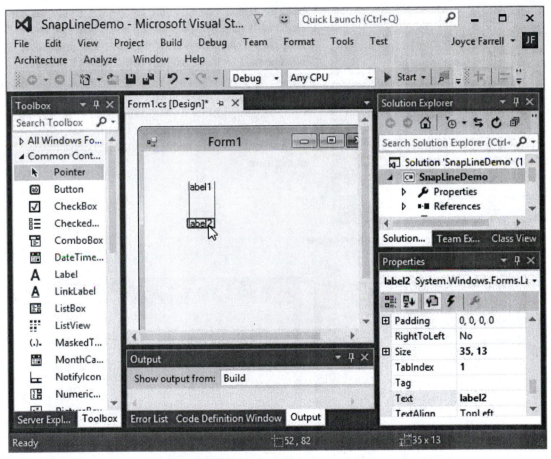

Figure 12-29   Snap lines in the Visual Studio Designer

You also can use the Location property in a Control's Properties list to specify a location. With either technique, code like the following is generated:

```
this.label1.Location = new System.Drawing.Point(23, 19);
```

Several other properties can help you to manage the appearance of a Form (or other ContainerControl). For example, setting the Anchor property causes a Control to remain at a fixed distance from the side of a container when the user resizes it. Figure 12-30 shows the Properties window for a Label that has been placed on a Form. The Anchor property has a drop-down window that lets you select or deselect the sides to which the label should be anchored. For most Controls, the default setting for Anchor is Top, Left.

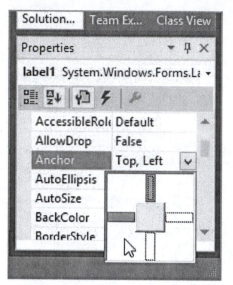

Figure 12-31 shows a Form with two Labels. On the Form, label1 has been anchored to the top left, and label2 has been anchored to the bottom right. The left side of the figure shows the Form as it first appears to the user, and the right side shows the Form after the user has resized it. Notice that in the resized Form, label1 is still the same distance from the top left as it originally was, and label2 is still the same distance from the bottom right as it originally was. Anchoring is useful when users expect a specific control to always be in the same general location in a container.

Figure 12-30 Selecting an Anchor property

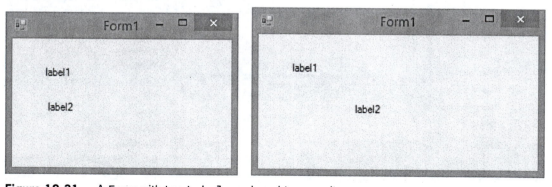

Figure 12-31 A Form with two Labels anchored to opposite corners

Setting the Dock property attaches a Control to the side of a container so that the Control stretches when the container's size is adjusted. Figure 12-32 shows the drop-down Dock Properties window for a Button. You can select any region in the window. Figure 12-33 shows a Button docked to the bottom of a Form before and after the Form has been resized.

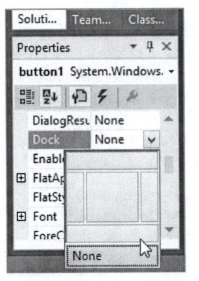

Figure 12-32 The Dock Properties window

Figure 12-33 A Form with a docked Button before and after resizing

A Form also has a MinimumSize property and a MaximumSize property. Each has two values—Width and Height. If you set these properties, the user cannot make the Form smaller or larger than you have specified. If you do not want the user to be able to adjust a Form's size at all, set the MinimumSize and MaximumSize properties to be equal.

Understanding GroupBoxes and Panels

Many types of ContainerControls are available to hold Controls. For example, a group box or panel can be used to contain a group of other controls and to move them as a group.

To create either of these Controls, you drag it from the Toolbox in the IDE and then drag the Controls you want on top of it. In C#, a **group box** and a **panel** differ in the following ways:

- A group box is created from the GroupBox class, and a panel is created from the Panel class.

- GroupBoxes can display a caption, but Panels cannot.

- Panels can include a scroll bar that the user can manipulate to view Controls; GroupBoxes do not have scroll bars.

You can anchor or dock Controls inside a GroupBox or Panel, and you can anchor or dock a GroupBox or Panel inside a Form. Doing this provides Control groups that can be arranged easily.

If you place several GroupBox Controls on a Form and several RadioButtons in each GroupBox, then a user can select one RadioButton from each GroupBox instead of being able to select just one RadioButton on a Form. In other words, each GroupBox operates independently.

When an application contains multiple GroupBox or Panel Controls on a Form, pressing Tab moves the focus to the next GroupBox or Panel. Then, within the GroupBox or Panel, you use arrow keys to progress to successive RadioButtons.

TWO TRUTHS & A LIE

Working with a Form's Layout

1. Setting the Anchor property causes a Control to remain at a fixed distance from the side of a container when the user resizes it.

2. Setting the Dock property attaches a Control to the side of a container so that the Control's size does not change when the container's size is adjusted.

3. The GroupBox and Panel controls are ContainerControls.

The false statement is #2. Setting the Dock property attaches a Control to the side of a container so that the Control stretches when the container's size is adjusted.

Adding a `MenuStrip` to a Form

Many programs you use in a Windows environment contain a **menu strip**, which is a horizontal list of general options that appears under the title bar of a `Form` or `Window`. When you click an item in a menu strip, you might initiate an action. More frequently, you see a list box that contains more specific options. Each of these might initiate an action or lead to another menu. For example, the Visual Studio IDE contains a horizontal menu strip that begins with the options File, Edit, and View. You have used word-processing, spreadsheet, and game programs with similar menus.

You can add a `MenuStrip` `Control` object to any `Form` you create. Using the Visual Studio IDE, you can add a `MenuStrip` to a `Form` by dragging it from the Toolbox onto the `Form`. This creates a menu bar horizontally across the top of the `Form`, just below the title bar. The strip extends across the width of the `Form` and contains a *Type Here* text box. When you click the text box, you can enter a menu item. Each time you add a menu item, new boxes are created so you can see where your next options will go, as shown in Figure 12-34.

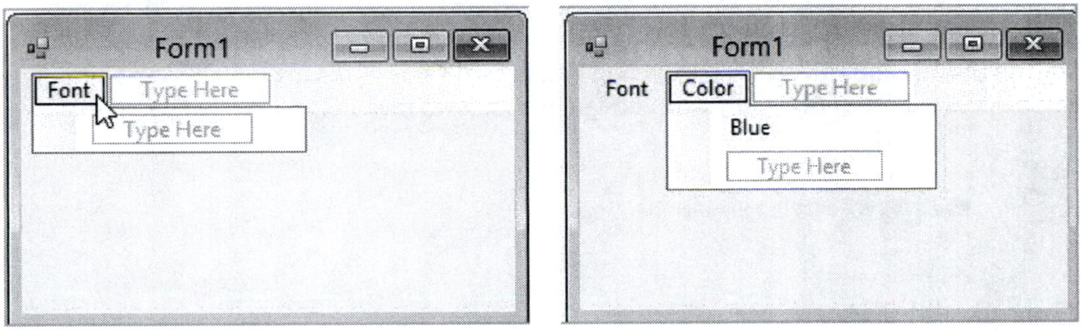

Figure 12-34   Creating a Form with a `MenuStrip`

If you do not see `MenuStrip` in your Toolbox, click the Menus & Toolbars group to expose it. You can click the `MenuStrip` icon at the bottom of the design screen to view and change the properties for the `MenuStrip`. For example, you might want to change the `Font` or `BackColor` for the `MenuStrip`.

If you create each menu item with an ampersand (&) in front of a unique letter, then the letter becomes an access key, and the user can press Alt and the letter to activate the menu choice. For example, if two choices were Green and Gray, you might want to type &Green and G&ray so the user could type Alt+G to select Green and Alt+R to select Gray.

When you double-click an entry in the `MenuStrip`, a `Click()` method is generated. For example, if you double-click *Blue* under *Color* in the menu being created in Figure 12-34, the method generated is `blueToolStripMenuItem_Click()`. As with all the other controls you have learned about, you can write any code statements within the method. For example, suppose that a Label named helloLabel has been dragged onto the Form. If choosing the *Blue* menu option should result in a blue forecolor for the label, you might code the method as follows:

```
private void blueToolStripMenuItem_Click(object sender, EventArgs e)
{
    helloLabel.ForeColor = Color.Blue;
}
```

You can work with the other menu items in this program in an exercise at the end of this chapter.

If possible, your main horizontal menu selections should be single words. That way, a user will not mistakenly think that a single menu item represents multiple items. Most applications do not follow this single-word convention for submenus. Also, users expect menu options to appear in conventional order. For example, users expect the far-left option on the main menu bar to be *File*, and they expect the *Exit* option to appear under *File*. Similarly, if an application contains a *Help* option, users expect to find it at the right side of the main menu bar. You should follow these conventions when designing your own menus.

Watch the video *Using a MenuStrip.*

TWO TRUTHS & A LIE

Adding a MenuStrip to a Form

1. When you click an item in a menu strip, the most common result is to initiate an action.

2. When you drag a MenuStrip Control object onto a Form using the Visual Studio IDE, the MenuStrip is added horizontally across the top of the Form, just below the title bar.

3. The default event for MenuStrip is Click().

The false statement is #1. When you click an item in a menu strip, you might initiate an action. More frequently, you see a list box that contains more specific options.

Using Other Controls

If you examine the Visual Studio IDE or search through the Visual Studio documentation, you will find many other Controls that are not covered in this chapter. If you click Project on the menu bar and click Add New Item, you can add extra Forms, Files, Controls, and other elements to your project. (In the next "You Do It" section, you create a project that adds new Forms that appear after selections are made from a primary Form.) New controls and containers will be developed in the future, and you might even design new controls of your own. Still, all controls will contain properties and methods, and your solid foundation in C# will prepare you to use new controls effectively.

You Do It

Adding CheckBoxes to a Form

In the next steps, you add two CheckBoxes to the BedAndBreakfast Form. These controls allow the user to select an available room and view information about it.

1. Open the BedAndBreakfast project in Visual Studio, if it is not still open on your screen.

2. In the Design view of the BedAndBreakfast project in the Visual Studio IDE, drag a CheckBox onto the Form below the *Check our rates* Label. (See Figure 12-35 for its approximate placement.) Change the Text property of the CheckBox to **BelleAire Suite**. Change the Name of the property to belleAireCheckBox. Drag a second CheckBox onto the Form beneath the first one. Change its Text property to **Lincoln Room** and its Name to lincolnCheckBox.

(continues)

(continued)

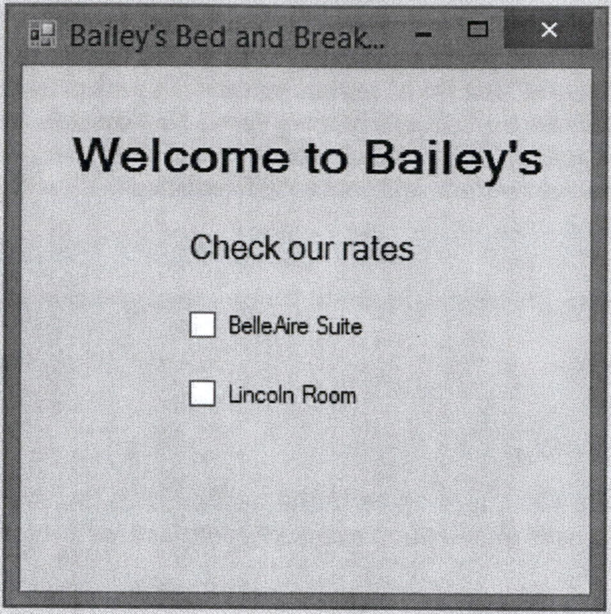

Figure 12-35 The BedAndBreakfast Form with two CheckBoxes

3. Next, you will create two new Forms: one that appears when the user selects the BelleAire CheckBox and one that appears when the user selects the Lincoln CheckBox. Click **Project** on the menu bar, and then click **Add New Item**. In the Add New Item window, click **Windows Form**. In the Name text box at the bottom of the window, type **BelleAireForm**. See Figure 12-36.

(continues)

(continued)

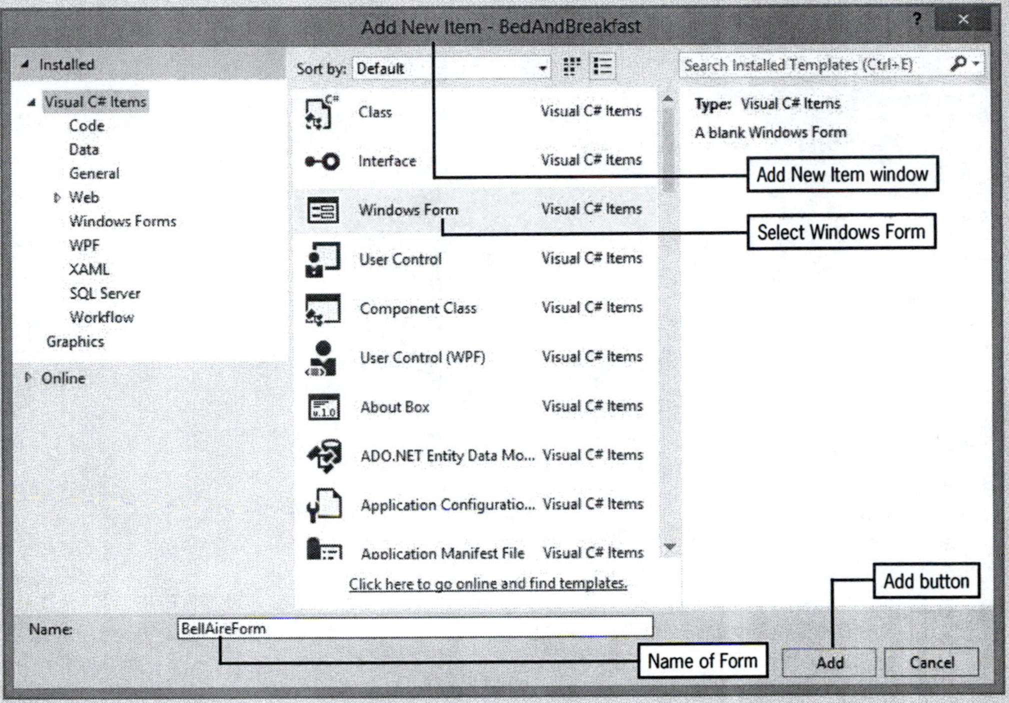

Figure 12-36 The Add New Item window

4. Click the **Add** button. A new Form is added to the project, and its Name and Text (title bar) properties contain *BelleAireForm*. Save the project (and continue to do so periodically).

5. Change the BackColor property of the Form to Yellow to match the color of BaileysForm.

6. Drag a Label onto the Form. Change the Name of the Label to **belleAireDescriptionLabel**. Change the Text property of the Label to contain the following: **The BelleAire suite has two bedrooms, two baths, and a private balcony**. Click the arrow on the text property to type the long label message on two lines. Adjust the size and position of the Label to resemble Figure 12-37. Drag a second Label onto the Form, name it **belleAirePriceLabel**, and type the price as the Text property: **$199.95 per night**.

(continues)

(continued)

Figure 12-37 The `BelleAireForm` with two `Labels`

7. Select the **Pointer** tool from the Toolbox at the left of the screen. Drag it to encompass both `Labels`. In the Properties list, select the **Font** property to change the `Font` for both `Controls` at once. Choose a suitable `Font`. Figure 12-38 shows **10-point Regular Papyrus**; you might choose a different font. Adjust the positions of the `Labels` if necessary to achieve a pleasing effect.

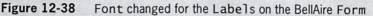

Figure 12-38 Font changed for the `Labels` on the BellAire `Form`

(continues)

(continued)

8. Click the **Form1.cs[Design]** tab at the top of the Designer screen to view the Bailey's Bed and Breakfast `Form`. Double-click the **BelleAire Suite CheckBox**. The program code (the method shell for the default event of a `CheckBox`) appears in the IDE main window. Within the `belleAireCheckBox_CheckedChanged()` method, add an `if` statement that determines whether the `BelleAire CheckBox` is checked. If it is checked, create a new instance of `BelleAireForm` and display it.

```
private void belleAireCheckBox_CheckedChanged(object sender,
    EventArgs e)
{
    if (belleAireCheckBox.Checked)
    {
        BelleAireForm belleAireForm = new BelleAireForm();
        belleAireForm.ShowDialog();
    }
}
```

When a new `Form` (or other `Windows` class) is instantiated, it is not visible by default. `ShowDialog()` shows the window and disables all other windows in the application. The user must dismiss the new `Form` before proceeding. A secondary window that takes control of a program is a **modal window**; the user must deal with this window before proceeding.

9. Save and then execute the program by selecting **Debug** from the menu bar, and then select **Start Without Debugging**. The main BedAndBreakfast `Form` appears. Click the **BelleAire Suite CheckBox**. The BelleAire `Form` appears. Dismiss the `Form`. Click the **Lincoln Room CheckBox**. Nothing happens because you have not yet written event code for this `CheckBox`. When you uncheck and then check the **BelleAire Suite CheckBox** again, the BelleAire form reappears. Dismiss the BelleAire `Form`.

10. When you dismiss the BelleAire `Form`, the BelleAire `CheckBox` remains checked. To see it appear as unchecked after its `Form` is dismissed, dismiss the program's main form (Bailey's Bed and Breakfast) to end the program. Then, add a third statement within the `if` block in the `CheckedChanged()` message as follows:

```
belleAireCheckBox.Checked = false;
```

That way, whenever the `CheckedChanged()` method executes because the `belleAireCheckBox` was checked, it will become unchecked. Save the project, and then execute it again. When you select the BelleAire `CheckBox`, view the `Form`, and dismiss it, the `CheckBox` appears unchecked and is ready to check again. Dismiss the BedAndBreakfast `Form`.

(continues)

(continued)

11. Click **Project** on the menu bar, and then click **Add New Item**. Click **Windows Form** and enter its Name: `LincolnForm`. When the new Form appears, its Name and Text properties will have been set to **LincolnForm**. Change the Text property to **Lincoln Room**. Then add two Labels to the Form, and provide appropriate Name properties for them. Change the Text on the first Label to **Return to the 1850s in this lovely room with private bath**. The second should be **$110 per night**. Change the Form's BackColor property to **White**. Change the Font to match the Font you chose for the BelleAire Form. See Figure 12-39.

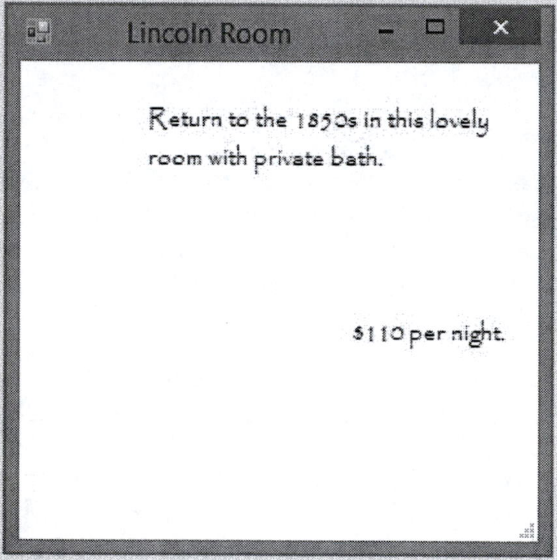

Figure 12-39   The LincolnForm

12. From the Toolbox, drag a PictureBox onto the Form. Select its **Image** property. A dialog box allows you to select a resource. Click **Local resource**, and then click the **Import** button to browse for an image. Find the AbeLincoln file in the Chapter.12 folder of your downloadable student files, and double-click it. (Alternately, you can import another image you prefer.) After the image appears in the Select Resource dialog box, click **OK**. The selected image appears in the PictureBox. Adjust the size of the Form and the sizes and positions of the labels and picture box so that the picture is fully visible and everything looks attractive on the Form. See Figure 12-40.

(continues)

(continued)

Figure 12-40 The `LincolnForm` with an Image in a `PictureBox`

The AbeLincoln file was obtained at www.free-graphics.com. You can visit the site and download other images to use in your own applications. You should also search the Web for "free clip art" and similar phrases.

13. In the Solution Explorer, double-click **Form1.cs** or click the **Form1.cs[Design]** tab at the top of the design screen. On the BedAndBreakfast `Form`, double-click the Lincoln Room `CheckBox`, and add the following `if` statement to the `lincolnCheckBox_CheckedChanged()` method:

```csharp
private void lincolnCheckBox_CheckedChanged(object sender,
    EventArgs e)
{
    if (lincolnCheckBox.Checked)
    {
        LincolnForm lincolnForm = new LincolnForm();
        lincolnForm.ShowDialog();
        lincolnCheckBox.Checked = false;
    }
}
```

(continues)

(continued)

14. Save the project and then execute it. When the BedAndBreakfast Form appears, click either CheckBox—the appropriate informational Form appears. Close it and then click the other CheckBox. Again, the appropriate Form appears.

15. Close all forms.

Adding *RadioButtons to a Form*

Next you add more Controls to the BedAndBreakfast Form. You generally use RadioButtons when a user must select from mutually exclusive options.

1. In the Design view of the main Form in the BedAndBreakfast project, add a Button near the bottom of the Form. Change the Button's Name property to **mealButton** and the Button's Text to **Click for meal options**. Adjust the size of the Button so that its text is fully visible.

2. From the menu bar, select **Project**, click **Add New Item**, and click **Windows Form**. Name the Form **BreakfastOptionForm**, and click **Add**. On the new Form, make the following changes:

   • Set the Form's BackColor to **Yellow**.

   • Drag a Label onto the Form. Name it appropriately, and set its Text to **Select your breakfast option**.

   • Drag three RadioButtons onto the Form. Set their respective Text properties to **Continental**, **Full**, and **Deluxe**. Set their respective Names to **contBreakfastButton**, **fullBreakfastButton**, and **deluxeBreakfastButton**.

   • Select an appropriate font for the Label and RadioButtons.

   • Drag a Label onto the Form, and then set its Text to **Price:** and its Name to **priceLabel**. Make the Font property a little larger than for the other Form components.

See Figure 12-41 for approximate placement of all these Controls.

(continues)

(continued)

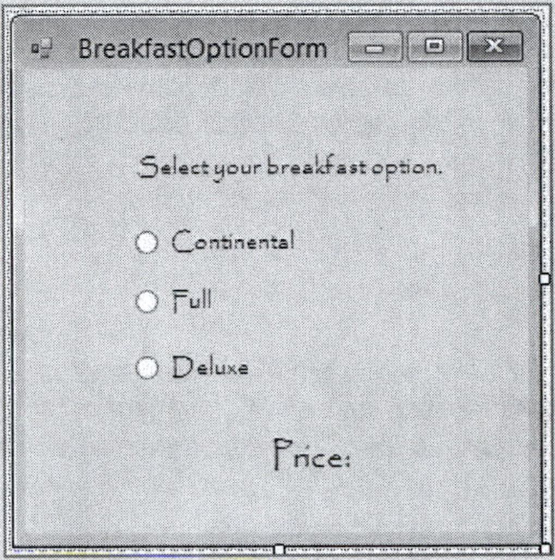

Figure 12-41   Developing the `BreakfastOptionForm`

3. Double-click the title bar of the `BreakfastOptionForm` to generate a method named `BreakfastOptionForm_Load()`. Within this method, you can type statements that execute each time the `Form` is created. Add the following statements within the `BreakfastOptionForm` class, which declare three constants representing prices for different breakfast options. Within the `BreakfastOptionForm_Load()` method, set the `priceLabel Text` property to the lowest price by default when the `Form` loads.

```
public partial class BreakfastOptionForm : Form
{
    private const double CONT_BREAKFAST_PRICE = 6.00;
    private const double FULL_BREAKFAST_PRICE = 9.95;
    private const double DELUXE_BREAKFAST_PRICE = 16.50;
    public BreakfastOptionForm()
    {
        InitializeComponent();
    }
    private void BreakfastOptionForm_Load
        (object sender, EventArgs e)
    {
        priceLabel.Text = "Price: " +
            CONT_BREAKFAST_PRICE.ToString("C");
    }
}
```

(continues)

(continued)

4. Return to the Design view for the BreakfastOptionForm, and double-click the **contBreakfastButton RadioButton**. When you see the generated CheckedChanged() method, add a statement that sets priceLabel to the continental breakfast price when the user makes that selection:

```
private void contBreakfastButton_CheckedChanged
    (object sender, EventArgs e)
{
    priceLabel.Text = "Price: " +
        CONT_BREAKFAST_PRICE .ToString("C");
}
```

5. Return to the Design view for the BreakfastOptionForm, double-click the **fullBreakfastButton RadioButton**, and add a statement to the generated method that sets the priceLabel to the full breakfast price when the user makes that selection:

```
private void fullBreakfastButton_CheckedChanged
    (object sender, EventArgs e)
{
    priceLabel.Text = "Price: " +
        FULL_BREAKFAST_PRICE.ToString("C");
}
```

6. Return to the Design view for the BreakfastOptionForm, double-click the **deluxeBreakfastButton RadioButton**, and add a statement to the generated method that sets the priceLabel to the deluxe breakfast price when the user makes that selection:

```
private void deluxeBreakfastButton_CheckedChanged
    (object sender, EventArgs e)
{
    priceLabel.Text = "Price: " +
        DELUXE_BREAKFAST_PRICE.ToString("C");
}
```

7. In the Solution Explorer, double-click the **Form1.cs file** to view the original Form. Double-click the **mealButton Button**. When the Click() method is generated, add the following code so that the BreakfastOptionForm is loaded when a user clicks the Button:

```
private void mealButton_Click(object sender,
    EventArgs e)
{
    BreakfastOptionForm breakfastForm = new
        BreakfastOptionForm();
    breakfastForm.ShowDialog();
}
```

(continues)

(continued)

8. Save the project and execute it. When the BedAndBreakfast Form appears, confirm that the BelleAire Suite and Lincoln Room CheckBoxes still work correctly, displaying their information Forms when they are clicked. Then click the **Click for meal options** Button. By default, the Continental breakfast option is chosen, as shown in Figure 12-42, so the price is $6.00. Click the other RadioButton options to confirm that each correctly changes the breakfast price.

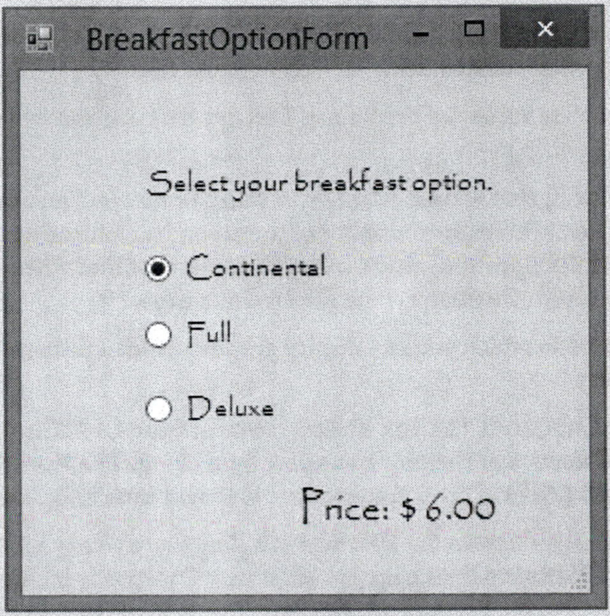

Figure 12-42 The BreakfastOptionForm with Continental breakfast RadioButton selected

9. Dismiss all the Forms, and close Visual Studio.

Chapter Summary

- The `Control` class provides definitions for GUI objects such as `Forms` and `Buttons`. There are 26 direct descendents of `Control` and additional descendents of those classes. Each `Control` has more than 80 `public` properties and 20 `protected` ones.

- When you design GUI applications using the Visual Studio IDE, much of the code is automatically generated.

- You use the `Font` class to change the appearance of printed text on your `Forms`.

- A `LinkLabel` is similar to a `Label`; it is a child of `Label`, but it provides the additional capability to link the user to other sources, such as Web pages or files.

- The `Color` class contains a wide variety of predefined `Colors` that you can use with your `Controls`.

- `CheckBox` objects are GUI widgets the user can click to select or deselect an option. When a `Form` contains multiple `CheckBox`es, any number of them can be checked or unchecked at the same time. `RadioButtons` are similar to `CheckBox`es, except that when they are placed on a `Form`, only one `RadioButton` can be selected at a time.

- A `PictureBox` is a `Control` in which you can display graphics from a bitmap, icon, JPEG, GIF, or other image file type.

- `ListBox`, `ComboBox`, and `CheckedListBox` objects descend from `ListControl` and enable you to display lists of items that the user can select by clicking. The `MonthCalendar` and `DateTimePicker Controls` allow you to retrieve date and time information.

- When you place `Controls` on a `Form` in the IDE, you can drag them to any location to achieve the effect you want. Blue snap lines help you align new `Controls` with others already in place. You also can use the `Location`, `Anchor`, `Dock`, `MinimumSize`, and `MaximumSize` properties to customize a `Form's` appearance. You can use a `GroupBox` or `Panel` to group related `Controls` on a `Form`.

- Many programs you use in a Windows environment contain a menu strip, which is a horizontal list of general options that appears under the title bar of a `Form` or `Window`. When a user clicks an item in a `MenuStrip Control`, a list box that contains more specific options is displayed frequently.

- If you examine the Visual Studio IDE or search through the Visual Studio documentation, you will find many `Controls`. If you click Project on the menu bar and click Add New Item, you can add extra `Forms`, `Files`, `Controls`, and other elements to a project.

Key Terms

Graphical control elements, or, more simply, **controls**, are the components through which a user interacts with a GUI program.

Widgets are GUI controls.

A **link label** is a control with text that links a user to other resources such as Web pages or files.

The **default event** for a `Control` is the one generated when you double-click the `Control` while designing it in the IDE and is the method you are most likely to alter when you use the `Control`, as well as the event that users most likely expect to generate when they encounter the `Control` in a working application.

A **check box** is a GUI widget the user can click to select or deselect an option.

A **radio button** is an option in a group in which only one can be selected at a time—selecting any radio button automatically deselects the others.

An **access key** provides a shortcut way to make a selection using the keyboard.

A **picture box** is a GUI element that can display graphics.

A **list box** is a GUI element that displays a list of items that the user can select by clicking.

A **combo box** is a GUI element that is a combination of a list box and an editing control that allows a user to select from the list or enter new text.

Snap lines appear in a design environment to help you align new `Control`s with others already in place.

A **group box** is a GUI element that contains other GUI elements; it is similar to a panel but does not have a scroll bar and can contain a caption.

A **panel** is a GUI element that contains other GUI elements; it is similar to a group box but does not have a caption and can contain a scroll bar.

A **menu strip** is a horizontal list of general options that appears under the title bar of a `Form` or `Window`.

A **modal window** is a secondary window that takes control from a primary window and that a user must deal with before proceeding.

Review Questions

1. `Labels`, `Buttons`, and `CheckBox`es are all _____ .

   a. GUI objects

   b. `Controls`

   c. widgets

   d. all of these

2. All `Control` objects descend from _____ .

   a. `Form`
   c. `ButtonBase`

   b. `Component`
   d. all of these

600

3. Which of the following is most like a `RadioButton`?

   a. `ListControl`
   c. `PictureBox`

   b. `CheckedListBox`
   d. `Button`

4. Which of the following is not a commonly used `Control` property?

   a. `BackColor`
   c. `Location`

   b. `Language`
   d. `Size`

5. The `Control` you frequently use to provide descriptive text for another `Control` object is a _____ .

   a. `Form`
   c. `CheckBox`

   b. `Label`
   d. `MessageBox`

6. Which of the following creates a `Label` named `firstLabel`?

   a. `firstLabel = new firstLabel();`

   b. `Label = new firstLabel();`

   c. `Label firstLabel = new Label();`

   d. `Label firstLabel = Label();`

7. The property that determines what the user reads on a `Label` is the _____ property.

   a. `Text`
   c. `Phrase`

   b. `Label`
   d. `Setting`

8. Which of the following correctly creates a `Font`?

   a. `Font myFont = new Font("Arial", 14F, FontStyle.Bold);`

   b. `Font myFont = new Font("Courier", 13.6);`

   c. `myFont = Font new Font("TimesRoman", FontStyle.Italic);`

   d. `Font myFont = Font(20, "Helvetica", Underlined);`

9. The default event for a `Control` is the one that _____ .

   a. occurs automatically whether or not a user manipulates the `Control`

   b. is generated when you double-click the `Control` while designing it in the IDE

   c. requires no parameters

   d. occurs when a user clicks the `Control` with a mouse

10. Assume that you have created a `Label` named `myLabel`. Which of the following sets `myLabel`'s background color to green?

   a. `myLabel = BackColor.System.Drawing.Color.Green;`

   b. `myLabel.BackColor = System.Drawing.Color.Green;`

   c. `myLabel.Green = System.DrawingColor;`

   d. `myLabel.Background = new Color.Green;`

11. What is one difference between `CheckBox` and `RadioButton` objects?

   a. `RadioButton`s descend from `ButtonBase`; `CheckBox`es do not.

   b. Only one `RadioButton` can be selected at a time.

   c. Only one `CheckBox` can appear on a `Form` at a time.

   d. `RadioButton`s cannot be placed in a `GroupBox`; `CheckBox`es can.

12. The `Checked` property of a `RadioButton` can hold the values _____ .

   a. `true` and `false`

   b. `Checked` and `Unchecked`

   c. `0` and `1`

   d. `Yes`, `No`, and `Undetermined`

13. The `Control` in which you can display a bitmap or JPEG image is a(n) _____ .

   a. `DisplayModule`   c. `BitmapControl`

   b. `ImageHolder`   d. `PictureBox`

14. `ListBox`, `ComboBox`, and `CheckedListBox` objects all descend from which family?

   a. `ListControl`   c. `ButtonBase`

   b. `List`   d. `ListBase`

15. Which of the following properties is associated with a **ListBox** but not a **Button**?

   a. **BackColor**

   b. **SelectedItem**

   c. **Location**

   d. **IsSelected**

16. With a **ListBox** you can allow the user to choose _____ .

   a. only a single option

   b. multiple selections

   c. either of these

   d. none of these

17. You can add items to a **ListBox** by using the _____ method.

   a. **AddList()**

   b. **Append()**

   c. **List()**

   d. **AddRange()**

18. A **ListBox**'s **SelectedItem** property contains _____ .

   a. the position of the currently selected item

   b. the value of the currently selected item

   c. a Boolean value indicating whether an item is currently selected

   d. a count of the number of currently selected items

19. When you create a **ListBox**, by default its **SelectionMode** is _____ .

   a. **Simple**

   b. **MultiExtended**

   c. **One**

   d. **false**

20. A horizontal list of general options that appears under the title bar of a **Form** or **Window** is a _____ .

   a. task bar

   b. subtitle bar

   c. menu strip

   d. list box

Exercises

Programming Exercises

1. Create a project named **DayNight**. Include a `Form` that contains two `Button`s, one labeled *Day* and one labeled *Night*. Add a `Label` telling the user to click a button. When the user clicks *Day*, change the `BackColor` of the `Form` to `Yellow`; when the user clicks *Night*, change the `BackColor` of the `Form` to `DarkBlue`.

2. Create a project named **FiveColors**. Its `Form` contains at least five `Button` objects, each labeled with a color. When the user clicks a `Button`, change the `BackColor` of the `Form` appropriately.

3. Create a project named **FiveColors2**. Its `Form` contains at least five `RadioButton` objects, each labeled with a color. When the user clicks a `RadioButton`, change the `BackColor` of the `Form` appropriately.

4. Create a project named **MyFlix**. Its `Form` contains a `ListBox` with the titles of at least six movies or TV shows available to purchase. Provide directions that tell users they can choose as many downloads as they want by holding down the Ctrl key while making selections. When the user clicks a `Button` to indicate the choices are final, display the total price, which is $1.99 per download. If the user selects or deselects items and clicks the button again, make sure the total is updated correctly.

5. Create a project named **FontSelector**. Its `Form` contains two `ListBox`es—one contains at least four `Font` names, and the other contains at least four `Font` sizes. Let the first item in each list be the default selection if the user fails to make a selection. Allow only one selection per `ListBox`. After the user clicks a `Button`, display *Hello* in the selected `Font` and size.

6. Create a project named **DavesDriveways** that contains a `Form` for a driveway installation company. Allow the user to choose a material (gravel, asphalt, cement, or brick) and a number of square feet. After the user makes selections, display the total price, which is $10 per square foot for gravel, $12 for asphalt, $14 for cement, and $17 for brick. Use the `Control`s that you think are best for each function. Label items appropriately, and use fonts and colors to achieve an attractive design.

7. Create a project named **VacationPlanner** for a tropical resort that offers all-inclusive vacation packages. The project contains a `Form` that allows the user to choose one option from at least three in each of the following categories—departure city, room type, and meal plan. Assign a different price to each selection, and display the total when the user clicks a `Button`. Use the `Control`s that you think are best for each function. Label items appropriately, and use fonts and colors to achieve an attractive design.

8. Create a project named **CarDealer** that contains a Form for an automobile dealer. Include options for at least three car models. After users make a selection, proceed to a new Form that contains information about the selected model. Use the Controls that you decide are best for each function. Label items on the Form appropriately, and use fonts and colors to achieve an attractive design.

9. Create a project named **AnnualBudget** that includes a Form with two LinkLabels. One opens a spreadsheet for viewing, and the other visits your favorite Web site. Include Labels on the Form to explain each link. You can create a spreadsheet with a few numbers that represent an annual budget, or you can use the AnnualBudget.xls file in the Chapter.12 folder of the downloadable student files.

10. Create a project named **NinasCookieSource** that includes a Form for a company named The Cookie Source. Allow the user to select from at least three types of cookies, each with a different price per dozen. Allow the user to select one-half, one, two, or three dozen cookies. Adjust the final displayed price as the user chooses cookie types and quantities. Also allow the user to select an order date from a MonthCalendar. Assuming that shipping takes three days, display the estimated arrival date for the order. Include as many labels as necessary so the user understands how to use the Form.

11. Create a project named **MenuStripDemo2** that is based on the MenuStripDemo project in the Chapter.12 folder of your downloadable student files. (See Figure 12-34 earlier in this chapter). Add appropriate functionality to the currently unprogrammed menu options (the two options in the Font menu and the three options in the Color menu). Add at least three other menu options to the program, either vertically, horizontally, or both.

12. Create a project named **LetsMakeADeal**. In this game, three prizes of varying value are assigned randomly to be hidden behind three "doors" that you can implement as Buttons. For example, the prizes might be a new car, a big-screen TV, and a live goat. The player chooses a Button, and then one of the two other prizes is revealed; the one revealed is never the most desirable prize. The user then has the option of changing the original selection to the remaining unseen choice. For example, consider these two game scenarios:

   • Suppose that the most valuable prize is randomly assigned to the first button. If the user chooses the first button, reveal either of the other two prizes, and ask the user if he wants to change his selection.

   • Suppose that the most valuable prize is assigned to the first button, but the user chooses the second button. Reveal the third prize so that the most valuable prize's location is still hidden, and then ask the user whether he wants to change his selection.

   After the user has chosen to retain his original selection or make a change, reveal what he has won.

Debugging Exercises

1. Each of the following projects in the Chapter.12 folder of your downloadable student files has syntax and/or logical errors. Immediately save the four project folders with their new names before starting to correct their errors. After you correct the errors, save each project using the same name preceded with *Fixed*. For example, DebugTwelve1 will become FixedDebugTwelve1.

   a. DebugTwelve1

   b. DebugTwelve2

   c. DebugTwelve3

   d. DebugTwelve4

Case Problems

1. Throughout this book, you have created programs for the Greenville Idol competition. Now create an interactive advertisement named **GreenvilleAdvertisement** that can be used to recruit contestants. Include at least three Controls that you studied in this chapter, and use at least two different Fonts and two different Colors.

2. Throughout this book, you have created programs for Marshall's Murals. Now create an interactive advertisement named **MarshallsAdvertisement** that can be used to advertise the available murals. Include at least three Controls that you studied in this chapter, and use at least two different Fonts and two different Colors.

CHAPTER 13

Handling Events

In this chapter you will:

- ◎ Learn about event handling
- ◎ Learn about delegates
- ◎ Declare your own events and handlers and use the built-in `EventHandler`
- ◎ Handle `Control` component events
- ◎ Handle mouse and keyboard events
- ◎ Manage multiple `Control`s
- ◎ Learn how to continue your exploration of `Control`s and events

608

Throughout this book, you have learned how to create interactive GUI programs in which a user can manipulate a variety of Controls. You have worked with several Controls that respond to a user-initiated event, such as a mouse click, and you have provided actions for Control default events. In this chapter, you will expand your understanding of the event-handling process. You will learn more about the object that triggers an event and the object that captures and responds to that event. You also will learn about delegates—objects that act as intermediaries in transferring messages from senders to receivers. You will create delegates and manage interactive events. You will learn to manage multiple events for a single Control and to manage multiple Controls for a project.

Event Handling

In C#, an **event** is a reaction to an occurrence in a program; an event transpires when something interesting happens to an object. When you create a class, you decide exactly what is considered "interesting." For example, when you create a Form, you might decide to respond to a user clicking a Button but ignore a user who clicks a Label—clicking the Label is not "interesting" to the Form.

A program uses an event to notify a client when something happens to an object. Events are used frequently in GUI programs—for example, a program is notified when the user clicks a Button or chooses an option from a ListBox. In addition, you can use events with ordinary classes that do not represent GUI controls. When an object's client might want to know about any changes that occur in the object, events enable the object to signal the client.

 The actions that occur during the execution of a program occur **at runtime**. The expression at *runtime* is used to distinguish execution-time activities from those that occur during development time and compile time. Events are runtime occurrences.

You have learned that when a user interacts with a GUI object, an event is generated that causes the program to perform a task. GUI programs are **event driven**—an event such as a button click "drives" the program to perform a task. Programmers also say that an action like a button click **raises an event**, **fires an event**, or **triggers an event**.

For example, Figure 13-1 shows a Form that contains a Label and a Button. The following changes are the only ones that have been made to the default Form in the IDE:

- The Size property of the Form has been adjusted to 500, 120.

- A Label has been dragged onto the Form, its Name property has been set to helloLabel, its Text property has been set to *Hello*, and its Font has been increased to 9.

- A Button has been dragged onto the Form, its Name property has been set to changeButton, and its Text property has been set to *Change Label*.

- When you double-click the button on the form, Visual Studio generates the following empty method in the program code:

```
private void changeButton_Click(object sender, EventArgs e)
{
}
```

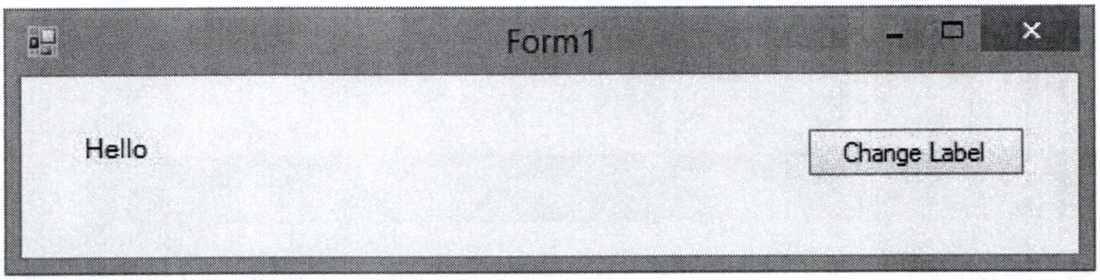

Figure 13-1   A Form with a Label and a Button

A method that performs a task in response to an event is an **event handler**. The changeButton_Click() method is an event handler. Although it is legal to create an event handler using any legal identifier, conventionally, event handlers are named using the identifier of the Control (in this case, changeButton), an underscore, and the name of the event type (in this case, Click).

Suppose that when a user clicks the button, you want the text on the label to change from *Hello* to *Goodbye*. You can write the following code for the event handler:

```
private void changeButton_Click(object sender, EventArgs e)
{
    helloLabel.Text = "Goodbye";
}
```

Then, when you run the application and click the button, the output appears as shown in Figure 13-2.

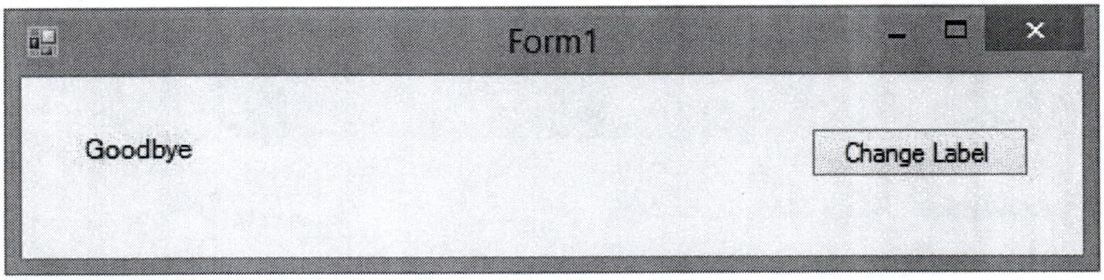

Figure 13-2   Output of the EventDemo application after the user clicks the button

The event-handler method is also known as an **event receiver**. The control that generates an event is an **event sender**. The first parameter in the list for the event receiver method is an object named sender; it is a reference to the object that generated the event. For example, if you code the event handler to display sender's information as follows, the output appears as in Figure 13-3.

```
private void changeButton_Click(object sender, EventArgs e)
{
    helloLabel.Text = sender.ToString();
}
```

610

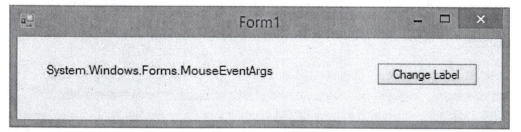

Figure 13-3   The EventDemo application modified to display sender information

The label in Figure 13-3 shows that the sender of the event is an instance of System.Windows.Forms.Button, whose Text property is *Change Label*.

The second parameter in the event-handler parameter list is a reference to an event arguments object of type EventArgs; in this method, the EventArgs argument is named e. EventArgs is a C# class designed for holding event information. If you change the code in the event handler to display the EventArgs ToString() value as in the following and then run the program and click the button, you see the output in Figure 13-4.

```
private void changeButton_Click(object sender, EventArgs e)
{
    helloLabel.Text = e.ToString();
}
```

Figure 13-4   The EventDemo application modified to display EventArgs information

In Figure 13-4, you can see that the **e** object is a `MouseEventArgs` object. That makes sense, because the user used the mouse to click the `Button`. (If the user has a touch screen, the user can also touch the `Button` to generate the event.)

When you open the Designer.cs file in the IDE, you can examine all the code generated for the application that creates the `Form` shown in Figure 13-4. Expanding the code generated by the Windows Form Designer lets you see comments as well as statements that set the `Controls'` properties. For example, the code generated for `changeButton` appears in Figure 13-5. You can recognize that such features as the button's `Location`, `Name`, and `Size` have been set.

```
//
// changeButton
//
this.changeButton.Location = new System.Drawing.Point(359, 24);
this.changeButton.Name = "changeButton";
this.changeButton.Size = new System.Drawing.Size(101, 23);
this.changeButton.TabIndex = 1;
this.changeButton.Text = "Change Label";
this.changeButton.UseVisualStyleBackColor = true;
this.changeButton.Click += new
    System.EventHandler(this.changeButton_Click);
```

Figure 13-5 Code involving `changeButton` generated by Visual Studio

 The code generated in Design mode in the IDE is not meant to be altered by typing. You should modify `Control` properties through the Properties window in the IDE, not by typing in the Designer.cs file.

All the code in Figure 13-5 was created by Visual Studio when the programmer clicked `changeButton` in the IDE. The most unusual statement in the section of `changeButton` code is shaded in Figure 13-5. This statement concerns a **click event**, which is an action fired when a user clicks a button during program execution. The shaded statement is necessary because `changeButton` does not automatically "know" what method will handle its events—C# and all other .NET languages allow you to choose your own names for event-handling methods for events generated by GUI objects. In other words, the event-handling method is not required to be named `changeButton_Click()`. You *could* create your program so that when the user clicks the button, the event-handling method is named `calculatePayroll()`, `changeLabel()`, or any other identifier for a method you could then write. Of course, you do not want to make such a change; using the name `changeButton_Click()` for the method that executes when `changeButton` is clicked is the clearest approach.

Connecting an event to its resulting actions is called **event wiring**. The event wiring for the `changeButton_Click()` method is accomplished in the shaded statement in Figure 13-5. The statement indicates that, for this program, the method named `changeButton_Click()` is the receiver for `changeButton`'s `Click` event; the method executes when a user clicks the button and an event is fired. Programmers say the statement creates a *delegate* or, more specifically, a *composed delegate*. The delegate's type is EventHandler, and it takes a reference to the changeButton_Click() method. You will learn about delegates in the next two sections of this chapter, and you will also learn why the += operator is used in the statement.

TWO TRUTHS & A LIE

Event Handling

1. An action such as a key press or button click raises an event.

2. A method that performs a task in response to an event is an event handler.

3. The control that generates an event is an event receiver.

The false statement is #3. The control that generates an event is an event sender.

Understanding Delegates

A **delegate** is an object that contains a reference to a method; object-oriented programmers would say that a delegate *encapsulates a method*. In government, a delegate is a representative that you authorize to make choices for you. For example, states send delegates to presidential nominating conventions. When human delegates arrive at a convention, they are free to make last-minute choices based on current conditions. Similarly, C# delegates provide a way for a program to take alternative courses that are not determined until runtime. When you write a method, you don't always know which actions will occur at runtime, so you give your delegates authority to run the correct methods.

 In Chapter 1, you learned that encapsulation is a basic feature of object-oriented programming. Recall that encapsulation is the technique of packaging an object's attributes and methods into a cohesive unit that can then be used as an undivided entity.

After you have instantiated a C# delegate, you can pass this object to a method, which then can call the method referenced within the delegate. In other words, a delegate provides a way to pass a reference to a method as an argument to another method. In other words, although you can't pass a method to a method, you *can* pass an object that is a reference to a method. For example, if del is a delegate that contains a reference to the method M1(), you can pass del to a new method named MyMethod(). Alternatively, you could create a delegate named del that contains a reference to a method named M2() and then pass this version to MyMethod(). When you write MyMethod(), you don't have to know whether it will call M1() or M2(); you only need to know that it will call whatever method is referenced within del. Perhaps the decision about which method will execute will be made as the result of user input the date of execution, or some other factor.

A C# delegate is similar to a function pointer in C++. A function pointer is a variable that holds a method's memory address. In the C++ programming language, you pass a method's address to another method using a pointer variable. Java does not allow function pointers because they are dangerous—if the program alters the address, you might inadvertently execute the wrong method. C# provides a compromise between the dangers of C++ pointers and the Java ban on passing functions. Delegates allow flexible method calls, but they remain secure because you cannot alter the method addresses.

You declare a delegate using the keyword `delegate`, followed by an ordinary method declaration that includes a return type, method name, and argument list. For example, by entering the following statement, you can declare a delegate named `GreetingDelegate()`, which accepts a `string` argument and returns nothing:

```
delegate void GreetingDelegate(string s);
```

Any delegate can encapsulate any method that has the same return type and parameter list as the delegate. So `GreetingDelegate` can encapsulate any method as long as it has a `void` return type and a single `string` parameter. If you declare a delegate and then write a method with the same return type and parameter list, you can assign an instance of the delegate to represent it. For example, the following `Hello()` method is a `void` method that takes a `string` parameter:

```
public static void Hello(string s)
{
    WriteLine("Hello, {0}!", s);
}
```

Because the `Hello()` method matches the `GreetingDelegate` definition, you can assign a reference to the `Hello()` method to a new instance of `GreetingDelegate`, as follows:

```
GreetingDelegate myDel = new GreetingDelegate(Hello);
```

Once the reference to the `Hello()` method is encapsulated in the delegate `myDel`, each of the following statements will result in the same output: "Hello, Kim!".

```
Hello("Kim");
myDel("Kim");
```

In this example, the ability to use the delegate `myDel` does not seem to provide any benefits over using a regular method call to `Hello()`. If you have a program in which you pass the delegate to a method, however, the method becomes more flexible; you gain the ability to send a reference to an appropriate method you want to execute at the time.

For example, Figure 13-6 shows a `Greeting` class that contains `Hello()` and `Goodbye()` methods. The `Main()` method declares two delegates named `firstDel` and `secondDel`. One is instantiated using the `Hello()` method, and the other is instantiated using the `Goodbye()` method. When the `Main()` method calls `GreetMethod()` two times, it passes a different method and string each time. Figure 13-7 shows the output.

614

```
using static System.Console;
delegate void GreetingDelegate(string s);
class Greeting
{
    public static void Hello(string s)
    {
        WriteLine("Hello, {0}!", s);
    }
    public static void Goodbye(string s)
    {
        WriteLine("Goodbye, {0}!", s);
    }
    static void Main()
    {
        GreetingDelegate firstDel, secondDel;
        firstDel = new GreetingDelegate(Hello);
        secondDel = new GreetingDelegate(Goodbye);
        GreetMethod(firstDel, "Cathy");
        GreetMethod(secondDel, "Bob");
    }
    public static void GreetMethod(GreetingDelegate gd, string name)
    {
        WriteLine("The greeting is:");
        gd(name);
    }
}
```

Figure 13-6   The Greeting program

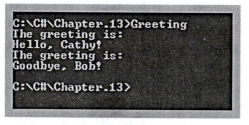

```
C:\C#\Chapter.13>Greeting
The greeting is:
Hello, Cathy!
The greeting is:
Goodbye, Bob!

C:\C#\Chapter.13>
```

Figure 13-7   Output of the Greeting program

 Delegates are useful in that a method reference can be passed to another method, so the receiving method can be customized. As with many other features of C# (and all other programming languages), you can use other techniques to accomplish the same result. For example, you certainly can produce simple output such as *Hello, Cathy* using other techniques. However, you should understand at least a little about delegates because they are used in the code that responds to events in C#'s GUI environment.

Creating Composed Delegates

You can assign one delegate to another using the = operator. You also can use the + and +=
operators to combine delegates into a **composed delegate** that calls the delegates from which
it is built. As an example, assume that you declare three delegates named del1, del2, and del3,
and that you assign a reference to the method M1() to del1 and a reference to method M2()
to del2. When the statement del3 = del1 + del2; executes, del3 becomes a delegate that
executes both M1() and M2(), in that order. Only delegates with the same parameter list can be
composed, and the delegates used must have a void return type. Additionally, you can use the –
and –= operators to remove a delegate from a composed delegate. A composed delegate is a
collection of delegates. The += and –= operators add and remove items from the collection.

Figure 13-8 shows a program that contains a composed delegate. This program contains only
two changes from the Greeting program in Figure 13-6: the class name (Greeting2) and the
shaded statement that creates the composed delegate. The delegate firstDel now executes
two methods, Hello() and Goodbye(), whereas secondDel still executes only Goodbye().
Figure 13-9 shows the output; *Cathy* is used with two methods, but *Bob* is used with only one.

```
using static System.Console;
delegate void GreetingDelegate(string s);
class Greeting2
{
    public static void Hello(string s)
    {
        WriteLine("Hello, {0}!", s);
    }
    public static void Goodbye(string s)
    {
        WriteLine("Goodbye, {0}!", s);
    }
    static void Main()
    {
        GreetingDelegate firstDel, secondDel;
        firstDel = new GreetingDelegate(Hello);
        secondDel = new GreetingDelegate(Goodbye);
        firstDel += secondDel;
        GreetMethod(firstDel, "Cathy");
        GreetMethod(secondDel, "Bob");
    }
    public static void GreetMethod
      (GreetingDelegate gd, string name)
    {
        WriteLine("The greeting is:");
        gd(name);
    }
}
```

Figure 13-8 The Greeting2 program

```
C:\C#\Chapter.13>Greeting2
The greeting is:
Hello, Cathy!
Goodbye, Cathy!
The greeting is:
Goodbye, Bob!

C:\C#\Chapter.13>
```

616

Figure 13-9　Output of the Greeting2 program

 Watch the video *Event Handling*.

TWO TRUTHS & A LIE

Understanding Delegates

1. A delegate is an object that contains a reference to a method.

2. Once you have created a delegate, it can encapsulate any method with the same identifier as the delegate.

3. A composed delegate can be created using the += operator; it calls the delegates from which it is built.

The false statement is #2. Once you have created a delegate, it can encapsulate any method with the same return type and parameter list as the delegate.

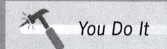 *You Do It*

Creating Delegates

To demonstrate how delegates work, you create two delegate instances in the next steps and assign different method references to them.

1. Open a new console project named **DiscountDelegateDemo**. Type the necessary using statements, and then create a delegate that encapsulates a void method that accepts a double argument:

```
using System;
using static System.Console;
delegate void DiscountDelegate(ref double saleAmount);
```

(continues)

(continued)

2. Begin creating a `Discount` class that contains a `StandardDiscount()` method. The method accepts a reference parameter that represents an amount of a sale. If the sale amount is at least $1,000, a discount of 5 percent is calculated and subtracted from the sale amount. If the sale amount is not at least $1,000, nothing is subtracted.

```
class DiscountDelegateDemo
{
    public static void StandardDiscount(ref double saleAmount)
    {
        const double DISCOUNT_RATE = 0.05;
        const double CUTOFF = 1000.00;
        double discount;
        if(saleAmount >= CUTOFF)
            discount = saleAmount * DISCOUNT_RATE;
        else
            discount = 0;
        saleAmount -= discount;
    }
```

3. Add a `PreferredDiscount()` method. The method also accepts a reference parameter that represents the amount of a sale and calculates a discount of 10 percent on every sale.

```
public static void PreferredDiscount(ref double saleAmount)
{
    const double SPECIAL_DISCOUNT = 0.10;
    double discount = saleAmount * SPECIAL_DISCOUNT;
    saleAmount -= discount;
}
```

4. Start a `Main()` method that declares variables whose values (a sale amount and a code) will be supplied by the user. Declare two `DiscountDelegate` objects named `firstDel` and `secondDel`. Assign a reference to the `StandardDiscount()` method to one `DiscountDelegate` object and a reference to the `PreferredDiscount()` method to the other `DiscountDelegate` object.

```
static void Main()
{
    double saleAmount;
    char code;
    DiscountDelegate firstDel, secondDel;
    firstDel = new DiscountDelegate(StandardDiscount);
    secondDel = new DiscountDelegate(PreferredDiscount);
```

(continues)

(continued)

5. Continue the Main() method with prompts to the user to enter a sale amount and a code indicating whether the standard or preferred discount should apply. Then, depending on the code, use the appropriate delegate to calculate the correct new value for saleAmount. Display the value and add closing curly braces for the Main() method and the class.

```
Write("Enter amount of sale ");
saleAmount = Convert.ToDouble(ReadLine());
Write("Enter S for standard discount,"
   + "or P for preferred discount ");
code = Convert.ToChar(ReadLine());
if(code == 'S')
   firstDel(ref saleAmount);
else
   secondDel(ref saleAmount);
WriteLine("New sale amount is {0}",
   saleAmount.ToString("C2"));
   }
}
```

6. Save the file, and then compile and execute it. Figure 13-10 shows the results when the program is executed several times.

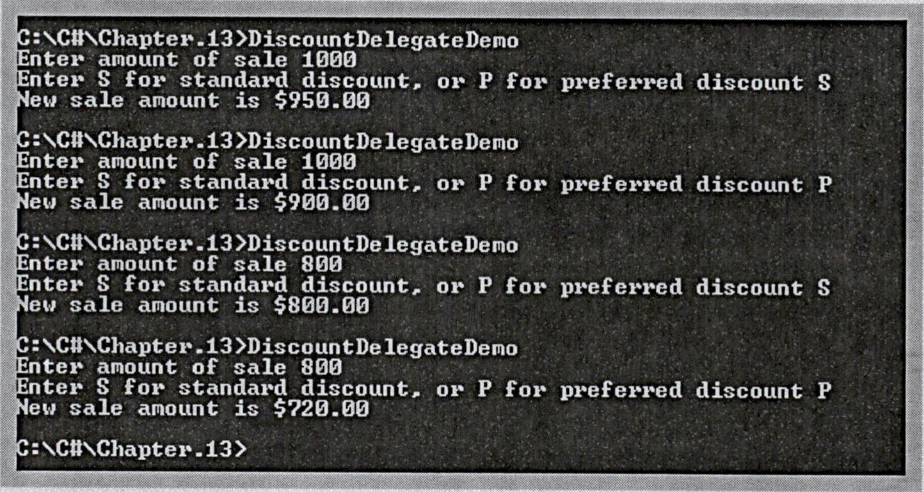

```
C:\C#\Chapter.13>DiscountDelegateDemo
Enter amount of sale 1000
Enter S for standard discount, or P for preferred discount S
New sale amount is $950.00

C:\C#\Chapter.13>DiscountDelegateDemo
Enter amount of sale 1000
Enter S for standard discount, or P for preferred discount P
New sale amount is $900.00

C:\C#\Chapter.13>DiscountDelegateDemo
Enter amount of sale 800
Enter S for standard discount, or P for preferred discount S
New sale amount is $800.00

C:\C#\Chapter.13>DiscountDelegateDemo
Enter amount of sale 800
Enter S for standard discount, or P for preferred discount P
New sale amount is $720.00

C:\C#\Chapter.13>
```

Figure 13-10   Sample executions of the DiscountDelegateDemo program

(continues)

(continued)

Creating a Composed Delegate

When you compose delegates, you can invoke multiple method calls using a single statement. In the next steps, you create a composed delegate to demonstrate how composition works.

1. Open the **DiscountDelegateDemo** file, and immediately save it as **DiscountDelegateDemo2**.

2. Within the `Main()` method, add a third `DiscountDelegate` object to the statement that declares the two existing versions, as follows:

```
DiscountDelegate firstDel, secondDel, thirdDel;
```

3. After the statements that assign values to the existing `DiscountDelegate` objects, add statements that assign the `firstDel` object to `thirdDel`, and then add `secondDel` to it through composition.

```
thirdDel = firstDel;
thirdDel += secondDel;
```

4. Change the prompt for the code, as follows, to reflect three options. The standard and preferred discounts remain the same, but the extreme discount (supposedly for special customers) provides both types of discounts, first subtracting 5 percent for any sale equal to or greater than $1,000, and then providing a discount of 10 percent more.

```
Write("Enter S for standard discount, "   +
    "P for preferred discount," +
    "\nor X for eXtreme  discount ");
```

5. Change the `if` statement so that if the user does not enter *S* or *P*, then the extreme discount applies.

```
if(code == 'S')
    firstDel(ref saleAmount);
else
    if(code == 'P')
        secondDel(ref saleAmount);
    else
        thirdDel(ref saleAmount);
```

(continues)

(continued)

6. Save the program, and then compile and execute it. For reference, Figure 13-11 shows the complete program. Figure 13-12 shows the output when the program is executed several times. When the user enters a sale amount of $1,000 and an *S*, a 5 percent discount is applied. When the user enters a *P* for the same amount, a 10 percent discount is applied. When the user enters X with the same amount, a 5 percent discount is applied, followed by a 10 percent discount, which produces a net result of a 14.5 percent discount.

```
using System;
using static System.Console;
delegate void DiscountDelegate(ref double saleAmount);
class DiscountDelegateDemo2
{
    public static void StandardDiscount(ref double saleAmount)
    {
        const double DISCOUNT_RATE = 0.05;
        const double CUTOFF = 1000.00;
        double discount;
        if(saleAmount >= CUTOFF)
            discount = saleAmount * DISCOUNT_RATE;
        else
            discount = 0;
        saleAmount -= discount;
    }
    public static void PreferredDiscount(ref double saleAmount)
    {
        const double SPECIAL_DISCOUNT = 0.10;
        double discount = saleAmount * SPECIAL_DISCOUNT;
        saleAmount -= discount;
    }
    static void Main()
    {
        double saleAmount;
        char code;
        DiscountDelegate firstDel, secondDel, thirdDel;
        firstDel = new DiscountDelegate(StandardDiscount);
        secondDel = new DiscountDelegate(PreferredDiscount);
        thirdDel = firstDel;
        thirdDel += secondDel;
        Write("Enter amount of sale ");
```

Figure 13-11   The DiscountDelegateDemo2 program *(continues)*

(continues)

(continued)

(continued)

```
        saleAmount = Convert.ToDouble(ReadLine());
        Write("Enter S for standard discount, " +
            "P for preferred discount, " +
            "\nor X for eXtreme discount ");
        code = Convert.ToChar(ReadLine());
        if(code == 'S')
            firstDel(ref saleAmount);
        else
            if(code == 'P')
                secondDel(ref saleAmount);
            else
                thirdDel(ref saleAmount);
        WriteLine("New sale amount is {0}",
            saleAmount.ToString("C2"));
    }
}
```

Figure 13-11   The DiscountDelegateDemo2 program

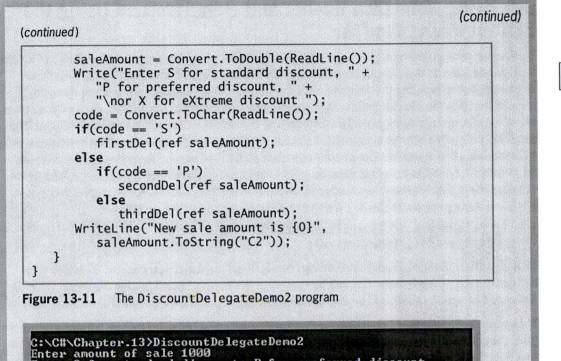

```
C:\C#\Chapter.13>DiscountDelegateDemo2
Enter amount of sale 1000
Enter S for standard discount, P for preferred discount,
or X for eXtreme discount S
New sale amount is $950.00

C:\C#\Chapter.13>DiscountDelegateDemo2
Enter amount of sale 1000
Enter S for standard discount, P for preferred discount,
or X for eXtreme discount P
New sale amount is $900.00

C:\C#\Chapter.13>DiscountDelegateDemo2
Enter amount of sale 1000
Enter S for standard discount, P for preferred discount,
or X for eXtreme discount X
New sale amount is $855.00

C:\C#\Chapter.13>
```

Figure 13-12   Three executions of the DiscountDelegateDemo2 program

For static methods like StandardDiscount and PreferredDiscount, a delegate object encapsulates the method to be called. When creating a class that contains instance methods, you create delegate objects that encapsulate both an instance of the class and a method of the instance. You will create this type of delegate in the next section.

Declaring Your Own Events and Handlers and Using the Built-in EventHandler

To declare your own event, you use a delegate. An event provides a way for the clients of a class to dictate methods that should execute when an event occurs. The clients identify methods to execute by associating the delegate with the method that should execute when the event occurs. Just like the event handlers that are automatically created in the IDE, each of your own event handler delegates requires two arguments: the object where the event was initiated (the sender) and an EventArgs argument. You can create an EventArgs object that contains event information, or you can use the EventArgs class static field named Empty, which represents an event that contains no event data. In other words, using the EventArgs.Empty field simply tells the client that an event has occurred, without specifying details. For example, you can declare a delegate event handler named ChangedEventHandler, as follows:

```
public delegate void ChangedEventHandler
    (object sender, EventArgs e);
```

The identifier ChangedEventHandler can be any legal identifier you choose. This delegate defines the set of arguments that will be passed to the method that handles the event. The delegate ChangedEventHandler can be used in a client program that handles events.

For example, Figure 13-13 contains the ChangedEventHandler delegate and a simple Student class that is similar to many classes you already have created. The Student class contains just two data fields and will generate an event when the data in either field changes.

```
public delegate void ChangedEventHandler(object sender, EventArgs e);
class Student
{
    private int idNum;
    private double gpa;
    public event ChangedEventHandler Changed;
    public int IdNum
    {
        get
        {
            return idNum;
        }
        set
        {
            idNum = value;
            OnChanged(EventArgs.Empty);
        }
    }
}
```

Figure 13-13 The Student class *(continues)*

(continued)

```
public double Gpa
{
    get
    {
        return gpa;
    }
    set
    {
        gpa = value;
        OnChanged(EventArgs.Empty);
    }
}
private void OnChanged(EventArgs e)
{
    Changed(this, e);
}
}
```

Figure 13-13   The Student class

The class in Figure 13-13 contains fields that hold an ID number and grade point average for a **Student**. The first shaded statement in the figure defines a third attribute of the **Student** class—an event named **Changed**. The declaration for an event looks like a field, but instead of being an **int** or a **double**, it is a **ChangedEventHandler**.

 Events usually are declared as **public**, but you can use any accessibility modifier.

The **Student** class event (**Changed**) looks like an ordinary field. However, you cannot assign values to the event as easily as you can to ordinary data fields. You can take only two actions on an event: You can compose a new delegate onto it using the **+=** operator, and you can remove a delegate from it using the **-=** operator. For example, to add **StudentChanged** to the **Changed** event of a **Student** object named **stu**, you would write the following:

```
stu.Changed += new ChangedEventHandler(StudentChanged);
```

In the **Student** class, each **set** accessor assigns a value to the appropriate class instance field. However, when either **idNum** or **gpa** changes, the method in the **Student** class named **OnChanged()** is also called, using **EventArgs.Empty** as the argument. The value of **EventArgs.Empty** is a read-only instance of **EventArgs**. You can pass it to any method that accepts an **EventArgs** parameter.

The **OnChanged()** method calls **Changed()** using two arguments: a reference to the **Student** object that was changed and the empty **EventArgs** object. Calling **Changed()** is also known as **invoking the event**.

623

If no client has wired a delegate to the event, the Changed field will be null, rather than referring to the delegate that should be called when the event is invoked. Therefore, programmers often check for null before invoking the event, as in the following example:

```
if(Changed != null)
    Changed(this, e);
```

For simplicity, the example in Figure 13-13 does not bother checking for null.

Figure 13-14 shows an EventListener class that listens for Student events. This class contains a Student object that is assigned a value using the parameter to the EventListener class constructor. The StudentChanged() method is added to the Student's event delegate using the += operator. The StudentChanged() method is the event-handler method that executes in response to a Changed event; it displays a message and Student data.

```
class EventListener
{
    private Student stu;
    public EventListener(Student student)
    {
        stu = student;
        stu.Changed += new ChangedEventHandler(StudentChanged);
    }
    private void StudentChanged(object sender, EventArgs e)
    {
        WriteLine("The student has changed.");
        WriteLine("ID# {0} GPA {1}",
            stu.IdNum, stu.Gpa);
    }
}
```

Figure 13-14   The EventListener class

Figure 13-15 shows a program that demonstrates using the Student and EventListener classes. The program contains a single Main() method, which declares a Student and an EventListener that listens for events from the Student class. Then three assignments are made. Because this program is registered to listen for events from the Student, each change in a data field triggers an event. That is, each field assignment not only changes the value of the data field, it also executes the StudentChanged() method that displays two lines of explanation. In Figure 13-16, the program output shows that an event occurs three times— once when IdNum becomes 2345 (and Gpa is still 0), again when IdNum becomes 4567 (and Gpa still has not changed), and a third time when Gpa becomes 3.2.

```
using System;
using static System.Console;
class DemoStudentEvent
{
    static void Main()
    {
        Student oneStu = new Student();
        EventListener listener = new EventListener(oneStu);
        oneStu.IdNum = 2345;
        oneStu.IdNum = 4567;
        oneStu.Gpa = 3.2;
    }
}
```

Figure 13-15   The DemoStudentEvent program

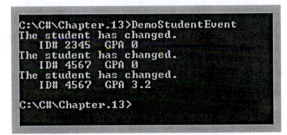

Figure 13-16   Output of the DemoStudentEvent program

Using the Built-in EventHandler

The C# language allows you to create events using any delegate type. However, the .NET Framework provides guidelines you should follow if you are developing a class that others will use. These guidelines indicate that the delegate type for an event should take exactly two parameters: a parameter indicating the source of the event, and an EventArgs parameter that encapsulates any additional information about the event. For events that do not use additional information, the .NET Framework has already defined an appropriate delegate type named EventHandler.

Figure 13-17 shows all the code necessary to demonstrate an EventHandler. Note the following changes from the classes used in the DemoStudentEvent program:

- No delegate is declared explicitly in the Student class.

- In the first statement with shading in the Student class, the event is associated with the built-in delegate EventHandler.

- In the second statement with shading, which appears in the EventListener class, the delegate composition uses EventHandler.

```
using System;
using static System.Console;
class Student
{
    private int idNum;
    private double gpa;
    public event EventHandler Changed;
    public int IdNum
    {
        get
        {
            return idNum;
        }
        set
        {
            idNum = value;
            OnChanged(EventArgs.Empty);
        }
    }
    public double Gpa
    {
        get
        {
            return gpa;
        }
        set
        {
            gpa = value;
            OnChanged(EventArgs.Empty);
        }
    }
    private void OnChanged(EventArgs e)
    {
        Changed(this, e);
    }
}
class EventListener
{
    private Student stu;
    public EventListener(Student student)
    {
        stu = student;
        stu.Changed += new EventHandler(StudentChanged);
    }
```

Figure 13-17   The Student, EventListener, and DemoStudentEvent2 classes *(continues)*

(continued)

```
    private void StudentChanged(object sender, EventArgs e)
    {
       WriteLine("The student has changed.");
       WriteLine("   ID# {0}   GPA {1}"
          stu.IdNum, stu.Gpa);
    }
}
class DemoStudentEvent2
{
    static void Main()
    {
       Student oneStu = new Student();
       EventListener listener = new EventListener(oneStu);
       oneStu.IdNum = 2345;
       oneStu.IdNum = 4567;
       oneStu.Gpa = 3.2;
    }
}
```

Figure 13-17   The `Student`, `EventListener`, and `DemoStudentEvent2` classes

When you compile and execute the program in Figure 13-17, the output is identical to that shown in Figure 13-16.

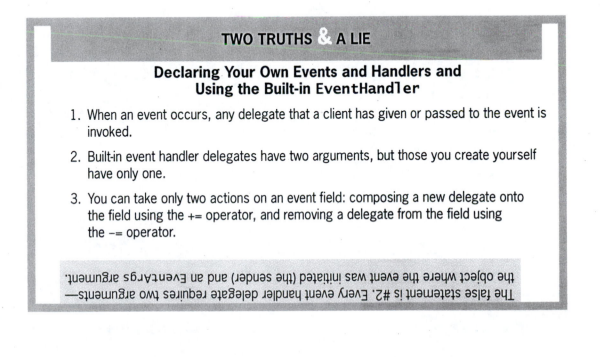

TWO TRUTHS & A LIE

Declaring Your Own Events and Handlers and Using the Built-in EventHandler

1. When an event occurs, any delegate that a client has given or passed to the event is invoked.

2. Built-in event handler delegates have two arguments, but those you create yourself have only one.

3. You can take only two actions on an event field: composing a new delegate onto the field using the += operator, and removing a delegate from the field using the -= operator.

The false statement is #2. Every event handler delegate requires two arguments—the object where the event was initiated (the sender) and an EventArgs argument.

You Do It

Creating a Delegate That Encapsulates Instance Methods

In the next set of steps, you create a simple `BankAccount` class that contains just two data fields: an account number and a balance. It also contains methods to make withdrawals and deposits. An event is generated after any withdrawal or deposit.

1. Open a project named **DemoBankEvent**. Type the `using` statements you need, and then begin a class named `BankAccount`. The class contains an account number, a balance, and an event that executes when an account's balance is adjusted.

```
using System
using static System.Console;
class BankAccount
{
    private int acctNum;
    private double balance;
    public event EventHandler BalanceAdjusted;
```

2. Add a constructor that accepts an account number parameter and initializes the balance to 0.

```
public BankAccount(int acct)
{
    acctNum = acct;
    balance = 0;
}
```

3. Add read-only properties for both the account number and the account balance.

```
public int AcctNum
{
    get
    {
        return acctNum;
    }
}
public double Balance
{
    get
    {
        return balance;
    }
}
```

(continues)

4. Add two methods. One makes account deposits by adding the parameter to the account balance, and the other makes withdrawals by subtracting the parameter value from the bank balance. Each uses the `OnBalanceAdjusted` event handler that reacts to all deposit and withdrawal events by displaying the new balance.

```
public void MakeDeposit(double amt)
{
    balance += amt;
    OnBalanceAdjusted(EventArgs.Empty);
}
public void MakeWithdrawal(double amt)
{
    balance -= amt;
    OnBalanceAdjusted(EventArgs.Empty);
}
```

5. Add the `OnBalanceAdjusted()` method that accepts an `EventArgs` parameter and calls `BalanceAdjusted()`, passing it references to the newly adjusted `BankAccount` object and the `EventArgs` object. (Earlier in the chapter, you learned that calling a method such as `OnBalanceAdjusted()` is also known as *invoking the event*.) Include a closing curly brace for the class.

```
public void OnBalanceAdjusted(EventArgs e)
{
    BalanceAdjusted(this, e);
}
}
```

6. Save the file.

Creating an Event Listener

1. When you write an application that declares a `BankAccount`, you might want the client program to listen for `BankAccount` events. To do so, you create an `EventListener` class.

2. After the closing curly brace of the `BankAccount` class, type the following `EventListener` class that contains a `BankAccount` object. When the `EventListener` constructor executes, the `BankAccount` field is initialized with the constructor parameter. Using the `+=` operator, add the `BankAccountBalanceAdjusted()` method to the event delegate. Next, write the `BankAccountBalanceAdjusted()` method to display a message and information about the `BankAccount`.

(continues)

(continued)

```
class EventListener
{
    private BankAccount acct;
    public EventListener(BankAccount account)
    {
        acct = account;
        acct.BalanceAdjusted += new EventHandler
            (BankAccountBalanceAdjusted);
    }
    private void BankAccountBalanceAdjusted(object sender,
        EventArgs e)
    {
        WriteLine("The account balance has been adjusted.");
        WriteLine(" Account# {0} balance {1}",
            acct.AcctNum, acct.Balance.ToString("C2"));
    }
}
```

3. Create a class to test the `BankAccount` and `EventListener` classes. Below the closing curly brace for the `EventListener` class, start a `DemoBankAccountEvent` class that contains a `Main()` method. Declare an integer to hold the number of transactions that will occur in the demonstration program. Also declare two variables: one can hold a code that indicates whether a transaction is a deposit or withdrawal, and one is the amount of the transaction.

```
class DemoBankAccountEvent
{
    static void Main()
    {
        const int TRANSACTIONS = 5;
        char code;
        double amt;
```

4. Declare a `BankAccount` object that is assigned an arbitrary account number, and declare an `EventListener` object so this program is registered to listen for events from the `BankAccount`. Each change in the `BankAccount` balance will not only change the balance data field, it will execute the `BankAccountBalanceAdjusted()` method that displays two lines of explanation.

```
BankAccount acct = new BankAccount(334455);
EventListener listener = new EventListener (acct);
```

(continues)

630

(continued)

5. Add a loop that executes five times (the value of TRANSACTIONS). On each iteration, prompt the user to indicate whether the current transaction is a deposit or withdrawal and to enter the transaction amount. Call the MakeDeposit() or MakeWithdrawal() method accordingly.

```
for(int x = 0; x < TRANSACTIONS; ++x)
{
    Write("Enter D for deposit or W for withdrawal ");
    code = Convert.ToChar(ReadLine());
    Write("Enter dollar amount ");
    amt = Convert.ToDouble(ReadLine());
    if(code == 'D')
        acct.MakeDeposit(amt);
    else
        acct.MakeWithdrawal(amt);
}
```

6. At the end of the for loop, add a closing curly brace for the Main() method and another one for the class.

7. Save the file, and then compile and execute it. Figure 13-18 shows a typical execution in which five transactions modify the account. The output shows that an event occurs five times—twice for deposits and three times for withdrawals.

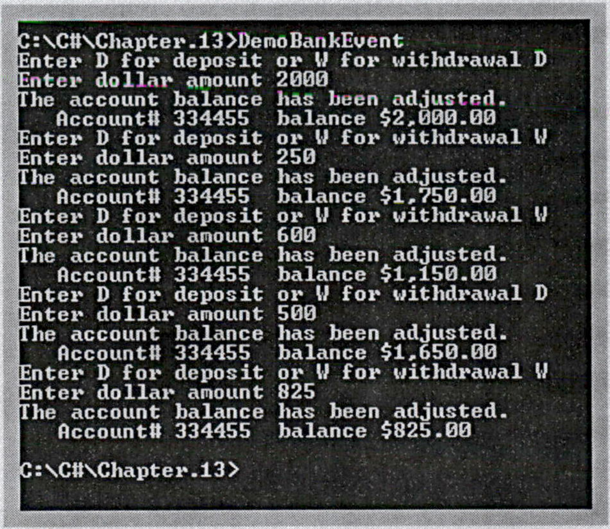

```
C:\C#\Chapter.13>DemoBankEvent
Enter D for deposit or W for withdrawal D
Enter dollar amount 2000
The account balance has been adjusted.
    Account# 334455   balance $2,000.00
Enter D for deposit or W for withdrawal W
Enter dollar amount 250
The account balance has been adjusted.
    Account# 334455   balance $1,750.00
Enter D for deposit or W for withdrawal W
Enter dollar amount 600
The account balance has been adjusted.
    Account# 334455   balance $1,150.00
Enter D for deposit or W for withdrawal D
Enter dollar amount 500
The account balance has been adjusted.
    Account# 334455   balance $1,650.00
Enter D for deposit or W for withdrawal W
Enter dollar amount 825
The account balance has been adjusted.
    Account# 334455   balance $825.00

C:\C#\Chapter.13>
```

Figure 13-18   Typical execution of the DemoBankEvent program

Handling Control Component Events

Handling events requires understanding several difficult concepts. Fortunately, you most frequently will want to handle events in GUI environments when the user will manipulate Controls, and the good news is that these events have already been defined for you. When you want to handle events generated by GUI Controls, you use the same techniques as when you handle any other events. The major difference is that when you create your own classes, like Student, you must define both the data fields and events you want to manage. However, existing Control components, like Buttons and ListBoxes, already contain fields and public properties, like Text, as well as events with names, like Click. Table 13-1 lists just some of the more commonly used Control events. You can consult the Visual Studio Help feature to discover additional Control events as well as more specific events assigned to individual Control child classes.

Event	Description
BackColorChanged	Occurs when the value of the BackColor property has changed
Click	Occurs when a control is clicked
ControlAdded	Occurs when a new control is added
ControlRemoved	Occurs when a control is removed
CursorChanged	Occurs when the Cursor property value has changed
DragDrop	Occurs when a drag-and-drop operation is completed
DragEnter	Occurs when an object is dragged into a control's bounds
DragLeave	Occurs when an object has been dragged into and out of a control's bounds
DragOver	Occurs when an object has been dragged over a control's bounds
EnabledChanged	Occurs when the Enabled property value has changed
Enter	Occurs when a control is entered
FontChanged	Occurs when the Font property value has changed
ForeColorChanged	Occurs when the ForeColor property value has changed
GotFocus	Occurs when a control receives focus
HelpRequested	Occurs when a user requests help for a control
KeyDown	Occurs when a key is pressed while a control has focus; event is followed immediately by KeyPress
KeyPress	Occurs when a key is pressed while a control has focus; event occurs just after KeyDown

Table 13-1 Some Control class public instance events (*continues*)

(continued)

Event	Description
KeyUp	Occurs when a key is released while a control has focus
Leave	Occurs when a control is left
LocationChanged	Occurs when the Location property value has changed
LostFocus	Occurs when a control loses focus
MouseDown	Occurs when the mouse pointer hovers over a control and a mouse button is pressed
MouseEnter	Occurs when the mouse pointer enters a control
MouseHover	Occurs when the mouse pointer hovers over a control
MouseLeave	Occurs when the mouse pointer leaves a control
MouseMove	Occurs when the mouse pointer moves over a control
MouseUp	Occurs when the mouse pointer hovers over a control and a mouse button is released
MouseWheel	Occurs when the mouse wheel moves while a control has focus
Move	Occurs when a control is moved
Resize	Occurs when a control is resized
TextChanged	Occurs when the Text property value has changed
VisibleChanged	Occurs when the Visible property value has changed

Table 13-1 Some Control class public instance events

You have already used the IDE to create some event-handling methods. These methods have been the default events generated when you double-click a Control in the IDE. For example, you have created a Click() method for a Button and a LinkClicked() method for a LinkLabel. A Form can contain any number of Controls that might have events associated with them. Additionally, a single Control might be able to raise any number of events. For example, besides creating a Button's default Click event, you might want to define various actions when the user's mouse rolls over the button. Table 13-1 lists only a few of the many events available with Controls; any Control could conceivably raise many of the available events.

Suppose you want to create a project that takes a different set of actions when the mouse is over a Button than when the mouse is clicked. Figure 13-19 shows a project that has been started in the IDE. The following actions have been taken:

- The Form was resized to 225, 150.

- A Button was dragged onto the Form, and its Text was set to *Click me*.

- A Label was added to the Form, its Text was set to *Hello*, and its Font was increased.

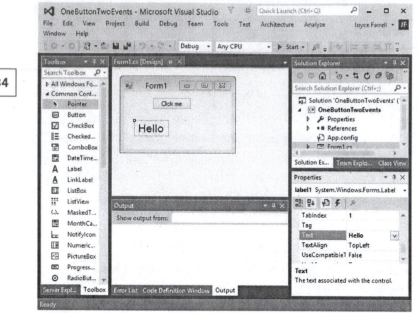

Figure 13-19   Start of the OneButtonTwoEvents project in the IDE

When you double-click the Button on the Form in the IDE, you generate the shell of a Click() method into which you can type a command to change the Label's text and color, as follows:

```
private void button1_Click(object sender, EventArgs e)
{
    label1.Text = "Button was clicked";
    label1.BackColor = Color.CornflowerBlue;
}
```

Color.CornflowerBlue is one of C#'s predefined Color properties. A complete list appears in Table 12-5 in Chapter 12.

With the Button selected on the design Form, you can click the Events icon in the Properties window at the right side of the screen. The Events icon looks like a lightning bolt. Figure 13-20 shows that the Properties window displays events instead of properties and that the Click event has an associated method.

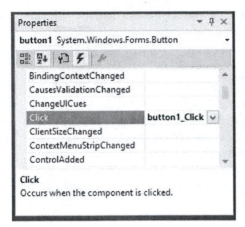

If you scroll through the Events listed in the Properties window, you can see a wide variety of Event choices. If you scroll down to MouseEnter and double-click, you can view the code for an event handler in the Form1.cs file as follows:

```csharp
private void button1_MouseEnter(object
    sender, EventArgs e)
{
}
```

 When you are viewing events in the Properties window, you can return to the list of properties by clicking the Properties icon. This icon is to the immediate left of the Events icon.

Figure 13-20   The Properties window displaying events

You can type any statements you want within this method. For example, you might write the following method:

```csharp
private void button1_MouseEnter(object sender, EventArgs e)
{
    label1.Text = "Go ahead";
    button1.BackColor = Color.Red;
}
```

When you run the program with the two new methods, two different events can occur:

- When you enter the button with the mouse (that is, pass the mouse over it), the Label's Text changes to *Go ahead*, and the button turns red, as shown on the left in Figure 13-21.

- After the button is clicked, the Label's Text changes again to *Button was clicked*, and the Label becomes blue, as shown on the right in Figure 13-21.

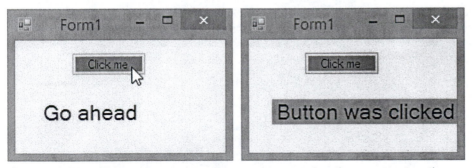

Figure 13-21   The OneButtonTwoEvents program when the mouse enters the button and after the button is clicked

If you examine the code generated by the Windows Form Designer, you will find the following two statements:

```
this.button1.Click += new System.EventHandler(this.button1_Click);
this.button1.MouseEnter += new
    System.EventHandler(this.button1_MouseEnter);
```

These EventHandler statements are similar to those in the Student class in Figure 13-17. The Click and MouseEnter delegates have been set to handle events appropriately for this application. You could have used the IDE to create these events just by selecting them from the Properties list and writing the action statements you want. The IDE saves you time by automatically entering the needed statement correctly. However, by knowing how to manually create a GUI program that contains events, you gain a greater understanding of how event handling works. This knowledge helps you troubleshoot problems and helps you create your own new events and handlers when necessary.

 Watch the video *Handling Control Component Events.*

TWO TRUTHS & A LIE

Handling Control Component Events

1. The default methods generated when you double-click a Control in the IDE are known as procedures.

2. A Form can contain any number of Controls that might have events associated with them, and a single Control might be able to raise any number of events.

3. You can type any statements you want within an automatically generated event method.

The false statement is #1. The default methods generated when you double-click a Control in the IDE are known as event handlers.

Handling Mouse and Keyboard Events

Users can interact with GUI applications in multiple ways. Certainly the most common tactics are to use a mouse or to type on a keyboard. Mouse and keyboard events are similar in that every mouse or key event-handling method must have two parameters: an object representing the sender and an object that holds information about the event.

Handling Mouse Events

Mouse events include all the actions a user takes with a mouse, including clicking, pointing, and dragging. Mouse events can be handled for any `Control` through an object of the class `MouseEventArgs`, which descends from `EventArgs`. The delegate used to create mouse event handlers is `MouseEventHandler`. Depending on the event, the type of the second parameter in the event-handling method is `EventArgs` or `MouseEventArgs`. Table 13-2 describes several common mouse events, and Table 13-3 lists some properties of the `MouseEventArgs` class.

Mouse event	Description	Event argument type
MouseClick	Occurs when the user clicks the mouse within the Control's boundaries	MouseEventArgs
MouseDoubleClick	Occurs when the user double-clicks the mouse within the Control's boundaries	MouseEventArgs
MouseEnter	Occurs when the mouse cursor enters the Control's boundaries	EventArgs
MouseLeave	Occurs when the mouse cursor leaves the Control's boundaries	EventArgs
MouseDown	Occurs when a mouse button is pressed while the mouse is within the Control's boundaries	MouseEventArgs
MouseHover	Occurs when the mouse cursor is within the Control's boundaries	MouseEventArgs
MouseMove	Occurs when the mouse is moved while within the Control's boundaries	MouseEventArgs
MouseUp	Occurs when a mouse button is released while the mouse is within the Control's boundaries	MouseEventArgs

Table 13-2   Common mouse events

A MouseDown event can occur without a corresponding MouseUp if the user presses the mouse but switches focus to another control or application before releasing the mouse button.

MouseEventArgs property	Description
Button	Specifies which mouse button triggered the event; the value can be Left, Right, Middle, or none
Clicks	Specifies the number of times the mouse was clicked
X	The x-coordinate where the event occurred on the control that generated the event
Y	The y-coordinate where the event occurred on the control that generated the event

Table 13-3 Properties of the MouseEventArgs class

 MouseClick and Click are separate events. The Click event takes an EventArgs parameter, but MouseClick takes a MouseEventArgs parameter. For example, if you define a Click event, you do not have the MouseEventArgs class properties.

Each part of Figure 13-22 contains a Form with a single Label named clickLocationLabel that changes as the user continues to click the mouse on it. The figure shows how the Label changes in response to a series of user clicks. Initially, the Label is empty (that is, the default Text property has been deleted and not replaced), but the following code was added to the Form.cs file:

```
private void Form1_MouseClick(object sender, MouseEventArgs e)
{
    clickLocationLabel.Text += "\nClicked at " + e.X +
        ", " + e.Y;
}
```

Every time the mouse is clicked on the Form, the Label is appended with a new line that contains "Clicked at" and the x- and y-coordinate position where the click occurred on the Form.

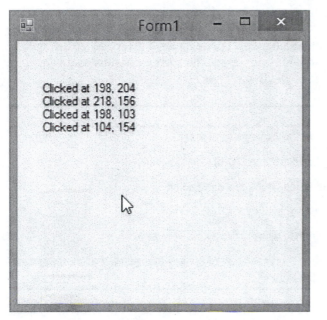

Figure 13-22   A Form that responds to clicks

When the programmer selects the MouseClick() event for Form1 from the Event list in the IDE, the following code is generated in the Designer.cs file. This code instantiates the MouseClick delegate.

```
this.MouseClick += new System.Windows.Forms.MouseEventHandler
    (this.Form1_MouseClicked);
```

Handling Keyboard Events

Keyboard events, also known as **key events,** occur when a user presses and releases keyboard keys. Table 13-4 lists some common keyboard events. Similar to the way mouse events work, every keyboard event-handling method must have two parameters. Depending on the event, the delegate used to create the keyboard event handler is either KeyEventHandler or KeyPressEventHandler and the type of the second parameter is KeyEventArgs or KeyPressEventArgs.

Keyboard event	Description	Event argument type
KeyDown	Occurs when a key is first pressed	KeyEventArgs
KeyUp	Occurs when a key is released	KeyEventArgs
KeyPress	Occurs when a key is pressed	KeyPressEventArgs

Table 13-4   Keyboard events

Table 13-5 describes KeyEventArgs properties, and Table 13-6 describes KeyPressEventArgs properties. An important difference is that KeyEventArgs objects include data about helper keys or modifier keys that are pressed with another key. For example, if you need to distinguish between a user pressing *A* and pressing *Alt+A* in your application, then you must use a keyboard event that uses an argument of type KeyEventArgs.

Property	Description
Alt	Indicates whether the Alt key was pressed
Control	Indicates whether the Control (Ctrl) key was pressed
Shift	Indicates whether the Shift key was pressed
KeyCode	Returns the code for the key
KeyData	Returns the key code along with any modifier key
KeyValue	Returns a numeric representation of the key (this number is known as the Windows virtual key code)

Table 13-5 Some properties of KeyEventArgs class

Property	Description
KeyChar	Returns the ASCII character for the key pressed

Table 13-6 A property of KeyPressEventArgs class

For example, suppose that you create a Form with a Label, like the Form in Figure 13-24. From the Properties window for the Form, you can double-click the KeyUp event to generate the shell for a method named Form1_KeyUp(). Suppose you then insert the statements into the method in the Form1.cs file, as shown in Figure 13-23. When the user runs the program and presses and releases a keyboard key, the Label is filled with information about the key. Figure 13-24 shows three executions of this modified program. During the first execution, the user typed *a*. You can see on the form that the KeyCode is *A* (uppercase), but you also can see that the user did not press the Shift key.

```
private void Form1_KeyUp(object sender, KeyEventArgs e)
{
    label1.Text += "Key Code " + e.KeyCode;
    label1.Text += "\nAlt " + e.Alt;
    label1.Text += "\nShift " + e.Shift;
    label1.Text += "\nControl " + e.Control;
    label1.Text += "\nKey Data " + e.KeyData;
    label1.Text += "\nKey Value " + e.KeyValue + "\n\n";
}
```

Figure 13-23 The KeyUp() method

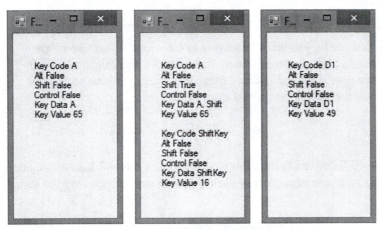

Figure 13-24   Three executions of the KeyDemo program

In the second execution in Figure 13-24, the user held down Shift, pressed *a*, and then released the Shift key. This causes two separate KeyUp events. The first has KeyCode *A* with Shift true, and the second has KeyCode ShiftKey. Notice that the Key values generated after typing *a* and *A* are the same, but the value after typing Shift is different.

In the third execution in Figure 13-24, the user pressed the number *1*, whose code is D1.

When you view the Form1.Designer.cs file for the KeyDemo program, you see the following automatically created statement, which defines the composed delegate:

```
this.KeyUp += new System.Windows.Forms.KeyEventHandler
    (this.Form1_KeyUp);
```

TWO TRUTHS & A LIE

Handling Mouse and Keyboard Events

1. The delegate used to create mouse event handlers is MouseEventHandler.

2. Keyboard events, also known as key events, occur when a user presses and releases keyboard keys.

3. Unlike mouse events, every keyboard event-handling method must be parameterless.

The false statement is #3. Like mouse events, every keyboard event-handling method must have two parameters: an object representing the sender, and an object that holds information about the event.

Managing Multiple Controls

When Forms contain multiple Controls, you often want one to have focus. You also might want several actions to have a single, shared consequence. For example, you might want the same action to occur whether the user clicks a button or presses the Enter key, or you might want multiple buttons to generate the same event when they are clicked.

Defining Focus

When users encounter multiple GUI Controls on a Form, usually one Control has **focus**. For example, when a Button has focus, a user expects that clicking the button or pressing the Enter key will raise an event.

TabStop is a Boolean property of a Control that identifies whether the Control will serve as a stopping place—that is, a place that will receive focus—in a sequence of Tab key presses. The default value for TabStop for a Button is true, but the default value for a Label is false because Labels are not expected to be part of a tabbing sequence. TabIndex is a numeric property that indicates the order in which the Control will receive focus when the user presses the Tab key. Programmers typically use small numbers for TabIndex values, beginning with 0. When a Control's TabStop value is true and the Control has the lowest TabIndex of a Form's Controls, it receives focus when the Form is initialized.

 Setting the TabIndex values of two or more Controls to 0 does not cause an error. Only one Control will receive focus, however.

Figure 13-25 shows a Form that contains three Buttons and a Label. Each Button has been associated with a Click() event such as the following:

```
private void button1_Click(object sender, EventArgs e)
{
    buttonInfoLabel.Text = "Button 1 selected";
}
```

Each Button has been assigned a TabIndex value in ascending order. When the application starts, the first Button (labeled *1*) has focus. Whether the user clicks that button or presses Enter, the message appears as shown on the left in Figure 13-25. In the next part of the figure, the user has pressed Tab and Enter to select button2, so it has focus, and the Label's Text property has changed. Alternatively, the user could have clicked button2 to achieve the same result. The user could then select either of the other Buttons by clicking them as usual or by pressing Tab until the desired button has focus and then pressing Enter.

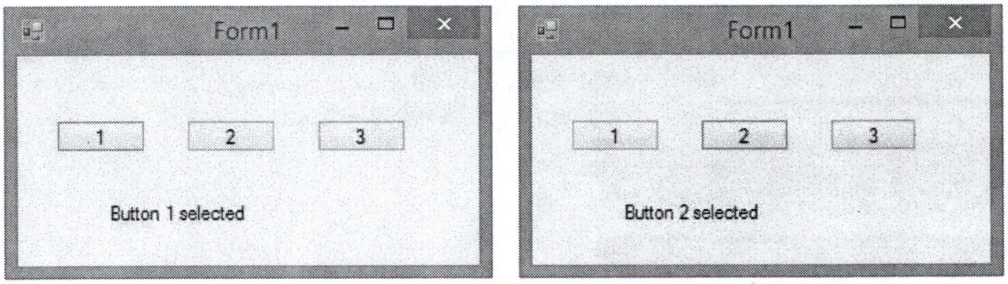

Figure 13-25   Execution of the FocusDemo application

Handling Multiple Events with a Single Handler

When a Form contains multiple Controls, you can create a separate event handler for each Control. However, you can also associate the same event handler with multiple Controls. For example, suppose you create a Form that contains three Buttons and a Label. The buttons have been labeled *A*, *B*, and *3*. Further suppose you want to display one message when the user clicks a letter button and a different message when the user clicks a number button. In the IDE, you can double-click the first Button and create an associated method such as the following:

```
private void button1_Click(object sender, EventArgs e)
{
    buttonInfoLabel.Text = "You clicked a letter button";
}
```

If you click the second button so its properties are displayed in the IDE's Properties list, you can click the Events icon to see a list of events associated with the second button. If no Click event has been chosen yet, a list box is available. This list contains all the existing events that have the correct signature to be the event handler for the event. Because the button1_Click() handler can also handle a button2_Click() event, you can select it as the event for button2. When you run the program, clicking either letter button produces the output shown in Figure 13-26.

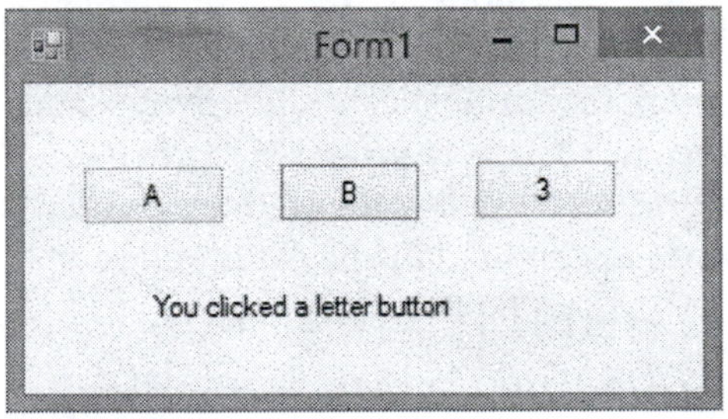

Figure 13-26   Output of the SingleHandler program after a letter button is clicked

Until you associate an event with the 3 button, nothing happens when the user clicks it. To complete the application that is running in Figure 13-26, you would want to associate an event with the 3 button to modify the Label's Text to *You clicked a number button*.

When two or more Controls generate the same event, many programmers prefer to generalize the event method name. For example, if button1 and button2 call the same method when clicked, it makes sense to name the event method letterButton_Click() instead of button1_Click().

Perhaps you have shopped online at a site that offers multiple ways to "buy now." For example, you might click a grocery cart icon, choose *Place order now* from a menu, or click a button. Often, *Place order now* buttons are displayed at several locations on the page. If you want to encourage a user's behavior, you should provide multiple ways to accommodate it.

 Watch the video *Managing Multiple Controls*.

TWO TRUTHS & A LIE

Managing Multiple Controls

1. The Control TabStop property can be set to true or false; it identifies whether the Control will serve as a stopping place in a sequence of Tab key presses.

2. On a Form with multiple Controls, one Control must have a TabIndex value of 0.

3. When a Form contains multiple Controls, you can associate the same event with all of them.

The false statement is #2. TabIndex is a numeric property that indicates the order in which the control will receive focus when the user presses the Tab key. Programmers typically use small numbers for TabIndex values, beginning with 0. However, you might choose not to use any TabIndex values, or if you do, you might choose not to start with 0.

Continuing to Learn about Controls and Events

If you examine the Visual Studio IDE, you will discover many additional Controls that contain hundreds of properties and events. No single book or programming course can demonstrate all of them for you. However, if you understand good programming principles and the syntax and structure of C# programs, learning about each new C# feature becomes progressively easier. When you encounter a new control in the IDE, you probably can use it without understanding all the code generated in the background, but when you do understand the background, your knowledge of C# is more complete.

Continue to explore the Help facility in the Visual Studio IDE. Particularly, read the brief tutorials there. Also, you should search the Internet for C# discussion groups. C# is a new, dynamic language, and programmers pose many questions to each other online. Reading these discussions can provide you with valuable information and suggest new approaches to resolving problems.

You Do It

Using TabIndex

In the next steps, you create a Form in the Visual Studio IDE and add four Buttons so you can demonstrate how to manipulate their TabIndex properties.

1. Open the Visual Studio IDE and start a new project. Define it to be a **Windows Forms Application** named **ManyButtons**.

2. Change the Size of the Form to **350, 130**. Change the Text property of Form1 to **Many Buttons**.

3. Drag four Buttons onto the Form, and place them so that they are similar to the layout shown in Figure 13-27. Change the Name properties of the buttons to redButton,

   Figure 13-27 Four Buttons on the Many Buttons Form

   whiteButton, blueButton, and favoriteButton. Change the Text on the Buttons to **Red**, **White**, **Blue**, and **My favorite color**, respectively. Adjust the size of the last button so its longer Text is fully displayed.

4. Examine the Properties list for the Red button. The TabIndex is 0. Examine the properties for the White, Blue, and My favorite color buttons. The IDE has set their TabIndex values to 1, 2, and 3, respectively.

5. Click the **Save All** button, and then run the program. When the Form appears, the Red button has focus. Press the **Tab** key, and notice that focus changes to the White button. When you press **Tab** again, focus changes to the Blue button. Press **Tab** several more times, and observe that the focus rotates among the four Buttons.

6. Dismiss the Form.

7. Change the TabIndex property of the Blue button to **0**, and change the TabIndex of the Red button to **2**. (The TabIndex of the White button remains 1, and the TabIndex of the My favorite color button remains 3.)

(continues)

(continued)

Save the program again, and then run it. This time, the Blue button begins with focus. When you press Tab, the order in which the Buttons receive focus is Blue, then White, then Red, then My favorite color. (Clicking the Buttons or pressing Enter raises no event because you have not assigned events to the Buttons.)

8. Change the TabIndex property for the Red button back to **0** and the TabIndex property for the Blue button back to **2**. Click the **Save All** button.

Associating One Method with Multiple Events

In the next steps, you add three methods to the Many Buttons Form and cause one of the methods to execute each time the user clicks one of the four Buttons.

1. If it is not still open, open the **ManyButtons** project in the Visual Studio IDE.

2. Double-click the **Red** button on the Form to view the code for the shell of a redButton_Click() method. Between the method's curly braces, insert a statement that will change the Form's background color to red as follows:

```
this.BackColor = Color.Red;
```

At first glance, you might think this refers to the Button that is clicked. However, if you examine the redButton_Click() code in the Form1.cs file in the IDE, you will discover that the method is part of the Form1 class. Therefore, this.BackColor refers to the Form's BackColor property.

3. Select the **Form1.cs [Design]** tab, and then double-click the **White** button. Add the following code to the whiteButton_Click() method that is generated:

```
this.BackColor = Color.White;
```

4. On the Form, double-click the **Blue** button. In its Click() method, add the following statement:

```
this.BackColor = Color.Blue;
```

5. On the form, click the **My favorite color** button. In its Properties list, click the **Events** button (the lightning bolt). Select the Click event. From the list box next to the Click event, select one of the three events to correspond to your favorite color of the three.

(continues)

(continued)

When you double-click a component on a Form in Design View, you move to the default method code. By clicking the component, however, you remain in Design View, and the correct set of properties appears in the Properties list.

6. Click the **Save All** button, and then execute the program. As you click Buttons, the Form's background color changes appropriately.

7. Dismiss the form, and exit Visual Studio.

Chapter Summary

- GUI programs are event driven—an event such as a button click "drives" the program to perform a task. Programmers also say a button click *raises an event, fires an event,* or *triggers an event.* A method that performs a task in response to an event is an event handler. The Click event is the event generated when a button is clicked.

- A delegate is an object that contains a reference to a method. C# delegates provide a way for a program to take alternative courses that are not predetermined; a delegate provides a way to pass a reference to a method as an argument to another method. You can assign one delegate to another using the = operator. You also can use the + and += operators to combine delegates into a composed delegate that calls the delegates from which it is built.

- To declare your own event, you use a delegate. A client identifies methods to execute by associating the delegate with the method that should execute when the event occurs. The .NET Framework provides guidelines that the delegate type for an event should take exactly two parameters: a parameter indicating the source of the event, and an EventArgs parameter that encapsulates any additional information about the event. For events that do not use additional information, the .NET Framework has already defined an appropriate type named EventHandler.

- When you use existing Control components like Buttons and ListBoxes, they contain fields and public properties like Text as well as events with names like Click. A Form can contain any number of Controls that might have events associated with them. Additionally, a single control might be able to raise any number of events.

- Every mouse or keyboard event-handling method must have two parameters: an object representing the sender, and an object that holds event information. Mouse events include all the actions a user takes with a mouse, including clicking, pointing, and dragging. Mouse events can be handled for any Control through an object of the class MouseEventArgs. The delegate used to create mouse event handlers is MouseEventHandler. Depending on the event, the type of the second parameter is EventArgs or MouseEventArgs. Keyboard events, also known as key events, occur when a user presses and releases keyboard keys. Depending on the event, the type of the second parameter is KeyEventArgs or KeyPressEventArgs.

- When users encounter multiple GUI Controls on a Form, usually one Control has focus. That is, if the user presses Enter, the Control will raise an event. When a Form contains multiple Controls, you can create a separate event for each Control. However, you can also associate the same event with multiple Controls.

- When you encounter a new control in the IDE, you probably can use it without understanding all the code generated in the background. However, when you learn about the background code, your knowledge of C# is more complete.

Key Terms

An **event** is a reaction to an occurrence in a program.

"At runtime" describes actions that occur during a program's execution.

Event-driven programs contain code that causes an event such as a button click to drive the program to perform a task.

A button click **raises an event, fires an event**, or **triggers an event**.

An **event handler** is a method that performs a task in response to an event.

An **event receiver** is another name for an event handler.

An **event sender** is the control that generates an event.

A **click event** is an action fired when a user clicks a button in a GUI environment.

Event wiring is the act of connecting an event to its resulting actions.

A **delegate** is an object that contains a reference to a method.

A **composed delegate** calls the delegates from which it is built.

Invoking the event occurs when you call an event method.

Key events are keyboard events that occur when a user presses and releases keyboard keys.

Focus is the property of a Control that causes an event to be raised when the user presses Enter.

Review Questions

1. In C#, events are _____ .

    a. triggered by actions

    b. handled by `catch` blocks

    c. Boolean objects

    d. only used in GUI programs

2. A delegate is an object that contains a reference to a(n) _____ .

    a. object

    b. class

    c. method

    d. `Control`

3. C# delegates provide a way for a program to _____ .

    a. take alternative courses that are not determined until runtime

    b. include multiple methods

    c. include methods from other classes

    d. include multiple `Control`s that use the same method

4. Which of the following correctly declares a `delegate` type?

    a. `void aDelegate(int num);`

    b. `delegate void aDelegate(num);`

    c. `delegate void aDelegate(int num);`

    d. `delegate aDelegate(int num);`

5. If you have declared a `delegate` instance, you can assign it a reference to a method as long as the method has the same _____ as the `delegate`.

    a. return type

    b. identifier

    c. parameter list

    d. two of the above

6. You can combine two delegates to create a(n) _____ delegate.

    a. assembled

    b. classified

    c. artificial

    d. composed

7. To combine two delegates using the + operator, the `delegate` objects must _____ .

    a. have the same parameter list

    b. have the same return type

    c. both of these

    d. neither of these

8. In C#, a(n) _____ is triggered when specific changes to an object occur.

   a. delegate

   b. event

   c. notification

   d. instantiation

9. An event handler delegate requires _____ argument(s).

   a. zero

   b. one

   c. two

   d. at least one

10. In an event-handler method, the sender is the _____ .

    a. delegate associated with the event

    b. method called by the event

    c. object where the event was initiated

    d. class containing the method that the event invokes

11. The `EventArgs` class contains a static field named _____.

    a. `Empty`

    b. `Text`

    c. `Location`

    d. `Source`

12. When creating events, you can use a predefined delegate type named _____ that is automatically provided by the .NET Framework.

    a. `EventArgs`

    b. `EventHandler`

    c. `EventType`

    d. `Event`

13. Which of the following is not a predefined `Control` event?

    a. `MouseEnter`

    b. `Click`

    c. `Destroy`

    d. `TextChanged`

14. A single `Control` can raise _____ event(s).

    a. one

    b. two

    c. five

    d. any number of

15. When you create `Forms` with `Control`s that raise events, an advantage to creating the code by hand over using the Visual Studio IDE is _____.

    a. you are less likely to make typing errors

    b. you save a lot of repetitious typing

    c. you are less likely to forget to set a property

    d. you gain a clearer understanding of the C# language

16. When a Form contains three Controls and one has focus, you can raise an event by
    _____.

    a. clicking any Control   c. either of these
    b. pressing Enter   d. none of these

651

17. The TabStop property of a Control is a(n) _____.

    a. integer value indicating the tab order
    b. Boolean value indicating whether the Control has a position in the tab
       sequence
    c. string value indicating the name of the method executed when the Control
       raises an event
    d. delegate name indicating the event raised when the user tabs to the Control

18. The TabIndex property of a Control is a(n) _____.

    a. integer value indicating the tab order
    b. Boolean value indicating whether the Control has a position in the tab
       sequence
    c. string value indicating the name of the method executed when the Control
       raises an event
    d. delegate name indicating the event raised when the user tabs to the Control

19. The Control that causes an event is the _____ argument to an
    event method.

    a. first   c. third
    b. second   d. fourth

20. Which of the following is true?

    a. A single event can be generated from multiple Controls.
    b. Multiple events can be generated from a single Control.
    c. Both of the above are true.
    d. None of the above are true.

Exercises

Programming Exercises

1. Create a project named **WordsOfWisdom** with a Form containing at least four Labels that hold "wise" quotes of your choice. When the program starts, the background color of the Form and each Label should be black. When the user passes a mouse over a Label, change its BackColor to white, revealing the text of the quote.

2. Create a project named **RecentlyVisitedSites** that contains a Form with a list of three LinkLabels that link to any three Web sites you choose. When a user clicks a LinkLabel, link to that site. When a user's mouse hovers over a LinkLabel, display a brief message that explains the site's purpose. After a user clicks a link, move the most recently selected link to the top of the list, and move the other two links down, making sure to retain the correct explanation with each link.

3. Create a project named **ClassicBookSelector** that contains a Form with a ListBox that lists at least five classic books that you think all educated people should have read. When the user places the mouse over the ListBox, display a Label that contains a general statement about the benefits of reading. The Label disappears when the user's mouse leaves the ListBox area. When the user clicks a book title in the ListBox, display another Label that contains a brief synopsis of the specific book. Also change the BackColor of the Form to a different color for each book.

4. Locate an animated .gif file on the Web. Create a project named **Animated** with a Form that contains a PictureBox. Display three different messages on a Label— one when the user's mouse is over the PictureBox, one when the mouse is not over the PictureBox, and one when the user clicks the PictureBox.

5. Create a project named **FlorencesFloralCreations** that allows a user to use a ListBox to choose an occasion for which to send a floral creation (for example *Get well*). When the user selects an occasion, the program should display a second ListBox that contains at least two main flower choices for each occasion type— for example, daisy or rose. After the user selects a flower type, the program should display a congratulatory message on a Label indicating that the choice is a good one, and the flower choice ListBox also becomes invisible. If the user makes a new selection from the occasion ListBox, the congratulatory message is invisible until the user selects a new flower option.

    Hint: You can remove the entire contents of a ListBox using the **Items.Clear()** method, as in **this.listBox1.Items.Clear();**.

6. Create a project named **GuessANumber** with a Form that contains a guessing game with five RadioButtons numbered 1 through 5. Randomly choose one of the RadioButtons as the winning button. When the user clicks a RadioButton, display a message indicating whether the user is right.

   Add a Label to the Form that provides a hint. When the user's mouse hovers over the label, notify the user of one RadioButton that is incorrect. After the user makes a selection, disable all the RadioButtons.

   You can create a random number that is at least min but less than max using the following statements:

   ```
   Random ran = new Random();
   int randomNumber;
   randomNumber = ran.Next(min, max);
   ```

7. Create a project named **PickLarger** with a Form that contains two randomly generated arrays, each containing 100 numbers. Include two Buttons labeled "1" and "2". Starting with position 0 in each array, ask the user to guess which of the two arrays contains the higher number and to click one of the two buttons to indicate the guess. After each button click, the program displays the values of the two compared numbers, as well as running counts of the number of correct and incorrect guesses. After the user makes a guess, disable the Buttons while the user views the results. After clicking a Next Button, the user can make another guess using the next two array values. If the user makes more than 100 guesses, the program should reset the array subscript to 0 so the comparisons start over but continue to keep a running score.

Debugging Exercises

1. Each of the following files or projects in the Chapter.13 folder of your downloadable student files has syntax and/or logical errors. Immediately save the two project folders with their new names before starting to correct their errors. After you correct the errors, save each file or project using the same filename preceded with *Fixed*. For example, the file DebugThirteen1.cs will become FixedDebugThirteen1.cs and the project folder for DebugThirteen3 will become FixedDebugThirteen3.

   a. DebugThirteen1.cs

   b. DebugThirteen2.cs

   c. DebugThirteen3

   d. DebugThirteen4

Case Problems

1. In Chapter 12, you created an interactive advertisement named **GreenvilleAdvertisement** that can be used to recruit contestants for the Greenville Idol competition. Now, modify that program to include at least one handled event using the techniques you learned in this chapter.

2. In Chapter 12, you created an interactive advertisement named **MarshallsAdvertisement** that can be used to advertise the available murals painted by Marshall's Murals. Now, modify that program to include at least one handled event using the techniques you learned in this chapter.

CHAPTER 14

Files and Streams

In this chapter you will:

◎ Learn about computer files and the `File` and `Directory` classes

◎ Understand file data organization

◎ Understand streams

◎ Write to and read from a sequential access text file

◎ Search a sequential access text file

◎ Understand serialization and deserialization

In the early chapters of this book, you learned that using variables to store values in computer memory provides programs with flexibility; a program that uses variables to replace constants can manipulate different values each time the program executes. However, when data values in a program are stored in memory, they are lost when the program ends. To retain data values for future use, you must store them in files. In this chapter, you will learn to create and manage files in C#.

Files and the `File` and `Directory` Classes

When data items are stored in a computer system, they can be stored for varying periods of time—temporarily or permanently.

Temporary storage is usually called computer memory, or **random access memory** (RAM). When you write a C# program that stores a value in a variable, you are using temporary storage; the value you store is lost when the program ends or the computer loses power. This type of storage is **volatile**.

Permanent storage, on the other hand, is not lost when a computer loses power; it is **nonvolatile**. When you write a program and save it to a disk, you are using permanent storage. Likewise, you use permanent storage when you write a program that saves data to a file.

 When discussing computer storage, *temporary* and *permanent* refer to volatility, not length of time. For example, a *temporary* variable might exist for several hours in a large program or one that the user forgets to end, but a *permanent* piece of data might be saved and then deleted within a few seconds.

A **computer file** is a collection of data stored on a nonvolatile device in a computer system. Files exist on **permanent storage devices**, such as hard disks, USB drives, reels of magnetic tape, and optical discs, which include CDs and DVDs.

You can categorize files by the way they store data:

- **Text files** contain data that can be read in a text editor because the data has been encoded using a scheme such as ASCII or Unicode. Text files might include facts and figures used by business programs; when they do, they are also called **data files**. The C# source programs you have written (with .cs extensions) are stored in text files.

- **Binary files** contain data that has not been encoded as text. Their contents are in binary format, which means that you cannot understand them by viewing them in a text editor. Examples include images, music, videos, and the compiled program files with an .exe extension that you have created using this book.

Although their contents vary, text and binary files have many common characteristics, as follows:

- Each has a name. The name often includes a dot and a file extension that describes the type of the file. For example, MyNotes.txt is a plain text file, and MyPicture.jpg is an image file in Joint Pictures Expert Group format.

- Each file has a specific time of creation and a time it was last modified.

- Each file occupies space on a section of a storage device; that is, each file has a size. Sizes are measured in bytes. A **byte** is a small unit of storage; for example, in a simple text file, a byte holds only one character. Because a byte is so small, file sizes usually are expressed in **kilobytes** (thousands of bytes), **megabytes** (millions of bytes), or **gigabytes** (billions of bytes).

When you use data, you never directly use the copy that is stored in a file. Instead, you use a copy that has been loaded into memory. Especially when data items are stored on a hard disk, their locations might not be clear to you—data just seems to be "in the computer." However, when you work with stored data, you must transfer copies from the storage device into memory. When you copy data from a file on a storage device into RAM, you **read from the file**. When you store data in a computer file on a persistent storage device, you **write to the file**. This means you copy data from RAM to the file.

Because you can erase data from files, some programmers prefer the term *persistent* storage to permanent storage. In other words, you can remove data from a file stored on a device such as a disk drive, so it is not technically permanent. However, the data remains in the file even when the computer loses power, so, unlike RAM, the data persists, or perseveres.

Computer files are the electronic equivalent of paper documents stored in file cabinets. In a physical file cabinet, the easiest way to store a document is to toss it into a drawer without a folder. When storing computer files, this is the equivalent of placing a file in the main or **root directory** of your storage device. However, for better organization, most office clerks place documents in folders; most computer users also organize their files into **folders** or **directories**. Users also can place folders within folders to form a hierarchy. The combination of the disk drive plus the complete hierarchy of directories in which a file resides is its **path**. For example, in the Windows operating system, the following line would be the complete path for a file named Data.txt on the C drive in a folder named Chapter.14 within the C# folder:

```
C:\C#\Chapter.14\Data.txt
```

The terms *directory* and *folder* are used synonymously to mean an entity that is used to organize files. *Directory* is the more general term; the term *folder* came into use in graphical systems. For example, Microsoft began calling directories *folders* with the introduction of Windows 95.

C# provides built-in classes named `File` and `Directory` that contain methods to help you manipulate files and their directories, respectively.

Using the File and Directory Classes

The File class contains methods that allow you to access information about files. Some of the methods are listed in Table 14-1.

Method	Description
Create()	Creates a file
CreateText()	Creates a text file
Delete()	Deletes a file
Exists()	Returns true if the specified file exists
GetCreationTime()	Returns a DateTime object specifying when a file was created
GetLastAccessTime()	Returns a DateTime object specifying when a file was last accessed
GetLastWriteTime()	Returns a DateTime object specifying when a file was last modified
Move()	Moves a file to the specified location

Table 14-1 Selected File class methods

DateTime is a structure that contains data about a date and time. In the chapter "Using Controls," you used the data from DateTime structures with MonthCalendar and DateTimePicker GUI objects. DateTime values can be expressed using Coordinated Universal Time (UTC), which is the internationally recognized name for Greenwich Mean Time (GMT). By default, DateTime values are expressed using the local time set on your computer. The property DateTime.Now returns the current local time. The property DateTime.UtcNow returns the current UTC time.

The File class is contained in the System.IO namespace. So, to use the File class, you can use its fully qualified name, System.IO.File, or you can just use File if you include the statement using System.IO; at the top of your program file as shown in the first shaded statement in Figure 14-1. Figure 14-1 shows a program which demonstrates several File class methods. The program prompts the user for a filename and then tests the file's existence in the second shaded statement. If the file exists, the creation time, last access time, and last write time are displayed. If the file does not exist, a message is displayed. Figure 14-2 shows two executions of the program. In the first execution, the user enters a filename that is not found. In the second execution, the file is found, and the three significant dates and times are displayed.

The System.IO.FileInfo class also allows you to access information about a file. See the Microsoft documentation at *http://msdn.microsoft.com* for more information.

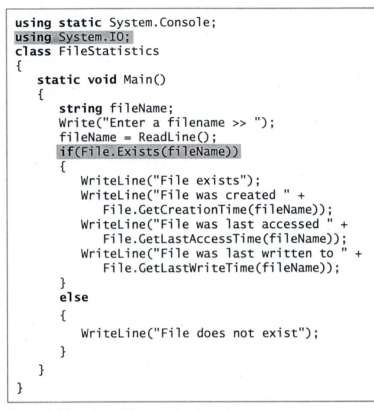

```
using static System.Console;
using System.IO;
class FileStatistics
{
   static void Main()
   {
      string fileName;
      Write("Enter a filename >> ");
      fileName = ReadLine();
      if(File.Exists(fileName))
      {
         WriteLine("File exists");
         WriteLine("File was created " +
            File.GetCreationTime(fileName));
         WriteLine("File was last accessed " +
            File.GetLastAccessTime(fileName));
         WriteLine("File was last written to " +
            File.GetLastWriteTime(fileName));
      }
      else
      {
         WriteLine("File does not exist");
      }
   }
}
```

Figure 14-1　The FileStatistics program

In the FileStatistics program in Figure 14-1, the file must be in the same directory as the program that is running.

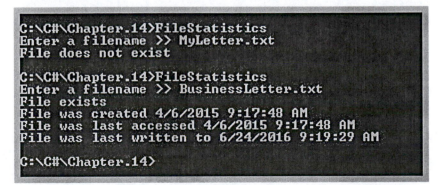

```
C:\C#\Chapter.14>FileStatistics
Enter a filename >> MyLetter.txt
File does not exist

C:\C#\Chapter.14>FileStatistics
Enter a filename >> BusinessLetter.txt
File exists
File was created 4/6/2015 9:17:48 AM
File was last accessed 4/6/2015 9:17:48 AM
File was last written to 6/24/2016 9:19:29 AM

C:\C#\Chapter.14>
```

Figure 14-2　Two typical executions of the FileStatistics program

The Directory class provides you with information about directories or folders. Table 14-2 lists some available methods in the Directory class.

Method	Description
CreateDirectory()	Creates a directory
Delete()	Deletes a directory
Exists()	Returns true if the specified directory exists
GetCreationTime()	Returns a DateTime object specifying when a directory was created
GetDirectories()	Returns a string array that contains the names of the subdirectories in the specified directory
GetFiles()	Returns a string array that contains the names of the files in the specified directory
GetLastAccessTime()	Returns a DateTime object specifying when a directory was last accessed
GetLastWriteTime()	Returns a DateTime object specifying when a directory was last modified
Move()	Moves a directory to the specified location

Table 14-2 Selected Directory class methods

Figure 14-3 contains a program that declares an array of string where filenames can be stored. (See the first shaded statement.) The program prompts a user for a directory and then fills the string array with a list of filename using the GetFiles() method. (See second shaded statement.) Then a for loop is used to display the list of files. Figure 14-4 shows two typical executions of the program.

```
using static System.Console;
using System.IO;
class DirectoryInformation
{
   static void Main()
   {
      string directoryName;
      string[] listOfFiles;
      Write("Enter a folder >> ");
      directoryName = ReadLine();
      if(Directory.Exists(directoryName))
      {
         WriteLine("Directory exists, " +
            "and it contains the following: ");
```

Figure 14-3   The DirectoryInformation program *(continues)*

(continued)

```
        listOfFiles = Directory.GetFiles(directoryName);
        for(int x = 0; x < listOfFiles.Length; ++x)
            WriteLine("    {0}", listOfFiles[x]);
    }
    else
    {
        WriteLine("Directory does not exist");
    }
  }
}
```

Figure 14-3   The DirectoryInformation program

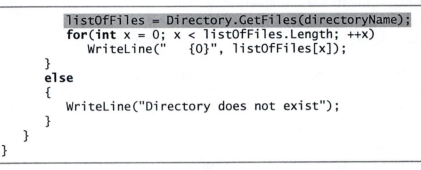

```
C:\C#\Chapter.14>DirectoryInformation
Enter a folder >> CustomerInfo
Directory does not exist

C:\C#\Chapter.14>DirectoryInformation
Enter a folder >> ClientMemos
Directory exists, and it contains the following:
    ClientMemos\ClientBillingWorksheet.xlsx
    ClientMemos\JohnsonMemo.txt
    ClientMemos\SmithMemo.txt

C:\C#\Chapter.14>
```

Figure 14-4   Two typical executions of the DirectoryInformation program

 Watch the video *File Handling*.

TWO TRUTHS & A LIE

Files and the File and Directory Classes

1. Temporary storage is nonvolatile; permanent storage is volatile.

2. When you write to a file, you copy data from RAM to a permanent storage device.

3. Most computer users organize their files into directories; the complete hierarchy of directories in which a file resides is its path.

The false statement is #1. Temporary storage is volatile; permanent storage is nonvolatile.

Understanding File Data Organization

Businesses store data in a relationship known as the **data hierarchy**, as described in Figure 14-5. For most users, the smallest useful piece of data is the character. A **character** is any one of the letters, numbers, or other special symbols (such as punctuation marks and arithmetic symbols) that constitute data. Characters are made up of bits (the zeros and ones that represent computer circuitry), but people who use data do not care whether the internal representation for an *A* is 01000001 or 10111110; rather, they are concerned with the meaning of *A*. For example, it might represent a grade in a course, a person's initial, or a company code.

 C# uses Unicode to represent its characters. You first learned about Unicode in Chapter 1. The set of all the characters used to represent data on a particular computer is that computer's **character set**.

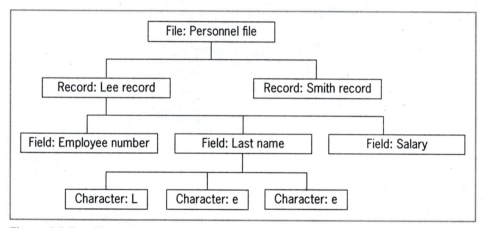

Figure 14-5 Hierarchical relationships of data components

 You can think of a character as a unit of information instead of data with a particular appearance. For example, the mathematical character *pi* (π) and the Greek letter *pi* look the same, but have two different Unicode values.

In computer terminology, a character can be any group of bits, and it does not necessarily represent a letter or number. Some characters do not correspond to those in natural language; for example, some "characters" produce a sound or control your display. You also have used the '\n' character to start a new line.

When businesses use data, they group characters into fields. A **field** is a character or group of characters that has some meaning. For example, the characters *T*, *o*, and *m* might represent your first name. Other data fields might represent items such as last name, Social Security number, zip code, and salary.

Fields are grouped together to form records. A **record** is a collection of fields that contain data about an entity. For example, the fields that hold a person's first and last names, Social Security number, zip code, and salary collectively are that person's record. When programming in C#, you have created many classes, such as an `Employee` class or a `Student` class. You can think of the data typically stored in each object that is an instance of these classes as a record. In other words, classes contain individual variables that represent data fields. A business's data records usually represent a person, item, sales transaction, or some other concrete object or event.

Records are grouped to create files. Data files consist of related records. For example, a company's personnel file contains many related records—one record for each company employee. Some files have only a few records; perhaps your professor maintains a file for your class with 25 records—one record for each student. Other files contain thousands or even millions of records. For example, a large insurance company maintains a file of policyholders, and a mail-order catalog company maintains a file of available items.

A data file is a **sequential access file** when each record is read in order from first to last in the file. Usually, the records are stored in order based on the value in some field; for example, employees might be stored in Social Security number order, or inventory items might be stored in item number order. The field used to uniquely identify each record in a sequential file is the **key field**. Frequently, records are sorted based on the key field. When records are not used in sequence, the file is used as a **random access file**, in which records can be accessed in any order.

Before an application can use a data file, it must open the file. A C# application **opens a file** by creating an object and associating a stream of bytes with that object. When you finish using a file, the program should **close the file**—that is, make the file no longer available to your application. Failing to close an input file (a file from which you are reading data) usually does not result in serious consequences; the data still exists in the file. However, if you fail to close an output file (a file to which you are writing data), the data might become inaccessible. You should always close every file you open, and you should close the file as soon as you no longer need it. Leaving a file open for no reason uses computer resources, and your computer's performance will suffer. Also, within a network, another program might be waiting to use the file. For example, if your program leaves the company's inventory file open after adding a new item, the program that fills orders for customers might fail to work correctly.

664

> ## TWO TRUTHS & A LIE
>
> ### Understanding File Data Organization
>
> 1. A field is a character or group of characters that has some meaning.
>
> 2. A record is a collection of data files that contain information about an entity.
>
> 3. A sequential access data file frequently contains records stored in order based on the value in some field.
>
> The false statement is #2. A record is a collection of fields that contain data about an entity. Data files consist of related records.

Understanding Streams

Whereas people view files as a series of records, with each record containing data fields, C# views files as just a series of bytes. When you perform an input operation in an application, you can picture bytes flowing into your program from an input device through a **stream**, which functions as a pipeline or channel. When you perform output, some bytes flow out of your application through another stream to an output device, as shown in Figure 14-6. A stream is an object, and like all objects, streams have data and methods. The methods allow you to perform actions such as opening, closing, and flushing (clearing) the stream.

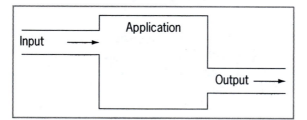

Figure 14-6 File streams

When you produce screen output and accept keyboard input, you use the `Console` class, which provides access to several standard streams:

- `Console.In` refers to the standard input stream object, which accepts data from the keyboard.

- `Console.Out` refers to the standard output stream object, which allows a program to produce output on the screen.

- `Console.Error` refers to the standard error stream object, which allows a program to write error messages to the screen.

You have been using Console.Out and its WriteLine() and Write() methods throughout this book. However, you may not have realized it because you do not need to refer explicitly to Out, so you have been writing the instruction as WriteLine(). Likewise, you have used Console.In with the ReadLine() and Read() methods.

Most streams flow in only one direction; each stream is either an input or output stream. You might open several streams at once within an application. For example, an application that reads a data disk and separates valid records from invalid ones might require three streams. The data arrives via an input stream, and as the program checks the data for invalid values, one output stream writes some records to a file of valid records, and another output stream writes other records to a file of invalid records.

When you read from or write to a file, you use a file-processing class instead of Console. Many file-processing classes are available in C#, including:

- StreamReader, for text input from a file

- StreamWriter, for text output to a file

- FileStream (which is used alone for bytes and with either StreamReader and StreamWriter for text), for either input from and output to a file

StreamReader and StreamWriter inherit from TextReader and TextWriter, respectively. Console.In and Console.Out are properties of TextReader and TextWriter, respectively.

When you write a program that stores data in a file, you create a FileStream object that defines a file's characteristics and abilities. Programmers say FileStream **exposes** a stream around a file. Table 14-3 lists some FileStream properties.

Property	Description
CanRead	Gets a value indicating whether current FileStream supports reading
CanSeek	Gets a value indicating whether current FileStream supports seeking
CanWrite	Gets a value indicating whether current FileStream supports writing
Length	Gets the length of the FileStream in bytes
Name	Gets the name of the FileStream
Position	Gets or sets the current position of the FileStream

Table 14-3   Selected FileStream properties

The FileStream class has 15 overloaded constructors. One that is used frequently includes the filename (which might include the complete path), mode, and type of access. For example, you might construct a FileStream object using the following statement:

```
FileStream outFile = new FileStream("SomeText.txt",
    FileMode.Create, FileAccess.Write);
```

In this example, the filename is *SomeText.txt*. Because no path is indicated, the file is assumed to be in the current directory. The mode is Create, which means a new file will be created even if one with the same name already exists. The access is Write, which means you can write data to the file but not read from it.

Another of FileStream's overloaded constructors requires only a filename and mode. If you use this version and the mode is set to Append, then the default access is Write; otherwise, the access is set to ReadWrite.

Table 14-4 describes the available file modes, and Table 14-5 describes the access types.

Member	Description
Append	Opens the file if it exists and seeks the end of the file to append new data
Create	Creates a new file; if the file already exists, it is overwritten
CreateNew	Creates a new file; if the file already exists, an IOException is thrown
Open	Opens an existing file; if the file does not exist, a System.IO. FileNotFoundException is thrown
OpenOrCreate	Opens an existing file; if the file does not exist, it is created
Truncate	Opens an existing file; once opended, the file is truncated so its size is zero bytes

Table 14-4 The FileMode enumeration

Member	Description
Read	Data can be read from the file.
ReadWrite	Data can be read from and written to the file.
Write	Data can be written to the file.

Table 14-5 The FileAccess enumeration

You can use a FileStream object as an argument to the StreamWriter constructor. Then you use WriteLine() or Write() with the StreamWriter object in much the same way you use it with Console.Out. The FileStream object must be created first, followed by the StreamWriter. At the end of the application, they must be closed in reverse order.

For example, Figure 14-7 shows an application in which a FileStream object named outFile is created, then associated with a StreamWriter named writer in the first shaded line. The writer object then uses WriteLine() to send a string to the FileStream file instead of sending it to the Console. Figure 14-8 shows a typical execution of the program, and Figure 14-9 shows the file as it appears in Notepad.

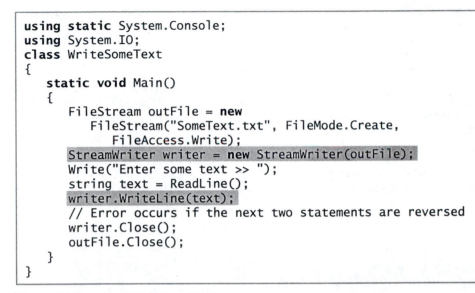

```
using static System.Console;
using System.IO;
class WriteSomeText
{
    static void Main()
    {
        FileStream outFile = new
            FileStream("SomeText.txt", FileMode.Create,
                FileAccess.Write);
        StreamWriter writer = new StreamWriter(outFile);
        Write("Enter some text >> ");
        string text = ReadLine();
        writer.WriteLine(text);
        // Error occurs if the next two statements are reversed
        writer.Close();
        outFile.Close();
    }
}
```

Figure 14-7   The WriteSomeText program

  Although the WriteSomeText application uses ReadLine() to accept user input, you could also create a GUI Form to accept input. You will create an application that writes to and reads from files using a GUI environment in a "You Do It" exercise at the end of this chapter.

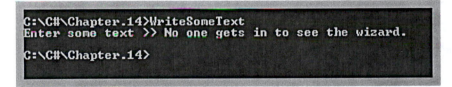

```
C:\C#\Chapter.14>WriteSomeText
Enter some text >> No one gets in to see the wizard.

C:\C#\Chapter.14>
```

Figure 14-8   Typical execution of the WriteSomeText program

SomeText - Notepad
File Edit Format View Help
No one gets in to see the wizard.

Figure 14-9   File created by the WriteSomeText program

In most applications that use files, you will want to place all the statements that open, write to, read from, and close files in a `try` block and then catch any `IOExceptions` that are thrown. Exception handling is eliminated from many examples in this chapter so that you can concentrate on the details of handling files without extra statements. In the "You Do It" section at the end of this chapter, you will add exception handling to an application.

The classes `BinaryReader` and `BinaryWriter` exist for working with binary files, which can store any of the 256 combinations of bits in any byte instead of just those combinations that form readable text. For example, photographs and music are stored in binary files.

The classes `XmlTextReader` and `XmlTextWriter` exist for working with XML files. **XML** is an abbreviation of eXtensible Markup Language, which is a standard for exchanging data over the Internet.

TWO TRUTHS & A LIE

Understanding Streams

1. When a file is opened in C#, an object is created, and a stream is associated with that object.

2. Most streams flow in only one direction; each stream is either an input or output stream.

3. You can open only one stream at a time within a C# application.

The false statement is #3. You might open several streams at once within an application.

Writing and Reading a Sequential Access File

Although people think of data files as consisting of records that contain fields, C# uses files only as streams of bytes. Therefore, when you write a program to store a data file or write a program to retrieve data from an already-created file, you must dictate the form in which the program will handle the file. Additionally, whether you are writing data to a file or reading data from one, you create a `FileStream` object.

Writing Data to a Sequential Access Text File

For example, suppose that you want to store `Employee` data in a file. Assume that an `Employee` contains an ID number, a name, and a salary that are respectively an `int`, a `string`, and a `double`. You could write stand-alone data for each of the three data types to a file, or you could create an `Employee` class that is similar to many you have seen throughout this book. Figure 14-10 shows a typical `Employee` class that contains three fields and properties for each.

```
class Employee
{
    public int EmpNum {get; set;}
    public string Name {get; set;}
    public double Salary {get; set;}
}
```

Figure 14-10   An `Employee` class

To store `Employee` data to a persistent storage device, you declare a `FileStream` object to define the characteristics of the stored file. For example:

```
FileStream outFile = new FileStream(FILENAME,
    FileMode.Create, FileAccess.Write);
```

The `FileStream` object is then passed to the constructor of a `StreamWriter` object so that text can be written. For example:

```
StreamWriter writer = new StreamWriter(outFile);
```

You can then use the `writer` object's `WriteLine()` method to write `Employee` data to the output stream. You can compose strings to write using text fields and commas. A block of text within a string that represents an entity or field is a **token**. Each comma that separates tokens is a **delimiter**, which is a character used to specify the boundary between data items in text files. Without a delimiter, the process of separating and interpreting tokens is more difficult. For example, suppose you define a delimiter as a comma using the following statement:

```
const string DELIM = ",";
```

Then, when you write data to a file, you can separate the fields with the comma delimiter using a statement such as the following:

```
writer.WriteLine(emp.EmpNum + DELIM + emp.Name + DELIM + emp.Salary);
```

A delimiter can be any character that is not needed as part of the data in a file, but a comma is commonly used. A file that contains comma-separated values is often called a **CSV file**. When a comma cannot be used as a delimiter because commas are needed as characters within the data, sometimes either the Tab character, the pipe character (|), or a comma within quotation marks is used as a delimiter.

The `WriteLine()` method ends output with a carriage return. When you use this method to create file output, the automatically appended carriage return becomes the *record delimiter*.

Figure 14-11 contains a complete program that opens a file and continuously prompts the user for Employee data. The first shaded statement in the figure is a **priming read**—an input statement that gets a first data item or record. In this case, the first item is an employee number. If the first input is the END value, the while loop is never entered. If a valid employee number value is entered, the rest of the record's data is retrieved within the loop, and the next employee number is entered in the second shaded statement at the bottom of the loop. When all three fields have been entered for an employee, the fields are written to the file, separated by commas. When the user enters the sentinel value 999 for an Employee ID number, the data entry loop ends, and the file is closed. Figure 14-12 shows a typical execution, and Figure 14-13 shows the contents of the sequential data file that is created.

```csharp
using System;
using static System.Console;
using System.IO;
class WriteSequentialFile
{
   static void Main()
   {
      const int END = 999;
      const string DELIM = ",";
      const string FILENAME = "EmployeeData.txt";
      Employee emp = new Employee();
      FileStream outFile = new FileStream(FILENAME,
         FileMode.Create, FileAccess.Write);
      StreamWriter writer = new StreamWriter(outFile);
      Write("Enter employee number or " + END +
         " to quit >> ");
      emp.EmpNum = Convert.ToInt32(ReadLine());
      while(emp.EmpNum != END)
      {
         Write("Enter last name >> ");
         emp.Name = ReadLine();
         Write("Enter salary >> ");
         emp.Salary = Convert.ToDouble(ReadLine());
         writer.WriteLine(emp.EmpNum + DELIM + emp.Name +
            DELIM + emp.Salary);
         Write("Enter next employee number or " +
            END + " to quit >> ");
         emp.EmpNum = Convert.ToInt32(ReadLine());
      }
      writer.Close();
      outFile.Close();
   }
}
```

Figure 14-11 The WriteSequentialFile class

In the `WriteSequentialFile` class, the delimiter is defined to be a `string` instead of a `char` to force the composed argument to `WriteLine()` to be a `string`. If the first data field sent to `WriteLine()` was a `string`, then `DELIM` could have been declared as a `char`.

 In the `WriteSequentialFile` program in Figure 14-11, the constant `END` is defined to be 999 so it can be used to check for the sentinel value. You first learned to use named constants in Chapter 2. Defining a named constant eliminates using a magic number in a program. The term **magic number** refers to the bad programming practice of hard-coding numbers (unnamed, literal constants) in code without explanation. In most cases, this makes programs harder to read, understand, and maintain.

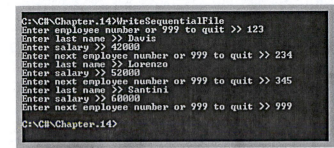

Figure 14-12 Typical execution of the `WriteSequentialFile` program

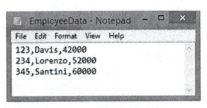

Figure 14-13 Contents of file created by the `WriteSequentialFile` program

Reading from a Sequential Access Text File

A program that reads from a sequential access data file contains many similar components to one that writes to a file. For example, a `FileStream` object is created, as in a program that writes a file. However, the access must be `FileAccess.Read` (or `ReadWrite`), as in the following statement:

```
FileStream inFile = new FileStream(FILENAME,
    FileMode.Open, FileAccess.Read);
```

Then, as data is being written, the `FileStream` object is passed to a `StreamReader` object's constructor, as in the following statement:

```
StreamReader reader = new StreamReader(inFile);
```

After the `StreamReader` has been defined, the `ReadLine()` method can be used to retrieve one line at a time from the data file. For example, the following statement gets one line of data from the file and stores it in a string named `recordIn`:

```
string recordIn = reader.ReadLine();
```

Using `ReadLine()` assumes a carriage return is the record delimiter, which is true, for example, if the records were created using `WriteLine()`.

If the value of `recordIn` is `null`, then no more data exists in the file. Therefore, a loop that begins `while(recordIn != null)` can be used to control the data entry loop.

After a record (line of data) is read in, the `Split()` method can be used to separate the data fields into an array of strings. The `Split()` method is a member of the `String` class; it takes a character delimiter parameter and separates a string into substrings at each occurrence of the delimiter. For example, the following code splits `recordIn` into the `fields` array at each `DELIM` occurrence. Then the three array elements can be stored as an `int`, `string`, and `double`, respectively.

```
string[] fields;
fields = recordIn.Split(DELIM);
emp.EmpNum = Convert.ToInt32(fields[0]);
emp.Name = fields[1];
emp.Salary = Convert.ToDouble(fields[2]);
```

Figure 14-14 contains a complete ReadSequentialFile application that uses the data file created in Figure 14-12. The records stored in the EmployeeData.txt file are read in one at a time, split into their `Employee` record components, and displayed. The first shaded statement is the priming read, and all subsequent records are input using the second shaded statement. Figure 14-15 shows the output.

```
using System;
using static System.Console;
using System.IO;
class ReadSequentialFile
{
    static void Main()
    {
        const char DELIM = ',';
        const string FILENAME = "EmployeeData.txt";
        Employee emp = new Employee();
```

Figure 14-14   The ReadSequentialFile program *(continues)*

(continued)

```
        FileStream inFile = new FileStream(FILENAME,
            FileMode.Open, FileAccess.Read);
        StreamReader reader = new StreamReader(inFile);
        string recordIn;
        string[] fields;
        WriteLine("\n{0,-5}{1,-12}{2,8}\n",
            "Num", "Name", "Salary");
        recordIn = reader.ReadLine();
        while(recordIn != null)
        {
            fields = recordIn.Split(DELIM);
            emp.EmpNum = Convert.ToInt32(fields[0]);
            emp.Name = fields[1];
            emp.Salary = Convert.ToDouble(fields[2]);
            WriteLine("{0,-5}{1,-12}{2,8}",
                emp.EmpNum, emp.Name, emp.Salary.ToString("C"));
            recordIn = reader.ReadLine();
        }
        reader.Close();
        inFile.Close();
    }
}
```

Figure 14-14   The ReadSequentialFile program

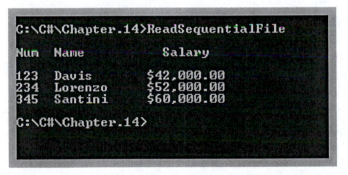

Figure 14-15   Output of the ReadSequentialFile program

  Watch the video *Sequential Access Files.*

674

TWO TRUTHS & A LIE

Writing and Reading a Sequential Access File

1. Although people think of data files as consisting of records that contain fields, C# uses files only as streams of bytes.

2. A comma is the default C# delimiter.

3. The Split() method can be used to separate data fields into an array of strings based on the placement of the designated delimiter.

The false statement is #2. A delimiter is any character used to specify the boundary between characters in text files. Although a comma is commonly used for this purpose, there is no default C# delimiter, and any character could be used.

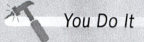

You Do It

Creating a File

In the next steps, you create a file that contains a list of names.

1. Open a new file named **CreateNameFile**, and write the first lines needed for a program that creates a file of names.

```
using System;
using System.IO;
class CreateNameFile
{
```

2. Start a Main() method that declares a FileStream you can use to create a file named Names.txt that is open for writing. Also create a StreamWriter to which you associate the file.

```
static void Main()
{
    FileStream file = new FileStream("Names.txt",
        FileMode.Create, FileAccess.Write);
    StreamWriter writer = new StreamWriter(file);
```

(continues)

(continued)

3. Add an array of names as follows. Each name is padded with spaces to make it 10 characters long so that you can easily demonstrate the `Seek()` method in a later exercise.

```
string[] names = {"Anthony   ",
                  "Belle     ",
                  "Carolyn   ",
                  "David     ",
                  "Edwin     ",
                  "Frannie   ",
                  "Gina      ",
                  "Hannah    ",
                  "Inez      ",
                  "Juan      "};
```

4. Declare a variable to use as an array subscript, then write each name to the output file.

```
int x;
for(x = 0; x < names.Length; ++x)
   writer.WriteLine(names[x]);
```

5. Close the `StreamWriter` and the `FileStream`. Also add two closing curly braces—one for the `Main()` method and one for the class.

```
      writer.Close();
      file.Close();
   }
}
```

6. Save the file, and then compile and execute it. Open the newly created **Names.txt** file in a text editor. The file contents appear in Figure 14-16.

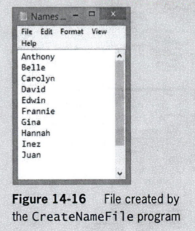

Figure 14-16 File created by the `CreateNameFile` program

(continues)

(continued)

Reading from a File

In the next steps, you read the text from the file created by the CreateNameFile program.

1. Start a new file named **ReadNameFile** as follows:

```
using static System.Console;
using System.IO;
class ReadNameFile
{
```

2. Start a Main() method that declares a FileStream that uses the same filename as the one created by the CreateNameFile program. Declare the file mode to be Open and the access to be Read. Declare a StreamReader with which to associate the file. Also declare an integer that counts the names read and a string that holds the names.

```
static void Main()
{
    FileStream file = new FileStream("Names.txt",
        FileMode.Open, FileAccess.Read);
    StreamReader reader = new StreamReader(file);
    int count = 1;
    string name;
```

3. Display a heading, and read the first line from the file. While a name is not null, display a count and a name, and increment the count.

```
WriteLine("Displaying all names");
name = reader.ReadLine();
while(name != null)
{
    WriteLine("" + count + " " + name);
    name = reader.ReadLine();
    ++count;
}
```

4. Close the StreamReader and the File, and add closing curly braces for the method and the class.

```
    reader.Close();
    file.Close();
}
}
```

(continues)

(continued)

5. Save the file, and then compile and execute it. The output appears in Figure 14-17.

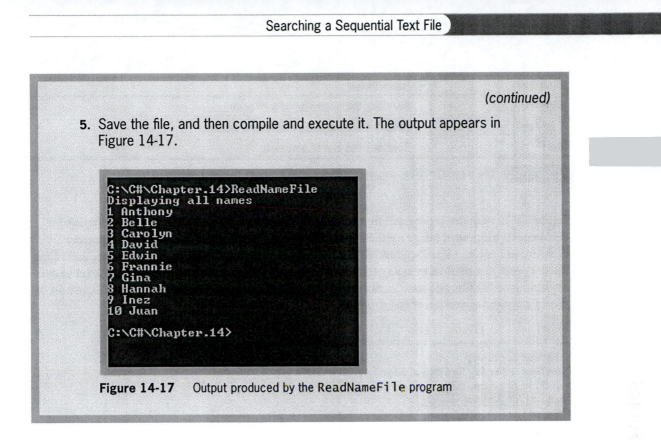

```
C:\C#\Chapter.14>ReadNameFile
Displaying all names
1  Anthony
2  Belle
3  Carolyn
4  David
5  Edwin
6  Frannie
7  Gina
8  Hannah
9  Inez
10  Juan

C:\C#\Chapter.14>
```

Figure 14-17   Output produced by the ReadNameFile program

Searching a Sequential Text File

When you read data from a sequential text file, as in the ReadSequentialFile program in Figure 14-14, the program starts at the beginning of the file and reads each record in turn until all the records have been read. Subsequent records are read in order because a file's **file position pointer** holds the byte number of the next byte to be read. For example, if each record in a file is 32 bytes long, then the file position pointer holds 0, 32, 64, and so on in sequence during the execution of the program.

Sometimes it is necessary to process a file multiple times from the beginning during a program's execution. For example, suppose you want to continue to prompt a user for a minimum salary and then search through a file for Employees who make at least that salary. You can compare the user's entered minimum with each salary in the data file and list those employees who meet the requirement. However, after one list is produced, the file pointer is at the end of the file, and no more records can be read. To reread the file, you could close it and reopen it, but that requires unnecessary overhead. Instead, you can just reposition the file pointer using the Seek() method and the SeekOrigin enumeration. For example, the following statement repositions the pointer of a file named inFile to 0 bytes away from the Begin position of the file:

```
inFile.Seek(0, SeekOrigin.Begin);
```

Table 14-6 lists the values in the SeekOrigin enumeration that you can use.

Member	Description
Begin	Specifies the beginning of a stream
Current	Specifies the current position of a stream
End	Specifies the end of a stream

Table 14-6 The SeekOrigin enumeration

Figure 14-18 contains a program that repeatedly searches a file to produce lists of employees who meet a minimum salary requirement. The shaded portions of the program represent differences from the ReadSequentialFile application in Figure 14-14. In this program, each time the user enters a minimum salary that does not equal 999, the file position pointer is set to the beginning of the file, and then each record is read and compared to the minimum. Figure 14-19 shows a typical execution of the program.

```
using System;
using static System.Console;
using System.IO;
class FindEmployees
{
    static void Main()
    {
        const char DELIM = ',';
        const int END = 999;
        const string FILENAME = "EmployeeData.txt";
        Employee emp = new Employee();
        FileStream inFile = new FileStream(FILENAME,
            FileMode.Open, FileAccess.Read);
        StreamReader reader = new StreamReader(inFile);
        string recordIn;
        string[] fields;
        double minSalary;
        Write("Enter minimum salary to find or " +
            END + " to quit >> ");
        minSalary = Convert.ToDouble(ReadLine());
        while(minSalary != END)
        {
            WriteLine("\n{0,-5}{1,-12}{2,8}\n",
                "Num", "Name", "Salary");
            inFile.Seek(0, SeekOrigin.Begin);
            recordIn = reader.ReadLine();
```

Figure 14-18 The FindEmployees program *(continues)*

(continued)

```
        while(recordIn != null)
        {
            fields = recordIn.Split(DELIM);
            emp.EmpNum = Convert.ToInt32(fields[0]);
            emp.Name = fields[1];
            emp.Salary = Convert.ToDouble(fields[2]);
            if(emp.Salary >= minSalary)
                WriteLine("{0,-5}{1,-12}{2,8}", emp.EmpNum,
                    emp.Name, emp.Salary.ToString("C"));
            recordIn = reader.ReadLine();
        }
        Write("\nEnter minimum salary to find or " +
            END + " to quit >> ");
        minSalary = Convert.ToDouble(ReadLine());
    }
    reader.Close(); // Error occurs if
    inFile.Close(); // these two statements are reversed
}
}
```

Figure 14-18   The FindEmployees program

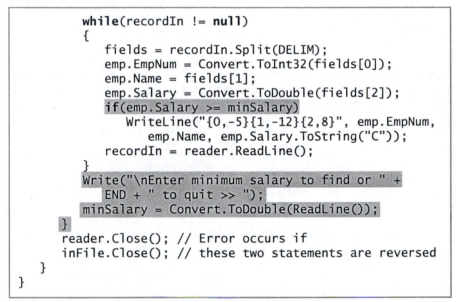

```
C:\C#\Chapter.14>FindEmployees
Enter minimum salary to find or 999 to quit >> 50000

Num  Name          Salary

234  Lorenzo       $52,000.00
345  Santini       $60,000.00

Enter minimum salary to find or 999 to quit >> 55000

Num  Name          Salary

345  Santini       $60,000.00

Enter minimum salary to find or 999 to quit >> 0

Num  Name          Salary

123  Davis         $42,000.00
234  Lorenzo       $52,000.00
345  Santini       $60,000.00

Enter minimum salary to find or 999 to quit >> 999

C:\C#\Chapter.14>_
```

Figure 14-19   Typical execution of the FindEmployees program

The program in Figure 14-18 is intended to demonstrate using the Seek() method. In a business setting, you might prefer to not leave a file open in one application if other users might be waiting for it. As an alternative, you could load all the records into an array and then search the array for desired records. Problems also exist with this approach because you would have to overestimate the number of records in the file to create an array large enough to hold them.

When you seek beyond the length of the file, you do not cause an error. Instead, the file size grows. In Microsoft Windows NT and later, any data added to the end of a file is set to zero. In Microsoft Windows 98 or earlier, any data added to the end of the file is not set to zero. This means that previously deleted data might become visible to the stream.

TWO TRUTHS & A LIE

Searching a Sequential Text File

1. When you read data from a sequential file, the program starts at the beginning of the file and reads each record in turn until all the records have been read.

2. When you read from a sequential file, its file position pointer holds the number of the record to be read.

3. To reread a file, you can close it and reopen it, or you can reposition the file pointer to the beginning of the file.

The false statement is #2. When you read from a sequential file, its file position pointer holds the byte number of the next byte to be read.

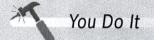

Using the Seek() Method

In the next steps, you use the Seek() method to reposition a file pointer so you can access a file from any location. The user will be prompted to enter a number representing a starting point to list the names in the Names.txt file. Names from that point forward will be listed, and then the user will be prompted for another selection.

1. Start a new program named **AccessSomeNames** that demonstrates how to access requested names from the Names.txt file you created in the CreateNameFile application.

(continues)

(continued)

```
using System;
using static System.Console;
using System.IO;
class AccessSomeNames
{
    static void Main()
    {
        FileStream file = new FileStream("Names.txt",
            FileMode.Open, FileAccess.Read);
        StreamReader reader = new StreamReader(file);
```

2. Declare a constant named END that represents an input value that allows the user to exit the program. Then declare other variables that the program will use.

```
const int END = 999;
int count = 0;
int num;
int size;
string name;
```

3. Read a line from the input file. While names are available, continue to read and count them. Then compute the size of each name by dividing the file length by the number of strings stored in it.

```
name = reader.ReadLine();
while(name != null)
{
    ++count;
    name = reader.ReadLine();
}
size = (int)file.Length / count;
```

4. Prompt the user for the number of the first record to read, and read the value from the Console.

```
Write("\nWith which number do you want to start? >> ");
num = Convert.ToInt32(ReadLine());
```

5. Start a loop that continues as long as the user does not enter the sentinel END value. Within the loop, display the user's number, and then use the Seek() method to position the file pointer at the correct file location. Because users enter numbers starting with 1 and file positions start with 0, you calculate the file position by first subtracting 1 from the user's entry. The calculated record number is then multiplied by the size of

(continues)

(continued)

each name in the file. For example, if each name is 10 bytes long, then the calculated starting position should be 0, 10, 20, 30, or some other multiple of the name size.

```
while(num != END)
{
    WriteLine("Starting with name " + num +": ");
    file.Seek((num - 1) * size, SeekOrigin.Begin);
```

6. Read and write the name at the calculated location. Then, in a nested loop, read and write all the remaining names until the end of the file.

```
name = reader.ReadLine();
WriteLine(" " + name);
while(name != null)
{
    name = reader.ReadLine();
    WriteLine(" " + name);
}
```

7. Finally, prompt the user for the next starting value for a new list, inform the user how to quit the application, and accept the next input value. Add a closing brace for the outer `while` loop.

```
    WriteLine("\nWith which number do you " +
        "want to start?");
    Write("   (Enter " + END + " to quit) >> ");
    num = Convert.ToInt32(ReadLine());
}
```

8. Close the `StreamReader` and `File` objects, and add closing braces for the method and the class.

```
    reader.Close();
    file.Close();
    }
}
```

9. Save the file, and then compile and execute it. Figure 14-20 shows a typical execution during which the user displays three sets of names starting at a different point each time.

(continues)

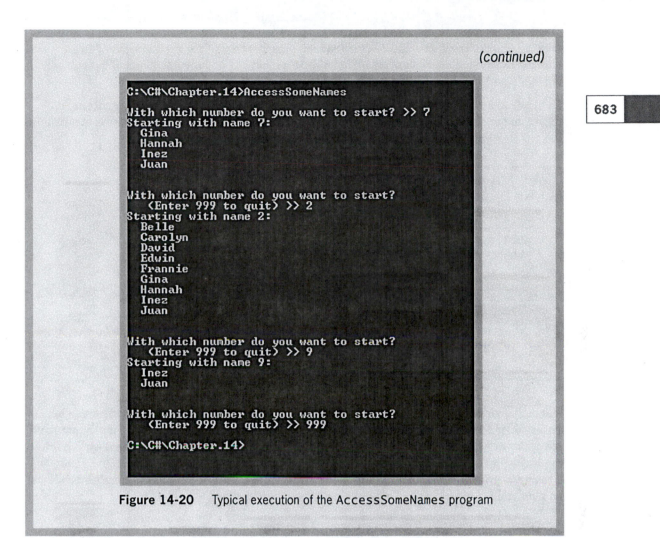

Figure 14-20 Typical execution of the AccessSomeNames program

Understanding Serialization and Deserialization

Writing to a text file allows you to store data for later use. However, writing to a text file does present two disadvantages:

- Data in a text file is easily readable in a text editor such as Notepad. Although this feature is useful to developers when they test programs, it is not a very secure way to store data.

- When a record in a data file contains many fields, it is cumbersome to convert each field to text and combine the fields with delimiters before storing the record on a disk. Similarly, when you read a text file, it is somewhat unwieldy to eliminate the delimiters, split the text into tokens, and convert each token to the proper data type. Writing an entire object to a file at once would be more convenient.

C# provides a technique called serialization that can be used for writing objects to and reading objects from data files. **Serialization** is the process of converting objects into streams of bytes. **Deserialization** is the reverse process; it converts streams of bytes back into objects.

To create a class that can be serialized, you mark it with the [Serializable] attribute, as shown in the shaded statement in Figure 14-21. The Employee class in the figure is identical to the one in Figure 14-10 except for the [Serializable] attribute.

```
[Serializable]
class Employee
{
    public int EmpNum {get; set;}
    public string Name {get; set;}
    public double Salary {get; set;}
}
```

Figure 14-21   The serializable Employee class

Attributes provide a method of associating information with C# code. They are always contained in square brackets. Search for *C# attributes* at *http://msdn.microsoft.com* for more details.

In a class marked with the [Serializable] attribute, every instance variable must also be serializable. By default, all C# simple data types are serializable, including strings. However, if your class contains fields that are more complex data types, you must check the declaration of those classes to ensure they are serializable. By default, array objects are serializable. However, if the array contains references to other objects, such as Dates or Students, those objects must be serializable.

If you create a class and want to be able to write its objects to a file, you can implement the ISerializable interface instead of marking a class with the [Serializable] attribute. When you use this approach, you must write a method named GetObjectData(). Marking the class with the attribute is simpler.

Two namespaces are included in programs that employ serialization:

- System.Runtime.Serialization.Formatters.Binary;

- System.Runtime.Serialization;

When you create a program that writes objects to files, you declare an instance of the BinaryFormatter class with a statement such as the following:

BinaryFormatter bFormatter = new BinaryFormatter();

Then, after you fill a class object with data, you can write it to the output file stream named outFile with a statement such as the following:

```
bFormatter.Serialize(outFile, objectFilledWithData);
```

The Serialize() method takes two arguments—a reference to the output file and a reference to a serializable object that might contain any number of data fields. The entire object is written to the data file with this single statement.

Similarly, when you read an object from a data file, you use a statement like the following:

```
objectInstance = (TypeOfObject)bFormatter.Deserialize(inFile);
```

This statement uses the Deserialize() method with a BinaryFormatter object to read in one object from the file. The object is cast to the appropriate type and can be assigned to an instance of the object. Then you can access individual fields. An entire object is read with this single statement, no matter how many data fields it contains.

Figure 14-22 shows a program that writes Employee class objects to a file and later reads them from the file into the program. After the FileStream is declared for an output file, a BinaryFormatter is declared in the first shaded statement. The user enters an ID number, name, and salary for an Employee, and the completed object is written to a file in the second shaded statement. When the user enters 999, the output file is closed.

```
using System;
using static System.Console;
using System.IO;
using System.Runtime.Serialization.Formatters.Binary;
using System.Runtime.Serialization;
class SerializableDemonstration
{
    static void Main()
    {
        const int END = 999;
        const string FILENAME = "Data.ser";
        Employee emp = new Employee();
        FileStream outFile = new FileStream(FILENAME,
            FileMode.Create, FileAccess.Write);
        BinaryFormatter bFormatter = new BinaryFormatter();
        Write("Enter employee number or " + END +
            " to quit >> ");
        emp.EmpNum = Convert.ToInt32(ReadLine());
        while(emp.EmpNum != END)
        {
            Write("Enter last name >> ");
            emp.Name = ReadLine();
            Write("Enter salary >> ");
            emp.Salary = Convert.ToDouble(ReadLine());
```

Figure 14-22 The SerializableDemonstration program *(continues)*

(continued)

```
        bFormatter.Serialize(outFile, emp);
        Write("Enter employee number or " + END +
            " to quit >> ");
        emp.EmpNum = Convert.ToInt32(ReadLine());
    }
    outFile.Close();
    FileStream inFile = new FileStream(FILENAME,
        FileMode.Open, FileAccess.Read);
    WriteLine("\n{0,-5}{1,-12}{2,8}\n",
        "Num", "Name", "Salary");
    while(inFile.Position < inFile.Length)
    {
        emp = (Employee)bFormatter.Deserialize(inFile);
        WriteLine("{0,-5}{1,-12}{2,8}",
            emp.EmpNum, emp.Name, emp.Salary.ToString("C"));
    }
    inFile.Close();
    }
}
```

Figure 14-22   The SerializableDemonstration program

After the output file closes in the SerializableDemonstration program in Figure 14-22, it is reopened for reading. A loop is executed while the Position property of the input file is less than its Length property. In other words, the loop executes while there is more data in the file. The last shaded statement in the figure deserializes data from the file and casts it to an Employee object, where the individual fields can be accessed. Figure 14-23 shows a typical execution of the program.

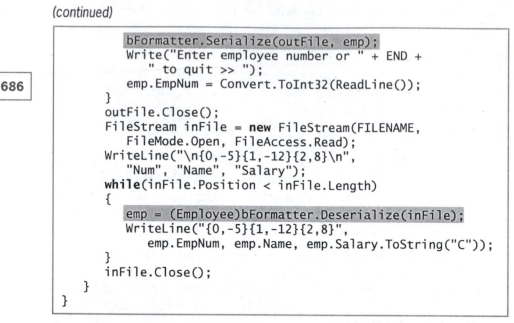

```
C:\C#\Chapter.14>SerializableDemonstration
Enter employee number or 999 to quit >> 333
Enter last name >> Garcia
Enter salary >> 42000
Enter employee number or 999 to quit >> 367
Enter last name >> Anderson
Enter salary >> 29000
Enter employee number or 999 to quit >> 412
Enter last name >> Jensen
Enter salary >> 51500
Enter employee number or 999 to quit >> 535
Enter last name >> Nance
Enter salary >> 70000
Enter employee number or 999 to quit >> 999

Num  Name        Salary

333  Garcia      $42,000.00
367  Anderson    $29,000.00
412  Jensen      $51,500.00
535  Nance       $70,000.00

C:\C#\Chapter.14>
```

Figure 14-23   Typical execution of the SerializableDemonstration program

The file created by the SerializableDemonstration program is not as easy to read as the text file created by the WriteSequentialFile program discussed earlier in the chapter (in Figure 14-11). Figure 14-24 shows the file contents displayed in Notepad (with some newline characters inserted so the output can fit on this page). If you examine the file carefully, you can discern the string names and some Employee class information, but the rest of the file is not easy to read.

```
                                        Data ser - Notepad                          _  □  ×
File  Edit  Format  View  Help
   ÿÿÿÿ              ⁹⌐    PSerializableDemonstration, Version=0.0.0.0, Culture=neutral,
PublicKeyToken=null|        ▐Employeeᴸ
┤<EmpNum>k__BackingFieldᴸ<Name>k__BackingField┤<Salary>k__BackingField    ▐⌐    M    -ᴸ   -Garcia      ,ª@♪
     ÿÿÿÿ              ⁹⌐    PSerializableDemonstration, Version=0.0.0.0, Culture=neutral,
PublicKeyToken=null|        ▐Employeeᴸ
┤<EmpNum>k__BackingField┤<Name>k__BackingField┤<Salary>k__BackingField    ▐⌐    o    -ᴸ   ▐Anderson
RÜ@♪     ÿÿÿÿ          ⁹⌐     PSerializableDemonstration, Version=0.0.0.0, Culture=neutral,
PublicKeyToken=null|        ▐Employeeᴸ
┤<EmpNum>k__BackingFieldᴸ<Name>k__BackingField┤<Salary>k__BackingField    ▐⌐    œ    -ᴸ   -Jensen     €%é@♪
     ÿÿÿÿ              ⁹⌐     PSerializableDemonstration, Version=0.0.0.0, Culture=neutral,
PublicKeyToken=null|        ▐Employeeᴸ
┤<EmpNum>k__BackingFieldᴸ<Name>k__BackingField┤<Salary>k__BackingField    ▐⌐    ┼⌐   -ᴸ   |Nance    ┤ñ@♪
```

Figure 14-24 Data file created using the SerializableDemonstration program

Watch the video *Understanding Serialization and Deserialization*.

TWO TRUTHS & A LIE

Understanding Serialization and Deserialization

1. An advantage of writing data to a text file is that the data is easily readable in a text editor such as Notepad.

2. Serialization is the process of converting objects into streams of bytes. Deserialization is the reverse process; it converts streams of bytes back into objects.

3. By default, all C# classes are serializable.

The false statement is #3. By default, all C# simple data types are serializable, including strings. However, if your class contains fields that are more complex data types, you must check the declaration of those classes to ensure they are serializable.

You Do It

Creating a Text File in a GUI Environment

The file writing and reading examples in this chapter have used console applications so that you could concentrate on the features of files in the simplest environment. However, you can write and read files in GUI environments as well. In the next steps, you create two applications. The first allows a user to enter invoice records using a Form and to store them in a file. The second application allows a user to view stored records using a Form.

1. Open the Visual Studio IDE, and start a new Windows Forms Application project named **EnterInvoices**.

2. Create a Form like the one shown in Figure 14-25 by making the following changes:

   - Change the Text property of the Form to **Invoice Data.**

   - Drag a Label onto the Form, and change its Text property to **Enter invoice data**. Increase the Label's Font to 12.

   - Drag three more Labels onto the Form, and change their Text properties to **Invoice number**, **Last name**, and **Amount**, respectively.

   - Drag three TextBoxes onto the Form next to the three descriptive Labels. Change the Name properties of the three TextBoxes to **invoiceBox**, **nameBox**, and **amountBox**, respectively.

   - Drag a Button onto the Form, change its Name to **enterButton**, and change its Text to **Enter record**. If necessary, resize **enterButton** so all of its text is visible.

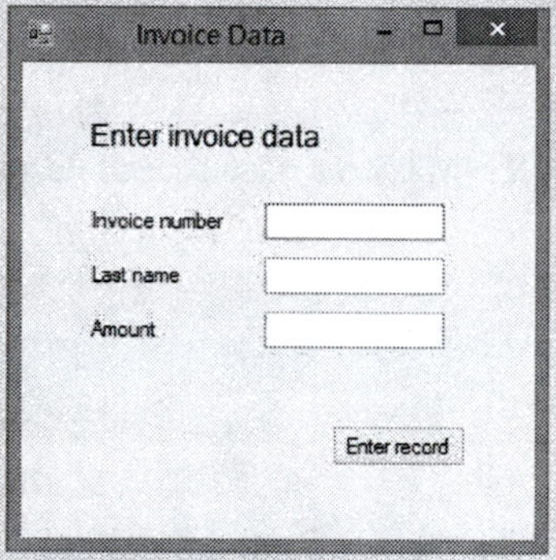

Figure 14-25   Designing the EnterInvoices Form

3. View the code for the Form. At the start of the class, before the Form1() constructor, add the shaded code shown in Figure 14-26. The new code contains statements that perform the following:

   - Declare a delimiter that will be used to separate records in the output file.

   - Declare a path and filename. You can change the path if you want to store the file in a different location on your system.

(continues)

(continued)

- Declare variables for the number, name, and amount of each invoice.
- Open the file, and associate it with a `StreamWriter`.

```
namespace EnterInvoices
{
    public partial class Form1 : Form
    {
        const string DELIM = ",";
        const string FILENAME =
            @"C:\C#\Chapter.14\Invoices.txt";
        int num;
        string name;
        double amount;
        static FileStream outFile = new
            FileStream(FILENAME, FileMode.Create,
            FileAccess.Write);
        StreamWriter writer = new StreamWriter(outFile);
        public Form1()
        {
            InitializeComponent();
        }
```

Figure 14-26   Partial code for the `EnterInvoices` program with typed statements shaded

Remember that placing an at sign (@) in front of a string indicates that its characters should be interpreted literally. The @ sign is used with the filename so that the backslashes in the path will not be interpreted as escape sequence characters.

4. At the top of the file, with the other `using` statements, add the following so that the `FileStream` can be declared:

   using System.IO;

5. Click **Save All** (and continue to do so periodically as you work). Return to Design view, and double-click the **Enter record** button. As shown in the shaded portions of Figure 14-27, add statements within the method to accept data from each of the three `TextBoxes`, and convert each field to the appropriate type. Then write each field to a text file, separated by delimiting commas. Finally, clear the `TextBox` fields to be ready for the user to enter a new set of data.

(continues)

(continued)

```
private void enterButton_Click(object sender, EventArgs e)
{
    num = Convert.ToInt32(invoiceBox.Text);
    name = nameBox.Text;
    amount = Convert.ToDouble(amountBox.Text);
    writer.WriteLine(num + DELIM + name + DELIM + amount);
    invoiceBox.Clear();
    nameBox.Clear();
    amountBox.Clear();
}
```

Figure 14-27   Code for the enterButton_Click() method of the
EnterInvoices program

6. Locate the Dispose() method, which executes when the user clicks the
Close button to dismiss the Form. A quick way to locate the method in the
Visual Studio IDE is to select **Edit** from the main menu, click **Find and
Replace**, click **Quick Find**, and type **Dispose** in the dialog box. (The Look
in: setting can be either Entire Solution or Current Project.) The method
appears on the screen. Add two statements to close writer and outFile,
as shown in the shaded statements in Figure 14-28.

```
protected override void Dispose(bool disposing)
{
    writer.Close();
    outFile.Close();
    if (disposing && (components != null))
    {
        components.Dispose();
    }
    base.Dispose(disposing);
}
```

Figure 14-28   The Dispose() method in the EnterInvoices program

7. Click **Save All**. Execute the program. When the Form appears, enter data
in each TextBox, and then click the **Enter record** button when you finish.

(continues)

(continued)

The TextBoxes clear in preparation for you to enter another record. Enter at least three records before dismissing the Form. Figure 14-29 shows data entry in progress.

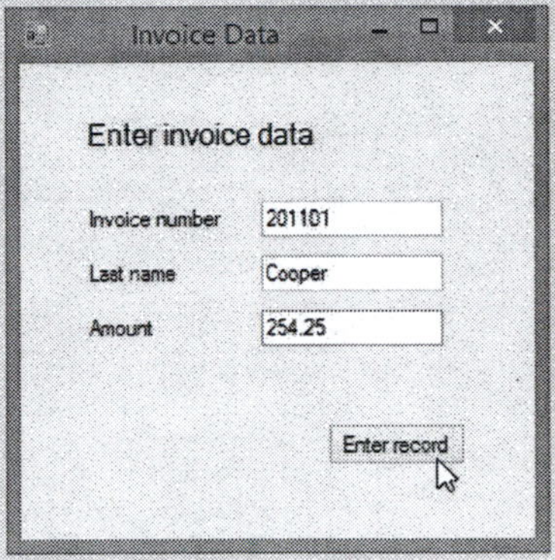

Figure 14-29 Entering data in the EnterInvoices application

Reading Data from a Text File into a Form

In the next steps, you create a Form that you can use to read records from a File.

1. Open a new Windows project in Visual Studio, and name it **ViewInvoices**.

2. Create a Form like the one shown in Figure 14-30 by making the following changes:

   • Change the Text of Form1 to **Invoice Data**.

   • Add four Labels with the text, font size, and approximate locations shown in Figure 14-30. (You can click the down arrow next to the Text property of a component to get a box into which you can type multiline text.)

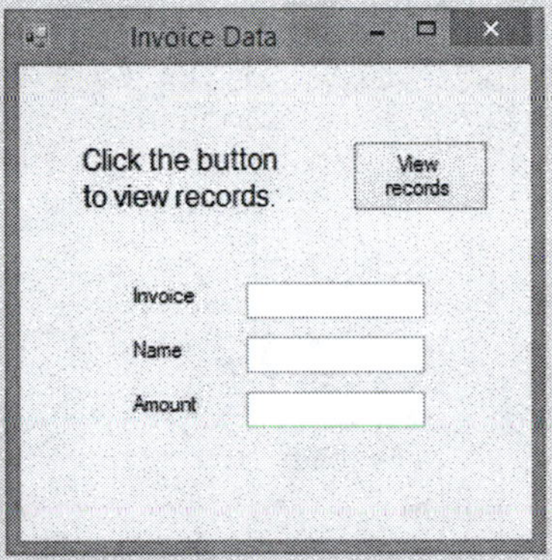

Figure 14-30 The ViewInvoices Form

   • Add a Button with the Text **View records**. Resize the Button if necessary. Name the Button **viewButton**.

   • Add three TextBoxes. Name them **invoiceBox**, **nameBox**, and **amountBox**, respectively.

3. In the IDE, double-click the **View records** Button to view the code.

(continues)

(continued)

4. Add the shaded statements shown in Figure 14-31. They include:

- A using System.IO statement

- Constants for the file delimiter character and the filename (change the path for your file if necessary)

- A string into which whole records can be read before they are split into fields

- An array of strings used to hold the separate, split fields of the entered string

- A FileStream and StreamReader to handle the input file

- Within the viewButton_Click() method, statements to read in a line from the file and split it into three components

```
using System;
using System.Collections.Generic;
using System.ComponentModel;
using System.Data;
using System.Drawing;
using System.Linq;
using System.Text;
using System.Windows.Forms;
using System.IO;
namespace ViewInvoices
{
    public partial class Form1 : Form
    {
        const char DELIM = ',';
        const string FILENAME = @"C:\C#\Chapter.14\Invoices.txt";
        string recordIn;
        string[] fields;
        static FileStream file = new FileStream(FILENAME,
            FileMode.Open, FileAccess.Read);
        StreamReader reader = new StreamReader(file);
        public Form1()
        {
            InitializeComponent();
        }
```

Figure 14-31   Partial code for the ViewInvoices application *(continues)*

(continues)

(continued)

```csharp
        private void viewButton_Click(object sender, EventArgs e)
        {
            recordIn = reader.ReadLine();
            fields = recordIn.Split(DELIM);
            invoiceBox.Text = fields[0];
            nameBox.Text = fields[1];
            amountBox.Text = fields[2];
        }
    }
}
```

Figure 14-31   Partial code for the `ViewInvoices` application

5. Add two `Close()` statements to the `Dispose()` method in the Form1Designer.cs file, as shown in Figure 14-32.

```csharp
        protected override void Dispose(bool disposing)
        {
            reader.Close();
            file.Close();
            if (disposing && (components != null))
            {
                components.Dispose();
            }
            base.Dispose(disposing);
        }
```

Figure 14-32   The `Dispose()` method for the `ViewInvoices` program

6. Save the project, and then execute it. When the Form appears, click the Button to view records. You see the data for the first record you entered when you ran the `EnterInvoices` application; your Form should look like the one in Figure 14-33. Click the Button again to display the next record.

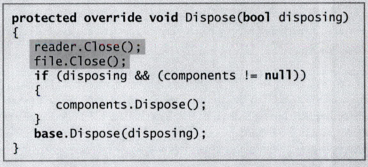

Figure 14-33   Typical execution of the `ViewInvoices` program

(continues)

(continued)

7. Continue to click the `Button` to view each record. After you view the last record you entered, click the `Button` again. An unhandled exception is generated, as shown in Figure 14-34, because you attempted to read data past the end of the input file.

Figure 14-34   Error message window displayed after user attempts to read past the end of the file

 Your error message might look different than the one in Figure 14-34 depending on the version of Visual Studio you are using.

8. Click the **Details** button in the `UnhandledException` window to view details of the error. Figure 14-35 shows that a `System.NullReferenceException` was thrown and not handled.

Figure 14-35   Details displayed by the unhandled exception window

(continues)

(continued)

9. Click **Quit** to close the unhandled exception window.

10. To remedy the unhandled `NullReferenceException` problem, you could take any number of actions. Depending on the application, you might want to do one or more of the following:

   - Display a message.
   - Disallow any more button clicks.
   - End the program.
   - Reposition the file pointer to the file's beginning so the user can view the records again.

   For this example, you take the first two actions: display a message and disallow further button clicks. Return to Visual Studio, and locate the code for the `viewButton_Click()` method. Add a `try...catch` block, as shown in Figure 14-36. Place all the record-handling code in a `try` block, and if a `NullReferenceException` is thrown, change the `Text` in `label1` and disable the View records `Button`.

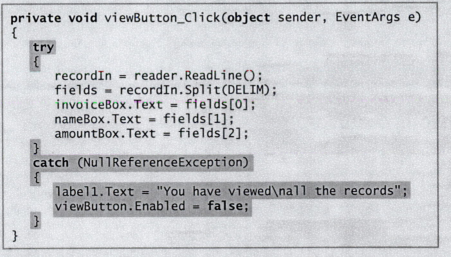

```
private void viewButton_Click(object sender, EventArgs e)
{
    try
    {
        recordIn = reader.ReadLine();
        fields = recordIn.Split(DELIM);
        invoiceBox.Text = fields[0];
        nameBox.Text = fields[1];
        amountBox.Text = fields[2];
    }
    catch (NullReferenceException)
    {
        label1.Text = "You have viewed\nall the records";
        viewButton.Enabled = false;
    }
}
```

Figure 14-36 The `viewButton_Click()` method modified to handle an exception

(continues)

(continued)

11. Save the project, and then execute it. This time, after you have viewed all the available records, the last record remains on the Form, an appropriate message is displayed, and the button is disabled, as shown in Figure 14-37.

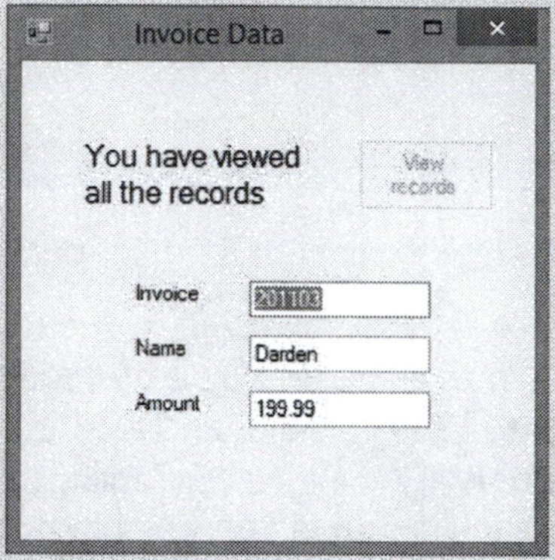

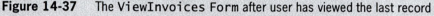

Invoice Data

You have viewed
all the records

View records

Invoice   201100

Name   Darden

Amount   199.99

Figure 14-37   The `ViewInvoices` Form after user has viewed the last record

12. Dismiss the Form. Close Visual Studio.

Chapter Summary

- A computer file is a collection of information stored on a nonvolatile, permanent storage device in a computer system. Computer users organize their files into folders or directories. The `File` class contains methods that allow you to access information about files. The `Directory` class provides you with information about directories or folders.

- Data items are stored in a hierarchy of character, field, record, and file. A data file is a sequential access file when each record is read in order from first to last. Usually, the records are stored in order based on the value in a key field. Before an application can use a data file, it must open the file by creating an object and associating a stream of bytes with that object. When you close a file, it is no longer available to your application.

- Bytes flow into and out of applications through streams. When you use the `Console` class, you have access to several standard streams: `Console.In`, `Console.Out`, and

`Console.Error`. When you read from or write to a file, you use a file-processing class instead of `Console`. Many file-processing classes are available in C#, including `StreamReader` for text input from a file, `StreamWriter` for text output to a file, and `FileStream` for both input and output.

- You can use a `StreamWriter` object to write objects to a file using the `WriteLine()` method. Fields should be separated by a delimiter. Data can be read from a file using a `StreamReader` object and the `ReadLine()` method. If the value of the returned string from `ReadLine()` is null, then no more data exists in the file. After a record (line of data) is read in, the `String` class `Split()` method can be used to separate the data fields into an array of strings.

- When you read data from a sequential file, subsequent records are read in order because a file's position pointer holds the byte number of the next byte to be read. To reread a file, you could close it and reopen it, or you can just reposition the file pointer using the `Seek()` method and the `SeekOrigin` enumeration.

- Serialization is the process of converting objects into streams of bytes. Deserialization is the reverse process; it converts streams of bytes back into objects. To create a class that can be serialized, you mark it with the `[Serializable]` attribute. A serializable object can be written to or read from a data file with a single statement.

Key Terms

Random access memory (RAM) is temporary storage in a computer.

Volatile describes storage in which data is lost when power is interrupted.

Nonvolatile storage is permanent storage; it is not lost when a computer loses power.

A **computer file** is a collection of information stored on a nonvolatile device in a computer system.

Permanent storage devices, such as hard disks, USB drives, reels of magnetic tape, and optical discs, are used to store files.

Text files contain data that can be read in a text editor because the data has been encoded using a scheme such as ASCII or Unicode.

Data files contain facts and figures.

Binary files contain data that has been encoded in binary format.

A **byte** is a small unit of storage; in a simple text file, a byte holds only one character.

A **kilobyte** is approximately one thousand bytes.

A **megabyte** is approximately one million bytes.

A **gigabyte** is approximately one billion bytes.

To **read from a file** is to copy data from a file on a storage device into RAM.

To **write to a file** is to store data in a computer file on a permanent storage device.

Persistent storage is nonvolatile storage.

The **root directory** is the main directory of a storage device.

Folders or **directories** are structures used to organize files on a storage device.

A **path** is composed of the disk drive in which a file resides plus the complete hierarchy of directories.

The **data hierarchy** is the relationship of characters, fields, records, and files.

A **character** is any one of the letters, numbers, or other special symbols (such as punctuation marks) that constitute data.

A **character set** is the group of all the characters used to represent data on a particular computer.

A **field** is a character or group of characters that has some meaning.

A **record** is a collection of fields that contain data about an entity.

A **sequential access file** is a data file in which each record is read in order based on its position in the file; usually the records are stored in order based on the value in some field.

The **key field** is the field used to control the order of records in a sequential file.

A **random access file** is one for which records can be accessed in any order.

Opening a file involves creating an object and associating a stream of bytes with it.

Closing a file means it is no longer available to an application.

A **stream** is a pipeline or channel through which bytes are input from and output to a file.

Programmers say `FileStream` **exposes** a stream around a file.

XML is an abbreviation of eXtensible Markup Language, which is a standard for exchanging data over the Internet.

A **token** is a block of text within a string that represents an entity or field.

A **delimiter** is a character used to specify the boundary between characters in text files.

A **CSV file** is one that contains comma-separated values.

A **priming read** is an input statement that gets a first data item or record.

The term **magic number** refers to the bad programming practice of hard-coding numbers in code without explanation.

A file's **file position pointer** holds the byte number of the next byte to be read.

Serialization is the process of converting objects into streams of bytes.

Deserialization is the process of converting streams of bytes back into objects.

Review Questions

1. Random access memory is _____.

   a. persistent

   b. volatile

   c. permanent

   d. sequential

2. A collection of data stored on a nonvolatile device in a computer system is a(n) _____.

   a. application

   b. computer file

   c. operating system

   d. memory map

3. Which of the following is not permanent storage?

   a. RAM

   b. a hard disk

   c. a USB drive

   d. all of these

4. When you store data in a computer file on a persistent storage device, you are _____.

   a. reading

   b. directing

   c. writing

   d. rooting

5. Which of the following is not a `File` class method?

   a. `Create()`

   b. `Delete()`

   c. `Exists()`

   d. `End()`

6. In the data hierarchy, a group of characters that has some meaning, such as a last name or ID number, is a _____.

   a. byte

   b. field

   c. file

   d. record

7. When each record in a file is stored in order based on the value in some field, the file is a(n) _____file.

   a. random access

   b. application

   c. formatted

   d. sequential

8. A channel through which data flows between a program and storage is a _____.

   a. path
   b. folder
   c. stream
   d. directory

9. Which of the following is not part of a `FileStream` constructor?

   a. the file size
   b. the file mode
   c. the filename
   d. the type of access

10. When a file's mode is `Create`, a new file will be created _____.

    a. even if one with the same name already exists
    b. only if one with the same name does not already exist
    c. only if one with the same name already exists
    d. only if the access is `Read`

11. Which of the following is not a `FileStream` property?

    a. CanRead
    b. CanExist
    c. CanSeek
    d. CanWrite

12. Which of the following is not a file `Access` enumeration?

    a. Read
    c. Write
    c. WriteRead
    d. ReadWrite

13. A character used to specify the boundary between data items in text files is a _____.

    a. sentinel
    b. stopgap
    c. delimiter
    d. margin

14. Which character can be used to specify a boundary between characters in text files?

    a. a comma
    b. a semicolon
    c. either of these
    d. neither of these

15. After a `StreamReader` has been created, the `ReadLine()` method can be used to _____.

   a. retrieve one line at a time from the file

   b. retrieve one character at a time from the file

   c. store one line at a time in a file

   d. split a `string` into tokens

16. The argument to the `String` class `Split()` method is _____.

   a. `void`

   b. the number of fields into which to split a record

   c. the character that identifies a new field in a `string`

   d. a `string` that can be split into tokens

17. The `String` class `Split()` method stores its results in _____.

   a. a `string`

   b. an array of `strings`

   c. an appropriate data type for each token

   d. an array of bytes

18. A file's _____ holds the byte number of the next byte to be read.

   a. index indicator

   b. position pointer

   c. header file

   d. key field

19. The process of converting objects into streams of bytes is _____.

   a. extrication

   b. splitting

   c. mapping

   d. serialization

20. Which of the following is serializable?

   a. an `int`

   b. an array of `ints`

   c. a `string`

   d. all of the above

Exercises

Programming Exercises

1. Create a program named **TestFileAndDirectory** that allows a user to continually enter directory names until the user types *end*. If the directory name exists, display a list of the files in it; otherwise, display a message indicating the directory does not exist. If the directory exists and files are listed, prompt the user to enter one of the filenames. If the file exists, display its creation date and time; otherwise, display a message indicating the file does not exist. Create as many test directories and files as necessary to test your program.

2. Create a program named **FileComparison** that compares two files. First, use a text editor such as Notepad to save your favorite movie quote. Next, copy the file contents, and paste them into a word-processing program such as Word. Then, write the file-comparison application that displays the sizes of the two files as well as the ratio of their sizes to each other. To discover a file's size, you can create a `System.IO.FileInfo` object using statements such as the following, where `FILE_NAME` is a string that contains the name of the file, and `size` has been declared as an integer:

```
FileInfo fileInfo = new FileInfo(FILE_NAME);
size = fileInfo.Length;
```

3. Using Visual Studio, create a `Form` like the one shown in Figure 14-38. Specify a directory on your system, and when the `Form` loads, list the files the directory contains in a `CheckedListBox`. (You first saw an example of a `CheckedListBox` in Chapter 12.) Allow the user to click a file's corresponding check box, and display the file's creation date and time. (Each time the user checks a new filename, display its creation date in place of the original selection.) Save the project as **TestFileAndDirectory2**. Create as many files as necessary to test your program.

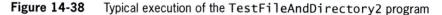

Figure 14-38   Typical execution of the `TestFileAndDirectory2` program

4. a. Create a program named **WriteCustomerRecords** that allows you to enter data for your business's customers and saves the data to a file. Create a `Customer` class that contains fields for ID number, name, and current balance owed.

   b. Create a program named **ReadCustomerRecords** that reads the file created in Exercise 4a and displays each customer's data on the screen.

   c. Create a program named **FindCustomerRecords** that prompts the user for a customer number, reads the file created in Exercise 4a, and displays data for the specified record.

   d. Create a program named **FindCustomerRecords2** that prompts the user for a minimum balance due, reads the file created in Exercise 4a, and displays all the records containing a balance greater than or equal to the entered value.

5. Create a program named **CustomizeAForm** that includes a `Form` for which a user can select options for the background color, size, and title. Change each feature of the `Form` as the user makes selections. After the user clicks a button to save the form settings, save the color, size, and title as strings to a file, and disable the button.

6. Design a program named **RetrieveCustomizedForm** that includes a `Form` like the one created in Exercise 5, except that instead of saving settings, the `Form`'s `Button` should retrieve the saved settings. When the user clicks the `Button`, read the saved settings from the file created in the CustomizeAForm project, and set the new `Form`'s color, size, and title appropriately.

7. Create a program named **HighScore** containing a `Form` that hosts a game in which the computer randomly selects one of three letters (A, B, or C) and the user tries to guess which letter was selected. At the start of the game, read in the previous high score from a data file. (Create this file to hold *0* the first time the game is played.) Display the previous high score on the `Form` to show the player the score to try to beat. Play continues for 10 rounds. As the player makes each guess, show the player's guess and the computer's choice, and award a point if the player correctly guesses the computer's choice. Keep a running count of the number of correct guesses. After 10 rounds, disable the game controls, and create a file that holds the new high score, which might be the same as before the game or a new higher number. When the player begins a new game, the high score will be displayed on the `Form` as the new score to beat.

Debugging Exercises

1. Each of the following files in the Chapter.14 folder of your downloadable student files has syntax and/or logical errors. In each case, determine the problem, and fix the program. After you correct the errors, save each file using the same filename preceded with *Fixed*. For example, save DebugFourteen1.cs as **FixedDebugFourteen.cs**.

    a. DebugFourteen1.cs

    b. DebugFourteen2.cs

    c. DebugFourteen3.cs

    d. DebugFourteen4.cs

Case Problems

1. In Chapter 11, you created the most recent version of the **GreenvilleRevenue** program, which prompts the user for contestant data for this year's Greenville Idol competition. Now, save all the entered data to a file that is closed when data entry is complete and then reopened and read in, allowing the user to view lists of contestants with requested talent types.

2. In Chapter 11, you created the most recent version of the **MarshallsRevenue** program, which prompts the user for customer data for scheduled mural painting. Now, save all the entered data to a file that is closed when data entry is complete and then reopened and read in, allowing the user to view lists of customer orders for mural types.

APPENDIX A

Operator Precedence and Associativity

When an expression contains multiple operators, their **precedence** controls the order in which the individual operators are evaluated. For example, multiplication has a higher precedence than addition, so the expression 2 + 3 * 4 evaluates as 14 because the value of 3 * 4 is calculated before adding 2. Table A-1 summarizes all operators in order of precedence from highest to lowest.

When you use two operators with the same precedence, the **associativity** of the operators controls the order in which the operations are performed.

- Except for the assignment and conditional operators, all binary operators (those that take two arguments) are **left-associative**, meaning that operations are performed from left to right. For example, 5 + 6 + 7 is evaluated first as 5 + 6, or 11; then 7 is added, bringing the value to 18.

- The assignment operators and the conditional operator (?:) are **right-associative**, meaning that operations are performed from right to left. For example, x = y = z is evaluated as y = z first, the result is then assigned to x.

- All unary operators (those that take one argument) are right-associative. If b is 5, the value of −++b is determined by evaluating ++b first (6), then taking its negative value (−6).

You can control precedence and associativity by using parentheses. For example, a + b * c first multiplies b by c and then adds the result to a. The expression (a + b) * c, however, forces the sum of a and b to be calculated first; then the result is multiplied by c.

Category	Operators	Associativity
Primary	x.y f(x) a[x] x++ x-- new typeof checked unchecked	left
Unary	+ -! ~ ++x -- x (T)x	right
Multiplicative	* / %	left
Additive	+ -	left
Shift	<< >>	right
Relational and type testing	< ><= >= is as	left
Equality	== !=	left
Logical AND	&	left
Logical XOR	^	left
Logical OR	|	left
Conditional AND	&&	left
Conditional OR	||	left
Conditional	?:	right
Assignment	= *= /= %= += = <<= >>= &= ^= |=	right

Table A-1 Operator precedence

Key Terms

The **precedence** of operators controls the order in which individual operators are evaluated in an expression.

The **associativity** of operators controls the order in which operations of equal precedence are performed in an expression.

With **left-associative** operators, operations are performed from left to right.

With **right-associative** operators, operations are performed from right to left.

Understanding Numbering Systems and Computer Codes

The numbering system you know best is the **decimal numbering system**, which is based on 10 digits, 0 through 9. Mathematicians call decimal system numbers *base 10 numbers*. When you use the decimal system to express positive whole numbers, no other symbols are available; if you want to express a value larger than 9, you must resort to using multiple digits from the same pool of 10, placing them in columns.

When you use the decimal system, you analyze a multicolumn number by mentally assigning place values to each column. The value of the rightmost column is 1, the value of the next column to the left is 10, the next column is 100, and so on, multiplying the column value by 10 as you move to the left. There is no limit to the number of columns you can use; you simply keep adding columns to the left as you need to express higher values. For example, Figure B-1 shows how the value 305 is represented in the decimal system. You simply sum the value of the digit in each column after it has been multiplied by the value of its column.

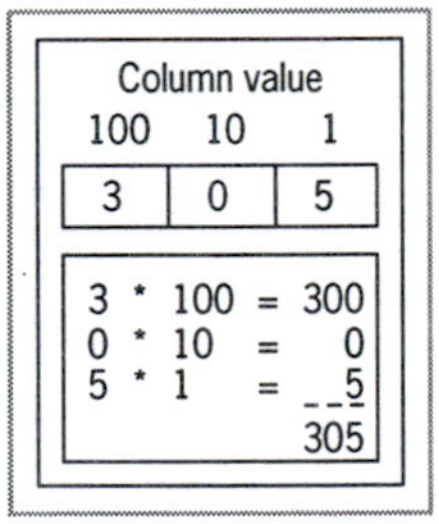

```
       Column value
  100    10     1
 ┌─────┬─────┬─────┐
 │  3  │  0  │  5  │
 └─────┴─────┴─────┘

  3 * 100  = 300
  0 * 10   =   0
  5 * 1    = _ _5
              305
```

Figure B-1   Representing 305 in the decimal system

The **binary numbering system** works in the same way as the decimal numbering system, except that it uses only two digits, 0 and 1. Mathematicians call these numbers *base 2 numbers*. When you use the binary system, if you want to express a value greater than 1, you must resort to using multiple columns, because no single symbol is available that represents any value other than 0 or 1. However, instead of each new column to the left being 10 times greater than the previous column, when you use the binary system, each new column is only two times the value of the previous column. For example, Figure B-2 shows how the numbers 9 and 305 are represented in the binary system. Notice that in both binary numbers and the decimal system, it is perfectly acceptable—and often necessary—to create numbers with 0 in one or more columns. As with the decimal system, the binary system has no limit to the number of columns; you can use as many as it takes to express a value.

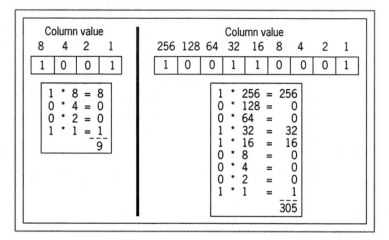

Figure B-2   Representing decimal values 9 and 305 in the binary system

A computer stores every piece of data it uses as a set of 0s and 1s. Each 0 or 1 is known as a **bit**, which is short for *binary digit*. Every computer uses 0s and 1s because all values in a computer are stored as electronic signals that are either on or off. This two-state system is most easily represented using just two digits.

Computers use a set of binary digits to represent stored characters. If computers used only one binary digit to represent characters, then only two different characters could be represented, because the single bit could be only 0 or 1. If computers used only two digits, then only four characters could be represented—the four codes 00, 01, 10, and 11, which in decimal values are 0, 1, 2, and 3, respectively. Many computers use sets of eight binary digits to represent each character they store, because using eight binary digits provides 256 different combinations. One combination can represent an *A*, another a *B*, still others *a* and *b*, and so on. Two hundred fifty-six combinations are enough so that each capital letter, small letter, digit, and punctuation mark used in English has its own code; even a space has a code. For example, in some computers 01000001 represents the character *A*. The binary number 01000001 has a decimal value of 65, but this numeric value is not important to ordinary computer users; it is simply a code that stands for *A*. The code that uses 01000001 to mean *A* is the **American Standard Code for Information Interchange**, or **ASCII**.

A set of eight bits is called a **byte**. Half a byte, or four bits, is a **nibble**. You will learn more about bytes later in this appendix.

ASCII is not the only computer code, but it is typical and is the one used in most personal computers. The **Extended Binary Coded Decimal Interchange Code**, or **EBCDIC**, is an eight-bit code that is used in IBM mainframe computers. In these computers, the principle is the same—every character is stored as a series of binary digits. However, the actual values used are different. For example, in EBCDIC, an *A* is 11000001, or 193. **Unicode** is another code used by languages such as Java and C#; with this code, 16 bits are used to represent each character. The character *A* in Unicode has the same decimal value (65) as the ASCII *A*, but it is stored as 0000000001000001. Using 16 bits provides many more possible combinations than using only eight bits—65,536 to be exact. Unicode has enough available codes for all English letters and digits and for characters from many international alphabets.

Ordinary computer users seldom think about the numeric codes behind the letters, numbers, and punctuation marks they enter from their keyboards or see displayed on a monitor. However, they see the consequence of the values behind letters when they see data sorted in alphabetical order. When you sort a list of names, *Andrea* comes before *Brian*, and *Caroline* comes after *Brian* because the numeric code for *A* is lower than the code for *B*, and the numeric code for *C* is higher than the code for *B*, no matter whether you are using ASCII, EBCDIC, or Unicode.

Table B-1 shows the decimal and binary values behind the most commonly used characters in the ASCII character set—the letters, numbers, and punctuation marks you can enter from your keyboard using a single key press. Most of the values not included in Table B-1 have a purpose. For example, the decimal value 7 represents a bell—a dinging sound your computer can make, often used to notify you of an error or some other unusual condition. Each binary number in Table B-1 is shown containing two sets of four digits; this convention makes the long eight-digit numbers easier to read.

Decimal number	Binary number	ASCII character	Decimal number	Binary number	ASCII character
32	0010 0000	Space	51	0011 0011	3
33	0010 0001	! Exclamation point	52	0011 0100	4
34	0010 0010	" Quotation mark, or double quote	53	0011 0101	5
35	0010 0011	# Number sign, octothorpe, pound sign, or hash	54	0011 0110	6
36	0010 0100	$ Dollar sign	55	0011 0111	7
37	0010 0101	% Percent	56	0011 1000	8
38	0010 0110	& Ampersand	57	0011 1001	9
39	0010 0111	' Apostrophe, single quote	58	0011 1010	: Colon
40	0010 1000	(Left parenthesis	59	0011 1011	; Semicolon
41	0010 1001	) Right parenthesis	60	0011 1100	< Less-than sign
42	0010 1010	* Asterisk	61	0011 1101	= Equal sign
43	0010 1011	+ Plus sign	62	0011 1110	> Greater-than sign
44	0010 1100	, Comma	63	0011 1111	? Question mark
45	0010 1101	- Hyphen or minus sign	64	0100 0000	@ At sign
46	0010 1110	. Period or decimal point	65	0100 0001	A
47	0010 1111	/ Slash or front slash	66	0100 0010	B
48	0011 0000	0	67	0100 0011	C
49	0011 0001	1	68	0100 0100	D
50	0011 0010	2	69	0100 0101	E

Table B-1 Decimal and binary values for common ASCII characters (continues)

(continued)

Decimal number	Binary number	ASCII character	Decimal number	Binary number	ASCII character
70	0100 0110	F	89	0101 1001	Y
71	0100 0111	G	90	0101 1010	Z
72	0100 1000	H	91	0101 1011	[Opening or left bracket
73	0100 1001	I	92	0101 1100	\ Backslash
74	0100 1010	J	93	0101 1101	] Closing or right bracket
75	0100 1011	K	94	0101 1110	^ Caret
76	0100 1100	L	95	0101 1111	_ Underline or underscore
77	0100 1101	M	96	0110 0000	` Grave accent
78	0100 1110	N	97	0110 0001	a
79	0100 1111	O	98	0110 0010	b
80	0101 0000	P	99	0110 0011	c
81	0101 0001	Q	100	0110 0100	d
82	0101 0010	R	101	0110 0101	e
83	0101 0011	S	102	0110 0110	f
84	0101 0100	T	103	0110 0111	g
85	0101 0101	U	104	0110 1000	h
86	0101 0110	V	105	0110 1001	i
87	0101 0111	W	106	0110 1010	j
88	0101 1000	X	107	0110 1011	k

Table B-1 Decimal and binary values for common ASCII characters (continues)

(continued)

Decimal number	Binary number	ASCII character	Decimal number	Binary number	ASCII character
108	0110 1100	l	118	0111 0110	v
109	0110 1101	m	119	0111 0111	w
110	0110 1110	n	120	0111 1000	x
111	0110 1111	o	121	0111 1001	y
112	0111 0000	p	122	0111 1010	z
113	0111 0001	q	123	0111 1011	{ Opening or left brace
114	0111 0010	r	124	0111 1100		Vertical line or pipe
115	0111 0011	s	125	0111 1101	} Closing or right brace
116	0111 0100	t	126	0111 1110	~ Tilde
117	0111 0101	u			

Table B-1 Decimal and binary values for common ASCII characters

The Hexadecimal System

The **hexadecimal numbering system** is a **base 16 system** because it uses 16 digits. As shown in Table B-2, the digits are 0 through 9 and A through F. Computer professionals often use the hexadecimal system to express addresses and instructions as they are stored in computer memory because hexadecimal provides convenient shorthand expressions for groups of binary values. In Table B-2, each hexadecimal value represents one of the 16 possible combinations of four-digit binary values. Therefore, instead of referencing memory contents as a 16-digit binary value, for example, programmers can use a 4-digit hexadecimal value.

Decimal value	Hexadecimal value	Binary value (shown using four digits)
0	0	0000
1	1	0001
2	2	0010
3	3	0011
4	4	0100
5	5	0101
6	6	0110
7	7	0111
8	8	1000
9	9	1001
10	A	1010
11	B	1011
12	C	1100
13	D	1101
14	E	1110
15	F	1111

 Table B-2   Values in the decimal and hexadecimal systems

In the hexadecimal system, each column is 16 times the value of the column to its right. Therefore, column values from right to left are 1, 16, 256, 4096, and so on. Figure B-3 shows how 171 and 305 are expressed in hexadecimal.

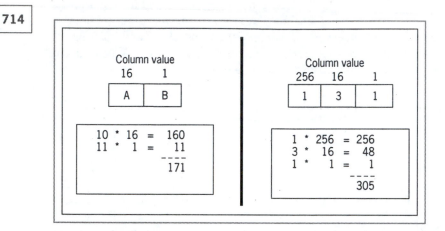

Figure B-3   Representing decimal values 171 and 305 in the hexadecimal system

Measuring Storage

In computer systems, both internal memory and external storage are measured in bits and bytes. Eight bits make a byte, and a byte frequently holds a single character (in ASCII or EBCDIC) or half a character (in Unicode). Because a byte is such a small unit of storage, the size of memory and files is often expressed in thousands or millions of bytes. Table B-3 describes some commonly used terms for storage measurement.

Term	Abbreviation	Number of bytes using binary system	Number of bytes using decimal system	Example
Kilobyte	KB or kB	1024	one thousand	This appendix occupies about 85 kB on a hard disk.
Megabyte	MB	1,048,576 (1024 × 1024 kilobytes)	one million	One megabyte can hold an average book in text format. A 3½-inch diskette you might have used a few years ago held 1.44 megabytes.
Gigabyte	GB	1,073,741,824 (1,024 megabytes)	one billion	The hard drive on a fairly new laptop computer might be 500 gigabytes. An hour of HDTV video is about 4 gigabytes.
Terabyte	TB	1024 gigabytes	one trillion	The entire Library of Congress can be stored in 10 terabytes.
Petabyte	PB	1024 terabytes	one quadrillion	Popular Web sites such as Google have 20 to 30 petabytes of activity per day.
Exabyte	EB	1024 petabytes	one quintillion	A popular expression claims that all words ever spoken by humans could be stored in text form in 5 exabytes.
Zettabyte	ZB	1024 exabytes	one sextillion	A popular expression claims that all words ever spoken by humans could be stored in audio form in 42 zettabytes.
Yottabyte	YB	1024 zettabytes	one septillion (a 1 followed by 24 zeros)	All data accessible on the Internet and in corporate networks is estimated to be 1 yottabyte.

Table B-3 Commonly used terms for computer storage

In the metric system, "kilo" means 1000. However, in Table B-3, notice that a kilobyte is 1024 bytes. The discrepancy occurs because everything stored in a computer is based on the binary system, so multiples of two are used in most measurements. If you multiply 2 by itself 10 times, the result is 1024, which is a little over 1000. Similarly, a gigabyte is 1,073,741,624 bytes, which is more than a billion.

Confusion arises because many hard-drive manufacturers use the decimal system instead of the binary system to describe storage. For example, if you buy a hard drive that holds 10 gigabytes, it actually holds exactly 10 billion bytes. However, in the binary system, 10 GB is 10,737,418,240 bytes, so when you check your hard drive's capacity, your computer will report that you don't quite have 10 GB, but only 9.31 GB.

Key Terms

The **decimal numbering system** is a numeric system that uses 10 digits, 0 through 9, arranged in columns to represent numbers.

The **binary numbering system** is a numbering system that uses two digits, 0 and 1, arranged in columns to represent numbers.

A **bit** is a binary digit.

The **American Standard Code for Information Interchange (ASCII)** is an eight-bit code that represents characters.

A **byte** is eight bits.

A **nibble** is four bits.

The **Extended Binary Coded Decimal Interchange Code (EBCDIC)** is an eight-bit code used in IBM mainframe computers.

Unicode is a 16-bit code used with languages such as C# and Java.

The **hexadecimal numbering system** is a number system that uses 16 digits, 0 through 9 and A through F, arranged in columns to represent numbers.

The **base 16 system** is the hexadecimal system.

Using the IDE Editor

The Visual C# Code Editor is like a word processor for writing source code. Just as a word-processing program provides support for spelling and grammar, the C# Code Editor helps ensure that your C# syntax is free from spelling and grammar errors. This support can be grouped into several categories that are described in this appendix.

IntelliSense

IntelliSense is Microsoft's name for the set of features designed to minimize the time you spend looking for help and to help you enter code more accurately and efficiently. The IntelliSense features provide basic information about C# language keywords, .NET Framework types, and method signatures as you type them in the editor. The information is displayed in ToolTips, list boxes, and Smart Tags. Features of IntelliSense include:

- Providing completion lists
- Providing quick information
- Providing parameter information
- Adding using statements

Providing Completion Lists

As you enter source code in the editor, IntelliSense displays a list box that contains all of the C# keywords, .NET Framework classes, and names you have defined in your program that fit the current circumstances. This feature is called **completion mode**. For example, Figure C-1 shows a list box that makes suggestions based on what the programmer has typed in the Code Editor. If you find a match in the list box for the name you intend to type, you can select the item. Alternatively, you can press the Tab key to have IntelliSense finish entering the name or keyword for you.

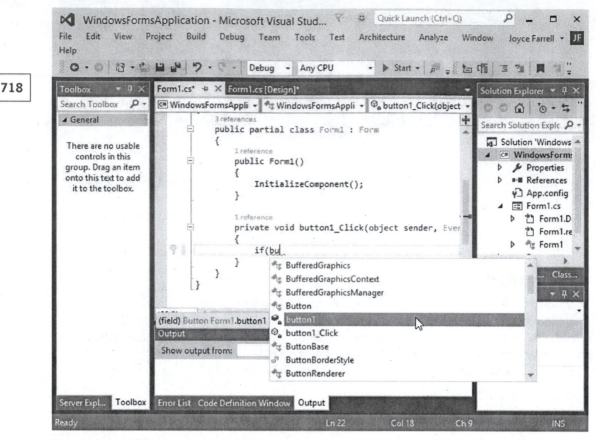

Figure C-1   A list displayed by IntelliSense

IntelliSense also supports a **suggestion mode**. In this mode, IntelliSense does not automatically complete identifiers, which makes it easier for you to type variable or method names without the completion list appearing. You can toggle between completion mode and suggestion mode by pressing Ctrl+Alt+Spacebar or by pointing to IntelliSense on the Edit menu and clicking Toggle Completion Mode.

Similarly, when you enter a .NET Framework type or an identifier of a specific type into the Code Editor and then type the dot operator (.), IntelliSense displays a list box that contains the members of that type. When you don't know what method or property you want for an object, typing its identifier and a dot can direct you to the appropriate choice. This technique sometimes teaches you about features you did not even realize were available.

Providing Quick Information

When you hover the cursor over a .NET Framework type, IntelliSense displays a Quick Info ToolTip that contains basic documentation about that type.

Providing Parameter Information

When you enter a method name in the Code Editor and then type an opening parenthesis, IntelliSense displays a Parameter Info ToolTip that shows the method's parameter list. If the method is overloaded, multiple method signatures are displayed, and you can scroll through them.

Adding using Statements

If you attempt to create an instance of a .NET Framework class without a sufficiently qualified name, IntelliSense displays a Smart Tag after the unresolved identifier. When you click the Smart Tag, IntelliSense displays a list of using statements to help you resolve the identifier. When you select a statement from the list, IntelliSense adds the using directive to the top of your source code file, and you can continue to write code at your current location.

Code Snippets

Code snippets are small units of commonly used C# source code that you can enter accurately and quickly with only a couple of keystrokes. To access the code snippet menu, right-click in the Code Editor, select Insert Snippet, and select Visual C#. Then, you can browse from the many available snippets, or you can create your own.

Wavy Underlines

Wavy underlines give you instant feedback about errors in your code as you type. A red wavy underline identifies a syntax error, such as a missing semicolon or mismatched braces. A green wavy underline identifies a potential compiler warning, and blue identifies an Edit and Continue issue. In Figure C-2, a wavy underline appears under button1 because the code in the statement is not yet complete.

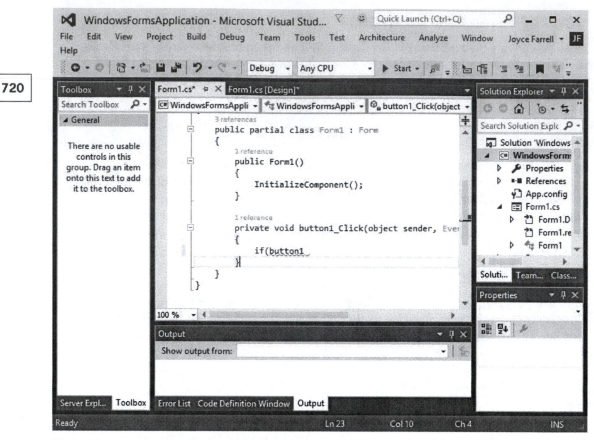

Figure C-2 Wavy underline in Code Editor

Readability Aids

The editor assigns different colors to various categories of identifiers in a C# source code file to make the code easier to read. For example, C# keywords are bright blue, classes are blue-green, and comments are green.

Key Terms

IntelliSense is Microsoft's name for the set of features designed to minimize the time you spend looking for help and to help you enter code more accurately and efficiently.

Completion mode is an IDE editing mode in which suggestions are automatically provided for your code based on context.

Suggestion mode is an IDE editing mode in which completion mode is turned off.

Code snippets are small units of commonly used C# source code that you can enter accurately and quickly with only a couple of keystrokes.

Glossary

A

abstract class—a class from which concrete objects cannot be instantiated but can serve as a basis for inheritance. Contrast with *concrete class*.

abstract method—a method that contains no statements and must be implemented by classes that derive from its class.

access key—a shortcut way to make a selection using the keyboard.

access specifier—a keyword that dictates which outside classes can use a method.

accessibility—describes limitations on how a method can be used.

accessors—methods in properties that specify how a class's fields are accessed. See *get accessors* and *set accessors*.

accumulated—describes totals that are added into a final sum by processing individual records one at a time in a loop.

actual parameters—arguments within a method call.

add and assign operator (+=)—an operator that adds the operand on the right to the operand on the left and assigns the results to the operand on the left in one step.

alias—an alternative name or pseudonym.

ambiguous—describes overloaded methods between which the compiler cannot distinguish.

American Standard Code for Information Interchange (ASCII)—an eight-bit code that represents characters.

ancestors—all the superclasses from which a subclass is derived.

AND operator—an operator that determines whether two expressions are both true; it is written using two ampersands (&&). Also called the *conditional AND operator*. Contrast with *Boolean logical AND operator*.

applicable methods—the collection of potential methods that could be used by a method call.

application classes—classes that contain a `Main()` method and are executable programs.

application software—programs that allow users to complete tasks, in contrast with system software that the computer needs to complete tasks.

argument—the expression passed to a method.

arithmetic operators are used to perform arithmetic; they include +, -, *, /, and %.

array—a list of data items that all have the same data type and the same name, but are distinguished from each other by a subscript or index.

array element—one object in an array.

assembly—a group of code modules compiled together to create an executable program.

assignment—a statement that provides a variable with a value.

assignment operator—the equal sign (=); any value to the right of the assignment operator is assigned to, or taken on by, the variable or constant to the left.

associativity—specifies the order in which a sequence of operations with the same precedence are evaluated.

at runtime—a phrase describing actions that occur during a program's execution.

attributes of an object—the characteristics of an object.

auto-implemented property—a property in which the code within the accessors is created automatically. The only action in the set accessor is to assign a value to the associated field, and the only action in the get accessor is to return the associated field value.

automatic properties—auto-implemented properties.

B

backing field—a field that has a property coded for it.

base 2 numbers—binary system numbers.

base 10 numbers—decimal system numbers.

base 16 system—a mathematical system that uses 16 symbols to represent numbers; hexadecimal.

base class—a class that is used as a basis for inheritance.

behaviors of an object—the methods associated with an object.

betterness rules—the rules that determine the best overloaded method to execute based on the arguments in a method call.

binary files—files that can store any of the 256 combinations of bits in any byte instead of just those combinations that form readable text.

binary numbering system—a numbering system that uses two digits, 0 and 1, arranged in columns to represent numbers.

binary operators—operators that use two operands: one value to the left of the operator and another value to the right of it.

binary search—an algorithm that attempts to find an item in a list by splitting the sorted list of objects in half repeatedly as the search gets closer to a match.

bit—a binary digit.

bitwise operators—operators that are used to manipulate the individual bits of values.

black box—any device that can be used without knowing how it works internally.

block—a collection of one or more statements contained within a pair of curly braces.

block comments—comments that start with a forward slash and an asterisk (/*) and end with an asterisk and a forward slash (*/). Block comments can appear on a line by themselves, on a line before executable code, or after executable code. They can also extend across as many lines as needed. Compare with *line comments*.

bool—a data type that holds a Boolean value.

Boolean logical AND operator—an operator that determines whether two expressions are both true; it is written using a single ampersand (&). Unlike the conditional AND operator, it does not use short-circuit evaluation.

Boolean logical inclusive OR operator—an operator that determines whether at least one of two conditions is true; it is written using a single pipe (|). Unlike the conditional OR operator, it does not use short-circuit evaluation.

Boolean variable—a variable that can hold only one of two values: true or false.

bugs—program errors.

byte—an integral data type that can hold an unsigned numeric value from 0 through 255.

C

C# programming language—a computer programming language developed as an object-oriented and component-oriented language. It exists as part of Visual Studio, a package used for developing applications for the Windows family of operating systems.

call—to invoke a method.

call stack—the memory location where the computer stores the list of locations to which the system must return after method calls.

called—describes a method that has been invoked.

called method—a method that has been invoked by another method.

calling method—a method that calls another method.

camel casing—a style of creating identifiers in which the first letter is not capitalized, but each new word is. Contrast with *Pascal casing*.

case label—identifies a course of action in a switch structure.

catch block—a block of code that can catch one type of Exception.

char—an integral data type that can store a character such as 'A', '4', or '$'.

character—any one of the letters, numbers, or other special symbols (such as punctuation marks) that comprise data.

character set—the group of all the characters used to represent data on a particular computer.

check box—a GUI widget that a user can click to select or deselect an option.

child class—a derived class; a subclass; a class that has inherited from a base class.

class—a category of objects or a type of object.

class access specifier—describes access to a class.

class client—a program or class that instantiates objects of another prewritten class. Also called a *class user*.

724

class definition—the first class line that describes a class; it contains an optional access specifier, the keyword `class`, and any legal identifier for the name of the class. Also known as *class definition*.

class header—the first class line that describes a class; it contains an optional access specifier, the keyword `class`, and any legal identifier for the name of the class. Also known as *class definition*.

class user—a program or class that instantiates objects of another prewritten class. Also called a *class client*.

click event—an action fired when a user clicks a button in a GUI environment.

client—a method that uses another method.

closing a file—the process of making a file no longer available to an application.

code bloat—describes unnecessarily long or repetitive program statements.

code refactoring—the process of changing a program's internal structure without changing the way the program works.

code snippets—small units of commonly used C# source code that are generated in the IDE using a few keystrokes.

combo box—a GUI element that is a combination of a list box and an editing control that allows a user to select from the list or enter new text.

command line—the operating system's text interface.

command prompt—a request for input that appears at the beginning of the command line.

comment out—to turn a statement into a comment so that the compiler will not execute its command.

comparison operator—an operator that compares two values.

compiler—a computer program that translates high-level language statements into machine code.

completion mode—an IDE editing mode in which suggestions are automatically provided based on context.

composed delegate—a delegate that calls the delegates from which it is built.

composition—the technique of using an object within another object.

computer file—a collection of information stored on a nonvolatile device in a computer system.

computer simulations—programs that attempt to mimic real-world activities to foster a better understanding of them.

concatenate—to join strings together in a chain.

concrete class—a nonabstract class from which objects can be instantiated. Contrast with *abstract class*.

conditional AND operator—an operator that determines whether two expressions are both true; it is written using two ampersands (&&). Also called the *AND operator*. Contrast with *Boolean logical AND operator*.

conditional operator—a ternary operator that is used as an abbreviated version of the `if-else` statement; it requires three expressions separated by a question mark and a colon.

conditional OR operator—an operator that determines whether at least one of two conditions is true; it is written using two pipes (||). Also called the *OR operator*. Contrast with *Boolean logical inclusive OR operator*.

constant—describes a data item when it cannot be changed after a program is compiled; in other words, when it cannot vary.

constructor—a method that instantiates (creates an instance of) an object.

constructor initializer—a clause that indicates another instance of a class constructor should be executed before any statements in the current constructor body.

contextual keywords—identifiers that act like keywords in specific circumstances.

control—a GUI component such as a text field, button, or check box that users can manipulate to interact with a program.

control statement—the part of a structure that determines whether the subsequent block of statements executes.

counted loop—a definite loop.

CSV file—a file that contains comma-separated values.

culture—a set of rules that determines how culturally dependent values such as money and dates are formatted.

D

data files—files that contain facts and figures; persistent collections of related records.

data hierarchy—the relationship of characters, fields, records, and files.

data type—a description of the format and size of a data item as well as the operations that can be performed on it.

dead code—statements that can never execute under any circumstances because the program logic "can't get there." Also see *unreachable*.

debugging—the process of removing all syntax and logical errors from a program.

decimal—a floating-point data type that has a greater precision and a smaller range than a `float` or `double`, which makes it suitable for financial and monetary calculations.

decimal numbering system—the system that uses 10 digits, 0 through 9, arranged in columns to represent numbers.

decision structure—a unit of program logic that involves choosing between alternative courses of action based on some value.

decrement operator (--)—an operator that reduces a variable's value by 1; there is a prefix and a postfix version.

decrementing—the act of decreasing the value of a variable, often by 1.

default constructor—a constructor that requires no parameters; it can be automatically supplied or written by a programmer.

default event—for a `Control`, the event or method generated when it is double-clicked in the IDE, as well as the event that users expect to generate when they encounter the `Control` in a working application.

default value of an object—the value initialized with a default constructor.

definite loop—a loop in which the number of iterations is predetermined. Also a *counted loop*. Contrast with *indefinite loop*.

delegate—an object that contains a reference to a method.

delimiter—a character used to specify the boundary between characters in text files.

derived class—a subclass; a class that has inherited from a base class.

deserialization—the process of converting streams of bytes back into objects.

design time—the period of time during which a programmer designs a program's interface and writes the code.

destructor—a method that contains the actions performed when an instance of a class is destroyed.

directories—structures used to organize files on a storage device; folders.

do loop—a type of posttest loop; a loop that is tested at the bottom of the loop after one repetition has occurred.

double—a data type that can hold a floating-point number with 15 or 16 significant digits of accuracy.

dual-alternative decisions—decisions that have two possible outcomes.

E

empty body—a block that has no statements in it.

encapsulation—the technique of packaging an object's attributes and methods into a cohesive unit that can be used as an undivided entity.

enhanced for loop—a version of the for loop that cycles through an array without specifying the starting and ending points for the loop control variable.

enumeration—a list of values in which names are substituted for numeric values.

Equals()—a method that determines equivalency. In the String class, it is the method that determines if two strings have the same value.

escape sequence—a single character composed of two symbols beginning with a backslash that represents a nonprinting character such as a tab.

event—an object generated when a user interacts with a GUI object, causing the program to perform a task.

event-driven programs—programs that contain code that causes an event such as a button click to perform a task.

event handler—a method that performs a task in response to an event; an event receiver.

event receiver—a method that performs a task in response to an event; an event handler.

event sender—the control that generates an event.

event wiring—the act of connecting an event to its resulting actions.

exception—an error condition or unexpected behavior in an executing program.

exception handling—the set of object-oriented techniques used to manage unexpected errors.

explicit cast—purposefully assigns a value to a different data type; it involves placing the desired result type in parentheses followed by the variable or constant to be cast.

explicitly—purposefully. Contrast with *implicitly*.

exposes—associates a FileStream with a file.

Extended Binary Coded Decimal Interchange Code (EBCDIC)—an eight-bit code that is used in IBM mainframe computers.

extended class—a derived class; a child class; a subclass; a class that has inherited from a base class.

extension methods—static methods that act like instance methods.

F

fault-tolerant—describes applications that are designed so that they continue to operate, possibly at a reduced level, when some part of the system fails.

field—in a class, an instance variable. In a file or database, a character or group of characters that has some meaning.

file position pointer—a variable that holds the byte number of the next byte to be read from a file.

finally block—a block of code that optionally follows a `try` block; the code within a `finally` block executes whether the preceding `try` block identifies any `Exceptions` or not.

fires an event—causes an event to occur. Also see *raises an event* and *triggers an event*.

fixed-pitch font—a font in which each character occupies the same width.

float—a data type that can hold a floating-point number with as many as seven significant digits of accuracy.

floating-point—describes a number that contains decimal positions.

flowchart—a tool that helps programmers plan a program's logic by writing program steps in diagram form, as a series of shapes connected by arrows.

focus—the state of a GUI component when the user's attention is drawn to it visually. When a component has focus, its action can be executed by pressing the Enter key.

folders—structures used to organize files on a storage device; directories.

for loop—a loop that contains the starting value for the loop control variable, the test condition that controls loop entry, and the expression that alters the loop control variable, all in one statement.

form—a GUI interface for collecting, displaying, and delivering information.

formal parameter—a parameter within a method header that accepts a value.

format specifier—one of nine built-in format characters in a format string that defines the most commonly used numeric format types.

format string—a string of characters that controls the appearance of output.

fragile—describes classes that depend on field names from parent classes because they are prone to errors; that is, they are easy to "break."

fully qualified—describes a name that includes the class name as well as the identifier.

G

garbage—an unknown memory value.

get accessors—methods in properties that allow retrieval of a field value by using a property name.

getter—another term for a class property's get accessor.

gigabyte—approximately a billion bytes.

governing type—in a `switch` statement, the type that is established by the `switch` expression. The governing type can be `sbyte`, `byte`, `short`, `ushort`, `int`, `uint`, `long`, `ulong`, `char`, `string`, or `enum`.

graphical control elements—the components through which user interacts with a GUI program.

graphical user interface (GUI)—an interface that employs graphical images representing controls the user manipulates.

group box—a GUI element that can be used to group controls on a form, it is similar to a panel but it can contain a caption and does not have a scroll bar.

H

hardware—the physical devices associated with a computer.

has-a relationship—the relationship created using composition, so called because one class "has an" instance of another.

hash code—a number that should uniquely identify an object.

hexadecimal numbering system—a mathematical system that uses 16 symbols to represent numbers; base 16.

hide—to override a parent class member in a child class, making the parent class member invisible.

high-level programming language—a language that uses a vocabulary of reasonable terms such as *read*, *write*, or *add* instead of referencing the sequence of on/off switches that perform these tasks.

I

identifier—the name of a program component such as a variable, class, or method.

if statement—a program statement used to make a single-alternative decision.

if-else statement—a statement that performs a dual-alternative decision.

immutable—unchangeable.

implementation hiding—the technique of keeping the details of a method's operations hidden.

implicit cast—the automatic transformation that occurs when a value is assigned to a type with higher precedence.

implicit conversion—the conversion that occurs when a type is automatically changed to another upon assignment.

implicit parameter—an undeclared parameter that gets its value automatically.

implicit reference conversion—the type of conversion that occurs when a derived class object is assigned to its ancestor's data type.

implicitly—automatically. Contrast with *explicitly*.

incrementing—the act of increasing the value of a variable, often by 1.

indefinite loop—a loop in which the number of iterations is not predetermined. Contrast with *definite loop*.

index—an integer contained within square brackets that indicates the position of one of an array's elements. Also see *subscript*.

infinite loop—a loop that (theoretically) never ends.

information hiding—a feature found in all object-oriented languages, in which a class's data is private and changed or manipulated only by its own methods.

inheritance—the ability to extend a class so as to create a more specific class that contains all the attributes and methods of a more general class; the extended class usually contains new attributes or methods as well.

initialization—an assignment made when a variable is declared.

initializer list—the list of values provided for an array.

inner loop—the loop in a pair of nested loops that is entirely contained within another loop.

instance methods—methods that are used with object instantiations.

instance of a class—an object; a tangible example of a class.

instance variables—data components of a class that exist separately for each instantiation. Also called *fields*.

instantiate—to create an object.

instantiation—a created object.

int—an integral data type that can hold a signed numeric value in four bytes.

integers—whole numbers.

integral data types—data types that store whole numbers; the nine integral types are byte, sbyte, short, ushort, int, uint, long, ulong, and char.

Integrated Development Environment (IDE)—a program development environment in which programmers select options from menus or by clicking buttons; an IDE provides helpful features such as color coding and automatic statement completion.

IntelliSense—Microsoft's name for the set of features designed to minimize program development time in the IDE.

interactive program—a program that allows user input.

interface—a collection of abstract methods (and perhaps other members) that can be used by any class as long as the class provides a definition to override the interface's abstract definitions..

intermediate language (IL)—the language into which source code statements are compiled.

internal—a class access modifier that means access is limited to the assembly to which the class belongs.

internal access—a level of method accessibility that limits method access to the containing program.

intrinsic types—basic, built-in data types; C# provides 15 intrinsic types.

invoke—to call a method.

invoking object—the object referenced by this in an instance method.

invoking the event—calling an event method.

iteration—one execution of any loop.

iteration variable—a temporary variable that holds each array value in turn in a `foreach` statement.

J

jagged array—a one-dimensional array in which each element is another array.

just in time (JIT)—the C# compiler that translates intermediate code into executable code.

K

key—a value that uniquely identifies a record.

key events—keyboard events that occur when a user presses and releases keyboard keys.

key field—the field used to uniquely identify records and to control the order of records in a sequential file.

keywords—predefined and reserved identifiers that have special meaning to the compiler.

kilobyte—approximately a thousand bytes.

L

label—a control that typically provides descriptive text for another control or displays other text information on a `Form`.

left-associative—describes operators whose operations are performed from left to right.

length field—a field that contains the number of elements in an array.

lexically—alphabetically.

line comments—comments that start with two forward slashes (//) and continue to the end of the current line. Line comments can appear on a line by themselves, or at the end of a line following executable code. Compare with *block comments*.

link label—a GUI control with text and that links the user to other sources, such as Web pages or files.

list box—a GUI element that displays a list of items the user can select by clicking.

literal constant—a value that is taken literally at each use.

literal string—a series of characters that is used exactly as entered.

local—describes a variable that is declared in the current method.

logic—the sequence of statements and methods that produce the desired results in a computer program.

long—an integral data type that can hold a signed numeric value in eight bytes.

loop—a structure that allows repeated execution of a block of statements.

loop body—the block of statements executed in a loop.

loop control variable—a variable that determines whether loop execution will continue on each iteration.

loop fusion—the technique of combining two loops into one.

lower camel casing—a style of creating identifiers in which the first letter is not capitalized, but each new word is. Also called *camel casing*. Contrast with *Pascal casing*.

M

machine language—the most basic circuitry-level language.

magic number—a hard-coded number.

menu bar—in the Visual Studio IDE, the list of choices that run horizontally across the top of the screen.

mandatory parameters—method parameters for which an argument is required in every method call.

megabyte—approximately a million bytes.

menu strip—a horizontal list of general options that appears under the title bar of a Form or Window.

method—an encapsulated series of statements that carry out a task.

method body—all the instructions contained within a pair of curly braces ({ }) following a method header.

method declaration—a method header or definition; it precedes a method and includes a return type, identifier, and an optional parameter list.

method definition—a method header or declaration; it precedes a method and includes a return type, identifier, and an optional parameter list.

method header—the first line of a method, which includes the method name and information about what will pass into and be returned from a method.

method's type—a method's return type.

mission critical—describes any process that is crucial to an organization.

modal window—a secondary window that takes control from a primary window and that a user must deal with before proceeding.

multidimensional arrays—arrays that require multiple subscripts to access the array elements.

multifile assembly—a group of files containing methods that work together to create an application.

multiple inheritance—the ability to inherit from more than one class.

N

named argument—a method argument that is preceded with the name of the called method's parameter to which it will be assigned.

named constant—an identifier whose contents cannot change.

namespace—a scheme that provides a way to group similar classes.

nested if—a statement in which one decision structure is contained within another.

nested method calls—method calls placed inside other method calls.

nibble—four bits; half a byte.

node—In the Visual Studio IDE, a box that appears on a vertical tree to the left of a list or a section of code and that can be expanded or condensed.

non-application classes—classes that do not contain a Main() method and therefore are not runnable programs; they provide support for other classes.

nonstatic—describes a method that requires an object reference.

nonvolatile—the type of computer storage that is permanent; it is not lost when a computer loses power.

NOT operator (!)—an operator that negates the result of any Boolean expression.

O

object—a concrete entity that has attributes and behaviors; an object is an instance of a class.

object (or object)—a class type in the System namespace that is the ultimate base class for all other types.

object initializer—a clause that assigns values to any accessible members or properties of a class at the time of instantiation without calling a constructor with parameters.

object-oriented approach—an approach to a problem that involves defining the objects needed to accomplish a task and developing classes that describe the objects so that each maintains its own data and carries out tasks when another object requests them.

object-oriented programming (OOP)—a programming technique that features objects, classes, encapsulation, interfaces, polymorphism, and inheritance.

one-dimensional array—an array whose elements are accessed using a single subscript. Also see *single-dimensional array*.

opening a file—the process of creating an object and associating a stream of bytes with it.

operands—the values that operators use in expressions.

operator precedence—rules that determine the order in which parts of a mathematical expression are evaluated. Also called *order of operation*.

optional parameter—a parameter to a method for which a default value is automatically supplied when no argument is supplied; a parameter is optional when it is given a value in the method declaration.

OR operator—an operator that determines whether at least one of two conditions is true; it is written using two pipes (||). Also called the *conditional OR operator*. Contrast with *Boolean logical inclusive OR operator*.

order of operation—rules that determine the order in which parts of a mathematical expression are evaluated. Also called *operator precedence*.

orphaned method—a method that never executes in an application, and thus serves no purpose.

out of bounds—describes a subscript that is not within the allowed range for an array.

out of scope—describes a variable that is not usable because it has ceased to exist.

outer loop—the loop in a pair of nested loops that contains another loop.

output parameter—a parameter to a method that receives the argument's address; it is not required to have an initial value. Contrast with *value parameter* and *reference parameter*.

overload resolution—the process of determining which of multiple applicable methods is the best match for a method call.

overloading—using one term to indicate diverse meanings. In C#, methods are overloaded when there are multiple versions with the same name but different parameter lists.

override—a keyword used in method headers when a derived class inherits an abstract method from a parent.

override—to take precedence over another method version.

P

panel—a GUI element that can be used to group controls on a Form; similar to a group box, but it does not have a caption and can have a scroll bar.

parallel array—an array that has the same number of elements as another array and holds corresponding data.

parameter array—a local array declared within a method header that can accept any number of elements of the same data type.

parameter list—the data types and parameter names that appear between parentheses in a method header.

parameter to a method—an object or reference that is declared in a method definition.

parameterless constructor—a constructor that takes no parameters; one that is called using no arguments.

parent class—a base class; a superclass; a class that is used as a basis for inheritance.

parse—to break an item into component parts.

Pascal casing—a style of creating identifiers in which the first letter of all new words in a variable name, even the first one, is capitalized. Contrast with *camel casing*.

passed by reference—describes how an argument is passed to a method when the method receives its memory address.

passed by value—describes how data is passed to a method when the method receives a copy of the argument passed to it.

path—the disk drive in which a file resides plus the complete hierarchy of directories.

permanent storage devices—hardware such as hard disks, USB drives, and compact discs that are used to store files.

persistent—describes storage that is nonvolatile.

picture box—a GUI element that displays graphics

polymorphism—the ability to create methods that act appropriately depending on the context.

populating an array—the act of providing values for all the elements in an array.

positional argument—an unnamed method argument that is assigned to a parameter list based on its position in the method call.

postfix increment operator—an operator that evaluates a variable and then adds 1 to it. This operator is represented by ++ after a variable.

posttest loop—a loop in which the loop control variable is tested after the loop body executes. Contrast with *pretest loop*.

precedence—a feature of operators that controls the order in which they are evaluated in an expression.

precision specifier—a specifier that controls the number of significant digits or zeros to the right of the decimal point in a format string.

prefix increment operator—an operator that increases the variable's value by 1 and then evaluates it. This operator is represented by ++ before a variable.

pretest loop—a loop in which the loop control variable is tested before the loop body executes. Contrast with *posttest loop*.

priming read—an input statement that gets a first data item or record.

private—an access specifier that indicates other classes may not use the method or variable that it modifies. When used as a class access specifier, it means access is limited to another class to which the class belongs.

private access—a level of method accessibility that limits method access to the containing class.

procedural program—a program created by writing a series of steps or operations to manipulate values.

program—a set of written computer instructions.

program comments—nonexecuting statements that document a program.

prompt—an instruction to the user to enter data.

propagating an exception—the act of transmitting an exception object unchanged through the call stack.

property—a member of a class that provides access to a field of a class; properties define how fields will be set and retrieved. The value of an object.

proportional font—a font in which different characters have different pitches or widths.

protected—a keyword that provides an intermediate level of security between public and private access.

protected access—a level of method accessibility that limits method access to the containing class or types derived from the containing class.

pseudocode—a tool that helps programmers plan a program's logic by writing plain English statements.

public—an access specifier that indicates other classes may use the method or variable it modifies.

public access—a level of method accessibility that allows unlimited access to a method by any class.

R

radio buttons—GUI widgets, similar to check boxes, except that when they are placed on a form, only one can be selected at a time and selecting any one automatically deselects the others.

raises an event—causes an event to occur. Also see *fires an event* and *triggers an event*.

random access file—a file from which records can be accessed in any order.

random access memory (RAM)—temporary storage in a computer.

range check—a series of statements that determine whether a value falls within a specified range.

range match—a process that determines whether a value falls between a pair of limiting values.

read from the file—to copy data from a file on a storage device into RAM.

read-only—describes a value, property, or file that can be accessed but not altered.

read-only property—a property that has only a get accessor, and not a set accessor.

record—a collection of fields that contain data about an entity.

rectangular array—an array in which each row has the same number of columns.

recursive—describes a method that calls itself.

reference equality—the type of equality that occurs when two reference type objects refer to the same object.

reference parameter—a parameter to a method that receives the argument's address; it is required to have an initial value. Contrast with *value parameter* and *output parameter*.

reference type—a data type that holds a memory address. Contrast with *value types*.

rethrow an Exception—to throw a caught Exception instead of handling it.

return statement—a method statement that causes a value to be sent back from a method to its calling method.

return type—the type of value a method will return to any other method that calls it.

right-associative—describes operators whose operations are performed from right to left.

robustness—describes the degree to which a system is resilient to stress, maintaining correct functioning even in the presence of errors.

root class—the ultimate or first base class in a hierarchical ancestry tree.

root directory—the main directory of a storage device.

run time—the period of time during which a program executes.

runnable—describes files that are executable.

S

sbyte—an integral data type that can hold a signed numeric value from −128 through 127.

scientific notation—a numeric expression format that includes an *E* (for exponent) and that specifies a number of implied decimal places.

scope—the area where a variable or constant is known and can be used.

sealed class—a class that cannot be extended.

searching an array—the process of comparing a value to a list of values in an array, looking for a match.

self-documenting—describes a program element that is self-explanatory.

sentinel value—a value that a user must supply to stop a loop.

sequence structure—a unit of program logic in which one step follows another unconditionally.

sequential access file—a data file in which each record is stored in order based on the value in some field.

sequential search—a search that is conducted by examining a list item-by-item in sequence.

serialization—the process of converting objects into streams of bytes.

set accessors—methods in properties that allow use of the assignment operator with a property name.

setter—another term for a class property's set accessor.

short—an integral data type that can hold a signed numeric value in two bytes.

short-circuit evaluation—the C# feature in which parts of an AND or OR expression are evaluated only as far as necessary to determine whether the entire expression is true or false.

side effect—an unintended consequence of an operation.

signature—a method's name and parameter list.

significant digits—specifies the mathematical accuracy of a value.

simple type—describes one of the following in C#: `byte`, `sbyte`, `short`, `ushort`, `int`, `uint`, `long`, `ulong`, `float`, `double`, `decimal`, `char`, and `bool`.

single-dimensional array—an array whose elements are accessed using a single subscript. Also see *one-dimensional array*.

snap lines—lines that appear in a design environment to help designers align new `Controls` with others that are already in place.

software—computer programs

source code—program statements.

standard numeric format strings—strings of characters expressed within double quotation marks that indicate a format for output.

state of an object—the collective value of all an object's attributes at any point in time.

static—a keyword that indicates that a method will be executed through a class and not by an object.

step value—the amount by which a loop control variable is altered on each iteration, especially in a `for` loop.

stream—a pipeline or channel through which bytes are input from and output to a file.

string—a data type that can hold a series of characters.

subclass—a derived class; a child class; a class that has inherited from a base class.

subscript—an integer contained within square brackets that indicates the position of one of an array's elements. Also see *index*.

suggestion mode—an IDE editing mode in which completion mode is turned off.

superclass—a base class; a parent class; a class that is the basis for inheritance.

switch structure—a structure that tests a single variable against a series of exact matches.

syntax—the set of grammar rules in a programming language.

syntax error—an error that occurs when a programming language is used incorrectly.

T

tab order—describes the sequence of controls selected when the user presses the Tab key in a program with a GUI interface.

ternary—describes an operator that requires three arguments.

TextBoxes—controls through which a user can enter input data in a GUI application.

text files—files that contain data that can be read in a text editor because the data has been encoded using a scheme such as ASCII or Unicode.

this reference—the reference to an object that is implicitly passed to an instance method of its class.

token—a block of text within a string that represents an entity or field.

transitive—inheriting all the members of one's ancestors.

triggers an event—causes an event to occur. Also see *fires an event* and *raises an event*.

truth tables—diagrams used in mathematics and logic to help describe the truth of an entire expression based on the truth of its parts.

try block—a block of code that might create exceptions that will be handled.

two-dimensional arrays—multidimensional arrays that have two or more columns of values for each row.

type precedence—a hierarchy of data types used to determine the unifying type in arithmetic expressions containing dissimilar data types.

U

uint—an integral data type that can hold an unsigned numeric value in four bytes.

ulong—an integral data type that can hold an unsigned numeric value in eight bytes.

unary operators—operators used with one operand.

Unicode—a 16-bit coding scheme for characters.

Unified Modeling Language (UML) diagrams—graphical tools that programmers and analysts use to describe systems.

unifying type—the type chosen for an arithmetic result when operands are of dissimilar types.

unreachable—describes program statements that can never execute under any circumstances because the program logic "can't get there." Also see *dead code*.

upper camel casing—a style of creating identifiers in which the first letter of all new words in a name is capitalized, even the first one; Pascal casing.

ushort—an integral data type that can hold an unsigned numeric value in two bytes.

using clause, or using directive—code that declares a namespace.

V

value parameter—a parameter to a method that receives a copy of the value passed to it. Contrast with *reference parameter* and *output parameter*.

value types—data types that hold a value; they are predefined types such as `int`, `double`, and `char`. Contrast with *reference type*.

variable—a named location in computer memory that can hold different values at different points in time.

variable declaration—the statement that names a variable; it includes a data type, an identifier, an optional assignment operator and assigned value, and an ending semicolon.

verbatim identifier—an identifier with an @ prefix.

virtual method—a method whose behavior is determined by the implementation in a child class.

visible—describes a class member that has not been hidden.

void—a keyword that indicates that a method does not return any value when called.

volatile—the type of computer storage that is lost when power is lost.

W

while loop—a structure that executes a body of statements continuously while some condition continues to be true; it uses the keyword `while`.

whitespace—any combination of spaces, tabs, and carriage returns (blank lines) in a program.

widgets—interactive controls such as labels, scroll bars, check boxes, and radio buttons.

write to a file—to store data in a computer file on a permanent storage device.

X

XML—an abbreviation of eXtensible Markup Language, which is a standard for exchanging data over the Internet.

XML-documentation format comments—comments that use a special set of tags within angle brackets to create documentation within a program.

Index

All bold page numbers indicate definitions

CPSIA information can be obtained
at www.ICGtesting.com
Printed in the USA
FFOW04n0838060517
35314FF